# Eating Disorders and Obesity

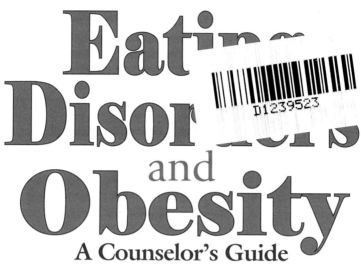

## A Counselor's Guide to Prevention and Treatment

Edited by Laura H. Choate

AMERICAN COUNSELING
ASSOCIATION
5999 Stevenson Avenue • Alexandria, VA 22304 • www.counseling.org

# Eating
# Disorders
## and
# Obesity
## A Counselor's Guide
## to Prevention and Treatment

10   9   8   7   6   5   4   3   2   1

**American Counseling Association**
5999 Stevenson Avenue • Alexandria, VA 22304

Director of Publications • Carolyn C. Baker

Production Manager • Bonny E. Gaston

Editorial Assistant• Catherine A. Brumley

Copy Editor • Kathleen Porta Baker

Cover and text design by Bonny E. Gaston.

**Library of Congress Cataloging-in-Publication Data**
Eating disorders and obesity: a counselor's guide to prevention and
  treatment/edited by Laura H. Choate.
    pages cm
  Includes bibliographical references and index.
  ISBN 978-1-55620-319-0 (alk. paper)
1. Eating disorders—Patients—Counseling of.   2. Obesity—Treatment.
I. Choate, Laura Hensley, editor of compilation.   II. American Counseling
  Association.
RC552.E18E28253   2013
616.85´2606—dc23                                          2012037876

# Contents

## Section 1   Foundations

## Section 2   Assessment and Practice Frameworks for Eating Disorders and Obesity

iii

## Section 3   Effective Prevention and Early Intervention for Eating Disorders and Obesity

## Section 4   Effective Treatments for Eating Disorders and Obesity

# Introduction

*Laura H. Choate*

The idea for this edited book, *Eating Disorders and Obesity: A Counselor's Guide to Prevention and Treatment,* originated from a variety of influences. First, my desire to compile this type of book stems from being a mother of elementary-age children who are exposed daily to harmful media images of and messages regarding narrow cultural definitions of how they "should" look and act. Because I want my children and all others to be equipped with the skills they need to stay healthy and resilient in the face of the cultural pressures surrounding eating, weight, and shape, this book is dedicated to assisting counselors and their clients to become empowered to effect positive change in this area within the multiple systems (family, school, community) in which they are embedded.

The origins of this book are also grounded in my professional experience as a licensed professional counselor and counselor educator. I have been involved in the prevention and treatment field in a variety of roles: I have counseled clients, supervised and taught graduate students, published articles regarding body image resilience and eating disorder (ED) treatment, and presented at local schools to adolescent girls as well as to professionals at state and national conferences. I have observed that counselors are often unclear as to their role in preventing EDs and obesity and in providing early intervention and treatment, and they often lack training in best practices in this field. Therefore, the overarching purpose of this book is to provide a much-needed resource specifically targeted to counselors that provides accessible information practitioners can implement in their daily work with clients across the continuum of care. The book strategically includes chapters that address assessment, prevention, and treatment, including information for working with children and adults as well as with clients from diverse cultural groups.

## Goals for the Book

I am not alone in acknowledging the pervasiveness of cultural pressures regarding eating, weight, and shape that leave very few individuals unscathed.

In fact, researchers have claimed that individuals in Western society currently live in a toxic culture that makes it increasingly difficult to maintain a healthy weight and a positive body image (Brownell & Horgan, 2004), and these negative forces have become even more intense in recent years. These pressures influence individuals to varying degrees depending on their genetic vulnerability and their exposure to environmental risks. The first goal of this book, therefore, is to provide a foundation for counselors who work with clients with initial problems in this area so that the typical progression toward increased symptom severity may be interrupted.

The spectrum of client concerns in the area of EDs and obesity is broad. Many people experience body dissatisfaction, and women in particular are said to have a "normative discontent" with their bodies (Rodin, Silberstein, & Striegel-Moore, 1984). Of these individuals, some might progress to engaging in disordered eating practices such as excessive dieting or binge eating that can lead to weight gain or obesity. At the other end of the continuum, others will have progressed to life-threatening EDs or obesity that significantly impairs their life functioning. Counselors need the preparation to recognize the signs and symptoms related to eating- and weight-related problems and the skills to respond according to client needs, whether it be a primary prevention program held in a school setting or a referral for inpatient hospitalization for a client who is emaciated from anorexia.

In addition to addressing client needs across the continuum, a second goal of the book is to provide essential information regarding a client population that is increasing not only in number but also in clinical severity and complexity, making it highly likely that counselors will work with clients who have these concerns. Despite increased awareness and research initiatives regarding EDs and obesity in recent years, rates of body dissatisfaction, disordered eating, rates of obesity, and problems with body weight and shape continue to increase across the life span. This increase is of concern in that the large number of individuals who experience current eating- and weight-related concerns are at risk for the future development of full-syndrome EDs and obesity. For example, the 2011 Youth Risk Behavior Surveillance survey found that 46% of all 9th to 12th graders and 61% of girls in particular were actively trying to lose weight (Centers for Disease Control and Prevention, 2012b). Binge eating has increased among adolescents in recent years, with between 20% and 60% in community samples reporting episodes of binge eating (Hudson, Hiripi, Pope, & Kessler, 2007). Young adult women are at particularly high risk for eating-related concerns; as many as 10% to 15% experience disordered eating such as excessive dieting and binge eating on a regular basis, and rates are even higher among college women (Hudson et al., 2007; Stice, Marti, Shaw, & Jaconis, 2009). Obesity rates are also increasing rapidly in the general population, with 69% of adults and one third of children in the United States being classified as overweight or obese (Ogden, Carroll, Kit, & Flegal, 2012). In addition, obesity rates among children and adolescents have more than tripled in the past 30 years (Centers for Disease Control and Prevention, 2012a).

These high rates are also concerning because both EDs and obesity are associated with significant medical and psychosocial impairment. EDs are chronic, putting clients at risk for future obesity, depression, suicide attempts, substance abuse, and morbidity risk (Crow et al., 2009; Swanson, Crow, Le Grange, Swendsen, & Merikangas, 2011), and obesity is related to an increased risk for a host of negative consequences in both childhood and adulthood, including cardiovascular disease, diabetes, and increased mortality risk (National Heart, Lung and Blood Institute, 1998). Therefore, these problems should remain a top priority for prevention and treatment.

A third goal of this book is to provide valuable information about assessment, prevention, and treatment of clients of diverse cultural backgrounds. Although once considered a problem exclusive to White middle-class girls and women, research has indicated that eating- and weight-related problems are not exclusive to any particular cultural group or gender; rather, they cut across gender, race, class, and sexual orientation. For example, African American and Latina women tend to experience binge eating at the same rates as White women (Alegria et al., 2007), and Asian American women report similar or higher rates of body dissatisfaction in comparison to White women (Grabe & Hyde, 2006). In addition, rates of excess weight or obesity are highest among Black (82%) and Latina (76%) women (Flegal, Carroll, Ogden, & Curtin, 2010) when compared with those of other cultural groups. Because individuals from diverse groups are often hesitant to seek out counseling services for their problems and because counselors might inadvertently overlook these problems in ethnic minority clients (Kelly et al., 2011), the chapters in this book include ways in which counselors can tailor traditional programs to better meet the prevention and treatment needs of all clients.

A final goal of this book is to provide foundational information for counselors, who typically receive minimal instruction in EDs and obesity prevention and treatment in their preparation programs. I regularly teach undergraduate and graduate courses on women's issues in counseling and supervise students in practicum settings serving young adult clients, and I have observed how problematic these issues are for clients and how unprepared student counselors feel to address these concerns because of the lack of training in their graduate preparation programs. In presenting at state and national conferences during the past 15 years, I have heard counselors describe their motivation to obtain information regarding best practices in the field, yet they often do not perceive themselves as prepared to work with clients experiencing disordered eating symptoms and are unclear regarding their role in prevention or early intervention that might circumvent the onset of full-syndrome EDs or obesity.

Despite the growing research base primarily established in the fields of psychiatry and clinical psychology, information on evidence-based prevention and treatment is clearly not well disseminated among counseling practitioners. This book, therefore, will provide assistance to the practitioner who might not have the resources to purchase numerous primary sources or locate research studies. As busy professionals, most practitioners do not have time to integrate existing information from these multiple resources and to use them to inform their work (e.g., treatment manuals, journal articles, chapters from handbooks in other fields). In this book, research, prevention strategies, and treatment methods are all synthesized in a highly practitioner-focused manner, with practical steps and language specifically tailored to counselors.

For all of these reasons, this is a book for all counselors, not just those for whom EDs or obesity are a specialty area of focus. All counselors need the knowledge to recognize and assess client problems related to eating, weight, and shape and the skills to provide research-based interventions based on the appropriate level of care. With proper training, counselors are ideally suited to implement the fundamental counselor competencies of prevention, early intervention, and treatments that are tailored to client needs. To be optimally successful, they need additional grounding in the literature, knowledge of research-based programs or treatments, and motivation to obtain supervised practice for their initial work with clients. My desire is that through this book, counselors can gain this knowledge and acquire the skills needed to provide effective interventions for clients across the continuum of care, regardless of their professional or clinical setting.

As the reader will discover as he or she reads this book, the chapters are specifically selected and designed to open these doors for students and practitioners alike. I invited a diverse and distinguished group of authors to participate in this book project, all of whom were excited to share their current research and clinical recommendations with professional counselors. The authors are a mix of seasoned practitioners, researchers, and faculty members from a variety of mental health and medical disciplines who are actively serving in the ED and obesity prevention and treatment field in the United States, Canada, and two different hospital-based treatment centers in Australia.

Several of the authors included in this volume also wrote articles included in the 2012 *Journal of Counseling & Development* special section on ED prevention and treatment. As the guest editor of that issue, I was excited to receive so many strong international contributions from participants. On the basis of the response, I decided that counselors would also benefit from a book specifically intended for their needs that could cover the special issue themes as well as other relevant areas. The issues raised in the special issue articles served as the book's foundation. Next, I sought out other multidisciplinary authors with expertise in EDs and obesity prevention and treatment. I was surprised at the enthusiasm and support for the book I received from almost every author I contacted. To paraphrase Margo Maine, McGilley, and Bunnell (2010), many authors have a similar interest in bridging the research–practice gap and possess a desire to present their research in a practical and easy-to-disseminate format. In this book, counselors now have highly accessible information regarding foundational knowledge, assessment and conceptualization, effective prevention programs, and best-practice treatments that span the continuum of care. To supplement their reading, recommended resources are included in every chapter, as well as a summary of the highlights of each chapter. More important, case examples are included to help counselors visualize what the theory or treatment would look like in practice. I should note that in the spirit of flexibility, some authors chose to incorporate case material throughout their chapters, and others included the case example to conclude the chapter.

# Book Overview

The book is divided into four sections: Section 1: Foundations; Section 2: Assessment and Practice Frameworks for Eating Disorders and Obesity; Section 3: Effective Prevention and Early Intervention for Eating Disorders and Obesity; and Section 4: Effective Treatments for Eating Disorders and Obesity.

## Section 1: Foundations

Section 1 provides information for understanding the sociocultural context in which EDs and obesity occur. Counselors need a firm understanding of cultural influences and risk factors to assist in the assessment, prevention, and treatment planning for these problems, including how interventions must account for environmental influences (e.g., media, family, peers) as well as for differences in gender and race and ethnicity. Ethical and legal considerations to increase counselor competence in this area are also explored.

First, Linda Smolak and Caitlin Chun-Kennedy address the role of sociocultural influences in the development of body image disturbance and disordered eating symptoms, two of the strongest risk factors for EDs and obesity. They discuss the influences of media, peers, and parents as three primary sociocultural agents operating to shape body image development and describe individual differences regarding individuals who are most vulnerable to these influences.

In Chapter 2, Margo Maine and Douglas Bunnell coauthor a chapter on gender and its impact on the prevention and treatment of both women and men with EDs. Because gender is a leading risk factor for the development of EDs, understanding how current gender role development affects an individual's risk and how gender-based factors can maintain and reinforce eating problems is important. Maine and Bunnell also address gender differences in the expression of EDs and provide counseling strategies for providing gender-sensitive treatment to both men and women who experience disordered eating.

Chapter 3 examines the importance of cultural influences through Regine M. Talleyrand's discussion of EDs and obesity in people of color. As discussed previously, eating- and weight-related problems are more common among people of color than previously thought, and counselors have an ethical responsibility to detect and assess for these problems in their clients. In her chapter, Talleyrand reviews existing research conducted with specific cultural groups and discusses cultural factors that might put a client at risk for the development of ED symptoms and obesity. She also provides counseling strategies to help counselors deliver more culturally sensitive assessment, prevention, and treatment for clients of color.

A final foundational chapter in Section 1 highlights important ethical and legal concerns when working with clients with EDs. Although clients with other mental health symptoms generally want to be rid of their problems, clients with EDs are frequently opposed to seeking treatment or altering disordered eating behaviors. In Chapter 4, I, Mary A. Hermann, and Leigh Pottle explore the ethical and legal complexities involved for counselors who work with clients who do not want to change life-threatening behaviors. Counselors must carefully balance the need to respect clients' ability to make their own life decisions while also fulfilling their own duty to protect clients from self-inflicted harm. The chapter also reviews counselors' ethical duty to increase their self-awareness and to practice within their own scope of competence. The authors also review the issue of client autonomy in detail, describing issues related to informed consent and treatment decision making. The use of an ethical decision-making model is also demonstrated through a case example authored by Jodi Manton, a master's degree candidate at Louisiana State University.

### Section 2: Assessment and Practice Frameworks for Eating Disorders and Obesity

Assessment of client concerns is critical in identifying problems, conceptualizing client concerns, and conducting effective prevention and treatment planning. This section includes criteria from the *Diagnostic and Statistical Manual of Mental Disorders* (4th ed., text rev., or *DSM–IV–TR*; American Psychiatric Association [APA], 2000) as well as the most recent proposed guidelines for the fifth edition of the *DSM* (*DSM–5*; American Psychiatric Association, 2012) to guide the discussion of assessment. Next, it includes chapters on two frameworks for guiding intervention decisions so that counselors can be more informed about determining where a client might need to enter the continuum of care, which ranges from prevention to intensive treatment.

In Chapter 5, Kelly C. Berg and Carol B. Peterson provide a careful overview of both the *DSM–IV–TR* and the *DSM–5* diagnostic criteria for the ED spectrum. Because eating- and weight-related concerns are so common, Berg and Peterson recommend that assessment for EDs be integrated into all initial intake interviews, and they provide detailed descriptions for incorporating screening questions into a clinical interview. They also address special considerations for assessment and diagnosis of EDs, including working with children (who might not be developmentally capable of understanding typical screening questions) and with clients of color.

Many eating- and weight-related problems emerge during the later childhood and adolescent years, indicating that youths experiencing these concerns spend most of their waking hours attending school. It makes sense, then, that school counselors can play an important role in detecting the early onset of eating issues and in serving as a resource to ensure that student needs are met. In Chapter 6, Jennifer Maskell Carney and Heather Lewy Scott provide information for school counselors on identifying, assessing, and intervening with students who have eating- and weight-related concerns. Specifically, they provide school counselors with a framework guided by the American School Counselor Association's National Model for conceptualizing and providing interventions for client concerns across the continuum of care, ranging from body image concerns, disordered eating (including binge eating, which leads to obesity), and EDs.

Although Carney and Scott's chapter focuses specifically on school-based intervention and referrals, in Chapter 7, Alan M. Schwitzer presents a framework for assessing and planning community-based interventions for young women with eating disorder not otherwise specified. Because this disorder is by far the most common ED, Schwitzer provides a model for working with clients who have it, including assessment guidelines, case conceptualization strategies, and a menu of counseling responses for prevention, early intervention, and treatment. Schwitzer's chapter is unique in that it is supplemented by journal entries and writings of contributor Constance Rhodes (author of *Life Inside the "Thin" Cage*; 2003), who writes vividly about her personal experience and recovery from ED not otherwise specified.

## Section 3: Effective Prevention and Early Intervention for Eating Disorders and Obesity

Because EDs and obesity are preventable public health concerns, this section of the book includes important chapters on prevention. Prevention is highly preferable to remediation and treatment in that prevention efforts can be successfully implemented in the childhood and adolescent period before serious problems occur. Prevention and early intervention are foundational to the practice of professional counseling, and counselors are well suited to provide prevention programs for schools and communities. This section includes two chapters on the prevention of EDs and obesity in children, two chapters on prevention in young adults and college students, and a final chapter regarding a culturally adapted guided self-help program that has demonstrated effectiveness with a community-based group of Mexican American women.

Janet A. Lydecker, Elizabeth Cotter, Rachel W. Gow, Nichole R. Kelly, and Suzanne E. Mazzeo's focus in Chapter 8 is on the prevention of obesity in children and adolescents. They provide evidence that the prevention of pediatric overweight and obesity should be a public health priority because of its potential short- and long-term medical and psychological consequences. In their chapter, the authors describe primary prevention interventions that can be implemented for all youths, including school-based interventions (changing school meals, vending machines, physical education), government policies (e.g., changing restrictions on media, food industry, pricing), and community-based interventions (e.g., food access and physical activity in local neighborhoods, addressing barriers related to culture and food or physical activity). They also examine secondary obesity prevention programs that target youths who are at risk of becoming overweight or obese. In particular, they describe the counselor's role as a behavioral specialist, using motivational interviewing strategies and family-based interventions in providing support for realistic goal setting in the areas of nutrition and physical activity.

In Chapter 9, Niva Piran discusses the importance of a counselor's role in preventing EDs in children. Because an increase in disordered eating symptoms and ED problems is occurring at younger ages, Piran asserts that preventing these problems from developing in children is far preferable to the complex treatment that is required when eating-related problems become entrenched in adolescence and early adulthood. Rather than focusing on the symptom level, Piran emphasizes the necessity of prevention programs that target the multiple systems in children's lives, including broader social forces that operate in the school and community environment. Piran details her emerging developmental theory of embodiment, which explicates the array of social experiences that shape the development of body image. After detailing this model, she then presents strategies for early intervention and prevention programs that are framed by an ecological developmental perspective.

In Chapter 10, Heather Shaw and Eric Stice address the prevention of EDs in older adolescents and young adults. After providing a thorough overview of ED prevention research, the authors highlight examples of effective universal, selective, and indicated prevention programs. Next they provide a detailed description of the Body Project, an empirically supported dissonance-based secondary prevention program in which young women at risk for EDs because of body image concerns spend four sessions critiquing the thin ideal for women through verbal, written, and behavioral exercises (Stice, Mazotti, Weibel, & Agras, 2000). The Body Project groups are highly applied and interactive, requiring participants to learn new skills through in-session exercises, homework, and increased commitment to change through participation in motivational enhancement exercises.

Deanne Zotter and Justine Reel (Chapter 11) turn readers' attention to the prevention of eating- and weight-related concerns in college and university settings. They provide a review of disordered eating behaviors and body image concerns in college and university populations, including those that occur in subpopulations most at risk for these problems: sorority women, college athletes, and students majoring in health and physical education. The authors describe research-supported prevention efforts designed specifically for university settings including Internet-based programs and tailored prevention programs for specific at-risk college-based groups.

Finalizing the section on prevention is a chapter on an indicated prevention program for individuals who have early-onset eating- or weight-related problems. In Chapter 12, Fary M. Cachelin, Munyi Shea, and Frances A.

Bono present a culturally sensitive indicated prevention program (cognitive–behavioral therapy guided self-help) for clients with early-onset bulimia nervosa and binge eating disorder. Cachelin and colleagues review the structure, contents, and counselor's role in these programs and describe how they adapted the program specifically for a group of Mexican American women. This type of early intervention is ideal for clients from diverse cultural groups who may have developed initial symptoms but might not be ready or willing to attend individual counseling.

## Section 4: Effective Treatments for Eating Disorders and Obesity

For clients who are in need of more intensive approaches than the prevention and early intervention programs described in the previous sections, Section 4 addresses the current evidence-based and recommended psychosocial outpatient treatments for EDs and obesity (APA, 2006; Wilfley et al., 2007), which are also those that are most likely to fall within counselors' scope of practice. EDs and obesity generally necessitate a multidisciplinary approach to treatment, including counseling, medical monitoring, medication, or even hospitalization. For children and adolescents, family involvement is also deemed essential (APA, 2006; Epstein, Wing, Koeske, & Valoski, 1987).

Despite these commonalities, and although many of the treatment approaches described in this section have theoretical concepts and treatment components that overlap, several distinct approaches to effective treatment exist; some require detailed attention to changing disordered eating patterns through monitoring and behavioral change projects (e.g., enhanced cognitive–behavioral therapy [CBT–E]), and others do not attend to the eating patterns at all but focus on the interpersonal problems that purportedly drive the behavior (e.g., interpersonal therapy, relational cultural therapy). It is therefore important for counselors to review the treatment approaches described here carefully, note the research findings regarding what works best for which particular subpopulation of clients, and implement the treatment only after obtaining additional reading and appropriate supervised practice.

In Chapter 13, Anthea Fursland and Hunna J. Watson focus on CBT–E (Fairburn, 2008), a treatment appropriate for all EDs because of its transdiagnostic nature. It has received strong research support in clinical and community trials, and the original cognitive–behavioral therapy (CBT) for bulimia nervosa (Fairburn, Marcus, & Wilson, 1993) is considered the gold standard treatment for bulimia nervosa and binge eating disorder (APA, 2006). In this chapter, the authors review the CBT–E model for conceptualizing EDs, describe specific strategies for addressing disordered eating (i.e., normalization of eating, elimination of diets and binges), and provide cognitive strategies to assist the client with decreasing the importance of weight and shape in determining his or her worth and value.

Heather L. Waldron, Marian Tanofsky-Kraff, and Denise E. Wilfley provide in Chapter 14 a detailed overview of interpersonal therapy as adapted for working with clients with bulimia nervosa and binge eating disorder.

Interpersonal therapy has a strong evidence base regarding its effectiveness, shows both short- and long-term effectiveness for the treatment of bulimia nervosa and binge eating disorder, and has outcomes comparable to those of CBT. The authors assert that social problems contribute to an environment in which EDs are initiated and maintained, so if a client is able to increase healthy interpersonal skills and relationships, eating-related pathology will subsequently decrease. Throughout the treatment, clients are taught to link their eating symptoms to their interpersonal functioning and then to address current interpersonal problems in one of the following four areas: interpersonal deficits, interpersonal role disputes, role transitions, and grief. The authors provide an outline of the phases of treatment, detailing the goals and techniques used during each phase.

Although other chapters also address binge eating, in Chapter 15 Kerri N. Boutelle and Stephanie Knatz address treatments specifically developed for obesity and aberrant overeating patterns (i.e., regularly eating for reasons that are not motivated by biological hunger) in overweight or obese children and adolescents. Youths who engage in these eating patterns often lack the ability to regulate their food intake, resulting in binge eating, loss-of-control eating, emotional eating, eating in secret, and eating in the absence of hunger. Boutelle and Knatz describe these categories of overeating and then provide a summary of current treatment programs for obesity and overeating that are specifically designed to address these patterns.

Many clients with EDs experience comorbid concerns such as depression, self-injury, and substance abuse (APA, 2006). The presence of multiple client issues can complicate treatment, resulting in the need for interventions designed specifically for clients with multiple mental health concerns. In Chapter 16, Anita Federici and Lucene Wisniewski, researcher and clinical director, respectively, of a dialectical behavior therapy (DBT) program in Ohio, provide an overview of treatment challenges associated with clients who present with multidiagnostic and complex EDs, many of whom have not experienced success in other treatment programs. Federici and Wisniewski provide a rationale for the use of DBT with this population, based on its affect regulation model, therapeutic stance, prioritization of clients' multiple problem behaviors, methods for increasing clients' commitment to recovery, and techniques for managing therapy-interfering behaviors. The authors highlight the implementation of their structured DBT program, providing a specific description of the program components and counseling strategies used.

Because of its typical onset in adolescence and its high potential for life-threatening medical complications, anorexia often requires an intensive treatment approach involving the entire family system. In Chapter 17, Kim Hurst and Shelly Read provide an overview of family-based therapy, the treatment approach for anorexia in children and adolescents that has garnered the most research support (APA, 2006; Bulik, Berkman, Brownley, Sedway, & Lohr, 2007; Lock, LeGrange, Agras, & Dare, 2001). The authors review family systems theory that undergirds the family-based therapy approach, including the importance of the parental executive subsystem, the reduction of blame for the disorder, and the importance of including all family members in treatment. Hurst and Read provide a practical review of treatment phases included in family-based therapy, applying the components to a case example that is woven throughout the chapter.

In the book's final chapter, Chapter 18, Heather Trepal, Ioana Boie, Victoria Kress, and Tonya Hammer review relational–cultural therapy, a feminist approach to treatment that posits that the foundation of development is connection and context, not individuation (Jordan, 2010). Relational–cultural therapy aims to heal chronic disconnection, which is proposed to be at the heart of many mental disorders, including EDs and excessive eating that can often contribute to obesity. The authors apply relational–cultural therapy's relationally focused strategies for working with clients with eating- and weight-related concerns and provide approaches for both prevention and treatment.

## Conclusion

Clearly, EDs and obesity are preventable public health concerns, and considerable efforts are necessary to prevent their initial onset and progression. Counselors are in a position to provide effective prevention programs in school, mental health, and college and university settings, and it is my hope that this book will provide them with essential resources for putting these programs into practice.

Counselors can also play a significant role in providing treatment. When prevention and early intervention is not enough, individuals who do experience EDs and obesity are in critical need of effective treatment; those who experience obesity are at risk for serious negative medical and psychosocial complications, both in childhood and in adulthood, and EDs may be fatal, are often chronic, and have high rates of remission (Wilson, Grilo, & Vitousek, 2007). Because of the frequency and potential severity of these concerns, I hope that counselors in all settings will be inspired to become actively involved in this field by seeking out additional training, professional development, and supervised practice. This book is meant to be a practical first step on this journey.

In closing, counselors can play a critical role in the prevention and treatment of EDs and obesity, and the field is certainly in need of our strong numbers, professional orientation, and clinical skills. Because we are foundationally oriented to work with clients in multiple systems and to maintain a holistic wellness focus, counselors can have a marked impact on reducing risk and ameliorating problems associated with EDs and obesity. Over time, we can help to create a healthier, balanced, and less toxic environment for future generations than the one in which we currently live.

# References

Alegria, M., Woo, M., Cao, Z., Torres, M., Meng, X. L., & Striegel-Moore, R. (2007). Prevalence and correlates of eating disorders in Latinos in the United States. *International Journal of Eating Disorders, 40*(Suppl.), S15–S21.

American Psychiatric Association. (2000). *Diagnostic and statistical manual of mental disorders* (4th ed., text rev.). Washington, DC: Author.

American Psychiatric Association. (2006). *APA practice guidelines: Treatment of patients with eating disorders, third edition.* Retrieved from http://www.psychiatryonline.com/content.aspx?aid=138866

American Psychiatric Association. (2012). *DSM–5 development.* Retrieved from http://www.dsm5.org/pages/default.aspx

Brownell, K. D., & Horgen, K. B. (2004). *Food fight: The inside story of the food industry, America's obesity crisis, and what we can do about it.* Chicago, IL: McGraw-Hill.

Bulik, C. M., Berkman, N. D., Brownley, K. A., Sedway, J. A., & Lohr, K. N. (2007). Anorexia nervosa treatment: A systematic review of randomized controlled trials. *International Journal of Eating Disorders, 40,* 310–320.

Centers for Disease Control. (2012a). *Adolescent and school health.* Retrieved from http://www.cdc.gov/healthyyouth/obesity/facts.htm

Centers for Disease Control and Prevention. (2012b). Youth Risk Behavior Surveillance—United States 2011. *MMWR: Surveillance Studies, 61*(4), 2–45.

Crow, S. J., Peterson, C. B., Swanson, S. A., Raymond, N. C., Specker, S., Eckert, E. D., & Mitchell, J. E. (2009). Increased mortality in bulimia nervosa and other eating disorders. *American Journal of Psychiatry, 166,* 1342–1346. doi:10.1176/appi.ajp.2009.09020247

Epstein, L. H., Wing, R. R., Koeske, R., & Valoski, A. (1987). Long-term effects of family-based treatment of childhood obesity. *Journal of Consulting and Clinical Psychology, 55,* 91–95.

Fairburn, C. G. (2008). *Cognitive behavior therapy and eating disorders.* New York, NY: Guilford Press.

Fairburn, C. G., Marcus, M. D., & Wilson, G. T. (1993). Cognitive–behavioral therapy for binge eating and bulimia nervosa: A comprehensive treatment manual. In C. G. Fairburn & G. T. Wilson (Eds.), *Binge eating: Nature, assessment, and treatment* (pp. 361–404). New York, NY: Guilford Press.

Flegal, K. M., Carroll, M. D., Ogden, C. L., & Curtin, L. R. (2010). Prevalence and trends in obesity among U.S. adults. *JAMA, 303,* 235–241.

Grabe, S., & Hyde, J. S. (2006). Ethnicity and body dissatisfaction among women in the United States: A meta-analysis. *Psychological Bulletin, 132,* 622–640.

Hudson, J., Hiripi, E., Pope, H. G., & Kessler, R. C. (2007). The prevalence and correlates of eating disorders in the National Comorbidity Survey replication. *Biological Psychiatry, 61,* 348–358.

Jordan, J. V. (2010). *Relational–cultural therapy*. Washington, DC: American Psychological Association.

Kelly, N. R., Mitchell, K. S., Gow, R. W., Trace, S. E., Lydecker, J. A., Bair, C. E., & Mazzeo, S. (2011). An evaluation of the reliability and construct validity of eating disorder measures in White and Black women. *Psychological Assessment, 24,* 608–617. doi:10.1037/a0026457

Lock, J., LeGrange, D., Agras, W. S., & Dare, C. (2001). *Treatment manual for anorexia nervosa: A family-based approach*. New York, NY: Guilford Press.

Maine, M., McGilley, B., & Bunnell, D. (Eds.). (2010). *Treatment of eating disorders: Bridging the research–practice gap*. New York, NY: Elsevier.

National Heart, Lung and Blood Institute. (1998). Clinical guidelines on the identification, evaluation, and treatment of overweight and obesity in adults: Executive summary. *American Journal of Clinical Nutrition, 68,* 899–917.

Ogden, C. L., Carroll, M. D., Kit, B. K., & Flegal, K. M. (2012). Prevalence of obesity and trends in body mass index among US children and adolescents, 1999–2010. *JAMA, 307,* 483–490.

Rhodes, C. (2003). *Life inside the "thin" cage: A personal look into the hidden world of the chronic dieter*. Colorado Springs, CO: Waterbrook Press.

Rodin, J., Silberstein, L., & Striegel-Moore, R. H. (1984). Women and weight: A normative discontent. In R. A. Dienstbier & T. B. Sonderegger (Eds.), *Nebraska Symposium on Motivation: Vol. 32. Psychology and gender* (pp. 267–304). Lincoln: University of Nebraska.

Stice, E., Marti, C. N., Shaw, H., & Jaconis, M. (2009). An 8-year longitudinal study of the natural history of threshold, subthreshold, and partial eating disorders from a community sample of adolescents. *Journal of Abnormal Psychology, 118,* 587–597.

Stice, E., Mazotti, L., Weibel, D., & Agras, W. S. (2000). Dissonance prevention program decreases thin-ideal internalization, body dissatisfaction, dieting, negative affect, and bulimic symptoms: A preliminary experiment. *International Journal of Eating Disorders, 27,* 206–217.

Swanson, S. A., Crow, S. J., LeGrange, D., Swendsen, J., & Merikangas, K. R. (2011). Prevalence and correlates of eating disorders in adolescents. *Archives of General Psychiatry, 68,* 714–723. doi:10.1001/archgenpsychiatry.2011.22

Wilfley, D. E., Tibbs, T. L., Van Buren, D. J., Reach, K. P., Walker, M. S., & Epstein, L. H. (2007). Lifestyle interventions in the treatment of childhood overweight: A meta-analytic review of randomized controlled trials. *Health Psychology, 26,* 521–532.

Wilson, G. T., Grilo, C. M., & Vitousek, K. M. (2007). Psychological treatment of eating disorders. *American Psychologist, 62,* 199–216.

# Acknowledgments

First, I thank the authors of all of the chapters in this book. They have truly been a pleasure to work with from start to finish, and I cannot overstate my gratitude for their cooperation and participation. Not only did they produce quality chapters that will highly benefit counselors, but they were also enthusiastic and professional in our correspondence through e-mail. I had not met most of them before this experience, but now I am very pleased to be able to call them professional colleagues.

Next, I acknowledge the writing group in which I have participated for the past 11 years. I would like to thank current members Petra Hendry and Jacqueline Bach for encouraging me to explore the idea for this book project and for supporting me throughout the process. Special thanks also go to the graduate assistants in the counselor education program at Louisiana State University who have helped with countless tasks along the way. Jennie Trocquet, the summer 2012 graduate assistant, was especially helpful in finalizing the project. I am also thankful for Carolyn Baker and her excellent team at the American Counseling Association for supporting the book from its inception to completion.

Finally, I extend my gratitude to my family, who always cheer me on in my work. I am forever grateful to my husband Michael, who is my role model and strongest supporter, and to my children Benjamin and Abigail, who try to be as understanding as possible when I spend a little too much time at the computer. I am definitely inspired by their ability to learn, write, and create on a daily basis. Benjamin and Abigail are both aspiring writers, and I am looking forward to reading their books one day!

• • •

# About the Editor

**Laura H. Choate** is an associate professor and counselor educator at Louisiana State University in Baton Rouge. Her research interests include eating disorders prevention and treatment, counseling issues and interventions for working with girls and women, college student wellness, and counselor preparation. She is the author of the 2008 book *Girls' and Women's Wellness: Contemporary Counseling Issues and Interventions*, published by the American Counseling Association. She has published numerous articles and book chapters on body image resilience and eating disorders and was the guest editor of the recent *Journal of Counseling & Development* theme issue on eating disorders prevention and treatment. She was the 2004–2006 editor of the *Journal of College Counseling* and is a three-term editorial board member of the *Journal of Counseling & Development*. She is a past recipient of the Louisiana State University Phi Kappa Phi Award for Outstanding Nontenured Faculty Member in the Humanities and Social Sciences and the American College Counseling Association Research Award. She is a licensed professional counselor in Louisiana and serves as the vice chair and the Discipline Committee chair of the Louisiana Licensed Professional Counselors Board of Examiners. She has also volunteered as an outreach presenter to more than 30 groups of girls and women in the Baton Rouge community on the topics of eating disorders prevention and sexual assault prevention. She is married to Michael Choate and is the mother of Benjamin (9) and Abigail (7). They live in Baton Rouge, Louisiana.

• • •

# About the Contributors

**Kelly C. Berg, PhD,** is a postdoctoral fellow with the Midwest Regional Postdoctoral Training Program in Eating Disorders Research and director of assessment for the Eating Disorders Research Program at the University of Minnesota. She received her doctorate in counseling psychology at the University of Minnesota after completing her predoctoral internship at the University of Chicago Medical School. Her research interests include the assessment and diagnosis of eating disorders as well as the development of innovative treatments for reducing binge eating and compensatory behaviors (Chapter 5).

**Ioana Boie, PhD,** is an assistant professor of counseling at Marymount University in Arlington, Virginia. Her clinical, research, and advocacy interests have revolved around treatment of eating disorders and body image, particularly related to multicultural issues. Other interests include clinical supervision, social justice, and immigration issues (Chapter 18).

**Frances A. Bono, MA,** has been a practicing registered dietitian for 16 years. Currently, she works as a health educator at Kaiser Permanente Hospital at the Panorama City Medical Center, Panorama City, California. Among her roles is to provide nutrition therapy to Kaiser members with eating disorders. She has also worked as a nutrition consultant for the Manick Program in Woodland Hills, California, an intensive outpatient treatment program for eating disorders, and for Clearview Treatment Programs in Westwood, California. Bono holds a Master of Arts in psychology from California State University, Los Angeles (Chapter 12).

**Kerri N. Boutelle, PhD,** is the psychological services and training director and director of behavioral services, Weight and Wellness Clinic, and associate professor of pediatrics and psychiatry at the University of California, San Diego. Boutelle has been working with youths and young adults who have weight- or eating-related issues for more than 12 years. Boutelle is the director of behavioral services of the Weight and Wellness Clinic, a clinic for youths (and their families) who struggle with their weight and leads parenting groups and provides individual and family therapy. Boutelle also sees patients in the eating disorders program for family-based and individual treatment of anorexia, bulimia, binge eating disorder, and eating disorder not otherwise specified. Boutelle's current research is focused on parenting children to reduce weight, parent and child skills for reducing binge eating, and epidemiological studies regarding adolescents who have been successful in weight loss (Chapter 15).

**Douglas Bunnell, PhD, FAED, CEDS,** is vice president of the Renfrew Center Foundation, Philadelphia, Pennsylvania, and editor of the Renfrew Center's professional journal *Perspectives*. Bunnell is a fellow of the Academy for Eating Disorders and a founder and past president of the National Eating Disorders Association. He is also a clinical advisor to the National Eating Disorders Association Navigator Program, which provides peer-to-peer support for families coping with eating disorders. A coeditor, with Margo Maine and Beth McGilley, of *Treatment of Eating Disorders: Bridging the Research–Practice Gap* (Academic Press, 2012), Bunnell maintains a private practice in Westport, CT (Chapter 2).

**Fary M. Cachelin, PhD,** received her Bachelor of Arts in psychology from Stanford University in 1988 and her doctorate in psychology from Harvard University in 1996. She has authored numerous publications on eating problems in ethnic minority populations and has received federal funding for her research to develop accessible treatments for Latinas with eating disorders. She currently is professor and chair of psychology at the University of North Carolina at Charlotte (Chapter 12).

**Jennifer Maskell Carney, PhD, LPC, NCC,** is an assistant professor of counselor education at Argosy University, Washington, DC. She has authored several articles on eating disorders advocacy and intervention and previously served as the coordinator for Eating Disorder Services at the University of Virginia Women's Center (Chapter 6).

**Caitlin Chun-Kennedy, MS,** is a doctoral student in counseling psychology at Pennsylvania State University. She has copublished several articles on college student mental health, most recently "Do Double Minority Students Face Double Jeopardy? Testing Minority Stress Theory" (*Journal of College Counseling*, 2011, with Jeffrey Hayes, Astrid Edens, and Benjamin Locke) (Chapter 1).

**Elizabeth Cotter, PhD,** is a postdoctoral research fellow at Virginia Commonwealth University. Her primary areas of interest include obesity prevention, eating disorders, and vocational psychology. She is particularly interested in the development of culturally sensitive obesity interventions that promote healthy eating and weight-related behaviors (Chapter 8).

**Anita Federici, PhD,** is a clinician and researcher in the Eating Disorder Programs at Credit Valley Hospital in Mississauga, Ontario, and St. Joseph's Healthcare in Hamilton, Ontario, Canada. She also serves as a research consultant and collaborator for the Cleveland Center for Eating Disorders, in Beachwood, Ohio. She has expertise in the application of dialectical behavior therapy and cognitive–behavioral therapy for patients with multidiagnostic eating disorder presentations, particularly those with comorbid borderline personality disorder and suicidal or self-injurious behaviors. Federici provides consultation training on dialectical behavior therapy and its adaptation to the treatment of eating disorders. Her work has been published in peer-reviewed journals and book chapters (Chapter 16).

**Anthea Fursland, PhD,** is principal clinical psychologist at the Centre for Clinical Interventions Eating Disorders Programme in Perth, Western Australia, Australia. She is a fellow of the international Academy for Eating Disorders and president of the Australia and New Zealand Academy for Eating Disorders. She also serves on the steering committee of the National Eating Disorders Collaboration and is a founding member of the Bridges Reference Group, which brings together local stakeholders in the field of eating disorders in Western Australia (Chapter 13).

**Rachel W. Gow, PhD,** is a research assistant professor in the Psychology Department at Virginia Commonwealth University. Gow's research interests are focused on the development, evaluation, and dissemination of obesity prevention and treatment interventions (Chapter 8).

**Tonya Hammer, PhD, LPC-S,** is an assistant professor of counseling at the University of Houston—Clear Lake. She has served in state leadership positions as well as national leadership positions within the American Counseling Association. Additionally, she is involved in leadership in an international organization addressing the issues of human dignity and humiliation. Among her presentations and publications are works on humiliation, controlling images, relational–cultural theory, and issues of social justice in counseling (Chapter 18).

**Mary A. Hermann, JD, PhD,** is an associate professor and chair of the Department of Counselor Education at Virginia Commonwealth University. She is a licensed attorney, a licensed professional counselor, a national certified counselor, and a certified school counselor. She has coedited two books and written numerous articles and book chapters on legal and ethical issues in counseling (Chapter 4).

**Kim Hurst, PhD,** is a senior psychologist with the Eating Disorder Program, Child and Youth Mental Health Service, on the Gold Coast, Queensland, Australia. Hurst is a founding member of the Eating Disorder Program and has been using Maudsley family-based treatment for the past 4 years. Before this, Hurst was a member of the multidisciplinary Burleigh Child and Youth Mental Health Service Continuing Care Team, Burleigh, Queensland, Australia, where she provided specialist mental health services in the areas of assessment, intervention, and treatment planning. She is currently completing her doctorate and has also published a journal article on family-based therapy for adolescent anorexia (Chapter 17).

**Nichole R. Kelly, MS,** is a doctoral student in counseling psychology at Virginia Commonwealth University. Kelly's research interests include ethnic and cultural variations in eating- and weight-related symptom-atology, binge eating etiology and treatment, and neuropsychological contributions to disordered eating (Chapter 8).

**Stephanie Knatz, PhD,** is an adolescent day treatment program therapist in the Eating Disorders Treatment and Research Program at the University of California, San Diego, Department of Psychiatry. Knatz is an advanced doctoral candidate in clinical psychology at Alliant International University. She currently provides individual, family, and group therapies to adolescents with eating disorders in the Adolescent Day Treatment Program. Her clinical and research work focuses on both eating disorders and pediatric obesity (Chapter 15).

**Victoria Kress, PhD,** is a clinic director, professor, and coordinator of the clinical mental health, addictions, and college counseling programs at Youngstown State University. She has more than 20 years of clinical experience in various settings including community mental health centers, hospitals, residential treatment facilities, private practice, and college counseling centers (Chapter 18).

**Janet A. Lydecker, MS,** is a doctoral student in counseling psychology at Virginia Commonwealth University. Her research interests include prevention and treatment of obesity and eating disorders. She is particularly interested in cognitive and cultural factors related to the development and maintenance of eating problems (Chapter 8).

**Margo Maine, PhD, FAED, CEDS,** cofounder of the Maine & Weinstein Specialty Group, is a clinical psychologist who has specialized in eating disorders and related issues for nearly 30 years. She is coeditor, with Beth McGilley and Douglas Bunnell, of *Treatment of Eating Disorders: Bridging the Research–Practice Gap* (Elsevier, 2010) and, with William Davis and Jane Shure, of *Effective Clinical Practice in the Treatment of Eating Disorders: The Heart of the Matter* (Routledge, 2009) and is author, with Joe Kelly, of *The Body Myth: Adult Women and the Pressure to Be Perfect* (Wiley, 2005); *Father Hunger: Fathers, Daughters and the Pursuit of Thinness* (Gurze, 2004); and *Body Wars: Making Peace With Women's Bodies* (Gurze, 2000). She is a senior editor of *Eating Disorders: The Journal of Treatment and Prevention.* Maine was a founding member, longtime board member, and vice president of the Eating Disorders Coalition for Research, Policy, and Action; a founding member and fellow of the Academy for Eating Disorders; and a member of the Founder's Council and past president of the National Eating Disorders Association. Maine is a member of the psychiatry departments at the Institute of Living/Hartford Hospital's Mental Health Network and Connecticut Children's Medical Center, having previously directed their eating disorders programs. Maine is the 2007 recipient of the Lori Irving Award for Excellence in Eating Disorders Awareness and Prevention, given by the National Eating Disorders Association. She lectures nationally and internationally on topics related to the treatment and prevention of eating disorders, female development, and women's health (Chapter 2).

**Jodi Manton** is a Master of Arts candidate in the Counselor Education program at Louisiana State University. She will graduate in August 2013 and plans to work with members of the military and their families (Chapter 4).

**Suzanne E. Mazzeo, PhD,** is a professor of psychology at Virginia Commonwealth University. Her research interests are in the areas of obesity and eating disorders. She has a particular interest in understanding more about environmental factors that influence expression of genetic predispositions to eating problems. She is also interested in the role of culture on eating behaviors and in developing culturally competent interventions to promote healthy eating and exercise behaviors (Chapter 8).

**Carol B. Peterson, PhD, LPC,** received her undergraduate degree from Yale University and her doctorate in clinical psychology from the University of Minnesota. She is currently a research associate and assistant professor in the Eating Disorders Research Program at the University of Minnesota, where her investigations have focused on the assessment, diagnosis, and treatment of bulimia nervosa, anorexia nervosa, binge eating disorder, and obesity. Peterson has authored more than 80 articles and book chapters and has served as an investigator on several federally funded grants. She is also an adjunct assistant professor in the Department of Psychology at the University of Minnesota and has a part-time private practice in which she specializes in the treatment of eating disorders (Chapter 5).

**Niva Piran, PhD,** professor of counseling psychology at the University of Toronto, is the recipient of the 2009 Florence Denmark Distinguished Mentorship Award from the Association of Women in Psychology. Piran's research is supported by the Social Sciences and Humanities Research Council of Canada. She is the author of three books, 40 book chapters, and 47 articles in refereed journals and guest editor of four journal special issues on eating disorders (Chapter 9).

**Leigh Pottle** is a Master of Education candidate in counselor education at Virginia Commonwealth University. She taught high school English in Williamsburg, Virginia, for 10 years and is currently an adjunct professor at Thomas Nelson Community College. She has extensive experience working with athletes at the high school level (Chapter 4).

**Shelly Read, PhD,** is a clinical psychologist and senior clinician working in the Eating Disorders Program, Child and Youth Mental Health Service, on the Gold Coast, Queensland, Australia. Since 2000, she has worked in various settings within mental health in London, England; Canberra, Australian Capital Territory, Australia; and the Gold Coast, Queensland, Australia. The majority of her clinical experience has been acquired through Child and Adolescent Mental Health, as both a clinician and team leader. Read has been specializing in the field of eating disorders for the past 5 years across two different eating disorder programs, providing specialist assessment and treatment to clients of all ages and their families. Read has also published journal articles in the areas of mental health recovery and Maudsley family-based treatment for adolescent anorexia (Chapter 17).

**Justine Reel, PhD, LPC, CC-AASP,** is an assistant professor in the Department of Health Promotion and Education at the University of Utah, a licensed professional counselor in the State of Utah, and a certified sport psychology consultant for college and Olympic athletes. She has treated clients with eating disorders across all levels of care and is currently implementing integrative eating disorder and obesity prevention programs for adolescents and their parents. She coauthored, with Katherine A. Beals, *Hidden Faces of Eating Disorders and Body Image* (2009; American Alliance for Health, Physical Education, Recreation and Dance) and was editor of *Eating Disorders: Encyclopedia of Causes, Treatment and Prevention* (2012; Greenwood), as well as 60 papers and 200 presentations on the topic of eating disorders and body image. She is the founder of and faculty advisor for SPEAK (Students Promoting Eating Disorder Awareness and Knowledge), a student organization at the University of Utah dedicated to promoting positive body image and health (Chapter 11).

**Constance Rhodes** is the author of *Life Inside the "Thin" Cage: A Personal Look Into the Hidden World of the Chronic Dieter* and *The Art of Being: Reflections on the Beauty and the Risk of Embracing Who We Are* (Waterbrook Press, 2003 and 2004, respectively). She is the founder and CEO of FINDINGbalance, Inc., a faith-based nonprofit dedicated to helping people address problematic eating and lifestyle needs. Her FINDINGbalance Web site serves nearly half a million people annually and her annual conference, Hungry for Hope, is the premiere Christian conference for eating disorders and body image issues. Rhodes previously worked in marketing and artist development in the music recording industry (Chapter 7).

**Alan M. Schwitzer, PhD,** is a licensed psychologist whose research encompasses more than 50 publications examining college and university student health and mental health needs. Schwitzer is a professor of counseling at Old Dominion University and previously worked at Virginia Commonwealth University, the University of Texas at Austin, Tulane University, and James Madison University. He has been editor of the *Journal of College Counseling* and chair of the American Counseling Association's Council of Journal Editors. Currently he is a department editor of *About Campus Magazine* and an expert reviewer for the *Journal of American College Health* and the *Journal of College Student Development*. He is the author, with Lawrence Rubin, of *Diagnosis and Treatment Planning for Mental Health Professionals: A Popular Culture Casebook Approach* (Sage, 2012) (Chapter 7).

**Heather Lewy Scott, MEd, NCC,** is a high school counselor for Fairfax County Public Schools in Virginia (Chapter 6).

**Heather Shaw, PhD,** trained at the University of Oregon and Arizona State University; she is currently a research associate at the Oregon Research Institute (Chapter 10).

**Munyi Shea, PhD,** completed her undergraduate studies at the University of Washington and received her doctorate in counseling psychology from Columbia University. She has published numerous journal articles and book chapters on ethnic minority immigrant mental health and on culturally responsive therapy and interventions. She is currently an assistant professor in the Department of Psychology at California State University, Los Angeles (Chapter 12).

**Linda Smolak, PhD,** graduated from Temple University in 1980 and is now Emerita Professor of Psychology at Kenyon College. She has published many articles on body image and eating disorders in children and adolescents. She coedited, with J. K. Thompson, *Body Image, Eating Disorders, and Obesity in Youth: Assessment, Prevention, and Treatment,* 2nd edition (American Psychological Association, 2009) and, with Thomas F. Cash, *Body Image: A Handbook of Science, Practice, and Prevention,* 2nd edition (Guilford Press, 2011) (Chapter 1).

**Eric Stice, PhD,** trained at the University of Oregon, Arizona State University, University of California, San Diego, and Stanford University; he is currently a senior research scientist at the Oregon Research Institute. His program of research focuses on understanding the risk factors for the development of eating disorders, obesity, and depression and the design of prevention programs for these public health problems (Chapter 10).

**Regine M. Talleyrand, PhD,** is an associate professor in the Counseling and Development Master of Education and Doctoral Programs in the College of Education and Human Development at George Mason University. Talleyrand's professional interests are studying mental and physical health disparities among women of color and developing culturally relevant counseling and vocational interventions for communities that have been underrepresented and underserved. She has published and presented in the areas of eating disorders in African American women, multicultural counseling, career counseling, and advising and mentoring relationships and has served as an ad hoc reviewer for the *Journal of Counseling Psychology, The Counseling Psychologist,* and the *Journal of Black Psychology* (Chapter 3).

**Marian Tanofsky-Kraff, PhD,** is an associate professor of medical and clinical psychology and clinical practicum coordinator at the Uniformed Services University of Health Sciences. Tanofsky-Kraff studies eating disorders and obesity in children and adolescents. Her research addresses the risks, protective factors, maintenance, and consequences of childhood eating disturbance and overweight, with a particular focus on binge eating and the prevention of excessive weight gain. Currently, she is studying binge eating behaviors in children and adolescents. In addition, she is piloting a psychotherapeutic program to prevent excessive weight in adolescent girls who are at high risk for adult obesity (Chapter 14).

**Heather Trepal, PhD, LPC-S,** is an associate professor in the Department of Counseling at the University of Texas at San Antonio. Her publications and clinical interests are in the areas of self-injurious behavior, relationships and relational development, gender issues in counseling, counselor preparation, supervision, and the use of technology in counseling and counselor training (Chapter 18).

**Heather L. Waldron, BS,** graduated summa cum laude from Northwestern University in 2011, with majors in psychology and journalism. She is currently clinical lab supervisor for Denise Wilfley, PhD, at Washington University in St. Louis and plans to pursue a doctorate in clinical psychology, studying treatments for eating and weight disorders (Chapter 14).

**Hunna J. Watson, PhD,** is senior research scientist at the Centre for Clinical Interventions and senior research psychologist at the eating disorders program at Princess Margaret Hospital for Children in Perth, Western Australia, Australia. She also serves on the steering committee of the National Eating Disorders Collaboration and on the management committee of Bridges, the peak eating disorders body in Western Australia, and is a past recipient of the Australian and New Zealand Academy for Eating Disorders' Peter Beumont Young Investigator Prize (Chapter 13).

**Denise E. Wilfley, PhD,** is professor of psychiatry, medicine, pediatrics, and psychology and the director of the Weight Management and Eating Disorders Program at Washington University in St. Louis. She has been awarded more than $25 million from the National Institutes of Health for a programmatic line of research examining the causes, prevention, and treatment of eating disorders and obesity among children, adolescents, and adults. She established the clinical significance of binge eating disorder and developed and tested novel interventions for recurrent binge eating and early intervention with eating disorders and obesity. She is the author of the empirically supported interpersonal therapy for binge eating disorder treatment manual and has also published more than 150 articles in the eating disorders and obesity fields (Chapter 14).

**Lucene Wisniewski, PhD, FAED,** is clinical director and cofounder of the Cleveland Center for Eating Disorders, Beachwood, Ohio, and is an adjunct assistant professor of psychology at Case Western Reserve University. Her research and clinical interests include using empirically founded treatments to inform clinical programs. She provides workshops on the cognitive–behavioral therapy and dialectical behavior therapy treatment of eating disorders nationally and publishes in peer-reviewed journals as well as invited book chapters. Wisniewski has been elected fellow and has served on the board of directors of the Academy for Eating Disorders; she is currently coleader of Academy for Eating Disorders' Borderline Personality Disorder special interest group (Chapter 16).

**Deanne Zotter, PhD,** is a professor of psychology at West Chester University of Pennsylvania. Her research interests focus on eating disorders and body image, especially the prevention of disordered eating and negative body image. She is the founder and director of the Sister to Sister Peer Mentor Program for the Prevention of Eating Disorders on the West Chester campus (Chapter 11).

Section 1

# Foundations

## Chapter 1

# Sociocultural Influences on the Development of Eating Disorders and Obesity

*Linda Smolak and Caitlin Chun-Kennedy*

Television, magazines, the Internet, and movies constantly expose people to ideal bodies, with girls and women being portrayed as thin and sexy (Levine & Murnen, 2009) and, somewhat less commonly, men as lean and muscular (McCreary, 2011). Appearance-related teasing is very common (Menzel et al., 2010). Even parents frequently comment on children's weight and body shape (Abraczinskas, Fisak, & Barnes, 2012; Fisher, Sinton, & Birch, 2009). Given all of these sources of information and perhaps pressure about what one's body should look like, it is not surprising that eating disorder (ED) researchers have investigated sociocultural factors as risk factors for the development of EDs. However, despite the ubiquitous images of ideal bodies, rates of overweight and obesity continue to increase in the United States (Ogden & Carroll, 2010). Thus, some people have wondered whether the cultural ideal has much relevance, raising the possibility that EDs are primarily biological in origin (Strober & Johnson, 2012; Sussman & Klump, 2011). However, even if genetic or neurochemical etiological factors are present in EDs, they certainly interact with environmental factors, including sociocultural influences, to shape the onset and maintenance of the disorders.

EDs, perhaps particularly anorexia nervosa, and obesity may seem like polar opposites. In fact, however, they have much in common. First, at least one form of ED, that is, binge eating disorder, is associated with an increased risk of obesity. Second, EDs and obesity share several risk factors, including body dissatisfaction and dieting, both of which are influenced by sociocultural messages. Indeed, certain sociocultural influences, including teasing about weight and parental comments, predict later overweight status among adolescents (Haines, Neumark-Sztainer, Wall, & Story, 2007; Neumark-Sztainer et al., 2006). Deeply embedded social messages about

3

the importance of being thin and the vilification of fat likely contribute to both problems. Thus, the sociocultural factors discussed in this chapter are relevant to both EDs and obesity.

In this chapter, we review the role of sociocultural influences in the development of body image disturbance and disordered eating, two of the primary risk factors for the development of EDs and obesity (Jacobi, Hayward, deZwaan, Kraemer, & Agras, 2004; Stice, 2002). *Disordered eating* refers to problematic attitudes and behaviors related to eating such as calorie-restrictive dieting, binge eating, and purging that are potentially dangerous to physical and mental health. Although we briefly discuss macro-level factors such as gender and ethnicity, our focus is media, peers, and parents as sociocultural agents. We also consider personal characteristics, particularly social comparison, thin-ideal internalization, and self-objectification, as possibly increasing the effect of these sociocultural risk factors. In the final sections of the chapter, we consider the application of the sociocultural risk factor research to counseling practice.

## Sociocultural Models of Eating Disorders and Body Image Dysfunction

In general, sociocultural models argue that culturally sanctioned messages and pressures from socialization agents are risk factors for the development of EDs. The most commonly discussed socialization agents are the media, parents, and peers. The models typically posit that there are mediating and moderating variables such as body dissatisfaction and thin-ideal internalization between the sociocultural messages and the ED outcomes. These variables allow the models to account for the fact that although most people are exposed to the messages, only some develop the problems.

Many specific models of EDs and body image disturbance (e.g., Halliwell & Harvey, 2006; Wertheim, Paxton, & Blaney, 2009) have included sociocultural variables. Most of these are revisions or expansions of Stice's (2001) Sociocultural Model or Thompson, Heinberg, Altabe, and Tantleff-Dunn's (1999) Tripartite Model. For example, the Tripartite Model suggests that three sources of thin-ideal messages (media, peers, parents) may directly contribute to disturbed body image and eating attitudes and behaviors. These sociocultural influences, which we explore in detail in this chapter, have been argued to actually help create body image and eating disturbances. Moreover, these sociocultural influences also facilitate the development of thin-ideal internalization and appearance comparisons that further heighten body image and eating dysfunction. Thin-ideal internalization and appearance comparisons therefore mediate the relationships between sociocultural variables and eating disturbances. Thus, the model includes both direct and mediated pathways. The Tripartite Model, then, helps one to understand why sociocultural factors are important and the ways in which sociocultural influences might work.

# Macro-Level Influences

Specific sources of ideal body shape information, such as the media, have certainly received the most attention in the sociocultural influences literature. However, increasing attention is being paid to what Bronfenbrenner (1977) referred to as *macro-level influences*. These influences reflect stereotypes and roles associated with social categories that shape the more specific, direct, proximal influences on development and behavior. So, for example, gender role stereotypes about the importance of attractiveness in women versus men would influence the nature of media messages (e.g., Murnen & Smolak, 2012). In addition to gender, ethnicity (Levine & Smolak, 2010) and sexual orientation (Morrison & McCutcheon, 2011) have been investigated as relevant to body image and disordered eating.

Women's gendered experience with sexual and gender harassment (e.g., Smolak & Piran, in press) as well as sexual objectification (Calogero, Tantleff-Dunn, & Thompson, 2011) have received considerable attention as relevant factors in creating both the societal messages about the ideal female body and women's vulnerability to them (see Chapter 2, this volume). Cross-cultural data have indicated that cultural definitions of an ideal body and its importance to women's identities influence body image and the likelihood of eating problems (Anderson-Fye, 2011). When these definitions begin to change, the rates of body dissatisfaction and disordered eating also change. For example, increases in bulimic, anorexic, and binge eating behavior among young women followed the introduction of Western television in Fiji (A. Becker, 2005). Apparently, the Fijian culture before Western television provided some protection against these eating disturbances. Similarly, the Black culture in the United States may be more accepting of a wider range of female body types, thus offering some protection against the restrictive EDs such as anorexia nervosa (e.g., Franko & Roehrig, 2011; see Chapter 3, this volume). However, this protection does not appear to apply to other U.S. ethnic groups (Levine & Smolak, 2010). Ethnicity and cross-cultural data have underscored the fact that different cultures may have different risks for developing eating problems. Such findings appear to be a prerequisite for arguing that sociocultural influences play a substantial etiological role in disordered eating.

Additional support for such cultural differences comes from findings concerning gay men and lesbian women. For example, gay men appear to develop eating problems more frequently than do heterosexual men. The increased rates of body dissatisfaction and disordered eating are associated with internalized homonegativity (discomfort with being gay). Stigma and discriminatory attacks may also contribute to gay men's body image disturbances (Morrison & McCutcheon, 2011). All of these factors are specific representations of broad cultural definitions and stereotypes of what it means to be gay.

# Specific Sociocultural Risk Factors

It is widely agreed that experimental or prospective data are needed to establish a characteristic or experience as a risk factor (Kraemer et al., 1997). Such data are available for media, parent, and peer influences on body image and disordered eating, although they are much more commonly found for media than for parental or peer factors. Thus, an empirical basis exists for arguing that these sociocultural factors play a role in the development and maintenance of body dissatisfaction, disordered eating, and EDs, although fewer data are available regarding their relationship with EDs.

## *Media*

*Media* is a broad term referring to television, magazines, Internet sites, and sometimes toys and games. If the media influence people's body image, then the evidence must suggest that Americans use media and absorb their messages (Levine & Murnen, 2009). Research has continued to indicate that Americans are exposed to television beginning in infancy and the preschool years. Most Americans watch television daily. For example, American children ages 8 years and younger watch about 1 hour and 44 minutes of television daily, and teens watch nearly 3.5 hours (Media Literacy Clearinghouse, 2012). Children age 8 years and younger play on the computer 25 minutes per day, and teens use either the computer or video games more than 1.5 hours daily (Media Literacy Clearinghouse, 2012). By early adolescence, at least 60% of girls are reading teen magazines that feature articles on being thin and sexy to attract boys (Field et al., 1999; Ward, 2003). Media use, then, is multifaceted, with the various sources (television, Internet, video games, magazines) reinforcing each other's messages. Moreover, use is common and extensive, beginning in early childhood.

Media images are unrealistic. Women are disproportionately portrayed as thin, tall, young, and White (Levine & Murnen, 2009). Such portrayals are evident even in media aimed at young children (e.g., Klein & Shiffman, 2006). Women in the media are also often sexually objectified, that is, presented as objects to be looked at and enjoyed by men for men's sexual pleasure (Murnen & Smolak, 2012; Stankiewicz & Rosselli, 2008). Women are encouraged to buy diet products, exercise programs, anti-aging products such as Botox, makeup, and other products to try to achieve this ideal. Thus, women (and men) are consistently given the impression that the ideal is not a fantasy but is rather an attainable reality for those who simply invest enough time, energy, effort, and money. The message is that women can control their appearance, and women with EDs may take this message very seriously.

Furthermore, heavier women are actively punished by the media. For example, Fouts and Burgraff (2000) found that heavier women were more likely to be disparaged in situation comedies, whereas female characters who are thinner than average receive more positive comments. In addition, heavier women make more negative comments about their own bodies and weight. These messages reflect and reinforce women's desire not to be fat. However, men's bodies are portrayed more diversely in the media, with some featured male actors being heavy and others quite thin. Many fall in the average size range. However, it is increasingly clear that lean muscularity is the ideal shape (McCreary, 2011). Indeed, entertainment magazines and television shows routinely feature male celebrities with six-pack abs.

Does exposure to these unrealistic media body ideals actually affect attitudes or behaviors? Several meta-analyses have documented small to moderate relationships between media use and various aspects of disordered eating attitudes and behavior among women. For example, Grabe, Ward, and Hyde (2008), examining 77 different studies, found significant relationships between media exposure and thin-ideal internalization, body dissatisfaction, and eating behaviors and beliefs (such as anorectic cognitions, dieting, and purging) among girls and women. The relationship between media exposure and body dissatisfaction was particularly consistent across studies. In another meta-analysis, girls and women with preexisting levels of body dissatisfaction were more susceptible to media effects in experimental studies (Want, 2009). Both the Grabe et al. and the Want (2009) meta-analyses found adolescent and adult women to be similarly influenced by the media in terms of appearance satisfaction. Furthermore, prospective research has found that girls as young as 5 years old may experience greater appearance dissatisfaction when they watch more appearance-oriented television (Dohnt & Tiggemann, 2006).

Exposure to such a consistent message starting at such a young age may lead people to assume that the content is normative (cultivation theory; Gerbner, Gross, Morgan, & Signorelli, 1994). In other words, girls and boys who grow up on thin-ideal messages come to believe that most women are thin and sexy and that virtually all women could look this way. They do not critique or even question this message. When women internalize this sexually objectified thin ideal and adopt it as a standard for judging themselves, their self-esteem is endangered and they are at increased risk of developing eating pathology and depression (Moradi & Yu-Ping, 2008). This image, then, becomes part of how girls and women process social and personal information. For example, innocent comments from parents and peers might be interpreted as indicative of how close a girl is to the ideal.

Men and boys are not immune to media effects. At least two relevant relationships between media and body image among boys and men deserve attention. First, boys see the same images of women that girls see. Thus, these images may contribute to boys' impression of what girls should look like; indeed, adolescent boys prefer thinner girls (Paxton, Norris, Wertheim, Durkin, & Anderson, 2005). Such exposure to the thin ideal might also increase the likelihood of peer teasing of girls by boys.

Second, media exposure to the ideal lean and muscular male body type has negative effects on men's and boys' body image. A meta-analysis of both experimental and correlational studies has indicated a significant relationship between media exposure and negative body image (Barlett, Vowels, & Saucier, 2008). The effect might be larger for college-age men than for teenage boys. Furthermore, exposure to the muscular ideal is associated with poorer self-esteem, more depression and EDs, and greater use of problematic body-change strategies such as taking food supplements or dieting (Barlett et al., 2008).

## Parents

It would be nice to title this section *Family,* thereby recognizing the influence of siblings, grandparents, and other important but nonparental family members. However, the sociocultural literature has clearly focused on parents and has largely neglected siblings and other family members. Studies have, of course, examined family dysfunction (e.g., conflicts, emotional atmosphere). Family dysfunction does not, however, necessarily involve socially sanctioned messages about the body and so is not generally considered part of sociocultural influences.

Two forms of parental influence have received considerable attention. Parents might model body image and eating problems. They might, for example, engage in dieting or make negative comments about their own bodies. Parents also comment on their children's bodies, with some evidence suggesting girls receive more remarks than boys, especially from their mothers (e.g., Smolak, Levine, & Schermer, 1999). A recent principal-components analysis using measures from numerous studies has confirmed the existence of these two separate forms of parental influence (Abraczinskas et al., 2012).

Both parental modeling and direct comments have been related to a wide range of body image and eating problems, including bulimic symptoms (e.g., Abraczinskas et al., 2012; Hanna & Bond, 2006; Smolak et al., 1999). The data have been more consistent in linking direct comments to eating pathology. Most of the data are cross-sectional, although some longitudinal data exist. More limited research has suggested that boys may also be affected by parental pressure to achieve a better body (e.g., Ricciardelli, McCabe, Lillis, & Thomas, 2006). For both boys and girls, some studies have found no relationship between parental influences and disordered eating or body image concerns (e.g., Byely, Archibald, Graber, & Brooks-Gunn, 2000; Smolak & Stein, 2010). Thus, although parents likely influence body image and disordered eating, the precise mechanism of this influence is unclear. Specifically, because not all children exposed to parental modeling or body-related comments develop body image or eating problems, variables must exist that mediate or moderate the parental influence–disordered eating relationship. These variables need to be better identified.

Fisher et al. (2009) also examined some data on parental control of young children's eating patterns. If parents try to limit what children eat or require children to eat certain foods or use food as a reward, research has suggested that the children may lose some of their ability to respond to natural hunger cues. These children are at greater risk for developing eating problems (e.g., overeating, becoming overweight) both in early childhood and later.

## Peers

Peer influence may take a variety of forms. Peers may model body dissatisfaction and pathological eating. Some of this is traditional modeling, with people observing and learning behavior, as when sorority sisters learn binge eating from each other (Crandall, 1988) or, more positively, when they observe peer role models who choose not to engage in problematic eating behavior (C. B. Becker, Ciao, & Smith, 2008). They may also model attitudes in conversations, including "fat talk." Peers also make direct comments to each other about weight and shape, including teasing. All of these phenomena have been related to body image concerns or disordered eating. However, the data are often limited (e.g., to particular age groups or to one gender), or the results are inconsistent. In the subsequent paragraphs, we describe these three primary forms of peer influence on body image and disordered eating: modeling, attitudes in conversations, and teasing.

Among girls, friends do tend to share body-related attitudes and so may encourage each other to diet or engage in other weight control behaviors (Wertheim et al., 2009). Girls who have friends who diet are more likely to diet. Friends may form a "peer appearance culture" that affects emphasis on appearance as well as the adoption of methods to attain a desired appearance (Jones, 2004). These trends have been found in preadolescent and adolescent samples. In fact, even 5- to 8-year-old girls who think their peers want to be thin are more likely to want to be thin themselves (Dohnt & Tiggemann, 2006). Cognitive schema, likely rooted in earlier experiences with appearance-related pressures, and social comparisons have been found to mediate the relationship between peer pressures and body concerns among girls.

Appearance-related conversations may also negatively influence girls' body image. Among young elementary school students, girls who participate in such discussions concurrently have lower appearance satisfaction (Dohnt & Tiggemann, 2006). Jones (2004) reported that conversations predicted body dissatisfaction 1 year later. However, Clark and Tiggemann (2008) did not find such a relationship. Research with primarily college women has demonstrated that fat talk is an expected behavior (Britton, Martz, Bazzini, Curtin, & LeaShomb, 2006). Salk and Engeln-Maddox (2011) reported that 93% of their university sample engaged in fat talk at least occasionally and that it was associated with higher body dissatisfaction and thin-ideal internalization.

Peer teasing has also been related to body dissatisfaction and disordered eating. For example, 10-year-old Swedish girls who were teased and bullied more frequently (including appearance teasing) tended to have lower weight esteem at age 13 (Lunde, Frisén, & Hwang, 2007) and more appearance monitoring and body shame at age 18 (Lunde & Frisén, 2011). Although heavier girls are more likely to be teased, the relationship between being teased and poorer body image exists independently of body mass index (Wertheim et al., 2009).

Boys, too, may be negatively affected by peer pressure and teasing. However, in studies that have included both genders, peer effects appear to be more limited for boys (e.g., Jones, 2004; Lunde & Frisén, 2011; Lunde et al., 2007). This finding may reflect methodological issues, especially when general body dissatisfaction measures are used as outcomes (Ricciardelli et al., 2006). Much more research is needed to understand how peers affect boys' body image and body change strategies.

### Mediators and Moderators

A mediator is a variable (e.g., internalization of the thin ideal) that develops from a preliminary predictor variable (e.g., media use) and then in turn influences the final outcome variable (e.g., body dissatisfaction). A moderator, however, predates the predictor variable. Ethnicity and gender are commonly used as moderators, but personal variables such as social comparison have also been investigated. Some variables, including social comparison and internalization of thin ideal, have been investigated as both mediators and moderators. The role of some characteristics may change during development or differ by context. So, for example, social comparison tendencies may increase girls' attention to media images but may also be intensified by watching television characters who compare themselves with others and magazines that offer to "improve" the readers' appearance.

Numerous characteristics have been shown to influence the relationships between sociocultural factors and eating dysfunction in at least some studies with both genders (e.g., Blashill, 2011; McCreary, 2011; Smolak & Stein, 2010; Wertheim et al., 2009). These characteristics include gender role, social comparison, body dissatisfaction, thin-ideal internalization, sexual orientation, self-esteem, perfectionism, and autonomy. Although the research on any one moderator or mediator is typically mixed, the literature has indeed supported the argument that the relationships between sociocultural variables and disordered eating are best understood as involving other psychosocial and demographic (and hence cultural) characteristics.

# Recommendations for Counselors

### Conceptualization of Eating Disorders

Debate is ongoing as to the role of genetic and neurochemical factors versus sociocultural factors in the development and maintenance of EDs. The evidence we review in this chapter has clearly suggested that cultural definitions of ideal body shape, as conveyed and enforced by the media, parents, and peers, contribute to EDs in many cases. Pressure from these social forces facilitates the development of important risk factors for EDs, especially body dissatisfaction and thin-ideal internalization (e.g., Wertheim et al., 2009). Sociocultural factors have been directly linked to symptoms of EDs (e.g., dietary restriction, binge eating, or purging). The idea that this perfect body is attainable may also mesh with the need for control that is part of many EDs. However, personality characteristics (e.g., high negative affect or high need for approval) and neurochemistry, both of which may be genetically influenced, also likely increase vulnerability to these messages (Kaye, Fudge, & Paulus, 2009; Strober & Johnson, 2012). Trauma, which may alter neurochemistry, may also make people more vulnerable to social messages emphasizing self-control of one's body (Smolak, 2011).

Thus, EDs are likely best conceptualized as having biological, psychological, social, and cultural risk factors and components. Because this chapter is focused on the sociocultural risk factors, we limit our comments concerning treatment to those factors. First, clients should be encouraged to examine their assumptions about the normative nature of thinness (or, for men, muscularity). As part of this, they should examine the sources of those beliefs. People often underestimate the influence of the media and particularly the media's impact on them. The evidence concerning media effects is especially strong for body image dysfunction. Thus, body image issues should be clearly integrated into ED treatment, an integration that is actually fairly rare in the existing literature. Cognitive–behavioral approaches may then be useful to undermine the belief system that thinness (or muscularity) is important to success and self-worth (Jarry & Cash, 2011).

Second, given that the environment fosters body image and eating problems, changes in the sociocultural milieu may be useful in treating or preventing EDs. For example, women might be encouraged to make conscious choices about watching television shows that glorify thinness or to at least recognize the unrealistic, damaging messages these shows send. In addition, feminist theorists have often suggested that women actually challenge these messages, an exercise that facilitates a sense of control in addition to possibly removing or limiting some of the toxic messages (Smolak & Piran, in press).

### Assessment

Several assessment tools are available to evaluate exposure to and investment in media, parent, or peer factors. By far the most commonly used media measure is the Sociocultural Attitudes Toward Appearance Questionnaire (Thompson, van den Berg, Roehrig, Guarda, & Heinberg, 2004). Its Internalization subscale is particularly widely used to measure how much someone has adopted the media standards as their own. Internalization is a more critical variable in the development of disordered eating than is sheer exposure (Thompson & Stice, 2001). Versions of this scale are available for use with women, men, adolescents, and athletes. It is short, the questions are easy to answer, and it is widely available.

The McKnight Risk Factor Survey (Shisslak et al., 1999) has subscales for parents and peers as well as media influences. Stice's 10-question measure of sociocultural pressures focuses on peer and parent influence (Stice &

Bearman, 2001). A relatively new scale to measure parental modeling and direct comments separately is also available (Abraczinskas et al., 2012). The Perception of Teasing Scale (Thompson, Cattarin, Fowler, & Fisher, 1995) can be used to retrospectively assess a client's exposure to teasing. It also measures the respondent's reaction to these experiences. This measure may be helpful in identifying people whose body image and body self-esteem were shaped by negative peer and parent comments about weight and shape.

# Case Example

Typically, the foci of ED treatment are individual pathologies such as body image distortion or impulse control problems. However, if sociocultural influences are major factors in the development and maintenance of EDs, then addressing these influences in therapy may facilitate recovery. In the case of Sarah, we illustrate the importance of sociocultural factors in the development and maintenance of an ED.

### Presenting Concern

Sarah is a White, female, heterosexual 1st-year college student who is majoring in psychology with a 3.5 GPA. Sarah is the youngest of three siblings, and she has two older sisters. Her parents are married and live together about an hour away from the university Sarah attends.

Sarah reports to her counselor that she is very upset about a recent break-up with her boyfriend. They had been dating for about 1 year, and they broke up after Sarah started becoming more distant and withdrawn. Sarah noted that this was her first romantic relationship, and she is devastated about its ending. She reports symptoms including decreased energy, difficulty concentrating, low motivation, and feelings of sadness and worthlessness. With some reluctance, Sarah also discloses that she has been dieting recently to lose weight, and she thinks it is becoming out of control. In addition to dieting, she also reports that she occasionally binges on ice cream, cookies, cereal, and pasta. Although Sarah denies purging through vomiting or laxatives, she reports that she will exercise obsessively after a binge.

### Background

Sarah's parents are married, and she reports having positive relationships with her parents and two older sisters. Sarah states that she was always an active child, and she played soccer and ran cross country in high school. Although Sarah was a strong athlete, her mother was concerned that Sarah was overweight and needed to slim down to be more competitive. In high school, Sarah's mother enrolled them both in Weight Watchers, and Sarah lost 15 pounds. Sarah's older sisters, who had always referred to her as their chubby little sister, stopped teasing her and complimented Sarah on her weight loss. When Sarah arrived at college, she had difficulty adjusting to a life without structure, family meals, and organized sports. As a 1st-year student, Sarah also struggled to transition to the college environment, including living with a roommate and learning to be more self-sufficient. She engaged in frequent social comparisons, particularly regarding weight, body image, and eating patterns. She began bingeing to comfort herself when she felt lonely at college and used exercise to compensate for her binges. Sarah's relationship with her boyfriend became strained by her disordered eating and negative body image, and she blames herself for their relationship ending. Sarah's perfectionistic tendencies helped her to excel in sports and academics but now seem to be contributing to her desire to lose weight and attain her vision of an ideal body.

## Sociocultural Model Applied to Client

Several examples of sociocultural influences are seen in Sarah's case. First, Sarah's interest in reading fashion magazines at the gym and watching reality shows about modeling may make her vulnerable to thin-ideal messages. In counseling, she reports that she has always enjoyed reading fashion magazines and that she often compares her body with those of the models and believes she comes up short. Second, Sarah's relationships with her siblings are characterized by criticism and competitiveness. Sarah describes her older sisters as successful, and she has always tried to prove herself to be as smart, athletic, and attractive as them. Sarah believes that her siblings have always been supportive of her, but she notes that when they teased her about being chubby she felt very hurt, lonely, and rejected. Third, Sarah's relationship with her mother is complicated because they were involved in dieting and weight loss efforts together. Although Sarah believes this brought her closer to her mother, it may also have contributed to her eating concerns by modeling unhealthy dieting behavior. Thus, Sarah has felt pressure from both the media and her family. Her tendency to be a perfectionist has likely contributed to her sensitivity to these pressures and to her desire to attain the ideal body.

## Recommendations for Treatment

Sarah may benefit from a cognitive–behavioral approach that examines her distorted thinking related to body image. This approach is currently the most popular one used to treat EDs (Fairburn, 2008; Jarry & Cash, 2011) and is also part of a very effective approach to prevention (e.g., C. B. Becker et al., 2008). Sarah appears to have developed some unhealthy ways of thinking about her body, she engages in frequent comparisons, and she has low self-esteem. A cognitive–behavioral approach can, for example, encourage Sarah to challenge and replace her negative beliefs about herself as the overweight runner or the chubby little sister. This approach can also help Sarah to critically examine the media sources she consumes and how these sociocultural influences affect her beliefs about her body and appearance.

Sarah may benefit from an interpersonal approach that examines her relationships with significant others and the counselor. Sarah's relationship with her boyfriend may have been characterized by anxiety about emotional closeness, and this pattern may also emerge in her relationship with her counselor. For example, an interpersonal approach could encourage Sarah to practice in counseling how to talk about her difficult emotions without fear of being rejected or dismissed, as she felt she was growing up in her family of origin.

Sarah may benefit from a family systems approach that addresses the family dynamics that have contributed to her eating concerns. A timeline approach might be helpful in determining how specific events and relationships may have made her more vulnerable to developing eating and body image concerns. For example, a family systems approach can encourage Sarah to examine how receiving negative messages about her body from her mother and sisters may have contributed to her body image disturbance.

## Conclusion

For many people, EDs are marked by an overwhelming desire to attain an ideal body shape, a body that they think self-control can provide. Sociocultural messages from the media, peers, and parents have been empirically demonstrated to contribute to beliefs about the importance and achievement of this perfect body. These ubiquitous messages are remarkable for how early they appear and how consistent they are. This is especially true for girls and women; an emphasis on appearance is part of the feminine gender role. Although sociocultural factors alone likely do not explain most cases of EDs, they probably play a significant role. More research is needed to specify how these processes work. Research is needed that examines the pathways of development from early exposure to the messages to the adoption of the ideal to body image disturbance and EDs. Investigators need to include a variety of ages and ethnic groups and both genders in their samples.

These messages are culturally constructed. Thus, they are not a necessary part of the human experience. They can be changed. This change can occur on an individual level, as when cognitive schema are altered in cognitive–behavioral therapy or when feminist therapy encourages active resistance to the messages. However, actually altering the culture to change the acceptability and presence of these portrayals of women and their bodies is also possible. Teasing can be stopped. Consumers can convince advertisers and companies to use different marketing techniques. Research on how such changes affect the development and maintenance of body image disturbance and EDs will be important.

## Chapter Highlights

- Cultural, ethnic group, gender, and sexual identification differences in rates and types of body image concerns, disordered eating patterns, and EDs all suggest that sociocultural factors play a role in the development of these psychological problems.

- Eating disorders and obesity share some risk factors, including body dissatisfaction, child sexual and physical abuse, and dieting that is designed and initiated without medical advice. In turn, factors that create body dissatisfaction and dieting may contribute to both EDs and obesity.
- Correlational, experimental, and longitudinal data have all supported a relationship between the media and risk factors for EDs, including thin-ideal internalization, body dissatisfaction, and weight control behaviors. Data have linked media and these problems among women, men, and adolescents. Black Americans may be less affected than other ethnic groups.
- Parental modeling and comments may affect children's body image and disordered eating. Although both boys and girls are affected, the effects may be greater for girls. Maternal comments may commonly be more influential. Parents' comments to children about their weight or shape seem more important than modeling.
- Parental attempts to exercise control over the child's eating may actually facilitate disordered (especially disinhibited) eating and obesity.
- Peers too may make direct comments or model disordered eating. Indeed, peers may form a culture in which body dissatisfaction, dieting, and other forms of body-change techniques are common.
- Peers frequently tease each other about appearance. Weight- and shape-related teasing is common. Research has linked such teasing to body image and eating problems.
- Fat talk is another form of peer interaction related to body image problems. Fat talk is socially expected among women, underscoring the link between appearance (including thinness) and feminine gender role.
- Some direct effects of media, parents, and peers on disordered eating likely exist. That many of the effects are moderated or mediated, particularly by tendencies toward social comparison or thin-ideal internalization, is also likely.
- Eating disorders are likely the result of complex interactions among biological (e.g., genetic), psychological (e.g., personality), and social (e.g., media influence) factors. The interplay among these contributors is currently poorly understood.
- Sociocultural factors should be integrated into the treatment and prevention of EDs, body image dysfunction, and disordered eating.

## Recommended Resources

### *Books*

Agras, W. S. (Ed.). (2010). *The Oxford handbook of eating disorders.* New York, NY: Oxford University Press.

Cash, T. F., & Smolak, L. (Eds.). (2011). *Body image: A handbook of science, practice, and prevention* (2nd ed.). New York, NY: Guilford Press.

Smolak, L., & Thompson, J. K. (Eds.) (2009). *Body image, eating disorders, and obesity in youth: Assessment, prevention, and treatment* (2nd ed.). Washington, DC: American Psychological Association.

### Web Sites

- Eating Disorders Coalition for Research, Policy, and Action
  http://www.eatingdisorderscoalition.org
- National Association of Anorexia Nervosa and Associated Disorders
  http://www.anad.org
- National Eating Disorders Association
  http://www.NationalEatingDisorders.org
  This group sponsors Eating Disorders Awareness Week.
- National Eating Disorder Information Center
  http://www.nedic.ca/ and http://www.nedic.caMirror-mirror.org

## References

Abraczinskas, M., Fisak, B., & Barnes, R. (2012). The relation between parental influence, body image, and eating behavior in a nonclinical female sample. *Body Image, 9,* 93–100.

Anderson-Fye, E. (2011). Body images in non-Western cultures. In T. F. Cash & L. Smolak (Eds.), *Body image: A handbook of science, practice, and prevention* (2nd ed., pp. 244–252). New York, NY: Guilford Press.

Barlett, C. P., Vowels, C. L., & Saucier, D. A. (2008). Meta-analyses of the effects of media images on men's body-image concerns. *Journal of Social and Clinical Psychology, 27,* 279–310.

Becker, A. (2005). *Body, self, and society: The view from Fiji.* Philadelphia: University of Pennsylvania.

Becker, C. B., Ciao, A., & Smith, L. (2008). Moving from efficacy to effectiveness in eating disorders prevention: The Sorority Body Image Program. *Cognitive and Behavioral Practice, 15,* 18–27.

Blashill, A. (2011). Gender roles, eating pathology, and body dissatisfaction in men: A meta-analysis. *Body Image, 8,* 1–11.

Britton, L., Martz, D., Bazzini, D., Curtin, L., & LeaShomb, A. (2006). Fat talk and self-presentation of body image: Is there a social norm for women to self-degrade? *Body Image, 3,* 244–250.

Bronfenbrenner, U. (1977). Toward an experimental ecology of human development. *American Psychologist, 32,* 513–531.

Byely, L., Archibald, A. B., Graber, J. A., & Brooks-Gunn, J. (2000). A prospective study of familial and social influences on girls' body image and dieting. *International Journal of Eating Disorders, 28,* 155–164.

Calogero, R., Tantleff-Dunn, S., & Thompson, J. K. (Eds.). (2011). *Self-objectification in women: Causes, consequences, and counteractions.* Washington, DC: American Psychological Association.

Clark, L., & Tiggemann, M.(2008). Sociocultural and individual psychological predictors of body image in young girls: A prospective study. *Developmental Psychology, 44,* 1124–1134.

Crandall, C. (1988). Social contagion of binge eating. *Journal of Personality and Social Psychology, 55,* 588–598.

Dohnt, H. K., & Tiggemann, M. (2006). The contribution of peer and media influences to the development of body satisfaction and self-esteem in young girls: A prospective study. *Developmental Psychology, 42,* 929–936.

Fairburn, C. (2008). *Cognitive behavior therapy and eating disorders.* New York, NY: Guilford Press.

Field, A., Cheung, L., Wolf, A., Herzog, D., Gortmaker, S., & Colditz, G. (1999). Exposure to the mass media and weight concerns among girls. *Pediatrics, 103,* e36.

Fisher, J. O., Sinton, M., & Birch, L. L. (2009). Early experience with food and eating: Influencing risk for the development of disordered eating and problems of energy balance. In L. Smolak & J. K. Thompson (Eds.), *Body image, eating disorders, and obesity in youth: Assessment, treatment, and prevention* (2nd ed., pp. 17–33*).* Washington, DC: American Psychological Association.

Fouts, G., & Burgraff, K. (2000). Television situation comedies: Female weight, male negative comments, and audience reactions. *Sex Roles, 42,* 925–932.

Franko, D., & Roehrig, J. (2011). African American body images. In T. F. Cash & L. Smolak (Eds.), *Body image: A handbook of science, practice, and prevention* (2nd ed., pp. 221–228). New York, NY: Guilford Press.

Gerbner, G., Gross, L., Morgan, M., & Signorelli, N. (1994). Growing up with television: The cultivation perspective. In J. Bryant & D. Zillmann (Eds.), *Media effects: Advances in theory and research* (pp. 17–41). Hillsdale, NJ: Erlbaum.

Grabe, S., Ward, L. M., & Hyde, J. S. (2008). The role of the media in body image concerns among women: A meta-analysis of experimental and correlational studies. *Psychological Bulletin, 134,* 460–476.

Haines, J., Neumark-Sztainer, D., Wall, M., & Story, M. (2007). Personal, behavioral, and environmental risk and protective factors for adolescent overweight. *Obesity, 15,* 2748–2760.

Halliwell, E., & Harvey, M. (2006). Examination of a sociocultural model of disordered eating about male and female adolescents. *British Journal of Health Psychology, 11,* 235–248.

Hanna, A. C., & Bond, M. J. (2006). Relationships between family conflict, perceived maternal verbal messages, and daughters' disturbed eating symptomatology. *Appetite, 47,* 205–211.

Jacobi, C., Hayward, C., deZwaan, M., Kraemer, H., & Agras, W. S. (2004). Coming to terms with risk factors for eating disorders: Application of risk terminology and suggestions for a general taxonomy. *Psychological Bulletin, 130,* 19–65.

Jarry, J., & Cash, T. (2011). Cognitive–behavioral approaches to body image change. In T. F. Cash & L. Smolak (Eds.), *Body image: A handbook of science, practice, and prevention* (2nd ed., pp. 415–423). New York, NY: Guilford Press.

Jones, D. C. (2004). Body image among adolescent girls and boys: A longitudinal study. *Developmental Psychology, 40,* 823–835.

Kaye, W., Fudge, J., & Paulus, M. (2009). New insights into symptoms and neurocircuit function of anorexia nervosa. *Nature Reviews Neuroscience, 10,* 573–584.

Klein, H., & Shiffman, K. (2006). Messages about physical attractiveness in animated cartoons. *Body Image, 3,* 353–363.

Kraemer, H. C., Kazdin, A. E., Offord, D. R., Kessler, R. C., Jensen, P. S., & Kupfer, D. J. (1997). Coming to terms with the terms of risk. *Archives of General Psychiatry, 54,* 337–343,

Levine, M. P., & Murnen, S. K. (2009). "Everybody knows that mass media are/are not (pick one) a cause of eating disorders": A critical review of evidence for a causal link between media, negative body image, and disordered eating in females. *Journal of Social & Clinical Psychology, 28,* 9–42.

Levine, M. P., & Smolak, L. (2010). Cultural influences on body image and the eating disorders. In W. S. Agras (Ed.), *The Oxford handbook of eating disorders* (pp. 223–246). New York, NY: Oxford University Press.

Lunde, C., & Frisén, A. (2011). On being victimized by peers in the advent of adolescence: Prospective relationships to objectified body consciousness. *Body Image, 8,* 309–314.

Lunde, C., Frisén, A., & Hwang, C. P. (2007). Ten-year-old girls' and boys' body composition and peer victimization experiences: Prospective associations with body satisfaction. *Body Image, 4,* 11–28.

McCreary, D. (2011). Body image and muscularity. In T. F. Cash & L. Smolak (Eds.), *Body image: A handbook of science, practice, and prevention* (2nd ed., pp. 198–205). New York, NY: Guilford Press.

Media Literacy Clearinghouse. (2012). *Media use statistics.* Retrieved April 24, 2012, from http://www.frankwbaker.com/mediause.htm.

Menzel, J., Schaefer, L., Burke, N., Mayhew, L., Brannick, M., & Thompson, J. K. (2010). Appearance-related teasing, body dissatisfaction, and disordered eating: A meta-analysis. *Body Image, 7,* 261–270.

Moradi, B., & Yu-Ping, H. (2008). Objectification theory and psychology of women: A decade of advances and future directions. *Psychology of Women Quarterly, 32,* 377–398.

Morrison, T. G., & McCutcheon, J. (2011). Gay and lesbian body images. In T. F. Cash & L. Smolak (Eds.), *Body image: A handbook of science, practice, and prevention* (2nd ed., pp. 214–220). New York, NY: Guilford Press.

Murnen, S. K., & Smolak, L. (2012). Social considerations related to adolescents girls' sexual empowerment. *Sex Roles, 66,* 725–735.

Neumark-Sztainer, D., Wall, M., Guo, J., Story, M., Haines, J., & Eisenberg, M. (2006). Obesity, disordered eating, and eating disorders in a longitudinal study of adolescents: How do dieters fare 5 years later? *Journal of the American Dietetic Association, 106,* 599–568.

Ogden, C., & Carroll, M. (2010). *Prevalence of overweight, obesity, and extreme obesity among adults: United States, trends 1960–1962 through 2007–2008.* Retrieved February 16, 2012, from http://www.cdc.gov/nchs/data/hestat/obesity_adult_07_08/obesity_adult_07_08.pdf

Paxton, S. J., Norris, M., Wertheim, E. H., Durkin, S. J., & Anderson, J. (2005). Body dissatisfaction, dating and importance of thinness to attractiveness in adolescent girls. *Sex Roles, 53,* 663–675.

Ricciardelli, L., McCabe, M., Lillis, J., & Thomas, K. (2006). A longitudinal investigation of the development of weight and muscle concerns among pre-adolescent boys. *Journal of Youth and Adolescence, 35,* 177–187.

Salk, R., & Engeln-Maddox, R. (2011). "If you're fat then I'm humongous!": Content and impact of fat talk among college women. *Psychology of Women Quarterly, 35,* 8–28.

Shisslak, C. M., Renger, R., Sharpe, T., Crago, M., McKnight, K. M., Gray, N., . . . Taylor, C. B. (1999). Development and evaluation of the McKnight Risk Factor Survey for assessing potential risk and protective factors for disordered eating in preadolescent and adolescent girls. *International Journal of Eating Disorders, 25,* 195–214.

Smolak, L. (2011). Sexual abuse and body image. In T. F. Cash & L. Smolak (Eds.). *Body image: A handbook of science, practice, and prevention* (2nd ed., pp. 119–128). New York, NY: Guilford Press.

Smolak, L., Levine, M. P., & Schermer, F. (1999). Parental input and weight concerns among elementary school children. *International Journal of Eating Disorders, 25,* 263–271.

Smolak, L., & Piran, N. (in press). Gender and the prevention of eating disorders. In G. McVey, B. Ferguson, M. Levine, & N. Piran (Eds.), *Improving the prevention of eating-related disorders: Collaborative research, advocacy, and policy change.* Waterloo, Ontario, Canada: Wilfred Laurier University Press.

Smolak, L., & Stein, J. A. (2010). A longitudinal investigation of gender role and muscle building in adolescent boys. *Sex Roles, 63,* 738–746.

Stankiewicz, J. M., & Rosselli, F. (2008). Women as sex objects and victims in print advertisements. *Sex Roles, 58,* 579–589.

Stice, E. (2001). A prospective test of the dual-pathway model of bulimic pathology: Mediating effects of dieting and negative affect. *Journal of Abnormal Psychology, 110,* 124–135.

Stice, E. (2002). Risk and maintenance factors for eating pathology: A meta-analytic review. *Psychological Bulletin, 128,* 825–848.

Stice, E., & Bearman, S. K. (2001). Body image and eating disturbances prospectively predict growth in depressive symptoms in adolescent girls: A growth curve analysis. *Developmental Psychology, 37,* 597–607.

Strober, M., & Johnson, C. (2012). The need for complex ideas in anorexia nervosa: Why biology, environment, and psyche all matter, why therapists make mistakes, and why clinical benchmarks are needed for managing weight correction. *International Journal of Eating Disorders, 45,* 155–178. doi: 10.1002/eat22005

Sussman, J., & Klump, K. (2011). Genetic and neuroscientific perspectives on body image. In T. F. Cash & L. Smolak (Eds.), *Body image: A handbook of science, practice, and prevention* (2nd ed., pp. 29–38). New York, NY: Guilford Press.

Thompson, J. K., Cattarin, J., Fowler, B., & Fisher, E. (1995). The Perception of Teasing Scale (POTS): A revision and extension of the Physical Appearance Related Teasing Scale (PARTS). *Journal of Personality Assessment, 65,* 146–157.

Thompson, J. K., Heinberg, L., Altabe, M., & Tantleff-Dunn, S. (1999). *Exacting beauty: Theory, assessment, and treatment of body image disturbance.* Washington, DC: American Psychological Association.

Thompson, J. K., & Stice, E. (2001). Thin-ideal internalization: Mounting evidence for a new risk factor for body image disturbance and eating pathology. *Current Directions in Psychological Science, 10,* 181–183.

Thompson, J. K., van den Berg, P., Roehrig, M., Guarda, A., & Heinberg, L. (2004). The Sociocultural Attitudes Towards Appearance Scale—3 (SATAQ–3): Development and validation. *International Journal of Eating Disorders, 35,* 293–304.

Want, S. C. (2009). Meta-analytic moderators of experimental exposure to media portrayals of women on female appearance satisfaction: Social comparisons as automatic processes. *Body Image, 6,* 257–269.

Ward, L. M. (2003). Understanding the role of entertainment media in the sexual socialization of American youth: A review of empirical research. *Developmental Review, 23,* 347–388.

Wertheim, E. H., Paxton, S. J., & Blaney, S. (2009). Body image in girls. In L. Smolak & J. K. Thompson (Eds.), *Body image, eating disorders, and obesity in youth: Assessment, prevention, and treatment* (2nd ed., pp. 47–76). Washington, DC: American Psychological Association.

## Chapter 2

# Gendered Considerations in the Treatment and Prevention of Eating Disorders

*Margo Maine and Douglas Bunnell*

Advances in the study of the genetics and neuroscience of eating disorders (EDs) threaten to marginalize considerations of the social and environmental factors that contribute to the etiology and maintenance of these complex conditions. Over the past decade, the EDs field has trended toward reductionism and biological determinism, significantly narrowing the scope of treatment and prevention models. In our opinion, however, any attempt to develop a meaningful conceptualization of EDs requires a biopsychosocial approach, carefully considering the many different factors that confer risk and vulnerability. Gender is only rarely mentioned in the current treatment or research literature, but it is, in fact, the most powerful risk factor for the development of an ED (Striegel-Moore & Bulik, 2007). In this chapter, we examine some of the ways in which gender still matters when considering how to prevent and treat women and men with EDs. Specifically, we review how gender development affects the risk for EDs, explore the role of sexualization and objectification, provide a brief overview of current perspectives on the gender-based factors that maintain and reinforce eating pathology, and begin to address some of the gender differences in the clinical features of EDs. We conclude with our view of how gender-informed clinicians can best work with their male and female patients with EDs.

## Scope of the Problem

EDs, disordered eating, and body image dissatisfaction are ubiquitous and debilitating. Now the third most common illness in adolescent girls (Fisher et al., 1995), after diabetes and asthma, EDs are a major public health issue,

**21**

appearing in every strata of U.S. culture and, as a result of globalization, in more than 40 countries worldwide (Gordon, 2001). Although multiple pathways may lead to an ED, virtually all involve a common factor: dieting. The act of dietary restriction can, for vulnerable men and women, be profoundly destabilizing. A recent survey in the United Kingdom found that nearly 25% of children younger than 10 diet and think they are overweight, with nearly 30% reporting dietary restriction. Nearly 50% reported that they had been teased and bullied about their weight and shape (Bates, 2012). Body image concerns, weight preoccupation, dieting, and weight-related teasing and bullying all increase the risk for EDs (Neumark-Sztainer, 2005). Also, although many people still consider EDs to be relatively benign problems of choice, the truth is abundantly and tragically clear. EDs are the most lethal illnesses with the highest rate of premature death of any psychiatric diagnosis (American Psychiatric Association, 2000; Sullivan, 2002). Even at the milder end of the clinical spectrum, these insidious disorders wreak physical and emotional havoc. For many women, and for an increasing number of men, weight, shape, and body image concerns are the sources of profound anxiety, self-criticism, and self-loathing that barely soften across the life span. Women in their 60s and 70s are as prone to the same levels of body image dissatisfaction as younger women (Lewis & Cachelin, 2001; Maine & Kelly, 2005).

Although EDs are not the only gendered psychiatric condition, the degree of gender disparity is much greater than with most diagnoses (Levine & Smolak, 2006). Past research has consistently found anorexia nervosa (AN) and bulimia nervosa to be 10 times more prevalent among females than males and binge eating disorder to be 3 times more common (Treasure, 2007). A national survey of psychiatric comorbidity reported that nearly one quarter of diagnosable cases of eating pathology occurred among males (Hudson, Hiripi, Pope, & Kessler, 2007), a substantial increase over other estimates of male prevalence. Men are clearly demonstrating increased body image concerns and more pressure to look young and competitive in contemporary society, so they may be more drawn to disordered eating and related behaviors. A substantial minority of men in the general community have significant levels of disordered eating and compensatory behaviors (Striegel-Moore et al., 2009). Yet, even with data suggesting an increase in EDs among males, the overall gender disparity remains pronounced. Gender plays an important role in shaping weight control attitudes and behaviors, and thus the prevention and treatment of EDs requires a thoughtful and nuanced appreciation of its influence.

## How Gender Unfolds: Developmental Considerations

From conception onward, gender is the product of the interaction of biological endowment and lived experience. Itself a biopsychosocial phenomenon, gender blends myriad influences including nature (biological differences that in turn create some vulnerabilities and risks for each sex) and nurture (the many interpersonal and social interactions that may reinforce feminine or masculine impulses). We believe that nature needs nurture and that the traditional delineations between the biological being and the lived experience are false dichotomies.

Biology, genetics, and environmental experience influence one another (Strober & Peris, 2011). Gender may be genetically coded, but its expression is equally, or even more so, affected by the socialization process and pressures in the family and culture. Although a virtual cottage industry has been created on the basis of the assumed differences between men and women, culminating in the construct of the war of the sexes and the popularity of books such as *Men Are From Mars, Women Are From Venus* (Gray, 1995) and *You Just Don't Understand: Men and Women in Conversation* (Tannen, 2001), the most comprehensive reviews of innate gender differences tell a vastly different and more complex story.

In their epic work *The Psychology of Sex Differences*, Maccoby and Jacklin (1974) reviewed more than 2,000 studies, identifying only four areas of sex-based difference: verbal ability, visuospatial ability, mathematical ability, and aggression. More recently, Hyde's (2005) meta-analysis of the gender difference literature reported that 78% of the differences are very small, actually close to zero, even in areas in which gender differences have been consistently considered strong. Eliot's (2009) exhaustive review of the gender difference literature concluded that there is "surprisingly little solid evidence of sex differences in children's brains" (p. 5), with the only consistent differences being brain size and brain maturity. Boys' brains are on average 8% to 11% larger at birth and throughout life, consistent with their higher weight and height. Girls' brains mature about 1 to 2 years earlier than boys', also mirroring the fact that they enter puberty earlier. Eliot reduced the discussion of gender differences to this:

> But actually growing a boy from those XY cells or a girl from those XX cells requires constant interaction with the environment, which begins in the prenatal soup and continues through all the dance recitals, baseball games, middle-school science classes, and cafeteria dramas that ceaselessly reinforce our gender-divided society. (p. 7)

One may be biologically male or female but one's cultural and social experiences affect how and when this affects one's life.

Regardless of some gender differences in the brain, neuroscience is now showing that people's brains are very malleable, especially in childhood (Eliot, 2009). People's hard wiring is not a finished and unchanging product because social experiences continually transform and mold the brain. With the advances in fetal testing available to those living in advanced nations, many, if not most, expectant parents (and their families and friends) already begin to relate to the fetus as a boy or a girl, buying blue or pink clothes and active and masculine or more passive and feminine toys, so gender identity begins to take shape very early. In fact,

23

as their first birthday approaches, infants have already begun to choose toys specific and stereotypically appropriate to their gender (Eliot, 2009), and by age 2, children begin to exhibit an internal sense of themselves as either male or female (Worell & Todd, 1996). Nature and nurture clearly go hand in hand to create a gendered identity with all the subsequent risk factors each gender brings.

Becoming a person, whether male or female, is a complicated business. Because women bear children and are generally the primary caretaker, at least during infancy, the mother–child relationship is a key to how identity and gendered identity unfold. For boys to develop a sense of self, they need to separate from their mother, both psychologically and physically, and move toward the father or other male figures. Girls must learn how to connect with fathers and other male figures while maintaining their connection to their mother. For girls, the developmental challenge places a premium on relational connections; for boys, the pressure is on separating. Girls begin to explore who they are and who they want to be by comparing themselves with peers, parents, siblings, and the cultural images available to them. Boys learn to harden themselves into self-sufficiency, fearful that dependence is shameful. The degree to which their familial and social environments are gendered will either reinforce stereotypic behavior or allow more room for difference or exploration (Maine & Bunnell, 2010). Children easily tune into what adults expect from them. For example, girls may act more typically feminine and boys more typically masculine to get approval or attention pending the cues and demands they perceive. In Western culture, the dominant values defining femininity reflect socioemotional and body image issues; masculine values are rooted in competence and autonomy. These stereotypes are powerful prescriptors: Women are to take care of others and attend to their appearance, and men are to take risks, assume leadership, and focus on success and work. For both sexes, the consequences are far reaching, creating vulnerabilities to EDs.

Every time they open their eyes, watch TV, see a billboard, play with their highly sexualized dolls, and watch the adults in their lives respond to media images and celebrities, girls learn that their bodies, if desirable enough, can give them power. Adolescents naturally begin to pay increased attention to the demands and expectations of the dominant culture, with girls, ready or not, leaving the safety of childhood and entering a world driven by factors outside the family such as peers, school, and the media, full of messages glorifying thinness and beauty and warning them about obesity and weight. At the same time, biologically dramatic hormonal changes usher in menstrual periods, breast development, and increased body fat. In fact, girls' bodies have to change drastically to continue their normal developmental trajectory. Between the ages of 10 and 14, a girl gains, on average, 10 inches of height and between 40 and 50 pounds, with most doubling their weight by the time they finish puberty (Friedman, 1997). Although increased body fat is essential to their physical development, it threatens their ability to succeed as females in a culture that idealizes slimness for women. Thus, a girl's natural body can be quite frightening, setting up the risk for significant body image and eating concerns that can pave the way to an ED.

As a girl transitions into puberty, she may feel as though she is falling down the proverbial rabbit hole, like Alice in Wonderland, landing in a place where things may look the same but feel very, very different. Gail, a young woman in recovery from bulimia, described that she went to bed at night after playing with dolls, woke up with breasts, and found that everyone treated her differently. She began to see herself differently as a result, becoming unhappy with her body, fearful of others' opinions and reactions to it and to her. Before she knew it, she was restricting her eating, losing weight, and then binging and purging as she wrestled with this new set of realities. Surrounded by messages about changing their bodies to look thinner, prettier, and more acceptable, girls like Gail soon begin to speak the language of fat in which all negative or difficult feelings become subsumed within feeling fat (Friedman, 1997). Constant diet ads and messages about the dangers of obesity, and a weight-loss industry that now accounts for approximately $60 billion per year in the United States (Marketdata Enterprises, 2007), only reinforce the language of fat, making dieting normative. For girls, the pressures to diet add to all the other developmental stressors of puberty; the gendered rite of passage instructs them to hate their bodies, to distrust their appetites, and to begin dieting, making early adolescence a peak time for girls to develop EDs.

Puberty is a great window onto how nature and nurture interact, as sexual maturation brings increased attention to the body, sexuality, and the developmental pressures of adolescence in a hypersexualized culture. Early puberty is an additional stressor. The age at which girls enter puberty has declined fairly rapidly: Just a century ago, the average age for menarche was 14.2, and now it is 12.3. In the 1970s, the average age of breast development was 11.5, but by 1997, it was younger than age 10 for Caucasian girls and age 9 for African American girls, with a significant number developing even before age 8 (Steingraber, 2009). The earlier a girl enters puberty, the more likely she is to have self-esteem issues, anxiety, depression, adjustment reactions, EDs, and suicide attempts (Graber, Seeley, Brooks-Gunn, & Lewinsohn, 2004) as well as use of drugs, alcohol, and tobacco; earlier sexual experiences; increased risk for physical violence; and, because of prolonged estrogen exposure, a higher incidence of breast cancer (Steingraber, 2009).

For boys, puberty also creates risk for body image and eating problems. Boys live in what some experts have called "a culture of cruelty" (Kindlon & Thompson, 1999) in which teasing and bullying are normative and profound experiences. Yet boys are taught to "man up," to never cry or act vulnerable, and to be fiercely independent. Teasing, bullying, competition, and conflict are important forces in male socialization, with many men who suffer EDs reporting specific and distinct memories of having been mocked and shamed about their bodies. Their road to body image and EDs may differ from that of women but be just as painful and dangerous.

Cultural ideals for boys emphasize that dependence is to be avoided; self-sufficiency is the ideal. Hardening the body, denying nourishment, and shame-based rules about eating cover up underlying fears that they are not sufficiently masculine and may be seen as weak and feminine. Boys and men with EDs tend to want a lean body rather than a thin body (Olivardia, 2007; Pope, Phillips, & Olivardia, 2000). Lean muscularity promises strength, competence, and "real" masculinity. Obviously, both boys' and girls' experiences can lead to body image obsessions as biological, social, psychological, and cultural factors collide in their lives.

## Risk Factors for Eating Disorders

Assessing risk for EDs requires that clinicians consider a wide range of possible etiological and maintaining factors. As clinicians' appreciation for these genetic, environmental, and epigenetic influences develops, they also need to consider how gender shapes their impact.

Temperament and brain circuitry are now seen as critical predisposing factors for AN and, to some lesser extent, bulimia nervosa and binge eating (Kaye, 2011; Kaye, Wagner, Fudge, & Paulus, 2011). Traits such as perfectionism and harm avoidance are associated with AN, and traits such as impulsivity are often associated with bulimia nervosa and binge eating. These traits, reflecting basic cognitive, emotional, and learning styles, are expressions of an individual's basic biological endowment. Emerging research has linked these traits to actual variations in brain circuitry (Kaye, 2011), but little is known regarding how gender influences these variations despite differences in the behavioral expressions of disruptions in the regulation of mood and anxiety. Males are more prone to externalizing expressions such as aggression; females are more likely to internalize, which may explain higher rates of mood disorders and EDs among females (Weinberg, Tronick, Cohn, & Olson, 1999).

Although the need for further research on the gender differences in the biological and temperamental risk factors for EDs is clear, social and cultural risk factors are essential to understanding how biological and temperamental vulnerabilities are exposed and expressed in actual pathological behavior. The internalization of a thin-body ideal is considered to be one of the most powerful environmental risk factors (Levine & Smolak, 2006; Stice, Marti, Spoor, Presnell, & Shaw, 2008). Men and boys are still decidedly less likely to report an idealization of a thin body type, which may help explain the lower incidence of male eating pathology. It is also clear that for most boys, the experience of being sexually objectified, another factor linked to ED risk, is less than for girls.

Biological, temperamental, and sociocultural risks often remain unexpressed and latent, and many exposed to these risks do not develop eating pathology. Models of risk require some precipitating event, and dieting is generally believed to be one of the most powerful triggers (Butryn, Lowe, Agras, & Safer, 2006; Fairburn, 2008; Schmidt, 2002; Stice, Nemeroff, &

Shaw, 1996). The fact that boys and men are much less likely to engage in dietary restriction as a means of weight loss can be a powerful factor insulating them from EDs.

## A Perfect Storm: The Media, Sexualization, Objectification, and Eating Disorders

Clinicians have long understood the critical role the media have played in the development of EDs, and a considerable body of literature research has now validated these impressions (Levine & Maine, 2010; Levine & Smolak, 2006). The media objectify women much more frequently than men and consistently portray them as unrealistically thin (Engeln-Maddox, 2006). Contemporary cultural experiences of girls and women contribute to both disordered body image and eating (Murnen & Smolak, 2009); exposure to mass media increases the risk for EDs (Groesz, Levine, & Murnen, 2002; Murnen, Levine, Smith, & Groesz, 2007), as do attempts to comply with traditional expectations regarding femininity (Murnen & Smolak, 1997).

The constant objectification and sexualization of the female body pushes girls to take an external view of themselves, so they lose the ability to identify, express, process, or respect their own emotions, thoughts, and instincts. They come to internalize the cultural standards regarding appearance, weight, and shape, disrupting awareness of their inner states. Dieting and denying themselves food, as well as other eating-disordered behaviors, can easily take hold, trumping girls' and women's appreciation of their natural bodies and paving the way for more serious body image preoccupation and eating pathology.

According to the American Psychological Association (2007), the consistent sexualization of girls and women comes at a high cost to their well-being, including impaired cognitive functioning resulting from intrusive and negative thoughts, emotional distress, body dissatisfaction, negative self-image, EDs, and health problems. Objectification theory (Frederickson & Roberts, 1997) explains the lasting harm of sexualization, especially the impact of media images and portrayals of women and the power of the sexual gaze. Girls come to see themselves as objects to be looked at and judged on the basis of their appearance. Internalizing an external standard leads to constant monitoring and self-scrutiny, compromising awareness of internal body states and experience. The culture thereby disrupts the connection to inner experience and contributes to a pervasive experience of disembodiment (Piran & Cormier, 2005), including denial of basic needs such as hunger and thirst.

Gender modulates the effects of objectification. Although children as young as age 7 idealize objectified media images, girls are more likely to internalize and try to meet these idealized standards (Murnen, Smolak, Mills, & Good, 2003). From early on, girls are exposed to criticisms and comments about their bodies, and not just in the media, because boys often disparage girls' bodies in their presence (Murnen & Smolak, 2000). According to research with children at age 11 and then at age 13, objectification appears to affect girls' emotional well-being but not boys' (Grabe, Hyde, & Lindberg, 2007). These experiences occur during critical developmental periods for girls in their relationship with their bodies. Enduring more self-objectification, body shame, rumination, and depression than their male peers, adolescent girls try to meet the external standards, hoping to find safety and self-acceptance. Instead, they become deeply disconnected from their bodies, creating fertile ground for EDs.

When people fail to meet cultural ideals, intrusive thoughts can undermine their cognitive functions (Bandura, 1991), and for women, this has a high price, literally and figuratively. Cultural standards for appearance, weight, and beauty are much more rigid for women, so they experience considerably more body image dissatisfaction than men (Ricciardelli & McCabe, 2004). Power and economic status are also at play. Women earn less than men, have less status and influence, and are more likely to be victims of abuse (Bordo, 2004). The intrusive and self-disparaging thoughts associated with objectification compromise their sense of self as well as their cognitive and emotional functioning.

Objectification leads to self-objectification, creating risk for three psychological issues: depression, sexual dysfunction, and EDs (Tiggemann & Slater, 2001). Not only do sexualization and objectification of girls harm girls individually, but they also foster a sexist or patriarchal culture that tolerates sexual harassment, violence, abuse, rape, and exploitation of girls and women (American Psychological Association, 2007). The two-edged sword (Sadker, Sadker, & Zittleman, 2009, p. 208) of sexism also victimizes boys and men. If girls must be objectified, boys must be objectifying, insensitive, and dismissive; if girls are to be harmed, then boys must harm through aggressive, insensitive, angry, and rejecting behaviors. With pressures to be independent, competitive, athletic, and disconnected from their own inner states much of the time, boys are also harmed by the culture's objectification of women.

## Maintaining Factors for Eating Disorders

Schmidt and Treasure (2006) have described four primary maintaining factors for EDs: the need to avoid negative emotion, perfectionistic and rigid temperamental traits, the responses of people in the individual's relational and cultural network, and pro-ED beliefs. The power of these factors is often quite different for male than for female clients.

Perfectionism and rule-bound thinking are risk factors for EDs among both men and women but may be less prominent among men (Elgin & Pritchard, 2006). Men also display less harm avoidance (Fernandez-Aranda et al., 2004). In addition, experience and articulation of emotional arousal and distress are influenced by both biology and cultural norms that inhibit emotional expression; men have less practice with and facility in the articulation of inner psychological experiences. Brain organization and emotional patterns reinforced by gender norms may insulate men from internalizing responses in the face of negative emotional experiences. The responses of family members to a boy or man with an ED can differ substantially from responses to female family members. According to conventional wisdom, boys and men do not get EDs, so they are less likely to be provided with validation and support. Finally, boys' and men's perceptions of the benefits of their EDs will often be quite different than the benefits perceived by girls and women. Although some of the benefits, such as a sense of discipline, control, strength, and uniqueness, are similar, men do not generally see themselves as enhanced by thinness. The goal is to defend against the fear of weight gain rather than to attain a particular level of thinness. Thinness for males is less socially desirable than it is for females. This critical difference may influence the male patient's experience of treatment and recovery. Men and boys are often less ambivalent than women and girls about weight restoration (Bunnell, 2010), and their EDs are typically more ego dystonic (Olivardia, Pope, Borowiecki, & Cohane, 2004)

## Gender, Symptom Manifestation, and Barriers to Treatment

The clinical features of AN, bulimia nervosa, ED not otherwise specified, and binge eating disorder (currently subsumed under the ED not otherwise specified category but a separate diagnosis in the forthcoming fifth edition of the *Diagnostic and Statistical Manual of Mental Disorders*; American Psychiatric Association, 2012) are quite similar across gender (Andersen, 1990, 2002; Fernández-Aranda et al., 2004; Hay, Loukas, & Philpott, 2005; Woodside et al., 2001). Comparisons of psychological functioning, including personality measures, have also revealed few differences; men show less harm avoidance, drive for thinness, and body dissatisfaction than women, but the statistical differences may not be clinically relevant (Fernández-Aranda et al., 2004). Woodside et al. (2001) concluded that male and female patients have similar psychosocial morbidities and that men with EDs are significantly different from healthy men on a variety of eating and psychological variables. The psychological distress associated with EDs is comparable for men and women (Striegel, Bedrosian, Wang, & Schwartz, 2012), and men with eating disorders are clearly more distressed on various dimensions than men without EDs (Striegel et al., 2012; Woodside et al., 2001), paralleling this same distinction between women with and without EDs. The variations in actual symptom constellations between men and women are less clear (Bunnell, 2010).

Despite core similarities, some differences exist in men's experiences of their bodies, expression of their illness, and access to treatment. As with women, even healthy men in nonclinical samples have exhibited increasing anxiety regarding their bodies (Pope, Olivardia, Boroweicki, & Cohane, 2001; Striegel-Moore et al., 2009), but their concerns focus on the upper torso, in contrast to women's concerns, which cluster around the hips and midsection. Compared with their female counterparts, men with EDs are less fearful of being fat and more fearful of being "soft" and small. Men are more likely to report that their motivation for restricting, overexercising, or binge eating and purging is a lean, muscular, and well-defined appearance rather than a thin appearance. They are also less likely to focus on specific weight loss goals (Olivardia, 2007; Pope et al., 2000). The ideal male body has less fat but requires more muscle so that the core motivation for men with EDs is a fear of softness rather than a fear of fatness. Despite being a highly desirable characteristic for most women, thinness represents weakness to men, leading the popular press to coin the term *reverse anorexia* and the professional literature, *muscle dysmorphia* (Olivardia, 2007) to describe the male pursuit of muscularity.

In our clinical experience, some female clients exercise excessively as a purging technique, but almost all men do so. Often, underweight male patients struggle with weight restoration; they are able to eat enough to sustain their weight but cannot eat enough to cover their exercise energy expenditure. In light of the cultural emphasis on male strength and prowess, both professionals and the public may see men with EDs as merely pursuing simple fitness, whereas a more informed look would reveal profound anxiety about smallness, softness, or flabbiness. Morgan (2008) has suggested that the fear of being small among men with EDs actually represents a deep dread of powerlessness and a fear of the feminine, exerting a profound impact on masculine psychology. Dependence is to be avoided; self-sufficiency is the ideal. Hardening the body, denying nourishment, and shame-based rules about eating all reflect this underlying fear. In the culture of cruelty mentioned earlier, teasing, bullying, competition, and conflict are important forces in male socialization and are less frequently reported among women with eating issues. Men with EDs often report specific and distinct memories of having been teased and shamed about their bodies, and the experience of humiliation often becomes concretized in the body (Bunnell, 2010).

Gay men appear to have higher rates of EDs than heterosexual men (Carlat, Camargo, & Herzog, 1997; Feldman & Meyer, 2007). The pressure to attract a male partner may be associated with these higher rates (Brown & Keel, 2012; Siever, 1994). Within the gay male community, different subgroups have different body image ideals, and these variations in group norms may influence motivation for weight loss and dietary restriction. In some groups, the idealized body is more muscular, whereas in others the ideal is defined by leanness and thinness (Olivardia, 2007). Although the evidence that the rate of EDs among gay men is substantially higher than the rate among heterosexual men is clear, the contrast between lesbian and heterosexual women is less distinct. Some research has suggested that lesbian women have a lower rate of EDs (Strong, Williamson, Netemeyer, & Geer, 2000) and that they may be insulated from some of the sociocultural pressures that contribute to EDs. Conflicting studies, however, have found no substantial differences in prevalence (Share & Mintz, 2002). Feldman and Meyer (2007) also reported no significant differences in rates of EDs in a large community sample of lesbian women and cautioned that clinicians should not assume that their lesbian patients are at decreased risk for disordered eating.

Gender biases color the identification of and referral for EDs. Even clinicians who are accustomed to working with female clients with EDs may underestimate the severity of the illness when they see a male client. AN may put male bodies at greater risk earlier in the weight loss process. In fact, a 10% loss of body weight in men is comparable to a 15% to 20% loss in women (Crisp & Burns, 1990). Similar to the impact of low estrogen in women, decreased testosterone levels in men increase the likelihood for osteopenia and osteoporosis (Andersen, Watson, & Schlechte, 2000; Mehler, Sabel, Watson, & Andersen, 2009). Although men may suffer a critical impact on their health earlier in the weight loss process, they often are not identified by health care professionals because of the belief that EDs are a woman's issue. Because overeating is more socially acceptable for men, the boundary between overeating and binge eating may be blurred, and binge eating disorder and bulimia may be underdiagnosed among men. Men are also less likely to be familiar with EDs in general and may not recognize the meaning and potential consequences of their weight-related behaviors. Their families may also ignore the onset of symptoms. Finally, virtually all of the assessment tools have been normed on girls and women, so very little is known about the symptomatic thresholds for EDs among boys and men (Darcy et al., 2012).

These factors create significant barriers to the identification of, referral for, and treatment of men. The greatest obstacle to diagnosis and treatment of men may in fact be the substantial stigma still associated with these disorders. Despite significant advances in public awareness, these disorders are seen as female illnesses and as relatively benign disorders of choice. To the extent that the culture still marginalizes people, and particularly women, with psychiatric illnesses, men with EDs are less likely to divulge difficulties with an illness associated with negative connotations of weakness, lack of control, and femininity.

With both sexes, early intervention is highly recommended, and all mental health professionals should be trained in diagnosis, treatment, and appreciation for gender differences in presentation to minimize the chances of failing to detect a serious illness.

## Gender-Informed Treatment of Eating Disorders

The treatment priorities for patients with EDs are essentially the same regardless of gender. Reestablishing a normal pattern of eating, decreasing restraint and restriction, and eliminating binge eating and compensatory behaviors set the stage for subsequent psychotherapeutic work (American Psychiatric Association, 2000). Because many of the psychological features associated with EDs are secondary expressions of the effects of inadequate or chaotic nutrition, normalization of eating is essential, with weight restoration critical for underweight and anorexic patients.

The barriers to normalization of nutritional intake are similar for men and women, with some qualitative differences. Men seeking treatment for an ED are generally less familiar with the diagnoses and likely treatment experiences than female patients. Despite usually exhibiting less drive for thinness and less explicit fear of weight restoration, shame can overpower their motivation to recover. Fear that exposure will reveal fundamental defects and that they may be violating the masculine imperative about self-sufficiency (Pleck, 1995) can amplify the ambivalence about recovery that always accompanies EDs. Men, raised to value self-sufficiency and autonomy and to fear dependence, may not be easily relieved by empathic connection (Blatt, 2008), with important implications for how clinicians conceptualize their treatment and how clinicians can best engage them. Most men with EDs will come to treatment with explicit memories of being teased, shamed, and humiliated about their bodies (Bunnell, 2010). These relational traumas reinforce a sense of "self in disconnection" and emotional compartmentalization that can consolidate in a focus on the body. Such experiences are likely to shape men's expectations in therapeutic relationships.

The feminist relational model is frequently used in the treatment of women with EDs (Maine, 2009), but it can be equally useful in working with men. First, it reframes healthy psychological development as a process of growth toward connection rather than toward separation and individuation (Jordan, 1997), offering new lessons about trust, empathy, and the comfort of relationships. For many boys and men who were pressured to disconnect emotionally from an early age, this model of listening and understanding may be a unique experience moving them out of a culture of cruelty and shame into a culture of connection and acceptance, creating the opportunity for true healing. The relational model equips both men and women with insight into how disconnection from their inner experience as well as from mutual relationships contributes to self-destructive behaviors such as EDs. A relational perspective also provides a language for discussing the connections among body perception, ED behaviors, and relational longings and needs. Ideally, a trusting and empathically attuned relationship is the foundation for more directive techniques for containing symptom use such as cognitive–behavioral therapy (Cloak & Powers, 2010).

A relational focus helps to place the individual's eating pathology in a broader context that explores how his or her symptoms are a response to unhealthy pressures, expectations, or roles (Sesan, 1994). By contextualizing the ED within the sociocultural environment, the relational paradigm helps the individual, male or female, to make sense of his or her struggle and often to feel less ashamed, less defective, and less alone. Treatment aims to explore and understand the meaning and function of individuals' behaviors, helping them to build other coping mechanisms to replace them. Another unique aspect of this model is the attempt to minimize the power differential between the therapist and the patient. Because women still have less economic power, authority, and status, and many mistakenly attempt to gain control through their bodies after being victims of abuse, the relational model is very sensitive to power in the therapeutic relationship. The emphasis is on collaboration instead of authority, with the goal of sharing power with rather than having power over (Bergman & Surrey, 1997). In one of the few books focusing on male eating and body image issues, Andersen, Cohn, and Holbrook (2000) echoed relational principles by stressing the importance of establishing trust and respect in the therapeutic relationship, developing a collaborative process, and empowering the patient to make decisions. The relational approach incorporates psychoeducation as a means of sharing power and knowledge with the patient, leveling the playing field, and engaging them as architects of their recovery process.

### Men in Psychotherapy

Most clinicians working with patients with EDs will see a limited number of male patients. Thus, most will need to make some adjustment to their standard approach to therapeutic engagement (Bunnell, 2010). A man's decision to seek treatment for his ED can reflect important attitudes about the need for assistance and support. The concerns about weakness and vulnerability that men often bring to therapy can be explored through careful and respectful examination of attitudes and beliefs about psychotherapy. Many therapists, male and female, are less likely to directly address relational issues with their male patients, in part because male patients may be less comfortable with direct explorations of the relationship. Englar-Calson (2006, p. 37) recommended an allied problem-solving stance with a focus on "action intimacy" because men may be more comfortable with directive techniques and may respond more favorably to cognitive–behavioral and similar therapies than female patients. Finally, therapists must also be willing to confront their own biases and gender stereotypes (see Bunnell, 2010, for further review). Countertransferential reactions to male patients may reflect clinicians' own biases about male vulnerability, also known as the "c'mon be a man" reaction. Do you as a clinician see men as less emotionally and relationally competent than your female patients? How do you as a therapist act differently with your male and female patients regarding issues of money, authority, psychological openness, self-disclosure, feelings of attraction, discussions about sex and intimacy, anger, flirtation, and power? Gender-competent therapists need to reflect on these questions and be mindful of their own blind spots and gender dynamics.

## Case Examples

### Case 1

This clinical vignette illustrates some of the issues specific to the treatment of male patients with EDs: deep shame about their bodies after teasing and bullying experiences, the maladaptive coping mechanism of excessive exercise, and a limited ability to express feelings verbally. Medical instability can develop quickly because of the metabolic needs of young male bodies and the severe limitations in intake in light of their energy expenditures. Psychotherapy must address these physical issues as well as the underlying conflicts regarding self-esteem and masculine identity.

Bob was a 16-year-old boy who lived at home with his two parents, both highly accomplished financial services professionals. Bob's dietary restriction started after a comment he heard at the pool about the size of his breasts, a long-standing source of shame for him, but this comment resulted in his first attempt to "do something." He lost weight rapidly and became medically unstable almost immediately. He started individual psychotherapy and family therapy after discharge.

Initial sessions revealed a long history of Bob's being teased about his body. Attempts at weight lifting and body building had not helped, and Bob was preoccupied with his upper body. He had no interest in weight loss per se, but his highly restrained eating served as his defense against the possibility of becoming soft again. In his mind, his dietary restraint not only countered his concerns about his upper body dissatisfaction but also represented a statement of his own self-sufficiency and denial of need. Bob also struggled with anxiety and panic, which were often provoked by variations in his eating, exercise, or weight. His worry and anxiety were often expressed somatically; he had only a limited vocabulary for feelings, with the exception of *guilty* or *worthless*.

Bob felt enormous pressure to be a man. The entire male side of his family tree was filled with prominent business executives, professors, and accomplished athletes. He would tell me on occasions that he felt like a "whining girl" when he explored these vulnerabilities, scanning my face for expected confirmation. His emerging relationship with me contained many of these same factors, including his fear of dependence and his questions about his masculinity.

### Treatment Considerations

The foundation for Bob's psychotherapeutic work was the reestablishment of his nutritional and medical stability. His profound anxiety and body image fears limited his ability to develop different perspectives about himself, his relationship with his family, and his concerns about his masculinity. Medical and nutritional stability, as noted earlier, may actually be more salient issues with male patients with EDs because they are more vulnerable to acute medical problems than female patients (Andersen, 2002).

As Bob's acute medical issues diminished, we were able to shift our focus to the psychological and relational factors that were supporting his ED. I (Douglas Bunnell) told Bob that it was essential that we keep pushing for a full recovery from his ED and that full recovery would require that he challenge many of his ED rules about the upper limit of his weight, the amount of exercise he did each day, and his long list of rules regarding the time, place, and menu variety he felt obligated to live with. This ongoing attention to pushing back against the rules helped him improve his sense of ownership of his treatment and recovery.

The history of teasing and criticism had a strong influence on Bob's experience of the treatment relationship. He was extremely ambivalent and prone to feelings of shame about his need for treatment. Shame-based reactions to emotional closeness and need will often shape the process of therapeutic engagement with male patients. Bob and I discussed these feelings openly, which gradually eased his concerns about our exploration of his body image and self-esteem worries, his sense of vulnerability to his father's criticism and implied disappointment, and his worries about his mother's distress regarding illness. We focused the psychotherapy on these core cognitive and interpersonal maintaining factors.

## Case 2

This case example demonstrates frequent themes in the treatment of adult women with EDs: history of body image and eating issues from early in development, a variation in ED symptoms over time, and motivation for treatment stimulated by a desire to not pass eating and body image issues along to their children. Parenting makes women's own recovery a more urgent issue and is often the stimulus for treatment.

At age 42, Jennifer first sought treatment for an ED that had started 30 years earlier when, in the midst of puberty and heavier than her body-conscious parents wanted her to be, they enrolled her in Weight Watchers. Although never diagnosed or treated, she developed AN in college, constantly being told how great she looked. After college, she regained some weight but always felt pressured by her family and the media to be thinner than her body seemed to want to be. After having her second child, Jennifer gradually reverted to anorexia, complicated by bulimic symptoms, first restricting her intake, later purging via exercise, and then vomiting multiple times a day. Although worn out emotionally and physically, Jennifer continued to be seduced by the constant compliments about her weight loss. Her daughter's emerging adolescence was what pushed Jennifer into therapy. Watching her daughter's body begin to add the fat that puberty requires and observing her fascination with fashion models and media images, Jennifer feared her daughter would succumb to the same pressures regarding weight, shape, and appearance, and she knew that the only way her daughter could escape an ED was for Jennifer to honestly face her own. She worked hard in individual therapy to build a stronger sense of herself, calm her perfectionistic and obsessive tendencies, and no longer rely on her appearance as a core part of her identity. Psychoeducation about the normal physical changes a girl's body experiences in puberty helped her to understand her own experience as well as to support her daughter.

### Treatment Considerations

Despite a chronic course of ED and body image issues, adult clients can still make major changes and restore their health when they access appropriate specialized care. Jennifer felt hopeless when she started treatment but was able to benefit from a gender-informed relational treatment approach relying on intense individual therapy with ancillary family and group therapy, dietary counseling, and medication. I (Margo Maine) accepted that her primary motivation was to prevent her daughter from suffering from an ED but gradually helped her to focus on her own needs and develop a healthy relationship with food and with her body for the first time in her life.

After a lifetime of people pleasing and deference to cultural expectations of how she should act and look as a woman, therapy empowered Jennifer to begin to act on her own needs and desires. This required her to break long-standing patterns in all of her relationships, especially in her family of origin, which had contributed tremendously to her ED through their shared emphasis on appearance, perfection, and conformity to family expectations. Although her body image concerns persist, Jennifer does not act on them and has been able to recover quite fully. Throughout treatment, Jennifer frequently noted that my critical perspective on the social and cultural pressures on women to look, think, and act in traditional female patterns enabled her to take the risks necessary to become the woman she wanted to be rather than the one her family and culture expected. The therapeutic relationship was critical to this process.

## Conclusion

Gender is a powerful factor in the experience of one's body, the ability to understand and meet its needs, and the degree to which it symbolizes nonphysical characteristics related to self-esteem, identity, and emotional well-being. It remains a major risk factor in the constellation of factors contributing to and sustaining EDs in both women and men. Although the clinical features of EDs are similar between men and women, awareness of how gender can affect the prevention, detection, diagnosis, and treatment of these disorders is growing. Clinicians working with these patients need to practice gender-informed care by incorporating knowledge of the unique features of eating pathology in men and women. They must also build a sophisticated appreciation for how their own gender beliefs and biases affect their clinical work.

## Chapter Highlights

- EDs are serious and pervasive illnesses that affect millions of men and women.
- More women than men have EDs, but the disparity is shrinking.
- A person's sense of gender is the product of a complex interaction between genetic endowment and lived experience. Culture shapes one's gender experience.
- Culture- and gender-based experiences are critical factors in the etiology and maintenance of ED psychopathology.

- Detection and diagnosis of EDs in boys and men can be complicated by differences in the nature of ED symptoms in men and women. For instance, the body image concerns of men with EDs often differ from those of women. Men's concerns focus on leanness and muscularity as opposed to thinness.
- For girls, the onset of puberty can radically alter body image. Virtually all girls in U.S. culture experience high levels of body dissatisfaction during their adolescence. For boys, teasing and shaming about body image are often important factors in the development of EDs.
- Most of the clinical features of EDs are similar in men and women, although subtle variations often occur in the nature of body image concerns, drive for thinness, and reluctance to gain weight. The treatment priorities for men and women with EDs are essentially similar. Weight restoration and normalization of eating are the most important treatment goals.
- Clinicians can use awareness of gender dynamics to foster engagement in psychotherapy. Understanding one's own gender-based beliefs, biases, and stereotypes is an important part of a counselor's professional development.

# Recommended Resources

## *Professional Organizations*

- Academy for Eating Disorders
  http://www.aedweb.org
  The Academy for Eating Disorders is a global professional association committed to leadership in ED research, education, treatment, and prevention. Special interest groups exist for a variety of specialized topics, including one for boys and men with eating disorders.
- International Association of Eating Disorder Professionals
  http://www.iaedp.com
  This association provides education and training to all disciplines involved in treating EDs.
- Jean Baker Miller Training Institute
  http://www.jbmti.org
  The Jean Baker Miller Training Institute at the Wellesley College Centers for Women has published more than 10 books and 100 scholarly working papers addressing issues such as culture and gender and provides a variety of learning opportunities including Webinars, intensive trainings, and a home-based course.
- National Eating Disorders Association
  http://www.nationaleatingdisorders.org
  The National Eating Disorders Association supports individuals and families affected by EDs and serves as a catalyst for prevention, cures, and access to quality care.

### Publications

- *AED Annual Review of Eating Disorders*
  http://www.aedweb.org
- *American Psychological Association Report on the Sexualization of Girls*
  http://www.apa.org/pi/women/programs/girls/report.aspx
- *Eating Disorders*
  http://www.taylorandfrancis.com
- *Eating Disorders Review*
  http://www.gurze.com
- *Effective Clinical Practice in the Treatment of Eating Disorders: The Heart of the Matter,* by M. Maine, W. N. Davis, and J. Shure (Routledge, 2009)
- *European Eating Disorders Review*
  http://www.aedweb.org
- *International Journal of Eating Disorders*
  http://www.aedweb.org
- *Treatment of Eating Disorders: Bridging the Research–Practice Gap,* edited by M. Maine, B. H. McGilley, and D. Bunnell (Elsevier, 2010)

# References

American Psychiatric Association. (2000). Practice guidelines for the treatment of patients with eating disorders (revision). *American Journal of Psychiatry, 157*(1, Suppl.), 1–39.

American Psychiatric Association. (2012). Eating disorders. Retrieved from http://www.dsm5.org/ProposedRevisions/Pages/EatingDisorders.aspx

American Psychological Association. (2007). *Report of the APA Task Force on the sexualization of girls.* Washington, DC: Author.

Andersen, A. E. (1990). *Males with eating disorders.* Philadelphia, PA: Brunner/Mazel.

Andersen, A. E. (2002). Eating disorders in males. In C. G. Fairburn & K. D. Brownell (Eds.), *Eating disorders and obesity* (pp. 188–192). New York, NY: Guilford Press.

Andersen, A. E., Cohn, L., & Holbrook, T. (2000). *Making weight: Men's conflicts with food, weight, shape, and appearance.* Carlsbad, CA: Gurze Books.

Andersen, A., Watson, T., & Schlechte, J. (2000). Osteoporosis and osteopenia in men with eating disorders. *Lancet, 355,* 1967–1968.

Bandura, A. (1991). Self-regulation through anticipatory and self-reactive mechanisms. In R. A. Dienstbier (Ed.), *Nebraska Symposium on Motivation: Vol. 38: Perspectives on motivation* (pp. 69–164). Lincoln: University of Nebraska Press.

Bates, C. (2012, January 5). A quarter of children under 10 diet because they think they are overweight and face bullying taunts, shocking survey finds. *The Daily Mail.* Retrieved from http://www.dailymail.co.uk/health/article-2082500/A-quarter-children-10-diet-think-overweight-face-bullying-taunts-shocking-survey-finds.html

Bergman, S. J., & Surrey, J. L. (1997). The woman–man relationship: Impasses and possibilities. In J. V. Jordan (Ed.), *Women's growth in diversity: More writings from the Stone Center* (pp. 260–87). New York, NY: Guilford Press,

Blatt, S. J. (2008). *Polarities of experience: Relatedness and self definition in personality, development, psychopathology and the therapeutic process.* Washington, DC: American Psychological Association.

Bordo, S. (2004). *Unbearable weight: Feminism, Western culture, and the body.* Berkeley: University of California Press.

Brown, T. A., & Keel, P. K. (2012). The impact of relationships on the association between sexual orientation and disordered eating in men. *International Journal of Eating Disorders, 45,* 792–799. doi:10.1002/eat.22013

Bunnell, D. W. (2010). Men with eating disorders: The art and science of treatment engagement. In M. Maine, B. McGilley, & D. Bunnell (Eds.), *Treatment of eating disorders: Bridging the research–practice gap* (pp. 301–316). New York, NY: Elsevier.

Butryn, M. L., Lowe, M. R., Agras, W. S., & Safer, D. L. (2006). Weight suppression as a predictor of outcome during cognitive–behavioral treatment of bulimia nervosa. *Journal of Abnormal Psychology, 115,* 62–67.

Carlat, D., Camargo, C., & Herzog, D. (1997). Eating disorders in males: A report on 135 patients. *American Journal of Psychiatry, 154,* 1127–1132.

Cloak, N., & Powers, P. (2010). Science or art: Integrating symptom management into psychodynamic treatment of eating disorders. In M. Maine, B. McGilley, & D. Bunnell (Eds.), *Treatment of eating disorders: Bridging the research–practice gap* (pp. 143–161). New York, NY: Elsevier.

Crisp, A., & Burns, T. (1990). Primary anorexia nervosa in the male and female: A comparison of clinical features and prognosis. In A. Andersen (Ed.), *Men with eating disorders* (pp. 77–99). Philadelphia, PA: Brunner/Mazel.

Darcy, A. M., Doyle, A. C., Lock, J., Peebles, R., Doyle, P., & Le Grange, D. (2012). The Eating Disorders Examination in adolescent males with anorexia nervosa: How does it compare to adolescent females? *International Journal of Eating Disorders, 45,* 110–114.

Elgin, J., & Pritchard, M. (2006). Gender differences in disordered eating and its correlates. *Eating and Weight Disorders, 11,* 96–101.

Eliot, L. (2009). *Pink brain blue brain: How small differences grow into troublesome gaps and what we can do about it.* New York, NY: Mariner Books.

Engeln-Maddox, R. (2006). Buying a beauty standard or dreaming of a new life? Expectations associated with media ideals. *Psychology of Women Quarterly, 30,* 258–266.

Englar-Carlson, M. (2006). Masculine norms and the therapy process. In M. Englar-Carlson & M. Stevens (Eds.), *In the room with men: A casebook of therapeutic change* (pp. 13–47). Washington, DC: American Psychological Association.

Fairburn, C. G. (2008). *Cognitive behavior therapy and eating disorders.* New York, NY: Guilford Press.

Feldman, M., & Meyer, I. (2007). Eating disorders in diverse lesbian, gay, and bisexual populations. *International Journal of Eating Disorders, 40,* 218–226.

Fernandez-Aranda, F., Aitken, A., Badia, A., Gimenez, L., Solano, D., Treasure, J., & Vallejo, J. (2004). Personality and psychopathological traits of males with an eating disorder. *European Eating Disorders Review, 12,* 367–374.

Fisher, M., Golden, N. H. , Katzman, D. K., Kreipe, R. E., Rees, J., Schebendach, J., . . . Hoberman, H. M. (1995). Eating disorders in adolescents: A background paper. *Journal of Adolescent Health, 16,* 420–437.

Frederickson, B. L., & Roberts, T. A. (1997). Objectification theory: Toward understanding women's lived experiences and mental health risks. *Psychology of Women Quarterly, 21,* 173–206.

Friedman, S. S. (1997). *When girls feel fat.* Toronto, Ontario, Canada: HarperCollins.

Gordon, R. A. (2001). Eating disorders East and West: A culture-bound syndrome unbound. In M. Nasser, M. A. Katzman, & R. A. Gordon (Eds.), *Eating disorders and cultures in transition* (pp. 1–23). New York, NY: Taylor & Francis.

Grabe, S., Hyde, J. S., & Lindberg, S. M. (2007). Body objectification and depression in adolescents: The role of gender, shame, and rumination. *Psychology of Women Quarterly, 31,* 164–75.

Graber, J. A., Seeley, J. R., Brooks-Gunn, J., & Lewinsohn, P. M. (2004). Is pubertal timing associated with psychopathology in young adulthood? *Journal of the American Academy of Child & Adolescent Psychiatry, 43,* 718–726.

Gray, J. (1995). *Men are from Mars, women are from Venus.* New York, NY: HarperCollins.

Groesz, L. M., Levine, M. P., & Murnen, S. K. (2002). The effects of experimental presentation of thin media images on body satisfaction: A meta-analytic review. *International Journal of Eating Disorders, 31,* 1–16.

Hay, P. J., Loukas, A., & Philpott, H. (2005). Prevalence and characteristics of men with eating disorders in primary care: How do they compare to women and what features may aid in identification? *Primary Care and Community Psychiatry, 10,* 1–6.

Hudson, J., Hiripi, E., Pope, H., & Kessler, R. (2007). The prevalence and correlates of eating disorders in the National Comorbidity Survey replication. *Biological Psychiatry, 61,* 348–358.

Hyde, J. S. (2005). The gender similarities hypothesis. *American Psychologist, 60,* 581–592.

Kaye, W. H. (2011). Neurobiology of anorexia nervosa. In D. Le Grange & J. Lock (Eds.), *Eating disorders in children and adolescents: A clinical handbook* (pp. 11–24). New York, NY: Guilford Press.

Kaye, W. H., Wagner, A., Fudge, J. L., & Paulus, M. (2011). Behavioral neurobiology of eating disorders. *Current Topics in Behavioral Neuroscience, 6,* 37–57.

Kindlon, D., & Thompson, M. (1999). *Raising Cain: Protecting the emotional life of boys.* New York, NY: Ballantine Books.

Jordan, J. (1997). A relational perspective for understanding women's development. In J. Jordan (Ed.), *Women's growth in diversity: More writings from the Stone Center* (pp. 9–24). New York, NY: Guilford Press.

Levine, M. P., & Maine, M. (2010). Are media an important medium for clinicians? Mass media, eating disorders, and the bolder model of treatment, prevention, and advocacy. In M. Maine, B. McGilley, & D. Bunnell (Eds.), *Treatment of eating disorders: Bridging the research–practice gap* (pp. 53–67). New York, NY: Elsevier.

Levine, M. P., & Smolak, L. (2006). *The prevention of eating problems and eating disorders: Theory, research and practice.* Mahwah, NJ: Erlbaum.

Lewis, D. M., & Cachelin, F. M. (2001). Body image, body dissatisfaction, and eating attitudes in midlife and elderly women. *Eating Disorders: The Journal of Treatment and Prevention, 9,* 29–39.

Maccoby, E. E., & Jacklin, C. N. (1974). *The psychology of sex differences.* Stanford, CA: Stanford University Press.

Maine, M. (2009). Beyond the medical model: A feminist frame for eating disorders. In M. Maine, W. M. Davis, & J. Shure (Eds.), *Effective clinical practice in the treatment of eating disorders: The heart of the matter* (pp. 3–17). New York, NY: Routledge.

Maine, M., & Bunnell, D. W. (2010). A perfect biopsychosocial storm: Gender, culture, and eating disorders. In M. Maine, B. McGilley, & D. Bunnell (Eds.), *Treatment of eating disorders: Bridging the research–practice gap* (pp. 3–16). New York, NY: Elsevier.

Maine, M., & Kelly, J. (2005). *The body myth: Adult women and the pressure to be perfect.* Hoboken, NJ: Wiley.

Marketdata Enterprises. (2007, April 19). *The U.S. weight loss & diet control market* (9th ed.). Rockville, MD: Author. Retrieved June 5, 2009, from http://www.prwebdirect.com/releases/2007/4/preweb520127.php

Mehler, P. S., Sabel, A. L., Watson, T., & Andersen, A. (2009). High risk of osteoporosis in male patients with eating disorders. *International Journal of Eating Disorders, 41,* 666–672.

Morgan, J. F. (2008). *The invisible man: A self help guide for men with eating disorders, compulsive exercise and bigorexia.* East Sussex, England: Routledge.

Murnen, S. K., Levine, M. P., Smith, J., & Groesz, L. (2007, August). *Do fashion magazines promote body dissatisfaction in girls and women? A meta-analytic review.* Paper presented at the 115th Annual Convention of the American Psychological Association, San Francisco, CA.

Murnen, S. K., & Smolak, L. (1997). Femininity, masculinity, and disordered eating: A meta-analytic review. *International Journal of Eating Disorders, 22,* 231–42.

Murnen, S. K., & Smolak, L. (2000). The experience of sexual harassment among grade-school students: Early socialization of female subordination? *Sex Roles, 43,* 1–17.

Murnen, S. K., & Smolak, L. (2009). Are feminist women protected from body image problems? A meta-analytic review of the relevant research. *Sex Roles, 60,* 186–197.

Murnen, S. K., Smolak, L., Mills, J. A., & Good, L. (2003). Thin, sexy women and strong, muscular men: Grade-school children's responses to objectified images of women and men. *Sex Roles, 43,* 1–17.

Neumark-Sztainer, D. (2005). Can we simultaneously work toward the prevention of obesity and eating disorders in children and adolescents? *International Journal of Eating Disorders, 38,* 220–227.

Olivardia, R. (2007). Body image and muscularity. In J. E. Grant, & M. N. Potenza (Eds.), *Textbook of men's mental health* (pp. 307–324). Washington, DC: American Psychiatric Publishing.

Olivardia, R., Pope, H., Borowiecki, J., & Cohane, G. (2004). Biceps and body image: The relationship between muscularity and self-esteem, depression, and eating disorder symptoms. *Psychology of Men and Masculinity, 5,* 112–120.

Piran, N., & Cormier, H. C. (2005). The social construction of women and disordered eating patterns. *Journal of Counseling Psychology, 52,* 549–58.

Pleck, J. H. (1995). The gender role strain paradigm: An update. In R. F. Levant & W. S. Pollack (Eds.), *A new psychology of men* (pp. 11–32). New York, NY: Basic Books.

Pope, H. G., Olivardia, R., Boroweicki, J., & Cohane, G. H. (2001). The growing commercial value of the male body: A longitudinal survey of advertising in women's magazines. *Psychotherapy and Psychosomatics, 70,* 189–192.

Pope, H., Phillips, K., & Olivardia, R. (2000). *The Adonis complex: The secret crisis of male body obsession.* New York, NY: Free Press.

Ricciardelli, L. A., & McCabe, M. P. (2004). A biopsychosocial model of disordered eating and the pursuit of muscularity in adolescent boys. *Psychological Bulletin, 130,* 179–205.

Sadker, D., Sadker, M., & Zittleman, K. (2009). *Still failing at fairness.* New York, NY: Scribner.

Schmidt, U. (2002). Risk factors for eating disorders. In C. G. Fairburn & K. D. Brownell (Eds.), *Eating disorders and obesity: A comprehensive handbook* (2nd ed., pp. 247–251). New York, NY: Guilford Press.

Schmidt, U., & Treasure, J. ( 2006). Anorexia nervosa: Valued and visible. A cognitive–interpersonal maintenance model and its implications for research and practice. *British Journal of Clinical Psychology, 45,* 343–366.

Sesan, R. (1994). Feminist treatment of eating disorders: An oxymoron? In P. Fallon, M. A. Katzman, & S. C. Wooley (Eds.), *Feminist perspectives on eating disorders* (pp. 251–271). New York, NY: Guilford Press.

Share, T. L., & Mintz, L. B. (2002). Differences between lesbians and heterosexual women in disordered eating and related attitudes. *Journal of Homosexuality, 42,* 89–106.

Siever, M. D. (1994). Sexual orientation and gender as factors in sociocultur-ally acquired vulnerability to body dissatisfaction and eating disorders. *Journal of Consulting and Clinical Psychology, 62,* 252–260.

Steingraber, S. (2009). Girls gone grown-up: Why are U.S. girls reaching puberty earlier and earlier? In S. Olfman (Ed.), *The sexualization of childhood* (pp. 51–62). Westport, CT: Praeger.

Stice, E., Marti, C., Spoor, S., Presnell, K., & Shaw, H. (2008). Dissonance and healthy weight eating disorder prevention programs: Long-term ef-fects from a randomized efficacy trial. *Journal of Consulting and Clinical Psychology, 76,* 329–334.

Stice, E., Nemeroff, C., & Shaw, H. E. (1996). Test of dual pathway model of bulimia nervosa: Evidence for dietary restraint and affect regulation mechanisms. *Journal of Social and Clinical Psychology, 15,* 340–363.

Striegel, R. H., Bedrosian, R., Wang, C., & Schwartz, S. (2012). Why men should be included in research on binge eating: Results from a compari-son of impairment in men and women. *International Journal of Eating Disorders, 45,* 233–240.

Striegel-Moore, R. H., & Bulik, C. M. (2007). Risk factors for eating dis-orders. *American Psychologist, 62,* 181–198.

Striegel-Moore, R., Rosselli, F., Perrin, N., DeBar, L., Wilson, G., May, A., & Kraemer, H. (2009). Gender difference in the prevalence of eating disorder symptoms. *International Journal of Eating Disorders, 42,* 471–474.

Strober, M., & Peris, T. (2011). Role of family environment in etiology: A neuroscience perspective. In D. Le Grange & J. Lock (Eds.), *Eating disorders in children and adolescents: A clinical* handbook (pp. 34–60). New York, NY: Guilford Press.

Strong, S. M., Williamson, D. A., Netemeyer, R. G., & Geer, J. H. (2000). Eating disorder symptoms and concerns about body differ as a func-tion of gender and sexual orientation. *Journal of Social and Clinical Psychology, 19,* 240–255.

Sullivan, P. (2002). Course and outcome of anorexia nervosa and bulimia nervosa. In C. G. Fairburn & K. D. Brownell (Eds.), *Eating disorders and obesity* (2nd ed., pp. 226–232). New York, NY: Guilford Press.

Tannen, D. (2001). *You just don't understand: Men and women in conversa-tion.* New York, NY: Harper.

Tiggemann, M., & Slater, A. (2001). A test of objectification theory in former dancers and non-dancers. *Psychology of Women Quarterly, 2,* 57–64.

Treasure, J. (2007). The trauma of self-starvation: Eating disorders and body image. In M. Nasser, K. Baistow, & J. Treasure (Eds.), *The female body in mind: The interface between the female body and mental health* (pp. 57–71). London, England: Routledge.

Weinberg, M., Tronick, E., Cohn, J., & Olson, K. (1999). Gender differ-ences in emotional expressivity and self regulation during early infancy. *Developmental Psychology, 35,* 175–188.

Woodside, D. B., Garfinkel, P. E., Lin, E., Goering, P., Kaplan, A. S., Goldbloom, D.S., & Kennedy, S. H. (2001). Comparisons of men with full or partial eating disorders, men without eating disorders, and women with eating disorders in the community. *American Journal of Psychiatry, 158,* 570–574.

Worell, J., & Todd, J. (1996). Development of the gendered self. In L. Smolak, M. P. Levine, & R. Striegel-Moore (Eds.), *The developmental psychopathology of eating disorders: Implications for research, prevention, and treatment* (pp. 135–156). Mahwah, NJ: Erlbaum.

## Chapter 3

# Clients of Color and Eating Disorders: Cultural Considerations

*Regine M. Talleyrand*

Eating disorder (ED) symptom rates among people of color have been increasing in recent years, yet the research in this area remains limited and plagued with inconsistencies. The lack of research examining people of color and EDs can be attributed to the fact that EDs have historically been considered to occur only among young, affluent White women (Andersen & Hay, 1985; Root, 2001). Yet, research reports have demonstrated that ED symptoms are experienced by women of color. In fact, African American and Latina women tend to experience binge eating rates comparable to those of their White counterparts (Alegria et al., 2007; George & Franko, 2010; Striegel-Moore, Wilfley, Pike, Dohm, & Fairburn, 2000), and Asian American women tend to experience similar or higher rates of body dissatisfaction in comparison to their White counterparts (George & Franko, 2010; Grabe & Hyde, 2006; Kronenfield, Reba-Harrelson, Von Holle, Reyes, & Bulik, 2010). In addition, obesity rates are highest among Black and Latina women, with four of five (80%) Black women experiencing excess weight or obesity and approximately three of four (75%) Latina women experiencing excess weight or obesity (Flegal, Carroll, Ogden, & Curtin, 2010).

Men, too, have traditionally been understudied in the ED literature on the basis of the belief that they are less likely to develop and engage in disordered eating behaviors (Mintz & Kashubeck, 1999). However, some evidence (albeit very limited) has shown that men of color do exhibit ED symptoms (Johnson, Rohan, & Kirk, 2002; Reyes-Rodriguez et al., 2010; Taylor, Caldwell, Baser, Faison, & Jackson, 2007). This research is highlighted in the next section of this chapter.

The reported incidences of ED symptoms and obesity in people of color underscore the need for counselors to know how to effectively assess and treat all individuals who struggle with eating, weight, and body image concerns. Because people of color may be less likely to receive referrals or to seek treatment for ED symptoms partially on the basis of prevailing stereotypes of traditional clients with EDs (Cachelin, Veisel, Barzengarnazari, & Striegel-Moore, 2000; Kelly et al., 2011), counselors have an ethical responsibility to provide culturally responsive assessment, prevention, and treatment to clients of color (Kempa & Thomas, 2000). In this chapter, I briefly highlight the research that has been conducted among people of color and review the unique sociocultural factors that may influence the presence of ED symptoms and obesity in clients of color. In addition, I provide specific counseling strategies to assist counselors in working with people of color who struggle with weight, eating, and body image concerns. A case study illustrating these strategies is also included at the end of the chapter.

# People of Color in the Eating Disorders Literature

As previously mentioned, EDs have been long documented to rarely occur among women of color in the United States because they are less likely to be exposed to key risk factors such as a thin beauty ideal or societal pressures to be thin (Chao et al., 2008; Nicdao, Hong, & Takeuchi, 2007; Root, 1990, 2001; Smolak & Striegel-Moore, 2001). However, the presence of increasing ED symptoms among women of color (Arriaza & Mann, 2001; Chao et al., 2008; Nicdao et al., 2007; Shaw, Ramirez, Trost, Randall, & Stice, 2004; Taylor et al., 2007) has prompted researchers to reconsider the belief that cultural factors protect women of color. Furthermore, the increased presence of racially and ethnically diverse celebrity female and male role models in the media may contribute to a rise in the rates of body and eating disturbances among women and men of color (Chao et al., 2008; Kempa & Thomas, 2000; Phan & Tylka, 2006; Smolak & Striegel-Moore, 2001).

## African American Women

African American women are the most studied group of women in the ED literature, with the majority of research studies comparing African American and White women's disordered eating attitudes and behaviors (Grabe & Hyde, 2006). Several researchers have argued that African American cultural factors may serve a protective role in the development of EDs among African American women because social pressures surrounding thinness may not exist in the African American community (Abrams, Allen, & Gray, 1993; Lynch, 2004; Rubin, Fitts, & Becker, 2003; Rucker & Cash, 1992; Smolak & Striegel-Moore, 2001; B. Thompson, 1994). Moreover, obesity may not be stigmatized in African American culture as in the dominant White American culture because, from a historical standpoint, being overweight was viewed as sign of wealth by the African community (Kumanyika, Wilson, & Guilford-Davenport, 1993; Smolak & Striegel-Moore, 2001).

Other researchers have noted that, from a historical standpoint, African American women have been exempt from traditional gender roles and have taken on the roles of caregivers, providers, and survivors as a result of the absence of husbands or male figures during the eras of slavery and post-Reconstruction (Malson, Mudimbe-Boyi, O'Barr, & Wyer, 1990). Consequently, African American women have been socialized to take care of others before taking care of themselves (Greene, 1994; Thomas, Witherspoon, & Speight, 2004; Villarosa, 1994). Understanding the portrayal of African American women as strong, resilient, and self-sufficient can potentially explain the additional stressors they may experience and the potentially risky eating behaviors (binge eating) they may use to cope with these stressors (Greene, 1994; Kempa & Thomas, 2000; Talleyrand, 2006).

Research studies have consistently supported the notion that African American women are, in general, less likely to be concerned about their size and body shape, less likely to view themselves as overweight, and less reliant on dieting or weight control behaviors, allegedly because of African American cultural beauty standards that support heavier body ideals (Arriaza & Mann, 2001; Chao et al., 2008; Grabe & Hyde, 2006; Kelly et al., 2011; Kronenfield et al., 2010; Roberts, Cash, Feingold, & Johnson, 2006; Root, 1990). However, several recent studies have suggested that prevalence rates of ED symptoms, in particular binge eating behaviors, among African American women are similar to or higher than rates among White women (Shaw et al., 2004; Striegel-Moore, Wilfley, Pike, Dohm, & Fairburn, 2000; Taylor et al., 2007). In addition, some researchers have claimed that Black women do experience pressures regarding beauty and body esteem, yet the traditional methods of evaluating these factors (e.g., use of weight, body parts) may not capture the real body appearance concerns of Black women (Kelly et al., 2011; Poran, 2006; Roberts et al., 2006). That is, additional factors such as hair, skin color, and social comparisons with other Black women may be more relevant when evaluating Black women's body esteem (Poran, 2006). Moreover, the high rates of obesity and binge eating behaviors among African American women highlight the need to look beyond traditional EDs (i.e., anorexia and bulimia) when working with African American women who struggle with problems with eating, weight, and shape.

## Asian American Women

Asian Americans are one of the most rapidly growing groups in the United States, yet Asian American women are largely underrepresented in the ED literature. This research gap has been suggested to be related to the stereotypical belief that Asian Americans do not experience psychological problems and their smaller body sizes protect them from experiencing body dissatisfaction (Phan & Tylka, 2006). In addition, Asian Americans' potential mistrust of the mental health care system, stigmatized view of mental health disorders, and cultural values, including the need for achievement, perfectionism, and family approval, may be reasons why they do not seek help for problems with symptoms of disordered eating (Nouri, Hill, & Orrell-Valente, 2011; Phan & Tylka, 2006; Sue & Sue, 2008). Finally, their label as the "model minority" (i.e., most highly achieving minority group) may also contribute to their pressure to succeed despite the fact that this label is in contrast to the true experiences of Asian Americans (Sue & Sue, 2008).

Although some cultural factors may prevent Asian American women from seeking treatment for their eating concerns, the growing consensus is that Asian American women are experiencing eating and body image disturbance and that research studies have underestimated these rates (Cummins, Simmons, & Zane, 2005; Grabe & Hyde, 2006; Nouri et al., 2011). Limited existing empirical research has produced contradictory findings regarding the presence of specific ED symptoms in female Asian American samples. Although some researchers have found that Asian American women exhibit higher rates of body dissatisfaction in comparison to women from other racial and ethnic groups (Mintz & Kashubeck, 1999), others have found little to no difference in reports of eating and body concerns among Asian American, African American, Latina, and White women (Arriaza & Mann, 2001; Grabe & Hyde, 2006; Shaw et al., 2004). In addition, some researchers have argued that Asian American women may experience body image dissatisfaction and low self-esteem because body parts and facial features specific to their racial and ethnic groups may not reflect the beauty ideal in the dominant culture (Grabe & Hyde, 2006; Mintz & Kashubeck, 1999; Nouri et al., 2011; Phan & Tylka, 2006). Thus, an evaluation of Asian American women's internalization of sociocultural pressures regarding beauty could be useful when working with Asian American women who display ED symptoms. Given the limited existing research and inconsistent findings, it is evident that additional ED research focused on Asian American women is warranted and could be instrumental in the development of culturally competent counseling strategies for Asian American women.

### Latina Women

Latina women represent another rapidly growing majority in the United States yet are also underrepresented in the ED research. Some researchers have believed that Latina women are protected from being dissatisfied with their bodies because, similar to African American cultural values, larger women are considered healthy and wealthy in Latino cultures (Kempa & Thomas, 2000). Other researchers have suggested that adherence to more traditional gender roles and a strong cultural focus on physical appearance may lead to higher prevalence rates of body dissatisfaction among Latina women. In addition, Latino cultural values, including the importance of machismo (dominance of men), religiosity, and *simpatia* (creating conflict-free situations), may explain why some Latina women may potentially engage in disordered eating behaviors as an expression of their anger and alleged lack of power within their cultural group (Grabe & Hyde, 2006; Kempa & Thomas, 2000).

A summary of the research on Latina women suggests that Latinas might not engage in dietary restraint behaviors, yet across all other measures of ED symptoms (e.g., weight and shape concerns), their rates of ED symptoms are similar to those of their White female counterparts (Alegria et al., 2007; Arriza & Mann, 2001; Shaw et al., 2004). Thus, whereas some have thought that Latina women may be protected from internalizing the thin ideal, they still appear to report body and eating behaviors and attitudes characteristic of anorexia, bulimia, and binge eating disorder that, again, reinforce the fact that cultural factors may no longer protect women of color.

Another important factor to consider when working with Latina women is the fact that Latina women have the second highest obesity rates in the United States. Some researchers have suggested that the acculturation process, a process of adjusting one's own cultural values and belief systems to accommodate the norms and values of a different, more dominant group (Kim & Abreu, 2001), is partially to blame for the obesity problem among Latina immigrants. That is, researchers have found that more time spent living in the United States has increased the potential for obesity among Latina women and children because they are exposed to unhealthy dietary patterns and sedentary lifestyles in the United States (Gordon-Larsen, Harris, Ward, & Popkin, 2003; Wolin, Colangelo, Chiu, & Gapstur, 2009). The acculturation process may also cause Latina immigrants to turn to ED symptoms to cope with the tension of living in a new culture that focuses on thinness versus the Latina culture's emphasis on being curvaceous (Franko & George, 2008). Thus, an exploration of the acculturation process may be helpful when working with Latina women who struggle with eating, body image, and weight concerns. A more in-depth discussion of acculturation as a risk factor for women of color is provided in a later section of the chapter.

## Men of Color

As previously stated, men are often not represented in research reports focused on the study of EDs. However, some reports have suggested that, compared with anorexia and bulimia, men and woman experience binge eating and binge eating disorder more equally (Mitchell & Mazzeo, 2004). The limited research on boys and men of color has suggested that male adolescents and adults of color do engage in binge eating behaviors and accompanying compensatory behaviors at rates that are comparable to those of their female counterparts. For example, Reyes-Rodriguez et al. (2010) studied ED symptoms among 1st-year college students and found that Latino college men engaged in more binge eating behaviors and compensatory behaviors (e.g., laxative use, excessive exercise) than their female Latina counterparts. In addition, Johnson et al. (2002) examined the prevalence and correlates of binge eating in a sample of 822 White and African American adolescents. These researchers found that African American boys reported the highest rate of binge eating (26%), whereas the binge eating rate for African American girls, White boys, and White girls was approximately 18%. In addition, depressive symptoms and consumption of high-fat foods served as the strongest predictors of binge eating behaviors. Finally, Taylor et al. (2007), in studying Black and African American adolescents and adults, found that male adolescents had more cases of anorexia nervosa, bulimia nervosa, and any binge eating than female adolescents. Thus, boys and men of color appear to experience ED symptoms at rates that are comparable to or higher than those of their female counterparts. Given these findings, additional investigations in this area are warranted to fully understand the severity and risk factors associated with these behaviors.

### Summary

It is evident from the limited body of research that the cultural factors once thought to protect clients of color from experiencing ED symptoms may no longer exist because women of color are displaying rates of ED symptoms similar to those of their White counterparts. In addition, some research reports have suggested that men of color also show ED symptoms. Furthermore, the traditional measures used to assess ED symptoms in clients of color may not provide an accurate portrayal of the eating and body appearance concerns experienced by clients of color. Thus, a more comprehensive and culturally relevant assessment of EDs among clients of color is needed to clear up the many inconsistencies that exist in the literature base (Chao et al., 2008; George & Franko, 2010; Kelly et al., 2011). Moreover, increased attention should be given to Asian American and Latina women because they represent a growing majority of the U.S. population and have been marginalized in the ED literature (George & Franko, 2010; Grabe & Hyde, 2006; Warren, Castillo, & Gleaves, 2010). Equally important is the need to explore the severity of ED symptoms across racially and ethnically diverse men because symptoms appear to be increasingly present in this segment of the population as well.

# Potential Risk Factors for Clients of Color

According to the *Diagnostic and Statistical Manual of Mental Disorders* (4th ed., text rev.; American Psychiatric Association, 2000), *anorexia nervosa* is defined as an ED characterized by a person's refusal to maintain her or his body weight, use of excessive dieting, and inaccurate perceptions of her or his body image on the basis of an obsessive fear of becoming fat. *Bulimia nervosa* is characterized by a person's excessive rapid bingeing followed by purging through the use of self-induced vomiting, laxatives, diuretics, restrained eating, or excessive exercise. Binge eating disorder, which falls under the ED not otherwise specified category, is defined by recurrent episodes of binge eating that occur in the absence of regular use of compensatory behaviors such as purging (Streigel-Moore et al., 2005). *Obesity* refers to having a body mass index of 30 or greater and being more than 20% above the upper limit for height, and *overweight* is defined as having a body mass index ranging from 25 to 29.9 (Centers for Disease and Prevention, 2012).

In spite of the increased awareness of disordered eating attitudes and behaviors among clients of color, counselors may have little or no experience treating clients of color who struggle with eating and body image concerns because clients of color may underuse the mental health system because of health care costs, stigma, fear of discrimination, and general mistrust of the mental health system (Kempa & Thomas, 2000; Sue & Sue, 2008; Smart, 2010b). In addition, counselors may miss diagnosing clients of color on the basis of prevailing stereotypes of clients with EDs. In this section, I discuss multiple contextual factors (e.g., acculturation, racial identity, intersection of race and gender) that may affect why and how clients of color struggle with their eating behaviors and weight (Polivy & Herman, 2002; Pumariega, Gustavson, Gustavson, Motes, & Ayers, 1994; Rucker & Cash, 1992; Smolak & Striegel-Moore, 2001; Talleyrand, 2006; Wood & Petrie, 2010).

## Acculturation and Immigration

Acculturation has often been viewed as the phenomenon that occurs when an individual comes into contact with more than one cultural system (Padilla, 1980). Thus, the acculturation process entails adjusting one's cultural values and belief systems to accommodate the norms and values of a different, more dominant group. Conversely, enculturation is a process through which an individual retains his or her own cultural values regardless of the dominant culture (Kim & Abreu, 2001). For example, a female immigrant from Ecuador living in the United States can be considered acculturated if she adopts the sociocultural pursuit of thinness embedded in the U.S. dominant culture but enculturated if she retains the cultural norms defining beauty and appearance from her country of origin.

Research studying the link between acculturation and the prevalence of EDs has yielded inconsistent results. Some researchers have found no link between levels of acculturation and reports of ED symptoms and obesity (Granillo, Jones-Rodriguez, & Carvajal, 2005; Nicdao et al., 2007; Nouri et al., 2011), whereas others have found some support for these relationships (Gowen, Hayward, Killen, Robinson, & Taylor, 1999; Liou & Bauer, 2007; Wolin et al., 2009). For example, Gowen et al. (1999) found that the more acculturated Latinas were to the dominant White American culture, the more likely they were to be diagnosed with a partial-syndrome ED than Latinas who were less acculturated to the dominant White American culture. Conversely, research has shown that the less acculturated Asian families are, the higher body image dissatisfaction they report, which may be indicative of traditional cultural norms regarding body image within

Asian ethnic groups (Gowen et al., 1999). Relatedly, more exposure to living in the United States has been found to be associated with the consumption of unhealthy American foods by Asian youths and with obesity among Latina women (Liou & Bauer, 2007; Wolin et al., 2009).

Although African Americans may not be considered immigrants in the United States, African American cultural values are different from those of the dominant culture, thus African Americans also undergo acculturation and enculturation processes to some extent (Landrine, Richardson, Klonoff, & Flay 1994). The few studies that have examined the relationship between cultural identity and ED symptoms among African American women have found that higher levels of cultural or ethnic identity have directly or indirectly protected African American women against some anorexia- and bulimia-related risk factors, including the internalization of societal messages about beauty (Pumariega et al., 1994; Shuttlesworth & Zotter, 2011; Wood & Petrie, 2010).

Given their identification with nondominant groups in the United States, one of the many challenges clients of color may face is the acculturation process. Assessing a client's level of acculturation could help counselors ascertain the level of risk in developing an ED. That is, cultural norms that promote larger body ideals may protect some individuals from engaging in severe weight- and body-related attitudes and behaviors (S. M. Harris, 1994; Root, 2001). However, others may struggle with competing cultural norms regarding appearance and experience more body dissatisfaction and eating disturbances because of this conflict (George & Franko, 2010; Root, 2001). Finally, it is important to recognize that some risk factors may be inherent in non-Western cultures (i.e., idealization of thinness in Asian cultures) that increase the risk of experiencing ED symptoms among non-Western groups (Gowan et al., 1999). I should also note that many inconsistencies do exist within these research findings, which can partially be explained by the conceptualization and measurement of acculturation (Nouri et al., 2011; Warren et al., 2010). For example, use of a language variable or racial or ethnic identity to measure acculturation may obscure the complexity of the acculturation process.

### Racial and Ethnic Identity

The concept of racial identity is related to the extent to which the person identifies with the racial group to which he or she supposedly belongs with the belief that commitment to one's racial group is necessary for healthy psychological functioning (Helms & Cook, 1999). *Ethnic identity* refers to the extent to which women accept, identify with, and affirm their ethnic heritage (Phinney, 1992). Researchers have suggested that high levels of ethnic and racial identity may assist ethnically diverse women in rejecting the societal beauty ideals of the dominant culture (S. M. Harris, 1994; Shuttlesworth & Zotter, 2011; Wood & Petrie, 2010). Only a few studies to date have examined the relationships between racial or ethnic identity and ED symptoms. A common finding using Helms's (1995) Black Racial Identity Model has been that African American women who idealize Whiteness or use White-identified schemas (e.g., preencounter) tend to engage in restrictive forms of disordered eating attitudes and behaviors (e.g., dietary restraint, body dissatisfaction; Abrams et al., 1993; S. M. Harris, 1994). Simply put, African American women's internalization of dominant White standards appears to be linked to anorexia- or bulimia-type symptoms. In studies of ethnic identity and ED symptoms, lower levels of ethnic identity among women of color have predicted higher rates of ED attitudes and behaviors among African American women (Shuttlesworth & Zotter, 2011; Wood & Petrie, 2010). Not surprisingly, high levels of ethnic identity among White women have been found to be related to high rates of both binge eating and global eating pathology (Shuttlesworth & Zotter, 2011).

Results from these studies have suggested that assessing racial or ethnic identity among clients of color may provide valuable information regarding the manner in which they may manifest ED symptoms (Talleyrand, 2006; Wood & Petrie, 2010). I should note that what is lacking in the ED and identity literature are measures that assess the identity process among individuals who identify with multiple racial or ethnic groups. Identifying with multiple racial or ethnic groups could cause additional stressors for clients of color, particularly if the cultural values of each group conflict.

## Racism and Oppression

Another risk factor for the development of EDs in clients of color is their simultaneous membership in two oppressed demographic identity groups (i.e., gender and race). This membership can heighten the possibility that women of color, in particular, will face unique challenges of racism and sexism, including feeling marginalized by and powerless in society (Greene, 1994; Kempa & Thomas, 2000; Myers, 1998; Thomas et al., 2004). That is, feelings of powerlessness and lack of control, which are common emotions in women who experience EDs, could drive women of color to use food (e.g., either restricting food or bingeing) as a mechanism to gain back control in their lives (Kempa & Thomas, 2000; B. Thompson, 1994, 1997). Given that women of color's eating and health concerns may be related to the double jeopardy of being a person of color and female, it is imperative that researchers assess levels of oppression and stress and coping behaviors when studying EDs and obesity among women of color. In addition, it is imperative that counselors understand how the interaction of racism and sexism may contribute to ED symptoms and obesity among women of color.

## Socioeconomic Status

Women of color in the United States experience classism (e.g., disparate effects of social policy on low-status groups) because they have less access to positions of power and authority than White men and women. Because a disproportionate number of African American and Latina women identify as low income, they are at risk for experiencing health concerns because they lack access to economic resources (Dounchis, Hayden, & Wilfrey, 2001; Downing, 2004; Paul,

2003). Results from research examining race, socioeconomic status, and disordered eating behaviors have been contradictory (O'Neill, 2003). Some findings have suggested that the risk of developing EDs such as anorexia nervosa and bulimia are higher among middle-class African American women who adopt White middle-class values (Polivy & Herman, 2002; Pumariega et al., 1994; Rucker & Cash, 1992; Smolak & Striegel-Moore, 2001). Yet, other researchers have found the link between socioeconomic status and ED symptoms to be nonsignificant (Besselieu, 1997; S. M. Harris, 1994; Reel, 2000).

With regard to poverty and obesity, there has been some agreement based on research that women of color of lower socioeconomic status seem to be at higher risk for becoming obese than those of higher socioeconomic status (O'Neill, 2003). For example, B. Thompson (1994) interviewed several women of color who struggled with eating problems and found that they used emotional overeating behaviors to cope with their experience of poverty-related stress. In addition, other researchers have argued that women who struggle with poverty may be malnourished or have diets high in fats and sugars (Dounchis et al., 2001; Paul, 2003). In fact, Kumanyika and Grier (2006) suggested that research has typically shown that low-income children typically live in areas that have a high concentration of unhealthy fast food restaurants than in predominately White and higher class neighborhoods. These low-income areas may present additional barriers, including unsafe and often dangerous streets and neighborhoods that provide inadequate area for children to play and exercise. Given the high rates of obesity among children and women of color, studying and understanding how poverty-related stress relates to eating behaviors and obesity in these groups continues to be important.

## Implications for Counseling

As noted in the previous section, multiple contextual factors such as acculturation, racism, and classism are potential realities in the lives of many women (and potentially men) of color. Yet, traditional risk factors such as body dissatisfaction are often used to evaluate the presence of ED symptoms among clients of color (Grabe & Hyde, 2006; Kempa & Thomas, 2000). Thus, their unique experiences as clients of color are rarely accounted for in the ED literature. Finally, clients of color who do struggle with eating concerns may not present in the same way as do their White counterparts. To that effect, counselors who are working with clients of color should be knowledgeable of their unique sociocultural experiences. The following are specific recommendations for assessing risk factors among clients of color and for providing culturally competent counseling when working with clients of color who present with concerns regarding body appearance, weight, or eating attitudes and behaviors.

1. Counselors should be aware that many potential barriers to mental health care exist among clients of color on the basis of their sociopolitical histories and cultural beliefs. For example, research has suggested that people of color may underuse treatment services for

EDs because of a lack of financial resources or insurance; strong distrust of the mental health system; fears that others may not be able to help; lack of awareness of resources; and feelings of shame and stigmatization (Alegria et al., 2007; Kempa & Thomas, 2000; Nicdao et al, 2007; Smart, 2010b; Sue & Sue, 2008). When working with clients of color, counselors need to be aware of these factors and address issues of trust and potential fears early on in the counseling session. Furthermore, the provision of psychoeducational workshops in local schools, community centers, and religious organizations may be a culturally appropriate method of providing access to useful resources for clients of color (Story et al., 2003).

2. University counseling centers and school and community agency counselors may want to use a more inclusive assessment system when working with clients of color who struggle with eating, weight, and body image concerns. Because researchers have shown that some ED measures may not assess the same constructs in women of color (Kelly et al., 2011), the use of traditional ED measures (e.g., EAT–26; Garner, Olmsted, Bohr, & Garfinkel, 1982) in combination with other data sources, including acculturation and racial identity measures, could provide a more comprehensive assessment system when working with clients of color. Consequently, use of a comprehensive assessment system could also improve rates of ED diagnosis and referrals among clients of color.

3. It is imperative for counselors to understand culture-specific themes and worldviews in the lives of clients of color (Kempa & Thomas, 2000). For example, Asian American cultural values, including the success myth, model minority myth, shame, and need for family approval (Sue & Sue, 2008), could also be important in understanding why and how Asian Americans manifest their ED symptoms. For Latinas, the importance of traditional gender roles, religiosity, and the notion of *simpatia* (creating conflict-free situations) may be relevant in understanding why and how Latina women present with ED symptoms and obesity. Finally, understanding African American women's multiple historic roles as caregivers, providers, and survivors can assist counselors in understanding the additional stressors they may experience and the potentially risky eating behaviors (binge eating) they may use to cope with these stressors (Greene, 1994; Kempa & Thomas, 2000; Talleyrand, 2006).

4. Understanding how clients' level of acculturation to their traditional culture or to the dominant culture influences their beliefs regarding food and physical appearance is critical. Therefore, assessing clients' level of acculturation and enculturation can provide useful information on how and why they present with weight concerns. Potential questions to pose with clients who have experienced the acculturation process could include migration status, generational status, rationale for coming to the United States, language acquisition, duration of time spent in the United States, lack of family presence, and ethnicity of social networks. A cultural genogram (Hardy & Laszloffy,

1995) could be an effective tool in eliciting information about the process clients and their families have gone through in coping with competing cultural demands involved in the acculturation process. In addition, a cultural genogram could potentially help clients uncover the messages related to the role of food, eating behaviors and attitudes, body image, and overall appearance that have been passed down in the family. Some questions could include "What kinds of messages regarding beauty and appearance were you raised with?" "What makes you aware of your body?" "How do you think being a client of color affects your experience of cultural messages regarding beauty and appearance?"

5. In addition to assessing levels of acculturation, counselors should assess the degree to which clients of color internalize racial and gender oppression (Kempa & Thomas, 2000; Talleyrand, 2006). More specifically, helping clients identify the conscious and unconscious methods they use to respond to stressors related to different oppressive forces in their lives could provide valuable information concerning ways they cope with their oppressed status (D. J. Harris & Kuba, 1997; Mastria, 2002; B. Thompson, 1994, 1997). For example, in Latino cultures, women occupy traditional gender roles and are less valued then men; this form of oppression and lack of power could serve as a risk factor for the development of EDs in Latina women (Kempa & Thomas, 2000). Use of a racial identity measure (e.g., Helms's People of Color Racial Identity Scale) could help counselors understand how clients of color internalize their racial oppression (Helms & Cook, 1999; Talleyrand, 2006). In addition, use of an ethnic identity measure (Phinney, 1992) could also provide insight into clients of color's identification with their ethnic heritage and the risk factors they may experience (Shuttlesworth & Zotter, 2011; Wood & Petrie, 2010). As mentioned earlier, when working with biracial and multiracial clients, assessing the strength of their identification with each of their racial or ethnic groups is important because it may affect their beliefs regarding appearance.

6. Counselors should consider referring to stress and coping models that address issues pertaining to clients of color to assist them in working with their clients. Limited extant research exists on the types of coping strategies that individuals use to respond to racism. Some theorists have suggested that the use of unhealthy coping strategies (e.g., avoidance, denial) to respond to racism may result in negative physical and mental health outcomes such as low self-esteem, hypertension, obesity, and suicide (e.g., Anderson, 1991; Clark et al., 1999; Landrine & Klonoff, 1996; Paul, 2003; B. Thompson, 1997; C. E. Thompson & Neville, 1999; Wyatt et al., 2003). For counselors, assessing the relationship between clients of color's appraisal of racial stressors and the enactment of subsequent coping strategies, particularly overeating, may be useful in evaluating how they manage

their racial stress and in evaluating whether negative physical health outcomes (e.g., obesity) are related to the use of particular coping strategies. Use of formal measures such as the Schedule of Racist Events (Landrine & Klonoff, 1996) or the Index of Race Related Stress (Utsey & Ponterotto, 1996) may help counselors assess the types and frequency of race-related stress experienced by African Americans. Informally, a counselor can ask clients of color to list the most salient stressors in their lives and then have them describe the types of coping mechanisms (e.g., active or passive) they use when they encounter these stressors.

In addition to the assessment of the above-mentioned factors when working with clients of color who struggle with eating and body concerns, counselors may also want to use the following counseling therapies and modalities when working with clients of color:

1. Cognitive–behavioral therapy is an evidence-based approach that has been found to be effective in the treatment of EDs, in particular in treating clients who struggle with bulimia (American Psychiatric Association, 2006; Smart, 2010a, 2010b; see also Chapter 13, this volume). The use of cognitive–behavioral therapy could be effective when working with clients of color because of its emphasis on a solution-focused, time-limited approach, educational and practical focus, collaborative action, and lack of emphasis on the past or family. These components of cognitive–behavioral therapy may be well accepted among groups that have been underrepresented and may distrust the mental health care system (Sue & Sue, 2008; Smart, 2010a, 2010b). Nonetheless, counselors may still need to adapt this approach to include an exploration of the contextual factors and cultural values that are relevant in understanding how a client perceives his or her problem (Smart, 2010a, 2010b; Sue & Sue, 2008). For example, assessing body satisfaction for women of color may include an evaluation of a client's facial features (skin color, nose) and hair (Grabe & Hyde, 2006; Mintz & Kashubeck, 1999; Smart, 2010b) in addition to body parts.

2. Feminist therapy techniques, which view problems in a sociopolitical and cultural context, could also be useful when working with clients of color given the sociopolitical histories of people of color. For example, viewing the presenting concerns of women of color in the context of a sexist and racist environment (McDonald, 2012) could inform the therapy process and give clients of color a voice with which to express their reactions (e.g., bingeing behaviors) to feeling the effects of sexism and racism (see also Chapter 18, this volume).

3. Interpersonal therapy is another evidence-based therapy that can be used with clients in individual or group settings (American Psychiatric Association, 2006; see also Chapter 14, this volume). Interpersonal therapy is a time-limited and semistructured form

of therapy that focuses on assisting clients to identify and cope with the interpersonal difficulties they face in their lives (Choate, 2010) rather than specifically on their disordered eating thoughts and behaviors. The assumption in interpersonal therapy is that women may use disordered eating behaviors to cope with the relational difficulties they may be experiencing, including lack of social support, conflict with peers, and family difficulties (Choate, 2010). Given that women of color, as members of two oppressed identity groups, may struggle with multiple life stressors (e.g., acculturation processes, role conflict, experiences of racism, racial identity) that could affect their interpersonal relationships, the use of interpersonal therapy could provide the contextual framework necessary when working with women of color who present with disordered eating attitudes and behaviors.

4. Group counseling may be an effective mode of service delivery when working with clients of color because of the nature of the experience—group counseling calls for close relationships among group members and a sense of community (Williams, Frame, & Green, 1999). The emphasis on close relationships and community is consistent with the collectivistic values embedded in African American, Latino, and Asian American cultures (Greene, 1994; Kempa & Thomas, 2000; Smart, 2010b). Moreover, use of group therapy versus traditional individual therapies with clients of color may feel less threatening given the potential barriers (e.g., distrust of the mental health system) to accessing mental health services among this population (George & Franko, 2010; Williams et al., 1999). Finally, the empowering and egalitarian nature of the group counseling process may also be appealing to clients of color who may face several forms of oppression on a daily basis (Coker, Meyer, Smith, & Price, 2010).

5. Family therapy has been considered another effective form of therapy for clients struggling with EDs because it deals with family relational problems that may contribute to the development of an ED (American Psychiatric Association, 2006). It is particularly helpful for adolescent clients (see Chapter 17, this volume). Given the strong value placed on family (including extended family members) in African American, Asian American, and Latino cultures, family therapy may be an effective and culturally relevant form of therapy when working with clients of color who present with eating and body concerns (Kempa & Thomas, 2000). That is, involving family members in the therapy process could potentially create a sense of unity among family members and the counselor, could allow counselors to educate family members about the general risk factors associated with the development of EDs, and could allow counselors to learn about specific cultural values in the family that could potentially contribute to the development of EDs.

# Case Example

Kathy is a 19-year-old who identifies as African American. Kathy has lived in a predominantly Black neighborhood for the first 19 years of her life and is currently completing her freshman year at a predominantly White university. Kathy is the oldest of three children—she has a younger brother and sister—and lived with her siblings and her parents before attending college. All of her childhood friends identify as Black, and she is the first from her neighborhood to leave her community and attend a university that is predominantly White and located far from her hometown. Everyone from her hometown was very excited about her move and has told her numerous times how proud they are of her. Kathy's roommate at school is White and has similar interests to Kathy—they both enjoy watching reality television shows, they love shopping for clothes, and both enjoy sports. Kathy enjoys spending time with her roommate but does not always feel comfortable in a large group of White peers. While living at home, Kathy was more concerned about her external appearance (e.g., hairstyle and clothes) and never worried about her weight. However, within the past few months Kathy has noticed that she has become more concerned with her weight and feels fat compared with her roommate. Her roommate has a slim build but is always dieting and goes to the gym on a daily basis. Kathy's build is heavier than her roommate's, yet her curvaceous figure was considered ideal when she lived at home. Kathy has been binge eating late at night on a daily basis to cope with her negative feelings regarding her body image. Because Kathy is not as invested in going to the gym and dislikes dieting, she has started to use laxatives and purging behaviors twice a week to deal with the weight she has gained from her nightly binges. Because she is focusing all of her attention on managing her weight, Kathy's grades are starting to suffer. She worries about going to see a counselor because she does not want to disclose her struggles with her weight. She has not talked to her family because she does not want to let them know she is struggling academically. After being called into her psychology professor's office for potentially failing her class, she informs her professor that she has been homesick, which has been stressing her out. Her instructor refers her to the University Counseling Center.

## Case Conceptualization of Client

On the basis of this client description, the counselor would attempt to understand Kathy's presenting concerns from a multicultural perspective given that she identifies as an African American woman and is experiencing a major cultural conflict given her new environment. In doing so, the counselor would examine the contextual factors that may be affecting her negative body image, use of unhealthy weight loss behaviors, and academic stress. Kathy reports several risk factors that could contribute to her experiencing ED symptoms. First, she has moved from a predominantly Black environment where she experienced family and peer support to a predominantly White environment where she seems to be part of an underrepresented group. This potential social isolation from a similar racial peer group could be contributing to her desire to fit in with her peers and minimize her feelings of being or looking different. Second, she seems to be receiving conflicting cultural messages regarding body image. At home, her curves were appreciated, yet a thinner body ideal seems to be the norm among her current peer group. This conflict regarding standards of beauty could be another source of stress for Kathy, and she may be using unhealthy weight management strategies to try to cope with this conflict. Third, her simultaneous membership in two oppressed demographic identity groups (i.e., gender and race) could heighten the possibility that Kathy is feeling marginalized and powerless in her new environment and is using negative coping strategies to gain control of her life. Finally, given that she is the first in her neighborhood to attend a school outside of her region and she is the first child in her family to attend college, she may be facing additional pressures to succeed.

## Course of Treatment

The first goal of counseling would be to establish rapport with Kathy because she is wary of disclosing her eating, body, and weight issues with anyone. The counselor should spend ample time explaining the therapy process to Kathy and creating a safe, egalitarian, and collaborative environment for her during the course of her treatment. It is also important that the counselor reduce any stigma regarding EDs with Kathy because she may be experiencing some sense of shame or lack of information regarding EDs and their related symptoms. What could be helpful during the initial phase of counseling would be use of literature discussing EDs among African American women (e.g., Covington Armstrong, 2009, Table 1).

Given the conflict Kathy may be experiencing in negotiating two different cultural contexts, the counselor may want to discuss how this shift in her environment has affected her. Use of a cultural genogram can assist with exploring the messages regarding standards of beauty she received at home versus those she is experiencing in school. Also, a discussion of the coping strategies she has used in the past to deal with stress may provide additional insight into her current behaviors.

During the course of treatment, the counselor should also administer a measure of EDs (e.g., EAT-26) to further assess the depth of Kathy's disordered eating behaviors and attitudes; however, the counselor should keep in mind that these measures may not be fully accurate with Kathy because they are based on White female norms. Use of a racial identity measure (Helms & Cook, 1999), ethnic identity measure (Phinney, 1992), or race-related stress measure (Schedule of Racist Events; Landrine & Klonoff, 1996) could help paint a more comprehensive picture of Kathy's experience.

Once rapport has been established between Kathy and the counselor, and Kathy has had the chance to explore her racial and cultural experiences, the use of cognitive–behavioral therapy to break the cycle of thinking and behaving that promotes poor self-image and uncontrolled binging and purging cycles could be effective. In addition, it would be beneficial to have Kathy self-monitor and record food intake, purging, thoughts, and feelings and explore her emotional struggles and how her disordered eating symptoms may be an expression of these struggles or an unhealthy way of managing them.

Conducting a depression inventory once more information has been gathered on Kathy to assess whether her feelings of social isolation are leaving her feeling depressed should also be considered. Exploration of Kathy's role in her family system could also be beneficial given the expectations she may feel have been placed on her. Given Kathy's close family ties, involving Kathy's family in the later stages of the therapy process may be another culturally relevant treatment alternative.

The counselor may also want to consider referring Kathy to an ED support group because group counseling calls for close relationships among group members and a sense of community. This lack of community may be what Kathy is missing at this point in her life. Finally, given Kathy's lack of interaction with African American peers, it may be necessary to link her with school resources such as affinity groups targeted toward minorities at her university. This linkage could provide Kathy with the support she used to receive at home.

## Conclusion

Although research focused on people of color and EDs has certainly increased in recent years, to date there continue to be few published studies that have examined the unique socialization experiences of African Americans and, to a lesser extent, Asian American and Latina women and men. Research with Native Americans and Arab Americans remains virtually nonexistent. Given the racial and ethnic composition of the United States and the presence of ED symptoms among women and men of color, additional investigations in this area can assist counselors, psychologists, counselor educators, and researchers to present a more comprehensive picture of the prevalence of and risk factors for eating concerns in all individuals. Furthermore, additional attention to this area can contribute to the provision of culturally competent assessment, prevention, treatment, and counselor training.

## Chapter Highlights

- Although EDs have historically been considered to occur only in young, affluent White women, the presence of increasing ED symptoms has recently been documented in women of color.
- The high rates of obesity and binge eating behaviors among African American women highlight the need to look beyond traditional EDs (i.e., anorexia and bulimia) when working with African American women who struggle with problems with eating, weight, and shape.

61

- Asian American women have been found to experience body image dissatisfaction and low self-esteem because body parts and facial features specific to their racial and ethnic groups may not reflect the beauty ideal in the dominant culture.
- Latina women may not engage in dietary restraint behaviors, yet across all other measures of ED symptoms (e.g., weight and shape concerns), the rate of ED symptoms among Latinas are similar to those among their White female counterparts.
- Potential sociocultural risk factors for clients of color experiencing ED symptoms include the acculturation and immigration process, racial and ethnic identity, acts of racism and oppression, and socioeconomic status.
- Traditional ED measures may not assess the same constructs in women of color; therefore, counselors should use a more comprehensive assessment system when working with clients of color.
- Cognitive–behavioral, feminist, and interpersonal therapy techniques along with group and family therapy modalities may be culturally sensitive therapeutic interventions for clients of color.

## Recommended Resources

Brown, L. (2009). *Feminist therapy: Theories of psychotherapy.* Washington, DC: American Psychological Association.

Comas-Díaz, L., & Greene, B. (1994). *Women of color: Integrating ethnic and gender identities in psychotherapy.* New York, NY: Guilford Press.

Covington Armstrong, S. (2009). *Not all Black girls know how to eat: A story of bulimia.* Chicago, IL: Lawrence Hill Books.

Roth, G. (2003). *Breaking free from emotional eating.* New York, NY: Plume.

Thompson, B. (1994). *A hunger so wide and so deep: A multiracial view of women's eating problems.* Minneapolis: University of Minnesota Press.

## References

Abrams, K. K., Allen, L. R., & Gray, J. J. (1993). Disordered eating attitudes and behaviors, psychological adjustment, and ethnic identity: A comparison of Black and White female college students. *International Journal of Eating Disorders, 14,* 49–57.

Alegria, M., Woo, M., Cao, Z., Torres, M., Meng, X. L., & Striegel-Moore, R. (2007). Prevalence and correlates of eating disorders in Latinos in the United States. *International Journal of Eating Disorders, 40* (Suppl. 3), S15–S21.

American Psychiatric Association. (2000). *Diagnostic and statistical manual of mental disorders* (4th ed., text rev.). Washington, DC: Author.

American Psychiatric Association. (2006). Practice guidelines for the treatment of patients with eating disorders (revision). *American Journal of Psychiatry, 157,* 1–39.

Andersen, A. E., & Hay, A. (1985). Racial and socioeconomic influences in anorexia and bulimia. *International Journal of Eating Disorders, 4,* 479–487.

Anderson, L. P. (1991). Acculturative stress: A theory of relevance to Black Americans. *Clinical Psychology Review, 11,* 685–702.

Arriaza, C. A., & Mann, T. (2001). Ethnic differences in eating disorder symptoms among college students: The confounding role of body mass index. *Journal of American College Health, 49,* 309–315.

Besselieu, L. D. (1997). *The meaning of weight and body image in African American women.* Unpublished doctoral dissertation, Auburn University.

Cachelin, F. M., Veisel, C., Barzengarnazari, E., & Striegel-Moore, R. H. (2000). Disordered eating, acculturation, and treatment-seeking in a community sample of Hispanic, Asian, Black, and White women. *Psychology of Women Quarterly, 24,* 244–253.

Centers for Disease Control and Prevention. (2012). *Defining overweight and obesity.* Retrieved from http://www.cdc.gov/obesity/defining.html

Chao, Y. M., Pisetsky, B. A., Dierker, L. C., Dohm, F., Rosselli, F., May A. M., & Striegel-Moore, R. H. (2008). Ethnic differences in weight control practices among U.S. adolescents from 1995–2005. *International Journal of Eating Disorders, 41,* 124–133.

Choate, L. H. (2010). Interpersonal group therapy for women experiencing bulimia. *Journal for Specialists in Group Work, 35,* 349–364.

Clark, R., Anderson, N. B., Clark, V. R., & Williams, D. R. (1999). Racism as a stressor for African Americans: A biopsychosocial model. *American Psychologist, 54,* 805–816.

Coker, A., Meyer, D., Smith, R., & Price, A. (2010). Using social justice group work with young mothers who experience homelessness. *Journal for Specialists in Group Work, 35,* 220–229.

Covington Armstrong, S. (2009). *Not all Black girls know how to eat: A story of bulimia.* Chicago, IL: Lawrence Hill Books.

Cummins, L. H., Simmons, A. M., & Zane, N. W. S. (2005). Eating disorders in Asian populations: A critique of current approaches to the study of culture, ethnicity, and eating disorders. *American Journal of Orthopsychiatry, 75,* 553–574.

Dounchis, J. Z., Hayden, H. A., & Wilfrey, D. E. (2001). Obesity, body image, and eating disorders in ethnically diverse children and adolescents. In J. K. Thompson & L. Smolak (Eds.), *Body image, eating disorders and obesity in youth* (pp. 67–91). Washington, DC: American Psychological Association.

Downing, R. A. (2004). *Perceptions of racism and classism in health care: Comparing the standpoints of poor and middle class women.* Unpublished doctoral dissertation, University of California, Santa Cruz.

Flegal, K. M., Carroll, M. D., Ogden, C. L., & Curtin, L. R. (2010). Prevalence and trends in obesity among U.S. adults. *JAMA, 303,* 235–241.

Franko, D. L., & George, J. B. E. (2008). A pilot intervention to reduce eating disorder risk in Latina women. *European Eating Disorders Review, 16,* 436–441.

Garner, D. M., Olmsted, M. P., Bohr, Y., & Garfinkel, P. E. (1982). The Eating Attitudes Test: Psychometric features and clinical correlates. *Psychological Medicine, 12,* 871–878.

George, J. B. E., & Franko, D. L. (2010). Cultural issues in eating pathology and body image among children and adolescents. *Journal of Pediatric Psychology, 35,* 231–242.

Gordon-Larsen, P., Harris, K. M., Ward, D. S., & Popkin, B. M. (2003). Acculturation and overweight-related behaviors among Hispanic immigrants to the U.S.: The National Longitudinal Study of Adolescent Health. *Social Science & Medicine, 57,* 2023–2034.

Gowen, L., Hayward, C., Killen, J. D., Robinson, T. N., & Taylor, C. (1999). Acculturation and eating disorder symptoms in adolescent girls. *Journal of Research on Adolescence, 9,* 67–83.

Grabe, S., & Hyde, J. S. (2006). Ethnicity and body dissatisfaction among women in the United States: A meta-analysis. *Psychological Bulletin, 132,* 622–640.

Granillo, T. G., Jones-Rodriguez, G., & Carvajal, S. C. (2005). Prevalence of eating disorders in Latina adolescents: Associations with substance use and other correlates. *Journal of Adolescent Health, 36,* 214–220.

Greene, B. (1994). African American women. In L. Comas-Díaz & B. Greene (Eds.), *Women of color: Integrating ethnic and gender identities in psychotherapy* (pp. 10–29). New York, NY: Guilford Press.

Hardy, K. V., & Laszloffy, T. A. (1995). The cultural genogram: Key to training culturally competent family therapists. *Journal of Marital and Family Therapy, 21,* 227–237.

Harris, D. J., & Kuba, S. A. (1997). Ethnocultural identity and eating disorders in women of color. *Professional Psychology: Research and Practice, 28,* 341–347.

Harris, S. M. (1994). Racial differences in predictors of college women's body image attitudes. *Women & Health, 21,* 89–104.

Helms, J. E. (1995). An update of Helms's White and people of color racial identity models. In J. G. Ponterotto, J. M. Casas, L. A. Suzuki, & C. M. Alexander (Eds.), *Handbook of multicultural counseling* (pp. 181–198). Thousand Oaks, CA: Sage.

Helms, J. E., & Cook, D. A. (1999). *Using race and culture in counseling and psychotherapy: Theory and process.* Upper Saddle River, NJ: Pearson/Allyn & Bacon.

Johnson, W. G., Rohan, K. J., & Kirk, A. A. (2002). Prevalence and correlates of binge eating in White and African American adolescents. *Eating Behaviors, 3,* 179–189.

Kelly, N. R., Mitchell, K. S., Gow, R.W., Trace, S. E., Lydecker, J. A., Bair, C. E., & Mazzeo, S. (2011). An evaluation of the reliability and construct validity of eating disorder measures in White and Black women. *Psychological Assessment, 24,* 608–617. doi:10.1037/a0026457

Kempa, M. L., & Thomas, A. J. (2000). Culturally sensitive assessment and treatment of eating disorders. *Eating Disorders, 8,* 7–12. doi:1064-0266/00

Kim, B. S. K., & Abreu, J. M. (2001). Acculturation measurement: Theory, current instruments, and future directions. In J. G. Ponterotto, J. M. Casas, L. A. Suzuki, & C. M. Alexander (Eds.), *Handbook of multicultural counseling* (2nd ed., pp. 394–424). Thousand Oaks, CA: Sage.

Kronenfeld, L. W., Reba-Harrelson, L., Von Holle, A., Reyes, M. L., & Bulik, C. M. (2010). Ethnic and racial difference in body size perception and satisfaction. *Body Image, 7,* 131–136.

Kumanyika, S., & Grier, S. (2006). Targeting interventions for ethnic minority and low-income populations. *Future of Children, 16,* 187–207.

Kumanyika, S., Wilson, J. F., & Guilford-Davenport, M. (1993). Weight-related attitudes and behaviors of African American women. *Journal of the American Dietetic Association, 93,* 416–422.

Landrine, H., & Klonoff, E. (1996). The Schedule of Racist Events: A measure of racial discrimination and a study of its negative physical and mental health consequences. *Journal of Black Psychology, 22,* 144–168.

Landrine, H., Richardson, J., Klonoff, E., & Flay, B. (1994). Cultural diversity in the predictors of adolescent cigarette smoking: The relative influence of peers. *Journal of Behavioral Medicine, 17,* 331–346.

Liou, D., & Bauer, K. (2007). Exploratory investigation of obesity risk and prevention in Chinese Americans. *Journal of Nutrition Education and Behavior, 39,* 134–141.

Lynch, S. L. (2004). *Eating disorders in African American women: Incorporating race into considerations of etiology and treatment.* Unpublished doctoral dissertation, Widener University, Delaware Campus.

Malson, M. R., Mudimbe-Boyi, E., O'Barr, J. F., & Wyer, M. (1990). *African American women in America: Social science perspectives.* Chicago, IL: University of Chicago Press.

Mastria, M. (2002). Ethnicity and eating disorders. *Psychoanalysis and Psychotherapist, 19,* 59–77.

McDonald, D. E. (2012). Impossible bodies, invisible battles: Feminist perspectives on the psychological research on and treatment of eating disorders in queer women. *Journal of Gay and Lesbian Social Services, 23,* 452–464.

Mintz, L. B., & Kashubeck, S. (1999). Body image and disordered eating among Asian American and Caucasian college students: An examination of race and gender differences. *Psychology of Women Quarterly, 23,* 781–796.

Mitchell, K. S., & Mazzeo, S. E. (2004). Binge eating and psychological distress in ethnically diverse undergraduate men and women. *Eating Behaviors, 5,* 157–169.

Myers, M. E. (1998). *An exploration of racial identity and social support in African American women.* Unpublished doctoral dissertation, California School of Professional Psychology, Alameda, CA.

Nicdao, E. G., Hong, S., & Takeuchi, D. T. (2007). Prevalence and correlates of eating disorders among Asian Americans: Results from the National Latino and Asian American Study. *International Journal of Eating Disorders, 40* (Suppl.), S22–S26.

Nouri, M., Hill, L. G., & Orrell-Valente, J. K. (2011). Media exposure, internalization of the thin ideal, and body dissatisfaction: Comparing Asian American and European American college females. *Body Image, 8,* 366–372.

O'Neill, S. K. (2003). African American women and eating disturbances: A meta-analysis. *Journal of Black Psychology, 29,* 3–16.

Padilla, A. (Ed.). (1980). *Acculturation: Theory, models, and some new findings.* Boulder, CO: Westview Press.

Paul, D. G. (2003). *Talkin' back.* Westport, CT: Praeger.

Phan, T., & Tylka, T. C. (2006). Exploring a model and moderators of disordered eating with Asian American college women. *Journal of Counseling Psychology, 53,* 36–47.

Phinney, J. S. (1992). The multigroup ethnic identity measure: A new scale for use with diverse groups. *Journal of Adolescent Research, 7,* 156–176. doi:10.1177/074355489272003

Polivy, J., & Herman, P. D. (2002). Causes of eating disorders. *Annual Review of Psychology, 53,* 187–213.

Poran, M. A. (2006). The politics of protection: Body image, social pressures, and the misrepresentation of young Black women. *Sex Roles, 55,* 739–755.

Pumariega, A. J., Gustavson, C., Gustavson, J. C., Motes, P. S., & Ayers, S. (1994). Eating attitudes in African-American women: The *Essence* eating disorders survey. *Eating Disorders, 2,* 5–16.

Reel, J. (2000). *Body image and physical self-perception among African American and Caucasian women across the adult life span.* Unpublished doctoral dissertation, University of North Carolina, Greensboro.

Reyes-Rodríguez, M. L., Franko, D. L., Matos-Lamourt, A., Bulik, C. M., Von Holle, A., Cámara-Fuentes, L. R., . . . Suárez-Torres, A. (2010). Eating disorder symptomatology: Prevalence among Latino college freshmen students. *Journal of Clinical Psychology, 66,* 666–679. doi:10.1002/jclp.20684

Roberts, A., Cash, T. F., Feingold, A., & Johnson, B. T. (2006). Are Black–White differences in females' body dissatisfaction decreasing? A meta-analytic review. *Journal of Consulting and Clinical Psychology, 74,* 1121–1131.

Root, M. P. P. (1990). Disordered eating in women of color. *Sex Roles, 22,* 525–535.

Root, M. P. P. (2001). Future considerations in research on eating disorders. *Counseling Psychologist, 29,* 754–762.

Rubin, L., Fitts, M., & Becker, A. (2003). Whatever feels good in my soul: Body ethics and aesthetics among African American and Latina women. *Culture, Medicine, and Psychiatry, 27,* 49–73. doi:10.1023/A:1023679821086

Rucker, C. E., & Cash, T. F. (1992). Body images, body-size perceptions, and eating behaviors among African-American and White college women. *International Journal of Eating Disorders, 12,* 291–299.

Shaw, H., Ramirez, L., Trost, A., Randall, P., & Stice, E. (2004). Body image and eating disturbances across ethnic groups: More similarities than differences. *Psychology of Addictive Behaviors, 18,* 12–18.

Shuttlesworth, M. E., & Zotter, D. (2011). Disordered eating in African American and Caucasian women: The role of ethnic identity. *Journal of Black Studies, 42,* 906–922. doi:10.1177/0021934710396368

Smart, R. (2010a). Counseling a bi-racial female college student with an eating disorder: A case study applying an integrative biopsychosocial cultural perspective. *Journal of College Counseling, 13,* 182–192.

Smart, R. (2010b). Treating Asian American women with eating disorders: Multicultural competency and empirically supported treatment. *Eating Disorders, 18,* 58–73. doi:10.1080/10640260903439540

Smolak, L., & Striegel-Moore, R. H. (2001). Challenging the myth of the golden girl: Ethnicity and eating disorders. In R. H. Striegel-Moore & L. Smolak (Eds.), *Eating disorders: Innovative directions in research and practice* (pp. 111–132). Washington, DC: American Psychological Association.

Story, M., Sherwood, N. E., Himes, J. H., Davis, M., Jacobs, D. R., Jr., Cartwright, Y., & Rochon, J. (2003). An after-school obesity prevention program for African-American girls: The Minnesota GEMS pilot study. *Ethnicity & Disease, 13*(1, Suppl. 1), S54–S64.

Striegel-Moore, R. H., Fairburn, C. G, Wilfley, D. E., Pike, K. M., Dohm, F., & Kraemer, H. C. (2005). Toward an understanding of risk factors for binge-eating disorder in Black and White women: A community-based case-control study. *Psychological Medicine, 35,* 907–917.

Striegel-Moore, R. H., Wilfley, D. E., Pike, K. M., Dohm, F., & Fairburn, C. G. (2000). Recurrent binge eating in Black American women. *Archives of Family Medicine, 9,* 83–87.

Sue, D. W., & Sue, D. (2008). *Counseling the culturally diverse: Theory and practice* (5th ed.). New York, NY: Wiley.

Talleyrand, R. M. (2006). Potential stressors contributing to eating disorders in African American women: Implications for mental health counselors. *Journal of Mental Health Counseling, 28,* 338–352.

Taylor, J. Y., Caldwell, C. H., Baser, R. E., Faison, N., & Jackson, J. S. (2007). Prevalence of eating disorders among Blacks in the National Survey of American Life. *International Journal of Eating Disorders, 40*(Suppl.), S10–S14.

Thomas, A. J., Witherspoon, K. M., & Speight, S. L. (2004). Toward the development of the Stereotypic Roles for Black Women Scale. *Journal of Black Psychology, 30,* 426–442.

Thompson, B. (1994). *A hunger so wide and so deep.* Minneapolis: University of Minnesota Press.

Thompson, B. (1997). Multiracial feminist theorizing about eating: Refusing to rank oppressions. *Eating Disorders: The Journal of Treatment & Prevention, 4,* 104–114.

Thompson, C. E., & Neville, H. A. (1999). Racism, mental health, and mental health practice. *The Counseling Psychologist, 27,* 155–223.

Utsey, S. O., & Ponterotto, J. G. (1996). Development and validation of the Index of Race-Related Stress (IRRS). *Journal of Counseling Psychology, 43,* 490–501.

Villarosa, L. (1994). *Body and soul: The African American women's guide to physical health and emotional well-being.* New York, NY: Harper Perennial.

Warren, C. S., Castillo, L. G., & Gleaves, D. H. (2010). The socio-cultural model of eating disorders in Mexican American women: Behavioral acculturation and cognitive marginalization as moderators. *Eating Disorders, 18,* 43–57. doi:10.1080/10640260903439532

Williams, C. B., Frame, M. W., & Green, E. (1999). Counseling groups for African American women: A focus on spirituality. *Journal for Specialists in Group Work, 24,* 260–273.

Wolin, K. Y., Colangelo, L. A., Chiu, B. C.-H., & Gapstur, S. M. (2009). Obesity and immigration among Latina women. *Journal of Immigrant Minority Health, 11,* 428–431.

Wood, N. A. R., & Petrie, T. A. (2010). Body dissatisfaction, ethnic identity, and disordered eating among African American women. *Journal of Counseling Psychology, 57,* 141–153.

Wyatt, S. B., Williams, D. R., Calvin, R., Henderson, F. C., Walker, E. R., & Winters, K. (2003). Racism and cardiovascular disease in African Americans. *American Journal of the Medical Sciences, 325,* 315–331.

## Chapter 4

# Ethical and Legal Issues in Counseling Clients With Eating Disorders

*Laura H. Choate, Mary A. Hermann, and Leigh Pottle,*
*With Jodi Manton*

Eating disorders (EDs) are serious biopsychosocial issues with severe consequences, including a range of potentially lethal medical complications. The rate of mortality in clients with anorexia nervosa (AN) is among the highest of all psychiatric conditions (American Psychiatric Association [APA], 2006). In addition, suicidality has been correlated with both AN and bulimia nervosa (BN; Swanson, Crow, LeGrange, Swendsen, & Merikangas, 2011) in that those with AN and BN have suicide attempt rates and overall mortality rates that are considerably higher than for those in the general population (Franko & Keel, 2006).

Despite these potentially lethal risks, clients with EDs are frequently not motivated to seek treatment or to alter their disordered eating behaviors (Tan, Hope, & Stewart, 2003). This reluctance poses several legal and ethical dilemmas for the counselor. From a legal perspective, a counselor's duty is to act in the public interest and to follow the treatment standards of the counseling profession as well as the legal codes of his or her particular state. From an ethical perspective, the standard of care is generally to provide the highest quality of care, to act in the client's best interest, to protect the client from harm, and to promote his or her autonomy. Therefore, EDs present unique legal and ethical challenges in determining what actions need to be taken to protect clients from potentially lethal self-harm (the ethical principles of beneficence and nonmaleficence) while also respecting their right to make their own life decisions (client autonomy). When working with clients with EDs, these principles may conflict, because providing autonomy can be challenging when the client does not want to change or become healthier (Bell, 2010; Carney, Ingvarson, & Tait, 2008; Werth, Wright, Archambault, & Bardash, 2003). Therefore, counselors need the training and experience to be able to discern when the principle of autonomy should yield to upholding the principles of beneficence and nonmaleficence to protect a client from self-harm (Werth et al., 2003).

Moreover, guidelines for ethical and legal decision making related to the treatment of EDs have not been well described in the literature. Fedyszyn and Sullivan (2007) found that in spite of the serious health risks related to EDs and the ethical challenges when working with this population of clients, the literature has presented a minimal amount of research regarding ethical clinical interventions. In addition, research has not adequately addressed legal and ethical issues when counseling a client who refuses treatment but who is also in declining health (Werth et al., 2003). Many counselors also claim a general lack of training, competency, and confidence in working with clients with EDs, so that when they do counsel these clients, counselors may be practicing beyond their scope of competence, which can ultimately be harmful to the client (Williams & Haverkamp, 2010). This is significant in that to work effectively with clients who have EDs, counselors need to be aware of relevant best-practice guidelines, codes of ethics, ethical principles, and state laws related to informed consent for both minors and adults (Bell, 2010; Carney et al., 2008; Fedyszyn & Sullivan, 2007; Werth et al., 2003).

As a step toward bridging this gap in the literature, we discuss specific issues related to promoting the well-being of clients with EDs, including counselor self-awareness, scope of practice, and practicing according to best-practice guidelines, which include the counselor's ethical duty to protect the client from self-harm. Next, we highlight the issue of client autonomy, describing issues related to informed consent and determining client competence to make rational treatment decisions. Finally, we explain the ethical decision-making process using a decision-making model and a case to illustrate the model's steps. Although both male and female clients experience EDs, for the purposes of simplification, we use terminology related to female clients throughout this chapter. We should note, therefore, that these ethical principles apply to both male and female clients.

## Promoting Client Well-Being and Protecting From Harm

The first area that a counselor should consider is his or her own personal and professional preparation for working with clients experiencing EDs. According to the *ACA Code of Ethics* (American Counseling Association [ACA], 2005), counselors must be aware of their own personal values, attitudes, and beliefs and not impose them on their clients (Standard A.4.b.). However, mental health professionals may have strong beliefs or values related to clients experiencing EDs, and they are obligated to spend considerable time in preparing to manage these personal values and biases.

For example, counselors should be aware of the impact of sociocultural influences on their own beliefs about self-worth and how strongly their self-worth is associated with their weight, shape, and appearance (Delucia-Waack, 1999). Counselors receive the same cultural messages about the importance of attractiveness and self-denial of food as their clients; therefore, counselors need to remain continuously aware of their body image behaviors and attitudes and take care not to inadvertently communicate them to their clients. Counselors should also be prepared to be personally scrutinized or even criticized by their clients with EDs; in one study, 83% of counselors reported that they felt their appearance was being monitored, examined, or evaluated by their clients or stated that they felt self-conscious about their appearance during treatment with a client with an ED, which can potentially trigger countertransference reactions (Warren, Crowley, Olivardia, & Schoen, 2009). In fact, when counselors do have their own struggles in these areas, they tend to overidentify with the client and run the risk of boundary crossings such as conflict avoidance, being overly nurturing, or having feelings of competition with the client (DeLucia-Waack, 1999).

In addition, because the ED often functions as a way for a client to establish power and control in her life, counselors may inadvertently become engaged in power struggles with clients when they refuse to change their disordered eating behaviors. Clients may also have difficulty establishing a trusting, open relationship with counselors because of their mistrust of others whom they perceive as demanding that they gain weight. In these types of relationships, counselors need to be aware of their reactions to clients, which may include frustration with clients who refuse to give up behaviors that are potentially life threatening, demoralization and lack of belief that clients can ever change, or an excessive need to rescue clients (APA, 2006). Indeed, it is often bewildering for counselors to grasp the ego-syntonic nature of clients' symptoms, how they prefer their emaciated state, or why they would knowingly continue self-starvation or purging behaviors that are self-harming. In sum, counselors need to be aware of their views regarding their own personal history with eating, weight, and appearance, as well as their reactions to working with clients who do not desire to change, and make proper referrals if their beliefs or values related to EDs are preventing clients from receiving appropriate care.

In addition to counselor self-awareness of personal values, counselors should be aware of their professional scope of competence. According to the *ACA Code of Ethics* (ACA, 2005), counselors should only practice within their boundaries of competence (Standard C.2.a.). or work to expand their knowledge and skills through education and training. While counselors are gaining the education, training, and supervised experience to work with clients with EDs, counselors take care to provide appropriate services and protect clients from harm (ACA, 2005, Standard C.2.b.). They should be aware that counseling clients with EDs is highly complex and requires that the counselor possess advanced, specialized training and high levels of supervised experience that are above and beyond what they might have received during their graduate preparation programs (Williams & Haverkamp, 2010).

Counselor competence is derived from working in settings in which clients with EDs are regularly seen while also receiving ongoing training, consultation, and supervision. To be effective, counselors need advanced-level skills in the areas of basic nutrition; they must know how to make proper referrals to medical professionals; how to work with an interdisciplinary team; and how to handle client challenges to the counseling relationship, including skills for managing clients' resistance to change (Williams & Kaverkamp, 2010).

Because many counselors will not be prepared to work with clients whose EDs are severe, counselors are expected to provide referrals to culturally and clinically appropriate practitioners (ACA, 2005, Standard A.11.b.) In this regard, it is incumbent on all counselors, regardless of their treatment expertise, to be able to assess for and identify potential EDs when they exist so that they can then make an appropriate referral. The 2009 American School Counselor Association position statement on the professional school counselor and student mental health exemplifies this ethical duty for identification and referral in that

> professional school counselors do not provide long-term therapy in schools to address psychological disorders; however, they must be prepared to recognize and respond to student mental health crises and needs, and to address these barriers to student success by offering education, prevention, and crisis and short-term intervention until the student is connected with available community resources. (p. 50)

The *Ethical Standards for School Counselors* (American School Counselor Association, 2010) clarify that "every attempt is made to find appropriate specialized resources for clinical therapeutic topics that are difficult or inappropriate to address in a school setting such as eating disorders" (Standard A5.b.). Even though they might not provide treatment for students with diagnosable EDs, school counselors can help identify, provide referrals, offer psychoeducational programs, and provide at-school support for students with EDs (see also Chapter 6, this volume).

A third area to consider when promoting client well-being is for counselors to draw from best-practice treatments when providing direct services for clients with EDs (Bell, 2010; Fedyszyn & Sullivan, 2007). Concern is growing that empirically supported treatments are not well used in clinical practice (Simmons, Milnes, & Anderson, 2008). According to the best-practice guideline published by the APA (2006), clients with EDs will require a thorough intake assessment and subsequent medical referral for ongoing monitoring of her medical condition and will necessitate an interdisciplinary team approach to treatment (e.g., physicians, dieticians, counselors) with ongoing consultation between team members (APA, 2006). The importance of ethical conduct in working as part of an interdisciplinary team is underscored in the *ACA Code of Ethics* (ACA, 2005, Standard D.1.c). For clients with AN, the initial goal of treatment is to provide nutritional rehabilitation to restore a healthy weight. Only once the effects of malnutrition are corrected can therapy begin to examine cognitive distortions related to self and others, developmental themes related to family and identity, how the disorder was used to cope with negative affect and cognitions, and how to develop more effective coping skills. The therapeutic approaches with the most empirical support for AN are family based, with Maudsley family-based therapy (Lock, LeGrange, Agras, & Dare, 2001) being the best studied (this approach is described in detail in Chapter 17, this volume).

In contrast, the goals of treatment for BN are to

- Reduce and eliminate binge eating and purging behavior.
- Treat physical complications related to binge–purge behaviors.
- Enhance client motivation or cooperation in treatment.
- Restore normal and healthy eating patterns.
- Provide education about nutrition and eating.
- Identify and replace core dysfunctional thoughts, attitudes, and feelings related to the ED.
- Provide treatment for associated psychiatric conditions.
- Enlist family support or use family counseling (strongly recommended in the case of children and adolescents).

The most effective treatment for BN to date is cognitive–behavioral therapy (Fairburn, 2008). This approach is described in detail in Chapter 13 (this volume). If clients do not respond to cognitive–behavioral therapy, interpersonal therapy is recommended (see Chapter 14, this volume). For those clients with binge eating disorder (BED), clients need many of the same treatment elements; in addition to the cognitive–behavioral therapy approach, interpersonal therapy and dialectical behavior therapy are also recommended (see Chapters 14 and 16, this volume; APA, 2006).

A final ethical issue in providing competent services for clients with EDs is to provide treatment in the least restrictive setting while also providing the highest quality of care possible. Services can range from outpatient weekly counseling to partial hospitalization programs, residential settings, and intensive inpatient programs in which the client receives specialized medical treatment, nutritional counseling, or individual, group, and family counseling (APA, 2006). Clients should begin treatment in the least restrictive setting and remain at this level unless they refuse to comply with treatment or continue to lose weight or their health becomes medically compromised. If a client does not comply with treatment, the team can first add an additional treatment modality (e.g., adding more frequent sessions, family counseling, nutritionist appointments, weight monitoring, activity restrictions) before proceeding to the next level of care (Werth et al., 2003). If the client refuses this step or her health continues to decline, a more intensive level will be needed. According to best-practice guidelines, the highest level of care (inpatient hospitalization) is deemed to be required when there is rapid or persistent decline in oral intake, a decline in weight, the presence of additional stressors that interfere with the client's ability to eat, co-occurring psychiatric problems that require hospitalization, and a high degree of client denial and resistance to participate in her own care in less intensively supervised settings (APA, 2006). Clients are rarely motivated to take this step. At this juncture, the client may need to be involuntarily hospitalized to receive the medical attention she needs to prevent further weight loss and to preserve her life, even though she may adamantly continue to refuse treatment. In making these decisions, the counselor must exercise reasonable care to promote client safety and protect the client from self-harm (APA, 2006; Manley, Smye, & Srika-meswaran, 2001).

## Duty to Protect Versus Client Autonomy

Promoting client well-being and protecting clients from harm involves counselor self-awareness, professional competence, and adequate decision-making skills for intervening when clients' lives are in danger. In addition to protecting client well-being, another ethical principle a counselor must consider is promoting clients' autonomy and clients' right to control their own lives and to make their own treatment decisions. To make the best treatment decisions, clients first need to be provided with information related to informed consent and the limits of confidentiality. The counselor should spend adequate time discussing client rights and the treatment services that will be provided. According to the *ACA Code of Ethics* (ACA, 2005), clients have the freedom to choose whether to enter into or remain in a counseling relationship. To make this decision, they require adequate information about the counseling process and the counselor (ACA, 2005, Standard A.2.a). Clients will also need to have knowledge of such issues as the goals of counseling, the procedures to be used, the potential risks associated with counseling, their right to refuse any services or modality changes, and their right to be informed of the consequences of such refusal (ACA, 2005, Standard A.2.b). Clients also need to know about their right to confidentiality (including how information will be shared between treatment team members) and its limitations.

However, these rights are questioned when clients' actions might be putting their lives in danger because of their low weight, unstable medical condition, or other related factors such as the presence of comorbid disorders. This dilemma places counselors in the position of having to decide whether to break confidentiality (ACA, 2005, Standard B.2.a.) and carry out their duty to protect the client from danger, because counselors are obligated to disclose information about clients and to act on their behalf to protect them from serious and foreseeable harm. The notion of overriding a client's autonomy is a topic debated in the literature, particularly with regard to AN. Although a client with BN or BED might be medically unstable and need to be hospitalized because of malnutrition or an overall unstable medical profile, most of the literature on involuntary hospitalization is related to severely underweight clients with AN and is the focus of our discussion.

Some ethicists have argued that an adult has the right to refuse any, even life-saving, treatment and that enforcing treatment goals without the client's consent is paternalistic and discriminatory (Tan, Stewart, Fitzpatrick, & Hope, 2006). Although this is a dilemma with adult clients, it can be even more difficult to manage with minor clients in that their parents have the right to give legal consent for counseling and treatment decisions for their minor children. Although in many cases, parents' right to make treatment decisions will help their child receive the necessary help, some parents may believe that forced hospitalization is intrusive or unnecessary and might refuse the counselor's treatment recommendations for their child. Parental refusal of treatment means the counselor may at times be called on to override not only the client's but also the family's autonomy in making treatment decisions, and many counselors may be hesitant to take this step.

Moreover, involuntary medical treatment has been argued to cause the client to feel violated and threatened, because it often involves a refeeding process that uses strict supervision, enforcement of prescribed dietary plans, prevention of exercising or purging, and forced nasogastric tube feeding (Giordano, 2005). Furthermore, involuntary treatment is viewed by some counselors as ineffective in that although clients might gain weight in the short term to be discharged from the hospital, they are not truly in remission and will relapse as soon as they are released (Griffiths & Russell, 1998). Therefore, the client may be temporarily medically stabilized, but the core of the ED remains unchanged (Giordano, 2005). Some authors have also viewed involuntary treatment as harmful to the efficacy of treatment in that distrust and hostility can develop in the therapy relationship and derail any progress and because the client, as a result of this experience, might be less willing to seek help in the future (Tan et al., 2006), thereby impeding any hopes of long-term recovery. In addition, if the family is not in agreement with the hospitalization decision, the treatment team's efforts for posttreatment care will likely be sabotaged when the client is released from hospital.

In contrast with the view that enforced treatment should always be avoided, best practices in the field currently state that compulsory treatment is justified, but only if the client lacks the capacity to make informed decisions and if the treatment is in the patient's best interest (APA, 2006). Therefore, issues related to client best interest and client capacity (also termed *client competence*) are critical in determining whether to enforce treatment against a client's will. Determining clients' best interests by taking measures to preserve their well-being (beneficence) and protecting them from harm (nonmaleficence) have already been discussed; therefore, here we focus the discussion on issues related to determining client competence. It is often quite difficult to determine whether a client with an ED is competent to make her own treatment decisions. Tan et al. (2006) found that current methods of ascertaining competence were inadequate when working with clients with EDs, in that clients might be highly functioning in other areas but unable to make rational decisions when it comes to their own eating, weight, and health.

Several things affect whether a client with an ED is competent to make the decision to refuse medical or psychological treatment: First, as stated previously, the symptoms of AN are ego syntonic in nature, so clients are reluctant to eliminate these attitudes and behaviors. Clients are proud of their symptoms and value the results of extreme weight loss. They rely on their symptoms to feel power and control and to organize and manage their lives (Werth et al., 2003). They may have knowledge about adequate nutrition and of the dangers of starvation, yet believe that they do not apply to them, or they may simply deny the extent or severity of their disorder (Carney et al., 2008; Honig & Bentovim, 1996; Manley et al., 2001; Tan et al., 2003). Because of the ego-syntonic nature of the ED, therefore, many clients clearly have no incentive to change and may in fact be highly defensive with others whom they perceive as a threat to the continuation of their symptoms.

A second area that potentially contributes to client incapacity is the presence of cognitive distortions that accompany self-starvation in clients with AN. In an emaciated state, clients will be unable to concentrate, which interferes with conceptualization, perceptions, judgment, and decision-making processes. Starvation may also affect clients' ability to realistically assess their medical situation or the severity of their impairment, and because they are not making sound assessments or judgments, they may become incapable of making decisions to preserve their own lives. Clearly, if a counselor tries to conduct therapy with a client in this state, the therapy will be ineffective and will be rendered meaningless because of the client's cognitive impairment, so no real progress can be made until her health is initially restored (Giordano, 2005). In sum, there is a synergy between the ego-syntonic nature of the disorder and the cognitive response to starvation that contributes to and sustains client cognitive impairment (Werth et al., 2003). This synergistic effect should be taken into account when making ethical and legal decisions regarding a client's right to autonomy.

In contrast, clients with BN or BED do not value their chronic dieting, binge, and purge symptoms but are highly distressed by them. However, many clients are reluctant to stop their behaviors because they believe they are the only means to effectively cope with negative emotions or to lose weight. They want to be free from the symptoms but are fearful of letting go of the mechanisms (e.g., dieting, avoidant coping strategies) that drive the disorder. In cases of BN and BED, therefore, counselors can assist clients in learning to recognize that to get what they want (to remain binge or purge free), they will have to replace their preferred methods for coping with more health-promoting behaviors. Because these clients are generally of normal or above-normal weight, they rarely have to be treated for the complications of self-starvation. In some cases, they might need medical treatment or hospitalization for nutritional restoration as a consequence of chronic dieting, bingeing, or purging, but because they are not emaciated, they do not have the severe problems with cognitive impairment that remain a significant problem for many clients with AN.

In sum, the counselor is placed in a highly challenging ethical dilemma when clients refuse to work toward treatment goals that are meant to promote their health and well-being. The counselor must ascertain whether they are able to make competent decisions for themselves or whether their decision making has been impaired by the extreme effects of self-starvation or the AN. The counselor must also consider the benefits and consequences of the intervention. On the one hand, clients who are medically unstable and malnourished can experience potentially lethal consequences if untreated and cannot benefit from psychosocial therapies until their medical restoration is well underway. On the other hand, forced hospitalization and treatment often impair therapy progress and may cause clients to leave treatment once they are released from the hospital.

# Ethical and Legal Decision-Making Processes

Clearly, counselors working with clients who have EDs would benefit from an ethical decision-making model to guide their decisions when they are faced with complex situations such as the ones described in this chapter. On the basis of recommendations from the *ACA Code of Ethics* (ACA, 2005) and common components of ethical decision-making models (Corey, Corey, & Callanan, 2007; Kitchener, 1984; Welfel, 2006), we present Remley and Herlihy's (2010) model here. The model incorporates steps drawn from principle and virtue ethics, feminist and multicultural ethics, and social constructivism. The model attends to both facts and counselor feelings (which is particularly important because EDs can produce strong countertransference reactions from the counselor) and tries to incorporate the client's perspective and involvement as much as possible. The steps of the model are presented next, followed by the application of the model to a case example.

## *Ethical Decision-Making Model (Remley & Herlihy, 2010)*

### *Identify the Problem*
The counselor should compile information related to the dilemma and determine relevant ethical codes and legal statutes that may apply, consulting an attorney, if necessary, concerning any legal matters. The counselor should consider the various aspects of the problem, because ethical and legal dilemmas are usually multifaceted and complex.

### *Consider Principles and Virtues*
Of particular relevance in cases of EDs are the moral principles of nonmaleficence (to do no harm), beneficence (which goes beyond nonmaleficence by being a benefit to the client), and autonomy (clients' right to make their own choices). The counselor should evaluate what precedence each principle takes in a specific case.

### Tune Into Feelings, Personal Values, and Emotions

As the counselor considers the situation and all possible interventions, he or she should attend to any emotions experienced such as fear, self-doubt, guilt, responsibility, or the need to rescue because awareness of emotions will help to inform the decision-making process. The counselor should also reflect on personal values and how they might affect his or her view of the client, problem, and judgment during the decision-making process.

### Obtain Consultation With Colleagues and Other Professionals, Particularly the Treatment Team Members

To make the most effective decisions, counselors should consult with the treatment team and with other professionals as part of the process (ACA, 2005, Standard B.2.a.). Consultation can provide a different perspective on the problem, helping the counselor to discover aspects of the problem that may not previously have been visible. Consultation is also an important part of supporting the counselor's actions in the event that he or she is brought before an ethical board or court of law.

### Involve the Client in the Decision-Making Process

The client should be included in the process as much as possible. If there are non-life-threatening treatment decisions to be made, it is in the client's best interest to be part of the process because she will be more receptive to treatment and will be more motivated to achieve treatment goals. Although in general the "counselor should avoid making decisions for the client when those decision can be made with the client" (Remley & Herlihy, 2010, p. 15), an exception might be made in the case of an impaired and emaciated client who is no longer able to make competent treatment decisions because of her emaciated state. This situation may also be complicated when the client is a minor, and the parent or legal guardian has the right to make any decisions on the minor's behalf. Even in these cases, offering the minor as much information as possible and providing her with choices whenever possible helps her to become more involved.

### Identify Desired Outcomes

Generally, any ethical dilemma has more than one outcome, but brainstorming possible outcomes is helpful in recognizing the goal of the decision-making process.

### Consider Possible Actions and Their Consequences, Enumerating the Consequences of Various Actions

As the counselor contemplates the desired outcomes, he or she should think about possible actions that might achieve those outcomes. Counselors should also anticipate the consequences of all potential actions, both positive and undesirable, and the implications those consequences might have for the client and for the counselor.

### Decide on the Best Course of Action

Once the counselor has carefully considered the options available, he or she should decide on a course of action on the basis of an analysis of each option.

As a final assessment of the decision, the counselor should apply four self-tests to ensure that he or she has selected the best course of action to achieve the most desired outcomes for the client: (a) justice: Would I treat others the same in this situation? (b) universality: Would I be willing to recommend this action to other counselors who are in a similar situation? (c) publicity: Would I be willing to have my actions come to light and be known by others? What if this decision were reported in the press? and (d) moral traces: lingering feelings of doubt, discomfort, or uncertainty after the decision (Stadler, 1986; Remley & Herlihy, 2010).

## Case Example

The following case example[1] demonstrates the difficulty a counselor with limited experience might have when working with a minor client experiencing symptoms of AN. Not only does the counselor have to manage the client's resistance to treatment, the counselor must also negotiate working with the minor client's parents to ensure that the client receives appropriate services for her symptoms.

You are a master's-level counselor with 3 years of experience. You have recently been hired at an outpatient agency that is affiliated with a local hospital. You have some limited experience in working with clients with EDs, but the field is relatively new to you. Ella, a 17-year-old high school senior, and her mother have come to see you after a recent visit to their family physician concerning Ella. The intake information indicates that at her last appointment, Ella's physician found that she was severely underweight and malnourished and had come into his office because she had fainted twice in the past month. Her menses have also ceased for the past 6 months. The physician had urged Ella's mother to bring her to the hospital for further evaluation, but she decided against this, insisting that Ella has simply been under extensive academic pressure to maintain her perfect GPA. Ella's mother thinks that because Ella's grades have been dropping lately, she would benefit most from seeing a counselor to address this issue. She is most troubled about Ella's anxiety and problems at school and does not seem to be overly concerned with Ella's medical condition. The physician referred the client and her mother to your agency because it is known to have outpatient counseling as well as access to a treatment team that specializes in EDs.

When she enters your office, Ella is noticeably thin, her bones visibly protruding. Your initial feelings are ones of discomfort because you notice how fragile and painfully thin she appears. You also feel some irritation with Ella's mother for not being concerned about Ella's medical condition. During the intake interview, Ella explains that she consumes no more than 600 calories daily and sometimes less, making certain she measures and weighs her food before consumption and then writes it down in her food journal. She goes on to say that even though she feels hungry, she is afraid she will gain weight if she consumes any additional calories and, as she pats

---

[1]*Note.* Case example contributed by Jodi Manton.

her sunken stomach, states, "I can't afford to add any more pounds to this fat body." She also asks, "Why are you people giving me such a hard time about my weight? It's my grades that are the problem!" When you ask her about the recent decline in her grades, she says that she has been having difficulty concentrating in class and when completing school assignments.

Ella goes on to describe what she calls "episodes" that she began having about 3 months ago in which she experiences sudden paniclike symptoms, such as a pounding heart, shortness of breath, dizziness, and chills. Because she fears that she might experience one of these episodes at any time, she has begun to avoid social situations and spends most of her time at home alone, reviewing her food journal and planning her meals so she does not risk pigging out. When you ask her to explain what she means by "pigging out," she says, "Like, having a slice of whole wheat bread. If I did that, I couldn't eat the whole next day to make up for it."

### Ethical Decision-Making Model

#### Identify the Problem

On the basis of the information available, Ella meets diagnostic criteria for AN and seems to be medically unstable. Also, she may have a comorbid anxiety disorder on the basis of her description of the paniclike symptoms she has been experiencing. The problem is that although Ella appears to need extensive medical evaluation and possible weight and nutritional restoration, the client and her mother are not concerned about her medical condition and only want treatment for anxiety and school-related problems. There might also be a problem with the counselor's lack of experience in treating severe AN. The relevant ethical codes are as follows:

A.2.b. TYPES OF INFORMATION NEEDED. Counselors explicitly explain to clients the nature of all services provided. They inform clients about issues such as, but not limited to, the following: the purposes, goals, techniques, procedures, limitations, potential risks, and benefits of services; the counselor's qualifications, credentials, and relevant experience; continuation of services upon the incapacitation or death of a counselor; and other pertinent information. Counselors take steps to ensure that clients understand the implications of diagnosis, the intended use of tests and reports, fees, and billing arrangements. Clients have the right to confidentiality and to be provided with an explanation of its limitations (including how supervisors and/ or treatment team professionals are involved); to obtain clear information about their records; to participate in the ongoing counseling plans; and to refuse any services or modality change and to be advised of the consequences of such refusal. (ACA, 2005)

A.2.d. INABILITY TO GIVE CONSENT. When counseling minors or persons unable to give voluntary consent, counselors seek the assent of clients to services, and include them in decision making as appropriate. Counselors recognize the need to balance the ethical rights of clients to make choices, their capacity to give consent or assent to receive services, and parental or familial legal rights and responsibilities to protect these clients and make decisions on their behalf. (ACA, 2005)

A.4.a. AVOIDING HARM. Counselors act to avoid harming their clients, trainees, and research participants and to minimize or to remedy unavoidable or unanticipated harm. (ACA, 2005)

A.4.b. PERSONAL VALUES. Counselors are aware of their own values, attitudes, beliefs, and behaviors and avoid imposing values that are inconsistent with counseling goals. Counselors respect the diversity of clients, trainees, and research participants. (ACA, 2005)

A.11.b. INABILITY TO ASSIST CLIENTS. If counselors determine an inability to be of professional assistance to clients, they avoid entering or continuing counseling relationships. Counselors are knowledgeable about culturally and clinically appropriate referral resources and suggest these alternatives. If clients decline the suggested referrals, counselors should discontinue the relationship. (ACA, 2005)

B.1.d. EXPLANATION OF LIMITATIONS. At initiation and throughout the counseling process, counselors inform clients of the limitations of confidentiality and seek to identify foreseeable situations in which confidentiality must be breached. (ACA, 2005)

B.2.a. DANGER AND LEGAL REQUIREMENTS. The general requirement that counselors keep information confidential does not apply when disclosure is required to protect clients or identified others from serious and foreseeable harm or when legal requirements demand that confidential information must be revealed. Counselors consult with other professionals when in doubt as to the validity of an exception. Additional considerations apply when addressing end-of-life issues. (See A.9.c.). (ACA, 2005)

B.3.b. TREATMENT TEAMS. When client treatment involves a continued review or participation by a treatment team, the client will be informed of the team's existence and composition, information being shared, and the purposes of sharing such information. (ACA, 2005)

B.5.a. RESPONSIBILITY TO CLIENTS. When counseling minor clients or adult clients who lack the capacity to give voluntary, informed consent, counselors protect the confidentiality of information received in the counseling relationship as specified by federal and state laws, written policies, and applicable ethical standards. (ACA, 2005)

B.5.b. RESPONSIBILITY TO PARENTS AND LEGAL GUARDIANS. Counselors inform parents and legal guardians about the role of counselors and the confidential nature of the counseling relationship. Counselors are sensitive to the cultural diversity of families and respect the inherent rights and responsibilities of parents/guardians over the welfare of their children/charges according to law. Counselors work to establish, as appropriate, collaborative relationships with parents/guardians to best serve clients. (ACA, 2005)

C.2.a. BOUNDARIES OF COMPETENCE. Counselors practice only within the boundaries of their competence, based on their education, training, supervised experience, state and national professional credentials, and appropriate professional experience. Counselors gain knowledge, personal awareness, sensitivity, and skills pertinent to working with a diverse client population. (See A.9.b., C.4.e., E.2., F.2.,

F.11.b.). (ACA, 2005)

C.2.b. NEW SPECIALTY AREAS OF PRACTICE. Counselors practice in specialty areas new to them only after appropriate education, training, and supervised experience. While developing skills in new specialty areas, counselors take steps to ensure the competence of their work and to protect others from possible harm. (See F.6.f.). (ACA, 2005)

### Consider the Principles and Virtues

*Nonmaleficence.* Because this client's medical condition is unstable, the counselor's priority should be to ensure her health and well-being, which may mean insisting on involuntary hospitalization, despite her and her mother's possible resistance to this course of action. Also, any treatment efforts conducted without medical attention will be in vain because of her cognitive impairment as illustrated in her recent decline in grades and inability to concentrate.

*Beneficence.* It is imperative that the counselor not only ensure the client's safety but also provide her with information regarding her condition, the effect it is having on her physical and mental health, treatment options, and potential consequences should she refuse treatment in order to encourage her progress toward achieving total wellness. The counselor should also be certain that he or she is within my scope of practice and is seeking appropriate supervision while treating this client.

*Autonomy.* As much as possible, the counselor wants to provide the client and her mother with choices because she will be more receptive and committed to treatment if she is a willing participant. However, because she is medically unstable and cognitively impaired, it may be necessary for the counselor to violate her autonomy to maintain her health in the event that she refuses treatment.

### Tune Into Feelings, Personal Values, and Emotions

Because of her frail appearance and distorted self-perception, the counselor initially feels the need to rescue the client and point out how dangerously thin she is. The counselor is also somewhat frustrated with Ella's mother for not being concerned about Ella's obvious medical instability. However, the counselor knows that her view of Ella would not be influenced by his or her simply pointing this out to her. Also, even though the counselor knows it is necessary for her to be medically stabilized, the counselor is afraid that she and her mother may react negatively if hospitalization is recommended.

### Obtain Consultation With Colleagues and Other Professionals, Particularly the Treatment Team Members

The counselor consults his or her direct supervisor and the staff psychiatrist. They both agree that because of the client's emaciated state and the fainting incidents she has already had it will be necessary to have the medical staff conduct a complete medical examination and perhaps hospitalize her to stabilize her medically and prevent further weight loss, even if the client, her mother, or both are not willing to voluntarily admit her. Because the counselor has only recently received training in treating EDs, the supervisor also advised the counselor to seek additional supervision, and the staff psychiatrist said that it would be vital to involve the treatment team to ensure adequate and complete care for this client.

### Involve the Client in the Decision-Making Process

Hospitalization may be required even if the client does not wish to begin treatment; however, the counselor wants to involve her in the process as much as possible and, the counselor hopes, encourage her to choose to enter a treatment program. The counselor can do this by discussing the results of the medical examination with the client and her mother and how they are the direct result of her ED. The counselor can then provide information to them about the dangers of AN. If the client is still reluctant, the counselor can further discuss with her the effects of starvation on her cognitive abilities, as exemplified by her declining grades. This step may be effective because her academic performance seems to be important to her and her mother.

### Identify Desired Outcomes

Ultimately, the counselor would like for the client to become medically stabilized and begin a treatment program that includes medical supervision, nutritional counseling, and individual counseling to address the psychological components of her AN and later the symptoms of anxiety she has been experiencing.

### Consider Possible Actions

*First possible course of action.* Consult with the client and her mother, encouraging hospitalization and a treatment program. In the event that the client or her mother refuses hospitalization, begin the process of involuntary hospitalization.

If Ella is hospitalized, a team of medical professionals can monitor her general health as she begins a nutritional program to prevent further weight loss and to help her gain weight in a safe manner, something that might be difficult to accomplish in an outpatient setting.

If the client agrees to hospitalization and treatment by her own choice, she will be more receptive to the process and may be more committed to making the changes necessary to deal with her ED.

If the client must be involuntarily hospitalized, she will be medically stabilized for the short term; however, she may be mistrusting of the treatment team, and the underlying psychological causes of her ED may not be resolved. Also, she may be reluctant to seek treatment in the future.

*Second possible course of action.* Consult with the client and her mother, encouraging the client to be hospitalized and enter a treatment program, but do not force the issue of involuntary hospitalization if they refuse. Encourage her to continue counseling.

As with the first course of action, the client will benefit from the holistic care offered with voluntary hospitalization and treatment and may be more committed to change.

It could be harmful to the client if the counselor does not force the issue of hospitalization because she is medically unstable and experiencing cognitive impairment because of her emaciated state, affecting her ability to make rational decisions. Also, the counselor could be held accountable if her medical condition worsens or if she dies as a result of her ED.

However, if the counselor is able to continue the counseling relationship with the client, he or she may be able to build a rapport and trust and eventually encourage the client to commit to hospitalization and treatment on her own.

*Third possible course of action.* Ask the client and her mother to allow the medical staff to conduct a thorough medical examination to determine the severity of her medical condition at this time. Once this has been completed, the counselor would discuss the results of the examination and the options of hospitalization and treatment with the client and her mother and make a determination about whether involuntary hospitalization may be required at that time.

By reviewing the results of the medical examination with the client and her mother, the counselor can demonstrate to them the severity of her condition and illustrate the direct effect her ED is having on her health.

The results of the medical exam will assist the counselor and the other members of the treatment team in deciding whether it will be necessary to move forward with involuntary hospitalization in the event that the client and her mother refuse or whether the counselor can continue the counseling relationship on an outpatient basis for a designated period of time to allow the client and her mother to agree to hospitalization on their own, which is the ideal situation.

*Fourth possible course of action.* Disregard the ED at this time because the client and her mother do not see it as an issue and treat the anxiety symptoms, which seem to be the main concern for the client's mother.

Because the client and her mother do acknowledge this as a problem, the client may be more receptive to treatment of these symptoms. This will also allow the counselor to build rapport with the client and possibly encourage her to seek treatment for her ED.

Although the anxiety symptoms described by the client may have a psychological or emotional component, they could also be the result of medical complications from her ED. Therefore, ignoring the ED could be harmful to the client, and treatment maybe not be beneficial if the symptoms are a physical reaction to her malnutrition and emaciated state.

### Decide on the Best Course of Action

After considering the pros and cons of each course of action, the third course of action seems to be the best intervention for this client. The results of the medical exam may be alarming enough to convince the client and her mother to acknowledge the presence of her ED and that hospitalization and treatment are in her best interest. In the event that the counselor has to involuntarily hospitalize the client, the results of the medical exam will be supporting evidence for my rationale in making this decision. Also, the counselor would be following the guidance provided by his or her supervisor and colleague during their consultation.

*Self-Tests Based on Ethical Principles*
- *Justice*: Would the counselor treat others the same in this situation? The counselor would follow the same course of action if another client were in this same situation.
- *Universality*: Would the counselor be willing to recommend this action to other counselors who are in a similar situation? Because the counselor is considering the best interest of the client and because his or her colleagues advised the counselor that they also believe this is the best course of action, the counselor would be willing to recommend this action to other counselors who are in similar situations.
- *Publicity*: Would the counselor be willing to have his or her actions come to light and be known by others? What if this decision were reported to the press? The counselor would stand by his or her decision if it were to be known by others or reported in the press because the counselor is placing the client's welfare at the forefront.
- *Moral traces*: Lingering feelings of doubt, discomfort, or uncertainty after a decision is made? The counselor is still a bit uncomfortable with the idea that he or she may have to involuntarily hospitalize the client. However, because the counselor has thoroughly evaluated all of the potential courses of action, the counselor is confident that he or she is making the decision that is in the best interest of the client as well as maintaining the ethical and moral standards of the profession.

# Conclusion

As is evidenced from the preceding example, working with clients with EDs can be highly complex and challenging. Counselors who engage in treatment with this population must have a strong desire and enthusiasm to pursue the additional training and personal examination necessary to conduct this work successfully. Counseling clients with EDs often enacts powerful countertransference reactions, high levels of frustration, and extreme stress because of ethical conflicts that can have life-threatening consequences. However, it can be highly rewarding to resolve ethical dilemmas that serve to preserve a client's life and well-being. When fully considering and balancing ethical principles, counselors can play an invaluable role in assisting clients to recover from a chronic and often devastating disorder.

# Chapter Highlights

- Be aware of relevant codes of ethics, ethical principles, and state laws related to informed consent for both minors and adults.

- Gain the knowledge and skill to recognize the disorder.
- Consult and make appropriate referrals when necessary and only work with specialized cases when sufficient training and supervision have been acquired.
- Consider a client's autonomy while addressing concerns regarding the client's health and overall well-being.
- The duty to protect may require the counselor to treat the individual even if treatment is unwanted.
- Do not consider the client to be incompetent simply because the client has a severe ED, but do specifically consider the client's decision making around food, eating, and weight.
- Consider your personal views on EDs and make proper referrals if those beliefs or values are preventing the client from receiving appropriate care.
- Be up to date on empirically supported interventions for this population, including working with a multidisciplinary treatment team.
- Refer to ethical decision-making models in making complex decisions related to clients with EDs.

## Recommended Resources

American Counseling Association. (2005). *ACA code of ethics*. Retrieved from http://www.counseling.org/Resources/CodeOfEthics/TP/Home/CT2.aspx

American Psychiatric Association. (2006). *Best practice guidelines for eating disorders* (3rd ed.). Retrieved from http://psychiatryonline.org/content.aspx?bookid=28&sectionid=1671334

American School Counselor Association. (2005). *ASCA position statements*. Retrieved from http://www.schoolcounselor.org/files/PositionStatements.pdf

Forester-Miller, H., & Davis, T. (1996). *A practitioner's guide to ethical decision making*. Alexandria, VA: American Counseling Association. Retrieved from http://www.counseling.org/Resources/CodeOfEthics/TP/Home/CT2.aspx

## References

American Counseling Association. (2005). *ACA code of ethics*. Retrieved from http://www.counseling.org/Resources/CodeOfEthics/TP/Home/CT2.aspx

American Psychiatric Association. (2006). Part A: Treatment recommendations for patients with eating disorders. In *Treatment of patients with eating disorders* (3rd ed.). Washington, DC: American Psychiatric Publishing. Retrieved from http://www.psychiatryonline.com/content.aspx?aid=138866

American School Counselor Association. (2009). The professional school counselor and student mental health. In *ASCA position statements* (pp. 50–51). Retrieved from http://www.schoolcounselor.org/files/PositionStatements.pdf

American School Counselor Association. (2010). Ethical standards for school counselors. Retrieved from http://www.schoolcounselor.org/files/EthicalStandards2010.pdf

Bell, K. (2010). Anorexia nervosa in adolescents: Responding using the Canadian code of ethics for psychologists. *Canadian Psychology, 51,* 249–256.

Carney, T., Ingvarson, M., & Tait, D. (2008). Experiences of "control" in anorexia nervosa treatment: Delayed coercion, shadow of law, or disseminated power and control? (Legal Studies Research Paper). Sydney, New South Wales, Australia: University of Sydney, Sydney Law School. Retrieved from http://ssrn.com/abstract=1080084

Corey, G., Corey, M., & Callanan, P. (2007). *Issues and ethics in the helping professions* (7th ed.). Pacific Grove, CA: Brooks/Cole.

Delucia-Waack, J. (1999). Supervision for counselors working with eating disorders groups: Countertransference issues related to body image, food, and weights. *Journal of Counseling & Development, 77,* 379–388.

Fairburn, C. G. (2008). *Cognitive behavior therapy and eating disorders.* New York, NY: Guildford Press.

Fedyszyn, I. E., & Sullivan, G. B. (2007). Ethical re-evaluation of contemporary treatments for anorexia nervosa: Is an aspirational stance possible in practice? *Australian Psychologist, 42,* 198–211.

Franko, D. L., & Keel, P. K. (*2006).* Suicidality in eating disorders: Occurrence, correlates, and clinical implications. *Clinical Psychology Review, 26,* 769–782

Giordano, S. (2005). *Understanding eating disorders: Conceptual and ethical issues in the treatment of anorexia and bulimia nervosa.* New York, NY: Oxford University Press.

Griffiths, R., & Russell, J. (1998). Compulsory treatment of anorexia nervosa patients. In W. Vandereycken & P. Beumont (Eds.), *Treating eating disorders: Ethical, legal, and personal issues* (pp. 127–150). New York, NY: New York University Press.

Honig, P., & Bentovim, M. (1996). Treating children with eating disorders: Ethical and legal issues. *Clinical Child Psychology and Psychiatry, 1,* 287–294.

Kitchener, K. S. (1984). Intuition, critical evaluation and ethical principles: The foundation for ethical decisions in counseling psychology. *Counseling Psychologist, 12,* 43–55.

Lock, J., LeGrange, D., Agras, W. S., & Dare, C. (2001). *Treatment manual for anorexia nervosa: A family-based approach.* New York, NY: Guilford Press.

Manley, R. S., Smye, V., & Srikameswaran, S. (2001). Addressing complex ethical issues in the treatment of children and adolescents with eating disorders: Application for a framework for ethical decision-making. *European Eating Disorders Review, 9,* 144–166.

Remley, T. P., & Herlihy, B. (2010). *Ethical, legal, and professional issues in counseling* (3rd ed.). Upper Saddle River, NJ: Pearson Education.

Simmons, A. M., Milnes, S. M., & Anderson, D. A. (2008). Factors influencing the utilization of empirically supported treatments for eating disorders. *Eating Disorders, 16,* 342–354.

Stadler, H. A. (1986). Making hard choices: Clarifying controversial ethical issues. *Counseling and Human Development, 66,* 258–260.

Swanson, S. A., Crow, S. J., LeGrange, D., Swendsen, J., & Merikangas, K. R. (2011). Prevalence and correlates of eating disorders in adolescents: Results from the National Comorbidity Survey Replication Adolescent Supplement. *Archives of General Psychiatry, 68,* 714–723.

Tan, J., Hope, T., & Stewart, A. (2003). Competence to refuse treatment in anorexia nervosa. *International Journal of Law and Psychiatry, 26,* 697–707.

Tan, J., Stewart, A., Fitzpatrick, R., & Hope, R. A. (2006). Competence to make treatment decisions in anorexia nervosa: Thinking processes and values. *Philosophy, Psychiatry, & Psychology, 13,* 267–282.

Warren, C. S., Crowley, M., Olivardia, R., & Schoen, A. (2009). Treating patients with eating disorders: An examination of treatment providers' experiences. *Eating Disorders, 17,* 27–45.

Welfel, E. R. (2006). *Ethics in counseling and psychotherapy: Standards, research, and emerging issues* (3rd ed.). Pacific Grove, CA: Brooks/Cole.

Werth, J. L., Wright, K. S., Archambault, R. J., & Bardash, R. J. (2003). When does the "duty to protect" apply with a client who has anorexia nervosa? *Counseling Psychologist, 31,* 427–450.

Williams, M., & Haverkamp, B. E. (2010). Identifying critical competencies for psychotherapeutic practice with eating disordered clients: A Delphi study. *Eating Disorders, 18,* 91–109.

Section 2

# Assessment and Practice Frameworks for Eating Disorders and Obesity

## Chapter 5

# Assessment and Diagnosis of Eating Disorders

*Kelly C. Berg and Carol B. Peterson*

The assessment and diagnosis of eating disorders (EDs) are critical for identifying EDs and associated symptoms, formulating an accurate understanding of the client's disorder, and planning effective treatment. When conducted with skill and empathy, assessment procedures can also enhance the counseling relationship and deepen therapeutic engagement (Peterson, 2005). Several factors can complicate the accurate assessment and diagnosis of ED symptoms, including the client's unintentional or deliberate misreporting of information as a result of fear of forced treatment or secondary effects of malnourishment; the co-occurrence of overlapping psychopathological and medical complications, including depression; and the complexity of several of the ED diagnostic constructs, including binge eating and the overevaluation of shape and weight that can lead to confusion for both the client and the clinician. In this chapter, we inform the accurate assessment and diagnosis of EDs by discussing (a) the diagnostic criteria for EDs, (b) strategies for integrating ED assessment into a clinical interview, and (c) special considerations for the assessment and diagnosis of EDs. We conclude with a case example, summary of important points, and a list of additional resources.

## Diagnostic Criteria for Eating Disorders

Two full-threshold EDs, anorexia nervosa (AN) and bulimia nervosa (BN), are formally identified in the *Diagnostic and Statistical Manual of Mental Disorders* (4th ed., text rev.; *DSM–IV–TR*; American Psychiatric Association [APA], 2000). A third ED category, labeled *eating disorder not otherwise specified* (EDNOS), is also included in *DSM–IV–TR* to identify individuals with clinically significant ED symptoms who did not meet criteria for either AN or BN (APA, 2000). The fifth edition of the *Diagnostic and Statistical Manual of Mental Disorders* (*DSM–5*) is set to be published in 2013 and will include several important changes to the diagnostic criteria for EDs. We describe the criteria sets for each *DSM–IV–TR* ED diagnosis next, along with details regarding how each criteria set will change in *DSM–5*.

For a diagnosis of AN, the *DSM–IV–TR* requires that the following four criteria be met: (A) minimal body weight for age, gender, and height; (B) fear of weight gain; (C) at least one symptom of cognitive dysfunction related to EDs (i.e., overevaluation of shape and weight, body image disturbance, or a denial of the seriousness of being at a low body weight); and (D) amenorrhea (i.e., missing three consecutive menstrual cycles; APA, 2000). Additionally, the *DSM–IV–TR* identifies two subtypes of AN. The restricting subtype is used to identify individuals who did not engage in regular binge eating or purging (i.e., self-induced vomiting, laxative misuse, diuretic misuse), and the binge eating/purging subtype is used to identify individuals who engaged in regular binge eating, regular purging, or both. *DSM–5* will include three major changes to the diagnostic criteria for AN (APA, 2012). First, the A criterion for *DSM–IV–TR* gives 85% ideal body weight as an example of what might be considered a minimally normal body weight. Although this ideal body weight is only provided to serve as an example, it has commonly been used in both research and clinical practice as a strict cutoff or threshold for body weight when diagnosing AN. *DSM–5* will eliminate this example from the A criterion and will require counselors to use more clinical judgment when determining whether an individual meets the underweight criterion for AN. Although the *DSM–5* text may include more specific guidelines to help clinicians determine what might be considered minimally normal body weight (e.g., body mass index [BMI], physical symptoms of semistarvation), these parameters have not been identified. Second, the B criterion for AN will be modified to read "intense fear of gaining weight or becoming fat, or persistent behavior that interferes with weight gain, even though at a significantly low weight" (American Psychiatric Association, 2012b, para. 2). Ultimately, this criterion means that if an individual denies fear of weight gain but regularly engages in behavior (e.g., dietary restriction, fasting, excessive exercise, purging) to prevent or avoid weight gain, that individual would still meet this criterion even if he or she denies an intense fear of gaining weight or becoming fat. Third, the D criterion will be eliminated, which means that amenorrhea or the loss of menstrual cycles will no longer be required for a diagnosis of AN. It is important to note that although amenorrhea will no longer be required for a diagnosis of AN, the loss of menstrual cycles can be used to determine whether an individual is underweight. Thus, assessment of amenorrhea will still be important when using *DSM–5* criteria.

The *DSM–IV–TR* criteria for BN are (a) the presence of binge eating, defined as the consumption of an unusually large amount of food coupled with a subjective sense of loss of control; (b) the presence of compensatory behaviors (i.e., self-induced vomiting, abuse of laxatives or diuretics, excessive exercise, or fasting); (c) the occurrence of both binge eating and compensatory behaviors at least twice per week for the past 3 months;

and (d) overevaluation of shape and weight (APA, 2000). Similar to AN, the *DSM–IV–TR* recognizes two subtypes of BN. The purging subtype identifies individuals who engage in regular purging compensatory behaviors (i.e., self-induced vomiting, abuse of laxatives or diuretics), and the nonpurging subtype identifies individuals who regularly engage in nonpurging compensatory behaviors (i.e., excessive exercise or fasting) but not purging behaviors. Additionally, we should note that in contrast to previous editions of the manual, the *DSM–IV–TR* does not allow an individual to be diagnosed with two EDs simultaneously. Rather, a diagnosis of AN trumps a diagnosis of BN, meaning that if an individual meets criteria for both AN and BN (e.g., an individual who is below a minimally normal weight, endorses fear of weight gain and overevaluation of shape and weight, who has amenorrhea, and who engages in binge eating and compensatory behaviors at least twice per week for 3 months), that person would be diagnosed with AN, binge eating/purging subtype, rather than BN according to the *DSM–IV–TR*. Given that the *DSM–IV–TR* criteria for AN and BN have substantial overlap (e.g., overevaluation of shape and weight), the most fundamental difference between AN and BN was the weight criterion. The *DSM–5* criteria for BN will largely remain the same (APA, 2012a); however, they will have two major changes. First, the frequency criterion for binge eating and compensatory behaviors will decrease from twice per week for 3 months to once per week for 3 months; second, BN will no longer include subtypes. The criteria will be the same as those described in the *DSM–IV–TR*, including the specification that AN trumps BN.

Last, the *DSM–IV–TR* provides the following examples of clinical presentations that would meet the criteria for EDNOS: (a) All criteria for AN are met, except amenorrhea; (b) all criteria for AN are met except that the individual is at a normal weight; (c) all criteria for BN are met except that the binge eating and compensatory behaviors occur less frequently than twice per week or for a shorter duration than 3 months; (d) regular purging without binge eating; (e) chewing and spitting food out without swallowing and no regular compensatory behaviors; (f) binge eating without the use of compensatory behaviors (i.e., binge eating disorder, or BED; APA, 2000). One of the primary goals for the *DSM–5* Eating Disorders Work Group was to address two important problems associated with the EDNOS category. First, as stated earlier, *DSM–IV–TR* EDNOS is meant to capture a small group of individuals with subthreshold EDs. However, research found that rates of *DSM–IV–TR* EDNOS were significantly higher than those for *DSM–IV–TR* AN and BN (e.g., Fairburn et al., 2007; Hoek, 2006). Additionally, the associated psychopathology, psychosocial impairment, treatment response, and medical–suicide risk of *DSM–IV–TR* EDNOS were comparable to those of *DSM–IV–TR* AN and BN (e.g., Crow et al., 2009; Fairburn et al., 2007), which suggests that individuals diagnosed with *DSM–IV–TR* EDNOS may not have been accurately described as having subthreshold symptoms.

The criteria for *DSM–5* will reduce the prevalence of EDNOS through several changes (APA, 2012a). First, as described earlier, the criteria for both AN and BN have been broadened (e.g., eliminating the amenorrhea requirement for AN, including behavioral indices of fear of weight gain for AN, reducing the required frequency of binge eating and compensatory behaviors for BN to once per week), with the goal of capturing some individuals who would have been diagnosed with *DSM–IV–TR* EDNOS. Second, a more dramatic change is that BED, one of the clinical syndromes included as an example of EDNOS, will be formally recognized by *DSM–5* as a full-threshold ED (discussed in the paragraphs to follow). Last, *DSM–5* EDNOS, which has been renamed *feeding and eating conditions not elsewhere classified,* describes five specific clinical presentations that could be considered for its diagnosis. These syndromes are (a) atypical AN (all criteria for AN are met except that the client is at or above normal weight), (b) subthreshold BN (all criteria for BN are met except that binge eating, purging, or both occurred less than once per week for 3 months), (c) subthreshold BED (all criteria for BED are met except that binge eating occurred less than once per week for 3 months), (d) purging disorder (regular purging in the absence of binge eating), and (e) night eating syndrome (recurrent night eating associated with distress or functional impairment that is not better accounted for by another medical or psychiatric disorder such as BED). Overall, research has demonstrated that these changes result in a substantial decrease in EDNOS (e.g., Berg et al., 2012; Keel, Brown, Holm-Denoma, & Bodell, 2011).

BED, which is provided as an example of EDNOS in *DSM–IV–TR*, is not formally recognized as a full-threshold ED in *DSM–IV–TR*. However, specific criteria for BED are included in Appendix B of the *DSM–IV–TR* (APA, 2000) for the purpose of encouraging research on the validity of the syndrome. The *DSM–IV–TR* criteria for BED are (a) the presence of binge eating, defined as the consumption of an unusually large amount of food accompanied by a sense of loss of control over eating during the episode; (b) the occurrence of binge eating at least twice per week for a duration of 6 months; (c) the presence of at least three features associated with binge eating (e.g., eating more rapidly than normal, eating until uncomfortably full, eating large amounts of food when not physically hungry, eating alone because of feeling embarrassed about how much one is eating, and feeling disgusted, depressed, or guilty after eating); (d) significant distress regarding binge eating; and (e) the absence of both AN and BN. As described earlier, the *DSM–IV–TR* does not allow for the diagnosis of two EDs simultaneously; therefore, the *DSM–IV–TR* also indicates that a diagnosis of either AN or BN trumps a diagnosis of BED. In *DSM–5*, BED will be included as a full-threshold ED, and the BED criteria will be modified such that binge eating must occur on average at least once per week for the past 3 months, which is consistent with the frequency and duration criteria for BN (APA, 2012a). Although the *DSM–IV–TR* and proposed *DSM–5* BED criteria do not specify a required weight threshold, epidemiological data have suggested that BED is associated with overweight and obesity (Wonderlich, Gordon, Mitchell, Crosby, & Engel, 2009).

The *DSM–5* ED section will also expand to include the following two feeding disorders, both of which are often diagnosed in childhood and were previously described in *DSM–IV–TR*: (a) pica, a disorder characterized by the eating of non-nutritive and nonfood substances, and (b) rumination disorder, which is characterized by the repeated regurgitation of food that is then rechewed, reswallowed, or spit out (APA, 2012a).

Additionally, *DSM–5* will include a new feeding disorder, avoidant/restrictive food intake disorder, to provide a diagnosis for individuals with significant feeding or eating disturbances other than AN and BN that are not related to concerns about body shape or weight. Although pica, rumination disorder, and avoidant/restrictive food intake disorder will be considered full-threshold EDs in *DSM–5*, individuals with these disorders are more likely to present to medical clinics than to mental health clinics. The *DSM–5* Eating Disorders Work Group also considered including obesity in the Feeding and Eating Disorders section of *DSM–5*, citing the significant health-related consequences of obesity and the fact that psychiatric disorders (e.g., depression, BED) can lead to weight gain. However, research has overall indicated that obesity is a heterogeneous condition and its etiology is multifaceted (Marcus & Wildes, 2009). Thus, given that little evidence has suggested that obesity is the direct result of mental dysfunction, the work group elected to not include obesity in *DSM–5*. In sum, the criteria for full-threshold EDs will change substantially from *DSM–IV–TR* to *DSM–5*. In this chapter, we provide recommendations and guidelines for the assessment and diagnosis of AN, BN, and BED using the *DSM–5* criteria.

## Integrating Eating Disorders Assessment Into an Unstructured Clinical Interview

Clinical interviews require counselors to balance the dual goals of obtaining a comprehensive assessment with developing and maintaining rapport with the client (Peterson, 2005). Given the serious medical and psychiatric complications associated with EDs (Academy for Eating Disorders' Medical Care Standards Task Force, 2011; Crow & Swigart, 2005), it is important for counselors to assess ED symptoms with all clients regardless of age, gender, race or ethnicity, or weight status. However, in general outpatient clinics, a comprehensive ED assessment may not be necessary or feasible. Therefore, we recommend that counselors conduct a screen for ED symptoms and follow up with a more comprehensive assessment if necessary.

### Screening for Eating Disorders

Unstructured clinical interviews that include assessment of general self-care lend themselves easily to ED screening. Specifically, questions about sleep and eating patterns can provide an effective segue into an ED screen.

General questions about a client's eating patterns such as "What is your general eating pattern?" and "Do you ever skip meals?" can introduce the topic of disordered eating behavior without causing initial discomfort. Counselors may choose to follow up with questions about the client's diet history (e.g., "Have you ever been on a diet?" "What kinds of diets have you tried?") and patterns of dietary restriction (e.g., "Are there any foods that you like that you're trying to avoid eating?" "Do you try to follow any rules regarding your eating?"). These questions can then lead into more specific questions about disordered eating behaviors such as binge eating (e.g., "Have you ever felt a sense of loss of control over your eating?") and compensatory behaviors (e.g., "Have you ever done anything to compensate for food you've consumed such as self-induced vomiting or laxative use?").

Questions about exercise may also be included in an unstructured interview in the context of assessing clients' self-care. The addition of several detailed questions regarding the quantity and quality of exercise can also provide information regarding the client's propensity for excessive exercise and disordered eating behaviors. If a client endorses exercise, it is recommended that counselors ask detailed questions about the type (e.g., "What kind of exercise do you typically do?"), duration (e.g., "On average, for how long do you typically exercise?"), and intensity (e.g., "How intense is the exercise you usually do?" "Do you ever feel that you exercise beyond what is physically healthy for you?"). The *DSM–IV–TR* and *DSM–5* describe problematic or disordered exercise as "excessive exercise"; however, determining what qualifies as excessive exercise can be difficult. For example, although frequent and intense exercise may reflect an underlying ED, these types of activity patterns may or may not be problematic in the context of athletic training. Research has suggested that the qualities of exercise that best differentiate normative exercise from disordered exercise are the following: (a) The exercise is motivated solely or primarily by shape or weight concerns and (b) feelings of guilt when exercise routines are not completed (Mond & Calogero, 2009; Mond, Hay, Rodgers, & Owen, 2006). Counselors may also choose to determine the extent to which the individual feels driven or compelled to exercise, whether exercise is completed even when the individual is sick or injured, and whether exercise is completed at the expense of other activities or commitments.

Finally, general questions about self-esteem, such as "How do you feel about yourself as a person?" can lead to more specific questions about body image, such as "Do you ever feel dissatisfied with your shape or weight?" These types of questions can be used to assess body image disturbance or overevaluation of shape and weight, which may be indicative of an ED.

### When to Follow Up Eating Disorders Screening With Additional Questions

Certain physical characteristics or the endorsement of certain behavioral or cognitive symptoms may indicate a possible ED and require further assessment. For example, counselors should always follow up with clients who present with low body weight or substantial weight changes because they can be indicative of a serious underlying medical or psychiatric condition, regardless of whether an ED is present. More important, low weight in children and adolescents may present as a failure to meet height and weight expectations or delays or interruptions to pubertal development (APA, 2012a). Furthermore, because of the possibility of associated medical complications, counselors should also follow up with clients who endorse any of the following: (a) recurrent binge eating, (b) purging behaviors (i.e., self-induced vomiting, misuse of laxatives, diuretics, enemas, insulin, thyroid medication), (c) regular fasting or extreme dietary restriction, or (d) exercise that interferes with psychosocial functioning, occurs in the context of illness or injury, or is primarily motivated by shape or weight concerns (Academy for Eating Disorders' Medical Care Standards Task Force, 2011; Crow & Swigart, 2005). Cognitive symptoms (e.g., extreme body dissatisfaction, overevaluation of shape or weight, or fear of weight gain) may also warrant further evaluation, even in the absence of physical or behavioral signs of an ED. However, it is important to note that body dissatisfaction is relatively common and may even be considered normative in Western culture. Therefore, counselors must balance the goal of adequately screening for EDs with that of being careful to not overpathologize clients whose weight and shape concerns fall within current cultural norms.

## Making Differential Diagnoses

When determining whether a pattern of symptoms is reflective of an ED, the first priority is establishing whether the problematic behavior, weight, or cognitions could be better explained by another medical or psychiatric condition. For example, although dramatic changes in weight can reflect an underlying ED, weight change is also a symptom of medical (e.g., hyperthyroidism, cancer, food allergies, gastrointestinal problems) and psychiatric (e.g., depression or substance dependence) problems. Determining the onset (e.g., "When did you or someone else first notice you had lost weight?" "What was going on in your life at the time?") and nature of symptoms (e.g., "Were you trying to lose weight?" "Did you notice any changes in your appetite?") can be helpful in determining the extent to which the weight change is reflective of an ED. In some cases, referral to a medical specialist may be necessary to rule out potential medical conditions. Other symptoms associated with EDs, such as anxiety when eating with others, avoidance of certain foods, and body checking, can be reflective of other psychiatric conditions (e.g., anxiety disorders, body dysmorphic disorder, paranoia). Detailed questions about the focus of the anxiety (e.g., is the individual's anxiety in social situations reflective of a fear of choking or a fear of judgment about what or how much food is consumed?), avoidance (e.g., not eating for fear of vomiting vs. not eating in an attempt to lose weight), or body checking (e.g., scrutinizing for signs of skin imperfections vs. scrutinizing for signs of weight gain) can help differentiate between EDs and other psychiatric disorders.

Once it becomes clear that the client's symptoms are not explained by other medical and psychiatric conditions, priority can be given to specifying the client's ED diagnosis. Differentiating among the ED diagnoses can be complicated, and using a decision tree can provide some guidance. First, the client's weight status should be assessed. Given that self-reported weights are often inaccurate, height and weight should ideally be measured using calibrated instruments. Accuracy of measurement can be further improved by weighing the client in a gown because the weight of a client's clothes can make it difficult to establish weight status at baseline, track weight changes over time, or both (Peterson, 2005). In addition, clients may put heavy objects such as coins in their pockets to increase their observed weight, usually motivated by fear of forced treatment or hospitalization. Although 85% ideal body weight is recommended as the threshold for underweight in *DSM–IV–TR* (APA, 2000), the proposed criteria for *DSM–5* will allow counselors to exercise more clinical judgment when defining underweight when diagnosing AN (APA, 2012a). For example, physical signs of malnutrition such as amenorrhea, low or irregular heart rate, dizziness, or fainting could be used as evidence that the client is at a significantly low body weight (Academy for Eating Disorders' Medical Care Standards Task Force, 2011; Crow & Swigart, 2005). If a client meets the weight criterion for AN, further probing can be used to determine whether the client meets the B criteria (i.e., fear of weight gain or persistent behaviors to avoid weight gain) and C criteria (i.e., body image disturbance, overevaluation of shape or weight, or lack of recognition of the seriousness of the low body weight).

Fear of weight gain can be determined by asking the client direct questions such as "How would you feel if you gained weight?" or "Are you afraid to gain weight?" Some clients may deny fear of weight gain or indicate that they are not afraid of gaining weight because they do not believe weight gain is a possibility given their current behaviors. In such cases, the *DSM–5* will allow counselors to assess for persistent behaviors that would prevent weight gain, such as dietary restriction, purging behaviors, fasting, or excessive exercise, to determine whether the client has an underlying fear of gaining weight (APA, 2012a). Fairburn (1995, 2008) has described three broad types of dietary restriction: (a) going for long periods of time without eating (e.g., skipping meals, fasting), (b) avoidance of certain types of foods (e.g., carbohydrates, chocolate, chips), and (c) overall caloric restriction (e.g., eating only 800 calories per day). Clients who engage in dietary restriction may endorse one type of restriction or a combination of these restrictive patterns.

The presence of cognitive disturbances associated with AN can be assessed through direct questions. For example, to assess body image disturbance, a counselor can ask questions including "Do you still feel as though your body is too large or as though you need to lose weight?" "Do you see your body as bigger or larger than others see your body?" "Do you feel that you look fat or overweight even when others tell you that you are at a normal weight or underweight?" Overvaluation of shape or weight can be a difficult construct to assess because it is a relatively abstract construct that requires clients to use meta-cognition to think about how they evaluate themselves and then determine the extent to which their shape or weight influences that evaluation (Fairburn & Cooper, 1993). Thus, counselors may find it useful to tailor their assessment of this construct to each individual client. For example, direct questions (e.g., "Does your body shape or weight have a large impact on how you feel about yourself?") may be an effective strategy for some clients, whereas others might benefit from the counselor's walking them through the meta-cognition required by this construct. Finally, to assess whether an individual lacks recognition of the seriousness of his or her low body weight, a counselor could ask, "Has anyone ever told you that there could be serious medical or physical conditions associated with being at your current weight?" (First, Spitzer, Gibbon, & Williams, 1995). If the client answers affirmatively, the counselor can follow up with a question to determine whether the client agrees. If the client denies that anyone has expressed concern, the counselor could pose a hypothetical question such as "If someone told you that there are serious medical or physical conditions associated with being at your current weight, what would you think of that?"

If a diagnosis of AN can be ruled out, the next diagnostic priority is to determine whether the client meets the criteria for BN, the hallmark symptoms of which are binge eating and the use of compensatory behaviors. As described earlier, *binge eating* is defined as the consumption of an unusually large amount of food accompanied by a sense of loss of control over the eating episode. Determining whether an eating episode would be categorized as "unusually large" can be surprisingly difficult because no universally accepted threshold exists for what constitutes an unusually large amount of food (Arikian et al., 2012). For example, although most people would agree that an entire family-size bag of chips (e.g., 16 ounces) would be an unusually large amount of food to consume in one sitting, disagreement may occur over the exact threshold for an "unusually large amount of chips" (e.g., 6 ounces? 8 ounces? 10 ounces?). To further complicate matters, clients may report consuming multiple types of food (e.g., chips, ice cream, and cereal) and determining whether such eating episodes would be considered unusually large may depend on a variety of factors such as the exact type (e.g., Was it cornflakes or granola? Was there milk on the cereal?) and amount (e.g., How many cups of cereal? One half cup? One cup? Two cups?) of each food consumed. Additionally, the environmental context and patient factors such as gender and BMI can affect whether an amount of food should be considered unusually large (Arikian et al., 2012; Fairburn, Cooper, & O'Connor, 2008). Thus, counselors are recommended to identify at least two specific examples of binge eating episodes, gather details about the type and quantity of food consumed and the context of the episode, and consult with other professionals when assessing binge eating to build consensus to determine whether a binge eating episode is large by *DSM–IV–TR* and *DSM–5* standards.

The experience of loss of control during eating episodes can also be difficult to assess because individual differences exist in the way loss of control is experienced as well as in the extent to which clients are aware that their eating is out of control. For example, some clients may either spontaneously report that their eating is out of their control or will respond affirmatively to direct questioning about loss of control (e.g., "Have you ever felt as though your eating was out of control?"). However, counselors may find that for other clients, describing the sensation of loss of control with different terminology is helpful (e.g., "Has it ever felt as though you couldn't stop or resist eating?" "Has your eating ever felt driven or compelled?"; Fairburn & Cooper, 1993; Fairburn et al., 2008). Some clients deny that their eating feels out of control because they plan their binges in advance. For example, a client may know that after class, she or he will stop at a convenience store and buy specific food for a binge. In such cases, additional questions (e.g., "Did you feel driven or compelled to go to the convenience store after class?" "Could you have resisted going to the convenience store?" "Could you have stopped eating the food that you bought at the convenience store once you started eating?") can be useful in determining the extent to which the subjective experience of loss of control was present during the eating episode. Clients will often indicate that once the plan for the binge was made, they felt driven or compelled to carry it out. In these circumstances, the subjective experience of lack of control is considered present even if the binge eating episode was planned (Fairburn, 2008).

Compensatory behaviors are also required for a diagnosis of BN. Both purging and nonpurging behaviors should be assessed. Purging behaviors include self-induced vomiting, laxative misuse, and diuretic misuse, whereas nonpurging behaviors include fasting and excessive exercise. Although relatively uncommon, use of ipecac to induce vomiting and misuse of insulin to prevent nutrient absorption should also be assessed. Once the counselor has established that a client is engaging in binge eating and compensatory behaviors, he or she needs to determine whether the frequency and duration of the episodes meet criteria for BN and whether overevaluation of shape or weight is present (see previous discussion, this section). As stated earlier, if a client meets criteria for AN and also engages in binge eating and purging, he or she would be given a diagnosis of AN (not BN).

If a client is engaging in binge eating but not compensatory behaviors, the counselor can consider a BED diagnosis. To confirm a BED diagnosis, the counselor needs to determine the following: (a) the frequency and duration of the binge eating episodes, (b) whether the binge eating episodes are characterized by at least three of the associated features of binge eating (see earlier discussion in the Diagnostic Criteria for Eating Disorders section), and (c) whether the client experiences significant distress regarding the binge eating. If a client endorses clinically significant ED symptoms but does not meet criteria for AN, BN, or BED, the counselor may consider a subthreshold ED diagnosis (feeding and eating conditions not elsewhere classified). Overall, assessment of the following variables is essential for the diagnosis of AN, BN, and BED as defined by the proposed *DSM–5* criteria: (a) weight status (as determined by height, weight, age, and gender), (b) fear of weight gain, (c) dietary restriction, (d) overevaluation of shape and weight, (e) body image disturbance, (f) presence and frequency of binge eating, and (g) presence and frequency of compensatory behaviors. If the client is underweight, determining whether the client is aware of the potential consequences associated with low weight may also be necessary.

### Structured Assessments

Several self-report questionnaires and structured interviews are available for the counselor to use in the assessment of EDs and associated symptoms (see Table 5.1). These measures can be used for different purposes depending on the needs of the counselor. For example, the Eating Disorders Diagnostic Scale (Stice, Telch, & Rizvi, 2000) is a brief screening instrument that can be used to determine the presence of self-reported ED symptoms as well as to make differential diagnoses between different types of EDs. Other instruments, including the Eating Disorder Examination Questionnaire (Fairburn & Beglin, 2008), can be used by the counselor to examine the severity of a wide range of ED symptoms (e.g., dietary restraint, eating concerns, weight concerns, and shape concerns) as well as specific behaviors including binge eating and purging. Given that the correlations between self-report questionnaires and structured clinical interviews are modest (e.g., Keel, Crow, Davis, & Mitchell, 2002), questionnaire data should be used along with information obtained during the clinical interview to ensure accurate assessment and diagnosis.

### Assessing Psychiatric Risk

High rates of co-occurring psychiatric disorders occur among individuals with both full and subthreshold EDs. Mood disturbances are particularly common (e.g., Wonderlich & Mitchell, 1997); however, the relationship between eating and mood disorders can be complex because EDs can exacerbate mood symptoms and vice versa. For example, many clients with AN also present with symptoms of depression because semistarvation can mimic symptoms associated with depression, including low mood, anhedonia, fatigue, and poor concentration (Keys, Brozek, Henschel, Mickelsen, & Taylor, 1950). In such cases, weight restoration will often lead to reductions in both eating and mood disturbances. Research has also demonstrated that ED behaviors such as binge eating and purging may function to mitigate negative affect (Smyth et al., 2007); thus, for some individuals, symptoms of depression may lead to the onset or exacerbation of eating disturbances. Although co-occurring bipolar disorder is less common, it is also observed in clients with EDs (e.g., Wonderlich & Mitchell, 1997). More important, although the *DSM–IV–TR* describes binge eating as one example of impulsive behavior associated with mania, binge eating should not be counted as a symptom of mania if a co-occurring ED is present.

Table 5.1
**Structured Assessment Tools Available to Professional Counselors**

| Instrument | Item Content | Information Provided | When to Use | Administration Time |
|---|---|---|---|---|
| Binge Eating Scale (Gormally, Black, Daston, & Rardin, 1982)[a] | Current ED symptoms, specifically related to binge eating | Derive diagnosis of BED; dimensional measure of binge eating severity | Intake; during course of treatment | < 5 minutes |
| Body Shape Questionnaire (Cooper, Taylor, Cooper, & Fairburn, 1987)[a] | Current ED symptoms, specifically related to body dissatisfaction | Dimensional measure of body dissatisfaction | During course of treatment | < 5 minutes |
| Dutch Eating Behavior Questionnaire (van Strien, Frijters, Bergers, & Defares, 1986)[b] | Current eating behaviors, specifically restraint, emotional eating, and external eating | Dimensional measure of ED symptom severity | During course of treatment | < 5 minutes |
| Eating Attitudes Test-26 (Garner, Olmsted, Bohr, & Garfinkel, 1982)[c] | Current ED symptoms | ED screening instrument; dimensional measure of ED symptom severity | Intake; during course of treatment | < 5 minutes |
| Eating Disorder Diagnostic Scale (Stice, Telch, & Rizvi, 2000)[a] | Current ED symptoms, based on *DSM-IV-TR* criteria for AN, BN, and BED | Derive ED diagnoses; dimensional measure of ED symptom severity | Intake; during course of treatment | < 5 minutes |
| Eating Disorder Examination Questionnaire (Fairburn & Beglin, 2008)[d] | Current ED symptoms, frequency of ED behaviors, restraint, and concerns about eating, shape, and weight | Derive ED diagnoses; dimensional measure of ED symptom severity | Intake; during course of treatment | 3–7 minutes |
| Eating Disorder Questionnaire (Mitchell, 2005)[e] | Current/lifetime ED symptoms; psychosocial, medical, and psychiatric history | Derive ED diagnoses; supplemental information garnered from a clinical interview | Intake | 20–45 minutes |

*(Continued)*

Table 5.1 (*Continued*)
**Structured Assessment Tools Available to Professional Counselors**

| Instrument | Item Content | Information Provided | When to Use | Administration Time |
|---|---|---|---|---|
| Night Eating Question-naire[a] (Allison et al., 2008) | Current ED symptoms, specifically related to NES | Screening instrument for NES; dimensional measure of NES symptom severity | Intake; during course of treatment | < 5 minutes |
| Questionnaire on Eating and Weight Patterns—Revised[a] (Spitzer et al., 1993) | Current ED symptoms, based on *DSM–IV–TR* criteria for BN and BED; dieting and weight history | Derive BN or BED diagnoses; supplement information garnered from a clinical interview | Intake | 3–7 minutes |
| Three-Factor Eating Questionnaire[a] (Stunkard & Messick, 1985) | Current eating behaviors, specifically restraint, disinhibition, and hunger | Dimensional measure of ED symptom severity | During course of treatment | 3–7 minutes |

*Note.* The primary reference for each instrument is presented in parentheses. ED = eating disorder; BED = binge eating disorder; *DSM–IV–TR = Diagnostic and Statistical Manual of Mental Disorders* (4th ed., text rev.; American Psychiatric Association, 2000); AN = anorexia nervosa; BN = bulimia nervosa; NES = night eating syndrome.
[a]Questionnaire is published in the primary reference. [b]Item content and scoring instructions are published in the primary reference. [c]Questionnaire can be downloaded from http://www.eat-26.com/permission.htm. [d]Questionnaire can be downloaded from http://www.psychiatry.ox.ac.uk/research/researchunits/credo/assessment-measures. [e]Questionnaire is published in Mitchell (2005).

Suicide and self-injury are also common and represent one of the leading causes of mortality among individuals with EDs. Thus, detailed questions about suicidal ideation (e.g., plan, means, and intent) and self-injury (e.g., location, type, and severity of self-harm) are critically important regardless of whether a co-occurring mood disorder is present.

Anxiety disorders, including obsessive–compulsive disorder, phobias, and posttraumatic stress disorder, are also common among individuals with EDs (e.g., Wonderlich & Mitchell, 1997). However, as with mood disorders, distinguishing between eating and anxiety symptoms can be difficult because anxiety symptoms often occur in the context of an ED. For example, panic attacks, rituals (e.g., cutting food into specific number of pieces), and phobias (e.g., fear of weighing, fear of specific foods) are common; however, these symptoms are often better explained by the ED. In such cases, a co-occurring anxiety disorder would not be diagnosed. If a client with an ED reports anxiety symptoms, a co-occurring anxiety disorder should only be diagnosed if the content of the anxiety is unrelated to eating, shape, weight, exercise, and so forth. Besides mood and anxiety disorders, substance use disorders (e.g., Holderness, Brooks-Gunn, & Warren, 1994; Wonderlich & Mitchell, 1997) and Axis II personality disorders (e.g., Wonderlich & Mitchell, 1997) are also common and should be assessed in all clients with ED symptoms.

### Assessing Medical Risk

Medical risk is significant across all ED diagnoses, including the subthreshold EDs described in feeding and eating conditions not elsewhere classified. Thus, if an ED is suspected or has been confirmed, referral should be made to a physician or other medical provider. In general, all clients with EDs should be referred for a physical examination, regardless of symptom severity; however, more immediate medical attention is warranted in certain situations. For example, if clients present with any of the following, they should immediately be referred for medical follow-up: (a) low BMI, (b) significant weight change, (c) purging (because of possible electrolyte disturbance), and (d) conditions that indicate cardiac abnormalities (e.g., fainting, dizziness). All medical examinations should assess (a) height and weight (see earlier discussion in the Making Differential Diagnoses section), (b) vital signs (e.g., pulse, orthostatic hypertension, blood pressure, electrocardiogram), (c) electrolytes (e.g., potassium, sodium, glucose, calcium, phosphorous), (d) bone density (e.g., dual-energy X-ray absorptiometry), and (e) menstrual status (Academy for Eating Disorders' Medical Care Standards Task Force, 2011; Crow & Swigart, 2005). Because of the high rates of obesity among individuals with BED, individuals who are obese should also be referred for a medical examination to evaluate disease risk including cardiological problems, Type 2 diabetes, and hypertension.

Often, clients with EDs require ongoing medical evaluation; thus, some clients may need to attend weekly physical examinations during the course of therapy. As a result, counselors who treat clients with EDs may find it useful to develop collaborative relationships with medical providers to whom they can refer clients in need of medical monitoring. Such relationships ensure clear, consistent communication with clients regarding treatment plans and goals. Regardless of whether clients with EDs are attending regular medical examinations, counselors should assess height and weight on an ongoing basis during the course of therapy to monitor weight status (particularly among clients who are underweight). As such, counselors who treat patients with EDs need to either maintain calibrated scales (e.g., in office or clinic) or collaborate with other health professionals who have access to calibrated scales and can obtain measurements (e.g., medical staff, dietitians). Among clients with AN or who present as underweight, menstrual status should also be assessed regularly in therapy because resumption of menses can be a useful indicator of recovery (e.g., Attia & Roberto, 2009).

### Determining Level of Care

Once an ED diagnosis has been established, the counselor will need to determine the level of care at which the client should be treated. Clients with EDs are treated at several different levels of care, including outpatient, intensive outpatient or partial day treatment, inpatient, and residential, and fluctuations in level of care are not uncommon. Clinics that specialize in EDs may offer multiple levels of care, and counselors who treat clients with EDs often find it helpful to maintain relationships with other clinics and providers to ensure continuity of care. In general, determining the appropriate level of care is an ongoing process that involves consideration of the severity of ED and co-occurring psychiatric symptoms, medical risk, and acute risk of self-injury or suicide. For example, clients with more severe symptoms (e.g., low BMI, suicide risk), medical instability, or symptoms that are unresponsive to outpatient counseling may require more intensive treatment. Client motivation is also important to consider in determining level of care. For example, highly motivated clients may be able to sustain weight gain procedures in an outpatient setting, whereas clients with more ambivalence about recovery may need more intensive treatment.

## Special Considerations for Eating Disorders Assessment

As in all psychological assessment, evaluation of clients with ED symptoms can be compromised by various biases, including inadvertent or deliberate minimization and recall biases. Assessment of diagnosis of EDs in children, adolescents, and racial or ethnic minority groups can also be particularly challenging.

### Inadvertent and Deliberate Minimization

Both inadvertent and deliberate minimization of symptoms are common among individuals with EDs. Inadvertent minimization may occur because some clients, especially children and adolescents, have limited capacity for self-awareness. Additionally, some ED symptoms are difficult to define (e.g., binge eating, overevaluation of shape and weight), which can lead to confusion and inadvertent minimization. Deliberate minimization is also common and often results from feelings of shame, desire to avoid hospitalization or treatment, or attachment to the ED symptoms (e.g., Vitousek, Watson, & Wilson, 1998). ED symptoms, particularly dietary restriction, purging, and underweight status, are often ego syntonic, with clients valuing these symptoms and seeing them as an aspect of their identity. The ego-syntonic nature of ED symptoms can make clients particularly guarded in the context of assessment because of the fear that revealing this information will result in forced treatment and the loss of their ED symptoms.

Accurate self-disclosure can be enhanced through the use of the following nonspecific therapeutic techniques: (a) demonstrating empathy, (b) conveying acceptance, (c) encouraging collaboration, (d) posing questions or statements in an open-ended format (e.g., "Tell me more about the rules you try to follow with regard to eating"), and (e) avoiding both verbal and nonverbal signals that imply criticism, judgment, lack of expertise, or fear (Miller & Rollnick, 2002). These nonspecific therapeutic factors are especially important when assessing topics that may be a source of shame or embarrassment (e.g., specific details about binge eating and purging). Moreover, when assessing abstract constructs including binge eating and overevaluation of shape and weight, counselors can help clients improve accuracy of self-disclosure by providing detailed and concrete information to the client about the constructs being assessed (e.g., "By binge eating, I mean eating an amount of food that other people may consider unusually large and feeling as though you're unable to control what or how much you're eating") and by obtaining detailed and concrete information from the client about the constructs being assessed (e.g., quantity and type of food consumed during a binge, measured rather than self-reported height and weight).

### Recall Biases

Even when clients intend to be forthcoming about their symptoms, the information they provide may be inaccurate because of a variety of recall biases resulting from both psychological and biological factors. For example, semistarvation can lead to cognitive impairments affecting concentration, memory, and decision making (Keys et al., 1950). Additionally, current mood and behavior have been found to influence the recollection of past events (Schacter, 1999). Finally, research has demonstrated that ED behaviors such as binge eating and purging may function as strategies to avoid negative affect (Smyth et al., 2007); thus, these symptoms may result in dissociation or cognitive narrowing (Heatherton & Baumeister, 1991). Recall biases may be minimized by using the timeline follow-back procedure (e.g., Fairburn & Cooper, 1993; L. C. Sobell, Maisto, Sobell, & Cooper, 1979), a structured interview in which patients are oriented to the past 12 weeks and then asked to recall the frequency of behaviors during that period. Asking detailed questions about the time period and obtaining specific examples can reduce potential overgeneralization (e.g., "I heard you mention there was a birthday party that week; was your eating any different on the day of the birthday party?"). This procedure has been successfully adapted for the assessment of both substance use and EDs.

## Assessment of Eating Disorders in Children and Adolescents

Although EDs may present similarly over the life span, the assessment and diagnosis of EDs in children and adolescents can be particularly difficult and may require one or more modifications to the procedures used with adults. For example, determining weight status for children and adolescents can be problematic because of individual differences in growth rates, which vary by gender, age, and pubertal stage (Bravender et al., 2011). Furthermore, weight status can be difficult to track over the course of treatment because children and adolescents may continue to grow in height while in treatment. Several methods have been identified for calculating weight status among adolescents; however, agreement between the methods is only moderate (Le Grange et al., 2012). Researchers have recommended that weight status for adolescents is determined using BMI percentiles, which can be calculated online (http://apps.nccd.cdc.gov/dnpabmi/) and take into account age, gender, and height. However, counselors should note that BMI percentiles do not account for developmental status, which may vary between same-aged individuals; thus, referral to a medical provider who can determine developmental status and modify weight status accordingly may be indicated.

Certain cognitive criteria for EDs such as overevaluation of shape or weight, body image disturbance, and loss of control over eating require clients to use abstract reasoning and meta-cognition. However, these advanced cognitive skills may not be fully developed in younger clients (Bravender et al., 2011). Comprehension may be enhanced by using age-appropriate metaphors (e.g., loss of control can be described as a car rolling down a hill with no brakes) and concrete examples (e.g., "Weight is what you see when you look at a scale and shape is what you see when you look in the mirror"; Bryant-Waugh, Cooper, Taylor, & Lask, 1996).

Binge eating can also be difficult to assess in children and adolescents for three reasons. First, most clients struggle to recall the type and quantity of food consumed during binge eating episodes; however, it can be a particularly difficult task for children and adolescents. As with adults, using the timeline follow-back procedure and obtaining concrete examples can be helpful. Clinicians may also find it useful to provide pictures of food or plastic models of food to help younger clients arrive at more accurate estimates of the quantity of food consumed. Second, because nutritional requirements vary by age, gender, height, and developmental status, determining whether the amount of food consumed was unusually large may be especially problematic when assessing children and adolescents (Tanofsky-Kraff, Yanovski, & Yanovski, 2011). Third, loss of control over eating, which is required for diagnosis of BN and BED, can be difficult to assess among children and adolescents because their eating (e.g., what they eat, when they eat) may be largely controlled by their parents, guardians, or school setting.

Finally, assessment of compensatory behaviors in children and adolescents can also be difficult because concepts such as self-induced vomiting and laxative or diuretic abuse may be inappropriate topics for younger clients. In such cases, asking more general questions about vomiting (e.g., "Do you remember the last time you threw up? When was that? Do you know why you threw up?") and medication use (e.g., "Some types of medicines make you go to the bathroom; have you ever taken any of those kinds of medicines?") may provide sufficient information to determine whether the symptom is present (Bryant-Waugh et al., 1996). Overall, when assessing ED symptoms in children and adolescents, consideration may be given to parental reports and behavioral indicators. For example, changes in food preferences (e.g., becoming vegetarian, declining favorite foods), eating behaviors (e.g., choosing to eat alone, sneaking food, going to the bathroom immediately after eating), or personality (e.g., interpersonal withdrawal, irritability) can be taken into account when assessing and diagnosing EDs in children and adolescents.

### Assessment of Eating Disorders With Diverse Client Groups

Historically, EDs have been thought of as conditions primarily affecting White females from high-socioeconomic-status households. However, recent epidemiological research in the United States has demonstrated that some EDs may be more common among racial and ethnic minorities than originally thought. For example, recent data have suggested that BN and BED may be more common among racial and ethnic minorities than among non-Hispanic White Americans (Swanson, Crow, Le Grange, Swendsen, & Merikangas, 2011). Although some EDs may be relatively common among racial and ethnic minorities compared with White Americans, special consideration should be given when assessing and diagnosing EDs in these groups. First, culturally normative behaviors may resemble ED symptoms (e.g., overeating, fasting); however, these behaviors would not be counted as a symptom of an ED (Becker, 2011). Second, researchers have noted that ED symptoms manifest differently across cultures. For example, researchers have observed the following variations: (a) Asian women with EDs do not universally endorse fear of gaining weight or drive for thinness (Lee, Ho, & Hsu, 1993), (b) the use of alternative compensatory behaviors such as herbal purgatives among Fijian women (Thomas, Crosby, Wonderlich, Striegel-Moore, & Becker, 2011), and (c) variability in the extent to which Native American women with EDs endorse overevaluation of shape and weight (Lynch, Crosby, Wonderlich, & Striegel-Moore, 2011). Third, a distinct possibility exists of miscommunication between the client and the counselor conducting the assessment. For example, clients from diverse cultures may misunderstand questions about concepts that do not exist in their culture of origin (Becker, 2011); in turn, counselors may misinterpret clients' responses. To enhance accurate ED assessment among culturally diverse client groups, counselors should take a flexible, curious approach; ask open-ended questions; provide concrete examples; and ask for clarification.

# Case Example

In this section, we provide an example of how an ED screen can be integrated into an unstructured clinical interview. In this case example, the client is a 20-year-old Asian American woman who is currently a junior in college and is seeking treatment for test anxiety. The following excerpt takes place in the middle of her intake assessment at a college counseling center.

*Counselor:* Now I'd like to ask you some questions about general self-care.
*Client:* Okay.
*Counselor:* Okay, what is your general pattern of eating?
*Client:* I usually have lunch and dinner.
*Counselor:* I see. Do you ever have breakfast?
*Client:* I'm usually too tired in the morning to fix breakfast. Or I'm running late and just don't have time.
*Counselor:* I see. Have you found yourself skipping other meals if you're tired or running late?
*Client:* Sometimes I'll skip lunch, but I always have dinner.
*Counselor:* So it sounds like you almost never have breakfast and sometimes skip lunch. How long has this been going on?
*Client:* It started sometime during my freshman year of college.
*Counselor:* Have there been any other changes in your eating patterns since you started college?
*Client:* Well, I decided to become a vegetarian after reading a book about the food industry.
*Counselor:* And when was that?
*Client:* I think I read that during the summer between my freshman and sophomore years.
*Counselor:* I see. And your motivation for becoming a vegetarian, was it primarily based on moral or ethical beliefs?
*Client:* Yes, primarily. Although, I also thought it might help me lose some of the weight I gained during freshman year.
*Counselor:* I see. So it sounds like the switch to vegetarianism was motivated by both moral and ethical reasons, but also by a desire to change your shape and your weight.
*Client:* Yes.
*Counselor:* What about skipping meals, like breakfast? I know you said that you don't eat breakfast because you don't have time or you're too tired, but I'm wondering if there's a part of you, even a very small part, that thinks that if you don't eat breakfast, it might also change your shape or weight?

*Client:* Well . . . yes, I suppose there's a part of me that thinks that.

*Counselor:* Have you made any other changes to try to influence your shape or weight?

*Client:* I've been exercising more. Some friends and I decided to train for a 5k to raise money for a charity that one of my friends is involved in. We had a lot of fun and I lost some weight, so after the race, I decided to keep running. I'm actually training for a marathon this spring.

*Counselor:* I see. How much weight have you lost?

*Client:* I was at my heaviest after freshman year of college. I weighed 155 pounds. I'm only 5 feet, 4 inches. I lost about 10 pounds training for the 5k—that was during my sophomore year—and now I'm down to about 105 pounds.

*Counselor:* Tell me more about your training.

*Client:* Well, I run every morning for 1 to 3 hours and sometimes longer on the weekends.

*Counselor:* It sounds like training for the marathon is a big commitment; do you ever feel guilty if you don't follow your training plan?

*Client:* Oh, definitely. I had to go home for a family reunion a couple weeks ago, so I couldn't train the same way I train while I'm here at school. I still ran a couple miles each morning, but we had so many family events, I couldn't run the longer distances that I was supposed to.

*Counselor:* Did you feel guilty that you couldn't run those longer distances?

*Client:* Oh, yes. Absolutely. I felt like my entire training was ruined. And it didn't help that there was so much food around!

*Counselor:* Tell me more about that.

*Client:* All of the family events were all potluck style, so there were always leftovers around. And my family is from the South, so none of the food is healthy at all. It's all fried and slathered with butter. It was a nightmare.

*Counselor:* In what way was it a nightmare?

*Client:* I just knew I couldn't eat any of it because I would gain all the weight back. So I tried to stay out of the kitchen and away from all of the food.

*Counselor:* So it sounds like you had a lot of concerns about having to eat more and exercise less during the weekend, and it made you really worried about gaining weight. Is that correct?

*Client:* Yes.

*Counselor:* Are you still worried about gaining weight?

*Client:* Yes, I really worry that I'll end up back at 155 pounds. I think about that a lot—it really helps me stay motivated to train for the marathon.

*Counselor:* I see. It sounds like this worry has a big impact on your life.

*Client:* Yes, it does.

*Counselor:* Does it feel like your shape or your weight influence your evaluation of yourself? That is, how you feel about yourself as a person?

*Client:* Yes, when I started to lose weight, I began feeling much better about myself. If I were to gain it all back, I think I would feel terrible about myself.

*Counselor:* It sounds like you've made a lot of changes to your eating and exercise to ensure that you don't gain weight.

*Client:* Yes, I have.

*Counselor:* Have you done anything else to prevent weight gain?

*Client:* Like what?

*Counselor:* Have you ever self-induced vomiting? Or used laxatives or diuretics?

*Client:* Well . . . I tried to throw up once, but it didn't work. So no, I haven't done those things.

*Counselor:* When was that?

*Client:* It was during my sophomore year. I had been at a party and had eaten some pizza. I just freaked out because I hadn't eaten pizza in a really long time.

*Counselor:* It sounds like eating the pizza really scared you.

*Client:* It did!

*Counselor:* Do you remember how much pizza you had?

*Client:* I had two pieces of a vegetarian pizza.

*Counselor:* Did you have anything else to eat that night?

*Client:* No, I was going to eat when I got home, but then I didn't because I had the pizza.

*Counselor:* Did you feel like your eating was out of control when you had the pizza?

*Client:* Yes, absolutely.

*Counselor:* Do you remember any other times when your eating was out of control?

*Client:* No, that was the only time.

### Discussion

Although the client did not present to therapy for ED treatment, because the counselor explored the client's eating and exercise patterns, the client's disordered eating behaviors were identified. By effectively transitioning from the topic of eating and exercise patterns to thoughts and feelings about shape and weight and, finally, to pointed questions about binge eating and purging, the counselor was able to obtain comprehensive information about the client's ED symptoms while strengthening rapport. Furthermore, the counselor's use of nonspecific therapeutic techniques such as empathy, unconditional positive regard, reflection, and collaboration may have enhanced the therapeutic alliance, creating a safe space for the client to disclose her ED symptoms.

# Conclusion

In sum, accurate assessment and diagnosis of EDs is particularly important given the serious medical and psychiatric risk associated with these disorders. Although a comprehensive ED assessment may not always be feasible, an ED screening assessment can easily be integrated into unstructured clinical assessments and should be conducted with all clients regardless of their age, gender, or race or ethnicity. Assessment of both cognitive (e.g., overevaluation of shape or weight) and behavioral (e.g., presence and frequency of binge eating episodes) symptoms should be included in ED assessments, no matter how brief the screening instrument may be. All ED assessments can be complicated by inadvertent or deliberate minimization; however, assessment of children, adolescents, and culturally diverse clients can be particularly complex. Counselors can enhance the accuracy of ED assessments by using therapeutic techniques such as conveying empathy and acceptance, asking open-ended questions, and providing clarification. Structured assessments such as semistructured interviews and self-report questionnaires can also improve the accuracy of ED assessments.

# Chapter Highlights

- ED assessment can not only provide information about ED symptoms but can also strengthen clinical rapport, inform treatment planning, and track therapy progress.
- All clients should be screened for ED symptoms regardless of age, gender, race, and so forth.
- Screening questions for EDs can easily be incorporated into questions about sleeping, eating, and exercise patterns that are already used to assess self-care behaviors.
- Further assessment is indicated when weight change, binge eating, purging behaviors, regular fasting or extreme restriction, or problematic exercise patterns are endorsed.
- Assessment of physical (e.g., weight status), behavioral (e.g., binge eating), and cognitive (e.g., fear of weight gain) characteristics is essential to assign an accurate diagnosis.
- If an ED is suspected, assessment of medical and psychiatric risk is important regardless of symptom severity, and referral to a medical provider is indicated.
- Inadvertent and deliberate minimization as well as recall biases can affect the accuracy of information collected in an ED assessment.
- The complexity of some of the diagnostic concepts can make ED assessment particularly challenging in children, adolescents, and culturally diverse clients.
- The accuracy of ED assessment can be enhanced through empathy, acceptance, open-ended questions, collaborative clarification, and concrete examples.
- The use of structured assessments can improve the reliability and scope of data gathered in an unstructured clinical interview.

# Recommended Resources

### Articles

Beglin, S. J., & Fairburn, C. G. (1992). What is meant by the term "binge"? *American Journal of Psychiatry, 149,* 123–124.

Vitousek, K., Watson, S., & Wilson, G. T. (1998). Enhancing motivation for change in treatment-resistant eating disorders. *Clinical Psychology Review, 18,* 391–420.

### Books

Fairburn, C. G. (1995). *Overcoming binge eating.* New York, NY: Guilford Press.

Lock, J., Le Grange, D., Agras, W. S., & Dare, C. (2001). *Treatment manual for anorexia nervosa: A family-based approach.* New York, NY: Guilford Press.

Mitchell, J. E., & Peterson, C. B. (Eds.). (2005). *Assessment of eating disorders.* New York, NY: Guilford Press.

### Web Sites

- Academy for Eating Disorders
  http://www.aedweb.org
- National Eating Disorders Association
  http://www.nationaleatingdisorders.org
- National Institutes of Heath
  http://www.nimh.nih.gov/health/publications/eating-disorders/complete-index.shtml
  Publications on EDs

# References

Academy for Eating Disorders' Medical Care Standards Task Force. (2011). *Critical points for early recognition and medical risk management in the care of individuals with eating disorders.* Deerfield, IL: Academy for Eating Disorders.

Allison, K. C., Lundgren, J. D., O'Reardon, J. P., Martino, N. S., Sarwer, D. B., Wadden, T. A., . . . Stunkard, A. J. (2008). The Night Eating Questionnaire (NEQ): Psychometric properties of a measure of severity of the night eating syndrome. *Eating Behaviors, 9,* 62–72

American Psychiatric Association. (2000). *Diagnostic and statistical manual of mental disorders* (4th ed., text rev.). Washington, DC: Author.

American Psychiatric Association. (2012a). *DSM–5 development.* Retrieved from http://www.dsm5.org

American Psychiatric Association. (2012b). *K 03 Anorexia nervosa.* Retrieved from http://www.dsm5.org/ProposedRevision/Pages/proposedrevision.aspx?rid=24

Arikian, A., Peterson, C. B., Swanson, S. A., Berg, K. C., Chartier, L., Durkin, N., & Crow, S. J. (2012). Establishing thresholds for unusually large binge eating episodes. *International Journal of Eating Disorders, 45,* 226.

Attia, E., & Roberto, C. A. (2009). Should amenorrhea be a diagnostic criterion for anorexia nervosa? *International Journal of Eating Disorders, 42,* 581–589.

Becker, A. E. (2011). Culture and eating disorders classification. In R. H. Striegel-Moore, S. A. Wonderlich, B. T. Walsh, & J. E. Mitchell (Eds.), *Developing an evidence-based classification of eating disorders: Scientific findings for DSM-5* (pp. 257–266). Washington, DC: American Psychiatric Publishing.

Berg, K. C., Stiles-Shields, E. C., Swanson, S. A., Peterson, C. B., Lebow, J., & Le Grange, D. (2012). Diagnostic concordance of the interview and questionnaire versions of the Eating Disorder Examination. *International Journal of Eating Disorders, 45,* 850–855.

Bravender, T. D., Bryant-Waugh, R., Herzog, D. B., Katzman, D., Kreipe, R. E., Lask, B., . . . Zucker, N. (2011). Classification of eating disturbance in children and adolescents. In R. H. Striegel-Moore, S. A. Wonderlich, B. T. Walsh, & J. E. Mitchell (Eds.), *Developing an evidence-based classification of eating disorders: Scientific findings for DSM-5* (pp. 167–184). Washington, DC: American Psychiatric Publishing.

Bryant-Waugh, R. J., Cooper, P. J., Taylor, C. L., & Lask, B. D. (1996). The use of the eating disorder examination with children: A pilot study. *International Journal of Eating Disorders, 19,* 391–397.

Cooper, P. J., Taylor, M. J., Cooper, Z., & Fairburn, C. G. (1987). The development and validation of the Body Shape Questionnaire. *International Journal of Eating Disorders, 6,* 485–494.

Crow, S. J., Peterson, C. B., Swanson, S. A., Raymond, N. C., Specker, S., Eckert, E. D., & Mitchell, J. E. (2009). Increased mortality in bulimia nervosa and other eating disorders. *American Journal of Psychiatry, 166,* 1346.

Crow, S., & Swigart, S. (2005). Medical assessment. In J. E. Mitchell & C. B. Peterson (Eds.), *Assessment of eating disorders* (pp. 120–128). New York, NY: Guilford Press.

Fairburn, C. G. (1995). *Overcoming binge eating.* New York, NY: Guilford Press.

Fairburn, C. G. (2008). *Cognitive behavior therapy and eating disorders.* New York, NY: Guilford Press.

Fairburn, C. G., & Beglin, S. (2008). Eating Disorder Examination Questionnaire. In C. G. Fairburn (Ed.), *Cognitive behavior therapy and eating disorders* (pp. 309–317), New York, NY: Guilford Press.

Fairburn, C. G., & Cooper, Z. (1993). The eating disorder examination (12th ed.). In C. G. Fairburn & G. T. Wilson (Eds.), *Binge eating: Nature, assessment, and treatment* (pp. 317–360). New York, NY: Guilford Press.

Fairburn, C. G., Cooper, Z., Bohn, K., O'Connor, M. E., Doll, H. A., & Palmer, R. L. (2007). The severity and status of eating disorder NOS: Implications for DSM-V. *Behaviour Research and Therapy, 45,* 1705–1715.

Fairburn, C. G., Cooper, Z., & O'Connor, M. (2008). Eating Disorder Examination, Edition 16.0D. In C. G. Fairburn (Ed.), *Cognitive behavior therapy and eating disorders* (pp. 265–308). New York, NY: Guilford Press.

First, M. B., Spitzer, R. L., Gibbon, M., & Williams, J. B. (1995). *Structured Clinical Interview for the DSM-IV Axis I Disorders—Patient Edition (SCID-I/P, Version 2)*. New York: New York State Psychiatric Institute, Biometrics Research Department.

Garner, D. M., Olmsted, M. P., Bohr, Y., & Garfinkel, P. E. (1982). The Eating Attitudes Test: Psychometric features and clinical correlates. *Psychological Medicine, 12*, 871–878.

Gormally, J., Black, S., Daston, S., & Rardin, D. (1982). The assessment of binge eating severity among obese persons. *Addictive Behaviors, 7*, 47–55.

Heatherton, T. F., & Baumeister, R. F. (1991). Binge eating as escape from self-awareness. *Psychological Bulletin, 110*, 86–108.

Hoek, H. W. (2006). Incidence, prevalence, and mortality of anorexia and other eating disorders. *Current Opinion in Psychiatry, 19*, 389–394.

Holderness, C. C., Brooks-Gunn, J., & Warren, M. P. (1994). Co-morbidity of eating disorders and substance abuse review of the literature. *International Journal of Eating Disorders, 16*, 1–34.

Keel, P. K., Brown, T. A., Holm-Denoma, J., & Bodell, L. P. (2011). Comparison of *DSM–IV* versus proposed *DSM–5* diagnostic criteria for eating disorders: Reduction of eating disorders not otherwise specified and validity. *International Journal of Eating Disorders, 44*, 553–560.

Keel, P. K., Crow, S., Davis, T., & Mitchell, J. E. (2002). Assessment of eating disorders: Comparison of interview and questionnaire data from a long term follow-up study of bulimia nervosa. *Journal of Psychosomatic Research, 53*, 1043–1047.

Keys, A., Brozek, J., Henschel, A., Mickelsen, O., & Taylor, H. L. (1950). *The biology of human starvation* (2 vols.). Minneapolis: University of Minnesota Press.

Lee, S., Ho, T. P., & Hsu, L. K. G. (1993). Fat phobic and non-fat phobic anorexia nervosa: A comparative study of 70 Chinese patients in Hong Kong. *Psychological Medicine, 23*, 999–1017. doi:10.1017/S0033291700026465

Le Grange, D., Doyle, P. M., Swanson, S. A., Ludwig, K., Glunz, C., & Kreipe, R. E. (2012). Calculation of expected body weight in adolescents with eating disorders. *Pediatrics, 129*, e438–e446.

Lynch, W. C., Crosby, R. D., Wonderlich, S. A., & Striegel-Moore, R. H. (2011). Eating disorder symptoms of Native American and White adolescents. In R. H. Striegel-Moore, S. A. Wonderlich, B. T. Walsh, & J. E. Mitchell (Eds.), *Developing an evidence-based classification of eating disorders: Scientific findings for DSM–5* (pp. 285–297). Washington, DC: American Psychiatric Publishing.

Marcus, M. D., & Wildes, J. E. (2009). Obesity: Is it a mental disorder? *International Journal of Eating Disorders, 42*, 739–753.

115

Miller, W. R., & Rollnick, S. (2002). *Motivational interviewing* (2nd ed.). New York, NY: Guilford Press.

Mitchell, J. E. (2005). A standardized database. In J. E. Mitchell & C. B. Peterson (Eds.), *Assessment of eating disorders* (pp. 59–78). New York, NY: Guilford Press.

Mond, J. M., & Calogero, R. M. (2009). Excessive exercise in eating disorder patients and in healthy women. *Australian and New Zealand Journal of Psychiatry, 43,* 227–234.

Mond, J. M., Hay, P. J., Rodgers, B., & Owen, C. (2006). An update on the definition of "excessive exercise" in eating disorders research. *International Journal of Eating Disorders, 39,* 147–153.

Peterson, C. B. (2005). Conducting the diagnostic interview. In J. E. Mitchell & C. B. Peterson (Eds.), *Assessment of eating disorders* (pp. 32–58). New York, NY: Guilford Press.

Schacter, D. L. (1999). The seven sins of memory: Insights from psychology and cognitive neuroscience. *American Psychologist, 54,* 182–203.

Smyth, J. M., Wonderlich, S. A., Heron, K. E., Sliwinski, M. J., Crosby, R. D., Mitchell, J. E., & Engel, S. G. (2007). Daily and momentary mood and stress are associated with binge eating and vomiting in bulimia nervosa patients in the natural environment. *Journal of Consulting and Clinical Psychology, 75,* 629–638.

Sobell, L. C., Maisto, S. A., Sobell, M. B., & Cooper, A. M. (1979). Reliability of alcohol abusers' self-reports of drinking behavior. *Behaviour Research and Therapy, 17,* 157–160.

Spitzer, R. L., Yanovski, S., Wadden, T., Wing, R., Marcus, M. D., Stunkard, A., . . . Horne, R. L. (1993). Binge eating disorder: Its further validation in a multisite study. *International Journal of Eating Disorders, 13,* 137–153.

Stice, E., Telch, C. F., & Rizvi, S. L. (2000). Development and validation of the Eating Disorder Diagnostic Scale: A brief self-report measure of anorexia, bulimia, and binge-eating disorder. *Psychological Assessment, 12,* 123–131.

Stunkard, A. J., & Messick, S. (1985). The Three-Factor Eating Questionnaire to measure dietary restraint, disinhibition, and hunger. *Journal of Psychosomatic Research, 1,* 71–83.

Swanson, S. A., Crow, S. J., Le Grange, D., Swendsen, J., & Merikangas, K. R. (2011). Prevalence and correlates of eating disorders in adolescents. *Archives of General Psychiatry, 68,* 714–723.

Tanofsky-Kraff, M., Yanovski, S. Z., & Yanovski, J. A. (2011). Loss of control over eating in children and adolescents. In R. H. Striegel-Moore, S. A. Wonderlich, B. T. Walsh, & J. E. Mitchell (Eds.), *Developing an evidence-based classification of eating disorders: Scientific findings for DSM-5* (pp. 221–236). Washington, DC: American Psychiatric Publishing.

Thomas, J. J., Crosby, R. D., Wonderlich, S. A., Striegel-Moore, R. H., & Becker, A. E. (2011). A latent profile analysis of the typology of bulimic symptoms in an indigenous Pacific population. In R. H. Striegel-Moore, S. A. Wonderlich, B. T. Walsh, & J. E. Mitchell (Eds.), *Developing an evidence-based classification of eating disorders: Scientific findings for DSM–5* (pp. 365–386). Washington, DC: American Psychiatric Publishing.

van Strien, T., Frijters, J. E. R., Bergers, G. P. A., & Defares, P. B. (1986). The Dutch Eating Behavior Questionnaire (DEBQ) for assessment of restrained, emotional, and external eating behavior. *International Journal of Eating Disorders, 5,* 295–315.

Vitousek, K., Watson, S., & Wilson, G. T. (1998). Enhancing motivation for change in treatment-resistant eating disorders. *Clinical Psychology Review, 18,* 391–420.

Wonderlich, S. A., Gordon, K. H., Mitchell, J. E., Crosby, R. D., & Engel, S. G. (2009). The validity and clinical utility of binge eating disorder. *International Journal of Eating Disorders, 42,* 687–705.

Wonderlich, S. A., & Mitchell, J. E. (1997). Eating disorders and comorbidity: Empirical, conceptual, and clinical implications. *Psychopharmacology Bulletin, 33,* 381–390.

## Chapter 6

# Assessment, Consultation, and Intervention for Eating Disorders in Schools

*Jennifer Maskell Carney and Heather Lewy Scott*

Mr. James is a school counselor at a large public high school. A few months into the school year, a teacher came to him with concerns about Elena, a freshman straight-A student. Mr. James knew Elena as a rather quiet and shy girl who kept to herself. The teacher said that she had heard from other students that Elena had lost a considerable amount of weight over the summer. One of the students also told the teacher that Elena had stopped coming to the cafeteria for lunch. Recently, the teacher noticed that Elena did not eat her cupcake when there was a celebration in the classroom. The teacher said she did not know whether there was a real problem but thought it might be a good idea to inform Mr. James about the situation.

As this brief vignette illustrates, knowledge about eating-related concerns in children and adolescents is essential for counselors who work in the school setting. These types of concerns in young people can range from body image issues to full-syndrome eating disorders (EDs) that threaten physical health and devastate self-esteem. Because anorexia nervosa most often occurs in young women between the ages of 15 and 19 (Keski-Rahkonen et al., 2007), and bulimia nervosa most often occurs in young women between the ages of 16 and 20 (Keski-Rahkonen et al., 2009), many individuals who develop EDs are students who spend significant time at school around their peers and school faculty. School counselors, therefore, are in a unique and important position to detect student eating issues in the early stages and to take steps to ensure student needs are being met. The purpose of this chapter is to provide a resource for school counselors to assist in identifying, assessing, and intervening with students who have eating-related concerns.

# Overview of Eating-Related Concerns in Schools

Isolating the prevalence of eating-related problems in the schools is difficult. Although anorexia and bulimia are relatively rare in the general population, the ED most often diagnosed is actually ED not otherwise specified (EDNOS), the category researchers know the least about (Striegel-Moore & Bulik, 2007). In addition, many adolescents are struggling with potentially serious eating issues that do not meet the diagnostic criteria for an ED. A recent nationally representative sample of U.S. high school students revealed a staggering 59.3% of girls and 30.5% of boys were trying to lose weight. Nearly 15% of girls and 7% of boys acknowledged engaging in unhealthy dieting behaviors within the past month (Centers for Disease Control and Prevention [CDC], 2010). Subclinical eating problems such as these can lead to the development of various mental health problems in young adulthood including depression, anxiety, and substance abuse disorders (Lewinsohn, Striegel-Moore, & Seeley, 2000).

Obesity is also a growing problem among school-age children. Since the 1970s, the prevalence of overweight among children and adolescents in the United States has nearly doubled (Jolliffe, 2004). Current research has indicated that 16.9% of U.S. children and adolescents are obese (Ogden, Carroll, Kit, & Flegal, 2012). Obesity, especially among adolescents, is tied to body image dissatisfaction, unhealthy weight-control practices, and myriad weight-specific psychosocial consequences that can continue into adulthood (Neumark-Sztainer & Haines, 2004).

These statistics likely do not capture all children and adolescents who in some way feel badly about their body size or shape. Research has indicated that between 40% and 70% of adolescent girls are dissatisfied with two or more aspects of their body (Levine & Smolak, 2004). Indeed, body dissatisfaction is so widespread among adolescent girls that it could even be considered a "normative discontent" (Levine & Smolak, 2004, p. 74).

## Role of the School Counselor

School counselors are often the first line of defense when it comes to identifying eating-related problems among children and adolescents. Although diagnosing students with specific mental disorders is outside of school counselors' scope, they have a critical role to play in assessment, support, referral, and follow-up services (Geroski, Rodgers, & Breen, 1997). The American School Counselor Association (ASCA; 2005) promotes a delivery system of programs in the schools to address the wide range of students' needs and concerns, including guidance curriculum, counseling, consultation, and referral. Thus, in this chapter we provide school counselors with a resource for assessing and managing eating issues in the schools, with an emphasis on the process of identification, consultation, and intervention with students who are struggling with eating-related problems.

This chapter is divided into sections covering eating-related issues on a continuum of severity, beginning with body image concerns, continuing to disordered eating, and concluding with EDs. Using the ASCA (2005) National Model as a guide, we provide and discuss suggestions for interventions at each level of assessment. We present a flexible framework that should be interpreted and applied depending on the individual needs of each student.

# Working With Students With Eating-Related Concerns

People often consider body image problems and EDs to be sensitive issues because they have their own personal experiences, vulnerabilities, and opinions related to the subject. Counselors should first examine their own attitudes and behaviors regarding body image and EDs before intervening with students. This examination could include one's own history with body image or struggles with weight, personal beliefs or prejudices regarding people with EDs and obesity, and current practices related to health, exercise, and diet. Some questions counselors can ask themselves include "Am I currently following a diet?" "How many times have I dieted in the past year?" "Has my physician recommended that I follow a diet for weight loss?" and "Do I weigh myself every day?" (Gabel & Kearney, 1998). Personal awareness is necessary to prevent an inadvertent endorsement of unhealthy habits and to give students the best chance for success (Akos & Levitt, 2002; Bardick, Bernes, McCulloch, Witko, & Roest, 2004).

# Body Image Dissatisfaction

*Body image dissatisfaction* is a term that indicates a distortion in the way in which an individual's body weight or shape is experienced, with undue influence of body weight or shape on self-evaluation (American Psychiatric Association, 2000). Poor body image has been linked to low self-esteem, depression, anxiety, dieting behaviors, and disordered eating in adolescents (Levine & Smolak, 2004; Wertheim, Paxton, & Blaney, 2004). It is also a primary risk factor for the development of EDs, including anorexia and bulimia (Polivy & Herman, 2002).

### Identification

Developmentally, most adolescents are to some extent conscious about how they appear to others, especially to their peers. Adolescence can be a tumultuous and uncertain time because identity is forming and dramatic physical changes are occurring as a result of the rapid growth and hormonal fluctuations of puberty. Socially, peers become the most important source of influence, and adolescents begin to compare themselves with others their age. Risk factors for body image dissatisfaction that may be especially relevant to the school setting include media influence, social comparison, and peer environment.

Sociocultural factors play a significant role in the development of body image in adolescence. Cultural standards of beauty portrayed through mass media create a "thin ideal" that is generally unattainable and yet universally promoted in Western society. The internalization of this ideal is a long-established risk factor for body image dissatisfaction, especially for girls and women (Striegel-Moore & Bulik, 2007). Students today are bombarded by unrealistic body images not only from television and magazines but also from the Internet. Many have laptops and smartphones and belong to social networking Web sites that are updated constantly. Instant connections to peers through these mediums allow images to be quickly and widely dispersed. Levine and Smolak (2004) posited that a connection exists between the cultural standards portrayed by mass media, making social comparisons, and experiencing body dissatisfaction.

Unfavorable social comparison has consistently been linked to body dissatisfaction among adolescents (Myers & Crowther, 2009). Although social comparison is a normal part of adolescent development, counselors should be mindful of students who use constant physical comparisons to measure their own self-worth. These students may compare themselves with their peers, celebrities, professional athletes, or other unrealistic ideals to make judgments about themselves. In general, when comparing themselves with others, girls tend to focus on weight in their hips, stomachs, buttocks, and thighs, and boys tend to focus on building muscle in their upper arms, chests, and shoulders (Levine & Smolak, 2004).

The overweight adolescent may have a particularly difficult time adjusting in school at this age and should not be overlooked by counselors. Longitudinal studies have indicated that increases in body mass index are related to higher body dissatisfaction among adolescents (Stice, 2002). Overweight students may be teased at school and feel badly about themselves as a result of society's prejudices regarding size (Melcher & Bostwick, 2001).

Behaviorally, students with body image difficulties may display a heightened self-consciousness about their bodies, especially in locker rooms and gym class, during hot weather months, and in other situations when bodies may be exposed. These situations can be difficult for girls as well as for boys, who may fear being teased for being too skinny or lacking in muscle development (Stout & Frame, 2004). Overweight students may be more likely to skip or fail gym class or resist wearing the required clothing. When working with students, school counselors may hear students express frustration about their weight or a particular body part.

In sum, body image is a concern for most adolescents. Although it is especially a concern of adolescent girls, adolescent boys also experience difficulties. Body image dissatisfaction is often related to developmental, peer, or sociocultural factors that can be managed effectively within the school setting with appropriate assessment, consultation, and intervention.

### School-Based Assessment and Prevention of Body Image Concerns

School counselors can take several steps to effectively assess and intervene to prevent body image concerns among students. A needs assessment should first be conducted to ascertain pressing eating-related issues among students in the school (ASCA, 2005). A needs survey can be distributed to students, parents, and school faculty via hard-copy letter or e-mail. Using survey Web sites such as Survey Monkey or Counseling Technology may increase response rate and efficiency of data collection.

School counselors can also consult with other professionals to gather input and determine what is needed. Classroom teachers, coaches, and other mental health professionals in the school can provide valuable insight regarding current student issues. Numerous interventions regarding body image can be effectively incorporated into schools, and consultation can also help school counselors research and develop evidence-based programs. Consultation with teachers in related subjects such as health or physical education presents valuable opportunities to collaborate on the planning and implementation of potential programs in the classroom.

Once all input has been gathered and student needs have been determined, a school counseling program should be designed to reach all relevant stakeholders to promote systemwide change. In alignment with the ASCA (2005) National Model, first garnering and managing system support is a key element of the school counseling program delivery system. Before beginning any type of intervention program, one suggestion is that the school counselor establish relationships with school administration, teachers, and parents with the ultimate goal of developing strong partnerships and support for program objectives. The school counselor is encouraged to initially meet with the school guidance department, physical education and health teachers, and key administrators to discuss a program proposal. Eventually, the school counselor would meet with the entire faculty to present the program objectives, rationale, procedures, and importance of adult modeling and to explore ways in which classroom teachers can reinforce learning (Rhyne-Winkler & Hubbard, 1994). Scheduling an open parents meeting or attending a parent–teacher association meeting can provide an opportunity to present the program as well as address any special concerns raised (Rhyne-Winkler & Hubbard, 1994). E-mails to parents and updates on the school Web site are additional ways to keep parents up to date about programs, promote visibility, and establish support.

An additional way to bolster system support for a school counseling program includes the provision of in-service training (ASCA, 2005). Trainings and workshops led by the school counselor can include important stakeholders such as faculty, staff, and parents (Neumark-Sztainer, 2011). Interventions that target and empower important adult role models in students' lives can enhance the overall effectiveness of school-based prevention efforts.

### Interventions for Faculty and Staff

Body image workshops for faculty and staff should focus on fostering an educational environment that supports the self-esteem and positive self-image of all students, regardless of their appearance (National Association of Anorexia Nervosa and Associated Disorders [ANAD], 2012). Teachers should be made aware of how comments about their own weight and diet can affect students and be empowered to act as examples for healthy eating. Teachers can be encouraged to provide diverse role models (in textbooks, videos, posters) who are recognized for their accomplishments rather than for the way they look. School faculty and staff can help combat size discrimination and bullying in classrooms, hallways, and school events and advocate for school policies that discourage stereotyping and prohibit sexual harassment, weight-based teasing, and bullying (ANAD, 2012; Bauer, Haines, & Neumark-Sztainer, 2009).

Several resources are available to counselors that can help facilitate school-based prevention efforts. Toledo and Neumark-Sztainer (1999) provided a training program for high school faculty and staff to help increase awareness of their own weight-related beliefs, knowledge of EDs, and how to support students with weight-related difficulties. McVey, Gusella, Tweed, and Ferrari (2006) offered Web-based training for teachers and parents to learn about factors affecting body image and how to prevent unhealthy dieting among children. ANAD (2012) has provided free school guidelines available for teachers, coaches, and parents that include tips for promoting positive body image in the classroom, recognizing potential eating-related problems, and making appropriate referrals.

### Interventions for Parents

Parents play an important role in shaping their children's body image, but they may be more challenging to access through school-based interventions because of logistical difficulties (Neumark-Sztainer, 2011). Counselors may most easily connect with parents by combining programming with existing school events (parent–teacher association meetings, back-to-school night, etc.). School counselors can also consider sending literature to parents via mail or e-mail or providing information or online resources linked from the school's Web site.

Many print and online materials are available to help parents instill positive body image and encourage healthy eating habits in their children. In her book, Neumark-Sztainer (2005) developed four cornerstones for parents to promote a healthy weight and positive body image in their children through behavior modeling, home environment, focus on overall health (rather than weight), and supporting techniques. The Weight-Control Information Network (2012), part of the National Institutes of Health, provides a free guidebook (print and online) for parents to promote healthy eating and regular physical activity in their families. The National Eating Disorders Association (2005) developed a list of 10 things that parents can do to help prevent EDs and promote positive body image in their children (available in print and online).

### Interventions for Students

School-based programs are often ideal interventions in that they have the potential to reach many children from diverse backgrounds who might otherwise have limited access to clinics or community-based programs (Neumark-Sztainer, 2011). One way in which counselors serve students in their schools is through the planning, design, implementation, and evaluation of school guidance curricula (ASCA, 2005). According to the ASCA (2005) National Model, a school guidance curriculum is a written instructional program that is comprehensive, preventive, and developmentally designed. Preventive intervention programs designed to engage a broad audience are an appropriate way to address body image concerns and work toward the prevention of EDs (Choate & Schwitzer, 2009).

Promotion of a healthy body image should be the main focus of school-based preventive programs (Akos & Levitt, 2002). Potential outcomes of such programs include the adoption of healthier eating and exercise behaviors, increased self-esteem, and enhanced resiliency skills (Bauer et al., 2009; Choate, 2007; O'Dea, 2004). Because these outcomes can be beneficial to all children, universal programs (targeting all students) can be used. In fact, programs that work toward the prevention of EDs as well as provide multiple healthy outcomes for students may be more likely to be implemented in time- or money-strapped schools (Neumark-Sztainer, 2011).

Research has indicated that successful prevention programs can vary widely in content (Stice & Hoffman, 2004), so it is important to keep in mind that there is no single best intervention to include in a guidance curriculum on body image. However, common themes across the existing school counseling literature include interventions that encourage students to adopt realistic beliefs regarding body size, enhance resiliency skills to cope with peer teasing and cultural pressures, understand healthy nutrition and exercise, and improve overall self-esteem and body acceptance (e.g., Choate, 2007; Gabel & Kearney, 1998; Rhyne-Winkler & Hubbard, 1994). It is possible for school-based programs to work simultaneously toward the prevention of both EDs and obesity because they share several similar risk factors (Neumark-Sztainer, 2011).

Rhyne-Winkler and Hubbard (1994) suggested that a classroom guidance program be implemented weekly and that each session last between 30 minutes and 1 hour. Although length of an ED prevention program does not necessarily affect outcome (Stice & Hoffman, 2004), this format may allow easier implementation in the classroom environment. Gabel and Kearney (1998) outlined an example prevention program for use by school counselors that provides suggestions for exercises, discussion topics, and guest speaker involvement. Sample lesson plans, exercises, and activities regarding positive body image and self-esteem are also available through the ASCA Web site (http://www.schoolcounselor.org). Counselors are encouraged to explore their school and county resources for additional support materials and sample guidance curricula (often available through Blackboard or other online platforms).

# Disordered Eating

Whereas *body image* refers to one's thoughts and beliefs, *disordered eating* refers to behaviors. *Disordered eating* is a term used to describe any abnormal eating behavior that may or may not be an indicator or component of an ED. Disordered eating may be chaotic or irregular and is done for reasons other than nourishment (McFarland & Tollerud, 1999). Some examples of disordered eating include skipping meals, fad dieting, emotional overeating, and binge eating. Dieting and body dissatisfaction have both been shown to predict risk for onset of EDs or worsening of eating pathology (Stice, 2002; Striegel-Moore & Bulik, 2007).

## Identification

When an individual moves from thinking about his or her body in a negative way into engaging in actual behaviors on the basis of these thoughts, she or he risks developing health problems that need to be taken seriously. Fluctuations in weight and diet can affect one's mood, energy, concentration, and overall physical health. In the school setting, counselors are advised to be mindful of social influences and individual behavioral clues that could be indicators of eating difficulties among students.

Friendship groups are extremely important to adolescents. Adolescent girls tend to mirror their friends in terms of their eating and dieting habits (Woelders, Larsen, Scholte, Cillessen, & Engels, 2010) and diet in part to gain approval from them (Mooney, Farley, & Strugnell, 2004). Girls may talk to their friends about the latest diet, comment on their need to lose weight, or discuss plans to restrict food to prepare for an upcoming social event. Many are aware of celebrity fad diets, and some try them out, engaging in short-term fasting or unhealthy dieting (Mooney et al., 2004). Aside from the obvious health risks, individuals who acutely restrict nutrition may also be more likely to binge eat when the restriction ends (Stice, 2002).

An athletic team is a different type of social group at risk for disordered eating behavior. Although high school athletic participation in and of itself is not necessarily associated with disordered eating and can even be considered a protective factor in some cases (Fulkerson, Keel, Leon, & Dorr, 1999), students involved in certain sports that emphasize thinness and a lean physique for peak performance (e.g., gymnasts, figure skaters, dancers, distance runners, swimmers, divers, cheerleaders) or extremes of weight loss (e.g., wrestlers) are considered more at risk (Female Athlete Triad Coalition, 2008; Weltzin et al., 2005).

Individual behavioral factors among students who engage in disordered eating may be visible to counselors, teachers, and coaches. For example, students at risk might be those who skip lunch, appear to favor particular foods (e.g., energy bars, diet drinks), or avoid certain types of food (e.g., carbohydrates). Students who are overeating will most likely do so in private and may therefore be difficult to identify unless they self-report. School counselors should not assume that an overweight student is overeating or necessarily concerned about food or weight (Melcher & Bostwick, 2001). These types of disordered eating practices may be able to be treated in the school or may be so serious as to require referral to community-based services. When a school counselor learns about a student who is engaging in disordered eating, he or she should first connect with the student of concern and then consider consultation.

## Assessment and Consultation

When disordered eating is suspected, the school counselor should meet with the student of concern. The counselor should arrange to speak to the student privately and reserve adequate time to avoid feeling rushed (ANAD, 2012). Eliciting general, open-ended conversation about what is happening in the student's life and then following up with more specific observations may help to build trust with the student and gather more information about the depth of the issue (ANAD, 2012).

After the initial assessment has been conducted, the school counselor will need to decide the necessary interventions to take next. Students who display disordered eating symptoms such as extreme dieting or occasional binge eating may not meet the criteria for an ED but do require a different approach to management and treatment than those with body image concerns only (Choate & Schwitzer, 2009). These symptoms could exist in isolation or be associated with other unhealthy weight control tactics such as self-induced vomiting or laxative or diuretic use. Given that the difference between those students who are preoccupied with weight and chronically diet and those who have partial- or full-syndrome EDs may only be a matter of degree (Scarano & Kalodner-Martin, 1994) and that the current *Diagnostic and Statistical Manual of Mental Disorders* (4th ed., text rev., or *DSM–IV–TR*; American Psychiatric Association, 2000) categorization for EDs will change in the forthcoming fifth edition (*DSM–5*; American Psychiatric Association, 2012), a significant amount of clinical judgment is involved in determining whether an ED is present. When repeated or escalating disordered eating behaviors are observed or suspected, expert consultation and collaboration are recommended to help assess these students and determine their needs.

Experts available to the school counselor may be a licensed clinician based in the school, such as a school psychologist or school-based licensed professional counselor or licensed clinical social worker. If such resources are not available, outside consultation can be sought with a licensed mental health professional specializing in EDs. Although there is no official qualification to become an ED specialist, appropriate referrals may be found through professional colleagues, conferences, training programs, or organizations. Local hospitals with ED units often maintain referral lists. The National Eating Disorders Association and ANAD maintain free hotlines that anyone may call for a referral in their local area. Specialists should have experience treating different types of eating problems and attend regular trainings, and they may be members of an ED organization. When consulting with an allied professional, the school counselor may be asked to describe the frequency, intensity, and duration of the student's eating-related thoughts and behaviors. Expert consultants will not be able to diagnose without seeing the student; however, they may be able to recommend whether a full clinical assessment and referral are warranted.

The consultant may also recommend a referral to a physician for a health evaluation. Whenever a student is known to be consistently restricting nutrition, a referral to a physician for an evaluation is needed before beginning treatment, regardless of body size (Bartlett, Hill, & Portrie-Bethke, 2007). Likewise, a student should have a medical evaluation if engaging in any self-induced vomiting or laxative or diuretic use. The evaluating physician can be the student's pediatrician, although ED experience is preferable.

### Interventions

The responsive services component of the school counseling program as described in the *ASCA National Model* (ASCA, 2005) consists of activities to meet students' immediate needs and concerns. If a student is referred (or self-referred) to the school counselor because of disordered eating, the school counselor can initiate interventions to address the presenting issue. Whereas guidance curricula can be universally applied, responsive services may be targeted to specific at-risk students or identified concerns.

Individual and small-group counseling are essential components of responsive services in the delivery system of school counseling programs and are initiated to meet students' immediate needs or concerns (ASCA, 2005). If the school counselor and expert consultant determine that a student with disordered eating may be managed in the school setting, both group and individual interventions designed to prevent full-syndrome EDs can be used. Individual and group counseling provided by the school counselor are planned, goal focused, and typically short term in nature (ASCA, 2005). These ongoing responsive services help students "identify problems, causes, alternative and possible consequences so they can take appropriate action" (ASCA, 2005, p. 42).

Small, single-gender groups emphasizing social support, psychoeducation, and cognitive–behavioral strategies are appropriate for those engaging in disordered eating behaviors (Choate & Schwitzer, 2009). Providing a safe space to discuss eating-related behaviors, values, and beliefs can help to reduce students' feelings of isolation and provide opportunities to receive support and feedback from peers. The counselor can help to promote safety and comfort among group members by keeping the group closed, setting flexible meeting times in collaboration with teachers to ensure maximum attendance, and facilitating ongoing discussion around confidentiality concerns and parameters. Psychoeducational elements can include discussion regarding the symptoms and dangers of EDs, cultural factors and influences on the development of eating problems in young people, and alternative ways of coping with stress. Cognitive–behavioral interventions can help group members learn to identify, challenge, and ultimately change irrational beliefs regarding the shoulds and musts about appearance, weight, and diet. Dissonance-based approaches, originated by Stice, Chase, Stormer, and Appel (2001), can help group members reduce disordered eating thoughts and behaviors by challenging them to take an active stance opposite to their internalized beliefs about body shape and weight. For example, a student could argue that being thin does not necessarily make someone healthier, more attractive, or more valuable. This stance would cause cognitive dissonance, which would lead one to make behavioral or attitudinal changes to relieve this inconsistency. Dissonance-based approaches have promising application in a school-based group because students could develop arguments, conduct role-plays, and brainstorm ways to mentor younger students or create classroom presentations.

Resources are available that can assist school counselors in developing group counseling interventions for students who display some symptoms of EDs but are below the diagnostic threshold. In their book, Stice and Presnell (2007) provided detailed guidelines for group counselors that emphasize dissonance-based exercises (see also Chapter 10, this volume). Rhyne-Winkler and Hubbard (1994) provided a topical outline for eight sessions of small-group counseling for students focusing on psychoeducation and cognitive–behavioral techniques. Diagneault (2000) offered an example of a 10-session counseling group for high school girls with disordered eating behaviors, including descriptions of techniques, sample activities, and tips for counselors starting a school-based group.

Although one-on-one counseling can also be an effective intervention for students with disordered eating behaviors, this approach should be considered with caution. School counselors considering this option would need to be prepared to schedule regular, uninterrupted meeting times with the student of concern. Furthermore, because school counselors do not engage in longer term therapy, they need be prepared to refer out to community resources if necessary (ASCA, 2005). Assuming time and resources are available, short-term counseling emphasizing cognitive–behavioral strategies, guided imagery, narrative techniques, exploration of family dynamics, and normalization of the student's experience is recommended (Bardick et al., 2004; Bartlett et al., 2007). Providing a student with a model of a healthy and supportive counseling relationship may help him or her develop more satisfying interpersonal relationships with others, which is important in that research has shown that interpersonal functioning may play an important role in the development and maintenance of EDs (Tantleff-Dunn, Gokee-LaRose, & Peterson, 2004).

# Eating Disorder

An *eating disorder* is a syndrome that meets the criteria for anorexia nervosa, bulimia nervosa, or EDNOS as defined by the *DSM–IV–TR* (APA, 2000). Anorexia nervosa is characterized by extreme low body weight (85% or less of expected weight), an intense fear of becoming fat, and severe body image disturbance. Bulimia nervosa is characterized by episodes of binge eating followed by purging (often self-induced vomiting) or other compensatory behavior to prevent weight gain (e.g., laxative or diuretic use, excessive exercise). Most school counselors are familiar with the general symptoms of these disorders (Price, Desmond, Price, & Mossing, 1990).

A third disorder, binge eating disorder, is currently listed under EDNOS and is expected to be included in the *DSM–5* (APA, 2000). Binge eating disorder is characterized by binge episodes without the compensatory behaviors that occur in bulimia. Besides binge eating disorders, the EDNOS category includes disorders of eating that do not meet the full criteria for anorexia or bulimia but have severe enough symptoms to warrant a diagnosis. As mentioned previously, EDNOS is probably the most common ED encountered in the school setting (Geroski et al., 1997). A common presentation of EDNOS includes a combination of anorexic and bulimic symptoms, for example, engaging in frequent binge eating and high levels of exercise for weight control but less purging or diet restriction than required for a diagnosis of anorexia or bulimia (Choate & Schwitzer, 2009).

## Identification

Familiarity with *DSM–IV–TR* criteria for EDs is an important start for identifying these problems in the school setting (Bardick et al., 2004; Bartlett et al., 2007; Geroski et al., 1997). However, many individuals with clinically significant EDs do not display symptoms perfectly in line with current diagnostic criteria (Striegel-Moore & Bulik, 2007). Counselor biases can also influence the identification of EDs. "Typical" people with EDs are often believed to be young White women from middle- to upper-class families who are obsessed with perfection and fitting into a Western societal ideal of slenderness. Beliefs such as these can cause professionals to miss warning signs in minority populations (Kalodner & Van Lone, 2001). Counselors must examine their own racial and cultural stereotypes and understand that eating concerns also affect children of color (Talleyrand, 2010; see also Chapter 3, this volume).

When identifying EDs among students, it is tempting to look for extreme binging and purging behaviors (Bardick et al., 2004) or excessive weight loss; however, other behavioral and psychological indicators may signal a problem. For example, a student might skip lunch and then make excuses for it, engage in food rituals, avoid certain foods such as high-fat foods and carbohydrates, engage in excessive exercise, dress in layers or baggy clothing (especially when inappropriate for the weather), constantly talk about food and weight, diet frequently, or need to use the bathroom immediately after eating (ANAD, 2012; Davis, 2000). Irrational food choices such as overindulging in diet foods, diet drinks, or high-fat foods might also indicate a problem (ANAD, 2012). Psychological indicators of a potential ED can include overconcern with body shape or weight and a need for constant reassurance of appearance, perfectionism, concern with pleasing others, rigidity related to food or body image, social withdrawal including isolation from family and friends, depressed mood, mood swings or irritability, high anxiety, obsessiveness, and decreased concentration (ANAD, 2012; Rogers & Petrie, 2001; Seligman, 1998). Counselors are encouraged to consider a cluster of behavioral and psychological factors when they suspect an ED in a student.

Moreover, it can be difficult to identify individuals with EDs because they tend to be extremely secretive and feel a great deal of shame about their behaviors. Perhaps for these reasons, school counselors are more likely to hear about students with EDs from their concerned friends and teachers rather than to notice symptoms firsthand (Price et al., 1990). If a school counselor suspects that a student has an ED, she or he should meet with the student, connect with the parents, and be prepared to provide referral and follow-up services.

## *Intervention*

Ideally, a student of concern should be approached by a counselor who has an established, positive relationship with the student (ANAD, 2012). If the student in question is female, she may be more responsive to a female counselor (Seligman, 1998). School counselors should be aware that denial and defensiveness are typical responses of people with EDs and that these reactions are not directed at them (Bardick et al., 2004). Loss of control, helplessness, and fear of gaining weight in treatment are all intensely threatening to people with EDs (Bardick et al., 2004; Seligman, 1998). Individuals with EDs tend to be extremely sensitive to criticism; therefore, approaching a student from a caring, honest, and supportive stance is crucial. Genuine support and approval may help the student disclose information that seems shameful and consider the options the counselor presents (Seligman, 1998). In addition to the ideas offered in the previous sections, school counselors meeting with a student to screen for a potential ED should include more specific observations, emphasize a serious concern for the student's health, and insist on enlisting help. If the student continues to deny the problem, the school counselor is advised to acknowledge that the student does not believe there is a problem but that her or his behaviors are still very concerning to the counselor and it is important to contact the parents. The counselor should encourage the student to be present and involved while parents are contacted.

Before parent contact is made, referrals for individual therapy and a medical evaluation should be prepared so that they can be offered to the student and her or his parents. In the parent meeting, the school counselor may offer observations, impressions, concerns expressed by others, and the appearance of the need for further diagnostic evaluation and therapeutic intervention (Geroski et al., 1997). Statements such as "I am concerned about your child's health and well-being and recommend further assessment by a professional" may be more palatable to parents than "Your child has a problem and needs help" (Bardick et al., 2004). The family may need referrals or may prefer to use service providers with whom they are already familiar. Typically, whomever the family chooses as the individual therapist will conduct a full assessment and provide referrals for family therapy, group therapy, nutrition counseling, and hospitalization options as needed.

If the student is determined to have an ED and needs to enter treatment, the school counselor can then serve in a consultant role. As a collaboration consultant (Dougherty, 2005), the school counselor works with the student, family, treating clinician, and physician throughout each step of the process but is not the primary treatment professional. Some examples of collaboration consultation activities include supporting the student and family in the decision to enter and the process of entering treatment, conferring with the treating clinician or physician to discuss the student's progress at school, and developing methods and procedures for continued communication between service providers. Apprehensive families may appreciate the school counselor setting up the initial appointment with the individual therapist or physician.

When communicating with other service providers, counselors uphold the guidelines of the profession regarding the release of confidential information and minimal disclosure (American Counseling Association, 2005). Before communicating with service providers, counselors must obtain consent from a parent or guardian of a minor child. It is recommended that school counselors use a reciprocal consent for release of information signed by the parent or guardian, the school counselor, and the service provider. Depending on the student's age and developmental level, she or he should also be encouraged to sign. A separate release form for each service provider is recommended. Release forms may be hand delivered (by the parent) or sent via fax or regular mail (Geroski et al., 1997). Fax may be the most effective mode of communication with physicians because they often have high scheduling demands during the day.

Geroski et al. (1997) recommended that a letter be sent to service providers along with the consent for release of information. This letter should include the school counselor's concerns, the student's behaviors, and the results of any assessments conducted, as well as an express interest in providing collaborative services and a request for follow-up information regarding diagnosis and treatment planning. Parents should be aware of the letter and support its contents. If they perceive school professionals to be open and honest, they may be more likely to participate collaboratively in treatment efforts.

### Reintegration

In rare cases, a student may need to be hospitalized because of the severity of the ED. The student is then temporarily withdrawn from school so that full focus may be given to treatment and recovery. When the student returns to school, challenges will inevitably occur as she or he adjusts back to a regular routine. The student may be behind on classwork, struggle socially, and be sensitive to triggers of the ED.

School counselors can play an important role in a student's successful reintegration into school. A conference among the student, parents, counselor, treating therapist, and teachers is recommended to help ease the transition back to regular school attendance. Focusing on the student's needs to construct creative solutions is encouraged. For example, support for the lunch hour, homeroom teacher assignment, nontraditional options for gym class, flexible scheduling, and a plan for catching up on missed assignments can all be discussed. A 504 plan or special education services may need to be considered for certain accommodations. Regular follow-up check-ins should be scheduled with the school counselor.

# Case Example

The following case is an example of a student referred to her school counselor for an eating-related problem.

Casey and Beth are 16-year-old sophomores who are best friends. Casey had been noticing changes in Beth over the past few months, so she went to see her school counselor, Ms. Madison, to discuss her concerns. Casey shared with Ms. Madison that 6 months ago, Beth's boyfriend ended their relationship and started dating someone new. Beth heard rumors that she was dumped because she was too fat. She also saw that her ex-boyfriend wrote on his Facebook page about how attractive his new girlfriend was. Casey said that Beth started complaining about her body and spending more and more time at the gym.

A few months later, Casey realized that Beth had lost a substantial amount of weight. Casey also noticed that Beth would eat only a few bites of her lunch and then either throw the rest away or make an excuse to use the restroom. When Casey tried to talk about her concerns, Beth became very defensive and accused Casey of being jealous. After that incident, Beth began canceling social plans with Casey and seemed to withdraw from their friendship. Casey expressed to Ms. Madison that she was very worried about her friend.

After listening to Casey's story, Ms. Madison decided to call Beth in to see how she was doing. She told Beth that someone was concerned about her weight loss. Beth immediately insisted that she ate three healthy meals a day and went to the gym for an hour each day. Beth also said she thought her friend Casey was jealous of all the attention she was getting from looking better. Ms. Madison noted that this defensive response was not a typical behavior for Beth. She could also tell that Beth looked quite thin, even though she chose to wear baggy clothing to school. Ms. Madison looked at Beth gently and shared that she had also heard Beth was not eating lunch at school and that she was concerned about Beth's health. Beth paused and then conceded she sometimes skipped lunch because she did not like the food. Ms. Madison nodded and said she understood that Beth did not believe there was a problem, but she was genuinely concerned about her health and so she needed to contact Beth's parents. Ms. Madison said that they could call together. Beth rolled her eyes but did not protest.

After consulting with another school counselor and a school-based licensed professional counselor about their thoughts and referral suggestions, Ms. Madison called Beth's parents. Beth's mother told Ms. Madison that she had just recently been wondering whether Beth was too thin. Beth's mother agreed with Ms. Madison that she should be seen by her doctor and would consider calling a therapist if the doctor was in favor of her doing so. A week later, Ms. Madison called Beth's mother to follow up. Beth's mom thanked Ms. Madison for urging her to seek help for Beth. After her doctor's appointment and consultation with a therapist, Beth was diagnosed with anorexia nervosa and would be in treatment after school for a while. Ms. Madison decided to follow up with both Casey and Beth to offer support. She also planned to follow up with Beth's family, teachers, and treatment providers so the school could implement accommodations recommended by her treatment plan.

# Conclusion

Body image, EDs, and obesity concerns are common and widespread among school-age children. School counselors provide essential services and support to students struggling with eating-related concerns, as well as to their families and other school-based professionals. After assessing student needs and determining the severity of the presenting difficulties, school counselors enlist system support and intervene by providing prevention programs, individual and group counseling, and referrals to appropriate community professionals.

# Chapter Highlights

- School counselors play a crucial role in the prevention and treatment of eating-related problems among children and adolescents.
- Because of the typical age of onset, many individuals who develop EDs are students, who spend a significant amount of time at school.
- School counselors can engage in prevention, assessment, intervention, ongoing case management, and professional consultation regarding EDs.
- The cooperation and support of the entire school faculty and staff are needed for successful implementation of school-based intervention programs. Counselors can facilitate support through collaborative meetings, presentations, and workshops.
- Consultation between the school counselor and allied professionals in the school and community is necessary for effective management and treatment of eating-related concerns among students.
- School counselors can promote positive body image and work toward the prevention of EDs through the development and delivery of guidance curricula for students and in-service workshops for faculty.
- Group and individual counseling may be effective school-based interventions for students with some disordered eating behaviors.
- Students with EDs should be referred out for treatment to community-based agencies or licensed mental health practitioners.
- School counselors provide follow-up services for students who are referred out of the school for community-based treatment.

# Recommended Resources

## Parents

National Eating Disorders Association. (2005). *Ten things parents can do to help prevent eating disorders.* Retrieved from http://www.nationaleatingdisorders.org/nedaDir/files/documents/handouts/10Parent.pdf

Neumark-Sztainer, D. (2005). *"I'm, like, SO fat!": Helping your teen make healthy choices about eating and exercise in a weight-obsessed world.* New York, NY: Guilford Press.

Weight Control Information Network. (2012). *Helping your child: Tips for parents* (NIH Pub. No. 04-4955). Retrieved from http://www.win.niddk.nih.gov/publications/PDFs/helpingyourchild.pdf

## School Counselors

American School Counselors Association. (2006–2012). Retrieved from http://www.schoolcounselor.org

Choate, L. H. (2007). Counseling adolescent girls for body image resilience: Strategies for school counselors. *Professional School Counseling, 10,* 317–326.

Daigneault, S. D. (2000). Body talk: A school-based group intervention for working with disordered eating behaviors. *Journal for Specialists in Group Work, 25,* 191–213.

Gabel, K. A., & Kearney, K. (1998). Promoting reasonable perspectives of body weight: Issues for school counselors. *Professional School Counseling, 1,* 32–35.

Rhyne-Winkler, M. T., & Hubbard, G. T. (1994). Eating attitudes and behavior: A school counseling program. *The School Counselor, 41,* 195.

Stice, E., & Presnell, K. (2007). *The body project: Promoting body acceptance and preventing eating disorders: Facilitator guide.* New York, NY: Oxford University Press.

## School Faculty and Staff

Female Athlete Triad Coalition. (2008). http://www.femaleathletetriad.org/for-athletes-coaches/

McVey, G., Gusella, J., Tweed, S., & Ferarri, M. (2006). *The student body: Promoting health at any size.* Retrieved from http://www.aboutkidshealth.ca/thestudentbody

National Association of Anorexia Nervosa and Associated Disorders. (2012). *ANAD school guidelines for educators.* Naperville, IL: Author.

Toledo, T., & Neumark-Sztainer, D. (1999). Weighting for you! Training for high school faculty and staff in the prevention and detection of weight-related disorders among adolescents. *Journal of Nutrition Education, 31,* 283–284.

# References

Akos, P., & Levitt, D. (2002). Promoting healthy body image in middle school. *Professional School Counseling, 6,* 138–144.

American Counseling Association. (2005). *ACA code of ethics.* Alexandria, VA: Author.

American Psychiatric Association. (2000). *Diagnostic and statistical manual of mental disorders* (4th ed., text rev.). Washington, DC: Author.

American Psychiatric Association. (2012). *Eating disorders.* Retrieved from http://www.dsm5.org/proposedrevisions/pages/eatingdisorders.aspx

American School Counselor Association. (2005). *The ASCA National Model: A framework for school counseling programs* (2nd ed.). Alexandria, VA: Author.

Bardick, A., Bernes, K., McCulloch, A., Witko, K., & Roest, A. (2004). Eating disorder intervention, prevention, and treatment: Recommendations for school counselors. *Professional School Counseling, 8,* 168–175.

Bartlett, J., Hill, N., & Portrie-Bethke, T. (2007). I'm too fat: Body images in childhood. In S. Duggar & L. Carleson (Eds.), *Critical incidents in counseling children* (pp. 317–327). Alexandria, VA: American Counseling Association.

Bauer, K. W., Haines, J., & Neumark-Sztainer, D. (2009). Obesity prevention: Strategies to improve effectiveness and reduce harm. In L. Smolak & J. Thompson (Eds.). *Body image, eating disorders, and obesity in youth: Assessment, prevention, and treatment* (pp. 241–260). Washington, DC: American Psychological Association.

Centers for Disease Control and Prevention. (2010). *Youth risk behavior surveillance 2009* (Pub. No. SS-5). Retrieved from http://www.cdc.gov/mmwr/

Choate, L. H. (2007). Counseling adolescent girls for body image resilience: Strategies for school counselors. *Professional School Counseling, 10,* 317–326.

Choate, L. H., & Schwitzer, A. (2009). Mental health counseling responses to eating-related concerns in young adult women: A prevention and treatment continuum. *Journal of Mental Health Counseling, 31,* 164–183.

Daigneault, S. D. (2000). Body talk: A school-based group intervention for working with disordered eating behaviors. *Journal for Specialists in Group Work, 25,* 191–213.

Davis, C. (2000). Exercise abuse. *International Journal of Sport Psychology, 31,* 278–289.

Dougherty, A. M. (2005). *Psychological consultation and collaboration in school and community settings: A casebook* (4th ed.). Belmont, CA: Thompson Brooks/Cole.

Female Athlete Triad Coalition. (2008). *Risk factors.* Retrieved from http://www.femaleathletetriad.org/for-athletes-coaches/risk-factors/

Fulkerson, J., Keel, P., Leon, G., & Dorr, T. (1999). Eating-disordered behaviors and personality characteristics of high school athletes and nonathletes. *International Journal of Eating Disorders, 26,* 73–79.

Gabel, K. A., & Kearney, K. (1998). Promoting reasonable perspectives of body weight: Issues for school counselors. *Professional School Counseling, 1*, 32–35.

Geroski, A., Rodgers, K., & Breen, D. (1997). Using the *DSM–IV* to enhance collaboration among school counselors, clinical counselors, and primary care physicians. *Journal of Counseling & Development, 75*, 231–239.

Jolliffe, D. (2004). Extent of overweight among US children and adolescents from 1971 to 2000. *International Journal of Obesity and Related Metabolic Disorders, 28*, 4–9.

Kalodner, C., & Van Lone, J. (2001). Eating disorders: Guidelines for assessment, treatment, and referral. In E. R. Welfel & R. E. Ingersoll (Ed.), *The mental health desk reference* (pp. 119–128). New York, NY: Wiley.

Keski-Rahkonen, A., Hoek, H., Linna, M., Raevuori, A., Sihvola, E., Bulik, C., Rissanen, A., & Kaprio, J. (2009). Incidence and outcomes of bulimia nervosa: A nationwide population-based study. *Psychological Medicine, 39*, 823–831.

Keski-Rahkonen, A., Hoek, H., Susser, E., Linna, M., Sihvola, E., Raevuori, A., Bulik, C., Kaprio, J., & Rissanen, A. (2007). Epidemiology and course of anorexia nervosa in the community. *American Journal of Psychiatry, 164*, 1259–1265.

Levine, M., & Smolak, L. (2004). Body image development in adolescence. In T. F. Cash & T. Pruzinski (Eds.), *Body image: A handbook of theory, research, & clinical practice* (pp. 74–82). New York, NY: Guilford Press.

Lewinsohn, P. M., Striegel-Moore, R. H., & Seeley, J. R. (2000). Epidemiology and natural course of eating disorders in young women from adolescence to young adulthood. *Journal of the American Academy of Child & Adolescent Psychiatry, 39*, 1284–1292.

McFarland, W., & Tollerud, T. (1999). Counseling children and adolescents with special issues. In A. Vernon (Ed.), *Counseling children and adolescents* (pp. 215–257). Denver, CO: Love.

McVey, G., Gusella, J., Tweed, S., & Ferarri, M. (2006). *The student body: Promoting health at any size.* Retrieved from http://www.aboutkidshealth.ca/thestudentbody

Melcher, J., & Bostwick, G. (2001). The fat client. In E. R. Welfel & R. E. Ingersoll (Ed.), *The mental health desk reference* (pp. 51–59). New York, NY: Wiley.

Mooney, E., Farley, H., & Strugnell, C. (2004). Dieting among females—Some emerging trends. *International Journal of Consumer Studies, 28*, 347–354.

Myers, T., & Crowther, J. (2009). Social comparison as a predictor of body dissatisfaction: A meta-analytic review. *Journal of Abnormal Psychology, 118*, 683–698.

National Association of Anorexia Nervosa and Associated Disorders. (2012). *ANAD school guidelines for educators.* Naperville, IL: Author.

National Eating Disorders Association. (2005). *Ten things parents can do to help prevent eating disorders.* Retrieved from http://www.nationaleatingdisorders.org/nedaDir/files/documents/handouts/10Parent.pdf

Neumark-Sztainer, D. (2005). *"I'm, like, SO fat!": Helping your teen make healthy choices about eating and exercise in a weight-obsessed world.* New York, NY: Guilford Press.

Neumark-Sztainer, D. (2011). Prevention of eating disorders in children and adolescents. In D. Le Grange & J. Lock (Eds.), *Eating disorders in children and adolescents: A clinical handbook* (pp. 421–439). New York, NY: Guilford Press.

Neumark-Sztainer, D., & Haines, J. (2004). Psychosocial and behavioral consequences of obesity. In J. K. Thompson (Ed.), *Handbook of eating disorders and obesity* (pp. 349–371). Hoboken, NJ: Wiley.

O'Dea, J. A. (2004). Evidence for a self-esteem approach in the prevention of body image and eating problems among children and adolescents. *Eating Disorders, 12,* 225–239.

Ogden, C. L., Carroll, M. D., Kit, B. K., & Flegal, K. M. (2012). Prevalence of obesity and trends in body mass index among US children and adolescents, 1999–2010. *JAMA, 307,* 483.

Polivy, J., & Herman, C. P. (2002). Causes of eating disorders. *Annual Review of Psychology, 53,* 187–213. doi:0084-6570/02/0201-0187

Price, J. A, Desmond, S., Price, J. H., & Mossing, A. (1990). School counselors' knowledge of eating disorders. *Adolescence, 25,* 945–957.

Rogers, R. L., & Petrie, T. A. (2001). Psychological correlates of anorexic and bulimic symptomatology. *Journal of Counseling & Development, 79,* 178–187.

Rhyne-Winkler, M. T., & Hubbard, G. T. (1994). Eating attitudes and behavior: A school counseling program. *The School Counselor, 41,* 195–198.

Scarano, G. M., & Kalodner-Martin, C. R. (1994). A description of the continuum of eating disorders: Implications for intervention and research. *Journal of Counseling & Development, 72,* 356–361.

Seligman, L. (1998). Disorders of behavior and impulse control. In *Selecting effective treatments* (pp. 238–303). San Francisco, CA: Jossey-Bass.

Stice, E. (2002). Risk and maintenance factors for eating pathology: A meta-analytic review. *Psychological Bulletin, 128,* 825–848. doi:10.1037//0033-2909.128.5.825

Stice, E., Chase, A., Stormer, S., & Appel, A. (2001). A randomized trial of a dissonance-based eating disorder prevention program. *International Journal of Eating Disorders, 29,* 247–262.

Stice, E., & Hoffman, E. (2004). Eating disorder prevention programs. In J. K. Thompson (Ed.), *Handbook of eating disorders and obesity* (pp. 33–57). Hoboken, NJ: Wiley.

Stice, E., & Presnell, K. (2007). *The Body Project: Promoting body acceptance and preventing eating disorders facilitator guide.* New York, NY: Oxford University Press.

Stout, E., & Frame, M. (2004). Body image disorder in adolescent males: Strategies for school counselors. *Professional School Counseling, 8,* 176–181.

Striegel-Moore, R., & Bulik, C. (2007). Risk factors for eating disorders. *American Psychologist, 62,* 181–198. doi:10.1037/0003-066X.62.3.181

Talleyrand, R. (2010). Eating disorders in African American girls: Implications for counselors. *Journal of Counseling & Development, 88,* 319–324.

Tantleff-Dunn, S., Gokee-LaRose, J., & Peterson, R. (2004). Interpersonal psychotherapy for the treatment of anorexia nervosa, bulimia nervosa, and binge eating disorder. In J. K. Thompson (Ed.), *Handbook of eating disorders and obesity* (pp. 163–185). Hoboken, NJ: Wiley.

Toledo, T., & Neumark-Sztainer, D. (1999). Weighting for you! Training for high school faculty and staff in the prevention and detection of weight-related disorders among adolescents. *Journal of Nutrition Education, 31,* 283–284.

Weight Control Information Network. (2012). *Helping your child: Tips for parents* (NIH Pub. No. 04-4955). Retrieved from http://www.win.niddk.nih.gov/publications/PDFs/helpingyourchild.pdf

Weltzin, T. E., Weisensel, N., Franczyk, D., Burnett, K., Klitz, C., & Bean, P. (2005). Eating disorders in men: Update. *Journal of Men's Health & Gender, 2,* 186.

Wertheim, E., Paxton, S., & Blaney, S. (2004). Risk factors for the development of body image disturbances. In J. K. Thompson (Ed.), *Handbook of eating disorders and obesity* (pp. 463–494). Hoboken, NJ: Wiley.

Woelders, L., Larsen, J., Scholte, R., Cillessen, A., & Engels, R. (2010). Friendship group influences on body dissatisfaction and dieting among adolescent girls: A prospective study. *Journal of Adolescent Health, 47,* 456–462.

## Chapter 7

# Assessment, Conceptualization, and Intervention With Young Adult Women With EDNOS: A Framework for Practice

*Alan M. Schwitzer With Constance Rhodes*

• • •

It became clear to me that this disorder of mine lacked a proper name. . . . I became increasingly disturbed with the fact that no one seemed to understand exactly what I was facing. . . . I [formed a belief] that there is a whole group of women and men who might not fit all the criteria for [anorexia or bulimia], but who have a unique and very real problem that needs to be addressed. . . . I referred to it as an "in-between" disorder.

[Then, in the *Diagnostic and Statistical Manual of Mental Disorders*], sandwiched between several pages of information on [anorexia and bulimia], I discovered a short little segment termed EDNOS (Eating Disorders Not Otherwise Specified). . . . Finally! In these paragraphs I found the exact problem I was struggling with. Those who have EDNOS—also called subclinical or subthreshold disorders—fit part but not all of the profiles of the better-known problems.

To better understand EDNOS, it is helpful to think of eating habits as being on a continuum. At one end of the continuum are the more extreme forms of eating disorders. . . . On the other end is healthy eating. Between these points are unhealthy behaviors that, while not considered extreme, can significantly affect the way we live our lives. In my case, I bounced from one end of the continuum to the other, finally ending up in the EDNOS category.

—Rhodes, 2003, pp. 17–19

• • •

The need for today's counselors and other practitioners to address gender-related health and mental health concerns has been well-established (Arnstein, 1995; Carter & Parks, 1996; Choate, 2008). Among these concerns, Park (2007) referred to eating disorders (EDs) as "one of the most troubling behavioral disorders in our society," especially for girls and women (p. 158), and among the eating-related disorders themselves, ED not otherwise specified (EDNOS) is by far the most common. In this chapter, we provide a framework for practice for counseling clients with EDNOS. In the sections that follow, we discuss the populations most affected by EDNOS; diagnostic criteria, assessment guidelines, and case conceptualization; and counseling responses for prevention, early intervention, and treatment. The framework presented in this chapter is based on a series of research studies by Alan M. Schwitzer and his colleagues. The approaches and interventions highlighted in the chapter include today's documented best mental health practices and evidence-based counseling recommendations. Throughout the chapter, aspects of the framework are illustrated by clinical snapshots drawn from the individual experiences of Constance Rhodes, who has written extensively about her own recovery from a subclinical eating disorder (Rhodes, 2003) and now directs a multifaceted nonprofit organization aimed at helping others with eating and body image issues.

# Young Adult Women and Eating Disorder Not Otherwise Specified

Adolescent boys and adult men certainly experience EDs (Ousley, Cordero, & White, 2008; Stout & Frame, 2004). In fact, Neumark-Sztainer (2005) reported that as many as 30% of the adolescent boys they studied expressed body dissatisfaction and were engaging in unhealthy weight management behaviors. However, boys and men with eating-related concerns are far outnumbered by girls and women (Hoek, 2006; Wittichen & Jacobi, 2005). Internationally, EDs are among the 10 most common causes of psychological distress among young adult women (Mathers, Vos, Stevenson, & Begg, 2000).

Previous authors have agreed that essentially all girls and women in the United States are pressured by factors associated with disordered eating (Peck & Lightsey, 2008; Striegel-Moore & Bulik, 2007), and counselors working in various settings are likely to find female clients with eating concerns in their caseloads (Choate & Schwitzer, 2009; Lewinsohn, Seeley, Moerk, & Striegel-Moore, 2000). For example, adolescent girls and young adult women in their 20s experience the highest risk for developing these types of problems (Stice, 2002; Striegel-Moore & Bulik, 2007). As follows, on college campuses, with large concentrations of young adult female students, the high incidence of EDs has been especially well documented (Gallagher, Golin, & Kelleher, 1992; Koszewski, Newell, & Higgins, 1990; G. A. Miller & Rice, 1993). Moreover, in the United States, although EDs were historically associated primarily with European American girls and women, these concerns are now seen with regularity among various ethnic populations (Becker, Franko, Speck, & Herzog, 2003; Cachelin & Striegel-Moore, 2006; Talleyrand, 2010; Tsai, Hoerr, & Song, 1998). Along these lines, Rich and Thomas (2008) found very few differences in disordered eating symptoms among African American, Latina, and White college women (Rich & Thomas, 2008; see also Chapter 3, this volume).

More important, although the major EDs—anorexia and bulimia—certainly occur among girls and women with some frequency, especially in clinical settings, the eating-related problems most likely to be seen by practitioners are, by far, the heterogeneous group of less severe problems diagnosed as EDNOS. For example, on college campuses, only 6% of female students reported concerns about anorexia or bulimia, whereas 25% to 40% reported moderate problems potentially falling into the EDNOS category—including body image worries, problems with weight management, out-of-control eating, and misperceiving normal versus disordered body size and eating and weight management behaviors (Bishop, Bauer, & Baker, 1998; Schwitzer, Rodriguez, Thomas, & Salimi, 2001; Tsai et al., 1998; Yost & Smith, 2012). Likewise, looking beyond collegiate populations, recent researchers have generally agreed that the large majority of young adult women with eating-related difficulties have disorders that fit into the EDNOS category (Fairburn & Bohn, 2005; Schwitzer et al., 2008; Shisslak, Crago, & Estes, 1995; Wilson, Grilo, & Vitousek, 2007; Wonderlich, Joiner, Keel, Williamson, & Crosby, 2007).

## Clinical Snapshot 7.1

In 2003, Constance Rhodes published *Life Inside the "Thin" Cage: A Personal Look Into the Hidden World of the Chronic Dieter.* She wrote the book to be self-reflective—an account of her own struggles with an ED—and to be a compelling resource that explains EDNOS to readers, especially female readers, who are concerned about their own problematic eating-related behavior. In this chapter, we use Rhodes's real-life experiences, borrowed from *Life Inside the "Thin" Cage,* to enliven the discussion by illustrating EDNOS dynamics.

At the time she wrote her book, Rhodes was a professionally successful adult woman who worked in marketing for the music recording industry. Her closest family relationships included her husband and son. Important resiliency factors included career success, a devoted husband, and faith-based supports centered on her participation in the Christian community. Today she leads FINDINGbalance, Inc., a faith-based nonprofit dedicated to helping people address eating and lifestyle needs.

Rhodes (2003) described first addressing thinness in her teens and then moving on to develop ED symptoms while in college. In fact, she said, "As a young girl, I don't recall ever being unhappy with my body." By contrast, "When I entered my teens . . . I began liking the way I looked in my clothes. Like most girls, once in a while I would worry that I had gained a little weight, so I'd go on a diet for a day or so" (Rhodes, 2003, p. 6). But a seed of food concerns had been planted earlier: "As I was growing up, my mother's struggles with weight and dieting were always present in my home. . . . At times Mom would be on a specific diet and would eat differently than the rest of us. She would also overeat quite frequently" (p. 68). Rhodes recalled her mother telling her she had only eaten "five hundred to seven hundred calories a day" while pregnant with her and stated "it was generally understood in our family that it was undesirable to be overweight" (p. 68). Rhodes's mother went on to experience her own "life-altering eating disorder" while Rhodes was a teen (p. 6).

Then, in college, Rhodes (2003) reported, "I put on weight for the first time in my life." She cited the academic, personal, and social stresses of being an unusually young 1st-year college student (she was 16 years old) and being underprepared for the practicalities of food shopping and cooking for herself as contributing factors: "[Adding] the stress of adjusting to living in an adult world . . . eating took on new meaning and purpose for me." She reported feeling "shock and terror" and being "devastated" at having gained 15 pounds during that 1st year (p. 8).

By her own estimation, Rhodes developed a range of disordered eating and weight management behaviors during college. She severely restricted her intake for awhile, telling herself, "This is all you get" (p. 9) and allowing herself meals only when "I felt I deserved to eat" (p. 9)—and believing that "if I could lose just a little more, I'd once again be happy with my body" (Rhodes, 2003, pp. 9–10). Likewise, she discovered that when she did allow herself a food treat, her "taste buds seemed to pop in delight," resulting in uncontrolled periods of bingeing such as when she finished "a entire pan of doughnuts." To compensate, on a few occasions, she "decided that throwing up was probably my best bet," along with trying diet pills and laxatives for a short while. Although she backed away from a regular habit of compensating, she "no longer had the power to resist the binges that were happening with alarming regularity." She recalled realizing she "was on the threshold of wreaking incredible havoc in my life" (pp. 11–12). Specifically, she was developing EDNOS.

• • •

## Eating Disorder Not Otherwise Specified: The *DSM–IV–TR* Diagnostic Criteria

Because of the diversity of individual presentations associated with any diagnostic class in the *Diagnostic and Statistical Manual of Mental Disorders* (4th ed., text rev., or *DSM–IV–TR*; American Psychiatric Association [APA], 2000a), including the EDs, it is impossible for the formal categories alone to cover every possible client situation (APA, 2000a; Schwitzer, Bergholtz, Dore, & Salimi, 1998). Therefore, each diagnostic class, including the EDs, offers at least one NOS category. The NOS category is used under several different conditions. Two of these conditions are especially relevant when identifying clients' eating-related difficulties. First, a person's presentation may conform to the general guidelines for the types of concerns covered in a diagnostic class but without fully meeting all of the exact criteria for a specific disorder. Second, symptoms may cause "clinically significant distress or impairment" (APA, 2000a, p. 4) but without conforming to any formal diagnostic category found in the manual.

Under these conditions—when a client's presentation does not fully meet the criteria for anorexia or bulimia but clearly consists of disordered eating patterns and experiences of distress or impairment in daily life—the EDNOS category is used (APA, 2000a; Schwitzer et al., 1998). For example, a person might be experiencing a scenario in which the behavioral features of a formal ED are only partially met. As an illustration, the EDNOS category is suggested when an individual exhibits normally expected body weight and normal menstrual patterns but is experiencing all of the other diagnostic features of anorexia (such as intense fear of gaining weight, disturbed body image, and severely restrictive dieting). Likewise, an individual might be experiencing a situation in which duration or frequency criteria are not met. As an illustration, the EDNOS category is again suggested when a person presents with all of the associated features of bulimia (self-evaluation that is unduly influenced by body and appearance considerations), but recurrent binging and compensating behaviors (purging, laxative use, etc.) occur at below-threshold levels (Schwitzer et al., 1998). A prominent example of the EDNOS category is the situation in which a client's behavior fits the criteria for binge eating disorder, a diagnosis currently under further study for possible future use in the *DSM,* indicating that the person is engaging in recurrent episodes of binge eating without regular use of the compensatory behaviors that would make up bulimia (APA, 2000a).

In sum, EDNOS is a moderate, heterogeneous group of "less severe problems centering on weight preoccupation and dissatisfaction with body image and sub-threshold problems with eating and compensatory behavior" (Schwitzer et al., 2008, p. 608; see also Ash & Piazza, 1995; Klemchuck, Hutchinson, & Frank, 1990;).

Naturally, counseling professionals should be aware of the current trends and future directions regarding ED best practices, including the trends concerning diagnosis. As readers can see, the framework for practice presented in this chapter is based on the *DSM–IV–TR's* criterion-referenced approach to the categorical diagnosis of EDs. Other writers have persuasively made the case for alternative approaches, including transdiagnostic and continuum methods of classifying eating-related concerns (Gleaves, Lowe, Green, Cororve, & Williams, 2000; Peck & Lightsey, 2008; Shisslak et al., 1995; Wonderlich et al., 2007). In turn, some readers may want to explore the benefits of these alternatives in comparison with, or as a supplement to, the approach used in this chapter.

In addition, some writers have raised a concern that overuse of the NOS approach has the potential to reduce diagnostic and predictive validity (Keel, Brown, Holm-Denoma, & Bodell, 2011). For practitioners, this means these writers believe overuse of EDNOS might possibly reduce the power of categorical diagnosis to meaningfully describe client situations. To address this potential problem, some of the new diagnostic criteria currently being proposed for the *DSM–5* include not only EDNOS, but also the addition of a formal binge eating disorder diagnosis (APA, 2010). Down the road, therefore, it is possible that offering both options (EDNOS and binge eating disorder), along with revised criteria sets for anorexia and bulimia, might reduce to some degree the prevalence of the EDNOS diagnosis. Practitioners with an interest in EDs should follow these developments; however, Keel et al. (2011), on the basis of their recent clinical trial studies, concluded that even though adding the binge eating disorder option would be a constructive step to take, "it appears likely that EDNOS may [still] continue to be the most common diagnosis" (p. 559).

# Clinical Snapshot 7.2

Constance Rhodes (2003) described making her first visit for evaluation of her eating-related health concerns at age 27. Her visit was with her primary care physician, who, interestingly, provided a diagnosis of anorexia. As Rhodes recalled, "A shock ran through me when I read the diagnosis the doctor wrote on the bottom of my slip: anorexia" (p. 17). Acknowledging that she was, in fact, confronting a problem that others in her life—her physician and family members—could recognize led to

> a moment of decision. And then the tears came . . . I was scared . . . to admit that I had a problem. Scared that everyone else had known about it all along and I had somehow been blind to it. It was an incredibly pivotal moment for me. (p. 17)

Still, Rhodes (2003) herself had the impression that the diagnosis was not quite an accurate fit with her symptoms. She agreed, "I had become so consumed with the fear of gaining weight that I was on an endless and unforgiving diet" and that her weight management had become unreasonable:

> Following my initial weight loss . . . I remained on this diet even though I was thin. . . . All I knew was that if I dared to eat just one forbidden bit, all would be lost, and I'd slip back into the frustrating weight gain I had experienced in college. (Rhodes, 2003, p. 15)

At the same time, she believed that she was not "an active anorexic" and "wasn't [even] practicing bulimia" at levels required by the diagnosis. Instead, she was someone whose behavior did not fit all the criteria, "though I realized I was highly anorexic in my thinking" and had "a very real problem in my life: an unhealthy obsession with weight" (p. 17).

Eventually, through personal research, she discovered the EDNOS diagnostic category. Her reaction was one of recognition: "Finally! . . . I found the exact problem I was struggling with" (Rhodes, 2003, p. 18). She recognized that she had some but not all of the symptoms of anorexia, which earlier in life she had taken as "a clear sign that I was not clinically [eating disordered]" (p. 18). She thought about "other disordered eaters [who] might be borderline bulimics or binge eaters, but [who,] since they don't fit all the criteria, . . . feel misunderstood and wrongly labeled" (p. 18). Considering the affirmation and sense of universality she felt on discovering the diagnosis, she said, "But the EDNOS category provides a home for us" (p. 18).

Thinking back, Rhodes (2003) said that "if someone had talked to me about this before, I probably would have been more willing to admit that I had a problem" (p. 18).

• • •

## Assessment and Conceptualization: What to Expect in Clients With Eating Disorders Not Otherwise Specified

Counseling professionals use assessment and conceptualization skills to evaluate, understand, organize, and make sense of the client's needs (Hinkle, 1994; Seligman, 2004). To paint a conceptual picture that will be useful during the course of therapy, practitioners must routinely first gain a comprehensive understanding of their client's presenting concerns and reason for referral. To be most effective, they must next cast a wider net to collect all of the clinically significant client data they can about such factors as additional issues pertaining to major life roles (including school, work, and additional major life roles), other relevant aspects of social and personal–emotional adjustment, and developmental and family history such as current and past family and parental relationships and previous peer and social experiences. Moreover, they should make observations about the person's help seeking and previous history with counseling during the session and collect relevant medical, psychiatric, substance use, suicidality, and other psychological assessment data (Schwitzer & Rubin, 2012).

To assist counseling professionals in knowing what to anticipate in an intake session, we discuss a comprehensive conceptual picture of clients with EDNOS. This conceptual model is drawn from a series of studies conducted as part of an ongoing clinical research program investigating EDNOS (Schwitzer et al., 1998, 2001, 2008; Schwitzer & Rodriguez, 2002). The model is consistent with the findings of other recent researchers (Peck & Lightsey, 2008).

## Eating Disorder Diagnostic Features

First and foremost, assessing for EDNOS means recognizing—and not overlooking—subthreshold eating syndromes when they are present. Counselors should take the lead, engaging clients in clinical exploration during screening, intake, and early sessions. Diagnostically, women with these problems present with combinations of anorexic and bulimic symptoms characterized by restrictive dieting, binging, or purging that occur at levels below minimum *DSM–IV–TR* requirements for a major ED. In other words, they might at times engage in severe dieting, but not often enough or for a long enough duration to cause severely low body weights; they might binge eat, characterized by discrete time periods of focused, excessive eating that feels out of control, but less frequently than twice per week or for a duration of less than 3 months; and they might compensate inappropriately with self-induced vomiting, misuse of laxatives, or excessive exercise but, once again, less frequently than twice per week or for duration of less than 3 months (APA, 2000a).

In fact, Schwitzer et al. (2001) found that more than 80% of college women in their ED treatment program had symptoms meeting these criteria. Regarding eating behavior, on the basis of two different studies with women in treatment and women not in treatment, about 80% of women with EDs reported occasionally bingeing, and their frequency was in the range of one to three times per month, compared with a mean of zero times per month for women without EDs (Schwitzer et al., 2001, 2008). Regarding anorexic behavior, although these women did report avoiding eating when hungry and engaging in dieting at greater rates than women without EDs, only a modest portion, 13%, reported the severely restrictive dieting often associated with a major ED diagnosis (Schwitzer et al., 2001, 2008). Instead, girls and women with EDNOS were more likely to use a mix of excessive exercise (or weekly exercise with ongoing rumination about the need to exercise more often), vomiting (at rates less than once per month), and laxative use (at rates less than once per month; Fairburn & Bohn, 2005; Shisslak et al., 1995; Wilson et al., 2007; Wonderlich et al., 2007). Taken together, the primary symptoms among those with EDNOS include

- eating binges in which one feels unable to stop;
- avoiding eating, and engaging in dieting and food intake control methods, at greater rates than peers without EDs; and
- managing weight, when it occurs, mostly through exercise augmented by occasional purging via vomiting, laxative use, and the like.

Characteristically, along with overt primary symptoms pertaining to eating and compensating, diagnosable EDs also consist of additional problematic cognitive, behavioral, and psychoemotional features. These features can include intense fears of gaining weight or becoming fat; undue negative influence of body appearance on self-evaluation; and misperceptions of body size, weight, or shape (APA, 2000a). These features are especially salient, and troubling, for girls and women with EDNOS. Here again, counselors should take the lead in inquiring about these symptoms. According to the evidence (Schwitzer et al., 2001, 2008), typical cognitive features of clients with EDNOS might include

- rumination about body appearance, thinness, and eating and weight management;
- preoccupation with food, becoming thinner, burning calories, and having body fat; and
- devotion of excessive amounts of time and thought to eating.

148

Looking at behavioral features beyond primary symptoms, clients

- are likely to be knowledgeable calorie, fat, and nutritional intake counters;
- might engage in food strategies such as secretive eating or eating meals unusually slowly; and
- are likely to have common fluctuations in their weight.

Looking at closely related psychoemotional features, these individuals generally feel tyrannized by their body and food preoccupations: They

- fear gaining weight;
- feel food controls their life;
- struggle to resist eating and compensatory urges; and
- work to stifle the effects of their preoccupations on their mood, stress levels, and sense of self.

## Co-Occurring Features: Depressive and Anxiety Symptoms

In addition, counselors must be aware that female clients with EDNOS are also likely to be experiencing collateral mood and anxiety problems. In turn, when investigating the presence of subthreshold eating problems, practitioners should be certain to evaluate for mood and anxiety symptoms. For example, Schwitzer et al. (2001) found that more than 40% of women in their ED programs had difficulties with moderate depression. Of these women, 14% reported periods of clinically significant suicidal ideation, and 8% said they had previously engaged at least once in some form of suicidal behavior (e.g., swallowing pills) or a form of self-harm (e.g., nonsuicidal cutting; Schwitzer & Rodriguez, 2002). Looking next at anxiety and stress, 75% of the ED clients reported difficulties with at least moderate symptoms of stress or anxiety. Although some of the stress occurred in relation to food and body image (e.g., women reported feeling pressure from other people to eat more), they also endorsed anxiety as a concern in arenas outside of eating and weight control, such as in response to managing various life pressures (Schwitzer et al., 2008; Schwitzer & Rodriguez, 2002). Because clients with EDNOS are relatively likely to have concurrent problems with mood and very likely to have concurrent problems with stress and anxiety, counselors should be certain that evaluation is extended to these areas.

## Common Themes and Stressors: Perfectionism, Low Self-Esteem, and Interpersonal Dependence

Moreover, girls and women with EDNOS share common psychological and developmental themes and certain psychosocial, environmental, and family stressors. As with mood and anxiety, these topics contribute to the conceptual picture, and therefore counselors should be sure to examine them as part of a thorough intake and evaluation process to identify critical targets for treatment.

149

Looking at psychological and developmental themes, clients with EDNOS often express a combination of low self-esteem, perfectionism across domains, and interpersonal dependency (Peck & Lightsey, 2008; Schwitzer et al., 1998, 2001, 2008; Schwitzer & Rodriguez, 2002). They consistently report problems with undue perfectionism associated with body appearance, irrational perfectionism about academic and work performance, and inability to meet the high expectations they set for themselves in personal and social roles such as girlfriend, roommate, and daughter. In fact, they typically experience strong pressure and anxiety about performing well academically in spite of clear objective evidence of their educational ability and track record of obvious success. Along the same lines as misjudging their specific abilities and personal qualities, their overall self-esteem may be unstable or fragile, too. Clients with EDNOS tend to make self-statements such as "I am my own worst critic," "I am too hard on myself," and I tend to judge myself too hard" (Schwitzer & Rodriguez, 2002, p. 53). Perhaps as a result, they sometimes tend to behave dependently in interpersonal relationships. They may give away power and decisions to others, be passive and avoid conflicts, or be overly emotionally dependent in their young adult relationships with parents (even considering today's norm of high parent involvement in the lives of their young adult children).

In sum, it is important to explore fears of being able to be psychologically and practically self-sufficient and doubts about effectively managing the pressures and demands of the young adult or adult world. In terms of family stressors, clients in the EDNOS population are likely to confront moderate interpersonal struggles with parents, often enacting the "perfect" role in their family of origin (Schwitzer et al., 1998, 2001, 2008; Schwitzer & Rodriguez, 2002, p. 51). Many clients say someone else in their family currently has an ED or had one in the past. Finally, to round out the topics for exploration, because some women with EDs do sometimes report past incidents of sexual victimization, clinicians should routinely check for (or rule out) this possible aspect of the person's psychological history (Schwitzer & Rodriguez, 2002). The clinician should explore with the client the general theme of parental and family pressures and roles and their influence on young adult psychological maturation.

### *Help-Seeking Characteristics of Clients With Eating Disorder Not Otherwise Specified: Ambivalence and Hesitation*

EDNOS falls into the general category of moderate counseling concerns (Choate & Schwitzer, 2009; Drum & Lawler, 1988; Schwitzer et al., 1998). Usually when concerns are moderate, the need for assistance is emerging or clearly present—meaning that a counseling problem exists, is causing difficulties, and has the potential to grow further in severity but at present falls short of severely impairing the person's adjustment or functioning (Choate & Schwitzer, 2009; Drum & Lawler, 1988; Schwitzer et al., 1998).

Ordinarily, people experiencing emerging and fully present moderate-level counseling concerns feel medium-high urgency to address or resolve their needs, medium-high interest in seeking help, moderately high urgency, and at least medium motivation for change (Drum & Lawler, 1988). By comparison, girls and women with EDNOS tend to be hesitant, ambivalent, or resistant help seekers despite the presence of their symptomatic difficulties (Schwitzer et al., 2001, 2008). In other words, although the level of concern they are experiencing is usually accompanied by some urgency and motivation for change, the help-seeking picture is more mixed with clients with EDNOS.

Specifically, although a portion of women dealing with EDNOS do seek psychotherapy on their own, most clients who arrive at clinicians' offices have been urged into counseling by friends or family or been referred by another professional (Schwitzer et al., 2001). Moreover, these girls and women are likely to (a) try out multiple helping relationships without engaging in an ongoing counseling relationship or commit to ongoing treatment and (b) terminate individual counseling or drop out of group programs prematurely (i.e., leave of their own accord without the professional agreement of their counselor). When they do seek assistance on their own, women with these concerns often enlist treatment from noncounseling adjunct services such as a primary care physician, nutritionist, health center, or support group rather than engage in ongoing individual mental health treatment from a counseling professional such as a professional counselor, psychologist, or psychiatrist (Schwitzer et al., 2001, 2008).

New clients presenting with EDNOS are relatively likely to have had previous counseling or tried out multiple professional help-seeking relationships with past counselors and adjunct services such as nutritionists. The visit is also likely to be the result of urging by family or friends or referral from another professional. Clinicians must look for ways to address the client's ambivalence if a therapeutic relationship is to be successfully established.

Additionally, clients who arrive for individual counseling with moderate EDs tend to initially discuss other counseling topics (Schwitzer et al., 2001, 2008; Schwitzer & Rodriguez, 2002). For example, their presenting concerns might at first center around feelings of moderate depression or anxiety, problematic perfectionism and self-esteem doubts, handling pressure, or dealing with relationships in which they feel uncomfortably dependent (such as with romantic partners, roommates, parents, or others). Alternatively, these clients might hint at eating concerns or describe eating-related behaviors as one of several presenting problems. They might report some version of the idea—"I don't have an eating disorder but I think about food all of the time"—or volunteer that they ruminate about eating, weight management, and body image (Schwitzer et al., 2001, p. 160). Likewise, they may disclose problems such as being "terrified about being overweight" or feeling "extremely guilty after eating" (Schwitzer et al., 2008, p. 611). Counselors should be cognizant of the importance of these problematic cognitions or associated weight control behaviors vis-à-vis

EDs—even if they are just hinted at or introduced tentatively—and alertly take the lead in exploring these issues along with the various presenting concerns the person endorses or reports.

## Clinical Snapshot 7.3

Constance Rhodes (2003) described the "shock and terror" she felt when she discovered during her 1st year in college that the "scale confirmed what the mirror had jeeringly suggested: I had gained about fifteen pounds" (p. 8). When confronted with her unexpected weight gain, Rhodes said she "did what any logical girl does. I headed for the diet books and frantically searched for one that promised quick results . . . I knew I liked being slim, and the idea of losing that status terrified me" (pp. 8–9). Rhodes said that at one point during college, "I didn't realize it at the time, but I was behaving like a textbook anorexic. Had I been aware of the danger of my actions though, I wouldn't have cared—I was now losing weight rapidly" (p. 10).

Along with her disordered eating symptoms, Rhodes also experienced perfectionism, depressed mood, and anxiety. These themes are captured in a diary entry Rhodes (2003) first shared in *Life Inside the "Thin" Cage*:

> Let me tell you about my life . . . it is dark place . . . everything is off-limits. Everything is based on performance. If I don't perform well or look good, then I am not good. I am not allowed to enjoy a piece of cake or a slice of pizza because if I do, tomorrow I will wake up fat. . . . Daily I complain to my husband . . . "Are you sure I'm not fat?" "I feel so gross . . . How can you love me?" . . . Since everything is about performance and appearance, a bad hair day can truly ruin me. If my performance ever slips, I am suddenly in the precarious position of losing my value to the world. Going anywhere . . . requires that I look my best, for people may not like me if they don't think I'm attractive and thin. (pp. 5–6)

Rhodes (2003) also describes in her book that her mother, "an educated . . . woman" who is a licensed psychologist, "had battled her weight since childhood" and confronted her own symptoms of bulimia (p. 7).

Although Rhodes (2003) first developed her concerns during her late teens, it was not until her late 20s that she was successfully urged by her father to seek assistance. When she did, she initially visited her primary care physician with health questions, reporting to her doctor, "I'm here because I think I might not be eating quite right" (p. 16). She then, only later, sought counseling.

• • •

## Clinical Action: Counseling Responses for Prevention, Early Intervention, and Treatment of Eating Disorder Not Otherwise Specified

Depending on their workplace setting, institutional context, or the composition of their client caseload, counseling professionals may have opportunities to engage in ED prevention programming, intermediate treatment for an EDNOS causing moderate distress or dysfunction, advanced psychotherapy with clients experiencing greater difficulties with EDNOS, or all of these. To help guide counseling responses across these contexts, Drum and Lawler (1988) developed a tripartite intervention approach that has been a very useful framework for clinical action with EDNOS (Choate & Schwitzer, 2009; Schwitzer et al., 1998; Schwitzer & Rodriguez, 2002). According to the approach,

- preventive interventions are the strategy of choice when, although no current counseling need exists, susceptibility to an EDNOS is possible or probable;
- intermediate interventions are used when symptoms cause some distress or disruptions and have the potential to increase but do not yet severely impair the client's daily life; and
- psychotherapeutic-level interventions are used at the end of the severity continuum, to address recurrent issues, full-syndrome disorders, and "entrenched dysfunctional life patterns" (Drum & Lawler, 1988, p. 13).

## Preventive Intervention: Responding to Susceptibility

Naturally, successfully mitigating the emergence of an ED seems to be a preferable first line of defense. Accordingly, preventive interventions are intended to "forestall the onset of problems or personal-emotional needs" (Schwitzer et al., 1998, p. 202). Prevention programs are aimed at populations who have no current need for assistance with EDs but who have susceptibility to eating-related difficulties (particularly, EDNOS; Choate & Schwitzer, 2009; Drum & Lawler, 1988; Schwitzer et al., 1998).

For counseling professionals who provide prevention services and programming, the special challenge is that the target audiences, because they are currently experiencing no distress, impairment, or other needs related to eating problems, feel no urgency and low or no motivation for assistance. In response, prevention uses strategies that engage individuals while keeping resistance low. Specifically, this means that prevention mainly relies on tactics that provide information and are aimed at increasing topical understanding, enhancing eating-related attitudes, and promoting healthier eating and weight management behaviors (Choate & Schwitzer, 2009; Drum & Lawler, 1988; Schwitzer et al., 1998).

Because prevention relies most heavily on information to improve understanding, preventive methods should usually involve educational formats such as lectures, discussion groups, and workshops; media presentations and written materials; and self-assessment. Counseling staff in a wide variety of settings—high schools, college and university campuses, community agencies, recreational centers, faith-based institutions, and other settings serving girls and women—can provide these types of psychoeducational experiences. Workshops pertaining to eating-related issues can be incorporated into high school orientations, 1st-year college orientations, sorority meetings, athletic team meetings, faith-based programs, summer camps, recreational sports events, and the like. Two common foundational models for EDNOS prevention programming are the health promotion model and the social–cognitive model. Professionals implementing the health promotion model attempt to "promote healthful eating and exercise habits . . . [and] provide information about normative physical development (e.g., weight gains that occur across a woman's life cycle), nutrition, and healthy weight control behaviors" (Choate & Schwitzer, 2009, p. 167). In contrast, counselors implementing the social cognitive model attempt to counteract "the powerful influence of current social and cultural forces on women's body images and development, [whereby] girls are taught at an early age that they should pursue the societal ideal of beauty" with its focus on "extreme thinness as central to beauty and necessary for women's social success and happiness" (Choate & Schwitzer, 2009, p. 166; see also American Psychological Association, 2007; Brazelton, Greene, Gynther, & O'Mell, 1998; Rodin, Silberstein, & Streigel-Moore, 1984).

## *Intermediate Intervention: Responding to Moderate Client Needs*

Intermediate intervention is implemented when a problem exists, causes moderate difficulties, and has the potential to grow, which means that practitioners rely on intermediate interventions with clients for whom ED symptoms are emerging or are currently being experienced but are as yet only modest or do not meet the criteria for a diagnosable ED. In turn, we suggest clinicians cast a wide net when identifying clients in need of intermediate ED intervention. Specifically, counselors should consider engaging their new, current, or ongoing female clients in intermediate interventions targeting the emergence of ED symptoms whenever their clients

- present with symptoms such as extreme dieting, excessive exercise, episodic binge eating, or occasional compensatory behaviors (e.g., vomiting or laxative use and diuretic misuse);
- express particular pressure to become thin and appear to heavily endorse the cultural thin ideal as their own standard for measuring their self-worth;
- are exposed to family members with body image and eating problems;
- appear to lack family and peer social support; and
- present with low self-esteem, negative affect, and problematic perfectionism (Choate & Schwitzer, 2009; Fairburn, 1995).

At the intermediate intervention level, clients usually express minimal motivation for change (Drum & Lawler, 1988). Therefore, intermediate counseling approaches aim to minimize client resistance, increase client engagement, and focus mostly on adding new skills to, building new dimensions into, and boosting resiliency factors in the individual's life. Brief or minimal individual counseling and an emphasis on group formats is recommended (Drum & Lawler, 1988). In other words, although individual counseling may also be needed, at the intermediate level short-term group counseling primarily is recommended as a treatment of choice (Choate & Schwitzer, 2009).

Intermediate-level group interventions for eating concerns should generally combine psychoeducational and cognitive–behavioral components (Choate & Schwitzer, 2009).

Intermediate ED counseling groups also capitalize on the benefits of social support among peers who might otherwise lack support in their natural interpersonal environments; create an ameliorative sense of universality with other girls and women confronting similar eating-related and body image struggles; and create interpersonal environments for learning new ways of coping (Stice, 2002; Stice & Hoffman, 2004). Moreover, groups can be used as efficient formats for providing topical information and new learning about self (Brown, 2011).

### Psychoeducation and Intermediate Intervention

When counseling group leaders provide psychoeducation, they should include themes such as the social–cognitive aspects of the thin ideal, especially as it is presented in societal media images portraying idealized female beauty; how the thin ideal and its portrayal in the media promote inappropriate and unrealistic standards for self-comparison, leading to poor self-evaluations unduly influenced by one's body image; and similar themes about beauty and women's self-esteem. Here, having group members realize the unattainability of the thin beauty ideal and recognize the role of media can serve as buffers against the negative influences of these factors (Coughlin & Kalodner, 2006; Yamamiya, Cash, Melnyk, Posavac, & Posavac, 2005). Furthermore, these groups can provide nutritional, eating, and weight management information emphasizing health promotion and use activities and homework leading to lifestyle changes (Stice, Gau, Presnell, & Shaw, 2007).

### Cognitive–Behavioral Strategies and Intermediate Intervention

When counselors use cognitive–behavioral strategies, EDNOS group members are generally challenged to change their beliefs and attitudes about the importance of weight and body shape on their self-evaluations and approval of self (Matusek, Wendt, & Wiseman, 2004; Stice, 2002; Yamamiya et al., 2005). More specifically, dissonance-based cognitive interventions are recommended. Dissonance-based strategies are based on the assumption that clients with intermediate needs have already internalized the thin ideal. On this basis, outcome goals are to heighten awareness about the cultural sources of the ideal, create cognitive dissonance and tension by encouraging clients to resist the ideal, and, in turn, lead to behavior change (Stice, Chase, Stormer, & Appel, 2001; see also Chapter 10, this volume). Clinicians can use role-plays, persuasive arguments, and other methods of cognitive confrontation to achieve these outcomes.

## Psychotherapeutic Intervention: Responding to Entrenched Needs

The tools most often suggested for psychotherapy with clients who have advanced EDNOS difficulties include three approaches: cognitive–behavioral therapy (CBT; APA, 2000b; Fairburn, 2008; Wilson et al., 2007), interpersonal therapy (IPT; APA, 2000b; Nevonen & Broberg, 2005; Wilson et al., 2007), and dialectical behavior therapy (DBT; Linehan, 1993; Telch, Agras, & Linehan, 2000; Wilson et al., 2007). CBT for EDs focuses closely on the belief systems and behaviors maintaining the disordered eating cycle (Fairburn, 2008). IPT focuses closely on the interpersonal areas of concern commonly reported by women with EDNOS, such as avoiding conflict, difficulty with independence or dependence, and concerns about meeting others' expectations. A distinctive feature of IPT is that the focus is on identifying and modifying the client's interpersonal difficulties rather than on disordered eating symptoms (Nevonen & Broberg, 2005; Wilson et al., 2007). DBT focuses closely on the client's eating symptoms as attempts to regulate strong emotions and to cope with stressors (Telch et al., 2000). A distinctive feature of DBT as it is applied to EDs is its use of skill training—including mindfulness, emotional regulation, distress tolerance, and interpersonal effectiveness—to address emotional regulation deficits (Linehan, 1993; Telch et al., 2000).

Among these approaches, CBT is considered the gold standard. Because CBT has the largest accumulation of evidence supporting its efficacy for the treatment of EDs, it is the most highly recommended psychotherapeutic approach (APA, 2000b; Wilson et al., 2007). Clinical trial outcomes suggest CBT is more effective than other counseling methods or treatment with medication (APA, 2000b, 2006; National Institute for Health and Clinical Excellence, 2004; Wilson et al., 2007). By comparison, recent researchers have suggested that IPT is a valuable approach as an alternative to CBT, particularly for those individuals who do not respond well to CBT and have pressing interpersonal issues (APA, 2000b; National Institute for Health and Clinical Excellence, 2004; Wilson et al., 2007), and DBT has garnered more recent support, especially when integrated with CBT (Wilson et al., 2007).

Because the CBT approach is the most highly recommended, our framework for practice emphasizes its use. In addition, because clients with EDs tend to feel low urgency, low motivation for change, and reservations about engaging in counseling relationships, motivational interviewing (MI) techniques are also suggested to augment CBT (Prochaska, DiClemente, & Norcross, 1992, W. R. Miller & Rollnick, 1991). The MI strategies most often used with CBT for eating concerns are also emphasized in our framework. In the short sections of this chapter that follow, we are constrained to provide just the basics pertaining to CBT and EDNOS. We provide additional resources for further study at the end of the chapter. Naturally, we also encourage readers who want more information about additional approaches, especially IPT and DBT, to seek other sources, including those included elsewhere in this volume (see Chapters 13 [CBT], 14 [IPT], and 16 [DBT]).

## Cognitive–Behavioral Therapy Strategies and Psychotherapeutic Intervention

Counseling professionals seeking practice methods for EDNOS should add to their counseling toolbox a specific form of CBT specially adapted to the psychotherapeutic treatment of EDs by Fairburn (2008). Fairburn's counseling approach, "enhanced cognitive behavior therapy for eating disorders (CBT-E)" (p. 23), is based on a structured series of stages used in sequence during the counseling process:

- Stage 1, emphasizing client–counselor engagement, client motivation, and education and orientation to the CBT-E approach;
- Stage 2, during which initial gains are reviewed, barriers to change are anticipated, and the counseling work to follow is formulated;
- Stage 3, during which the main counseling work occurs and the cognitive and behavioral mechanisms maintaining the client's ED are fully confronted; and
- Stage 4, during which progress is reviewed and consolidated and methods whereby the client can manage future relapse risk are introduced.

## Motivational Interviewing Strategies and Psychotherapeutic Intervention

Interwoven among Fairburn's (2008) four stages are motivational strategies, cognitive change strategies, and behavioral change strategies. However, we should highlight characteristics of client engagement and motivation that require special attention early in EDNOS treatment—and that benefit from MI strategies. Specifically, during the first phase of counseling, corresponding to the initial formation stages of the helping relationship, clinicians must emphasize engaging and motivating the client because—as we discussed earlier pertaining to EDNOS help-seeking characteristics—the individual is typically precontemplative, has low motivation, and expresses little intent to change attitudes or improve behaviors. MI techniques are seen as most effective when engaging such clients (W. R. Miller & Rollnick, 1991). With the goal of increasing a client's leanings toward change, counseling includes

- using reflection and open-ended questions to clarify and make explicit the client's beliefs about the eating problem and fears about losing control of his or her eating, weight, and body shape;
- comparing the costs and benefits, and short-term versus long-term effects, of current versus healthier eating and weight management behavior;
- providing psychoeducation about eating-related disorders and their detrimental psychological and emotional patterns; and
- providing health education about the negative consequences of unhealthy eating and weight habits (such as the cyclic effects of dieting and ineffectiveness of severe dieting or vomiting for long-term weight control; Choate & Schwitzer, 2009; Fairburn, Marcus, & Wilson, 1993; W. R. Miller & Rollnick, 1991; Vitousek, Watson, & Wilson, 1998).

When these tactics are successful, the client outcomes resulting from use of MI together with CBT-E during this phase are a client's increasing openness to the notion that change is in his or her best long-term interest and clearer understanding of what current attitudes and behaviors he or she might want to keep unchanged versus those he or she is motivated to alter (W. R. Miller & Rollnick, 1991; Vitousek et al., 1998). Psychotherapy then proceeds through CBT-E's subsequent stages of reviewing initial gains, next confronting the problematic cognitive and behavioral mechanisms maintaining the client's EDNOS symptoms, and then consolidating gains to create resiliency against future relapse.

## Clinical Snapshot 7.4

Reading *Life Inside the Thin Cage* (Rhodes, 2003), clinicians may notice a missed opportunity for preventive intervention. Rhodes described being involved in college life on her campus; because of her young age, she was under the watchful attention of the dean's office, and she was connected to the college's singing group. Ideally, counseling, health education, or student development programming at the institution might have used some of the health promotion strategies or social–cognitive approaches we have described to reach susceptible populations of college women on its campus.

Likewise, once she pursued counseling, Rhodes (2003) raised a concern that her initial therapists were underinformed about EDNOS:

> When I finally did begin to seek counseling for my problem, no one seemed to know what to do with me . . . [I wasn't anorexic or bulimic], but it seemed that therapists were looking for me to be one extreme or the other. (p. 18)

Whereas in this chapter, we described CBT, especially CBT-E combined with MI, as the evidence-based gold standard for ED treatment and suggested IBT and DBT as reasonable alternatives, Rhodes (2003) reported that her earliest therapists variously prescribed fluoxetine and recommended rapid eye movement therapy to address her EDNOS concerns. As a counseling client, she wondered, "How was I supposed to get help if people didn't 'get' the problem?" (p. 18).

Ultimately, Rhodes persevered and did find a successful, productive counseling relationship with a counselor who was "equipped to give sound advice while maintaining healthy professional boundaries" (Rhodes, 2003, p. 217). She made substantial gains in counseling and, through her efforts and those of her counselor, reached many of her outcome goals. On reflection, Rhodes said that "looking back, I can see that if it hadn't been for [my counselor] and our weekly sessions, I would never be where I am today" (p. 216).

At first, Rhodes (2003) remembered her ambivalence about counseling and her counselor's responses:

> When I first met [my counselor], it was after a few years of coming to terms not only with my eating but also with some other issues in my life. One day I told [my counselor] it was hard for me not to feel selfish when spewing out all my problems to her, and she gently reminded me that this process was not only acceptable but necessary to my recovery. And she was right. (pp. 215–216)

Once the psychotherapeutic relationship was well established, Rhodes was able to productively address the faulty thinking processes and unhealthy behaviors making up her EDNOS symptoms. She confronted such cognitive themes and schema as "Will my clothes still fit me today?" (p. 27), "The mirror is my enemy," "Oh, those scales" (p. 28), "warped body image," "What size am I?" (p. 29), "Thin equals control equals power!" "Look at me! I am thin!" (p. 30), and others. Likewise, she successfully confronted the "weird eating habits [that] can become so much a part of our lives that we don't even notice them" (p. 47) and triggers (she said, "One of my triggers used to be fashion magazines. If I came across a copy of *Vogue* or *W*, I would find myself unhappy with my body"; p. 223).

Eighteen months into her recovery journey, Rhodes reflected on how life is "different now that I'm no longer consumed with dieting" and "about all the changes that have occurred since I've been able to see myself as more than just a 'body" (p. 193). In that regard, she noted, "I suppose one of the primary differences is that I am not so consumed with always having to look perfect" (p. 193). However, she saw "many more positive changes" (p. 193) beyond eating and body image, too. For example, she found that intrapersonally and interpersonally, "I'm a lot more even-tempered, . . . I have so much more 'brain time' now for being creative, . . . [and] I am learning to see others for who they are, not what they look like" (p. 194).

"I would be lying if I said I no longer struggle . . . it's important to know that leaving a life of disordered eating and weight obsession is a process, not a quick fix" (p. 229). Still, the process is worth it: "When we choose to break free from the cage we are in, the happiness we will find far outweighs the perceived benefits of our unhealthy lifestyle" (p. 193).

• • •

# Conclusion

In this chapter, we presented a suggested framework for practice with clients with EDNOS. First, the framework relies on the categorical approach to diagnosis and encourages clinicians to not overlook EDNOS presentations among their clients. Next, the framework uses clinical evidence to develop a full conceptual picture of the most likely EDNOS client scenarios. Then, the framework offer three points of intervention: prevention emphasizing health promotion and social–cognitive strategies, intermediate counseling emphasizing psychoeducation and cognitive strategies, and psychotherapeutic treatment using CBT-E augmented by MI.

## Chapter Highlights

Some of this chapter's most important considerations for clinicians regarding EDNOS are the following:

- The majority of young adult women with eating-related difficulties experience disorders that fit into the EDNOS category.

- EDNOS is moderate, heterogeneous, and involves less severe concerns centering on weight preoccupation, body image dissatisfaction, and subthreshold problems with eating and compensatory behavior.
- The primary symptoms of EDNOS include eating binges, avoiding eating and engaging in dieting and other food control, and weight management through exercise plus occasional purging.
- Clients with EDNOS commonly present with cognitive features including rumination about body appearance and preoccupation with food and thinness; are knowledgeable about calories, fat, and nutrition; and fear gaining weight and feel food controls their lives.
- Clients with EDNOS commonly experience co-occurring mood problems and concurrent stress and anxiety problems.
- Young adult clients with EDNOS express difficulties with problematic perfectionism, feeling adequate to meet the challenges and pressures of the adult world, and establishing psychological autonomy.
- New clients with EDNOS have typically tried out previous professional help-seeking relationships, arrive at the urging of family or friends or by professional referral, and are ambivalent about ED treatment.
- Preventive interventions are the strategy of choice and emphasize psychoeducation, health promotion, and social–cognitive strategies.
- Intermediate interventions address emerging and moderate EDNOS client scenarios and—although individual counseling may also be needed—emphasize short-term group counseling as a treatment of choice.
- Psychotherapeutic-level interventions are used to respond to advanced, entrenched problems.
- CBT, especially CBT-E, is the gold standard for the psychotherapeutic-level treatment of EDNOS and may be combined with MI.
- Additional suggested approaches for the psychotherapeutic-level treatment of EDNOS, especially when CBT is ineffective, are IPT and DBT.
- Counseling professionals should be cautious to avoid overlooking the moderate problems of EDNOS in their everyday practices.

# Recommended Resources

### Books

Choate, L. H. (2008). *Girls' and women's wellness: Contemporary counseling issues and interventions.* Alexandria, VA: American Counseling Association.

Fairburn, C. G. (2008). *Cognitive behavior therapy and eating disorders.* New York, NY: Guilford Press.

Jongsma, A. E., Peterson, L. M., & Bruce, T. J. (2006). *The complete adult psychotherapy treatment planner* (4th ed.). Hoboken, NJ: Wiley.

Miller, W. R., & Rollnick, S. (2002). *Motivational interviewing: Preparing people to change* (2nd ed.). New York, NY: Guilford Press.

Rhodes, C. (2003). *Life inside the "thin" cage: A personal look into the hidden world of the chronic dieter.* Colorado Springs, CO: Waterbrook Press.

Schwitzer, A. M., & Rubin, L. C. (2012). *Diagnosis and treatment planning skills for mental health professionals: A popular culture casebook approach.* Thousand Oaks, CA: Sage.

### Web Sites

- FINDINGbalance, Inc.
  http://www.findingbalance.org
  Nonprofit; a variety of client resources can be retrieved.
- Media Education Foundation
  http://www.mediaed.org
  A variety of psychoeducational media can be retrieved, including *Killing Us Slowly 4: Advertising's Image of Women* (DVD).

## References

American Psychiatric Association. (2000a). *Diagnostic and statistical manual of mental disorders* (4th ed., text rev.). Washington, DC: Author.

American Psychiatric Association. (2000b). Practice guidelines for the treatment of patients with eating disorders (revision). *American Journal of Psychiatry, 157,* 1–39.

American Psychiatric Association. (2010). *Eating disorders.* Retrieved April 9, 2010, from http://www.dsm5.org/ProposedRevisions/Pages/EatingDisorders.aspx.2010

American Psychological Association. (2007). Guidelines for psychological practice with girls and women. *American Psychologist, 62,* 949–979.

Arnstein, R. I. (1995). Mental health on the campus revisited. *Journal of American College Health, 43,* 243–251.

Ash, J. B., & Piazza, E. (1995). Changing symptomatology in eating disorders. *International Journal of Eating Disorders, 18,* 27–28.

Becker, A., Franko, D. L., Speck, A., & Herzog, D. B. (2003). Ethnicity and differential access to care for eating disorder symptoms. *International Journal of Eating Disorders, 33,* 205–212.

Bishop, J. B., Bauer, K. W., & Baker, E. T. (1998). A survey of counseling needs of male and female college students. *Journal of College Student Development, 39,* 205–210.

Brazelton, E. W., Greene, K. S., Gynther, M., & O'Mell, J. (1998). Femininity, bulimia, and distress in college women. *Psychological Reports, 83,* 355–363.

Brown, N. (2011). *Psychoeducational groups: Process and practice* (3rd ed.). New York, NY: Routledge.

Cachelin, F. M., & Striegel-Moore, R. H. (2006). Help seeking and barriers to treatment in a community sample of Mexican American and European American women with eating disorders. *International Journal of Eating Disorders, 39,* 154–161.

161

Carter, R. T., & Parks, E. E. (1996). Womanist identity and mental health. *Journal of Counseling & Development, 74,* 484–489.

Coughlin, J. W., & Kalodner, C. (2006). Media literacy as a prevention intervention for college women at low- or high-risk for eating disorders. *Body Image, 3,* 35–41. Retrieved from ScienceDirect database.

Choate, L. H. (2008). *Girls' and women's wellness: Contemporary counseling issues and interventions.* Alexandria, VA: American Counseling Association.

Choate, L. H., & Schwitzer, A. M. (2009). Mental health counseling responses to eating-related concerns in young adult women: A prevention and treatment continuum. *Journal of Mental Health Counseling, 31,* 161–183.

Drum, D. J., & Lawler, A. C. (1988). *Developmental interventions: Theories, principles, and practice.* Columbus, OH: Merrill.

Fairburn, C. G. (1995). *Overcoming binge eating.* New York, NY: Guilford Press.

Fairburn, C. G. (2008). *Cognitive behavior therapy and eating disorders.* New York, NY: Guilford Press.

Fairburn, C. G., & Bohn, K. (2005). Eating disorder NOS (EDNOS): An example of the troublesome "not otherwise specified" (NOS) category in *DSM–IV. Behavior Research and Therapy, 43,* 691–701.

Fairburn, C. G., Marcus, M. D., & Wilson, G. T. (1993). Cognitive–behavior therapy for binge eating and bulimia nervosa: A comprehensive treatment manual. In C. G. Fairburn & G. T. Wilsons (Eds.), *Binge eating nature, assessment, and treatment* (pp. 361–404). New York, NY: Guilford Press.

Gallagher, R. P., Golin, A., & Kelleher, K. (1992). The personal, career, and learning skills needs of college students. *Journal of College Student Development, 33,* 301–309.

Gleaves, D., Lowe, M. R., Green, B. A., Cororve, M. B., & Williams, T. L. (2000). Do anorexia and bulimia nervosa occur on a continuum? A taxometric analysis. *Behavior Therapy, 31,* 195–219.

Hinkle, S. (1994). The *DSM–IV*: Prognosis and implications for mental health counselors. *Journal of Mental Health Counseling, 16,* 174–183.

Hoek, H. W. (2006). Incidence, prevalence and mortality of anorexia nervosa and other eating disorders. *Current Opinion in Psychiatry, 19,* 389–394.

Klemchuck, H. P., Hutchinson, C. B., & Frank, R. I. (1990). Body dissatisfaction and eating-related problems on campus: Usefulness of the Eating Disorder Inventory with a nonclinical population. *Journal of Counseling Psychology, 37,* 292–305.

Keel, P. K., Brown, T. A., Holm-Denoma, & Bodell, L. P. (2011). Comparison of *DSM–IV* versus proposed *DSM–5* diagnostic criteria for eating disorders: Reduction of eating disorder not otherwise specified and validity. *International Journal of Eating Disorders, 44,* 553–560.

Koszewski, W. M., Newell, G. K., & Higgins, J. J. (1990). Effect of a nutrition education program on the eating attitudes and behaviors of college women. *Journal of College Student Development, 31,* 203–210.

Lewinsohn, P. M., Seeley, J. R., Moerk, K. C., & Striegel-Moore, R. H. (2002). Gender differences in eating disorder symptoms in young adults. *International Journal of Eating Disorders, 32,* 426–440.

Linehan, M. (1993). *Skills training manual for treating borderline personality disorder.* New York, NY: Guilford Press.

Mathers, C. D., Vos, E. T, Stevenson, C. E., & Begg, S. J. (2000). The Australian Burden of Disease Study: Measuring the loss of health from diseases, injuries, and risk factors. *Medical Journal of Australia, 172,* 592–596

Matusek, J. A., Wendt, S. J., & Wiseman, C. V. (2004). Dissonance thin-ideal and didactic healthy behavior eating disorder prevention programs: Results from a controlled trial. *International Journal of Eating Disorders, 36,* 376–388.

Miller, G. A., & Rice, K. G. (1993). A factor analysis of a university counseling center problem checklist. *Journal of College Student Development, 34,* 98–102.

Miller, W. R., & Rollnick, S. (1991). *Motivational interviewing: Preparing people to change addictive behavior.* New York, NY: Guilford Press.

National Institute for Health and Clinical Excellence. (2004). *Eating disorders—Core interventions in the treatment and management of anorexia, bulimia nervosa, and related eating disorders* (Clinical Guideline No. 9). London, England: Author. Retrieved from www.nice.org.uk/guidance/CG9

Neumark-Sztainer, D. (2005). Can we simultaneously work toward the prevention of obesity and eating disorders in children and adolescents? *International Journal of Eating Disorders, 38,* 220–227.

Nevonen, L., & Broberg, A. G. (2005). A comparison of sequenced individual and group psychotherapy for eating disorder not otherwise specified. *European Eating Disorders Review, 13,* 29–27.

Ousley, L., Cordero, E. D., & White, S. (2008). Eating disorders and body image of undergraduate men. *Journal of American College Health, 56,* 617–621.

Park, D. C. (2007). Eating disorders: A call to arms. *American Psychologist, 62,* 158.

Peck, L. D., & Lightsey, O. R., Jr. (2008). The eating disorder continuum, self-esteem, and perfectionism. *Journal of Counseling & Development, 86,* 184–192.

Prochaska, J. O., DiClemente, C. C., & Norcross, J. C. (1992). In search of how people change: Applications to addictive behaviors. *American Psychologist, 47,* 1102–1114.

Rhodes, C. (2003). *Life inside the "thin" cage: A personal look into the hidden world of the chronic dieter.* Colorado Springs, CO: WaterBrook Press.

Rich, S. S., & Thomas, C. R. (2008). Body mass index, disordered eating behavior, and acquisition of health information: Examining ethnicity and weight-related issues in a college population. *Journal of American College Health, 56,* 623–628.

Rodin, J., Silberstein, L. R., & Streigel-Moore, R. H. (1984). Women and weight: A normative discontent. In T. B. Sonderegger (Ed.), *Nebraska Symposium on Motivation: Vol. 32. Psychology and gender* (pp. 267–307). Lincoln: University of Nebraska Press.

Schwitzer, A. M., Bergholtz, K., Dore, T., & Salimi, L. (1998). Eating disorders among college women: Prevention, education, and treatment responses. *Journal of American College Health, 46,* 199–207.

Schwitzer, A. M., Hatfield, T., Jones, A. R., Duggan, M. H., Jurgens, J., & Winninger, A. (2008). Confirmation among college women: The eating disorders not otherwise specified diagnostic profile. *Journal of American College Health, 56,* 607–615.

Schwitzer, A. M., & Rodriguez, L. E. (2002). Understanding and responding to eating disorders among college women during the first-college year. *Journal of the First-Year Experience & Students in Transition, 14,* 41–64.

Schwitzer, A. M., Rodriguez, L. E., Thomas, C., & Salimi, L. (2001). The eating disorders NOS diagnostic profile among college women. *Journal of American College Health, 49,* 157–166.

Schwitzer, A. M., & Rubin, L. C. (2012). *Diagnosis and treatment planning skills for mental health professionals: A popular culture casebook approach.* Thousand Oaks, CA: Sage.

Seligman, L. (2004). *Diagnosis and treatment planning in counseling* (3rd ed.). New York, NY: Plenum Press.

Shisslak, C. M., Crago, M., & Estes, L. (1995). The spectrum of eating disturbances. *International Journal of Eating Disorders, 18,* 209–219.

Stice, E. (2002). Risk and maintenance factors for eating pathology: A meta-analytic review. *Psychological Bulletin, 128,* 825–848.

Stice, E., Chase, A., Stormer, S., & Appel, A. (2001). A randomized trial of a dissonance-based eating disorder prevention program. *International Journal of Eating Disorders, 29,* 247–262.

Stice, E., Gau, J., Presnell, K., & Shaw, H. (2007). Testing mediators of intervention effects in randomized controlled trials: An evaluation of two eating disorder prevention programs. *Journal of Consulting and Clinical Psychology, 75,* 20–32.

Stice, E., & Hoffman, E. (2004). Eating disorder prevention programs. In J. K. Thompson (Ed.), *Handbook of eating disorders and obesity* (pp. 33–57). Hoboken, NJ: Wiley.

Stout, E. J., & Frame, M. W. (2004). Body image disorder in adolescent males: Strategies for school counselors. *Professional School Counseling, 8,* 176–181.

Striegel-Moore, R. H., & Bulik, C. M. (2007). Risk factors for eating disorders. *American Psychologist, 62,* 181–198.

Talleyrand, R. M. (2010). Eating disorders in African American girls: Implications for counselors. *Professional School Counseling, 8,* 176–181.

Telch, C. F., Agras, W., & Linehan, M. M. (2000). Group dialectical behavior therapy for binge-eating disorder: A preliminary, uncontrolled trial. *Behavior Therapy, 31,* 569–582.

Tsai, C.-Y., Hoerr, S. L., & Song, W. O. (1998). Dieting behavior of Asian college women attending a U.S. university. *Journal of American College Health, 46,* 163–168.

Vitousek, K., Watson, S., & Wilson, G. T. (1998). Enhancing motivation for change in treatment-resistant eating disorders. *Clinical Psychology Review, 18,* 391–420.

Wilson, G. T., Grilo, C. M., & Vitousek, K. M. (2007). Psychological treatment of eating disorders. *American Psychologist, 62,* 199–216.

Wittichen, H. U., & Jacobi, F. (2005). Size and burden of mental disorders in Europe—A critical review and appraisal of 27 studies. *European Neuropsychopharmacology,* 15, 357–376.

Wonderlich, S. A., Joiner, T. E., Jr., Keel, P., Williamson, D. A., & Crosby, R. D. (2007). Eating disorder diagnoses: Empirical approaches to classification. *American Psychologist, 62,* 167–180.

Yamamiya, Y., Cash, T. F., Melnyk, S. E., Posavac, H. D., & Posavac, S. S. (2005). Women's exposure to thin-and-beautiful media images: Body image effects of media-ideal internalization and impact-reduction interventions. *Body Image, 2,* 74–80.

Yost, M. R., & Smith, L. A. (2012). When does it cross the line? College women's perceptions of the threshold between normal eating and eating disorders. *Journal of College Student Development, 53,* 163–167.

165

Section 3

# Effective Prevention and Early Intervention for Eating Disorders and Obesity

## Chapter 8

# Preventing
# Childhood Obesity

*Janet A. Lydecker, Elizabeth Cotter, Rachel W. Gow,*
*Nichole R. Kelly, and Suzanne E. Mazzeo*

Nearly one third of youths in the United States are overweight and, of these, 17% are obese (Ogden, Carroll, Curtin, Lamb, & Flegal, 2010). Among youths, overweight and obesity are defined using body mass index (BMI) percentiles. Values above the 85th percentile are classified as overweight, and those above the 95th percentile are considered obese (Barlow, 2007). Obesity in children and adolescents is associated with negative physical and psychosocial comorbidities that decrease quality of life and increase risk for adult obesity and associated chronic health conditions, including coronary heart disease, Type 2 diabetes, certain cancers, hypertension, stroke, liver disease, and sleep apnea (National Heart, Lung and Blood Institute, 1998). Approximately 70% of obese youths have at least one risk factor for heart disease (Freedman, Zuguo, Srinivasan, Berenson, & Dietz, 2007) and are more likely than their peers to have prediabetes or diabetes (Centers for Disease Control and Prevention, 2011b). In addition to these physical comorbidities, pediatric obesity is linked to psychosocial issues that include depression, anxiety, and disordered eating. Moreover, the number of overweight and obese individuals has increased dramatically in the past few decades. To address the pediatric obesity epidemic, prevention efforts are urgently needed.

Biological, psychological, sociocultural, and environmental factors influence whether an individual is at risk for becoming overweight or obese. For example, metabolic mechanisms, endocrine disorders, stress, or neighborhood safety might increase or decrease an individual's relative risk of becoming overweight. Environmental factors are among the most important to consider for prevention because of their widespread influence. The U.S. culture creates a toxic environment for maintaining a healthy weight (i.e., with food

169

and activity conditions that make it difficult to avoid weight gain; Brownell & Horgen, 2004). Furthermore, providing effective interventions is difficult in that dieting and weight loss treatments are generally not effective over the long term and may lead to disordered eating, weight cycling, or failure to lose sufficient weight to mitigate physical comorbidities (Brownell, Schwartz, Puhl, Henderson, & Harris, 2009). Prevention assumes that individuals have some degree of susceptibility to obesity and would benefit from medical and psychosocial interventions to counter that susceptibility. Prevention has multiple levels: primary, secondary, and tertiary. Primary prevention is universal treatment: all individuals receive the programming. For example, primary prevention occurs in schools when all students receive information about nutritional guidelines. Policy can serve as a primary prevention strategy when state or federal policies seek to promote healthful behavior. Secondary prevention addresses subsamples of the population who are at greater risk for becoming overweight or obese or who are at risk for negative medical or psychosocial consequences of obesity. For example, borderline overweight BMI, less healthy dietary or physical activity habits, or a strong family history of obesity are risk factors (Daniels et al., 2005). Tertiary prevention comes after the problem and seeks to prevent worsening severity or negative consequences. In this chapter, we focus on primary and secondary prevention.

Cultural factors play a role in pediatric obesity and are addressed throughout this chapter. These factors include race, ethnicity, socioeconomic status, age and gender, among others, and must be considered in pediatric obesity prevention (Freedman, Khan, Serdula, Ogden, & Dietz, 2006). For example, African American youths may value traditional soul foods high in fat and salt and might view more healthful eating as giving up a part of their cultural heritage (Airhihenbuwa et al., 1996; James, 2004). Likewise, various cultural factors may influence the financial resources that families can invest in food and activity, neighborhood safety, patient–provider communication efficacy and style, perceived norms about physical activity, and ideal body size and shape, among others. Because the nature of prevention programming is far reaching, providers must proactively seek to include culturally relevant material targeted to their intended recipients.

In this chapter, we describe current prevention programming for pediatric obesity and offer effective strategies for counselors working with individuals, families, and schools. We focus on prevention rather than treatment because prevention can be more far reaching than treatment and aims to avoid health problems that occur with obesity. First, we address primary prevention, or universal prevention programming aimed at improving the health of all children. The primary prevention section covers strategies that occur in public settings including schools, government, and the community. Next, we address secondary prevention, or prevention programming that targets youths at risk for becoming obese or developing obesity-related health problems. In this section, we review the interdisciplinary approach to prevention and specific strategies for counselors working with individuals, groups, and families. We review motivational interviewing and parental role modeling in depth. Last, we present clinical considerations and a list of resources for counselors who are engaged in preventing pediatric obesity.

# Primary Prevention

Given the potential health risks associated with obesity (Ballard-Barbash, Berrigan, Potischman, & Dowling, 2010; Ogden et al., 2010) and the link between youth overweight and adult obesity (Freedman et al., 2005; Guo, Wu, Chumlea, & Roche, 2002), prevention of pediatric overweight and obesity should be a key public health focus. The World Health Organization (2012) has recommended that obesity be seen as a population concern, as opposed to an individual problem, and suggested that effective prevention will involve all sectors of society (e.g., schools, family, media, community organizations).

## Public Perceptions of Obesity Prevention Efforts

A shift in public attitudes appears to be ongoing regarding obesity prevention efforts. Public perceptions of the seriousness of pediatric obesity are rising, leading to increased support for obesity prevention (Brownell, 2005; Evans, Finkelstein, Kamerow, & Renaud, 2005; Morin & Roy, 2011). The public particularly supports policies involving the promotion of healthy foods in school vending machines, increased time for physical education (PE), increased education about healthy eating and physical activity, restriction of advertisements geared toward youths that promote unhealthy foods, and mandated placement of health ratings and nutrition information on restaurant menus (Evans et al., 2005). Individuals' beliefs about the primary causes of obesity also play a role in their level of support for obesity policy (Barry, Brescoll, Brownell, & Schlesinger, 2009; Oliver & Lee, 2005). For example, individuals who perceive obesity as a problem with self-control or a lack of personal responsibility are less likely to support public policy prevention than those who see obesity as resulting from societal problems, such as a toxic food and physical activity environment.

## Role of School Systems

Schools are positioned to play an integral role in primary obesity prevention efforts. Schools have access to many students and have the capacity to change policies that affect youths' nutrition and physical activity. Schools can also provide education for their students about eating and exercise and provide outreach to parents. In this section, we review primary prevention related to school meals, physical activity, and BMI screening information for parents and review existing programs that use a comprehensive approach to prevention.

### School Meals

Most youths do not consume diets that meet the recommended nutritional guidelines (Krebs-Smith, Guenther, Subar, Kirkpatrick, & Dodd,

2010). Access to energy-dense foods and sugar-sweetened beverages may facilitate eating habits that increase obesity risk. The Healthy, Hunger Free Kids Act of 2010 is one primary prevention effort designed to enhance the nutritional standards of school meals. This act requires school meals to be consistent with the latest dietary recommendations, including availability of fruits and vegetables, offering whole grains, and preparation of foods without trans fat. Counselors can work with policymakers on laws such as this one, which increase the presence of healthy food choices in the school environment.

Students participating in school-based nutrition intervention programs (examples of which are discussed in the following paragraph) eat more fruits and vegetables than their peers (Howerton et al., 2007), supporting the link between availability of fruits and vegetables and their consumption (Howerton et al., 2007; Jago, Baranowski, & Baranowski, 2007). For instance, introducing salad bars as a lunch option in schools increased overall fruit and vegetable intake among youths over a 2-year period (Joshi & Beery, 2007; Slusser, Cumberland, Browdy, Lange, & Neumann, 2007). The Fresh Fruit and Vegetable Program in Texas schools, which provided fresh snacks, led to significant increases in consumption of fruit and 100% fruit juice but yielded no differences in vegetable intake (Davis, Cullen, Watson, Konarik, & Radcliffe, 2009). Garden-based nutrition education programs in schools also have the potential to increase fruit and vegetable consumption (McAleese & Rankin, 2007; Morris & Zidenberg-Cherr, 2002), although more research is needed on their efficacy (Robinson-O'Brien, Story, & Heim, 2009). Counselors can play a role in increasing youths' motivation to eat fruits and vegetables and encourage more regular consumption of these foods.

Vending machines remain widely available in schools, particularly middle and high schools (Finkelstein, Hill, & Whitaker, 2008). Unfortunately, youths tend to choose less healthy options from vending machines, even when healthier options are available (Park, Sappenfield, Huang, Sherry, & Bensyl, 2010). In addition, youths are less likely to buy school lunch when they have access to vending machine snacks, particularly youths who identify as African American or Hispanic (Park et al., 2010). Removal of vending machines that offer unhealthy items or replacing these items with only healthy products could be included in school-based obesity prevention programs. As with encouraging consumption of fruits and vegetables, counselors can also work with youths to facilitate healthy food choices when vending machines are accessible.

*Physical Activity*
Youths between the ages of 6 and 17 should get at least 60 minutes of physical activity daily (Centers for Disease Control and Prevention, 2011a). Schools can help ensure youths meet these recommendations through regular PE classes. Currently, no federal laws require PE in schools, although a majority of states mandate it (National Association for Sport and Physical Educa-

tion & American Heart Association, 2010). One barrier to offering more frequent physical activity in schools is concern that PE classes and recess interfere with academic curricula. However, evidence has suggested that regular PE does not negatively affect academic performance (Trudeau & Shephard, 2008), but does improve youths' physical fitness level (Sallis et al., 1997; Strong et al., 2005; Zaza, Briss, & Harris, 2005). Moreover, PE classes effectively increase physical activity for students of both genders and across all races and socioeconomic groups (Khan et al., 2009).

### BMI Screening

In 2005, the Institute of Medicine recommended schools calculate youths' BMI and report the information to parents as a method of preventing obesity. This practice originated to track the effectiveness of ongoing school obesity prevention programming and to engage with overweight children and their families (Ikeda, Crawford, & Woodward-Lopez, 2006; Nihiser et al., 2007; Story, Nanney, & Schwartz, 2009). However, opinions on BMI screening are mixed because of their unclear effectiveness (Nihiser et al., 2007) and concerns about potential stigmatization (Ikeda et al., 2006). Specifically, peers might tease youths about their BMI status, youths might self-stigmatize and have lowered self-esteem, or parents might shame children and promote unhealthy dieting behaviors. If BMI screenings are conducted at schools, safeguards should be in place so that information is shared in a sensitive, confidential, and nonstigmatizing manner (Nihiser et al., 2009). Alternatively, measuring the health of the school environment as a whole, as opposed to focusing on individual youths, could avoid this harm (Maclean et al., 2010). School health assessment could include whether school meals meet federal dietary requirements, whether all youths have 30 minutes of physical activity per day, whether other physical activity opportunities are available (e.g., after-school programs, intramurals, recess), and whether sales of unhealthy foods as part of school fundraising and the use of food as a reward in the classroom or at special school events are avoided (e.g., ice cream parties for completing testing). Schools with policies that promote healthy dietary intake and limit availability of high-calorie foods of low nutritional quality are less likely to have overweight students (Coffield, Metos, Utz, & Waitzman, 2011; Foster et al., 2008; Seo & Lee, 2012).

### Comprehensive Programming

School programs that address nutrition, physical activity, and psychosocial factors offer the most comprehensive prevention content. For example, the CATCH program (Coleman et al., 2005; Hoelscher et al., 2010), an intervention targeting schools with a large number of Hispanic students, included a focus on nutrition, physical education, and health curriculum. After 2 years, youths who participated in CATCH had significantly less weight gain than peers and were less likely to become overweight. Similarly, a school-based intervention in the Mid-Atlantic that consisted of school self-assessment, nutrition education and policy, social marketing, and parent outreach led to a 50% decrease in the number of youths who became overweight compared with control schools over the same 2-year time period (Foster et al., 2008).

In addition to the intervention content, several other factors influence the effectiveness of school-based obesity prevention programs. Gender appears to influence outcomes; girls respond better to programs based on social learning, and boys respond better to programs that enable physical activity (Kropski, Keckley, & Jensen, 2008). Age differences are also evident; older children (ages 10–14) have better outcomes than younger children (ages 7–10), perhaps because older children may have increased control over their lifestyle behaviors. School prevention programs should be culturally adapted for their specific population to be most effective (Caballero et al., 2003; Peña, Dixon, & Taveras, 2012). Finally, given the strong influence of the home on children's weight-related behaviors, future directions for school-based programs should include an emphasis on the home environment as well.

## Role of Government Policy

The use of policy to alter the environments in which individuals make food choices can have a significant impact on the healthfulness of these decisions. A three-pronged approach for tackling obesity prevention at the policy level is recommended, involving "altering relative food prices, shifting exposure to food, and improving the image of healthy food while making unhealthy food less attractive" (Frieden, Dietz, & Collins, 2010, p. 357). Policies with these aims can target various aspects of the environment, including the media, food industry, and pricing.

### Media

Youths and adolescents are prime targets of food and beverage advertising in the United States. Advertisers spend an estimated $10 billion on food marketing to youths annually (McGinnis, Gootman, & Kraak, 2006). Most of this marketing is contrary to recommendations for a healthy diet and instead focuses on energy-dense junk foods. More than half of the advertisements youths view promote foods, particularly fast food, sugar-sweetened beverages, and low-nutrient snack foods (McGinnis et al., 2006; Story & French, 2004), which is particularly troublesome because youths have difficulty distinguishing between entertainment, information, and the persuasive intent behind advertisements (Kunkel et al., 2004). Government policy interventions for obesity prevention could include restrictions on child-targeted advertisements for unhealthy junk foods (Graff, Kunkel, & Mermin, 2012) or the implementation of media messages that promote healthier physical activity and nutrition behaviors.

### Food Industry

Policy could also mandate that the food industry take steps to promote healthier eating. Fast food and other restaurants could include nutrition information on all food products, and the number of healthier options could be expanded. Indeed, although more research is needed on the impact of nutrition information labeling, some studies have indicated that individuals choose meals with significantly fewer calories when nutrition information is displayed (Bassett et al., 2008; Roberto, Larsen, Agnew, Baik, & Brownell, 2010), although other research has found no change (Elbel, Kersh, Brescoll, & Dixon, 2009). In addition, food labels could be changed to represent the actual amounts contained in the package (e.g., an entire bottle of soda). These policies would be beneficial to counselors, who could use nutrition information as tools to empower youths to make healthy decisions about dietary intake.

### Pricing

Individuals' consumption patterns are largely dependent on the cost of foods. Currently, the price per calorie of foods containing excess dietary fat and sugar is less expensive than the cost per calorie of healthful foods such as fruits and vegetables (Drewnowski & Darmon, 2005). Implementing food taxes on less healthy, energy-dense foods could significantly affect youths' weight (Powell & Chaloupka, 2009). Junk food taxes are comparable to cigarette taxes, which have led to decreased adult smoking (Levy, Nikolayev, Mumford, & Compton, 2005). Brownell, Fairley, et al. (2009) supported taxes on sugar-sweetened beverages, such as soda. They suggested that revenue generated through these taxes could support obesity prevention programming or health care costs for those who are uninsured. Older children may be particularly affected by this taxation because they are likely to use their limited income on snack foods and leisure. Counselors could also work with youths to enhance awareness of the financial and physical costs of energy-dense, low-nutrient foods compared with the costs of healthy foods.

## Community Interventions

Families' access to healthy food and adequate physical activity can depend in part on their neighborhood. Primary prevention at the community level aims to increase the availability of fresh fruits and vegetables and increase the safety of surroundings. Counselors can also aid in prevention that aims to help families think of solutions to these barriers.

### Food Access

A major barrier to successful obesity prevention is community access to grocery stores. When healthier food options found at larger food retailers or farmers' markets are not readily available, community members may shop primarily at convenience stores or fast food restaurants, where they are likely to purchase energy-dense foods high in sugar and fat. This is particularly common in low-income neighborhoods, which are sometimes referred to as *food deserts* (Beaulac, Kristjansson, & Cummins, 2009). Assisting older children and caregivers with making healthy food choices within the accessible options could lessen this barrier.

### Physical Activity Access

A barrier to physical activity is neighborhood safety. Unsafe neighborhoods lead to decreased opportunity for youths to be physically active outside

175

and increased screen time (Burdette & Whitaker, 2005). Programs such as Safe Routes to School (Watson & Dannenberg, 2008) focus on removing the barriers that prevent youths from walking or biking to school. Helping youths and parents to establish safe times and spaces where youths can play or brainstorming active alternatives to screen time within the accessible options could help prevent pediatric obesity.

## Multicultural Considerations

Multicultural factors are important to consider when providing primary obesity prevention because of the universal nature of this prevention. Although all individuals can benefit from improving healthy eating and increasing physical activity, counselors should know the audience receiving their intervention and adapt the prevention effort so that it is relevant for the youths receiving the programming. We review cultural factors related to food and physical activity in subsequent paragraphs because of their particular relevance to obesity prevention.

### Culture and Food

Racial and ethnic minorities in the United States are disproportionately affected by obesity, which may be related to risk factors that occur in childhood (Dixon, Peña, & Taveras, 2012). African American and Hispanic youths eat more fast food and drink more sugar-sweetened beverages than their White peers. Socioeconomic status also plays a role: Families of low socioeconomic status may have less access to healthier food options in their neighborhood or be unable to afford healthier foods because of their generally higher cost. Obesity prevention programming must be culturally relevant to be effective, and healthy, low-cost alternatives to typical food choices should be placed within a family's cultural framework (Davis, Ventura, Cook, Gyllenhammer, & Gatto, 2011; Peña et al., 2012). Traditional meals can be modified to reduce sugar, calories, and total fat while still including culturally relevant items. For example, families can participate in a taste test that compares a favorite food such as banana bread when it is traditionally prepared with the same food with healthy substitutions such as applesauce instead of oil.

### Culture and Physical Activity

Risk factors related to physical activity and culture include youths' television viewing practices and sedentary behavior (Dixon et al., 2012). Another central cultural factor related to physical activity is access to recreational facilities. Families who do not perceive their neighborhoods to be safe for children to play outside are likely to encourage sedentary leisure activities. Safety concerns often include exposure to violence, proximity of sex offenders, or heavy traffic. Likewise, perceptions that recreational facilities are not accessible or affordable are often a barrier to physical activity (Gordon-Larsen et al., 2004). Obesity prevention programming must address these barriers with individuals, families, and communities so that realistic goals and solutions can be developed collaboratively. For example, counselors can recommend low- or no-cost physical activities such as hopscotch, jump rope, or dancing to the radio (Gordon-Larsen et al., 2004). Other cultural considerations include perceptions of whether one's ethnic or racial group traditionally participates in sports or physical activities (Kumanyika, 2008). Perceptions about whether physical activity is leisure or work also warrant attention so that providers can work within youths' cultural framework. Other factors, such as aversion to sweating and the complexity of hair styling and care (Barnes et al., 2007) can also be a barrier to physical activity that can be misperceived as a lack of motivation. Working to develop collaborative, culturally relevant solutions to these barriers can help counselors understand youths' ambivalence and empower them to find alternative solutions.

## Secondary Obesity Prevention

Secondary obesity prevention includes individual- and group-oriented programs that target youths who are more likely than their peers to become overweight or obese (Daniels et al., 2005). This programming can occur in various settings, including medical or mental health settings, churches, schools, and after-school care. Although secondary prevention may be more time and cost intensive than primary prevention, it provides an opportunity to individualize treatment and barriers. Because pediatric obesity is linked to many psychosocial concerns, it is critical for secondary prevention to begin with an evaluation of medical, psychosocial, family, cultural, and community factors that may facilitate or impair prevention. For example, sleep difficulties and fatigue may discourage youths from regular physical activity or healthy eating, and sleep hygiene could warrant inclusion in prevention programming. Similarly, psychosocial impairments such as social anxiety, body dissatisfaction, or depression may prevent youths from exercising around others. Youths and families may also benefit from skills to prepare culturally traditional foods in a healthier manner, assertiveness to navigate eating and exercise barriers, or strategies to cope with weight-related teasing.

Goals of secondary prevention depend, in part, on BMI status. Goals for youths at risk for overweight are to improve lifestyle factors that influence weight, including energy consumption and expenditure. For overweight youths, recommended goals include weight maintenance until BMI is below the 85th percentile or until weight gain slows (Barlow, 2007; Daniels et al., 2005; Spear et al., 2007). Obese youths and youths with comorbid health concerns would benefit from a more structured weight management approach (e.g., a program with a prescribed diet and regular weigh-ins). We do not review these approaches in this chapter because they are generally beyond the scope of secondary prevention.

### Interdisciplinary Approach

Given the complex array of factors that contribute to obesity (e.g., genetic, environmental, psychological, physiological), prevention approaches involving multiple professions are recommended (Grimes-Robison & Evans, 2008; McGovern et al., 2008). An interdisciplinary obesity prevention team typically includes a registered dietician, exercise physiologist, medical physician, and mental health professional such as a counselor. The registered dietician and exercise physiologist provide education and skill building (e.g., improving food choices, meal preparation, type and intensity of exercise). Medical evaluations can determine whether genetic or endocrine disorders contribute to a youth's weight and also track obesity-related medical comorbidities (e.g., hypertension, hypercholesterolemia). Although an interdisciplinary approach is recommended, it may not always be feasible, and counselors may need to provide education in addition to behavioral support. Recommended resources are included at the end of this chapter, which may aid in education about nutrition and physical activity. The role of counselors is critical in addressing any gaps between recommendations made by medical, nutrition, and exercise experts and engagement of the patient in those health behaviors (Grimes-Robison & Evans, 2008). Education alone is insufficient to produce sustainable change among individuals and families with overweight and obese youths (Wilfley et al., 2007). Counseling techniques are the focus of this section; however, they are most effective when they complement prevention efforts from nutrition, exercise, and medical disciplines (Kamath et al., 2008).

Counselors meet with individuals, groups, or families regularly to focus on goal setting, monitoring, skill building, and evaluating progress and readiness to change (Wilfley, Kass, & Kolko, 2011). In this context, an individual can also identify barriers to behavioral change and develop solutions most suitable for his or her specific family. Health behavior change succeeds when counselors assist individuals to address environmental and personal factors that influence behavior (Bandura, 1986; Han, Lawlor, & Kimm, 2010). These factors include knowledge, expectancies, modeling, reinforcement, and self-efficacy. Counselors also assess for social problems such as teasing, rejection and loneliness, and develop appropriate goals and strategies to increase social support because youths' social functioning is a critical factor in promoting and sustaining health behavior change (Wilfley et al., 2011).

### Counseling Support for Nutrition

Nutrition experts provide education about youths' dietary needs, portion sizes, and food choices (e.g., decreasing availability of fast food and sugar-sweetened beverages). Behavioral support can help individuals or families make the changes recommended by the dietician. One technique focuses on making specific, measurable, achievable, realistic, and timely (SMART) goals ("What Would You Do," n.d.). For example, when addressing a 13-year-old girl who wants to lose 20 pounds, a provider might say, "That seems like a good long-term goal but let's think about shorter term goals that focus on what you'll actually do to lose the weight and keep you healthy." Then, he or she would help the adolescent create a realistic, behavior-focused goal such as increasing fruit and vegetable intake by one serving per day. SMART goals help to encourage youths and create confidence that long-term goals can be met because they achieve reinforcing goals en route to the long-term goal. Another goal-setting strategy breaks goals into steps that need to be in place to reach the goal. Counselors should encourage youths to keep an open mind and be flexible about goals so they can be changed if the current goal is not feasible.

One of the most effective behavioral interventions for individuals making dietary changes is self-monitoring. When youths and families track the food they eat on paper diaries or online logs, they increase their awareness of their eating and have a record of their progress. Self-monitoring has been linked to BMI reduction in pediatric obesity at 12-month follow-up (Jelalian et al., 2010). Stimulus control is another strategy that is particularly helpful in reducing consumption of calorie-dense foods. For example, counselors might help families reduce the amount of unhealthy foods kept in the house or increase the accessibility of healthy foods (e.g., keeping cut vegetables ready in the refrigerator). Counselors can also help youths and families to avoid all-or-nothing thinking about foods and, rather, consider all foods as acceptable in moderation. This approach can help youths avoid feelings of hopelessness and get back on track during times when they are not following their behavioral plan. This approach also avoids dieting or restrictive eating, which can lead to overeating (Stice, Davis, Miller, & Marti, 2008). Similarly, to avoid eating-related shame, counselors can avoid referring to good and bad foods, instead referring to foods' health quality. Encouraging healthy food consumption reduces the potential stigma associated with making unhealthy foods off limits and also reduces cravings for unhealthy foods that can lead to overeating.

*Counseling Support for Physical Activity*

Exercise experts provide education and recommendations about the time and intensity of physical activity. Many of the techniques described for nutrition goals also apply to physical activity goals. For example, SMART goals can structure a series of physical activity–related challenges that gradually increase in duration and intensity (Daniels, Jacobson, McCrindle, Eckel, & Sanner, 2009; Epstein, Myers, Raynor, & Saelens, 1998). This approach will also help prevent injury or undue fatigue (Gutin, 2008). Counselors can also assist youths and families in selecting age-appropriate physical activities. Younger children may prefer active games, whereas some adolescents may do well with the adult model of exercising on machines or jogging (Daniels et al., 2005). An example of stimulus control might be storing a dog leash at the front door as a reminder to take walks.

One of the primary areas for mental health support is addressing barriers to physical activity goals. For example, one barrier to physical activity for youths might be peer involvement. Peers play a significant role in adolescents' decisions about trying out for a sport or engaging in regular physical activity (Ali, Amialchuk, & Heiland, 2011). Activity barriers for youths and families are often related to time and safety. The counselor can assist youths and families in developing solutions to these barriers. For example, if a family is busy with many evening activities, they can brainstorm ways to increase lifestyle activities, or opportunities for activity during regular daily events (e.g., taking the stairs instead of the elevator, parking further away from a store). Families can also create rules about screen time, or the amount of time youths spend looking at electronics (e.g., television, computer, games). Reducing sedentary behavior may be particularly important for young children, because adolescents are more resistant to changing this behavior (Kamath et al., 2008). Another barrier to following experts' physical activity and nutrition recommendations may be motivation to change. We review one strategy to address motivation in the following section.

## *Motivational Interviewing*

Motivational interviewing (MI) techniques are preferred interventions to increase and maintain motivation for healthy lifestyle behaviors (Miller & Rollnick, 2002). Motivation has three components: readiness to change a specific behavior, importance of making the change, and confidence in one's ability to make a change. In the area of pediatric obesity, parents' reported confidence is most predictive of completing prevention programming and reducing youths' BMI (Gunnarsdottir, Njardvik, Olafsdottir, Craighead, & Bjarnason, 2011). Mental health professionals such as counselors are ideally suited to provide MI interventions within interdisciplinary teams because of their training in goal setting and behavior change (Wilfley et al., 2011).

Applications of MI to pediatric obesity prevention programs appear efficacious (Pollak et al., 2009; Walpole, Dettmer, Morrongiello, McCrindle, & Hamilton, 2011; Wilson et al., 2002). MI is an empathetic style of counseling that can be incorporated into counselors' existing approaches. Skills include reflective listening, shared decision making, rolling with resistance, and eliciting change talk. Providers can use MI, together with clinical judgment about age-appropriate approaches, to increase youths' and families' readiness to change health-related behaviors and motivation to stick with those changes. In the subsequent paragraphs, we briefly review the three stages of the MI approach as applied to pediatric obesity prevention. Links to complete manuals and intervention strategies are provided in the Recommended Resources section at the end of this chapter.

### *Following*

Counselors begin prevention programming by assessing youths' and families' readiness to change. This stage of MI is termed *following* because the youth or family takes the lead in the identification of changes and concerns. Individuals may seek obesity prevention programming from a counselor at any stage of change and may move fluidly among precontemplation (not thinking about change), contemplation (thinking about it), action (actually changing), and maintenance (Prochaska & DiClemente, 2005). Open-ended questions and reflective listening allow youths and their families to communicate how ready they are to change. For example, a counselor may greet a child by asking, "What brings you here today?"; listening to the child's response; and reflecting, "You are here because your pediatrician expressed concerns about your health and now you're concerned as well" or "You don't particularly want to be here but your parents thought it might be a good idea." Reflection can take several forms. Simple reflection is the most basic technique; reflecting the youth's thoughts and feelings communicates acknowledgement and permits further exploration rather than enhancing defensiveness. Amplified reflection exaggerates the thoughts or feelings using empathy, not sarcasm, to further encourage exploration and questioning whether the thoughts or feelings are in line with the youth's values. Double-sided reflection communicates both the good and the not-so-good aspects of change to widen the youth's perspective.

If the youth does not express concern about obesity or his or her health behaviors, the counselor can raise awareness of potential problems. The counselor does this using a light and positive approach, focusing on unhealthy behaviors related to obesity. If the youth expresses concerns about obesity, the counselor can explore ambivalence to change (e.g., the good and not-so-good things about changing). When addressing ambivalence, the counselor "rolls with resistance." The reflection skills described previously can assist with this. Additionally, the counselor can shift the youth's focus away from a barrier to an issue he or she is more amenable to discussing. The counselor can reframe ambivalence by empathically acknowledging the validity of the youth's thoughts and feelings and offering a new meaning or interpretation (e.g., "Walking with your mom several times a week will certainly be tough, and there is no doubt that you will miss spending time with your friends after school. I also know, based on what you said earlier, that it really means a lot to you to overcome difficulties and meet goals you set for yourself. Like when you raised your C in math to an A; meeting this goal really helped you feel more confident"). Alternatively, the counselor can defend the counterchange side of ambivalence to encourage the youth to consider the pro-change side and feel heard. Ultimately, the youth, family, and counselor work together to identify what behaviors can be addressed, thereby moving into the guiding phase of MI.

### Guiding

The purpose of the guiding phase is to facilitate youths' and families' adoption of goals and to increase self-efficacy for change. Individuals are more likely to change their behavior if they voice plans to do so themselves (Miller & Rollnick, 2002). To encourage this change talk, counselors can use activities that help youths think about where they are in readiness to change and what would have to occur for them to increase their readiness (e.g., importance–confidence rulers). Another example of a guiding activity is having youths write their values on index cards and sort them according to how important each is to them (i.e., personal values card sort). This form of self-assessment elicits change talk when youths perceive the discrepancy between stated values and unhealthy behaviors; it is also a helpful tool for counselors to return to when they confront subsequent ambivalence to change.

### Directing

After the youth has made a behavioral decision, the focus shifts toward helping him or her make concrete action plans, set goals, explore the next steps, problem solve, and identify barriers, solutions, and facilitators to goals. As with earlier phases, the counselor first reflects what he or she heard from the youth and then asks permission to give information or advice. For example, a counselor might say, "You had one really great idea. Do you mind if I share a few more that have worked for some of my patients in the past?" Any information or advice offered uses the youth's words and ideas as much as possible to keep him or her involved and central to the change process. Suggestive phrasing (e.g., "could work" or "might consider") rather than definitive phrasing facilitates youths' playing more active and autonomous roles in their own change process.

## Group and School Approaches

Many of the techniques described previously function in individual or group formats. A group format reduces the opportunity to individualize material but is more cost effective and easily disseminated. A group also offers a developmentally appropriate forum for adolescents to learn from peers with similar health behavior change goals (Jelalian et al., 2010). Obesity prevention groups have been conducted in churches (Resnicow, Taylor, Baskin, & McCarty, 2005), school theater programs (Neumark-Sztainer et al., 2009), and after-school programs (Klesges et al., 2010). Although school-based secondary prevention programming is increasing in popularity, success rates are variable (American Dietetic Association, 2006). Moreover, although pediatric obesity is a widespread problem, concerns about (unintentionally) stigmatizing overweight and obese youths in prevention programs remain (Daníelsdóttir, Burgard, & Oliver-Pyatt, 2009). Thus, primary prevention programming (vs. secondary prevention) focused on health, not weight, is recommended for school settings (American Dietetic Association, 2006; Caballero, 2004; Fowler-Brown & Kahwati, 2004).

## Family Approaches

Family-based pediatric overweight prevention programs are more successful than those that target youths exclusively (Epstein, Wing, Koeske, Andrasik, & Ossip, 1981; Epstein, Wing, Koeske, & Valoski, 1987; Golan & Crow, 2004b). Including parents is important because children depend on them to structure daily routines and the home environment. In particular, permissive and restrictive parenting styles have been associated with pediatric obesity risk (Faith et al., 2003; Gable & Lutz, 2000; Moens,

Braet, & Soetens, 2007). For example, when parents restrict food type and quantity, children have poorer self-regulation skills and are more likely to overeat (Birch, 2006; Birch & Davison, 2001). However, when parents are more permissive (i.e., monitor eating and activity levels less frequently), children eat fewer vegetables (Vereecken, Rovner, & Maes, 2010), consume more low-nutrient and energy-dense food (De Bourdeaudhuij, 1997; Klesges et al., 1983), engage in less physical activity (Arredondo et al., 2006), and are more sedentary (Gentile & Walsh, 2002). Parents and their children both appear to benefit from psychoeducation about parenting styles and discussion about contexts and developmental stages when different styles are appropriate in eating and physical activity-related situations (Daniels et al., 2005). In particular, counselors can discuss parenting styles related to the feeding relationship or the relationship between parent and child that centers on eating. Using the approach popularized by Satter (1996), providers should encourage parents to view their responsibilities as providing the meals and creating a healthy and welcoming eating environment. In turn, their children's responsibilities are to decide the amount of food they want to eat. This approach is thought to reduce stress at mealtimes and encourage learning through role modeling and trust.

*Role Modeling*

Children watch and learn from their parents' eating and exercise behaviors. Parental role modeling of healthy behaviors is one of the strongest predictors of weight reduction among overweight youths (Wrotniak, Epstein, Paluch, & Roemmich, 2005). Moreover, parents' modeling of fruit and vegetable consumption predicts youths' fruit and vegetable intake (Fisher, Mitchell, Smiciklas-Wright, & Birch, 2002; Wardle, Carnell, & Cooke, 2005). Problematic eating behaviors, such as restraint and disinhibition, can also be modeled by parents and linked to children's eating behaviors (Birch & Fisher, 2000; Contento, Zybert, & Williams, 2005). Parents create routines for the entire family that can include the presence or absence of structured family meals. Evidence has suggested that children who eat meals with their parents have healthier dietary intake than children who do not (Neumark-Sztainer, Hannan, Story, Croll, & Perry, 2003). Given the many barriers to regular family mealtimes, such as conflicting and busy schedules, television viewing, and media that encourage fast food meals (Brownell & Horgen, 2004), several successful prevention programs have helped parents establish regular meal schedules and provided strategies to prepare easy, healthy meals (Mazzeo, Gow, Stern, & Gerke, 2008; Wrotniak et al., 2005).

Similarly, parents model sedentary and active behaviors. Parents who exercise are more likely to have children who participate in physical activities (Neumark-Sztainer, Story, Hannan, Tharp, & Rex, 2003). Parental support is a powerful factor in increasing the activity levels of inactive children. Patterns of sedentary behavior are similar such that children of overweight parents show a preference for sedentary activities and are more likely than their peers to be sedentary (Sallis, Patterson, McKenzie, & Nader, 1988). Counselors can help parents increase their own physical activity and reduce sedentary behaviors to prevent pediatric obesity (Mazzeo et al., 2008). In particular, physical activity-related prevention should focus on young children, because activity decreases significantly, particularly among girls, during the transition to adolescence (Hampson, Andrews, Peterson, & Duncan, 2007; Kimm et al., 2002). Role modeling establishes positive images of physical activity for youths, which may help children maintain their athleticism over time (Hampson et al., 2007).

### Parents as Primary Targets for Prevention

Targeting parents exclusively for pediatric obesity prevention promotes health behavior change for the entire family rather than solely for the at-risk child (Golan & Crow, 2004a). If an overweight child becomes the "identified patient" in a family, this experience can have a negative impact on self-esteem (Golan, Weizman, Apter, & Fainaru, 1998). In contrast, when the whole family is involved, youths are less likely to resist change and more likely to adopt sustainable eating and activity patterns (Golan, Fainaru, & Weizman, 1998). Parent-only interventions offer the additional benefit of greater cost efficiency because resources are not needed for child interventionists (Golan, Kaufman, & Shahar, 2006).

One example of a parent-only pediatric obesity prevention program is Nourishing Our Understanding of Role modeling to Improve Support and Health (NOURISH; Mazzeo et al., 2008). NOURISH emphasizes role modeling healthy eating and exercise behaviors to foster the development of these behaviors in overweight youths. Caregivers participate in an intensive 6-week parent skills training group designed to be culturally relevant and address unique challenges facing lower socioeconomic status and primarily African American families. Pilot data have shown that families who participated in NOURISH had small but significant reductions in children's BMI percentile, whereas families in the control group showed increases in children's BMI percentile, which suggests that NOURISH may be a successful secondary prevention program.

Many of the techniques used in the NOURISH program are consistent with those described for individual youth, groups, and school settings. The benefit to a group setting for a parent-only intervention is the collaborative atmosphere this modality encourages. Parents empathize with each other and learn from others' challenges and successes. Parents in NOURISH have identified several barriers to adopting healthy eating and exercise behaviors. Common barriers include competing demands for limited resources such as time and money. For example, parents generally report knowing that they should eat fruits and vegetables but cite as barriers the expense of these items and their children's frequent refusal to eat them. Counselors can encourage parents to collectively brainstorm solutions or share successful experiences with one another. Providers present ideas for inexpensive, healthy meals and approaches for feeding selective eaters.

Parents also learn strategies described previously for individual and group prevention programming, such as stimulus control, goal setting, and self-monitoring. Additionally, parents learn limit setting around meals, aiming to establish regular family meals and snacks and discourage grazing behaviors. Limits around screen time are also set, with alternative activities encouraged instead. Consistent with prevention recommendations, parents also consult with nutrition experts during the group.

### Other Clinical Considerations for Prevention

In addition to the recommendations provided for individual, group, and family approaches, counselors should keep in mind several other clinical considerations while working to prevent pediatric obesity. In the following paragraphs, we address weight bias, technology, and working with adolescents.

#### Weight Bias

Weight bias is pervasive, even among professionals working in the obesity prevention sector (Bertakis & Azari, 2005; Washington, 2011) and may deter individuals and families from engaging in obesity prevention (Olson, Schumaker, & Yawn, 1994). Thus, providers must increase their awareness of their own biases regarding weight, which might include reflecting on whether they make assumptions about overweight individuals and those who have a history of unsuccessful health behavior change, and taking steps to challenge and change any such biases so they are not communicated to patients. Likewise, acknowledging societal weight bias increases empathy and facilitates discussion of how weight bias might influence youths and their families. With established obesity prevention programming, providers can minimize environmental weight bias by having furnishings and medical equipment that accommodate a range of body sizes and by using materials with images of youths of all sizes engaging in healthy behavior, among other strategies. Links to more information on these strategies are in the Recommended Resources section at the end of this chapter.

In addition to the counselor's efforts to decrease weight bias when interacting with youths and families, direct interventions related to media literacy can reduce perceived weight bias and increase youths' body image (Daníelsdóttir et al., 2009). Interventions with families or youths can focus on education about changes the media make to images (e.g., computerized editing), looking at advertisements to notice the discrepancy between the product being sold and the message being communicated, and talking about how the media do not show healthy people of all sizes.

#### Role of Technology

Researchers are beginning to investigate whether technology can assist with pediatric obesity prevention. Game-related technology has the potential to transform inactivity into education, motivation, and activity (Baranowski, Baranowski, Thompson, & Buday, 2011). For example, in one intervention, replacing sedentary video games with active games increased physical activity and reduced sedentary behavior and mindless snacking (Maddison et al., 2011). Internet-based prevention programming is another innovative format to investigate. The anonymity of the Internet may appeal to some youths, and accessibility could widen the dispersion of programming in rural settings. Text messaging and social networking sites may provide youth-friendly designs that facilitate self-monitoring and social support, which is particularly important among adolescents (Dowda, Dishman, Pfeiffer, & Pate, 2007; Salvy et al., 2009). Texting is teens' preferred means of communication, and nearly 73% of teens use social networking sites (Lenhart, Ling, Campbell, & Purcell, 2010; Lenhart, Purcell, Smith, & Zickuhr, 2010).

*Working With Adolescents*

Secondary obesity prevention may differ for adolescents compared with younger children. Developmentally, adolescents' drive for independence is increasing. Counselors can foster confidence regarding health behavior engagement by recognizing and supporting adolescents' emerging autonomy and maturity (e.g., encourage self-monitoring) while continuing to set limits and define boundaries. Teens are particularly vulnerable to media and peer messages regarding an ideal appearance as they undergo significant physical and social changes, and they describe the media as a key source of body image and appearance pressure (Peterson, Paulson, & Williams, 2007). Thus, secondary prevention efforts with adolescents need to be proactive in fostering positive body image and discouraging unhealthy weight control behaviors. Prevention for adolescents can also, as with that for younger children, involve the family to avoid stigmatization and facilitate behavior change. However, unlike pediatric obesity prevention with young children, adolescents need to be involved as well as their parents because of adolescents' developing autonomy (Barlow, 2007).

# Conclusion

Pediatric obesity is a public health issue of major concern to mental health providers. Currently, nearly one third of youths in the United States are overweight or obese, putting them at higher risk for various serious health problems (Ogden et al., 2010), emotional and psychological issues (Stern et al., 2006), and social stigmatization (Latner & Stunkard, 2003). Moreover, overweight youths are more likely to become obese adults, increasing their risk for obesity-related health concerns later in life (Ballard-Barbash et al., 2010; Eckel & Krauss, 1998). In addition, significant racial and ethnic disparities exist in pediatric obesity rates, necessitating the development of culturally relevant prevention efforts (Freedman et al., 2006). Given the prevalence of pediatric obesity in the United States, along with the associated negative health and psychosocial consequences, prevention efforts are greatly needed, and counselors must play an integral role in these efforts for prevention to be effective.

Prevention of pediatric obesity is clearly complex because a number of factors influence youths' eating and weight-related behaviors, including the environment, individual differences, cultural factors, and familial patterns. Therefore, singular approaches that focus only on one aspect of obesity or address only one system in which a child functions (e.g., school, family) might not be successful. Indeed, educational approaches alone, which may not have the flexibility to integrate barriers and motivational factors that prohibit change, are generally ineffective (Wilfley et al., 2007). Moreover, obesity prevention is complicated by the toxic societal environment that can derail even the most motivated youth or family (Brownell & Horgen, 2004; Brownell, Schwartz, et al., 2009). Therefore, given the complexity of pediatric obesity prevention, an integrative, multisystem approach will likely provide the best outcome. At the individual, group, family, or school level, this approach could involve an interdisciplinary prevention plan involving a registered dietician, exercise physiologist, medical physician, and counselor. At the societal level, it might involve government regulations improving the nutrition of school meals and increasing opportunities for physical activity, subsidies on fresh produce, or restrictions on food marketing to youths.

Moving forward, we offer recommendations to counselors that we believe can enhance pediatric obesity prevention efforts. First, it is imperative that prevention be culturally adapted to fit the needs of youths and their families. Examples of cultural adaptations could include creating healthier versions of culturally traditional foods, maintaining awareness of cultural variations in ideal body types and perceptions of health, incorporating culturally relevant forms of exercise, and including members of extended family or salient community institutions. Prevention programming should also be tailored to meet the needs of lower socioeconomic status youths and families because this group is not only disproportionately affected by obesity (Singh, Kogan, Van Dyck, & Siahpush, 2008) but is also more likely to face co-occurring barriers such as unsafe neighborhoods and a dearth of easily accessible fruit and vegetable retailers. Second, we recommend that counselors incorporate parents into pediatric obesity prevention whenever possible, particularly with younger children. Parental support and role modeling of healthy behaviors can have a powerful impact on youths' eating and weight-related behaviors. In addition, targeting parents helps improve the entire family's health be-haviors and avoids stigmatizing children as the identified patient. Finally, we want to highlight the importance of behavioral support. We believe that consulting regularly with individuals and families to set goals, identify and problem solve barriers, and build on existing skills can enhance the odds that prevention efforts will be successful.

## Chapter Highlights

- Primary prevention takes the perspective that pediatric obesity is a societal public health concern, and all youths would benefit from prevention programming.

- Primary prevention can reduce barriers to healthy eating and physical activity through information and access.
- An interdisciplinary approach to pediatric obesity prevention is recommended; teams should include nutrition, exercise, and medical experts, as well as counselors.
- Education alone does not produce sustainable change; counselors address the gap between expert recommendations and patient engagement in these health behaviors.
- MI assesses youths' and families' readiness to change and joins with them through collaboration and empathy to increase motivation and self-efficacy.
- Family approaches seek to change the family environment and behaviors rather than identify the overweight youth as the patient, which can be damaging to self-esteem and willingness to change.
- Parental role modeling of healthy eating and physical activity encourages children to engage in similar behaviors and increases self-efficacy for those behaviors as they get older.

## Recommended Resources

### Journal Articles

Barlow, S. E., & the Expert Committee. (2007). Expert committee recommendations regarding the prevention, assessment, and treatment of child and adolescent overweight and obesity: Summary report. *Pediatrics, 120*(Suppl. 4), S164–S192. doi:10.1542/peds.2007-2329C.

This article reviews guidelines for the prevention, assessment, and treatment of pediatric obesity.

Davis, M. M., Gance-Cleveland, B., Hassink, S., Johnson, R., Paradis, G., & Resnicow, K. (2007). Recommendations for prevention of childhood obesity. *Pediatrics, 120*(Suppl. 4), S229–S253. doi:10.1542/peds.2007-2329E

This article on motivational interviewing for pediatric obesity prevention offers providers a 15-minute protocol and sample language.

Mazzeo, S. E., Kelly, N. R., Stern, M., Gow, R. W., Serdar, K., Evans, R. K., . . . Bulik, C. M. (2012). Nourishing Our Understanding of Role Modeling to Improve Support and Health (NOURISH): Design and methods. *Contemporary Clinical Trials, 33*, 515–522. doi:10.1016/j.cct.2012.01.003

This article reviews the NOURISH program in depth.

### Web Sites

- Academy for Eating Disorders
  http://www.aedweb.org/media/Guidelines.cfm
  Recommendations for pediatric obesity prevention, including how to minimize weight stigmatization.
- Centers for Disease Control and Prevention
  http://www.cdc.gov/obesity/childhood

Information about pediatric obesity in the United States, including statistics and suggested strategies.

- MINT
    http://www.motivationalinterviewing.org
    A resource for counselors that offers a library of audio, visual, and written resources and information on training events.
- MyPlate
    http://www.choosemyplate.gov
    Published by the U.S. Department of Agriculture; has information about healthy eating, physical activity, and weight management and handouts that counselors or individuals could print, interactive diet-tracking tools, and many other features.
- U.S. Department of Agriculture Center for Nutrition Policy and Promotion
    http://www.cnpp.usda.gov/DietaryGuidelines.htm
    Current dietary guidelines.
- World Health Organization
    http://www.who.int/mediacentre/factsheets/fs311/en/
    Information on worldwide overweight and obesity and recommendations for how they can be reduced.
- Yale University's Rudd Center for Food Policy and Obesity
    http://www.yaleruddcenter.org
    Strategies for combatting weight bias, information on policy obesity prevention efforts, and headlines about current obesity news.

# References

Airhihenbuwa, C. O., Kumanyika, S., Agurs, T. D., Lowe, A., Saunders, D., & Morssink, C. B. (1996). Cultural aspects of African American eating patterns. *Ethnicity & Health, 1,* 245–260. doi:10.1080/1355785 8.1996.9961793

Ali, M. M., Amialchuk, A., & Heiland, F. W. (2011). Weight-related behavior among adolescents: The role of peer effects. *PLoS One, 6,* e21179. doi:10.1371/journal.pone.0021179

American Dietetic Association. (2006). Position of the American Dietetic Association: individual-, family-, school-, and community-based interventions for pediatric overweight. *Journal of the American Dietetic Association, 106,* 925–945.

Arredondo, E. M., Ayala, G. X., Baquero, B., Campell, N. R., Duerksen, S., & Elder, J. P. (2006). Is parenting style related to children's healthy eating and physical activity in Latino families? *Health Education Research, 21,* 862–871. doi:10.1093/her/cyl110

Ballard-Barbash, R., Berrigan, D., Potischman, N., & Dowling, E. (2010). Obesity and cancer epidemiology. In N. A. Berger (Ed.), *Cancer and energy balance, epidemiology and overview* (pp. 1–44). New York, NY: Springer-Verlag.

Bandura, A. (1986). *Social foundations of thought and action. A social cognitive theory.* Englewood Cliffs, NJ: Prentice-Hall.

Baranowski, T., Baranowski, J., Thompson, D., & Buday, R. (2011). Behavioral science in video games for children's diet and physical activity change: Key research needs. *Journal of Diabetes Science and Technology, 5,* 229–233.

Barlow, S. E. (2007). Expert committee recommendations regarding the prevention, assessment, and treatment of child and adolescent overweight and obesity: Summary report. *Pediatrics, 120* (Suppl. 4)., S164–S192. doi:10.1542/peds.2007-2329C

Barnes, A. S., Goodrick, G. K., Pavlik, V., Markesino, J., Laws, D. Y., & Taylor, W. C. (2007). Weight loss maintenance in African-American women: Focus group results and questionnaire development. *Journal of General Internal Medicine, 22,* 915–922.

Barry, C. L., Brescoll, V. L., Brownell, K. D., & Schlesinger, M. (2009). Obesity metaphors: How beliefs about the causes of obesity affect support for public policy. *Milbank Quarterly, 87,* 7–47.

Bassett, M. T., Dumanovsky, T., Huang, C., Silver, L. D., Young, C., Nonas, C., . . . Frieden, T. R. (2008). Purchasing behavior and calorie information at fast-food chains in New York City, 2007. *American Journal of Public Health, 98,* 1457–1459.

Beaulac, J., Kristjansson, E., & Cummins, S. (2009). A systematic review of food deserts, 1966–2007. *Preventing Chronic Disease, 6,* A105.

Bertakis, K. D., & Azari, R. (2005). The impact of obesity on primary care visits. *Obesity Research, 13,* 1615–1623.

Birch, L. L. (2006). Child feeding practices and the etiology of obesity. *Obesity, 14,* 343–344.

Birch, L. L., & Davison, K. K. (2001). Family environmental factors influencing the developing behavioral controls of food intake and childhood overweight. *Pediatric Clinics of North America, 48,* 893–907.

Birch, L. L., & Fisher, J. O. (2000). Mothers' child-feeding practices influence daughters' eating and weight. *American Journal of Clinical Nutrition, 71,* 1054–1061.

Brownell, K. D. (2005). The chronicling of obesity: Growing awareness of its social, economic, and political contexts. *Journal of Health Politics, Policy and Law, 30,* 955–964.

Brownell, K. D., Farley, T., Willett, W. C., Popkin, B. M., Chaloupka, F. J., Thompson, J. W., & Ludwig, D. S. (2009). The public health and economic benefits of taxing sugar-sweetened beverages. *New England Journal of Medicine, 361,* 1599–1605.

Brownell, K. D., & Horgen, K. B. (2004). *Food fight: The inside story of the food industry, America's obesity crisis, and what we can do about it.* Chicago, IL: McGraw-Hill.

Brownell, K. D., Schwartz, M. B., Puhl, R. M., Henderson, K. E., & Harris, J. L. (2009). The need for bold action to prevent adolescent obesity. *Journal of Adolescent Health, 45* (Suppl.), S8–S17. doi:10.1016/j.jadohealth.2009.03.004

Burdette, H. L., & Whitaker, R. C. (2005). A national study of neighbor-hood safety, outdoor play, television viewing, and obesity in preschool children. *Pediatrics, 116,* 657–662.

Caballero, B. (2004). Obesity prevention in children: Opportunities and challenges. *International Journal of Obesity and Related Metabolic Disorders, 28*(Suppl. 3), S90–S95.

Caballero, B., Clay, T., Davis, S. M., Ethelbah, B., Rock, B. H., Lohman, T., . . . Stevens, J. (2003). Pathways: A school-based, randomized controlled trial for the prevention of obesity in American Indian schoolchildren. *American Journal of Clinical Nutrition, 78,* 1030–1038.

Centers for Disease Control and Prevention. (2011a). *How much physical activity do you need?* Retrieved June 2012 from http://www.cdc.gov/physicalactivity/everyone/guidelines/index.html

Centers for Disease Control and Prevention. (2011b). *National diabetes fact sheet: National estimates and general information on diabetes and prediabetes in the United States.* Atlanta, GA: Author.

Coffield, J. E., Metos, J. M., Utz, R. L., & Waitzman, N. J. (2011). A multivariate analysis of federally mandated school wellness policies on adolescent obesity. *Journal of Adolescent Health, 49,* 363–370.

Coleman, K. J., Tiller, C. L., Sanchez, J., Heath, E. M., Sy, O., Milliken, G., & Dzewaltowski, D. A. (2005). Prevention of the epidemic increase in child risk of overweight in low-income schools: The El Paso coordinated approach to child health. *Archives of Pediatrics and Adolescent Medicine, 159,* 217.

Contento, I. R., Zybert, P., & Williams, S. S. (2005). Relationships of cognitive restraint of eating and disinhibition to the quality of food choices of Latina women and their young children. *Preventive Medicine, 40,* 326–336.

Daniels, S. R., Arnett, D. K., Eckel, R. H., Gidding, S. S., Hayman, L. L., Kumanyika, S., . . . Williams, C. L. (2005). Overweight in children and adolescents: Pathophysiology, consequences, prevention, and treatment. *Circulation, 111,* 1999–2012. doi:10.1161/01.CIR.0000161369.71722.10

Daniels, S. R., Jacobson, M. S., McCrindle, B. W., Eckel, R. H., & Sanner, B. M. (2009). American Heart Association Childhood Obesity Research Summit report. *Circulation, 119,* e489–e517. doi:10.1161/CIRCULATIONAHA.109.192216

Daníelsdóttir, S., Burgard, D., & Oliver-Pyatt, W. (2009). *Academy for Eating Disorders guidelines for childhood obesity prevention programs.* Retrieved June 2012 from http://www.aedweb.org/AM/Template.cfm?Section=Advocacy&Template=/CM/ContentDisplay.cfm&ContentID=1659

Davis, E. M., Cullen, K. W., Watson, K. B., Konarik, M., & Radcliffe, J. (2009). A fresh fruit and vegetable program improves high school students' consumption of fresh produce. *Journal of the American Dietetic Association, 109,* 1227–1231. doi:10.1016/j.jada.2009.04.017

Davis, J. N., Ventura, E. E., Cook, L. T., Gyllenhammer, L. E., & Gatto, N. M. (2011). LA sprouts: A gardening, nutrition, and cooking intervention for latino youth improves diet and reduces obesity. *Journal of the American Dietetic Association, 111,* 1224–1230.

De Bourdeaudhuij, I. (1997). Family food rules and healthy eating in adolescent. *Journal of Health Psychology, 2,* 45–56.

Dixon, B., Peña, M. M., & Taveras, E. M. (2012). Lifecourse approach to racial/ethnic disparities in childhood obesity. *Advances in Nutrition: An International Review Journal, 3,* 73–82.

Dowda, M., Dishman, R. K., Pfeiffer, K. A., & Pate, R. R. (2007). Family support for physical activity in girls from 8th to 12th grade in South Carolina. *Preventive Medicine, 44,* 153–159.

Drewnowski, A., & Darmon, N. (2005). The economics of obesity: Dietary energy density and energy cost. *American Journal of Clinical Nutrition, 82,* 265S–273S.

Eckel, R. H., & Krauss, R. M. (1998). American Heart Association call to action: Obesity as a major risk factor for coronary heart disease. *Circulation, 97,* 2099–2100.

Elbel, B., Kersh, R., Brescoll, V. L., & Dixon, L. B. (2009). Calorie labeling and food choices: A first look at the effects on low-income people in New York City. *Health Affairs, 28,* w1110–w1121.

Epstein, L. H., Myers, M. D., Raynor, H. A., & Saelens, B. E. (1998). Treatment of pediatric obesity. *Pediatrics, 101,* 554–570.

Epstein, L. H., Wing, R. R., Koeske, R., Andrasik, F., & Ossip, D. J. (1981). Child and parent weight loss in family-based behavioral modification programs. *Journal of Consulting and Clinical Psychology, 49,* 674–685.

Epstein, L. H., Wing, R. R., Koeske, R., & Valoski, A. (1987). Long-term effects of family-based treatment of childhood obesity. *Journal of Consulting and Clinical Psychology, 55,* 91–95.

Evans, W. D., Finkelstein, E. A., Kamerow, D. B., & Renaud, J. M. (2005). Public perceptions of childhood obesity. *American Journal of Preventive Medicine, 28,* 26–32.

Faith, M. S., Heshka, S., Keller, K. L., Sherry, B., Matz, P. E., Pietrobelli, A., & Allison, D. B. (2003). Maternal-child feeding practices and child body weight: Findings from a population-based sample. *Archives of Pediatrics & Adolescent Medicine, 157,* 926–932.

Finkelstein, D. M., Hill, E. L., & Whitaker, R. C. (2008). School food environments and policies in US public schools. *Pediatrics, 122,* e251–e259.

Fisher, J. O., Mitchell, D. C., Smiciklas-Wright, H., & Birch, L. L. (2002). Parental influences on young girls' fruit and vegetable, micronutrient, and fat intakes. *Journal of the American Dietetic Association, 102,* 58–64.

Foster, G. D., Sherman, S., Borradaile, K. E., Grundy, K. M., Vander Veur, S. S., Nachmani, J., . . . Shults, J. (2008). A policy-based school intervention to prevent overweight and obesity. *Pediatrics, 121,* e794–802. doi:10.1542/peds.2007-1365

Fowler-Brown, A., & Kahwati, L. C. (2004). Prevention and treatment of overweight in children and adolescents. *American Family Physician, 69,* 2591–2598.

Freedman, D. S., Khan, L. K., Serdula, M. K., Dietz, W. H., Srinivasan, S. R., & Berenson, G. S. (2005). The relation of childhood BMI to adult adiposity: The Bogalusa Heart Study. *Pediatrics, 115,* 22–27.

Freedman, D., Khan, L. K., Serdula, M. K., Ogden, C. L., & Dietz, W. H. (2006). Racial and ethnic differences in secular trends for childhood BMI, weight, and height. *Obesity, 14,* 301–308.

Freedman, D. S., Zuguo, M., Srinivasan, S. R., Berenson, G. S., & Dietz, W. H. (2007). Cardiovascular risk factors and excess adiposity among overweight children and adolescents: The Bogalusa Heart Study. *Journal of Pediatrics, 150,* 12–17.

Frieden, T. R., Dietz, W., & Collins, J. (2010). Reducing childhood obesity through policy change: Acting now to prevent obesity. *Health Affairs, 29,* 357–363.

Gable, S., & Lutz, S. (2000). Household, parent, and child contributions to childhood obesity. *Family Relations, 49,* 293–300.

Gentile, D. A., & Walsh, D. S. (2002). A normative study of family media habits. *Applied Developmental Psychology, 23,* 157–178.

Golan, M., & Crow, S. (2004a). Parents are key players in the prevention and treatment of weight-related problems. *Nutrition Reviews, 62,* 39–50.

Golan, M., & Crow, S. (2004b). Targeting parents exclusively in the treatment of childhood obesity: Long-term results. *Obesity Research, 12,* 357–361.

Golan, M., Fainaru, M., & Weizman, A. (1998). Role of behaviour modification in the treatment of childhood obesity with the parents as the exclusive agents of change. *International Journal of Obesity, 22,* 1217–1224.

Golan, M., Kaufman, V., & Shahar, D. R. (2006). Childhood obesity treatment: Targeting parents exclusively versus parents and children. *British Journal of Nutrition, 95,* 1008–1015.

Golan, M., Weizman, A., Apter, A., & Fainaru, M. (1998). Parents as the exclusive agents of change in the treatment of childhood obesity. *American Journal of Clinical Nutrition, 67,* 1130–1135.

Gordon-Larsen, P., Griffiths, P., Bentley, M. E., Ward, D. S., Kelsey, K., Shields, K., & Ammerman, A. (2004). Barriers to physical activity: Qualitative data on caregiver–daughter perceptions and practices. *American Journal of Preventive Medicine, 27,* 218–223. doi:10.1016/j.amepre.2004.05.002

Graff, S., Kunkel, D., & Mermin, S. E. (2012). Government can regulate food advertising to children because cognitive research shows that it is inherently misleading. *Health Affairs, 31,* 392–398.

Grimes-Robison, C., & Evans, R. R. (2008). Benefits and barriers to medically supervised pediatric weight-management programs. *Journal of Child Health Care, 12,* 329–343. doi:10.1177/1367493508096319

Gunnarsdottir, T., Njardvik, U., Olafsdottir, A. S., Craighead, L. W., & Bjarnason, R. (2011). The role of parental motivation in family-based treatment for childhood obesity. *Obesity, 19,* 1654–1662.

Guo, S. S., Wu, W., Chumlea, W. C., & Roche, A. F. (2002). Predicting overweight and obesity in adulthood from body mass index values in childhood and adolescence. *American Journal of Clinical Nutrition, 76,* 653–658.

Gutin, B. (2008). Child obesity can be reduced with vigorous activity rather than restriction of energy intake. *Obesity, 16,* 2193–2196. doi:10.1038/oby.2008.348

Hampson, S. E., Andrews, J. A., Peterson, M., & Duncan, S. C. (2007). A cognitive–behavioral mechanism leading to adolescent obesity: Children's social images and physical activity. *Annals of Behavioral Medicine, 34,* 287–294. doi:10.1080/08836610701677402

Han, J. C., Lawlor, D. A., & Kimm, S. Y. (2010). Childhood obesity. *Lancet, 375,* 1737–1748. doi:10.1016/S0140-6736(10)60171-7

Healthy, Hunger-Free Kids Act of 2010, Pub. L. No. 111–296 124 Stat. 3183 (2010).

Hoelscher, D. M., Springer, A. E., Ranjit, N., Perry, C. L., Evans, A. E., Stigler, M., & Kelder, S. H. (2010). Reductions in child obesity among disadvantaged school children with community involvement: The Travis County CATCH trial. *Obesity, 18*(Suppl. 1), S36–S44.

Howerton, M. W., Bell, B. S., Dodd, K. W., Berrigan, D., Stolzenberg-Solomon, R., & Nebeling, L. (2007). School-based nutrition programs produced a moderate increase in fruit and vegetable consumption: Meta and pooling analyses from 7 studies. *Journal of Nutrition Education and Behavior, 39,* 186–196.

Ikeda, J. P., Crawford, P. B., & Woodward-Lopez, G. (2006). BMI screening in schools: Helpful or harmful. *Health Education Research, 21,* 761–769.

Institute of Medicine. (2005). *Preventing childhood obesity: Health in the balance.* Washington, DC: National Academies Press.

Jago, R., Baranowski, T., & Baranowski, J. C. (2007). Fruit and vegetable availability: A micro environmental mediating variable? *Public Health Nutrition, 10,* 681–689.

James, D. C. (2004). Factors influencing food choices, dietary intake, and nutrition-related attitudes among African Americans: Application of a culturally sensitive model. *Ethnicity & Health, 9,* 349–367. doi:10.1080/1355785042000285375

Jelalian, E., Lloyd-Richardson, E. E., Mehlenbeck, R. S., Hart, C. N., Flynn-O'Brien, K., Kaplan, J., . . . Wing, R. R. (2010). Behavioral weight control treatment with supervised exercise or peer-enhanced adventure for overweight adolescents. *Journal of Pediatrics, 157,* 923–928. doi:10.1016/j.jpeds.2010.05.047

Joshi, A., & Beery, M. (2007). *A growing movement: A decade of farm to school in California.* Los Angeles, CA: Center for Food & Justice, Urban and Environmental Policy Institute.

Kamath, C. C., Vickers, K. S., Ehrlich, A., McGovern, L., Johnson, J., Singhal, V., . . . Montori, V. M. (2008). Clinical review: Behavioral interventions to prevent childhood obesity: A systematic review and metaanalyses of randomized trials. *Journal of Clinical Endocrinology and Metabolism, 93,* 4606–4615. doi:10.1210/jc.2006-2411

Khan, L. K., Sobush, K., Keener, D., Goodman, K., Lowry, A., Kakietek, J., & Zaro, S. (2009). Recommended community strategies and measurements to prevent obesity in the United States. *MMWR Recommendations and Reports, 58,* 51–26.

Kimm, S. Y., Glynn, N. W., Kriska, A. M., Barton, B. A., Kronsberg, S. S., Daniels, S. R., . . . Liu, K. (2002). Decline in physical activity in Black girls and White girls during adolescence. *New England Journal of Medicine, 347,* 709–715. doi:10.1056/NEJMoa003277

Klesges, R. C., Coates, T. J., Brown, G., Sturgeon-Tillisch, J., Moldenhauer-Klesges, L. M., Holzer, B., . . . Vollmer, J. (1983). Parental influences on children's eating behavior and relative weight. *Journal of Applied Behavior Analysis, 16,* 371–378.

Klesges, R. C., Obarzanek, E., Kumanyika, S., Murray, D. M., Klesges, L. M., Relyea, G. E., . . . Slawson, D. L. (2010). The Memphis Girls' Health Enrichment Multi-Site Studies: An evaluation of the efficacy of a 2-year obesity prevention program in African American girls. *Archives of Pediatrics and Adolescent Medicine, 164,* 1007–1014. doi:10.1001/archpediatrics.2010.196

Krebs-Smith, S. M., Guenther, P. M., Subar, A. F., Kirkpatrick, S. I., & Dodd, K. W. (2010). Americans do not meet federal dietary recommendations. *Journal of Nutrition, 140,* 1832–1838.

Kropski, J. A., Keckley, P. H., & Jensen, G. L. (2008). School-based obesity prevention programs: An evidence-based review. *Obesity, 16,* 1009–1018.

Kumanyika, S. K. (2008). Environmental influences on childhood obesity: Ethnic and cultural influences in context. *Physiology & Behavior, 94,* 61–70. doi:10.1016/j.physbeh.2007.11.019

Kunkel, D., Wilcox, B. L., Cantor, J., Palmer, E., Linn, S., & Dowrick, P. (2004*). Report of the APA task force on advertising and children.* Washington, DC: American Psychological Association.

Latner, J. D., & Stunkard, A. J. (2003). Getting worse: The stigmatization of obese children. *Obesity, 11,* 452–456.

Lenhart, A., Ling, R., Campbell, S., & Purcell, K. (2010). *Teens and mobile phones.* Washington, DC: Pew Internet & American Life Project.

Lenhart, A., Purcell, K., Smith, A., & Zickuhr, K. (2010). *Social media and mobile Internet use among teens and young adults.* Washington, DC: Pew Internet & American Life Project.

Levy, D. T., Nikolayev, L., Mumford, E., & Compton, C. (2005). The Healthy People 2010 smoking prevalence and tobacco control objectives: Results from the SimSmoke tobacco control policy simulation model (United States). *Cancer Causes and Control, 16,* 359–371.

Maclean, L. M., Clinton, K., Edwards, N., Garrard, M., Ashley, L., Hansen-Ketchum, P., & Walsh, A. (2010). Unpacking vertical and horizontal integration: Childhood overweight/obesity programs and planning: A Canadian perspective. *Implementation Science, 5,* 36. doi:10.1186/1748-5908-5-36

Maddison, R., Foley, L., Ni Mhurchu, C., Jiang, Y., Jull, A., Prapavessis, H., . . . Rodgers, A. (2011). Effects of active video games on body composition: A randomized controlled trial. *American Journal of Clinical Nutrition, 94,* 156–163. doi:10.3945/ajcn.110.009142

Mazzeo, S., Gow, R., Stern, M., & Gerke, C. K. (2008). Developing an intervention for parents of overweight children. *International Journal of Child and Adolescent Health, 1,* 355–363.

McAleese, J. D., & Rankin, L. L. (2007). Garden-based nutrition education affects fruit and vegetable consumption in sixth-grade adolescents. *Journal of the American Dietetic Association, 107,* 662–665.

McGinnis, J. M., Gootman, J. A., & Kraak, V. I. (2006). *Food marketing to children and youth: Threat or opportunity?* Washington, DC: National Academies Press.

McGovern, L., Johnson, J. N., Paulo, R., Hettinger, A., Singhal, V., Kamath, C., . . . Montori, V. M. (2008). Clinical review: Treatment of pediatric obesity: A systematic review and meta-analysis of randomized trials. *Journal of Clinical Endocrinology and Metabolism, 93,* 4600–4605.

Miller, W. R., & Rollnick, S. (2002). *Motivational interviewing: Preparing people for change.* New York, NY: Guilford Press.

Moens, E., Braet, C., & Soetens, B. (2007). Observation of family functioning at mealtime: A comparison between families of children with and without overweight. *Journal of Pediatric Psychology, 32,* 52–63.

Morin, P., & Roy, M. A. (2011). Perceptions of employed parents about early childhood obesity and the need for prevention strategies. *Health Promotion Practice.* Advance online publication. doi:10.1177/1524839911405843

Morris, J. L., & Zidenberg-Cherr, S. (2002). Garden-enhanced nutrition curriculum improves fourth-grade school children's knowledge of nutrition and preferences for some vegetables. *Journal of the American Dietetic Association, 102,* 91–93.

National Association for Sport and Physical Education & American Heart Association. (2010). *Shape of the nation report: Status of physical education in the USA.* Reston, VA: Author.

National Heart, Lung and Blood Institute. (1998). Clinical guidelines on the identification, evaluation, and treatment of overweight and obesity in adults: Executive summary. *American Journal of Clinical Nutrition, 68,* 899–917.

Neumark-Sztainer, D., Haines, J., Robinson-O'Brien, R., Hannan, P. J., Robins, M., Morris, B., & Petrich, C. A. (2009). "Ready. Set. ACTION!" A theater-based obesity prevention program for children: A feasibility study. *Health Education Research, 24,* 407–420. doi:10.1093/her/cyn036

Neumark-Sztainer, D., Hannan, P. J., Story, M., Croll, J., & Perry, C. (2003). Family meal patterns: Associations with sociodemographic characteristics and improved dietary intake among adolescents. *Journal of the American Dietetic Association, 103,* 317–322.

Neumark-Sztainer, D., Story, M., Hannan, P. J., Tharp, T., & Rex, J. (2003). Factors associated with changes in physical activity: A cohort study of inactive adolescent girls. *Archives of Pediatrics and Adolescent Medicine, 157,* 803–810.

Nihiser, A. J., Lee, S. M., Wechsler, H., McKenna, M., Odom, E., Reinold, C., . . . Grummer-Strawn, L. (2007). Body mass index measurement in schools. *Journal of School Health, 77,* 651–671. doi:10.1111/j.1746-1561.2007.00249.x

Nihiser, A. J., Lee, S. M., Wechsler, H., McKenna, M., Odom, E., Reinold, C., . . . Grummer-Strawn, L. (2009). BMI measurement in schools. *Pediatrics, 124*(Suppl. 1), S89–S97. doi:10.1542/peds.2008-3586L

Ogden, C. L., Carroll, M. D., Curtin, L. R., Lamb, M. M., & Flegal, K. M. (2010). Prevalence of high body mass index in US children and adolescents, 2007–2008. *JAMA, 303,* 242–249.

Oliver, J. E., & Lee, T. (2005). Public opinion and the politics of obesity in America. *Journal of Health Politics, Policy and Law, 30,* 923–954.

Olson, C. L., Schumaker, H. D., & Yawn, B. P. (1994). Overweight women delay medical care. *Archives of Family Medicie, 3,* 888–892.

Park, S., Sappenfield, W. M., Huang, Y., Sherry, B., & Bensyl, D. M. (2010). The impact of the availability of school vending machines on eating behavior during lunch: The Youth Physical Activity and Nutrition Survey. *Journal of the American Dietetic Association, 110,* 1532–1536.

Peña, M. M., Dixon, B., & Taveras, E. M. (2012). Are you talking to me? The importance of ethnicity and culture in childhood obesity prevention and management. *Childhood Obesity, 7,* 36–37. doi:abs/10.1089/chi.2011.0109

Peterson, K. A., Paulson, S. E., & Williams, K. K. (2007). Relations of eating disorder symptomatology with perceptions of pressures from mother, peers, and media in adolescent girls and boys. *Sex Roles, 56,* 629–639. doi:10.1007/s11199-007-9296-z

Pollak, K. I., Alexander, S. C., Ostbye, T., Lyna, P., Tulsky, J. A., Dolor, R. J., . . . Bravender, T. (2009). Primary care physicians' discussions of weight-related topics with overweight and obese adolescents: Results from the Teen CHAT Pilot study. *Journal of Adolescent Health, 45,* 205–207. doi:10.1016/j.jadohealth.2009.01.002

Powell, L. M., & Chaloupka, F. J. (2009). Food prices and obesity: Evidence and policy implications for taxes and subsidies. *Milbank Quarterly, 87,* 229–257.

Prochaska, J. O., & DiClemente, C. C. (2005). The transtheoretical approach. In J. C. Norcross & M. R. Goldfried (Eds.), *Handbook of psychotherapy integration* (2nd ed., pp. 147–171). New York, NY: Oxford University Press.

Resnicow, K., Taylor, R., Baskin, M., & McCarty, F. (2005). Results of "Go Girls": A weight control program for overweight African-American adolescent females. *Obesity Research, 13,* 1739–1748.

Roberto, C. A., Larsen, P. D., Agnew, H., Baik, J., & Brownell, K. D. (2010). Evaluating the impact of menu labeling on food choices and intake. *American Journal of Public Health, 100,* 312–318. doi:10.2105/AJPH.2009.160226

Robinson-O'Brien, R., Story, M., & Heim, S. (2009). Impact of garden-based youth nutrition intervention programs: A review. *Journal of the American Dietetic Association, 109,* 273–280.

Sallis, J. F., McKenzie, T. L., Alcaraz, J. E., Kolody, B., Faucette, N., & Hovell, M. F. (1997). The effects of a 2-year physical education program (SPARK) on physical activity and fitness in elementary school students. Sports, Play and Active Recreation for Kids *American Journal of Public Health, 87,* 1328–1334.

Sallis, J. F., Patterson, T. L., McKenzie, T. L., & Nader, P. R. (1988). Family variables and physical activity in preschool children. *Journal of Developmental and Behavioral Pediatrics, 9,* 57–61.

Salvy, S. J., Roemmich, J. N., Bowker, J. C., Romero, N. D., Stadler, P. J., & Epstein, L. H. (2009). Effect of peers and friends on youth physical activity and motivation to be physically active. *Journal of Pediatric Psychology, 34,* 217–225.

Satter, E. (1996). Internal regulation and the evolution of normal growth as the basis for prevention of obesity in children. *Journal of the American Dietetic Association, 96,* 860–864. doi:10.1016/s0002-8223(96)00237-4

Seo, D. C., & Lee, C. G. (2012). Association of school nutrition policy and parental control with childhood overweight. *Journal of School Health, 82,* 285–293. doi:10.1111/j.1746-1561.2012.00699.x.

Singh, G. K., Kogan, M. D., Van Dyck, P. C., & Siahpush, M. (2008). Racial/ethnic, socioeconomic, and behavioral determinants of childhood and adolescent obesity in the United States: Analyzing independent and joint associations. *Annals of Epidemiology, 18,* 682–695. doi:10.1016/j.annepidem.2008.05.001

Slusser, W. M., Cumberland, W. G., Browdy, B. L., Lange, L., & Neumann, C. (2007). A school salad bar increases frequency of fruit and vegetable consumption among children living in low-income households. *Public Health Nutrition, 10,* 1490–1496.

Spear, B. A., Barlow, S. E., Ervin, C., Ludwig, D. S., Saelens, B. E., Schetzina, K. E., & Taveras, E. M. (2007). Recommendations for treatment of child and adolescent overweight and obesity. *Pediatrics, 120*(Suppl. 4), S254–S288. doi:10.1542/peds.2007-2329F

Stern, M., Mazzeo, S. E., Gerke, C., Porter, J. S., Bean, M. K., & Laver, J. (2006). Gender, ethnicity, and psychosocial factors and quality of life among participants in a multidisciplinary program targeting adolescent overweight. *Journal of Pediatric Psychology, 32,* 90–94.

Stice, E., Davis, K., Miller, N. P., & Marti, C. N. (2008). Fasting increases risk for onset of binge eating and bulimic pathology: A 5-year prospective study. *Journal of Abnormal Psychology, 117,* 941–946.

Story, M., & French, S. (2004). Food advertising and marketing directed at children and adolescents in the US. *International Journal of Behavioral Nutrition and Physical Activity, 1,* 3.

Story, M., Nanney, M. S., & Schwartz, M. B. (2009). Schools and obesity prevention: Creating school environments and policies to promote healthy eating and physical activity. *Milbank Quarterly, 87,* 71–100. doi:10.1111/j.1468-0009.2009.00548.x

Strong, W. B., Malina, R. M., Blimkie, C. J., Daniels, S. R., Dishman, R. K., Gutin, B., . . . Trudeau, F. (2005). Evidence based physical activity for school-age youth. *Journal of Pediatrics, 146,* 732–737. doi:10.1016/j.jpeds.2005.01.055

Trudeau, F., & Shephard, R. J. (2008). Physical education, school physical activity, school sports and academic performance. *International Journal of Behavioral Nutrition and Physical Activity, 5,* 10.

Vereecken, C., Rovner, A., & Maes, L. (2010). Associations of parenting styles, parental feeding practices and child characteristics with young children's fruit and vegetable consumption. *Appetite, 55,* 589–596. doi:10.1016/j.appet.2010.09.009

Walpole, B., Dettmer, E., Morrongiello, B., McCrindle, B., & Hamilton, J. (2011). Motivational interviewing as an intervention to increase adolescent self-efficacy and promote weight loss: Methodology and design. *BMC Public Health, 11,* 459.

Wardle, J., Carnell, S., & Cooke, L. (2005). Parental control over feeding and children's fruit and vegetable intake: How are they related? *Journal of the American Dietetic Association, 105,* 227–232.

Washington, R. L. (2011). Childhood obesity: Issues of weight bias. *Preventing Chronic Disease, 8,* A94.

Watson, M., & Dannenberg, A. (2008). Investment in safe routes to school projects: Public health benefits for the larger community. *Preventing Chronic Disease, 5,* 1–7.

*What would you do if you knew you couldn't fail? Creating S.M.A.R.T. goals.* (n.d.). Retrieved from http://www.oma.ku.edu/soar/smartgoals.pdf

Wilfley, D. E., Kass, A. E., & Kolko, R. P. (2011). Counseling and behavior change in pediatric obesity. *Pediatric Clinics of North America, 58,* 1403–1424.

Wilfley, D. E., Tibbs, T. L., Van Buren, D. J., Reach, K. P., Walker, M. S., & Epstein, L. H. (2007). Lifestyle interventions in the treatment of childhood overweight: A meta-analytic review of randomized controlled trials. *Health Psychology, 26,* 521–532.

Wilson, D. K., Friend, R., Teasley, N., Green, S., Reaves, I. L., & Sica, D. A. (2002). Motivational versus social cognitive interventions for promoting fruit and vegetable intake and physical activity in African American adolescents. *Annals of Behavioral Medicine, 24,* 310–319.

World Health Organization. (2012). *Obesity and overweight* (Fact Sheet 311). Retrieved from who.int/mediacentre/factsheets/fs311/en/

Wrotniak, B. H., Epstein, L. H., Paluch, R. A., & Roemmich, J. N. (2005). The relationship between parent and child self-reported adherence and weight loss. *Obesity Research, 13,* 1089–1096.

Zaza, S., Briss, P. A., & Harris, K. W. (2005). *The guide to community preventive services: What works to promote health?* New York, NY: Oxford University Press.

## Chapter 9

# Prevention of Eating Disorders in Children: The Role of the Counselor

*Niva Piran*

This chapter equips counselors with the background knowledge and tools to help prevent negative body image and disordered eating patterns among children through age 14. I begin by describing the importance of engaging in the prevention of negative body image and disordered eating patterns in children and continue by delineating social factors that shape the development of negative body image and discuss their expression in a child's environment. A description of early identification and intervention follows. I conclude the chapter by delineating several prevention programs a counselor may want to examine and use and by highlighting key points related to the prevention of eating disorders with children in school and community settings.

## Prevalence and Phenomenology of Body Weight and Shape Preoccupation, Disordered Eating Patterns, and Eating Disorders Among Children

For many girls, the experience of the body as being a personal site of deficiency, limitations, and low self-worth starts in childhood, is accentuated during puberty, and continues to be a burden throughout their lives. This experience is present, although less common, among some boys and men. More important, during the childhood phase, research has documented a progression from attitudinal disruptions, such as body dissatisfaction or preoccupation with thinness, to engagement in disordered eating behaviors and then to full-blown eating disorders (EDs). For example, by age

*Note.* This work was supported by the Social Sciences and Humanities Research Council of Canada.

5, girls are already more concerned with being thin than boys (Lowes & Tiggemann, 2003). By ages 10–12, about 40% of girls worry about their weight and are aware of dieting and purging methods (Hill, Weaver, & Blundell, 1990; Murnen, Smolak, Mills, & Good, 2003). By ages 13–14, after the onset of puberty, 40% to 44% of girls engage in dieting attempts, a rate 2 to 3 times higher than that of boys (e.g., Field et al., 1999; French et al., 1997). In a recent study with a nationally representative sample of adolescents (ages 13–18) in the United States, Swanson, Crow, Le Grange, Swendsen, and Merikangas (2011) reported a prevalence of anorexia and subthreshold anorexia of 1.8% in girls and 0.4% in boys. Similarly, the prevalences of bulimia nervosa and subthreshold bulimia and of binge eating disorder are 3.6% and 2.3%, respectively, among girls and 3.1% and 0.8%, respectively, among boys. Not only do these numbers translate to a very large number of affected children in the United States, but Swanson et al. found that the age of onset of these disorders was younger than in other studies that have often relied on retrospective recall. In particular, Swanson et al. reported that the median age of onset ranged between 12.3 and 12.6 for the different types of EDs. The high rates of EDs and the young age of onset clearly suggest the urgency of implementing prevention interventions with children.

A second reason that prevention interventions are important is that if children develop body dissatisfaction by the time they are in middle school (ages 13–14), they are at risk for a variety of psychological and health challenges. First, body dissatisfaction in middle school predicts the development of dieting and eating difficulties, including clinical-level EDs, that are associated with a high rate of health complications (Wertheim, Paxton, & Blaney, 2009). Second, body dissatisfaction predicts the development of consumption of substances aimed at weight control, such as tobacco smoking (Neumark-Stzainer, Paxton, Hannan, Haines, & Story, 2006). Third, body dissatisfaction and dieting in middle school leads to weight gain and reduced engagement in physical activities (Neumark-Stzainer et al., 2006; Stice, Cameron, Hayward, Taylor, & Killen, 1999). Fourth, body dissatisfaction in middle school predicts the development of depression (Stice & Bearman, 2001). Moreover, Bearman and Stice (2008) suggested that the well-documented lifelong higher rates of depression among women than men are also predicted by body dissatisfaction among middle school girls.

Overall, then, research has suggested that during childhood and early adolescence, children, and girls in particular, commonly acquire negative attitudes about their bodies, followed by engagement in disordered eating patterns, as well as the occurrence of full-blown clinical EDs among a sizable minority of young adolescents. The whole range of disruption, from body dissatisfaction to EDs, is associated with considerable impairment and morbidity. All significant adults in children's lives, and counselors in particular, need to keep the goal of prevention of negative body image, disordered eating patterns, and EDs a priority.

# Understanding Negative Body Image in Context: The Developmental Theory of Embodiment as a Guide for Counselors

A comprehensive understanding of the social experiences that shape body image development can help guide the work of counselors toward the goal of prevention of EDs. However, the complexity of this task cannot be underestimated. In his seminal article, "Toward an Experimental Ecology of Human Development," Bronfenbrenner (1977) described human development as

> [the] progressive accommodation, throughout the life span, between the growing human organism and the changing environments in which it actually lives and grows. The latter include not only the immediate settings containing the developing person but also the larger social contexts, both formal and informal, in which these settings are embedded. (p. 513)

In this description and in his seminal article, Bronfenbrenner (1977) emphasized the hierarchical structure of social contexts, with higher level organizations, such as the media, or higher level variables, such as gender and social class, shaping the experiences at lower level institutions, such as schools. In particular, the field of EDs has been faced with the challenge of explaining the higher rate of body dissatisfaction among girls, especially at the onset of puberty and beyond (Smolak & Piran, 2012). As Smolak and Piran (2012) suggested, integrated developmental models are needed that can address the challenge of body image development at multiple levels of social influence. Working both as an academic researcher and as a school consultant in the area of body image and EDs, I have repeatedly emphasized the importance of transforming the school and community environment into one aimed at prevention (e.g., Piran, 1999a, 1999c). Indeed, prevention programs with children that target students without initiating concurrent changes in their schools, homes, and neighborhoods have shown limited efficacy that has tended to fade over time (Piran, 2010). Furthermore, I have emphasized that environmental changes aimed at prevention need to be guided by the broad range of social experiences that shape body image. Because existing programs for the prevention of EDs typically address only a narrow range of social experiences (typically, pressures for thinness and media literacy), it is useful for counselors to be informed by the range of experiences that affect body image and disordered eating patterns.

In a series of studies involving prospective qualitative studies with girls, including a participatory action project in a school with girls and boys aimed at the prevention of EDs (Piran, 2001), an interview study with young women (e.g., Piran, Carter, Thompson, & Pajouhandeh, 2002), a 5-year prospective qualitative study with girls (e.g., Piran, 2009; Piran et al., 2006, Piran & Teall, 2012), and a series of quantitative studies with young women (Piran & Cormier, 2005; Piran & Thompson, 2008), I have derived a developmental model, the developmental theory of embodiment, that delineates a complex array of social experiences that shape the development of body image, examining both protective and risk factors (Piran & Teall, 2012). The developmental theory of embodiment suggests that the broad range of social experiences that girls describe as affecting their body experiences can be grouped into three domains: the physical domain, the mental (or social stereotypes) domain, and the social power domain (Piran & Teall, 2012). I use this research-based theory here to provide counselors key dimensions to address in transforming children's social environment into one aimed at the prevention of negative body image.

### Physical Domain

In the physical domain, the counselor should look for experiences in the community and school that disrupt students' experiences of respectful ownership and care of their bodies and that limit their experience of body agency and competence.

#### Physical Violations

One type of disruption of positive body image, particularly in school, relates to physical violations, such as sexual harassment. Sexual harassment has been found to be associated with disordered eating patterns in several cross-sectional studies among girls (Murnen & Smolak, 2000; Piran, 2009, 2011) and women (Harned, 2000; Harned & Fitzgerald, 2002; Piran & Thompson, 2008). Murnen and Smolak (2000) further reported that girls were significantly more likely than boys to believe that victims of cross-gender sexual harassment would be scared. The following exchange with a 12-year-old participant in a 5-year prospective interview study with girls (Piran, 2009, 2011) reflects the disruptive experience of body-based harassment; this participant stopped eating in school in relation to this harassment:

> *There's something at our school . . . but I kinda get like, uncomfortable with it . . .*
> *Like guys go around like they slap those asses . . . .*
> [Interviewer: what would your body say?]
> *it'll be like part of me, I don't want to be here.*
> [Interviewer: What do you think it [harassment] makes a girl feel about herself?]
> *Like it makes her nervous, kind of sad, sometimes scared if they'll do it again . . .*
> *Maybe being afraid to go outside. Stay in her house.* (Piran, 2009, p. 110)

Similarly, Legge (2010) reported on a 17-year-old girl battling anorexia, with repeated hospitalizations for 3 years, who made no progress until her experience of pervasive sexual harassment in school was revealed and addressed. In developing anorexia, the girl hoped to disappear at school and, through that, control these ongoing violations.

With the goal of prevention of negative body image, counselors have an important role in initiating and monitoring the implementation of sexual and other body-based harassment policies (Piran, 1999c). In addition, school counselors in particular can address these phenomena through educational sessions with students aimed at changed norms of safety at the school. Counselors in school and in the community should validate sexual harassment and other body violations as significant disruptions in body experience and body image; in other words, what is normative or common is not necessarily benign.

## Movement and Competence

Active and joyful physical engagement in acting on the world enhances a sense of functional connection with the body and works against the self-objectification of the body (looking at one's body as an object of gaze by others; Fredrickson & Roberts, 1997; Piran & Teall, 2012; Theberge, 2003; Young, 1990). Although the reduced involvement in physical activities among both boys and girls throughout childhood is worrisome, the reduction in pubertal girls' involvement in vigorous physical activities is particularly marked (Bradley, McMurray, Harrell, & Deng, 2000; Falgairette, Deflandre, & Gavarry, 2004), as is the associated reduced sense of physical competence (Biddle, 1993; Richman & Shaffer, 2000). Counselors are likely familiar with the gradual reduction in the use of the physical space of the school campus by girls as they change from active participants with boys in physical activities in the lower grades to observers of boys' physical games by puberty.

Several factors shape girls' reduced engagement in physical activities. For example, sports are often perceived as not fitting with an acceptable feminine comportment, and girls may be teased for not complying with this norm (Ewing & Seefeldt, 1996; Piran & Teall, 2012). Even clothing and sports uniforms can affect girls' freedom and joy in being physically active. In a 5-year prospective interview study with girls (Piran, 2009), girls repeatedly described the problem of being expected to wear tight and exposing clothing:

> A popular girl wears a halter top, tight skirt, high heels, they just make you look
> taller . . . she can't play sports . . . she can't climb without people looking . . . She
> can walk around . . . She could sit on a bench
> [Interviewer. How does she feel?]
> Not comfortable . . . her skin is showing . . . [10-yr-old] (p. 57)

Indeed, in 2007, when the uniform for netball (the fourth most popular organized sport for girls and women in Australia) changed from shorts and a shirt to a Lycra bodysuit, a countrywide reduction of 35,000 occurred in the number of girls and women who engaged in this sport.

With the goal of prevention of negative body image, counselors should work in collaboration with the school administration and local recreation leagues to facilitate students' continued joyful engagement in physical activities. Because girls tend to withdraw from physical activities on the school campus over time, setting specific times for girls-only (and parallel

**205**

boys-only) use of the school gym during recess can work toward this goal. Similarly, low-cost and accessible community-based after-school programs for girls and boys that promote joyful engagement in physical activities are important for increasing children's participation in sports as well as their sense of body functionality and competence (Dwyer et al., 2006). Parents', teachers', or counselors' support for engagement in physical activities increases children's sport participation as well (Biddle, Whitehead, O'Donovan, & Nevill, 2005). Norms for school clothing, including during physical education or swimming classes, should support girls' comfortable engagement in physical activities. For example, in a dance school where I worked, students requested to come to class (at least once a week) dressed in clothes that inspired them and made them feel comfortable and in tune with their internal experience of dance. As I described (Piran, 2001), counselors can support students in their requests of school administration. Counselors in community settings have an opportunity to educate parents and children themselves about the importance of listening to and respecting the experience of comfort in the choice of clothing.

### Desires: Appetite and Sexuality

Counselors are likely to face disruption in students' body image and eating patterns related to cultural prejudices about, and stigmatization of, appetite and weight in all children (more so in girls) and sexuality in girls. Regarding appetite and eating, it is most unfortunate that biased attitudes about weight are also conveyed through anti-obesity educational programs and widely disseminated messages (for a detailed and important discussion of this challenge, see O'Dea, 2005). Examining girls' narratives prospectively has revealed a common shift in girls from a narrative of connection to appetite at prepuberty (e.g., "I like pasta with salmon and broccoli. I like chips. I hate cheese") to a narrative of disruption to appetite postpuberty (e.g., "It's like I can't eat in the mornings, like I don't eat at lunch. I have to be in the mood to eat"; Piran, 2009, p. 64). Counselors, with the aid of professional nutritionists and health educators who are aware of existing prejudices (see, e.g., Brownell, Puhl, Schwartz, & Rudd, 2005) and who have a broader concept of health and of the nutritional needs of growing children often need to engage in "repair work" (Piran, 1999b, 1999c). Students are frequently overwhelmed by the experience of puberty. They often need to be reminded and reassured that puberty is a natural and healthy process that includes weight gain, growth spurts, and the physiological effects of growth and sex hormones. They need to know that these healthy and natural processes are disrupted during nutritional deprivation (Piran, 1999b). In a 1999 publication (Piran, 1999b), I reported on two 15-year-old students with bulimia nervosa whose growth was stunted because of the development of anorexia at the age of 11; they were both put on a diet by their health practitioners at that age and were encouraged to diet by their parents. Experiencing loss because of their stunted growth, they both sadly claimed to have never been exposed to knowledge about nutritional deprivation and growth until age 15. Community-based counselors can also inform parents about the importance of regular family meals in preventing the development of EDs (Neumark-Sztainer, Wall, Story, & Fulkerson, 2004).

Sexuality is another dimension of desire that is experienced as problematic, especially by girls, affecting comfort with the body and body esteem (e.g., Crisp, 1995, Piran & Teall, 2012). Similar to appetite, the pre- or early pubertal connection to sexual desire (e.g., "There's this one guy that I like and he likes me, too. He's got the cutest face and he's adorable") shifts to disrupted connection postpuberty ("Well, I try to ignore it [sexual desire]. Like 'cause like I know that I am not a whore and I am not a slut"; Piran, 2009, p. 105). Girls sometimes attempt to control their desire and experiences in the sexual social arena by changing their body shape (e.g., Crisp, 1995; Piran, 2009). The natural connection to desire among girls is often disrupted because of sexual violations, prejudicial treatment of girls' sexuality, expectations that girls should contain boys' desire, and negative labeling (such as *slut*; Piran, 2009; Tolman, 2002). Counselors should therefore not be surprised if the topic of sexuality emerges in body image groups with girls or boys. As a counselor, I have encouraged girls' discussion about their own desire, including respecting female desire, who is responsible for boys' desire, the problem of sexual behavior without desire, and self-care in desire (Piran, 2009).

## Social Stereotypes Domain

As with all members of society, students and counselors alike internalize societal prejudices and stereotypes related to gender, social class, ethnicity, sexual orientation, health, and other aspects of social location. Stereotypes of femininity have an adverse effect on girls' body image (Murnen & Smolak, 2009; Piran & Teall, 2012). Girls learn to view their own bodies as objects to be looked at rather than as sites of freedom, function, competence, and joy (Fredrickson & Roberts, 1997; Piran, 2009; Piran & Teall, 2012). Moreover, as they get to the early pubertal stage and beyond, girls aim to embody the idealized image of "perfect" femininity and concurrently experience their own natural appearance as deficient (Piran, 2009). In addition to being thin (yet voluptuous), among other physical characteristics, the "ideal" female is also demure, passionless, and desireless while being a sexualized object (Tolman, 2002) and competing with other girls for boys' attention (Brown, 2003). Girls who are judged to deviate from this ideal often experience social exclusion and negative social labeling (e.g., *butch, bitch, slut, nerd*; Piran, 2009; Piran & Teall, 2012). This social pressure on girls to live in their body as a deficient site needing ongoing repair to achieve perfection has a powerful adverse effect on girls' body image. Boys similarly experience the pressure of stereotypes, for example, to look muscular, sometimes leading them to use steroids (Ricciardelli, McCabe, Mussap, & Holt, 2009).

Familiarity with restrictive gender molds of femininity and masculinity can help counselors in their work with children, supporting them in developing a critical look at stereotyped gender roles, reframing their understanding, and encouraging them to live in their bodies in a way not constrained by these stereotypes. Here is an example from Piran and Teall's (2012) research interviews with girls. In line with the feminine stereotype of the natural female body as deficient, the 12-year-old girl claims that "pretty girls don't sweat":

> It's weird to think about girls sweating. I try to avoid it . . . I think it's more like boys are having so much fun because they don't care what they look like . . . If I didn't sweat I will be playing sports like every day.
> [Interviewer: Is there another way to think about sweat?]
> Everybody does that. It's normal.
> [Interviewer: Is there a way to think about sweat as a strength?]
> That I am trying so hard. I am trying super hard. I am playing really well.
> (Piran, 2009, p. 92)

### Social Power Domain

Experiencing equitable social power with others, as well as a connection to others and to desired groups or communities, enhances positive self- and body image (Piran & Teall, 2012). Gender, ethnocultural group membership, socioeconomic status, sexual orientation, health, education, and other aspects of social location determine social power. Often, individuals who hold positions of less privilege experience body-based prejudices, teasing, and harassment, all centrally related to body image (Larkin & Rice, 2005; Piran & Thompson, 2008). For example, the prejudice against higher weight, which children experience from a young age, is related to prejudices about low social class. In most Western countries, lower social class is statistically associated with higher weight (O'Dea, 2005). Research has found this association to relate to multiple environmental factors, such as the high price and limited accessibility of fresh produce and more limited access to physical activities and physical safety in low-income neighborhoods. Although not often recognized, the association of heavier weight with low social class shapes social prejudices about weight. In addition, higher weight has been associated with individual characterological flaws (e.g., lazy, poor control). Weight-based teasing is as much a social justice issue as any form of prejudice; however, it is often not recognized as such (Steiner-Adair & Vorenberg, 1999). Social class teasing is also expressed through the targeting of other body-based aspects, such as non–brand-name clothing and references to poorer students' hygiene (Piran, 2009).

Although body-based prejudices and harassment exist along different dimensions of social location, it is important to examine the intersection of these dimensions in the representation of the idealized feminine image. In a 5-year prospective study with a group of girls from diverse backgrounds in terms of ethnicity, social class, and other factors (Piran, 2009), the "ideal girl" was consistently described (with minor variations) as having "a skirt and a tight top. Long hair and really pretty shoes. [Body] Like long and thin . . . blond hair in pigtails, long eyelashes. Great smile . . . Pretty blue eyes. White sparkly teeth . . . makeup everywhere and designer clothes. [12-yr-old]" (p. 148).

This commonly shared internalized image of the ideal girl embodies prejudices about gender (thin, not too big, perfect, sexualized, objectified), ethnicity (blond, blue eyed, straight hair), social class (designer clothes, likely expensive makeup, thin), and sexual orientation (heterosexual). This idealized image of femininity is portrayed amply in the media and shapes social relations in all social systems. Embodying this idealized image yields ample social rewards; for example, on school campuses it may translate to access to dates and popularity (see student quote, Social Power Domain section; Piran, 2009; Piran & Teall, 2012).

The pervasiveness of the idealized image of femininity has led to a strong emphasis on the prevention of EDs in the development of a critical stance toward media-generated images that reinforce this idealized image and its internalization (e.g., Neumark-Sztainer, Sherwood, Coller, & Hannon, 2000; Stice, Mazotti, Weibel, & Agras, 2000). Indeed, counselors should promote programs that develop a critical stance toward media-generated idealized images, and several such programs are available and are discussed in the next section. In addition, however, counselors should be involved in examining the impact of these idealized images on social life in the school, home, and community in terms of rewards and teasing (Haines, Neumark-Sztainer, Perry, Hannan, & Levine, 2006; Piran, 2001, 2011). Workshops or groups that invite students to examine body-based prejudices should be encouraged. For example, a discussion of the idealized feminine image often clarifies the associated social rewards of getting dates and popularity but also suggests the ultimate deprecation of this ideal as *dumb blond, ditsy,* or *mean,* reflecting the inherent lower social status of girls and women (ir-respective of how perfect they aim to be; Piran, 2009; Piran & Teall, 2012). In the 5-year prospective qualitative research with girls, I found that they recognized that the idealized appearance indeed gives them social rewards but not real power, because "It [looking like the ideal image] makes us feel that we are part of a group, but I think you lose part of who you are, part of your power" (16-year-old girl; Piran, 2009, p. 155).

Schools, families, and counselors can provide youths with ample oppor-tunities to engage in critical dialogues about adverse stereotypes, freeing them from trying to pursue an elusive ideal. When a critical perspective becomes normative among peers and in families, youths are more free from having to comply with adverse stereotypes, such as those regarding body size and body monitoring (Becker, Smith, & Ciao, 2006; Piran, 2001). Youths should be supported in connecting to communities that can support a resistant stance toward inequitable treatment. Even virtual communities can be used, such as the Hardy Girls Healthy Women Web site for girls (http://www.hghw.org). Counselors can encourage youths to be active participants in transforming their school (or other community-based) environment through poster campaigns, self-generated plays, and daily dialogues (Haines et al., 2006; McVey, Tweed, & Blackmore, 2007; Piran, 2001). In school, a counselor can support administration and teachers in examining their own stereotypes regarding femininity, social class, ethnicity, and other social factors and examine the impact of these prejudices on, for example, who is invited to speak and represent the school in different public forums (Brownell, Puhl, Schwartz, & Rudd, 2005; O'Dea, 2005; Piran, 1999b, 1999c, 2004). Students are sensitive to norms disseminated by school personnel at school. Moreover, the school, with the support of the school counselor, can engage in a critical review of its curriculum and its representation of women and girls and individuals of diverse weights, of different ethnicities, and other groups. Also, the school may agree to have its staff participate in educational sessions that examine staff's own prejudices (e.g., about weight and gender) and the impact of these prejudices on their behaviors with students (Piran, 2004).

## Early Identification and Intervention

Considering the multiple domains of influence on students' body experiences, some children and early adolescents will inevitably not only develop a negative body image but start to engage in a disordered eating pattern in an effort to alter their body shape. Counselors in community-based settings need to be aware of the high prevalence of negative body image, as well as disordered eating patterns, among children. Therefore, the initial assessment should include inquiries about such challenges among children. School-based counselors have a unique role in the early identification of the development of disordered eating patterns and can be a resource for teachers in that domain. In moving toward the goal of early identification and intervention, it is important for counselors to work against the negative stigma associated with EDs and frame negative body image and disordered eating patterns as understandable reactions to multiple pressures that exist in and outside of the school and community environment (Piran, 1999b). In the context of experienced pressures, students may view altering their body as their only way of coping.

Counselors need to make themselves accessible to youths expressing distress about body weight and shape and other body concerns. By removing the stigma of EDs, and by being accessible to students who are preoccupied with body image issues, counselors make it more likely that students will seek out help and approach them at the earlier phases of preoccupation and before disordered eating patterns (such as starvation or bingeing and purging) have become entrenched as central coping strategies in these students' lives. A longer duration of difficulties has been well established as being associated with poorer outcome (Katzman, 1999).

Students approaching the counselor themselves (rather than being mandated by a teacher or parent) is much more preferable, and it may indeed happen if the counselor becomes known as a source of support in relation to body image issues. Students can then be invited by the counselor to examine challenges they experience in their lives at that time and decide collaboratively on an action plan. Unless the counselor has had special training in treating disorders of body shape and eating, it is vital that the student be referred to a health professional for a comprehensive assessment and intervention. EDs are associated with significant medical complications and, in particular during puberty, several consequences are irreversible (such as stunted growth; Katzman, 1999).

## Resources for Counselors

Counselors have varied resources in this area. In this section, I describe a sample of such resources rather than provide a comprehensive review of all available resources. First, counselors can consult Web sites that aim to educate about EDs, their identification, and ways to address EDs in students. For example, the provincial government of British Columbia constructed a useful online resource for school personnel (http://www.bced.gov.bc.ca/specialed/edi/12.htm). A similar resource for school personnel has been devised by the Hincks Dellcrest Centre for the treatment of a range of mental difficulties in children, including EDs (http://www.hincksdellcrest.org/ABC/Welcome.aspx). Another educational interactive Web site for school personnel and parents, The Student Body, was developed by Sick Kids hospital in Toronto (http://research.aboutkidshealth.ca/thestudentbody/home.asp). The advantage of this latter resource is that it addresses biases in significant adults in children's lives, including teachers and parents, so that adults are better able to provide children with a constructive developmental environment in the domain of the body. In addition, national community-based organizations, such as the National Eating Disorders Association, located in New York, have developed Web-based information for educators and coaches (http://www.nationaleating-disorders.org/information-resources/educators-and-coaches.php). All of these Web sites are useful for counselors regarding the phenomenology of EDs and their management.

The prevention of EDs requires multiple changes in the lives of children, as described earlier. Nonetheless, the counselor may opt to implement varied packaged programs that aim at the prevention of EDs by focusing on a particular source of adverse social influence. One promising trend in prevention programs for EDs are media literacy programs that enhance the development of critical resistance skills in students to media-generated presentations regarding body shape and thinness. For example, Wilksch and Wade (2009) devised an eight-lesson co-ed media literacy program for eighth-grade students called "Media Smart." A randomized controlled evaluation of the program revealed that it led to positive outcomes for girls on measures of shape and weight concerns and dieting, even 30 months after administration. Neumark-Sztainer et al. (2000) developed a media literacy program, "Free to Be Me," that was implemented in Girl Scout

211

troops. Participants engaged in tasks that focused on the critical evaluation of real and virtual body types and of advertisements. They also engaged in writing tasks, such as writing letters about the media, and writing skits for parents to share what they have learned. The program seemed to change media-related attitudes and choice of leisure magazines, but not participants' dieting behavior. Steiner-Adair and Vorenberg (1999) described a media literacy program for third-grade students in which students engage in media creation. This interesting program has not been evaluated in a research study; however, students' recorded comments during these activities reveal a developing critical stance toward the media. Other prevention programs that aim at addressing a broader range of issues that could contribute to EDs include components of media literacy. For example, O'Dea and Abraham's (2000) prevention program, which aims to enhance students' self-esteem, has a strong unit about social stereotypes and the media.

Outcome evaluation research has suggested that didactic programs with children that focus on delivering information about healthy eating and the media do not seem to be effective in preventing EDs. However, the program developed by Kater (2004, 2005) is particularly strong in conveying to elementary school children the natural diversity in weight. Kater, an experienced clinician, avoided weight biases that are common in programs that promote healthy eating. Counselors can also use children's books that represent the natural range of body weights and sizes. Parents and schools should be encouraged to use reading material that enhances a positive body image in children. For example, Dohnt and Tiggemann (2008) evaluated the impact of a children's book titled *Shapesville* aimed at promoting positive body image in young children (ages 5–9) and found that reading it to children was associated with increased appearance satisfaction in girls and with reduced stereotyping on the basis of weight.

Other programs were designed to address a range of factors that challenge youths in the area of body image. The Full of Ourselves: Advancing Girl Power, Health, and Leadership program by Steiner-Adair and Sjostrom (Sjostrom & Steiner-Adair, 2005; Steiner-Adair & Sjostrom, 2006; Steiner-Adair et al., 2002) is a program designed specifically for middle school girls. This program involves multiple interactive activities such as discussions, art projects, role plays, and guided mediation. The program emphasizes dialoging with the body, such as experiential learning through body scanning and writing a journal to the body, and actions that counteract restrictions put on girls (such as a bioenergetic punching activity, physical exercises, and assertive training). It addresses weightism as a social issue, identifying and resisting unhealthy media messages, and how to be an activist at home and at school. In a controlled evaluation, the program was found to lead to positive changes in participants' body image, a result not often found in a primary prevention program, that was maintained at the 6-month follow-up. However, changes in eating behaviors were only marginally significant (Steiner-Adair et al., 2002). Steiner-Adair et al. recognized that a stronger maintenance of gains could be achieved through environmental change involving parents, teachers, and administrators.

In addition to implementing specific packaged prevention programs with students, several ecologically based programs are particularly well suited to schools. For example, counselors can be facilitators of ecological changes in the school environment that aim at enhancing constructive experiences for students in the body domain. In the Understanding Negative Body Image in Context section, I delineated facets of the school environment that could be targeted for change toward the goal of prevention. However, school counselors may find it useful to read about several programs that have targeted such schoolwide changes. The whole-school approach may help sustain program-related gains among children.

I implemented the Dance School Participatory Prevention Program in a competitive residential dance school (Piran, 1999a, 1999b, 1999c, 2001). In implementing this program, I emphasized a participatory, feminist–relational approach. Conducting body image groups with students, I invited the students to bring forward elements of their school environment that disrupted (or that enhanced) their body experiences. I then worked with the students and staff to change the school environment. Facets of change in the school environment included peer norms, such as the norms of no teasing, harassment, or mutual body evaluations; school policies, such as anti-harassment policies or no comments by teachers on students' body shape; curriculum, such as a greater emphasis on safety during training, as well as allocating time for body image groups centered on students' concerns regarding body shape; staff training and hiring, such as identifying staff who could be onsite sources of support for students regarding body issues; and the physical setting, such as allowing more privacy in changing rooms (Piran, 2001). Repeated all-school surveys during a 10-year period revealed a significant reduction in disordered eating patterns at the school (Piran, 1999c).

Haines et al. (2006) implemented a program, Very Important Kids, in an inner-city school in the United States that focused on an issue, weight teasing, identified by students as disruptive to their body experience at the school. The program used different methods to address teasing, including schoolwide training, a no-teasing school campaign, and a theater production, which focused on changing social norms regarding teasing. Parents were invited to the theater production. In addition, students participated in training regarding responses to teasing. Haines et al. found that the program was associated with reduced weight- and appearance-related teasing.

McVey et al. (2007) implemented a prevention program in middle schools (ages 11–14) that followed the Comprehensive School Health model. The program included a specific curriculum, a school play, a workshop and newsletter for parents, small-group discussions, and staff training. McVey et al. found significant positive effects in intervention schools compared with controlled schools.

213

# Chapter Highlights

This chapter leads to several conclusions regarding the counselor's role in preventing negative body shape and EDs among children and adolescents:

- Prevention of negative body image and EDs is an important aspect of counselors' role.
- Counselors should become familiar with the range of social experiences that contribute to the development of negative body image and disordered eating.
- The developmental theory of embodiment addresses a range of social experiences that shape body image development:
  a. Experiences of safety, engagement in physical activities, respect for bodily needs and care, freedom from constraining and demeaning social stereotypes, and equitable connection to others facilitate the development of positive body image within the child's environment.
  b. Experiences of violations, restrictions in physical activities or needs, and exposure to negative labeling, prejudices, or harassment, as well as to pressures to attain idealized (yet demeaned) stereotypes of perfection (specifically of femininity among girls) are adverse influences that contribute to the development of negative body image.
- Counselors can choose to work toward the prevention of EDs by addressing facets of the school environment or by implementing existing prevention programs in communities or schools, especially programs that aim to enhance media literacy and a critical and social justice perspective among students.
- Counselors should be familiar with the expressions of EDs, including anorexia, bulimia nervosa, and binge eating disorder, with the goal of early identification and should learn to approach students who may develop disordered eating patterns. Moreover, counselors should have a network of health and mental health professionals to whom students with EDs could be referred.

# References

Bearman, S. K., & Stice, E. (2008). Testing a gender additive model: A longitudinal study of risk factors for adolescent depression. *Journal of Abnormal Child Psychology, 36,* 1251–1263.

Becker, C. B., Smith, L. M., & Ciao, A. C. (2006). Peer-facilitated eating disorder prevention: A randomized effectiveness trial of cognitive dissonance and media advocacy. *Journal of Counseling Psychology, 53,* 550–555.

Biddle, S. J. (1993). Children, exercise, and mental health. *International Journal of Sport Psychology,24,* 200–216.

Biddle, S. J. H., Whitehead, S. H., O'Donovan, T. M., & Nevill, M. E. (2005). Correlates of participation in physical activity for adolescent girls: A systematic review of recent literature. *Journal of Physical Activity and Health, 2,* 423–34.

Bradley, C. B., McMurray, R. G., Harrell, J. S., & Deng, S. (2000). Changes in common activities of 3rd through 10th graders: The CHIC study. *Medicine & Science in Sports & Exercise, 32,* 2071–2078.

Bronfenbrenner, U. (1977). Toward an experimental ecology of human development. *American Psychologist, 32,* 513–531.

Brown, L. M. (2003). *Girlfighting: Betrayal and rejecting among girls.* New York: New York University Press.

Brownell, K. D., Puhl, R., Schwartz, M. B., & Rudd, L. (Eds.). (2005). *Weight bias: Nature, consequences, and remedies.* New York, NY: Guilford Press

Crisp, A. H. (1995). *Anorexia nervosa: Let me be.* Mahwah, NJ: Erlbaum.

Dohnt, H. K., & Tiggeman, M. (2008). Promoting positive body image in young girls: An evaluation of Shapesville. *European Eating Disorders Review, 16,* 222–233.

Dwyer, J. J. M., Allison, K. R., Goldenberg, E. R., Fein, A. J., Yoshida, K. K. & Boutilier, M. A. (2006). Adolescent girls' perceived barriers to participation in physical activity. *Adolescence, 41,* 75–89.

Ewing, M., & Seefeldt, V. (1996). Patterns of participation and attrition in American agency-sponsored youth sports. In F. Smoll & R. E. Smith (Eds.), *Children and youth in sport: A biopsychosocial perspective* (pp. 31–45). Madison, WI: Brown & Benchmark.

Falgairette, G., Deflandre, A., & Gavarry, O. (2004). Habitual physical activity, influences of gender and environmental factors. *Science & Sports, 19,* 161–173.

Field, A., Camargo, C., Taylor, C., Berkey, C., Frazier, L., Gillman, M., & Colditz, G. (1999). Overweight, weight concerns, and bulimic behaviors among girls and boys. *Journal of the American Academy of Child & Adolescent Psychiatry, 38,* 754–760.

Fredrickson, B. L., & Roberts, T. (1997). Objectification theory: Toward understanding women's lived experiences and mental health risks. *Psychology of Women Quarterly, 21,*173–206.

French, S. A., Story, M., Neumark-Sztainer, D., Downes, B., Resnick, M., & Blum, R. (1997). Ethnic differences in psychosocial and health behavior correlates of dieting, purging, and binge eating in a population-based sample of adolescents. *International Journal of Eating Disorders, 22,* 315–322.

Haines, J., Neumark-Sztainer, D., Perry, C. L., Hannan, P. J., & Levine, M. P. (2006). V.I.K. (Very Important Kids): A school-based program designed to reduce teasing and unhealthy weight-control behaviors. *Health Education Research: Theory and Practice, 21,* 884–895

Harned, M. S. (2000). Harassed bodies: An examination of the relationships among women's experiences of sexual harassment, body image, and eating disturbances. *Psychology of Women Quarterly, 24,* 336–348.

Harned, M. S., & Fitzgerald, L. F. (2002). Understanding a link between sexual harassment and eating disorder symptoms: A mediational analysis. *Journal of Consulting and Clinical Psychology, 70,* 1170–1181.

Hill, A. J., Weaver, C., & Blundell, J. E. (1990). Dieting concerns of 10-year-old girls and their mothers. *British Journal of Clinical Psychology, 29,* 346–348.

Kater, K. (2004). *Real kids come in all sizes.* New York, NY: Broadway Books.

Kater, K. J. (2005). *Healthy body images: Teaching kids to eat, and love their bodies, too!* (2nd ed.). Carlsbad, CA: Gürze Books. Retrieved from http://www.nationaleatingdisorders.org

Katzman, D. K. (1999). Prevention of medical complications in children and adolescents with eating disorders. In N. Piran, M. P. Levine, & C. Steiner-Adair (Eds.), *Preventing eating disorders: A handbook of interventions and special challenges* (pp. 304–318). Philadelphia, PA: Brunner/Mazel.

Larkin, J., & Rice, C. (2005). Beyond "healthy eating" and "healthy weights": Harassment and the health curriculum in middle school girls. *Body Image, 2, 219–232.*

Legge, R. (2010, June). *If I am thin, I am safe: Speaking through the body following trauma.* Paper presented at the 4th Critical Multicultural Counselling and Psychotherapy Conference, Ontario Institute for Studies in Education, University of Toronto, Toronto, Ontario, Canada.

Lowes, J., & Tiggemann, M. (2003). Body dissatisfaction, dieting awareness and the impact of parental influence in young children. *British Journal of Health Psychology, 8,* 135–147.

McVey, G., Tweed, S., & Blackmore, E. (2007). Healthy Schools–Healthy Kids: A controlled evaluation of a comprehensive universal eating disorder prevention program. *Body Image, 4,* 115–136.

Murnen, S. K., & Smolak, L. (2000). The experience of sexual harassment among grade-school students: Early socialization of female subordination? *Sex Roles, 43,* 1–17.

Murnen, S. K., & Smolak, L. (2009). Are feminist women protected from body image problems? A meta-analytic review of relevant research. *Sex Roles, 60,* 186–197.

Murnen, S. K., Smolak, L., Mills, J. A., & Good, L. (2003). Thin, sexy women and strong, muscular men: Grade-school children's responses to objectified images of women and men. *Sex Roles, 49,* 427–437.

Neumark-Sztainer, D., Paxton, S. J., Hannan, P. J., Haines, J., & Story, M. (2006). Does body satisfaction matter? Five-year longitudinal associations between body satisfaction and health behaviors in adolescent females and males. *Journal of Adolescent Health, 39,* 244–251.

Neumark-Sztainer, D., Sherwood, N. E., Coller, T., & Hannon, P. J. (2000). Primary prevention of disordered eating among preadolescent girls: Feasibility and short-term effect of a community-based intervention. *Journal of the American Dietetic Association, 100,* 1466–1473.

Neumark-Sztainer, D., Wall, M., Story, M., & Fulkerson, J. A. (2004). Are family meal patterns associated with disordered eating behaviors among adolescents? *Journal of Adolescent Health, 35,* 350–359.

O'Dea, J. A. (2005) Prevention of child obesity: "First, do no harm." *Health Education Research, 20,* 259–265.

O'Dea, J. A., & Abraham, S. (2000). Improving the body image, eating attitudes, and behaviors of young male and female adolescents: A new educational approach that focuses on self-esteem. *International Journal of Eating Disorders, 28,* 43–57.

Piran, N. (1999a). Eating disorders: A trial of prevention in a high risk school setting. *Journal of Primary Prevention, 20,* 75–90.

Piran, N. (1999b). On the move from tertiary to secondary and primary prevention: Working with an elite dance school. In N. Piran, M. P. Levine, & C. Steiner-Adair (Eds.), *Preventing eating disorders: A handbook of interventions and special challenges* (pp. 256–269). Philadelphia, PA: Brunner/Mazel.

Piran, N. (1999c). The reduction of preoccupation with body weight and shape in schools: A feminist approach. In N. Piran, M. P. Levine, & C. Steiner-Adair (Eds.), *Preventing eating disorders: A handbook of interventions and special challenges* (pp. 148–150). Philadelphia, PA: Brunner/Mazel.

Piran, N. (2001). Re-inhabiting the body from the inside out: Girls transform their school environment. In D. L. Tolman & M. Brydon-Miller (Eds.), *From subjects to subjectivities: A handbook of interpretive and participatory methods* (pp. 218–238). New York: New York University Press.

Piran, N. (2004). Teachers: On "being" prevention. *Eating Disorders: The Journal of Treatment and Prevention, 12,* 1–9.

Piran, N. (2009). *The body journey of girls: Stories of disruption and resilience delineate paths for constructive changes.* Unpublished manuscript.

Piran, N. (2010). A feminist perspective on risk factor research and on the prevention of eating disorders. *Eating Disorders: The Journal of Treatment and Prevention, 18,* 183–198.

Piran, N. (2011, May). *How can schools promote positive body image and prevent eating disorders among students?* Invited workshop presented to the Assembly of Teachers of the Viennese School Board, Vienna, Austria.

Piran, N., Antoniou, M., Legge, R., McCance, N., Mizevich, J., Peasley, E., & Ross, E. (2006). On girls' disembodiment: The complex tyranny of the "ideal girl." In D. L. Gustafson & L. Goodyear (Eds.), *Women, health, and education: CASWE 6th bi-annual international institute proceedings* (pp. 224–229). St. John's, Newfoundland, Canada: Memorial University.

Piran, N., Carter, W., Thompson, S., & Pajouhandeh, P. (2002). Powerful girls: A contradiction in terms? Young women speak about the experience of growing up in a girl's body. In S. Abbey (Ed.), *Ways of knowing in and through the body: Diverse perspectives on embodiment* (pp. 206–210). Welland, Ontario, Canada: Soleil.

Piran, N., & Cormier, H. (2005). The social construction of women and disordered eating patterns. *Journal of Counseling Psychology, 52,* 549–558.

Piran, N., & Teall, T. (2012). The developmental theory of embodiment. In G. McVey, M. P. Levine, N. Piran, & H. B. Ferguson (Eds.), *Preventing eating-related and weight-related disorders: Collaborative research, advocacy, and policy change* (pp. 171–199). Waterloo, Ontario, Canada: Wilfred Laurier University Press.

Piran, N., & Thompson, S. (2008). A study of the adverse social experiences model to the development of eating disorders. *International Journal of Health Promotion and Education, 46,* 65–71.

Ricciardelli, L., McCabe, M., Mussap, A., & Holt, K. E. (2009). Body image in preadolescent boys. In L. Smolak & J. K. Thompson (Eds.), *Body image, eating disorders, and obesity in youth: Assessment, prevention, and treatment* (2nd ed., pp. 77–96). Washington, DC: American Psychological Association.

Richman, E. L., & Shaffer, D. R. (2000). If you let me play sports: How might sport participation influence the self-esteem of adolescent females? *Psychology of Women Quarterly, 24,* 189–199.

Sjostrom, L. A., & Steiner-Adair, C. (2005). Full of ourselves: A wellness program to advance girl power, health & leadership: An eating disorder prevention program that works. *Journal of Educational Behavior, 37*(Suppl. 2), S141–S144.

Smolak, L., & Piran, N. (2012). Gender and the prevention of eating disorders. In G. McVey, M. P. Levine, N. Piran, & H. B. Ferguson (Eds.), *Preventing eating-related and weight-related disorders: Collaborative research, advocacy, and policy change* (pp. 200–222). Waterloo, Ontario, Canada: Wilfred Laurier University Press.

Steiner-Adair, C., & Vorenberg, A. P. (1999). Resisting weightism: Media literacy for elementary school children. In N. Piran, M. P. Levine, & C. Steiner-Adair (Eds.), *Preventing eating disorders: A handbook of interventions and special challenges* (pp. 105–121). Philadelphia, PA: Brunner/Mazel.

Steiner-Adair, C., & Sjostrom, L. A. (2006). Full of ourselves: A wellness program to advance girl power, health & leadership. New York, NY: Teachers College Press.

Steiner-Adair, C., Sjostrom, L., Franko, D.L., Pai, S., Tucker, R., Becker, A., & Herzog, D. (2002). Primary prevention of risk factors for eating disorders in adolescent girls: Learning from practice. *International Journal of Eating Disorders, 32,* 401–411.

Stice, E., & Bearman, S. K. (2001). Body image and eating disturbances prospectively predict increases in depressive symptoms in adolescent girls: A growth curve analysis. *Developmental Psychology, 37,* 597–607.

Stice, E., Cameron, R., Hayward, C., Taylor, C. B., & Killen, J. (1999). Naturalistic weight-reduction efforts prospectively predict growth in relative weight and onset among female adolescents. *Journal of Consulting and Clinical Psychology, 67,* 967–974.

Stice, E., Mazotti, L., Weibel, D., & Agras, W. S. (2000). Dissonance prevention program decreases thin-ideal internalization, body dissatisfaction, dieting, negative affect, and bulimic symptoms: A preliminary experiment. *International Journal of Eating Disorders, 27,* 206–217.

Swanson, S. A., Crow, S. J., Le Grange, D., Swendsen, J., & Merikangas, K. R. (2011). Prevalence and correlates of eating disorders in adolescents: Results from the National Comorbidity Survey Replication Adolescent Supplement. *Archives of General Psychiatry, 68,* 714–723.

Theberge, N. (2003). "No fear comes": Adolescent girls, ice hockey, and the embodiment of gender. *Youth and Society, 34,* 497–516.

Tolman, D. (2002). *Dilemmas of desire: Teenage girls talk about sexuality.* Boston, MA: Harvard University Press.

Wertheim, E., Paxton, S., & Blaney, S. (2009). Body image in girls. In L. Smolak & J. K. Thompson (Eds.), *Body image, eating disorders, and obesity in youth: Assessment, prevention, and treatment* (2nd ed., pp. 47–76). Washington, DC: American Psychological Association.

Wilksch, S. M., & Wade, T. D. (2009). Reduction of shape and weight concern in young adolescents: A 30-month controlled evaluation of a media literacy program. *Journal of the American Academy of Child & Adolescent Psychiatry, 48,* 652–661.

Young, I. M. (1990). Throwing like a girl: A phenomenology of feminine body comportment, mobility, and spatiality. In I. M. Young (Ed.), *Throwing like a girl and other essays in feminist philosophy and social theory* (pp. 141–159). Bloomington: Indiana University Press.

## Chapter 10

# Eating Disorders Prevention With Adolescents and Young Adults

*Heather Shaw and Eric Stice*

Approximately 10% of young women have anorexia nervosa, bulimia nervosa, or eating disorder not otherwise specified (EDNOS), which includes binge eating disorder and subthreshold eating disorders (EDs; Hudson, Hiripi, Pope, & Kessler, 2007; Stice, Marti, Shaw, & Jaconis, 2009; Wade, Bergin, Tiggemann, Bulik, & Fairburn, 2006). Threshold EDs and EDNOS are marked by chronicity, relapse, distress, functional impairment, and risk for future obesity, depression, suicide attempts, anxiety disorders, substance abuse, and morbidity (Arcelus, Mitchell, Wales, & Nielsen, 2011; Crow et al., 2009; Le Grange et al., 2006; Schmidt et al., 2008; Swanson, Crow, Le Grange, Swendsen, & Merikangas, 2011). The standardized mortality ratio (observed deaths in a population divided by expected deaths on the basis of demographics) was 1.7 for anorexia nervosa, 1.6 for bulimia nervosa, and 1.8 for EDNOS (comparable increases for suicide were 4.7, 6.5, and 3.9, respectively; Crow et al., 2009). Indeed, EDs show stronger relations to suicide attempts, outpatient and inpatient treatment, and functional impairment than virtually all other psychiatric disorders (Newman et al., 1996).

## Importance of Prevention

Although most individuals with EDs have some contact with mental health services (80% of those with threshold EDs; 67% of those with EDNOS), few seek ED treatment (20% with threshold ED; 3% with EDNOS; Swanson et al., 2011). Furthermore, treatments of choice result in lasting symptom remission for only 35% to 45% of treated patients (e.g., Agras, Walsh, Fairburn, Wilson, & Kraemer, 2000; Lock et al., 2010), and treatments are typically less effective when delivered in real-world clinical settings

(Weersing & Weisz, 2002), where dropout rates are higher (Merrill, Tolbert, & Wade, 2003). ED treatment is also very expensive, often costing more than $10,000 (Striegel-Moore et al., 2000), with residential treatment costs estimated at an average of $956 per day with an average stay of 83 days (Frisch, Herzog, & Franko, 2006). These issues surrounding treatment point to why preventing EDs is at the forefront of considerable research efforts. Prevention programs may be particularly successful for EDs, relative to other psychiatric conditions, because the peak risk period for onset of these disorders occurs between the ages of 16 and 19 (Hudson et al., 2007; Lewinsohn et al., 2000; Stice, Marti, et al., 2009). These data imply that if efficacious programs were widely implemented during this period, they could reduce the incidence of EDs. Moreover, it is more ethical to prevent the emergence of these debilitating disorders than to wait for them to develop and attempt treatment. Thus, broadly implementing effective ED prevention programs is a public health priority.

Prevention scientists recognize three qualitatively different types of prevention programs: universal, selective, and indicated. Universal prevention describes interventions that are offered to all individuals in a particular population, such as high school students. Selective prevention programs are offered only to individuals at elevated risk for a particular psychiatric condition, such as young women or those with established risk factors for eating pathology (e.g., body image or weight concerns). Indicated prevention programs are offered to individuals with initial symptoms of the psychiatric condition, such as those who endorse binge eating or other ED symptoms. Although several prevention programs have significantly reduced putative risk factors for EDs, such as body dissatisfaction, only a small handful have significantly reduced ED symptoms or disorders through follow-up.

In the following sections, we provide an overview of research evaluating ED prevention programs and describe examples of effective universal, selective, and indicated programs. We then describe the Body Project, a dissonance-based eating disorder prevention program, in greater detail, because it has received the most empirical support of the ED prevention programs that have been evaluated to date.

## Overview of Effective and Efficacious Eating Disorder Prevention Programs

A recent meta-analytic review found that 51% of ED prevention programs reduced ED risk factors and 29% reduced current or future eating pathology (Stice, Shaw, & Marti, 2007), although fewer produced effects that persisted through follow-up (reviewed later when specific interventions are discussed). Larger intervention effects tended to occur for programs that were selected (vs. universal), interactive (vs. didactic), multisession (vs. single session), solely offered to female participants (vs. both sexes), offered to participants older than age 15 (vs. younger ones), and delivered by professional interventionists (vs. endogenous providers). Programs with body acceptance and dissonance-induction content and without psychoeducational content and programs evaluated in trials using validated measures also produced larger effects.

## Universal Prevention Programs

To our knowledge, three universal prevention programs have produced reductions in select ED symptoms that have persisted through at least 6-month follow-up relative to assessment-only control conditions. Neumark-Sztainer, Butler, and Palti (1995) evaluated a didactic psychoeducational intervention that presented information on healthy weight control behaviors, body image, EDs, putative causes of EDs, and social pressure resistance skills. Their intervention significantly reduced the frequency of self-reported binge eating relative to an assessment-only control condition but did not affect other eating-disordered behaviors (Neumark-Sztainer et al., 1995).

Stewart, Carter, Drinkwater, Hainsworth, and Fairburn (2001) evaluated an interactive program focused on resisting cultural pressures for thinness, determinants of body weight, body acceptance, effects of cognitions on emotions, nature and consequences of EDs, self-esteem enhancement, stress management, and healthy weight control behaviors. Their intervention produced significant effects for ED symptoms at both posttest and 6-month follow-up relative to an assessment-only control group.

Austin, Field, Wiecha, Peterson, and Gortmaker (2005) evaluated a 26-hour universal prevention program that promotes less media use, a healthy diet, and regular exercise. Their intervention significantly reduced unhealthy weight control behaviors (e.g., vomiting, diet pill use) and body mass index scores among female, but not male, preadolescents relative to controls (Austin et al., 2005).

Although the effects of universal ED prevention programs are encouraging, a meta-analytic review found that universal prevention programs typically produce smaller intervention effects than selective prevention programs (Stice, Shaw, & Marti, 2007). Moreover, the effects of these three universal prevention programs have not been replicated by the original investigators or by independent investigators, nor have these prevention programs been shown to significantly outperform credible alternative interventions. As such, the empirical support for these three prevention programs is very limited.

## Selective and Indicated Prevention Programs

Empirical support has also emerged for several selective ED prevention programs. McVey, Lieberman, Voorberg, Wardrope, and Blackmore (2003) evaluated a 10-hour targeted program that promoted critical media use, body acceptance, healthy weight control behaviors, and stress management skills and provided information regarding body mass determinants. Their program produced significantly greater decreases in body dissatisfaction, dieting, and bulimic symptoms than observed in assessment-only controls at both termination and 3-month follow-up. However, these effects did not replicate in a second trial (McVey, Lieberman, Voorberg, Wardrope, Blackmore, & Tweed, 2003).

Our research group found that a brief 3-hour Healthy Weight selective prevention program, which promotes incremental lasting healthy improvements in dietary intake and physical activity in young women with body image concerns, reduced ED symptoms and body mass index relative to assessment-only controls and alternative interventions through 3-year follow-up, reduced ED onset relative to assessment-only controls through 3-year follow-up (7% vs. 15%), and reduced obesity onset relative to assessment-only controls and an alternative intervention at 1-year follow-up (1% vs. 12% and 9%, respectively) and assessment-only controls at 3-year follow-up (8% vs. 18%; Stice, Marti, Spoor, Presnell, & Shaw, 2008). A follow-up trial evaluated a version of the Healthy Weight intervention that incorporated principles that should facilitate healthy changes to dietary intake drawn largely from nutrition research (Ello-Martin, Roe, & Rolls, 2004), including (a) replacing high energy-dense foods with low energy-dense foods, (b) eating complex carbohydrates with high water content at the start of meals (e.g., soup, fruit, salad), (c) reducing portion sizes, (d) eating meals with less variety in the types of foods, and (e) keeping only healthy foods in the living area (e.g., not having unhealthy snacks in the home or dorm). Compared with controls, intervention participants showed significantly greater reductions in ED symptoms and greater increases in physical activity at posttest and significantly greater reductions in body mass index and self-reported dieting at 6-month follow-up (Stice, Rohde, Shaw, & Marti, 2012).

Greater empirical support has emerged for a selective dissonance-based ED prevention program (the Body Project) in which young women at risk for EDs because of body image concerns critique the thin ideal espoused for women in verbal, written, and behavioral exercises (Stice, Mazotti, Weibel, & Agras, 2000). Our research has focused on women because they are at much higher risk for eating pathology than men (Hudson et al., 2007). These activities theoretically cause cognitive dissonance that motivates participants to reduce pursuit of the thin ideal, decreasing body dissatisfaction, unhealthy weight control behaviors, negative affect, and ED symptoms. Efficacy trials have found that the Body Project produces greater reductions in ED risk factors (e.g., thin-ideal internalization, body dissatisfaction, negative affect), ED symptoms, functional impairment, and future onset of EDs over a 3-year follow-up than assessment-only or alternative-intervention control conditions (e.g., Stice et al., 2000, 2008; Stice, Shaw, Burton, & Wade, 2006). Efficacy trials conducted by independent researchers have also found that dissonance-based prevention programs produce greater reductions in risk factors and ED symptoms relative to an assessment-only control condition (Mitchell, Mazzeo, Rausch, & Cooke, 2007) and an alternative intervention (Becker, Smith, & Ciao, 2005).

Consistent with the intervention theory for the Body Project, reducing thin-ideal internalization appears to mediate the effects of the intervention on change in the outcomes (Seidel, Presnell, & Rosenfield, 2009; Stice, Marti, Rohde, & Shaw, 2011; Stice, Presnell, Gau, & Shaw, 2007). Moreover, completing the Body Project offsets the most potent risk factor for ED onset in a high-risk sample—denial of the costs of pursuing the thin ideal—which had an odds ratio of 5.0 (Stice, Rohde, Gau, & Shaw, 2012). Supporting the thesis that dissonance induction contributes to the effects of this intervention, participants assigned to high-dissonance versions of this program have shown significantly greater reductions in ED symptoms than those assigned to low-dissonance versions (Green, Scott, Diyankova, Gasser, & Pederson, 2005; McMillan, Stice, & Rohde, 2011).

In contrast to efficacy trials, which carefully standardize intervention implementation with homogeneous samples in tightly controlled research settings, effectiveness trials examine the effects of interventions that are delivered by real-world providers to heterogeneous samples in ecologically valid settings. Effectiveness trials have also confirmed that the Body Project produces similar effects when high school counselors recruit at-risk young women with body image concerns and deliver the intervention under ecologically valid conditions, including significant reductions in ED symptoms that persist through 3-year follow-up (Stice, Rohde, Gau, & Shaw, 2009; Stice, Rohde, Shaw, & Gau, 2011). Even larger effects are emerging in an ongoing effectiveness trial (Stice, Rohde, Shaw, Butryn, & Marti, 2011), in which college counselors recruit young women with body image concerns and deliver an enhanced-dissonance program. The enhanced-dissonance program adds elements that putatively increase dissonance induction, including components that (a) underscore the voluntary nature of participation in the sessions, (b) increase public accountability for counter–thin-ideal perspectives, and (c) make in-session and home exercises more effortful.

To our knowledge, in trials conducted by independent laboratories only the dissonance-based prevention program has produced significant intervention effects for ED symptoms and significantly outperformed active alternative interventions, which are both necessary for a prevention program to be considered efficacious (American Psychological Association, 1995). Furthermore, this ED prevention program is the only one that has produced effects that persist through 3-year follow-up and that has significantly reduced future onset of EDs.

Indicated ED prevention programs are those that are offered to individuals with subthreshold EDs or recently emerged full-threshold EDs. Although no group-based indicated ED prevention programs have yet been evaluated, our suspicion is that they may also be highly effective. One facilitator-supported version of the Internet-based Student Bodies prevention program, which is largely based on cognitive–behavioral interventions that have been developed for body dissatisfaction, did produce significant reductions in ED symptoms relative to a wait-list control condition (Jacobi, Volker, Trockel, & Taylor, 2012), which is an effect that has not been observed in trials that involved only young women free of EDs.

225

# Guidelines for Counselors Interested in Preventing Eating Disorders

Our review of the literature suggests that, to date, the strongest evidence base has emerged for the Body Project, which has also been adapted for use and widely disseminated in university sororities as Reflections. In addition to garnering the most empirical support, the Body Project has been found to be successful in effectiveness trials in which professionals such as counselors, nurses, or teachers are responsible for recruitment and delivery. After receiving training, such professionals can also train others to recruit for and deliver the intervention. In the next sections, we review the Body Project intervention, summarizing session content and materials. We then discuss the training process for professional facilitators, as well as how to recruit participants and deliver this intervention. A revision of the facilitator's guide for the Body Project will be published in 2012. Although these issues are discussed within the context of the Body Project, many of the principles would apply to other ED intervention programs that are delivered in a group format.

The Body Project was originally developed as a four-session, 4-hour program, designed to accommodate college students' schedules, although the targeted age range has broadened over the years to include girls and women aged 13 to 22. We have also developed a six, 45-minute-session version of the Body Project to deliver in settings in which the sessions need to be shorter, such as college counseling centers. We review the four-session, 4-hour version here because it is the most widely studied and implemented.

Several principles guided the development of the Body Project intervention. We minimized didactic presentation because psychoeducational interventions are less effective than those that actively engage participants (Stice, Shaw, & Marti, 2007). We included exercises that require participants to apply the skills taught in the program to facilitate skill acquisition and homework to reinforce the skills taught in the sessions and help participants learn how to apply them. We used motivational enhancement exercises to maximize motivation to use the new skills (e.g., reviewed costs of body image concerns) and activities to foster group cohesion.

In Session 1, we inform participants that the intervention is based on the idea that discussing the costs of the thin ideal perpetuated by society can improve body satisfaction. We ask them whether they would be willing to try this approach and solicit verbal affirmation of their commitment. Participants discuss the definition and origins of the thin ideal; how it is perpetuated; the impact of messages about the thin ideal from family, peers, dating partners, and the media; and how corporations profit from this unrealistic standard. For homework, we ask participants to write a letter to a hypothetical younger girl that discusses the costs of pursuing the thin ideal and to examine their reflection in a full-length mirror, recording their positive aspects.

In Session 2, we discuss participants' reactions to writing the letter regarding the costs of pursuing the thin ideal and the main costs each participant generated. Second, participants discuss the self-affirmation exercise and the feelings and thoughts they had during this exercise. We ask them to share what they like about themselves. Third, we conduct a counterattitudinal role-play, in which each participant attempts to dissuade the group leaders from pursuing the thin ideal. For homework, we ask participants to provide three examples from their lives concerning pressures to be thin and generate verbal challenges to these pressures. We also ask them to produce a top-10 list of things girls and women can do to resist the thin ideal.

In the third session, participants discuss an example from their lives concerning pressure to be thin and how they might verbally challenge this pressure. Next, they generate quick comebacks that challenge thin-ideal statements made by peers. Participants then discuss the reasons they signed up for the class and identify their body image concerns. We ask them to challenge themselves with a behavioral experiment related to body image concerns in the next week (e.g., wearing shorts if they have avoided doing so because of body dissatisfaction). Next, we ask them to share items from their top-10 list of things girls and women can do to resist the thin ideal. For a second homework assignment, we ask them to enact one of their body activism ideas.

In Session 4, each participant shares her experiences with and reaction to her behavioral challenge. We encourage members to continue to challenge themselves and their body-related concerns in the future. Next, participants' experiences with the body activism exercise are discussed. Then, more subtle ways in which the thin ideal is perpetuated are discussed (e.g., joining in when friends complain about their bodies). We give participants a list of these types of subtle statements and ask them to identify how each perpetuates the thin ideal. We next review difficulties participants might encounter in resisting the thin ideal, as well as how each could be addressed. To further increase awareness, we ask participants to explore future pressures to conform to the thin ideal and ways of responding to those pressures. Next, group members discuss how to talk about one's body in a positive, rather than a negative, way. For homework, we ask participants to write a letter to another hypothetical younger girl about how to avoid developing body image concerns and select a self-affirmation exercise to complete at home (e.g., when given a compliment, practice saying "Thank you" rather than objecting, "No, I'm so fat,"). We ask them to e-mail the facilitator about their experiences with these exercises.

### Recruiting Participants

We have focused on recruiting female students with body image concerns because they are at elevated risk for eating pathology and effects for prevention programs tend to be larger for this population. However, several trials have found that the Body Project program is also efficacious for young women without body image concerns (Becker et al., 2005; Becker,

Bull, Schaumberg, Cauble, & Franco, 2008). We have found that recruiting approximately eight participants with body image concerns per group works well, because smaller groups may not evoke sufficient public accountability, particularly if one or two participants drop out, and larger groups do not allow enough time for all attendees to participate in all of the session exercises.

Body Project recruitment tends to be more successful when potential participants know that the program is being offered in their schools and the program is presented as a fun and interesting opportunity rather than just another class with homework. Removing potential attendance barriers is important. For example, conducting the sessions at school, rather than requiring participants to travel to another location, facilitates participation. Moreover, the best times to hold sessions for students appear to be immediately after school (generally, within 30 minutes of school dismissal) or at times that do not conflict with class schedules (during study hall for high school students or in the evenings for college students) or compete with popular extracurricular activities (e.g., sorority meetings, band practice). Holding sessions no more than once per week can also help increase attendance and avoid potential scheduling conflicts.

We have used a range of recruitment methods, including mass mailings, mass e-mail messages, posters, leaflets, announcements on the school public address system, class announcements, ads in the school paper, and announcements on school Web sites (e.g., Blackboard). We typically invite all female students at a particular school or college, usually via mass mailings or e-mail messages, to sign up for these body acceptance classes. This recruitment approach is by far the most effective. We often find it useful to send a second mailing or e-mailing 2 weeks after the first. The second most effective recruitment strategy is to hang recruitment posters in the student union, the student health center, the student recreation center, the counseling center, sororities, dorms, large lecture halls, and other places with a high volume of student traffic. Using flyers with rip-off tabs containing the relevant contact telephone number or e-mail address on the inside of stalls in women's bathrooms or other locations where individuals can access the information with some privacy is also useful, because body image concerns are often a sensitive topic among adolescents. Recruitment materials should not create unrealistic expectations for potential participants and should include accurate descriptions of the facilitator's qualifications and a clear description of the intervention and its purpose. Including images of minority women on the recruitment posters helps ensure that the students are more ethnically diverse. We have also found it helpful to ask teachers or professors to announce the program in classes and to encourage the school counselors or nurses to mention the body acceptance classes to individuals they feel may be appropriate for the intervention. These recruitment procedures can be effective, resulting in as many as 15% of all female students at some schools and colleges completing this intervention. Former Body Project participants have also been a significant source of referrals.

## Screening and Evaluation of Potential Participants

Interested participants are first screened by telephone. During the initial phone screen, it is important to answer any questions the young women may have about the class and to reassure them that they will have a positive experience (our exit interviews with participants show that their experiences are usually very positive). As part of the phone screen, we ask the following question to screen for the presence of body dissatisfaction in potential participants: "This project is designed for young women who have some concerns about their bodies. Would you say that you have concerns or dissatisfaction with your body?" Participants who answer with some type of affirmative response are enrolled. This approach is our preferred one because it does not involve labeling students as high risk, and it is considerably easier and less expensive.

Allotting adequate time for recruitment is also important. If this is the first time the Body Project is being offered, it usually takes at least a month to generate interest in the class, screen potential participants, and begin the first class.

## Facilitator Recruitment, Training, and Supervision

Dozens of group facilitators have been trained as part of the numerous efficacy and effectiveness studies that have evaluated the Body Project. Because these groups have been conducted for research purposes, we have developed training and supervision requirements for our staff for quality assurance. The success of the Body Project is likely due in part to the effort we have put into carefully selecting, training, and supervising group leaders.

### Recruiting Facilitators

We consider several issues when selecting group leaders for the Body Project and any ED prevention program. First, we have found that the most successful facilitators are those who are enthusiastic and engaging and incorporate humor into the discussions. Second, a clear understanding and commitment to the underlying theory (cognitive dissonance) behind this intervention is very important, as is knowledge about EDs and cultural pressures for thinness. Third, previous experience conducting group-based interventions is valuable, because general therapeutic issues important in conducting effective interventions are not covered in detail in the manual. Thus, individuals who have a background in counseling, social work, psychology, or nursing or who are trainees in these areas may be particularly good candidates for group leaders. Fourth, we have found that having expertise in EDs and cultural factors that appear to contribute to these disorders is also useful. People with this type of background can interject interesting research findings at opportune times, which increases the participants' level of interest. We developed a Facilitator Fact Sheet for the Body Project that details some interesting findings that facilitators may wish to mention during the sessions, which can be accessed at www.bodyprojectsupport.org/resources/materials. We encourage all facilitators to review this fact sheet carefully before leading groups.

Body Project leaders should also be informed that this intervention is not intended to be an open-ended discussion or therapy group; its success depends on facilitators adhering closely to the manual. It is possible that any significant deviation from the manual could render the intervention ineffective, or potentially even iatrogenic. Improvements to the intervention have relied heavily on feedback from facilitators and participants, but any changes occur after the program has been delivered in its entirety (see the Body Project Support Web page, http://www.ori.org/thebodyproject/).

We recommend that two facilitators deliver the intervention together when possible. Cofacilitating is preferable so that leaders can demonstrate role-plays and work together to make sure that all of the material is being covered clearly within the allotted time frame. If one facilitator is sick, having another allows the session to proceed as scheduled. Finally, we have also found it preferable to have women lead the groups because participants might feel freer to discuss sensitive material and experiences, and the facilitators might be better able to relate to the program theory and content. However, male therapists who are sensitive to the experiences of young women in Western culture can deliver the intervention effectively.

### *Training Facilitators*

Body Project facilitator training includes several steps. First, facilitators should familiarize themselves with dissonance theory and all of the material included in the published facilitator's guide (Stice & Presnell, 2007). Second, they should watch the 1-hour training video on the Body Project Support Web page (http://www.ori.org/thebodyproject/) that showcases clinicians from our trials successfully implementing each intervention component. If possible, observing all four sessions conducted by an experienced leader is also very useful. The most important component of training, however, is to practice conducting all of the exercises in each session with other facilitators in training or with mock participants, preferably from the beginning of the session to the end. Practicing the role-play activities is particularly important because it helps facilitators anticipate the many possible responses that might occur in a session regarding ways in which the thin ideal has been internalized. Memorizing as much of the script as possible is also encouraged, because reading the script verbatim can stifle the flow of the group discussion.

If possible, we also recommend that new group leaders first cofacilitate a group with an experienced leader. It is ideal if the facilitator and cofacilitator train together and meet briefly before each session to plan, establish rapport, and anticipate any unforeseen problems. Having a cofacilitator is also useful for time management purposes. While one person leads a section, the cofacilitator can focus on time management. In the beginning, the experienced leader takes more responsibility for running most of the session, and the trainee primarily observes. Gradually, the trainee can take an increasingly active role in leading the sessions. After each session, the experienced leader reviews the trainee's performance and discusses possible solutions to the different clinical issues encountered during the session. We strongly recommend that each session be videotaped to maximize accountability, and therefore dissonance induction, among participants. Videotaping also provides an excellent opportunity for facilitators to view themselves delivering the intervention, which invariably leads to more effective implementation in the future. At the conclusion of the first four-session intervention, the trainee is generally ready to lead the course independently, provided that some supervision is available.

It is also important for new facilitators to be aware of some of the common implementation problems that can arise, which can include participants missing sessions and not completing home exercises and dealing with participants who are particularly invested in the thin ideal. Occasionally group management can be an issue, especially with participants ages 11 to 13. Missing sessions should be strongly discouraged because the Body Project relies on group dynamics to induce cognitive dissonance. However, sometimes a participant has to miss a session because of illness or some other extraneous circumstance. In these instances, a brief make-up session can be scheduled to cover the main points of the session. Because homework assignments are designed to be fun and engaging, we have found that most participants complete them. Reminding participants to complete homework through text messages and e-mails has proven successful. When a participant has a difficult time challenging the thin ideal, clearly differentiating between the thin ideal (an unrealistic standard attained through unhealthy means) and the healthy ideal (a healthy body that includes fat and muscle), which is addressed in the first session, has proven successful. This difference sometimes needs to be restated in subsequent sessions.

## Supervision

Supervising new facilitators in their first few Body Project groups is also important for quality assurance. This process allows more experienced facilitators to provide input on challenges that may arise in sessions (e.g., participants may not do the home exercises or might think there is nothing wrong with the thin ideal). However, if an experienced counselor wants to deliver the Body Project independently and does not have the resources or time to receive supervision, we have found that they can conduct the sessions if they adhere to the script closely.

As noted, we recommend videotaping all sessions because it enhances dissonance induction and therefore the effects of the intervention. We encourage facilitators to watch the videotapes of the first full group they conduct because this provides an opportunity to ensure all session components were delivered with fidelity. Information from the taped sessions can be of particular importance in research studies, wherein independent raters can assess adherence to the intervention manual in the taped sessions, as well as the clinical competence exhibited while delivering the materials.

When providing supervision is possible, the supervisor should review the videotape to ensure that all components of the intervention were delivered as described in the script and were allotted the recommended amount of time. The supervisor can also note more subtle therapeutic qualities of the facilitator, such as whether the facilitator solicited feedback from participants well or allowed everyone a chance to participate. Ideally, supervision should be provided in person, although we have supervised group leaders successfully via e-mail in several of our multisite studies that are based on the review of videotaped sessions. If supervision is to be provided via e-mail, we recommend that supervisors first talk with the trainees (either in person or by telephone) to discuss the supervision process and review expectations of both the supervisor and the trainee. We have found the e-mail supervision process viable and efficient, although it can require occasional check-ins to clarify misunderstandings or discuss more complicated clinical issues that occasionally emerge in the session.

### Securing Administrative Approval

Securing administrative approval for the Body Project should be fairly straightforward for counselors working in schools or university counseling centers. In general, school administrators are most receptive to offering prevention programs such as the Body Project when (a) it is demonstrated that research supports the beneficial effects of the intervention for participants, (b) implementing this program does not interfere with regular school activities (e.g., classes), and (c) the program reduces rather than increases the burden on school administrative staff by preventing future cases of EDs.

Informing administrators of the benefits of the Body Project (e.g., reduced risk for current and future ED symptoms, reduced risk for future obesity, and improved psychosocial functioning) should increase the chances of gaining approval. It can also be useful to point out that offering ED prevention programs can serve as an important public relations tool for the school. Given that EDs affect 1 of every 10 young women, it is likely that there are students in high schools or universities with serious EDs, which can be fatal. Many students with EDs are not identified by school clinicians. Parents of students with EDs are typically relieved to know that prevention programs are being provided. It might also be useful to highlight that data suggest that for every 100 high-risk young women who complete the intervention, approximately nine fewer cases of EDs should occur (Stice et al., 2008). Thus, offering effective ED prevention programs may actually reduce the clinic load of those who treat EDs.

Student trainees, such as school psychology interns and counselors completing practicum or internship placements, welcome the opportunity to offer the Body Project, which provides valuable clinical experience and the chance to be part of an empirically supported prevention program. Because it may be somewhat more difficult to secure approval for trainees to offer this intervention, it might be necessary to make a more formal presentation regarding the beneficial effects of the program in school settings. Providing empirical data regarding EDs and support for this dissonance-based prevention program should be sufficient for such a presentation.

### Participant Retention

Retaining group members is also crucial to the success of this and other ED prevention programs. Holding groups in a relaxed atmosphere, such as a conference room or other comfortable space, where participants can face each other in a circle or around a table and sit in a comfortable, casual setting, helps facilitate retention. Regularly reminding participants about the sessions and home exercises and having facilitators send all participants a text or e-mail the day before each scheduled session helps improve attendance. We have sometimes included prize drawings (e.g., a $10 iTunes gift card) for those who attend all groups in some of our prevention trials, which is a fun way to promote attendance. Also, in the beginning of each session, group members publicly commit to actively participating, which we believe increases the odds that they will attend subsequent sessions. Making the sessions fun and engaging, particularly the first one, seems to facilitate attendance.

Emphasizing to Body Project participants the confidentiality of their personal information will also increase the likelihood that they will attend the sessions. Occasionally, participants discuss personal situations that involve other students or friends outside the group. When doing so, they should be instructed to omit any personally identifying information (i.e., names). Ensuring that sensitive information disclosed during sessions remains confidential can promote group cohesion and trust, as well as encourage continued participation. Finally, for facilitators in school settings, we recommend that the full group be offered during the course of a single semester or quarter. Students might have to drop out of the intervention if their course schedule changes across quarters or semesters or if they are starting a new sport or job at this transition point. Furthermore, the flow of the cumulative learning that is crucial to this program is disrupted if sessions are not conducted weekly.

### Developmental Factors

The delivery of the Body Project should be tailored to the population to whom it is delivered. For this reason, we recommend that groups consist of participants who are in a relatively narrow age range. Pressures to be thin likely vary depending on the age of the young woman. For example, high school students are generally still living in a fairly stable food environment, and their issues may be related more to looking slim for their school prom or pressure they receive from athletic coaches to maintain a particular weight, and college students may be more focused on avoiding the "freshman 15." The social environments of high school and college students also differ. Most high school participants live at home and may encounter substantial pressure to be thin (either intentional or uninten-

233

tional) from family members. We also recommend not including young women with significant developmental delays or learning problems, because experience has suggested that they do not benefit much from the sessions, which involve abstract concepts.

### Web-Based Support

To facilitate implementation of the Body Project, we have also created a Web page that provides support for clinicians (http://www.ori.org/the-bodyproject/). This Web page includes an intervention delivery training video, a video that depicts delivery of each component of the intervention, and a forum for consultation regarding questions clinicians may have about recruitment and intervention delivery.

# Resources and Referral Information for Eating Disorders

EDs are serious health conditions that require trained professional help, and early diagnosis and intervention can improve the chances of recovery. In the event that participants experience significant ED symptoms during the course of the intervention, it is essential that facilitators identify and refer them to more intensive treatment programs. The Body Project is intended as a prevention intervention and should not be used in place of an empirically supported treatment intervention for EDs.

Although the *Diagnostic and Statistical Manual of Mental Disorders* (4th ed., text rev.; American Psychiatric Association, 2000) outlines formal guidelines for the diagnosis of EDs, these behaviors exist on a continuum. Clearly, any individual who meets the diagnostic criteria for an ED should be identified and referred to treatment. However, even individuals who do not meet the full criteria for an ED may experience significant distress and engage in behaviors that put their physical and psychological health at risk. For example, research has suggested that individuals who engage in binge eating (defined as an episode in which the person consumes an objectively large amount of food accompanied by a sense of loss of control) an average of once a week do not differ from those who binge more often in terms of functional impairment (Le Grange et al., 2006). Therefore, those who meet all other criteria for bulimia nervosa or binge eating disorder but fail to meet the frequency or duration requirement for binge eating may be viewed as subthreshold cases that warrant referral for treatment. Similarly, individuals who meet all criteria for anorexia nervosa but whose weight is marginally above the threshold or who do not meet the amenorrhea requirement should be referred. Other cases that should be referred for more intensive intervention include individuals who engage in repeated purging or other inappropriate compensatory behaviors in the absence of objective binge episodes or repeated chewing and spitting out of large amounts of food without swallowing.

# Conclusion

Numerous ED prevention programs have been developed and evaluated in controlled trials. At present, the Body Project has the most empirical support, which has emerged from independent research studies. It has been successfully delivered to thousands of young female high school and college students in efficacy trials, effectiveness trials, and dissemination efforts. The program is based on providing an opportunity for young women to challenge the thin ideal. Adopting a new attitude toward this unattainable ideal appears to induce dissonance, thereby resulting in attitudinal and behavioral shifts away from this ideal and ultimately in reductions in ED symptoms and onset. In this chapter, we have provided general information for clinicians who would like to offer the Body Project in local high schools, colleges, or other settings, with a focus on recruitment, intervention delivery, and participant retention. Although we discussed these issues within the framework of the Body Project, some of the suggestions can also be applied to implementing other ED programs.

# Chapter Highlights

- Because EDs affect 1 in 10 young women, are rarely treated and are difficult to treat, prevention of these conditions is a vital public health priority.
- It is crucial for school clinicians to implement empirically supported ED prevention programs because they are optimally positioned to deliver programs at the correct developmental age.
- Although dozens of ED prevention programs have been developed and evaluated, the Body Project, a four-session group-based intervention aimed at young women with body image concerns, has amassed the most empirical support.
- Key to the success of the Body Project and other ED prevention programs is the successful recruitment of participants through a variety of methods, such as fliers, mailings, and community presentations.
- Proper training and supervision (when possible) of group leaders also contributes to the successful implementation of ED programs.
- When possible, it is ideal to have two facilitators lead the sessions.

# Recommended Resources

- Academy for Eating Disorders
  http://www.aedweb.org
- National Eating Disorders Association
  http://www.nationaleatingdisorders.org
- Oregon Research Institue, The Body Project
  http://www.ori.org/thebodyproject/
- Student Bodies
  http://www.beyondblackboards.com/StudentBodies
  Computer-delivered undergraduate-level course exploring body image, eating problems, and social concepts of beauty

# References

Agras, W. S., Walsh, B. T., Fairburn, C. G., Wilson, G. T., & Kraemer, H. C. (2000). A multicenter comparison of cognitive-behavioral therapy and interpersonal psychotherapy for bulimia nervosa. *Archives of General Psychiatry, 57,* 459–466.

American Psychiatric Association. (2000). *Diagnostic and statistical manual of mental disorders* (4th ed., text rev.). Washington, DC: Author.

American Psychological Association Task Force on Psychological Intervention Guidelines. (1995). *Template for developing guidelines: Interventions for mental disorders and psychological aspects of physical disorders.* Washington, DC: American Psychological Association.

Arcelus, J., Mitchell, A., Wales, J., & Nielsen, S. (2011). Mortality rates in patients with anorexia nervosa and other eating disorders: A meta-analysis of 36 studies. *Archives of General Psychiatry, 68,* 724–731.

Austin, S. B., Field, A. E., Wiecha, J., Peterson, K. E., & Gortmaker, S. L. (2005). The impact of a school-based obesity prevention trial on disordered weight-control behaviors in early adolescent girls. *Archives of Pediatric Medicine, 159,* 225–230.

Becker, C. B., Bull, S., Schaumberg, K., Cauble, A., & Franco, A. (2008). Effectiveness of peer-led eating disorders prevention: A replication trial. *Journal of Consulting and Clinical Psychology, 76,* 347–354.

Becker, C. B., Smith, L., & Ciao, A. C. (2005). Reducing eating disorder risk factors in sorority members: A randomized trial. *Behavior Therapy, 36,* 245–254.

Crow, S. J., Peterson, C. B., Swanson, S. A., Raymond, N. C., Specker, S., Eckert, E. D., & Mitchell, J. E. (2009). Increased mortality in bulimia nervosa and other eating disorders. *American Journal of Psychiatry, 166,* 1342–1346.

Ello-Martin, J., Roe, L., & Rolls, B. (2004). A diet reduced in energy density results in greater weight loss than a diet reduced in fat. *Obesity Research, 12,* A23–A23.

Frisch, M. J., Herzog, D. B., & Franko, D. L. (2006). Residential treatment for eating disorders. *International Journal for Eating Disorders, 39,* 434–442.

Green, M., Scott, N., Diyankova, I., Gasser, C., & Pederson, E. (2005). Eating disorder prevention: An experimental comparison of high level dissonance, low level dissonance, and no-treatment control. *Eating Disorders, 13,* 157–169.

Hudson, J., Hiripi, E., Pope, H., & Kessler, R. (2007). The prevalence and correlates of eating disorders in the National Comorbidity Survey Replication. *Biological Psychiatry, 61,* 348–358.

Jacobi, C., Volker, U., Trockel, M. T., & Taylor, C. B. (2012). Effects of an Internet-based intervention for subthreshold eating disorders: A randomized controlled trial. *Behavior Research and Therapy, 50,* 93–99.

Le Grange, D., Binford, R., Peterson, C., Crow, S., Crosby, R., Klein, M., . . . Wonderlich, S. (2006). *DSM-IV* threshold versus sub-threshold bulimia nervosa. *International Journal of Eating Disorders, 39,* 462–467.

Lewinsohn, P. M., Striegel-Moore, R. H., & Seeley, J. R. (2000). Epidemiology and natural course of eating disorders in young women from adolescence to young adulthood. *Journal of the American Academy of Child & Adolescent Psychiatry, 39,* 1284–1292.

Lock, J., Le Grange, D., Agras, W. S., Moye, A., Bryson, S., & Jo, B. (2010). Randomized clinical trial comparing family-based treatment with adolescent-focused individual therapy for adolescents with anorexia nervosa. *Archives of General Psychiatry, 67,* 1025–1032.

McMillan, W., Stice, E., & Rohde, P. (2011). High- and low-level dissonance-based eating disorder prevention programs with young women with body image concerns: An experimental trial. *Journal of Consulting and Clinical Psychology, 79,* 129–134.

McVey, G. L., Lieberman, M., Voorberg, N., Wardrope, D., & Blackmore, E. (2003). School-based peer support groups: A new approach to the prevention of disordered eating. *Eating Disorders, 11,* 169–185.

McVey, G. L., Lieberman, M., Voorberg, N., Wardrope, D., Blackmore, E., & Tweed, S. (2003). Replication of a peer support program designed to prevent disordered eating: Is a life skills approach sufficient for all middle school students? *Eating Disorders, 11,* 187–195.

Merrill, K. A., Tolbert, V. E., & Wade, W. A. (2003). Effectiveness of cognitive therapy for depression in a community mental health center: A benchmarking study. *Journal of Consulting and Clinical Psychology, 71,* 404–409.

Mitchell, K. S., Mazzeo, S. E., Rausch, S. M., & Cooke, K. L. (2007). Innovative interventions for disordered eating: Evaluating dissonance-based and yoga interventions. *International Journal of Eating Disorders, 40,* 120–128.

Neumark-Sztainer, D., Butler, R., & Palti, H. (1995). Eating disturbances among adolescent girls: Evaluation of a school-based primary prevention program. *Journal of Nutritional Education, 27,* 24–31.

Newman, D. L., Moffitt, T. E., Caspi, A., Magdol, L., Silva, P. A., & Stanton, W. R. (1996). Psychiatric disorder in a birth cohort of young adults: Prevalence, comorbidity, clinical significance, and new case incidence from ages 11 to 21. *Journal of Consulting and Clinical Psychology, 64,* 552–562.

Schmidt, U., Lee, S., Perkins, S., Eisler, I., Treasure, J., Berelowitz, M., . . . Yi, I. (2008). Do adolescents with "eating disorder not otherwise specified" (EDNOS) or full-syndrome bulimia nervosa differ in clinical severity, comorbidity, risk factors, or treatment outcome? *International Journal of Eating Disorders, 41,* 498–504.

Seidel, A., Presnell, K., & Rosenfield, D. (2009). Mediators in the dissonance eating disorder prevention program. *Behaviour Research and Therapy, 47,* 645–653.

Stewart, D. A., Carter, J. C., Drinkwater, J., Hainsworth, J., & Fairburn, C. G. (2001). Modification of eating attitudes and behavior in adolescent girls: A controlled study. *International Journal of Eating Disorders, 29,* 107–118.

Stice, E., Marti, C. N., Shaw, H., & Jaconis, M. (2009). An 8-year longitudinal study of the natural history of threshold, subthreshold, and partial eating disorders from a community sample of adolescents. *Journal of Abnormal Psychology, 118,* 587–597.

Stice, E., Marti, C. N., Spoor, S., Presnell, K., & Shaw, H. (2008). Dissonance and healthy weight eating disorder prevention programs: Long-term effects from a randomized efficacy trial. *Journal of Consulting and Clinical Psychology, 76,* 329–340.

Stice, E., Mazotti, L., Weibel, D., & Agras, W. S. (2000). Dissonance prevention program decreases thin-ideal internalization, body dissatisfaction, dieting, negative affect, and bulimic symptoms: A preliminary experiment. *International Journal of Eating Disorders, 27,* 206–217.

Stice, E. & Presnell, K. (2007). *The body project: Promoting body acceptance and preventing eating disorders facilitators guide.* New York: Oxford University Press.

Stice, E., Presnell, K., Gau, J., & Shaw, H. (2007). Testing mediators of intervention effects in randomized controlled trials: An evaluation of two eating disorder prevention programs. *Journal of Consulting and Clinical Psychology, 75,* 20–32.

Stice, E., Rohde, P., Gau, J., & Shaw, H. (2009). An effectiveness trial of a dissonance-based eating disorder prevention program for high-risk adolescent girls. *Journal of Consulting and Clinical Psychology, 77,* 825–834.

Stice, E., Rohde, P., Gau, J., & Shaw, H. (2012). Effect of a dissonance-based prevention program on risk for eating disorder onset in the context of eating disorder risk factors. *Prevention Science, 13,* 129–139.

Stice, E., Rohde, P., Shaw, H., Butryn, M., & Marti, C. N. (2011, September). *Effectiveness trials of a dissonance eating disorder prevention program are producing large and persistent effects.* Paper presented at the Eating Disorder Research Society Meeting, Edinburgh, Scotland.

Stice, E., Rohde, P., Shaw, H., & Gau, J. (2011). An effectiveness trial of a selected dissonance-based eating disorder prevention program for female high school students: Long-term effects. *Journal of Consulting and Clinical Psychology, 79,* 500–508.

Stice, E., Rohde, P., Shaw, H., & Marti, N. (2012). Efficacy trial of a selected prevention program targeting both eating disorder symptoms and unhealthy weight gain among female college students. *Journal of Consulting and Clinical Psychology, 80,* 164–170.

Stice, E., Shaw, H., Burton, E., & Wade, E. (2006). Dissonance and healthy weight eating disorder prevention programs: A randomized efficacy trial. *Journal of Consulting and Clinical Psychology, 74,* 263–275.

Stice, E., Shaw, H., & Marti, C. N. (2007). A meta-analytic review of eating disorder prevention programs: Encouraging findings. *Annual Review of Clinical Psychology, 3,* 233–257.

Striegel-Moore, R. H., Leslie, D., Petrill, S. A., Garvin, V., & Rosenheck, R. A. (2000). One-year use and cost of inpatient and outpatient services among female and male patients with an eating disorder: Evidence from a national database of health insurance claims. *International Journal of Eating Disorders, 27,* 381–389.

Swanson, S. A., Crow, S. J., Le Grange, D., Swendsen, J., & Merikangas, K. R. (2011). Prevalence and correlates of eating disorders in adolescents: Results from the National Comorbidity Survey Replication Adolescent Supplement. *Archives of General Psychiatry, 68,* 714–723.

Wade, T. D., Bergin, J. L., Tiggemann, M., Bulik, C. M., & Fairburn, C. G. (2006). Prevalence and long-term course of eating disorders in an adult Australian cohort. *Australian and New Zealand Journal of Psychiatry, 40,* 121–128.

Weersing, V. R., & Weisz, J. R. (2002). Mechanisms of action in youth psychotherapy. *Journal of Child Psychology and Psychiatry, 43,* 3–29.

Winzelberg, A. J., Eppstein, D., Eldredge, K. L., Wilfley, D., Dasmahapatra, R., Dev, P., & Taylor, C. (2000). Effectiveness of an Internet-based program for reducing risk factors for eating disorders. *Journal of Consulting and Clinical Psychology, 68,* 346–350.

## Chapter 11

# Effective Prevention Programs in College and University Settings

*Deanne Zotter and Justine Reel*

Although eating disorders (EDs) and disordered eating can occur at any age (Reel, SooHoo, Summerhays, & Gill, 2008), college students tend to be more vulnerable than their older counterparts. Estimates are that 10% to 30% of college women appear to be at risk for developing an ED over the course of their college years (Franko et al., 2005). EDs are associated with significant impairment in functioning. Furthermore, disordered eating can increase the risk for depressive and anxiety disorders, substance abuse, health problems, and obesity (Johnson, Cohen, Kasen, & Brook, 2002; Stice, Cameron, Killen, Hayward, & Taylor, 1999). Given the poor to modest treatment outcomes, prevention of EDs has become a well-recognized public health goal.

Targeting college students for prevention efforts makes sense for many reasons. College students have been identified as an at-risk group, and specific groups of college students (e.g., sorority women, athletes, health and physical education [H&PE] majors) are believed to be at higher risk than college students in general. Effective prevention programs may not only help the students themselves, but the positive effects of such programs (i.e., producing healthier attitudes and behaviors in the college participants) have the potential to benefit students, and those they come in contact with, well beyond their college years. If healthy body attitudes and weight management behaviors can be instilled in these individuals through effective prevention programs during their career preparation years, they will be in a position to be positive role models for their future communities, students, patients, consumers, and, perhaps most important, their future children.

In this chapter, we review the prevalence of EDs, disordered eating behaviors, and body image concerns in college and university populations. Attention is given to groups believed to be at higher risk, including

241

sorority women, college athletes, and those majoring in health and physical education. Prevention programs developed and administered on college campuses are then discussed. Given that even well-intentioned efforts can have negative outcomes such as normalizing eating-disordered behaviors (Mann et al., 1997), we focus on prevention efforts in university settings that have received research support for their effectiveness. First, we review the findings from literature reviews of prevention programs across all settings and then examine findings specific to university settings. Next, we provide information on an Internet-based prevention program, two programs aimed at preventing EDs among sorority women, and suggestions for the prevention of disordered eating in college athletes. A summary of a recent study examining prevention among H&PE students is also provided. Finally, we discuss important considerations for prevention efforts with university students, including directions for further research.

## Prevalence of Body Image Concerns and Eating Disorders in College Settings

Body size, shape, and appearance concerns and body-related dissatisfaction are widespread among college-age women and men. For women, pressures to achieve an ultra-thin figure are pervasive in Western society with messages from the media, family members, and peers (Fitzsimmons-Craft et al., 2012) that lead to the internalization of a thin ideal and the desire to change one's body. For example, 80% of college women reported intense body dissatisfaction, the strongest predictor for disordered eating and EDs (Krahn, Kurth, Gomberg, & Drewnowski, 2005). Body dissatisfaction should not be dismissed as normative for college students (Neighbors & Sobal, 2007) because a determination to "fix" one's physique can lead to inappropriate dieting, disordered eating, and other unhealthy practices (e.g., excessive exercise) among college women (Fitzsimmons-Craft et al., 2012).

Dieting and the desire to change one's weight or shape are also common among college men. In several studies of undergraduate students in the United States and Australia, 16% to 28.9% of college men were found to engage in dieting for the purposes of gaining weight and exhibited disordered behaviors such as excessive weight lifting and body building (Yager & O'Dea, 2008). The drive for muscularity (i.e., the desire to achieve a more muscular body) was observed among 91% of college-age men (Jacobi & Cash, 1994). Kyrejto, Mosewich, Kowalski, Mack, and Crocker (2008) found that college men were significantly more likely to demonstrate drive-for-muscularity attitudes than their female counterparts. Of men, 74.6% reported using physical activity, and 33.8% used dieting in their attempts to achieve their desired physique. The desire to be larger while maintaining low body fat has been associated with disordered eating behaviors such as excessive exercise, weight lifting, restricting, and supplementation (Galli & Reel, 2009).

242

The reported prevalence of clinical EDs among college students ranges from 1% to 3% (Franko et al., 2005) to 4% to 9% (Fitzsimmons-Craft et al., 2012). However, eating-disordered behaviors, some of which may meet the diagnostic criteria for eating disorder not otherwise specified (EDNOS), have been reported as occurring in as many as 34% to 67% of college women (Fitzsimmons-Craft et al., 2012). Less research has been done with college men, but one study found 9% of university men reported disordered eating, with 2% meeting the diagnostic criteria for bulimia nervosa (O'Dea & Abraham, 2002).

College students are thought to be particularly vulnerable to unhealthy weight control practices because of normative dieting, a body-shaming culture, fear of weight gain, and increased depression and stress (i.e., negative affect) because many are also experiencing the pressures associated with leaving home for the first time. Factors such as weight gain, dating pressures, and achievement threats have long been recognized as contributing to the development of EDs (Levine & Smolak, 1992). Developmentally, young adults are seeking romantic partners. Because of the association between attractiveness and heterosocial popularity and the emphasis on the thin beauty ideal for women, pressure is placed on college women where weight is concerned. Moreover, college women may invest more of their identity in relationships than do college men and may therefore be more vulnerable to negative affect when relationships fail. Additionally, heterosexual relations carry more risks for college women in the form of date rape, unwanted pregnancy, and threats to reputation. In addition to social pressures, academic pressures (e.g., increased workload, making career choices, fear of failure) can heighten negative emotion. In sum, the cumulative stressors of leaving home, social pressures, and academic pressures, can lead to increased negative affect, a well-established risk factor for EDs (Stice, 2001). Furthermore, the college years are often associated with the infamous "freshman 15" (i.e., the expected weight gain of 15 pounds during one's 1st year of college). Although 51% to 72% of 1st-year students gain some weight, most studies (e.g., Mihalopoulos, Auinger, & Klein, 2008; Jung, Bray, & Ginis, 2008) have found that the actual weight gain averages 4.6 to 7.4 pounds, and one study found that only 5.4% of participants gained 15 pounds during their 1st year in college (Delinsky & Wilson, 2008). Despite the scientific evidence that the freshman 15 is a myth, college students battle the fear of weight gain by engaging in unhealthy eating behaviors, such as dieting, excessive exercise, and restricting certain foods. Unfortunately, a dieting mentality and restricting behavior have been shown to increase tendencies for binge eating episodes and weight cycling (Bacon & Aphramor, 2011). Meanwhile, students have also reported having decreased access to healthy foods and limited ability to cook with fresh ingredients (Smith-Jackson & Reel, 2012), while relying heavily on processed foods (e.g., chips) to satisfy hunger. Therefore, educational programs are needed for college students to promote positive body image and health, with the goal of preventing disordered eating and EDs.

243

### Sorority Women

Although evidence is mixed, most studies have supported the idea that sorority women are at increased risk for EDs (e.g., Alexander, 1998). Sorority women have been found to have higher scores than nonsorority women on measures of drive for thinness and body dissatisfaction (Schulken, Pinciaro, Sawyer, Jensen, & Hoban, 1997) and disordered eating attitudes and behaviors (Prouty, Protinsky, & Canady, 2002). Sorority members report more awareness of pressure to be thin and attractive, higher levels of thin-ideal internalization, and higher frequencies of dieting than nonsorority women (Cashel, Cunningham, Landeros, Cokley, & Muhammad, 2003). It is not clear, however, whether these attitudes preexist and serve as a selection factor for women who choose to join sororities, or whether there is a cultural emphasis within sororities that supports increased risk for disordered eating attitudes and behaviors. In support of a social contagion effect, a prospective study of college women found that although women who joined sororities were similar to those who did not join in baseline levels of disordered eating, sorority women maintained their preoccupation with weight throughout their college years, whereas this preoccupation decreased in nonsorority women (Allison & Park, 2004). Furthermore, researchers who found increased bulimic symptomatology in sorority women also found that sorority women knew more women who binged and purged than nonsorority women (Kashubeck, Marchand-Martella, Neal, & Larsen, 1997). Additionally, these researchers found sorority women were more likely to read fashion magazines and perceived greater pressure to date than nonsorority women. Greater pressure to date may result from sorority–fraternity mixers, date parties, and formals, all of which are regular events on sorority calendars. The desire to attract a man leads to greater appearance pressure that, given the societal thin beauty ideal, translates to the belief in the importance of having a slender body. Thin-ideal internalization is a known risk factor for the development of EDs (Stice, 2002).

Aside from actual risk, targeting sorority women for prevention programs makes sense for a variety of reasons. Large numbers of college women participate in sororities and express genuine concern about EDs among their members. Additionally, Greek organizations have a highly organized social structure, and sororities can mandate attendance at programs. Finally, those who join sororities value sisterhood, service, and leadership, making sorority women an appropriate and highly receptive group for ED prevention efforts (Becker, Bull, Smith, & Ciao, 2008).

### Athletes and Eating Disorders

College athletes may experience pressure to meet sports-related body expectations associated with stronger performance, which can lead to dieting behaviors, disordered eating behaviors, and clinical EDs such as anorexia nervosa, bulimia nervosa, and EDNOS (Reel, 2012). Lifetime prevalence rates for anorexia nervosa, bulimia nervosa, and binge eating disorder have been estimated at 0.9%, 1.5%, and 3.5%, respectively among women in the general population, compared with 0.3%, 0.5%, and 2.0%, respectively, among men (Hudson, Hiripi, Pope, & Kessler, 2007). In contrast, prevalence rates for EDs among the athletic population range from 1% to 62%, depending on the competitive level and type of sports represented (aesthetic vs. ball sports), sensitivity of ED measures used, and the way EDs are defined (Sherman & Thompson, 2009). Estimates for college female athletes who engage in disordered eating (i.e., engaging in unhealthy weight control methods that do not fit full clinical criteria for EDs) have been between 15% and 25%, compared with estimates of between 0% and 3% for female athletes who have full-syndrome EDs (Reel, SooHoo, Doetsch, Carter, & Petrie, 2007; Sanford-Martens et al., 2005). Petrie, Greenleaf, Reel, and Carter (2008) found that 19% of college male athletes reported ED symptoms (e.g., excessive exercise, restricting) and 14% admitted to fasting and dieting with the intention to lose weight.

The female athlete triad was originally described by the American College of Sports Medicine (2011) in 1997 as a condition involving the relationship of three interrelated components (i.e., disordered eating, menstrual dysfunction, and low bone mass) among women who exercised. The original position statement identified disordered eating as a spectrum of harmful behaviors designed to lose weight that contributed to menstrual dysfunction. Beals and Manore (2002), who studied the female athlete triad symptoms among female college athletes ($N = 425$), found that 15.2% of athletes reported being at risk for disordered eating, 31% reported menstrual irregularities, and 34.4% sustained bone injuries. For a separate sample of female college athletes ($N = 451$), 6.7% of athletes met the criteria for EDNOS, 19.2% of athletes exhibited disordered eating symptoms, 17.3% reported menstrual dysfunction, 65% reported muscle injuries, and 35% reported skeletal injuries (Reel et al., 2007).

More recently, the American College of Sports Medicine (2011) revised its position statement for the female athlete triad, and it has been redefined as the interrelationship between energy availability (i.e., the amount of "unused" dietary energy available after exercise training for all other metabolic processes), menstrual function, and bone mineral density, in which each component represents a continuum from a healthy to unhealthy status. Although some athletes suffer from low energy availability unintentionally, other athletes strategically engage in dietary restriction to keep weight low in an attempt to achieve athletic success (Zach, Machin & Hoch, 2011).

The pressure to lose weight, gain weight, or change weight might lead an athlete to believe that dieting behavior is necessary to facilitate performance achievement. For example, Pritchard, Milligan, Elgin, Rush, and Shea (2007) found that 36% of female athletes engaged in disordered eating compared with only 13% of their nonathlete counterparts. Sundgot-Borgen and Torstveit (2010) reported that elite athletes engaged in more disordered eating than nonathletes and that as many as 70% of elite athletes were dieting and using abnormal eating behaviors to reduce weight before competition.

245

Although each sport has a unique set of demands, certain sports (e.g., gymnastics, distance running, ski jumping) may present a higher risk for disordered eating and body image disturbances because they are inherently more focused on appearance or body weight (Thompson & Sherman, 2010). Athletes in lean or aesthetic sports (e.g., figure skating) have reported more disordered eating than either nonathletes (Smolak, Murnen, & Ruble, 2000) or athletes participating in endurance or ball-game sports (Hausenblas & Carron, 1999). For example, competitive synchronized swimmers reported greater body dissatisfaction than athletes in sports that did not demand leanness or nonathlete controls (Ferrand, Magnan, Rouveix, & Filaire, 2007). Similarly, Torstveit, Rosenvinge, and Sundgot-Borgen (2008) reported that a higher number of female elite athletes in leanness sports (46.7%) met the criteria for clinical EDs than athletes in nonleanness sports (19.8%) or controls (21.4%; Torstveit et al., 2008). Similarly, Reinking and Alexander (2005) found that female college athletes in leanness-demand sports exhibited greater body dissatisfaction, drive for thinness, and risk for disordered eating than athletes in non–leanness-demand sports. Athletes from a variety of sports who perceive performance improvements from changing their body shape or weight are clearly at risk for disordered eating, and prevention efforts should target college athletes across all sports (Selby & Reel, 2011).

### Health and Physical Education Majors

Students majoring in H&PE are a less studied group of individuals at risk for disordered eating and dieting behaviors. Because their eventual profession (i.e., health or physical education teacher) focuses on health and being physically active, it is meaningful to note that lifetime prevalence of EDs was higher among H&PE men (12.5%) than non-H&PE men (0%) and among H&PE women (7.7%) than non-H&PE women (6%; Yager & O'Dea, 2009). Moreover, dieting to lose weight was more common among female H&PE students than among non-H&PE students (55% vs. 42%). Prevention efforts that instill healthy attitudes and behaviors toward body weight and shape are useful pursuits for this group of college students, given their future role as teachers and therefore as role models for their students.

## Prevention in College and University Settings

Efforts to increase awareness of EDs with the goal of prevention have expanded exponentially since the formation of National Eating Disorder Awareness Week in 1987. Each year, a large number of universities offer programming during this week sponsored annually by the National Eating Disorders Association. The stated goals of National Eating Disorder Awareness Week are to "prevent eating disorders and body image issues while reducing the stigma surrounding eating disorders and improving access to treatment" (National Eating Disorders Association, 2012, para. 2). Although these goals are important ones, it is imperative that the prevention efforts being implemented are those known to be effective. Researchers have noted the unintentional negative effects that can result from uninformed interventions that may serve to reduce the stigma to the point of normalizing eating-disordered behaviors (Mann et al., 1997). Furthermore, programming on campuses requires resources, both monetary and human. Investing valuable resources in ineffective programs wastes time, energy, and money. Additionally, fewer resources are likely to be dedicated to future ED prevention efforts if the current programs are seen to not work (Becker, 2011).

Meta-analytic reviews of ED prevention programs across a variety of settings (Stice & Shaw, 2004; Stice, Shaw, & Marti, 2007; Yager & O'Dea, 2008) have provided information on program features that have the most support in the research literature. These reviews suggested that secondary (or selected) prevention programs provide more benefits than primary (or universal) programs. Interactive programs and those that take place across multiple sessions have shown larger effects than didactic programs and those that rely on a single session. Programs offered to participants older than age 15 and only to girls and women have also been supported. Finally, programs without psychoeducational content seem to be more effective. Specific content that has been supported includes programs focusing on body acceptance and dissonance induction (Stice et al., 2007; see Chapter 10, this volume). Although the results of these meta-analytic reviews are important for informing prevention programs in general, looking specifically at studies conducted on college campuses is useful to understand effective prevention aimed at college and university students.

In their review, Yager and O'Dea (2008) identified aspects of ED prevention efforts found to be successful with the college population. These aspects include the use of dissonance-based approaches, including a dissonance approach to teaching media literacy. Yager and O'Dea also pointed to success with computer-based prevention programs, such as Student Bodies (Winzelberg et al., 2000) and Food, Mood, and Attitude (Franko et al., 2005). Additionally, they suggested health promotion activities aimed at building self-esteem as promising avenues to explore. Similar to Stice and colleagues' (Stice & Shaw, 2004; Stice & Presnell, 2007) findings, Yager and O'Dea did not find support for didactic, psychoeducational, and cognitive–behavioral interventions.

The Body Project, a dissonance-based program (Stice, Rohde, Shaw, & Marti, 2012) has high levels of research support among both college and young adult women and is reviewed extensively elsewhere in this volume. In this chapter, we review Student Bodies (Winzelberg et al., 2000), a well-supported Internet-based prevention program and then highlight programs designed specifically for sorority women, athletes, and H&PE majors.

### Internet-Based Prevention Programs

Internet-based prevention is appealing for many reasons. Computer-delivered interventions are relatively inexpensive and can reach large numbers of individuals. Furthermore, Internet-based programs can be accessed in the privacy of a dormitory room, reducing the potential fear of stigmatization related to seeking help. Finally, with the explosion of social media (e.g., Facebook, Twitter), college students spend a considerable amount of time online and are comfortable with using the Internet to obtain information and interact with others.

Student Bodies is the most widely researched of the Internet-based interventions for ED prevention aimed at college students. Developed by researchers from Stanford University, Student Bodies is an 8-week, Internet-based cognitive–behavioral intervention. Content focuses on psychoeducational material covering EDs, cultural determinants of beauty, the role of the media, nutrition, exercise, and cognitive–behavioral strategies for improving body dissatisfaction. The program is interactive, with online self-monitoring journals, behavior change exercises to be completed each week, and an online discussion board that is monitored by a clinical moderator (Winzelberg et al., 2000). Variations in the Student Bodies program have been studied, including adding face-to-face sessions (Celio et al., 2000), the use of an unmonitored online discussion board (Low et al., 2006), and adding booster sessions after the 8-week intervention (Taylor et al., 2006). Studies examining the effectiveness of Student Bodies have resulted in some promising findings. In general, Student Bodies appears to be most effective with high-risk participants and in reducing weight and shape concerns (Taylor et al., 2006). The Student Bodies program can be accessed via the National Association of Anorexia Nervosa and Related Disorders, Inc., Web site (http://www.anad.org/get-help/online-program/).

## Eating Disorder Prevention in Sororities

### Reflections Body Image Program

The most well-known intervention for sorority women is the Reflections Body Image Program, codeveloped by Carolyn Becker and Tri Delta (national sorority). Reflections is based on Becker and colleagues' research (e.g., Becker, Bull, Schaumberg, Cauble, & Franco, 2008; Becker, Smith, & Ciao, 2005, 2006) demonstrating the effectiveness of a dissonance-based prevention program to reduce thin-ideal internalization in sorority women. Becker's program is based largely on the initial dissonance-based prevention studies of Stice, Mazotti, Weibel, and Agras (2000). Becker modified Stice and Presnell's (2007) protocol, which in its current form is titled the Body Project. In modifying the Body Project to meet the needs of sorority women, Becker reduced the number of intervention sessions to two and geared the program to all sorority women, regardless of their risk status. She also introduced the use of peer leaders, who are trained to implement the program. The cognitive dissonance exercises remain much the same. Tri Delta has been instrumental in closing the research–practice gap by disseminating the Reflections Body Image Program nationally.

As with the Body Project, the Reflections Body Image Program includes activities designed to induce cognitive dissonance around thin-ideal internalization. These activities include discussions and writing assignments on how the thin ideal is maintained in U.S. society, who benefits from the thin ideal, and the costs of pursuing the thin ideal. Counterattitudinal exercises are included, such as a mirror exposure activity (done as homework) in which participants stand in front of a mirror, wearing as little clothing as possible, and note their positive qualities, both physical and emotional. Additionally, participants engage in role-plays in which they attempt to convince the group leader to give up pursuit of the thin ideal. Participants also develop a list of strategies to resist the thin ideal. At the conclusion of the program, participants choose a self-affirmation homework activity, such as making a pact to stop "fat talk." Research has supported the effectiveness of this intervention for reducing thin-ideal internalization, dieting, eating pathology, and body dissatisfaction, with effects lasting at 8-month follow-up (Becker, Bull, Schaumberg, et al., 2008; Becker et al., 2005, 2006).

The Reflections program is designed to be peer led. It is implemented among participants in two 2-hour sessions using an interactive approach. The goals of the program are to learn to embrace a healthy body ideal, reduce body dissatisfaction, decrease fat talk in daily life, and give more recognition to non–appearance-related aspects of self and others (Center for Living, Learning, and Leading, 2012). In 2008, Tri Delta formally launched the Reflections program nationwide and held their first Reflections: Body Image Academy to train sorority members to be peer leaders. The Body Image Academy has since been opened to campus professionals for training on how to implement the Reflections program, including how to recruit and train sorority women to be peer leaders. According to Tri Delta's Web site, the Reflections program has been implemented by more than 80 campuses across North America (Center for Living, Learning, and Leading, 2012).

### Sister to Sister

Another prevention program developed for sororities is the Sister to Sister (S2S) program (Zotter, 2009). This program was developed in an attempt to improve on the reduction in positive outcomes at follow-up commonly found in the prevention literature. Even with cognitive dissonance interventions, which continue to show some positive effects at 2- and 3-year follow-ups, most effects are found to lessen sooner (Stice, Marti, et al., 2008), which may be a result of most interventions being time limited (e.g., two or four sessions). The S2S program was designed on the basis of an empowerment–relational model (Levine & Smolak, 2001), with the idea that long-term change requires a consistent and constant effort on the part of sorority women to shift away from the appearance-focused climate that supports dieting, thinness idealization, and disordered eating behaviors. The S2S program was also inspired by the work of Piran (1999). Piran successfully reduced EDs in an elite dance school over the course of 13 years by emphasizing systemic change and students' empowerment. The S2S program was designed with the support of the university's Panhellenic Council to use peer leaders to provide a constant presence of healthy attitudes in each sorority. Peer mentors work to continually educate, support, and empower sorority women, specifically focusing on issues relevant to the risk of EDs (e.g., body dissatisfaction, dieting, thin-ideal internalization).

Based loosely on a program developed on the campus of the University of Maryland (Sigall, 1999), the S2S program originated at West Chester University of Pennsylvania in 2000. The stated mission of the S2S program is to improve body image, self-esteem, and feelings of empowerment among sorority women. Goals for improving body image include increasing acceptance of all body shapes and sizes, improving body satisfaction, learning to respect one's body and to treat one's body well, and focusing more on health than on appearance. Activities geared toward this goal include teaching media literacy, increasing awareness of genetic influences on body shape and weight (e.g., set point theory), understanding weightism (i.e., discrimination based on weight), and learning to live a healthy lifestyle (e.g., intuitive eating and regular exercise). Goals for improving self-esteem include decreasing the emphasis on appearance in the evaluation of self-worth and increasing the emphasis on other, less superficial characteristics. Goals for increasing empowerment include learning to recognize and take steps to change those things that perpetuate body dissatisfaction and body obsession among women.

S2S recruits and selects sorority women to serve as peer mentors each spring. All peer mentors complete an intensive training program during the first half of the following fall semester (totaling roughly 20 hours) and continue to meet as a group throughout the entire academic year. After their training, peer mentors are required to conduct at least one formal program per month (often during their chapter meetings), targeting some aspect of dieting, body image, or self-esteem. These programs are listed in the S2S training manual (available from Deanne Zotter). Many of these programs are designed to induce cognitive dissonance, increase feelings of empowerment, and lead to collective social action focused on reducing appearance pressures. Peer mentors are also instructed to serve as role models for positive body image on a day-to-day basis. In addition, peer mentors take an active role in ED awareness activities on campus. They are also trained in how to appropriately intervene when a potential ED is suspected in a sorority member to assist that member in receiving a professional evaluation and referral for treatment if necessary. After their 1st year with the program, peer mentors have the option of continuing for a 2nd (or 3rd) year as a senior peer mentor. Senior peer mentors play a large role in training new peer mentors and take on leadership roles in the program.

Research using a quasi-experimental design and examining the effectiveness of the S2S program has demonstrated positive outcomes on measures of eating-disordered behaviors and attitudes and body image. All of the dependent measures improved in the sorority group, whereas they generally remained remarkably similar in the nonsorority control group from Time 1 (preintervention) to Time 2 (8 years after the introduction of the S2S program; Zotter, 2009). These findings underscore the importance of a long-term, continuous intervention. Changing the thin-ideal, weight-conscious climate among young women takes a consistent effort. Data gathered after the 1st year of the S2S program showed no benefits, whereas more recent data have provided promising results. These findings also support the use of peers in ED prevention. Sorority peer mentors are likely to be especially effective because of their frequent interactions with other sorority women and their resulting ability to facilitate changes in the social milieu in which they live. Although S2S has been shown to be effective on the campus of West Chester University, results need to be replicated on other campuses to fully evaluate the S2S program.

# Eating Disorder Prevention in College Sports

Researchers and practitioners should address weight pressures in college sports to prevent disordered eating and body image disturbances. Health professionals and counselors need to become more aware of the weight pressures most frequently identified by male and female athletes. Whenever possible, attempts should be made to influence change in the existing sport-specific weight pressures (e.g., weight limits) that have become normalized within the sport structure (Reel, 2012). We describe weight-related pressures in sports (i.e., uniforms, teammates, weight requirements and weigh-ins, and coaches), along with recommendations for addressing these pressures within college athletics. In addition to addressing pressures frequently reported in sports, educational programs are needed to promote healthy habits and prevent disordered eating attitudes and behaviors among college athletes.

### Uniforms

Across studies with athletic populations, uniforms have consistently been a frequent sport-specific pressure for male and female athletes (e.g., Reel, 2012; Reel & Gill, 1996, 2001). For example, 54% of female college cheerleaders and 41% of male college cheerleaders reported that the revealing team uniform created body image distress (Reel & Gill, 1998), and Torres-McGehee (in press) found that uniforms that displayed midriffs were more highly associated with body dissatisfaction. Similarly, 45% of female college swimmers and 99% of female college dancers reported that the uniform or costume served as a negative body image influence (Reel & Gill, 2001; Reel, SooHoo, Gill, & Jamieson, 2005).

Therefore, we recommend that college athletes choose team uniforms that are comfortable and do not hinder performance demands (e.g., jumps). Athletes should receive a custom fitting, or at least be able to select an appropriate size, rather than feel the need to lose weight to fit into a previous player's uniform or smaller size. The motivation to wear extremely revealing uniforms should be evaluated across sports (Reel, 2012).

### Teammates

Social comparison theory underscores the importance placed on comparing one's body to others. For an athlete, one's teammates provide a salient basis

251

for comparison related to size, shape, and weight. Male and female athletes from diverse sports, including cross-country runners, divers, and gymnasts, overwhelmingly reported teammate pressures at the college level (Galli, Reel, Petrie, Greenleaf, & Carter, 2011; Reel, SooHoo, Petrie, Greenleaf, & Carter, 2010). We recommend that athletes be discouraged from making weight-related or appearance-oriented comments about themselves or other athletes. For example, stunt partners should avoid criticizing their partners for weight changes (Selby & Reel, 2011). Of course, this type of climate needs to be supported and encouraged from the top down (i.e., by coaches and athletic directors).

### Weight Requirements and Weigh-Ins

To participate in their sport, some college athletes face weight limits (e.g., cheerleading) or weight classes (e.g., wrestling) that require regular weigh-ins. More than half (54%) of college cheerleaders reported try-out weight limits for their squad, with 40% of women and 41% of men being weighed in throughout the season. Male athletes in sports such as fencing (50%), wrestling (50%), and football (33%) also identified sport-related weight requirements (Galli et al., 2011).

We recommend that health professionals and counselors work with college athletic directors and sports federations to eliminate weight requirements and weigh-ins. Weight limits may set athletes up for unhealthy dieting practices. A registered dietician should challenge unrealistic weight-loss or weight-gain goals, discourage weight-based goal setting on teams, and monitor weight-related goal setting only when absolutely necessary (Reel, 2012). Similarly, weigh-ins should be avoided to discourage an overemphasis on weight, but medical weigh-ins should be conducted privately by a medical professional (Selby & Reel, 2011).

### Coaches

Coaches can exert influence over athletes regarding body size, weight, and shape expectations through their comments and actions (e.g., team weigh-ins). Female (70%) and male (88%) college cheerleaders identified their coach as an important source of weight-related pressure in sport. The existence of this coaching pressure was reinforced by Kerr, Berman, and De Souza's (2006) finding that 44% of current gymnasts reported receiving negative comments about their bodies from coaches and that 71% of those gymnasts were more likely to feel they should lose weight than those who had not received a negative body comment (Kerr et al., 2006). Similar to coaching pressure, more than half (57%) of college dancers reported that their choreographer noticed weight gain or loss and selected the thinnest dancers for the most important performance roles (Reel et al., 2005).

Coaches should receive education regarding performance and nutritional requirements, especially as they relate to matching food intake requirements to energy expenditure. Coaches and support staff should have a referral network of professionals who specialize in EDs, substance abuse, and mental health treatment in case a problem arises (Whisenhunt, Williamson, Drab-Hudson, & Walden, 2008). Coaches and athletic directors are increasingly taking the initiative to address disordered eating among athletes, and universities are establishing on-campus wellness teams to provide mental health services. However, coaches who are more resistant to changing weight policies can be reminded of both the health-related and the performance consequences associated with negative body image and disordered eating. For example, malnourished athletes may be more at risk for stress fractures. Likewise, athletes who are focused on body flaws may experience decreased concentration, increased anxiety, and less focus related to technique and performance demands of sport (Selby & Reel, 2011).

### Perceived Performance Advantages

Another challenge across sports relates to a perceived performance improvement associated with body weight loss or gain. For example, athletes in endurance sports, such as cross-country running and swimming, have reported the desire to shed pounds to run or swim faster, a practice that is commonly supported by coaches (Thompson & Sherman, 2010). Policies that discourage unhealthy dieting can be effective. For example, ski jumpers have notoriously lost weight for the purpose of being lighter in the air. However, in advance of the 2006 Winter Olympics, the Fédération Internationale de Ski established weight-minimum standards for male ski jumpers that penalized dropping weight too low. Dubbed the "anorexic rule," when a ski jumper drops below the minimum body mass index of 18.5 (nude) or 20 (in gear), his skis are shortened 2% for each kilogram of weight below the standard, resulting in a distinct performance disadvantage (Thompson & Sherman, 2010). This policy effectively eliminated extreme weight loss for male ski jumpers and reinforced the need for policies that discourage unhealthy and extreme weight loss and gain across collegiate sports. Additionally, educational programs for athletes and sport professionals should be developed, implemented, and evaluated with college athletes.

### ATHENA

Despite the evidence of weight-related pressures and disordered eating risks for athletes, few prevention studies have been implemented with athletes. One exception is the Athletes Targeting Health Exercise and Nutrition Alternatives (ATHENA) program, designed to prevent disordered eating among female high school athletes (Elliot et al., 2004). Specifically, ATHENA, a coach-led and peer-led format, was developed to teach a broad array of topics including sports nutrition, effective exercise training, depression prevention, self-esteem, media images and societal pressures to be thin, and drug use and other unhealthy behaviors' effects on performance. ATHENA engages participants to become activists to fight EDs and drug use by means of public service campaigns.

ATHENA was implemented with high school athletes ($N = 928$) from 40 teams using peer-led sessions incorporated into the 8 weeks of team practice. Participants reported significantly greater improvements in healthy eating, as well as decreased intention to use diet pills, vomiting, or tobacco to lose weight compared with the control group (Elliot et al., 2004). Although this prevention program was developed for high school athletes, it shows promise for modification with college students. Efficacious prevention programs have occurred in a team setting, and programs with an interactive format (rather than a didactic one) and peer led by a trained member of the competitive team yielded the strongest effects (Stice et al., 2007; Torres-McGehee et al., 2011).

### Female Athlete Body Project

Becker, McDaniel, Bull, Powell, and McIntyre (2012), after their successful intervention studies with college sorority women, have recently explored using similar prevention programs with female college athletes. Specifically, they implemented the Female Athlete Body Project with female college athletes ($N = 168$) across nine sports teams and the varsity cheerleading squad. They compared dissonance-based prevention (DBP) with a healthy weight intervention, both of which were tailored to athletes' needs and held within teams to address sport-specific concerns. Healthy weight intervention (HWI) encourages participants to make small lifestyle changes in eating and exercise behaviors with the goal of maintaining a healthy weight. HWI has garnered some support in reducing thin-ideal internalization, body dissatisfaction, negative affect, and bulimic pathology in at-risk adolescent girls (Stice, Chase, Stormer, & Appel, 2001; Stice, Shaw, Burton, & Wade, 2006) and among female sorority members (Becker et al., 2010).

Interventions consisted of three sessions over a 3-week period. Similar to other intervention programs, peer leaders who were athletes from the team received 6 hours of training in advance of the program and facilitated group sessions. Both the DBP and the HWI groups were given information on the female athlete triad and discussed the cultural thin ideal as well as sport-specific body image pressures using language relevant to the athletes. This dual body image pressure (i.e., the traditional thin ideal plus sport performance concerns) is thought to make female athletes a particularly challenging population for prevention, and it was addressed in both conditions. Athletes in the DBP group were exposed to dissonance-inducing activities (e.g., role-plays), modified to focus on the body image concerns of athletes. Athletes in the HWI group discussed the benefits of pursuing an athlete-specific healthy ideal, appropriate energy intake–output balance, society's effect on food choices, ways to make healthier food choices, the benefits of physical activity, and the importance of sleep. They were also asked to keep food and exercise logs and to identify specific exercise, sleep, and eating goals to complete.

In this exploratory study with female college athletes, athletes from both DBP and HWI groups reported decreased thin-ideal internalization, dietary restraint, bulimic pathology, shape and weight concerns, and negative affect at

6 weeks and bulimic pathology, shape concerns, and negative affect at 1 year. Furthermore, several students spontaneously sought medical attention for the triad. Although both groups produced similar outcomes, participants indicated a strong preference for the HWI. The HWI, with its emphasis on performance and health, is thought to have more face validity for athletes (Becker et al., 2012). Although this study is promising, several limitations restrict the generalizability of the findings, and more research using HWI with college athletes is needed.

# Eating Disorder Prevention for Health and Physical Education Majors

Yager and O'Dea (2010) implemented and evaluated two 12-week interventions to promote healthy body image, decrease eating-disordered behaviors, and prevent excessive exercise among H&PE university students. This study is one of the few in the prevention literature that has included male participants. The two interventions examined were similar with the addition of a stronger dissonance approach and the use of online activities in Intervention 2. Intervention 2 produced the strongest results, so we describe this program. This program used a combined self-esteem, dissonance, and media literacy health education program using online and computer-based activities. Program content was aimed at building knowledge about adolescent growth and development (e.g., puberty), weight issues, nutrition, self-esteem, and media literacy. For example, during the weight issues session, program participants discussed the limitations of using the body mass index and how to promote size acceptance. Participants then used an online discussion board to address how to best measure and promote health (not weight) within the schools.

Women showed significant reductions in drive for thinness, reduced levels of excessive exercise, and improved self-esteem after the intervention. Men showed decreases in eating-disordered behaviors and attitudes, reductions in drive for muscularity, and improved self-esteem. Yager and O'Dea (2010) concluded that the superior results in Intervention 2 stemmed from the stronger dissonance approach and the online discussions that increased the amount of exposure to the material and required public displays of counterattitudinal thoughts. Although the study's sample size was small, it appears that an ED prevention program that combines self-esteem, dissonance, and media literacy using a variety of interactive delivery formats (e.g., online discussion boards) shows promise for H&PE college students (Yager & O'Dea, 2010).

## Conclusion

Efforts to prevent EDs on college campuses have increased exponentially over the past 2 decades. There is much variability in the content of successful programs; however, programs that have received the strongest research support with college populations are those that rely less on psychoeducation and more on promoting attitude and behavioral change. Strategies such as inducing cognitive dissonance around the pursuit of the thin ideal and promoting body acceptance and healthier weight control behaviors seem to be the most promising. Successful prevention programs have been implemented with low-risk and high-risk college women and with select groups such as sorority women, athletes, and H&PE majors. Online prevention programs have also shown some success and deserve further exploration given their cost effectiveness and ease of dissemination and the Internet immersion of the present generation of college students. Whereas broad meta-analytic studies on effective ED prevention suggest the need for professional interventionists, much success has been found using peer leaders on college campuses. Similarly, although meta-analyses have suggested better results when targeting high-risk groups (secondary or selected prevention), primary or universal prevention is effective and sometimes preferred with university populations. That is, sorority members and athletes reported a desire to foster group or team cohesion and therefore wanted programs to be given to all members (Stice, Shaw, et al., 2008). Although much progress in understanding effective prevention has been made, continued research is needed.

With the increased concern with obesity rates in the U.S. population, more research is needed on healthy weight interventions. Promising results from healthy weight interventions have been found in studies using adolescents (Stice, Marti, Spoor, Presnell, & Shaw, 2008) and college athletes (Becker et al., 2012). However, limited success was found using an HWI with a sample of high-risk university women (Stice et al., 2012). Recent findings have suggested the importance of matching the prevention program to the population of interest. For example, college athletes were more receptive to an HWI as opposed to a DBP (Becker et al., 2012). More research is needed to determine which programs are most effective with which groups.

Additionally, most ED prevention research at the college level has been conducted with White women. More needs to be done to develop and test programs with other populations, including men and individuals of other races or ethnicities.

## Chapter Highlights

- College women are considered at risk for EDs, with specific groups (i.e., sorority women, athletes, H&PE majors) believed to be at higher risk than college students in general.
- When introducing prevention efforts on college and university campuses, it is imperative to use methods shown to be effective in reducing risk factors to avoid unintentional negative effects (e.g., normalizing disordered eating behaviors).
- The content of successful prevention programs varies, but the programs that are most effective on college campuses include those using interactive, multisession, dissonance-based approaches. The least effective are those using single-session, didactic, psychoeducational interventions.

- Internet-based prevention programs deserve further exploration as potentially effective methods of reaching large numbers of college students in a cost-effective way.
- Peer leaders are effective in implementing prevention programs on college campuses and present advantages to the groups they serve over professional interventionists.
- Interventions need to be tailored to the specific population of interest. For example, when working with college athletes, coaches may need to be targeted, and structural changes in terms of weight requirements and uniforms may be needed. Likewise, athletes may be more receptive to programs that focus on performance and health rather than body image.

## Recommended Resources

- National Eating Disorders Association
  http://www.nationaleatingdisorders.org/
- Reflections: Body Image Program
  http://www.tridelta.org/thecenter/ourinitiatives/
  reflectionsbodyimageprogram
- Sister to Sister training manual
  Available from Deanne Zotter, PhD, West Chester University of Pennsylvania (dzotter@wcupa.edu)
- Student Bodies Internet-based prevention program
  http://www.anad.org/get-help/online-program/

## References

Alexander, L. A. (1998). The prevalence of eating disorders and eating disordered behaviors in sororities. *College Student Journal, 32,* 66–75.

Allison, K. C., & Park, C. L. (2004). A prospective study of disordered eating among sorority and nonsorority women. *International Journal of Eating Disorders, 35,* 354–358.

American College of Sports Medicine. (2011). *The female athlete triad.* Retrieved from http://www.acsm.org/access-public-information/articles/2011/10/04/the-female-athlete-triad

Bacon, L., & Aphramor, L. (2011). Weight science: Evaluating the evidence for a paradigm shift. *Nutrition Journal, 10*(9),1–13.

Beals, K. A., & Manore, M. M. (2002). Disorders of the female athlete triad among collegiate athletes. *International Journal of Sport Nutrition and Exercise Metabolism, 12,* 281–293.

Becker, C. B. (2011). Prevention of eating disorders: A top 10 list of things we should not do. *Perspectives: A Professional Journal of the Renfrew Center Foundation, Summer,* 1–6.

Becker, C. B., Bull, S., Schaumberg, K., Cauble, A., & Franco, A. (2008). Effectiveness of peer-facilitated eating disorders prevention: A replication trial. *Journal of Consulting and Clinical Psychology, 76,* 347–354.

Becker, C. B., Bull, S., Smith, L. M., & Ciao, A. C. (2008). Effects of being a peer-leader in an eating disorder prevention program: Can we further reduce eating disorder risk factors? *Eating Disorders, 16*, 444–459.

Becker, C. B., McDaniel, L, Bull, S., Powell, M., & McIntyre, K. (2012). Can we reduce eating disorder risk factors in female college athletes? A randomized exploratory investigation of two peer-led interventions. *Body Image, 9*, 31–42. doi:10.1016/j.bodyim.2011.09.005

Becker, C. B., Smith, L. M., & Ciao, A. C. (2005). Reducing eating disorder risk factors in sorority members: A randomized trial. *Behavior Therapy, 36*, 245–253.

Becker, C. B., Smith, L. M., & Ciao, A. C. (2006). Peer facilitated eating disorder prevention: A randomized effectiveness trial of cognitive dissonance and media advocacy. *Journal of Counseling Psychology, 53*, 550–555.

Becker, C. B., Wilson, C., Williams, A., Kelly, M., McDaniel, L., & Elmquist, J. (2010). Peer-facilitated cognitive dissonance versus healthy weight eating disorders prevention: A randomized comparison. *Body Image, 7*, 280–288

Cashel, M. L., Cunningham, D., Landeros, C., Cokley, K. O., & Muhammad, G. (2003). Sociocultural attitudes and symptoms of bulimia: Evaluating the SATAQ with diverse college groups. *Journal of Counseling Psychology, 50*, 287–296. doi:10.1037/0022-0167.50.3.287

Celio, A., Winzelberg, A., Wilfley, D., Eppstein-Herald, D., Springer, E., Dev, P., & Taylor, C. B. (2000). Reducing risk factors for eating disorders: Comparison of an Internet and a classroom-delivered psychoeducational program. *Journal of Consulting and Clinical Psychology, 68*, 650–657.

Center for Living, Learning, and Leading. (2012). *Reflections: Body image program*. Retrieved from http://www.tridelta.org/thecenter/ourinitiatives/reflectionsbodyimageprogram

Delinsky, S. S., & Wilson, G. T. (2008). Weight gain, dietary restraint, and disordered eating in the freshman year of college. *Eating Behaviors, 9*(1), 82–90.

Elliot, D. L., Goldberg, L., Moe, E. L., DeFrancesco, C. A., Durham, M. B., & Hix-Small, H. (2004). Preventing substance use and disordered eating: Initial outcomes of the ATHENA (Athletes Targeting Healthy Exercise and Nutrition Alternatives) program. *Archives of Pediatrics & Adolescent Medicine, 158*, 1043–1049.

Ferrand, C., Magnan, C., Rouveix, M., & Filaire, E. (2007). Disordered eating, perfectionism and body esteem of elite synchronized swimmers. *European Journal of Sport Science, 7*, 223–230.

Fitzsimmons-Craft, E. E., Harney, M. B., Koehler, L. G., Danzi, L. E., Riddell, M. K., & Bardone-Cone, A. M. (2012). Explaining the relation between thin ideal internalization and body dissatisfaction among college women: The roles of social comparison and body surveillance. *Body Image, 9*, 43–49. doi:10.1016/j.bodyim.2011.09.002

Franko, D. L., Mintz, L. B., Villapiano, M., Green, T. C., Mainelli, D., Folensbee, L., . . . Budman, S. H. (2005). Food, mood and attitude: Reducing risk for eating disorders in college women. *Health Psychology, 24*, 567–578. doi:10.1037/0278-6133.24.6.567

Galli, N., & Reel, J. J. (2009). Adonis or Hephaestus? Exploring body image in male athletes. *Psychology of Men & Masculinity, 10,* 95–108. doi:10.1037/a0014005

Galli, N., Reel, J. J., Petrie, T. P., Greenleaf, C., & Carter, J. (2011). Preliminary development and validation of the Weight Pressures in Sport Scale for male athletes. *Journal of Sport Behavior, 34,* 47–68.

Hausenblas, H. A., & Carron, A. V. (1999). Eating disorder indices and athletes: An integration. *Journal of Sport & Exercise Psychology, 21,* 230–258.

Hudson, J. I., Hiripi, E., Pope, H. G., & Kessler, R. C. (2007). The prevalence and correlates of eating disorders in the National Comorbidity Survey replication. *Biological Psychiatry, 61,* 348–358.

Jacobi, L., & Cash, T. F. (1994). In pursuit of the perfect appearance: Discrepancies among self-ideal perceptions of multiple physical attributes. *Journal of Applied Social Psychology, 24,* 379–396.

Johnson, J. G., Cohen, P., Kasen, S., & Brook, J. S. (2002). Eating disorders during adolescence and the risk for physical and mental disorders during early adulthood. *Archives of General Psychiatry, 59,* 545–552.

Jung, M. E., Bray, S. R., & Ginis, K. A. M. (2008). Behavior change and the freshman 15: Tracking physical activity and dietary patterns in 1st-year university women. *Journal of American College Health, 56,* 523–530.

Kashubeck, S., Marchand-Martella, N., Neal, C., & Larsen, C. (1997). Sorority membership, campus pressures, and bulimic symptomatology in college women: A preliminary investigation. *Journal of College Student Development, 38,* 40–48.

Kerr, G., Berman, E., & De Souza, M. J. (2006). Disordered eating in women's gymnastics: Perspectives of athletes, coaches, parents and judges. *Journal of Applied Sport Psychology, 18,* 28–43.

Krahn, D. D, Kurth, C. L, Gomberg, E., & Drewnowski, A. (2005). Pathological dieting and alcohol use in college women: A continuum of behaviors. *Eating Behaviors, 6,* 43–52.

Kyrejto, J. W., Mosewich, A. D., Kowalski, K. C., Mack, D. E., & Crocker, P. R. E. (2008). Men's and women's drive for muscularity: Gender differences and cognitive and behavioral correlates. *International Journal of Sport & Exercise Psychology, 6,* 69–84.

Levine, M. P., & Smolak, L. (1992). Toward a model of the developmental psychopathology of eating disorders: The example of early adolescence. In J. H. Crowther, D. L. Tennenbaum, S. E. Hobfoll, & M. A. P. Stephens (Eds.), *The etiology of bulimia nervosa: The individual and familial context* (pp. 59–80). Washington, DC: Hemisphere.

Levine, M. P., & Smolak, L. (2001). Primary prevention of body image disturbances and disordered eating in childhood and early adolescence. In J. K. Thompson & L. Smolak (Eds.), *Body image, eating disorders, and obesity in youth: Assessment, prevention, and treatment* (pp. 237–260). Washington, DC: American Psychological Association.

Low, K. G., Charanasomboon, S., Lesser, J., Reinhalter, K., Martin, R., Jones, H., . . . Taylor, C. B. (2006). Effectiveness of a computer-based interactive eating disorders prevention program at long-term follow-up. *Eating Disorders, 14,* 17–30. doi:10.1080/10640260500403816

259

Mann, T., Nolen-Hoeksema, S., Huang, K., Burgard, D., Wright, A., & Hanson, K. (1997). Are two interventions worse than none? Joint primary and secondary prevention of eating disorders in college females. *Health Psychology, 16,* 215–225.

Mihalopoulos, N. L., Auinger, P., & Klein, J. D. (2008). The freshman 15: Is it real? *Journal of American College Health, 56,* 531–533.

National Eating Disorders Association. (2012). *NEDAwareness: National Eating Disorders Awareness Week.* Retrieved from http://www.nationaleatingdisorders.org/programs-events/nedawareness-week-info.php

Neighbors, L. A., & Sobal, J. (2007). Prevalence and magnitude of body weight and shape dissatisfaction among university students. *Eating Behaviors, 8,* 429–439.

O'Dea, J., & Abraham, S. F. (2002). Eating and exercise disorders in young college men. *Journal of American College Health, 50,* 273–278.

Petrie, T., Greenleaf, C., Reel, J. J., & Carter, J. E. (2008). Prevalence of eating disorders and disordered eating behaviors among male collegiate athletes. *Psychology of Men and Masculinity, 9,* 267–277.

Piran, N. (1999). On the move from tertiary to secondary and primary prevention: Working with an elite dance school. In N. Piran, M. P. Levine, & C. Steiner-Adair (Eds.), *Preventing eating disorders: A handbook of interventions and special challenges* (pp. 256–269). Philadelphia, PA: Brunner/Mazel.

Pritchard, M. E., Milligan, B., Elgin, J., Rush, P., & Shea, M. (2007). Comparisons of risky health behaviors between male and female college athletes and non-athletes. *Athletic Insight, 9,* 67–78.

Prouty, A. M., Protinsky, H. O., & Canady, D. (2002). College women: Eating behaviors and help-seeking preferences. *Adolescence, 37,* 353–363.

Reel, J. J. (2012). Identification and prevention of weight pressures and body image concerns among athletes. *Latin American Journal of Sport Psychology, 6,* 203–216.

Reel, J. J., & Gill, D. L. (1996). Psychosocial factors related to eating disorders among high school and college female cheerleaders. *Sport Psychologist, 10,* 195–206.

Reel, J. J., & Gill, D. L. (1998). Weight concerns and disordered eating attitudes among male and female college cheerleaders. *Women in Sport and Physical Activity Journal, 7,* 79–94.

Reel, J. J., & Gill, D. L. (2001). Slim enough to swim? Weight pressures for competitive swimmers and coaching implications. *Sport Journal, 4.* Retrieved from http://www.thesportjournal.org/article/slim-enough-swim-weight-pressures-competitive-swimmers-and-coaching-implications

Reel, J. J., SooHoo, S., Doetsch, H., Carter, J. E., & Petrie, T. A. (2007). The female athlete triad: Is the triad a problem among division I female athletes? *Journal of Clinical Sport Psychology, 1,* 358–370.

Reel, J. J., SooHoo, S., Gill, D. L., & Jamieson, K. M. (2005). Femininity to the extreme: Body image concerns among college female dancers. *Women in Sport and Physical Activity Journal, 14,* 39–51.

Reel, J. J., SooHoo, S., Petrie, T. A., Greenleaf, C., & Carter, J. E. (2010). Slimming down for sport: Developing a weight pressures in sport measure for female athletes. *Journal of Clinical Sport Psychology, 4,* 99–111.

Reel, J. J., SooHoo, S., Summerhays, J., & Gill, D. L. (2008). Age before beauty: An exploration of body image in African-American and Caucasian adult women. *Journal of Gender Studies, 17,* 321–330. doi:10.1080/09589230802419963

Reinking, M. F., & Alexander, L. E. (2005). Prevalence of disordered-eating behaviors in undergraduate female collegiate athletes and nonathletes. *Journal of Athletic Training, 40,* 47–51.

Sanford-Martens, T. C., Davidson, M. M., Yakushko, O. F., Martens, M. P., Hinton, P., & Beck, N. (2005). Clinical and subclinical eating disorders: An examination of collegiate athletes. *Journal of Applied Sport Psychology, 17,* 79–86.

Schulken, E. D., Pinciaro, P. J., Sawyer, R. G., Jensen, J., & Hoban, M. T. (1997). Sorority women's body size perceptions and their weight-related attitudes and behaviors. *Journal of American College Health, 46,* 69–74.

Selby, C., & Reel, J. J. (2011). A coach's guide to identifying and helping athletes with eating disorders. *Journal of Sport Psychology in Action, 2,* 100–112.

Sherman, R. T., & Thompson, R. A. (2009). Body image and eating disturbance in athletes: Competing to win or to be thin? In J. J. Reel & K. A. Beals (Eds.), *The hidden faces of eating disorders and body image* (pp. 9–38). Reston, VA: National Association for Girls and Women in Sports.

Sigall, B. A. (1999). The Panhellenic Task Force on Eating Disorders: A program of primary and secondary prevention for sororities. In N. Piran, M. P. Levine, & C. Steiner-Adair (Eds.), *Preventing eating disorders: A handbook of interventions and special challenges* (pp. 222–235). Philadelphia, PA: Brunner/Mazel.

Smith-Jackson, T., & Reel, J. J. (2012). Freshman women and the "freshmen 15": Perspectives on prevalence and causes of college weight gain. *Journal of American College Health, 60,* 14–20.

Smolak, L., Murnen, S. K., & Ruble, A. E. (2000). Female athletes and eating problems: A meta-analysis. *International Journal of Eating Disorders, 27,* 371–380.

Stice, E. (2001). A prospective test of the dual pathway model of bulimic pathology: Mediating effects of dieting and negative affect. *Journal of Abnormal Psychology, 110,* 124–135.

Stice, E. (2002). Risk and maintenance factors for eating pathology: A meta-analytic review. *Psychological Bulletin, 128,* 825–848.

Stice, E., Cameron, R., Killen, J. D., Hayward, C., & Taylor, C. B. (1999). Naturalistic weight reduction efforts prospectively predict growth in relative weight and onset of obesity among female adolescents. *Journal of Consulting and Clinical Psychology, 67,* 967–974.

Stice, E., Chase, A., Stormer, S., & Appel, A. (2001). A randomized trial of a dissonance-based eating disorder prevention program. *International Journal of Eating Disorders, 29,* 247–262.

261

Stice, E., Marti, N., Spoor, S., Presnell, K., & Shaw, H. (2008). Dissonance and healthy weight eating disorder prevention programs: Long-term effects from a randomized efficacy trial. *Journal of Consulting and Clinical Psychology, 76,* 329–340.

Stice, E., Mazotti, L., Weibel, D., & Agras, W. S. (2000). Dissonance prevention program decreases thin-ideal internalization, body dissatisfaction, dieting, negative affect, and bulimic symptoms: A preliminary experiment. *International Journal of Eating Disorders, 27,* 206–217.

Stice, E., & Presnell, K. (2007). *The body project: Promoting body acceptance and preventing eating disorders facilitator guide.* New York, NY: Oxford University Press.

Stice, E., Rohde, P., Shaw, H., & Marti, C. N. (2012). Efficacy trial of a selective prevention program targeting both eating disorder symptoms and unhealthy weight gain among female college students. *Journal of Consulting and Clinical Psychology, 80,* 164–170.

Stice, E., & Shaw, H. (2004). Eating disorder prevention programs: A meta-analytic review. *Psychological Bulletin, 130,* 106–227.

Stice, E., Shaw, H., Becker, C. B., & Rohde, P. (2008). Dissonance-based interventions for the prevention of eating disorders: Using persuasion principles to promote health. *Prevention Science, 9,* 114–128.

Stice, E., Shaw, H., Burton, E., & Wade, E. (2006). Dissonance and healthy weight eating disorder prevention programs: A randomized efficacy trial. *Journal of Consulting and Clinical Psychology, 74,* 263–275.

Stice, E., Shaw, H., & Marti, C. N. (2007). A meta-analytic review of eating disorder prevention programs: Encouraging findings. *Annual Review of Clinical Psychology, 3,* 207–231. doi:10.1146/annurev.clinpsy.3.022806.091447

Sundgot-Borgen, J., & Torstveit, M. K. (2010). Aspects of disordered eating continuum in elite high-intensity sports. *Scandinavian Journal of Medicine & Science in Sports, 20,* 112–121. doi:10.1111/j.1600-0838.2010.01190.x

Taylor, C. B., Bryson, S., Luce, K. H., Cunning, D., Doyle, A. C., Abascal, L. B., . . . Wilfley, D. E. (2006). Prevention of eating disorders in at-risk college-age women. *Archive of General Psychology, 63,* 881–888.

Thompson, R. A., & Sherman, R. T. (2010). *Eating disorders in sport.* New York, NY: Routledge.

Torres-McGehee, T. M. (in press). Eating disorder risk and the role of clothing on body image in collegiate cheerleaders. *Journal of Athletic Training.*

Torres-McGehee, T. M., Green, J. M., Leaver-Dunn, D., Leeper, J. D., Bishop, P. A., & Richardson, M. T. (2011). Attitude and knowledge changes in collegiate dancers following a short-term, team-centered prevention program on eating disorders. *Perceptual and Motor Skills, 3,* 711–725.

Torstveit, M. K., Rosenvinge, J. H., & Sundgot-Borgen, J. (2008). Prevalence of eating disorders and the predictive power of risk models in female elite athletes: A controlled study. *Scandinavian Journal of Medicine & Science in Sports, 18,* 108–118.

Whisenhunt, B. L., Williamson, D. A., Drab-Hudson, D. L., & Walden, H. (2008). Intervening with coaches to promote awareness and prevention of weight pressures in cheerleaders. *Eating and Weight Disorders, 13,* 102–110.

Winzelberg, A. J., Eppstein, D., Eldredge, K. L., Wilfley, D., Dasmahapatra, R., Dev, P., & Taylor, C. B. (2000). Effectiveness of an Internet-based program for reducing risk factors for eating disorders. *Journal of Consulting and Clinical Psychology, 68,* 346–350.

Yager, Z., & O'Dea, J. (2008). Prevention programs for body image and eating disorders on university campuses: A review of large, controlled interventions. *Health Promotion International, 23,* 173–189. doi:10.1093/heapro/dan004

Yager, Z., & O'Dea, J. (2009). Body image, dieting and disordered eating and activity practices among teacher trainees: Implications for school-based health education and obesity prevention programs. *Health Education Research, 24,* 472–482. doi:10.1093/her/cyn044

Yager, Z., & O'Dea, J. (2010). A controlled intervention to promote a healthy body image, reduce eating disorder risk and prevent excessive exercise among trainee health education and physical education teachers. *Health Education Research, 25,* 841–852. doi:10.1093/her/cyq036

Zach, K. N., Machin, A. L. S., & Hoch, A. Z. (2011). Advances in management of the female athlete triad and eating disorders. *Clinics in Sports Medicine, 30,* 551–573.

Zotter, D. (2009, August). *Evaluation of a sorority-based eating disorders prevention program.* Paper presented at the 117th American Psychological Association, Toronto, Ontario, Canada.

263

# Cognitive–Behavioral Therapy Guided Self-Help for Binge Eating: A Culturally Sensitive Minimal or Early Intervention Program

*Fary M. Cachelin, Munyi Shea, and Frances A. Bono*

Research has demonstrated that eating disorders (EDs) such as bulimia nervosa (BN) and binge eating disorder (BED) regularly occur among ethnic minority women and pose serious mental and physical health risks (Cachelin, Phinney, Schug, & Striegel-Moore, 2006; Cachelin, Schug, Juarez, & Monreal, 2005; Cachelin, Veisel, Striegel-Moore, & Barzegarnazari, 2000). For example, among Hispanic women lifetime prevalence estimates for BN and BED range from 1.9% to 2.0% and from 2.3% to 2.7%, respectively (Alegria et al., 2007; Marques et al., 2010); these numbers are similar to those reported for the general female population of the United States (Granillo, Jones-Rodriguez, & Carvajal, 2005). Despite their chronicity and severity, EDs largely go undetected and untreated (Becker, Hadley Arrindell, Perloe, Fay, & Striegel-Moore, 2010; Cachelin, Rebeck, Veisel, & Striegel-Moore, 2001; Cachelin, Striegel-Moore, & Regan, 2006). Moreover, ethnic minority women, especially those from lower income backgrounds, continue to be underrepresented in therapy, treatment trials, and research (Garvin & Striegel-Moore, 2001) because of a variety of help-seeking barriers including feelings of shame, fear of stigmatization, minimization of eating problems, financial constraints, language barriers, limited knowledge and access to health care services, and logistical challenges such as lack of child care (Cachelin et al., 2001; Cachelin &

*Note.* This work was funded by the National Institute of Mental Health (Grant 1SC-1MH087975). Fary M. Cachelin and Munyi Shea contributed equally to this chapter.

Striegel-Moore, 2006). These findings underscore the great need to develop and deliver accessible treatment to this population.

In this chapter, we illuminate the utility of a culturally sensitive cognitive–behavioral early intervention program for BN and BED. We first provide an overview of the cognitive–behavioral therapy guided self-help (CBT–GSH) program: its structure, contents, and the role of the supporter, the person who facilitates and provides support throughout the guided self-help program. We then discuss the importance of cultural adaptation and the effectiveness of the culturally adapted CBT–GSH program. Next, we present a case study to illustrate the step-by-step implementation of the culturally adapted CBT–GSH program with a Mexican American woman with BED. We close the chapter by highlighting available literature and resources for counselors and clinicians. Through these discussions, we hope to provide clinicians and counselors with a relatively low-cost, accessible, yet evidence-supported intervention for working with clients with BN and BED.

## Overview of Cognitive-Behavioral Therapy and Guided Self-Help

CBT is widely considered to be the treatment of choice for BN and BED (Wilson, Grilo, & Vitousek, 2007). According to the cognitive–behavioral model, the core psychopathology of binge eating is a negative overconcern with body shape and weight that leads to dysfunctional dieting and other unhealthy weight control behaviors. The dysfunctional dieting in turn predisposes an individual to binge eating. CBT consists of cognitive and behavioral procedures designed to enhance motivation for change, replace dysfunctional dieting with a regular and flexible pattern of eating, decrease undue concern with body shape and weight, and prevent relapse. CBT for EDs involves three basic stages: In Stage 1, self-monitoring of eating and techniques to help the client establish normalized eating patterns are introduced. Coping mechanisms are also taught to deal with emotional distress. Stage 2 focuses on cognitive restructuring, including identifying and challenging maladaptive cognitions such as the overvaluation of weight and shape. In Stage 3, relapse prevention techniques are taught to promote the maintenance of change after treatment (Fairburn, 1995; Grilo, 2006). CBT requires specialized training and expertise for delivery, making it less readily available to a wide range of clients. Hence, implementation science researchers have begun to examine the effectiveness of CBT-based guided self-help (GSH) as a more easily disseminable intervention or first step in the treatment of binge eating–related problems (DeBar et al., 2011; Lynch et al., 2010; Striegel-Moore et al., 2010). CBT-GSH is a low-intensity intervention in which clients use a self-help manual with only limited support and instruction from either a specialist or a nonspecialist in clinical or nonclinical settings. A typical CBT-GSH program consists of following a self-help manual with programmatic steps based in CBT and attending regular guidance and support sessions with a coach or supporter. A few such programs have been developed with similar components (e.g., Masheb & Grilo, 2008; Traviss, Heywood-Everett, & Hill, 2011). The most commonly evaluated CBT-GSH program is the one developed by Fairburn (1995), Overcoming Binge Eating. This program consists of following six steps of a self-help manual accompanied by eight guidance and support sessions (25 minutes in duration each), with more sessions clustered early in the treatment period: four weekly sessions followed by four biweekly sessions. The program is designed to be delivered by personnel with no background in the use of CBT or expertise in the treatment of BN or BED. The book is available in English and Spanish and has two sections. The first section is educational and summarizes current knowledge about binge eating, BED, and BN and provides the rationale for the self-help program. The second section of the book presents the program itself, which consists of six steps on how to change eating habits or other associated problems. The steps are additive and meant to be followed in sequence: Step 1, getting started—self-monitoring and weekly weighing; Step 2, establishing a pattern of regular eating and stopping vomiting and laxative misuse; Step 3, substituting alternative activities for binge eating; Step 4, practicing problem solving and reviewing progress; Step 5, tackling dieting and other forms of avoidance of eating; and Step 6, preventing relapse and dealing with other problems. The program's primary focus is to develop a regular pattern of moderate eating using self-monitoring, self-control strategies, and problem solving. Additionally, relapse prevention is emphasized to promote maintenance of behavioral change.

The principal role of the guide or supporter is to explain the rationale for using the self-help book, generate a reasonable expectancy for a successful outcome, and motivate the participant to use the book as a guide for proceeding through the program steps. The support sessions are program led and follow the therapist's manual developed by Fairburn (1998). The manual specifies the length and tone of the sessions, how the supporters should prepare in advance for them, and the elements that should be followed in each session. It is important to note that the role of the supporter is not to provide education or skills training to the participant (which would undermine the self-help nature of the program). Prior research has demonstrated the effectiveness of nonspecialists as supporters for such CBT–GSH programs (Bailer et al., 2004; Dunn, Neighbors, & Larimer, 2006).

CBT–GSH is most appropriate for adult men and women ages 18 and older whose primary symptom is binge eating, who have less severe eating pathology, and who have lower levels of psychiatric comorbidity. As a minimal or first-step intervention, it is not indicated for those with anorexia nervosa, who need medical and clinical attention to address low weight; those who are morbidly obese and need targeted behavioral weight loss strategies; or those with more serious clinical concerns (such as suicidality or severe depression). In a specialty clinic setting, CBT–GSH can be used as the first step in a stepped care approach and can even prime response to further treatment (Wilson, Wilfley, Agras, & Bryson, 2010). In nonspecialty settings, it can be delivered by nonspecialists (e.g., nurses, primary care physicians) to individuals who would otherwise not be able to access care.

Given the collaborative nature of guided self-help, the time-limited modality, and the lower implementation cost, this CBT intervention is suitable for use in school, college, and community mental health settings where counselors can play an important role as the guide or supporter. Because the program can be completed in a less formal and nonstigmatizing setting (e.g., student's home) and on a more flexible schedule, it reduces or eliminates some of the help-seeking barriers faced by clients (such as shame, stigma, long commute to and from health care services), making it a more feasible choice for those who would not consider or seek professional psychological services. Moreover, the emphasis on self-help may enhance clients' understanding of their disordered eating and empower them with a sense of self-efficacy in coping and problem solving. If the program is successfully implemented, it may also provide a positive framework for clients with regard to psychological interventions and encourage them to seek further treatment and services if needed.

Research conducted primarily with White women has demonstrated that CBT–GSH is effective in reducing binge eating and vomiting, decreasing shape and weight concerns and related eating disorder pathology, and improving depression and self-esteem (Sysko & Walsh, 2008; Wilson et al., 2007). Reported remission rates from binge eating range from 24% to 74%, and improvement is typically maintained at 12- and 18-month follow-ups (Bailer et al., 2004; Grilo, 2006). It has also been shown to be as effective as specialty interpersonal therapy and significantly superior to behavioral weight loss in treating BED (Grilo & Masheb, 2005; Wilson et al., 2010). Despite its promise, experts have agreed that considerably more community-based research is needed before CBT–GSH can be disseminated widely (Grilo, 2006; Sysko & Walsh, 2008). Most notable is the lack of ethnic or cultural representation in these treatment studies.

## Cultural Adaptation for Treatment of Eating Disorders

Cultural adaptation involves the process of modifying aspects of a treatment approach or intervention program to tailor it to a specific ethnic or cultural group's worldviews, values, and stylistic preferences (Falicov, 2009). Research and case studies have shown that incorporating cultural components into existing treatment approaches can be beneficial for ethnic minority clients and is likely to increase their treatment engagement (Flaskerud & Nyamanthi, 2000; Hwang, 2006; Shea & Leong, 2013; Shea, Yang, & Leong, 2010; Vega et al., 2007).

The need for cultural adaptation for treatment of EDs is also supported by anthropological literature demonstrating that eating behaviors and practices are culturally and socially determined (Logue, 1991) and by empirical research demonstrating ethnic differences in presentation of ED symptoms (Brown, Cachelin, & Dohm, 2009). For example, Black and Hispanic women report less drive for thinness than do White women, presumably because of cultural differences in the valuation of thinness. Similarly, perceptions of both food amount and body size may be influenced by ethnicity (Cachelin, 2001; Dohm, Cachelin, & Striegel-Moore, 2005). Specifically, Latino culture tends to place a high degree of importance on food and eating and at the same time on women's physical appearance.

Resnicow, Soler, Braithwaite, Ahluwalia, and Butler (2000) suggested that cultural sensitivity and adaptation occur on two levels. Surface structure adaptation includes matching intervention programs and materials to the superficial characteristics of a target population, such as providing treatment in clients' native language and matching clients with an ethnically similar therapist. Deep structure adaptation involves understanding and incorporating cultural and contextual factors—such as cultural values, gender role expectations, socioeconomic status, political and historical environments—into treatment consideration. For instance, Latinas are typically taught that taking care of their bodies and their health should be secondary to taking care of others (Lozano-Vranich & Petit, 2003). This belief is likely to shape their help-seeking behavior and treatment engagement.

We recently completed a series of studies to adapt the CBT–GSH intervention for binge eating to Latinas' cultural beliefs and values and to pilot test its feasibility and effectiveness in a community sample. Using the focus group methodology, we evaluated the acceptability of the CBT–GSH program among Mexican American women and identified the cultural themes that need to be considered (Shea et al., 2012). Overall, all the focus group participants reported that they liked the CBT–GSH program, would follow it, and would recommend it to a friend. They also believed that—with some modifications—the program would be feasible and acceptable for Latinas with BED. Specific themes and considerations for treating Latinas with EDs were identified:

- *Navigating cultural expectations and acculturation differences:* Participants experienced tensions and conflicts with others in their family, with their community, and within themselves regarding their eating problems because of different cultural beliefs, values, and acculturation levels. Participants reported that their family members, particularly those from older generations, tended to be less acculturated and less knowledgeable about EDs. As such, family members were sometimes unable to identify with participants' experience and might impede or hinder the treatment.
- *Involving the family:* Participants identified two areas in which family can potentially influence their treatment engagement: (a) family's attitudes toward their weight and shape concerns and (b) family's involvement in the treatment process. Family can be a detriment to recovery and to relapse prevention because they are not sufficiently knowledgeable about

269

eating issues as health problems. For example, eating larger meals is the norm in Latino families and having a curvy appearance is a positive attribute; therefore, the need for or purpose of the intervention might be misunderstood. With adequate education and communication, the family can be a source of support; for example, they can assist with healthier grocery shopping and choice of restaurants.

- *Incorporating cultural eating patterns and foods:* Participants expressed that food carries multiple social and emotional meanings in Latino culture, which can pose challenges to women's ability to manage their eating problems and treatment success. Participants also described that food symbolizes abundance and hospitality in their community. Therefore, social gatherings and activities tend to revolve around food, and serving portions are large. These culturally prescribed eating patterns may increase Latinas' vulnerabilities to overeating. Therefore, the intervention should address how to maneuver at social gatherings that frequently involve food, and the emphasis should be on portion control rather than on food avoidance.

- *Overcoming feelings of guilt and shame:* Participants identified their own emotions as being a barrier to treatment success in the CBT–GSH program. They often experienced guilt and shame about their disordered eating. Participants emphasized the need for ongoing encouragement and validation from supporters throughout the treatment process.

- *Using culturally meaningful scenarios and activities:* Participants suggested that the presentation of the CBT–GSH manual should be contextualized to reflect Latinas' life experiences, preferences, and needs and that the intervention lacks culturally relevant resources and references. For example, some of the scenarios and suggestions for alternate coping activities, such as going for a drive or taking a walk, are not appropriate for Latina women (who may not be allowed to go driving alone or who cannot exercise outdoors because of unsafe neighborhoods).

- *Empowerment through self-help:* Participants reported experiencing loneliness and alienation as a result of the shame and secrecy over their eating problems. Most participants preferred seeking help from informal sources such as friends, family, church, and community resources. Participants expressed concerns and reluctance to seek professional help because of the cultural stigma attached to psychological problems. The self-help nature of the intervention, therefore, appealed to all participants.

On the basis of these themes and suggestions emerging from the focus groups, a number of modifications to the original CBT-GSH program were indicated and implemented: (a) Coping strategies and mechanisms for dealing with family's lack of support and negative feedback were provided through vignettes and role playing; (b) an ethnic-specific food guide (e.g., Mexican food) was added to provide objective information on normal food portions and on healthy distribution of macronutrients using both American and Mexican foods; (c) encouragement and hope were instilled throughout the support sessions; and (d) supporters' sensitivity toward clients' worldviews, life experience, and social context was emphasized.

In the next stage of this research program, we conducted a pilot study to test the feasibility and effectiveness of the culturally adapted CBT–GSH program with a community sample of Mexican American women with BN and BED. These participants were recruited directly from the greater Los Angeles area, via ads and flyers posted at local colleges and community organizations asking for Mexican American women who had problems with overeating to participate in a study on women's health. The support sessions were conducted over the phone by nonspecialists. We examined the intervention's acceptability, feasibility, and efficacy by assessing program acceptability, attrition, adherence, reduction in binge eating, and evaluation of each program step:

- *Program acceptability:* Of eligible participants, 30 of 49 (61%) agreed to enroll in the CBT–GSH program. This ratio indicates program acceptability by this population.
- *Program attrition:* Of these 30 participants, 10 (30%) dropped out at some point after enrolling in the program. In past studies, attrition between baseline and posttreatment has ranged from 6% to 42%, with attrition in most studies at around 25%.
- *Program efficacy:* We examined initial treatment efficacy as a reduction in the primary outcome of binge eating between baseline and post-treatment. The 20 participants who completed the program reported a significant decrease in frequency of binge eating over the 12 weeks ($Ms$ = 42.4 episodes at baseline and 8.1 episodes posttreatment, $p$ = .000). All participants except 1 experienced a reduction in overeating, and 11 of 20 (55%) were completely symptom free at posttreatment.
- *Program adherence:* Adherence to the GSH program was high for program completers. Program completers attended 97% of support phone sessions and completed 92% of weekly monitoring assignments.
- *Program evaluation:* The participants reported each step of the program to be "somewhat helpful" to "very helpful."

In conclusion, our findings supported that this culturally adapted self-help intervention may have been effective in reducing binge eating in a community sample of Mexican American women with BED and was viewed positively by those who completed it. In the next section, we present the case of Ms. A, a participant in our pilot study, to elucidate the implementation of the CBT–GSH program. The program consisted of eight sessions that spanned 12 weeks. Ms. A's supporter was a nutritionist who did not have formal training in clinical psychology or in counseling; however, the supporter was supervised by two clinical researchers throughout the program implementation. The support sessions were conducted over the phone. Participants were asked to enter their daily and weekly food monitoring records on a secure Web site so that their supporters could access the records and go over them during the phone sessions.

# Case Example

Ms. A was a second-generation Mexican American woman in her 20s.[1] She was attending college and majored in drama and theater arts at the time of intervention. She also held a job in a related field. Ms. A resided in a predominantly Mexican American neighborhood with her partner.

Diagnostic assessments revealed that Ms. A had recurrent BED and depressive disorder. Ms. A engaged in binge eating 2 to 5 days a week and sometimes binged more than once a day. She did not engage in any compensatory behaviors (e.g., self-induced vomiting, laxative or diuretic use, overexercise) and was mostly concerned about the effects of her binging on her physical health rather than on her appearance. Ms. A's binge eating predated dieting. Her first attempt at dieting to lose weight was at age 15, but this and subsequent attempts were unsuccessful. Eventually, Ms. A gave up dieting and calorie restriction. Ms. A reported a weight gain of 5 to 10 pounds per year over the past 5 years. She weighed herself daily and sometimes more than once per day. Her body mass index was in the overweight category.

Since adolescence, Ms. A had had several episodes of depression. At the time of the CBT–GSH intervention, Ms. A was not receiving any psychological treatment, in part because she could not drive. However, she expressed a desire to receive help and make behavioral changes. Under the care and supervision of a psychiatrist, Ms. A had been taking medications to manage symptoms associated with depression.

## CBT–GSH Intervention

### Orientation Session

The supporter introduced Ms. A to the CBT–GSH intervention program and discussed with her the confidentiality agreement, the structure and schedule of the phone meetings, and the Web-based food logging and self-monitoring system. In addition, the supporter explored with Ms. A her expectations about the CBT–GSH program and the process of doing an intervention over the phone. Ms. A was concerned about logging her food intake on the home computer that everyone could access and decided that she would update the online records via a hand-held device.

The supporter then introduced role-playing vignettes, designed as part of the cultural adaptation to prepare participants for potential challenging interpersonal and family interactions. Ms. A chose to role-play a college student who struggles with her binge eating and is confronted by her intrusive family members. However, Ms. A stated that she could not identify

---

[1]*Note.* The details of the case have been changed in significant ways to protect the client's confidentiality.

with the character because her family—contrary to the one depicted in the vignette—was respectful and highly supportive of her decision to seek treatment. The supporter acknowledged Ms. A's ability to assert herself and to communicate the need for treatment with her family members. The session concluded with the understanding that Ms. A was to start Step 1 in the following week.

### Session 1

Step 1, getting started, addresses self-monitoring and weekly weighing. Before this session, Ms. A was asked to log her food intake daily and complete a weekly summary online. In this session, the supporter guided Ms. A in identifying her eating patterns and triggers for binge eating according to her self-monitoring records. Ms. A noted that food logging had helped her become more mindful of her food choices (what she was eating) and her portion size (how much she was eating). However, mindless eating, such as grazing at night and lack of meal planning, often led to disruptions in her eating (e.g., skipped breakfast) and binge eating. In terms of weighing, Ms. A had made progress in not weighing herself more than once in the past week. She also identified the detrimental effects of constant weighing, which had contributed to her dissatisfaction and anxiety about her weight and discouraged her from focusing on positive behavior changes such as making healthy food choices. The supporter commended Ms. A for her efforts and encouraged her to start Step 2, regular eating, which emphasizes meal planning. The supporter also introduced the Mexican American food guide to help Ms. A gauge the portion size and nutrition of specific ethnic foods.

In this session, Ms. A expressed concern about her ability to make lasting changes to her eating because of prior unsuccessful attempts. The supporter validated Ms. A's feelings and suggested that abstinence from binge eating was not the only indicator of successful treatment. The supporter then guided Ms. A to identify other beneficial outcomes that could result from participating in the CBT–GSH program.

### Session 2

Step 2 focuses on establishing a regular pattern of eating and discontinuing any maladaptive compensatory behaviors (e.g., use of laxatives). Because Ms. A did not have a history of compensatory behaviors, the session mainly focused on regular eating and meal planning.

The supporter reviewed Ms. A's self-monitoring records and guided her to identify barriers to regular eating. Ms. A reported some success in eating breakfast regularly; however, she continued to struggle with eating regular meals for the rest of the day because of her long and inconsistent school and work schedules. Moreover, Ms. A came to realize that the triggers of her binge eating tended to revolve around two themes: (a) budget planning and (b) dining with other people who overeat. Ms. A stated that when she had extra cash in her pocket, she would go buy junk food or treat herself to a meal at a restaurant on a whim. She also noticed that she tended to

273

overeat during family gatherings at which food was plentiful and overeating was the norm. Dining with her boyfriend could also trigger binge eating because both of them gravitated toward junk food and consumed large amounts of food. When asked about her planned course of action to resolve these issues, Ms. A stated that she needed to communicate to her partner that they can still enjoy each other's company even if they need to place separate orders or make healthier food choices.

Another problem that arose in this session was related to food logging. Ms. A was out of town celebrating the Christmas holiday with her extended family, which resulted in her skipping a few days of logging. Nevertheless, Ms. A resumed self-monitoring as soon as she returned home. The supporter commended Ms. A's willingness to persist in self-monitoring after the temporary interruptions.

### Session 3

Step 3 focuses on alternatives to binge eating. Ms. A stated that passive alternative activities such as studying, watching TV, or taking a bath had not been effective in the past; rather, they had triggered binge eating. However, active activities—such as painting her fingernails or doing her hair—had been helpful because these activities required using her hands and made eating incompatible. Ms. A found it particularly difficult to elicit or engage in alternative activities when she was drinking and socializing with others in a bar because "drinking and eating go hand in hand." Yet, she did not want to give up bar outings because they were a source of enjoyment for her. The supporter provided Ms. A with a few alternatives to binge eating during bar outings (such as calling her partner, taking a brisk walk around the block) and asked her to evaluate the feasibility of each alternative.

### Session 4

Step 4 focuses on practicing problem solving and taking stock of progress. At first, Ms. A indicated that Step 4 was not applicable to her because she did not practice the six-tier approach to problem solving, which includes the following components: (a) identifying the problem, (b) accurately specifying the trigger, (c) considering multiple solutions, (d) evaluating the implications and consequences of each solution, (e) choosing the best solution, and (f) acting on the solution. As the supporter pointed out the recent improvements Ms. A had made, she came to realize that she had been using the problem-solving strategies, albeit informally. It also appeared that Ms. A was rather astute in identifying specific triggers and brainstorming solutions, although she did not always evaluate the pros and cons of each solution or act on the solution. The supporter encouraged Ms. A to continue exploring other problem areas and generate ideas for targeted problems by following the six-tier approach.

In reviewing her overall progress, Ms. A reported that her experience with the CBT–GSH program had been very positive. Initially, she was skeptical about the program and her ability to change. Nevertheless, she began to see the benefits of the steps once she started practicing them.

Her consistency in self-monitoring had increased her awareness of various problem areas and her confidence in successfully managing her eating problem. Some of her behavioral changes included reduced frequency of nonstop snacking and weighing, eating breakfast daily, and endorsing a more flexible perspective on her behavior. Ms. A stated, "This is a big deal . . . because I used to feast or famine . . . all-or-nothing." Among all improvements, Ms. A was most surprised by and proud of her attitudinal change: She had become less critical of herself and more open minded and accepting of others' suggestions. For example, she accepted an invitation to attend Overeaters Anonymous meetings, a treatment opportunity she would not have entertained in the past. Ms. A reported that she felt reassured during the Overeaters Anonymous meetings.

Regular eating and meal planning remained the biggest challenge for Ms. A. She attributed the lack of planning to her inconsistent work and school schedules. Additionally, she was surrounded by finger foods at her workplace and by colleagues who also grazed on these foods. As a result, she found it difficult to resist the culture and ended up snacking constantly. The supporter commended Ms. A for her insight and acknowledged the challenges presented by her job environment. The supporter encouraged Ms. A to continue identifying factors that influence her binge eating and to apply the problem-solving approach to tackle the issue of erratic eating.

### Sessions 5 and 6 (Combined)

Step 5 addresses dieting and other forms of avoidance, such as avoiding eating foods with high-calorie content. Ms. A had never avoided any types of foods; her diet always included the foods that she enjoyed and found palatable. Thus, the supporter and Ms. A spent the rest of the session discussing body checking or body avoidance, not exploring healthy alternatives to fast food.

Body checking or body avoidance was the topic of discussion in Session 6. Ms. A stated that she did not engage in body avoidance, nor did she check her body excessively. Therefore, much of the session was spent discussing Ms. A's appraisal of her body image and physical health. She related that she became more self-conscious about her body when she was surrounded by well-dressed women in dancing clubs. Unlike those women, Ms. A dressed for comfort rather than for style. Ms. A was also aware that she was larger than many of her peers. Nevertheless, she felt content with her body and did not consider herself unattractive.

What troubled Ms. A, however, was her rapid weight gain over the past few years and the ill effects on her physical health. For instance, she constantly complained about pain in her feet. Ms. A identified stress and lack of exercise as the main contributors to her steady weight gain. Although she enjoyed physical activities, she had not been consistent in exercising. Moreover, she tended to engage in stress-related eating when she took on too many responsibilities at work. The supporter validated Ms. A's concerns about her physical health and asked Ms. A how she might use the skills discussed in previous sessions, including regular eating, to address her weight gain.

*Session 7*

Step 6 emphasizes relapse prevention. Ms. A discussed the areas in which she would like to improve and shared her thoughts and feelings about the program. Ms. A had experienced a few binges during the past few weeks, which had been triggered by grazing on junk food (e.g., at her workplace) or by social outings (e.g., bar hopping). However, she identified self-monitoring and meal planning as the most effective preventive strategies; both had helped her become more mindful of her eating habits and adapt to unexpected events.

Since she had started the program, Ms. A had gained a strong awareness of her personal shortcomings in problem recognition and problem solving. For instance, she did not initially realize that being around family members who eat large amounts of food could make her vulnerable to binge eating. She also realized that she still lacked alternatives to overeating in situations that triggered bingeing such as bar outings and dining with her partner. Ms. A said, "I have a tendency of letting life get in the way of things that I really want [healthy eating], and this is something that I need to work on." The supporter validated Ms. A's struggles and encouraged her to continue using problem solving to address factors that perpetuate her binge eating.

*Session 8*

This session is the termination of the CBT–GSH intervention. The supporter encouraged Ms. A to discuss her thoughts and feelings about ending the program and discontinuing the guided support. Ms. A stated that she had expected to get "a complete handle" on her binge eating and weight gain by participating in this program; she did not quite meet her expectations. However, in hindsight, she realized that her expectations were unrealistic and that she should see her recovery as a work in progress. Ms. A related that one of her future goals was to maintain a positive attitude and not dwell on things that she was not doing well, including regular eating. Ms. A remained concerned about her weight gain: "I want to lose weight, but dieting won't work now. It's like pouring liquid into a cup that has a crack." The supporter concurred with Ms. A's perspective and encouraged her to pursue her weight management goal by taking part in a gradual, sensible weight loss program that emphasizes healthy eating and regular physical activity.

Ms. A felt confident that she would continue applying the skills she had learned. However, she was nervous about being discouraged by potential relapses, which would lead her to completely quit the program. The supporter pointed out that Ms. A had been persistent in tackling her eating problems in spite of multiple challenges (e.g., no computer access, inconsistent work schedule), to which Ms. A responded, "Yes, I need to keep in mind that recovery is a life-long process, and life is not all or nothing." Ms. A stated that she was tremendously grateful for the profound impact the CBT–GSH program had made on her life.

### Discussion

The case of Ms. A illustrates the structure and course of the CBT–GSH program (i.e., 12 weeks, 8 sessions, 6 steps), the nature of guided support, and the content of typical sessions. Overall, Ms. A had made significant progress and improvements. Although she was not completely free of binge eating, the frequency of her bingeing had been reduced. She also began eating more regularly toward the end of the intervention. Through self-monitoring, Ms. A had identified several situational and emotional triggers to her binge eating, including bar outings, family gatherings, eating with her partner, stress, work environment, and poor planning. In terms of weighing, Ms. A was successful in decreasing the frequency of weighing from multiple times a day to once every 4 days, which reduced her anxiety about her weight gain.

Ms. A did experience challenges and setbacks during the 12-week course of the CBT–GSH intervention. For instance, her self-monitoring was erratic during and after the holidays because of limited access to her online records. When Ms. A started a new job, she took a short hiatus from the program and did not return any of the supporter's phone calls. She attributed her disengagement to feeling overwhelmed by multiple responsibilities and getting discouraged after failed attempts to follow the program steps. Ms. A also missed several phone sessions without prior notice of cancellation, which prompted the supporter to make last-minute changes to accommodate rescheduled sessions and to combine two sessions into one at one time to stay within the 12-week program timeframe.

Ms. A faced tremendous barriers to seeking professional psychological help because of her feelings of shame, school and work hours, and lack of financial resources. The self-help intervention reduced or eliminated most of these barriers to treatment seeking. Self-help programs are brief, inexpensive, nonstigmatizing, and empowering and can be tailored to meet individual needs (Apfel, 1996; Garvin, Striegel-Moore, Kaplan, & Wonderlich, 2001), making it a feasible and appealing treatment option for clients such as Ms. A, who tend to underuse professional psychological services.

The culturally sensitive CBT–GSH program ensured that the contents and delivery of the intervention strategies (e.g., the nutrition guide, alternative activities to binge eating) were congruent and relevant to Ms. A's worldview and life experiences. Although Ms. A initially did not find the vignettes and role-playing exercise helpful, she later acknowledged the challenge of negotiating cultural norms and interpersonal dynamics that influence her eating patterns and food choices and alluded to wanting more concrete examples to help her address these interpersonal dilemmas.

As discussed earlier, the focus of the support sessions was not to clinically resolve or work through any issues. Rather the supporter guided, encouraged, and motivated Ms. A to apply the knowledge and self-regulation skills acquired from the self-help manual. In addition, the supporter was responsive to the role of sociocultural factors in the development and maintenance of Ms. A's eating problem, as well as in her treatment engagement. For instance, many of our pilot study participants, including Ms. A, came from low-income backgrounds; their life circumstances were marred by limited resources such as lack of healthy food options or safe places to exercise in their neighborhoods. Hence, our supporters had to be aware of the implications of these realistic challenges on Latinas' treatment trajectory and be creative in exploring alternative options (such as joining a low-cost food co-op that provides healthy food, starting a walking group with family members) that are not offered by the self-help manual.

## Conclusion

Through a case presentation, we illustrated how to integrate culturally relevant factors in an innovative, evidence-based treatment—the CBT–GSH program—to provide a low-cost, accessible service for socioeconomically disadvantaged and underserved clients. The CBT–GSH program is most appropriate as a first-step intervention for clients with lower levels of psychopathology. With culturally appropriate modifications and accommodations, the CBT–GSH program can be tailored to address the needs of clients from diverse ethnic and cultural groups. We hope that the discussion in this chapter will provide counselors with an additional intervention tool to consider, assess, and use to treat binge eating–related disorders and engender interest in using a guided self-help treatment modality in practice.

## Chapter Highlights

- BN and BED do occur in ethnic minority women. Latinas report a prevalence rate of BN and BED similar to that of White women (Alegria et al., 2007; Marques et al., 2010). However, they are less likely to seek professional psychological help because of a variety of social, cultural, and financial barriers (Cachelin & Striegel-Moore, 2006).
- CBT, which targets irrational beliefs, dysfunctional dieting, and unhealthy weight control behaviors, is the treatment of choice for BN and BED (Wilson et al., 2007). However, CBT requires specialized training, making it a costly and less accessible treatment option.
- CBT–GSH is a low-intensity intervention in which clients use a self-help manual with minimal guidance from either a specialist or a nonspecialist in clinical or nonclinical settings. The CBT–GSH program can be completed at the client's choice of location (e.g., home) and tailored to meet individual needs (Garvin et al., 2001). By its nature, the CBT–GSH program is brief, inexpensive, and nonstigmatizing (Apfel, 1996), making it a more accessible intervention or first step in the treatment of binge eating–related problems (Striegel-Moore et al., 2010).
- The CBT–GSH program is most appropriate for individuals whose primary symptom is binge eating and who have less severe eating pathology and lower levels of psychiatric comorbidity. Considerable research evidence has supported the effectiveness of CBT–GSH in reducing symptoms associated with binge eating–related disorders in White women (Wilson et al., 2007).

- Research and case studies have demonstrated that incorporating cultural components into evidence-based treatment can enhance treatment engagement and effectiveness for ethnic minority clients (Shea et al., 2010; Vega et al., 2007). Cultural adaptation of intervention programs requires (a) matching the materials and program contents to the characteristics of a target population, such as using clients' language and culturally relevant examples, and (b) acknowledging and accommodating the role of cultural and contextual factors (e.g., acculturation, socioeconomic status) in clients' understanding of problem behaviors, symptom expression, and help-seeking behavior.
- On the basis of the focus group interviews, we adapted the CBT–GSH program to ensure its congruence with Latinas' cultural values and life experiences (Shea et al., 2012). Preliminary studies examining the feasibility and efficacy of the culturally adapted CBT–GSH revealed that this treatment option was both feasible and effective for Latinas with BN and BED.
- Counselors and clinicians who would like to implement such self-help programs with ethnic minority clients will want to consider several cultural adaptations, as appropriate, including providing ethnic food guides, using role-playing exercises, addressing family and social issues, and incorporating multicultural competence training for professional staff.

## Recommended Resources

We recommend Fairburn's (1995) book *Overcoming Binge Eating*, published by Guilford Press, whose appendix contains a rather comprehensive list of readings for counselors, clinicians, and clients. Here, we provide some additional resources pertinent to binge eating–related disorders, self-help interventions, and culturally sensitive therapy and treatment:

Constantine, M. G., Miville, M. L., Kindaichi, M. M., & Owens, D. (2010). Case conceptualizations of mental health counselors—Implications for the delivery of culturally competent care. In M. M. Leach & J. D. Aten (Eds.), *Culture and the therapeutic process—A guide for mental health professionals* (pp. 99–115). New York, NY: Routledge

Cooper, P. J. (1995). *Bulimia nervosa and binge eating: A guide to recovery.* London, England: Robinson.

Fairburn, C. G., Marcus, M. D., & Wilson, G. T. (1993). Cognitive behaviour therapy for binge eating and bulimia nervosa: A treatment manual. In C. G. Fairburn & G. T. Wilson (Eds.), *Binge eating: Nature, assessment and treatment.* New York, NY: Guilford Press.

Franko, D. L., Thompson-Brenner, H., Thompson, D. R., Boisseau, C. L., Davis, A., Forbush, K. T., . . . Wilson, G. (2012). Racial/ethnic differences in adults in randomized clinical trials of binge eating disorder. *Journal of Consulting and Clinical Psychology, 80,* 186–195. doi:10.1037/a0026700

Hays, P. A., & Iwamasa, G. Y. (2006). *Culturally responsive cognitive-behavioral therapy: Assessment, practice, and supervision.* Washington, D.C.: American Psychological Association.

Leong, F. T., & Lee, S. (2006). A cultural accommodation model for cross-cultural psychotherapy: Illustrated with the case of Asian Americans. *Psychotherapy: Theory, Research, Practice, Training, 43,* 410–423. doi:10.1037/0033-3204.43.4.410

Lewis-Fernández, R., & Díaz, N. (2002). The cultural formulation: A method for assessing cultural factors affecting the clinical encounter. *Psychiatric Quarterly, 73,* 271–295. doi:10.1023/A:1020412000183

Trace, S. E., Thornton, L. M., Root, T. L., Mazzeo, S. E., Lichtenstein, P., Pedersen, N. L., & Bulik, C. M. (2012). Effects of reducing the frequency and duration criteria for binge eating on lifetime prevalence of bulimia nervosa and binge eating disorder: Implications for *DSM-5. International Journal of Eating Disorders, 45,* 531–536. doi:10.1002/eat.20955

Wilfley, D. E., Wilson, G. T., & Agras, W. S. (2003). The clinical significance of binge eating disorder. *International Journal of Eating Disorders, 34*(Suppl.), S96–S106. doi:10.1002/eat.10209

Zweig, R. D., & Leahy, R. L. (2012). *Treatment plans and intervention for bulimia and binge-eating disorder.* New York, NY: Guilford Press.

Sue, W. G., & Sue, D. (2008). *Counseling the culturally diverse: Theory and practice* (5th ed.). Hoboken, NJ: Wiley.

# References

Alegria, M., Woo, M., Cao, Z., Torres, M., Meng, X., & Striegel-Moore, R. (2007). Prevalence and correlates of eating disorders in Latinos in the United States. *International Journal of Eating Disorders, 40*(Suppl.), S15–S21. doi:10.1002/eat

Apfel, R. (1996). "With a little help from my friends I get by": Self-help books and psychotherapy. *Psychotherapy, 59,* 309–321.

Bailer, U., de Zwaan, M., Leisch, F., Strnad, A., Lennkh-Wolfsberg, C., El-Giamal, N., Kasper, S. (2004). Guided self-help vs. cognitive-behavioral group therapy in the treatment of bulimia nervosa. *International Journal of Eating Disorders, 35,* 522–537. doi:10.1002/eat.20003

Becker, A. E., Hadley Arrindell A., Perloe, A., Fay, K., & Striegel-Moore, R. H. (2010). A qualitative study of perceived social barriers to care for eating disorders: Perspectives from ethnically diverse health care consumers. *International Journal of Eating Disorders, 43,* 633–647. doi:10.1002/eat.20755

Brown, M., Cachelin, F. M., & Dohm, F. A. (2009). Eating disorders in ethnic minority women: A review of the emerging literature. *Current Psychiatry Reviews, 5,* 182–193. doi:10.2174/157340009788971119

Cachelin, F. M. (2001). Ethnic differences in body size preferences: Myth or reality? *Nutrition, 17,* 353–356.

Cachelin, F. M., Phinney, J., Schug, R. A., & Striegel-Moore, R. H. (2006). Acculturation and eating disorders in a Mexican American community sample. *Psychology of Women Quarterly, 30,* 340–347. doi:10.1111/j.1471-6402.2006.00309.x

Cachelin, F. M., Rebeck, R., Veisel, C., & Striegel-Moore, R. H. (2001). Barriers to treatment for eating disorders among ethnically diverse women. *International Journal of Eating Disorders, 30,* 269–278. doi:10.1002/eat.1084

Cachelin, F. M., Schug, R. A., Juarez, L. L., & Monreal, T. K. (2005). Sexual abuse and eating disorders in a community sample of Mexican American women. *Hispanic Journal of Behavioral Sciences, 27,* 533–546. doi:10.1177/0739986305279022

Cachelin, F. M., & Striegel-Moore, R. H. (2006). Help seeking and barriers to treatment in a community sample of Mexican American and European American women with eating disorders. *International Journal of Eating Disorders, 39,* 1544–1561. doi:10.1002/eat.20213

Cachelin, F. M., Striegel-Moore, R. H., & Regan, P. C. (2006). Factors associated with treatment seeking in a community sample of European American and Mexican American women with eating disorders. *European Eating Disorders Review, 14,* 422–429. doi:10.1002/erv.720

Cachelin, F. M., Veisel, C., Striegel-Moore, R. H., & Barzegarnazari, E. (2000). Disordered eating, acculturation and treatment seeking in a community sample of Hispanic, Asian, Black, and White women. *Psychology of Women Quarterly, 24,* 244–253. doi:10.1111/j.1471-6402.2000.tb00206.x

DeBar, L. L., Striegel-Moore, R. H., Wilson, G. T., Perrin, N., Yarborough, B. J., Dickerson, J., & Kraemer, H. C. (2011). Guided self-help treatment for recurrent binge eating: Replication and extension. *Psychiatric Services, 62,* 367–373. doi:10.1176/appi.ps.62.4.367

Dohm, F. A., Cachelin, F. M., & Striegel-Moore, R. H. (2005). Factors that influence food amount ratings by White, Hispanic, and Asian samples. *Obesity Research, 13,* 1061–1069. doi:10.1038/oby.2005.124

Dunn, E. C., Neighbors, C., & Larimer, M. E. (2006). Motivational enhancement therapy and self-help for binge eaters. *Psychology of Addictive Behaviors, 20,* 44–52. doi:10.1037/0893-164X.20.1.44

Fairburn, C. G. (1995). *Overcoming binge eating.* New York, NY: Guilford Press.

Fairburn, C. G. (1998). *Guided self-help for bulimia nervosa: Therapist's manual for use in conjunction with* Overcoming Binge Eating *(Fairburn, 1995).* Oxford, England: University of Oxford, Department of Psychiatry.

Falicov, C. J. (2009). On the wisdom and challenges of culturally attuned treatments for Latinos. *Family Process, 48*(2), 295–312. doi:10.1111/j.1545-5300.2009.01282.x

Flaskerud, J. H., & Nyamanthi, A. M. (2000). Collaborative inquiry with low income Latina women. *Journal of Health Care for the Poor and Underserved, 11,* 326–342.

Garvin, V., & Striegel-Moore, R. H. (2001). Health services research for eating disorders in the United States: A status report and a call to action. In R. H. Striegel-Moore & L. Smolak (Eds.), *Eating disorders: Innovative directions in research and practice* (pp. 135–152). Washington, DC: American Psychological Association. doi:10.1037/10403-007

Garvin, V., Striegel-Moore, R. H., Kaplan, A., & Wonderlich, S. (2001). The potential of professionally developed self-help interventions for the treatment of eating disorders. In R. H. Striegel-Moore & L. Smolak (Eds.), *Eating disorders: Innovative directions in research and practice* (pp. 153–172). Washington, DC: American Psychological Association.

Granillo, T., Jones-Rodriguez, G., & Carvajal, S. C. (2005). Prevalence of eating disorders in Latina adolescents: Associations with substance use and other correlates. *Journal of Adolescent Health, 36,* 214–220. doi:10.1016/j.jadohealth.2004.01.015

Grilo, C. M. (2006). *Eating and weight disorders.* New York, NY: Psychology Press.

Grilo, C. M., & Masheb, R. M. (2005). A randomized controlled comparison of guided self-help cognitive behavioral therapy and behavioral weight loss for binge eating disorder. *Behaviour Research and Therapy, 43,* 1509–1525. doi:10.1016/j.brat.2004.11.010

Hwang, W. (2006). The Psychotherapy Adaptation and Modification Framework (PAMF): Application to Asian Americans. *American Psychologist, 61,* 702–715.

Logue, A. W. (1991). *The psychology of eating and drinking* (2nd ed.). New York, NY: Freeman.

Lozano-Vranich, B., & Petit, J. (2003). *The seven beliefs: A step-by-step guide to help Latinas recognize and overcome depression.* New York, NY: HarperCollins.

Lynch, F. L., Striegel-Moore, R. H., Dickerson, J. F., Perrin, N., DeBar, L., Wilson, G. T., & Kraemer, H. C. (2010). Cost-effectiveness of guided self-help treatment for recurrent binge eating. *Journal of Consulting and Clinical Psychology, 78,* 322–333. doi:10.1037/a0018982

Marques, L., Alegria, M., Becker, A. E., Chen, C.-N., Fang, A., Chosak, A., & Diniz, J. B. (2010). Comparative prevalence, correlates of impairment, and service utilization for eating disorders across US ethnic groups: Implications for reducing ethnic disparities in health care access for eating disorders. *International Journal of Eating Disorders, 44*(5), 1–9. doi:10.1002/eat.20787

Masheb, R. M., & Grilo, C. M. (2008). Examination of predictors and moderators for self-help treatments of binge eating disorder. *Journal of Consulting and Clinical Psychology, 76,* 900–904. doi:10.1037/a0012917

Resnicow, K., Soler, R., Braithwaite, R. L., Ahluwalia, J. S., & Butler, J. (2000). Cultural sensitivity in substance use prevention. *Journal of Community Psychology, 28,* 271–290. doi:10.1002/(SICI)1520-6629(200005)28:3<271::AID-JCOP4>3 .0.CO;2-I

Shea, M., Cachelin, F., Uribe, L., Striegel-Moore, R., Thompson, D., & Wilson, G. T. (2012). Cultural adaptation of a cognitive behavior therapy guided self-help program for Mexican American women with binge eating disorders. *Journal of Counseling & Development, 90,* 308–318.

Shea, M., & Leong, F. T. L. (2013). Working with a Chinese immigrant with severe mental illness: An integrative approach of cognitive–behavioral therapy and multicultural conceptualization. In S. Poyrazli & C. E. Thompson (Eds.), *International case studies in mental health* (pp. 205–223). Thousand Oaks, CA: Sage.

Shea, M., Yang, L. H., & Leong, F. T. L. (2010). Loss, psychosis, and chronic suicidality in a Korean American immigrant man: Integration of cultural formulation model and multicultural case conceptualization approach. *Asian American Journal of Psychology, 1*, 212–223. doi:10.1037/a0020951

Striegel-Moore, R. H., Wilson, G. T., DeBar, L., Perrin, N., Lynch, F., Rosselli, F., Kraemer, H. C. (2010). Cognitive behavioral guided self-help for the treatment of recurring binge eating. *Journal of Consulting and Clinical Psychology, 78*, 312–321. doi:10.1037/a0018915

Sysko, R., & Walsh, T. (2008). A critical evaluation of the efficacy of self-help interventions for the treatment of bulimia nervosa and binge eating disorder. *International Journal of Eating Disorders, 41*, 97–112. doi:10.1002/eat.20475

Traviss, G. D., Heywood-Everett, S., & Hill, A. (2011). Guided self-help for disordered eating: A randomized control trial. *Behaviour Research and Therapy, 49*, 25–31. doi:10.1016/j.brat.2010.10.007

Vega, W. A., Karno, M., Alegria, M., Alvidrez, J., Bernal, G., Escamilla, M., & Loue, S. (2007). Research issues for improving treatment of U.S. Hispanics with persistent mental disorders. *Psychiatric Services, 58*, 383–394. doi:10.1176/appi.ps.58.3.385

Wilson, G. T., Grilo, C., & Vitousek, K. M. (2007). Psychological treatment of eating disorders. *American Psychologist, 62*, 199–216. doi:10.1037/0003-066X.62.3.199

Wilson, G. T., Wilfley, D. E., Agras, S., & Bryson, S. W. (2010). Psychological treatments of binge eating disorder. *Archives of General Psychiatry, 67*, 94–101. doi:10.1001/archgenpsychiatry.2009.170

Section 4

# Effective Treatments for Eating Disorders and Obesity

## Chapter 13

# Enhanced Cognitive–Behavioral Therapy Approach to Counseling Clients With Eating Disorders

*Anthea Fursland and Hunna J. Watson*

In this chapter, we introduce counselors to an evidence-based treatment that can be applied to all eating disorder (ED) diagnoses in adults. Enhanced cognitive–behavioral therapy (CBT–E) is a relatively new treatment that has shown promising results in research and community settings.

## Why Do Counselors Need to Know About Eating Disorders Treatment?

Treatment of EDs is notoriously difficult, and many counselors are hesitant to treat people with such conditions, especially those with anorexia nervosa (AN) because of the high prevalence and seriousness of medical comorbidities. Bulimia nervosa (BN) also carries health risks, and atypical variations of these diagnoses (eating disorder not otherwise specified, or EDNOS) have similar levels of morbidity and pathology to AN and BN (Fairburn et al., 2007; Ricca et al., 2001). AN, BN, and EDNOS are the three categories of EDs recognized in the *Diagnostic and Statistical Manual of Mental Disorders* (4th ed., text rev.; *DSM–IV–TR*; American Psychiatric Association, 2000). Binge eating disorder is currently categorized as a form of EDNOS, although inclusion as a standalone ED in its own right is anticipated in the forthcoming fifth edition.

It is widely accepted that EDs, especially AN, are relatively rare. Yet recent population studies have shown that they are more prevalent than previously thought, with one study showing lifetime prevalences for AN and atypical AN of 2.2% and 4.2%, respectively (Keski-Rahkonen et al., 2007).

Approximately 15% of women will need clinical treatment for a diagnosable ED in their lifetime (Wade, Bergin, Tiggemann, Bulik, & Fairburn, 2006). Although it has been accepted that only 10% of individuals with AN or BN are male, a recent community study of more than 10,000 teenagers found equal numbers of male and female teens with AN (Swanson, Crow, Le Grange, Swendsen, & Merikangas, 2011).

Furthermore, unhealthy weight control methods, including disordered eating, are common (Neumark-Sztainer, Wall, Larson, Eisenberg, & Loth, 2011), and behaviors falling under the criteria for EDNOS are increasing among men and women (Hay, Mond, Buttner, & Darby, 2008; White, Reynolds-Malear, & Cordero, 2011). Counselors working in general practice settings will likely encounter adults with disordered eating and full-syndrome EDs, even if these clients were referred for other reasons. In fact, many individuals with EDs do not disclose the ED and instead seek help from health and mental health professionals for related issues or secondary consequences of the ED (e.g., depression, anxiety, gastrointestinal problems, weight loss). The low rate of help seeking among people with EDs stems from many factors, such as shame and poor self-recognition of disordered eating. It is thus incumbent on all counselors to screen for and be prepared to treat EDs (see Chapter 5, this volume). A useful tool for screening EDs is the five-question SCOFF questionnaire (Morgan, Reid, & Lacey, 1999), which is akin to the CAGE for screening alcohol problems:

1. Do you make yourself vomit because you feel uncomfortably full?
2. Do you worry you have lost control over how much you eat?
3. Have you lost over 14 lbs. in a three month period?
4. Do you believe yourself to be fat when others say you are too thin?
5. Would you say that food dominates your life? (Morgan et al., 1999, p. 1467)

(Two or more "yes" answers are suggestive of possible anorexia nervosa or bulimia nervosa and indicate the need for further questioning.)

Being alert and ready to respond to EDs can be a very professionally rewarding experience and bring substantial scope to counselors to contribute meaningfully to clients' long-term physical and mental health.

## Why Enhanced Cognitive–Behavioral Therapy?

Because counselors are likely to encounter clients with EDs and because of the seriousness of these conditions, it is important that they have access to evidence-based protocols for ED treatment. In this chapter, we focus on CBT–E, a single treatment suitable for all EDs. CBT–E is transdiagnostic and is therefore highly suitable for a range of individuals, both male and female, including those who have a clinically significant eating problem that does not meet diagnostic criteria for AN or BN. CBT–E is efficacious for adults with EDs, as shown in a randomized controlled trial (Fairburn et al., 2009), and effective in community settings (Byrne, Fursland, Allen, & Watson, 2011;

Fairburn et al., in press). Two easy-to-read treatment guides are available: one by the developer of CBT–E (Fairburn, 2008) and another, describing a similar version of transdiagnostic CBT, by a long-standing proponent of CBT for EDs (Waller et al., 2007). CBT–E was developed for and is generally used with adults with EDs. Both manuals provide chapters on modifying the treatment for adolescents with EDs, although CBT–E has not yet been scientifically validated with individuals younger than age 18. For youths with AN, the strongest evidence to date has supported family-based treatment (American Psychiatric Association, 2006; National Institute for Health and Clinical Excellence, 2004). For youths with BN, research into efficacious treatment is in its infancy, yet preliminary data have supported family-based treatment modified for BN. For further information on family-based treatment for youths, counselors may wish to consult available treatment manuals for AN (Lock, Le Grange, Agras, & Dare, 2001) and BN (Le Grange & Lock, 2007).

## What Is the Basis for Enhanced Cognitive–Behavioral Therapy?

The transdiagnostic model of CBT was developed from the cognitive–behavioral theory of BN (Fairburn, 1981; Fairburn, Marcus, & Wilson, 1993). Individuals with BN evaluate their worth almost exclusively in terms of controlling their weight and shape rather than in terms of other life domains (e.g., work, family relationships). This overvaluation of weight and shape is considered the core psychopathology of EDs and leads to a resolute pursuit of weight and shape attainment, typically thinness for females and muscularity with leanness for males. Efforts to reach these goals involve dietary restriction, which can include avoidance of high-calorie foods and certain food groups (e.g., carbohydrates), and keeping strict rules (e.g., never eating more than others). Over time, these efforts at dietary restriction can set off binge eating through two mechanisms: physiological (hunger) and psychological (black-and-white thinking that leads to beliefs such as "I've already broken my rule, I might as well continue eating"). Binge eating often leads to compensatory attempts to rid the body of excess calories by purging (self-induced vomiting, laxative and diuretic misuse), fasting, excessive exercising, and misuse of weight loss drugs. Moreover, binge eating often results in a sense of shame and failure (to keep up dietary restriction) and a further resolve to try even harder to maintain the restriction. The binge eating thus reinforces a focus on the overvalued control over eating, weight and shape, and dieting efforts, resulting in the vicious cycle (restrict → binge → purge) typical of BN.

From this theory came the development of cognitive–behavioral therapy for BN (CBT–BN). CBT–BN focuses on reducing disordered behaviors (dietary restriction, binge eating, purging) and distorted body weight- and shape–related cognitions. It has been empirically validated among adults with EDs and is endorsed by the National Institute for Health and Clinical Excellence (2004) and the American Psychiatric Association (2006).

However, even the creators of the original BN theory and treatment acknowledged that CBT–BN only provided a full and lasting response in 50% of clients (Fairburn, Cooper, & Shafran, 2003). Consequently, they extended CBT–BN into an enhanced version, CBT–E (Fairburn, 2008; Fairburn et al., 2003). This enhanced model applies to all types of EDs, including the symptoms associated with AN: severe dietary restriction resulting in loss of body weight and the starvation state with symptoms that are psychological (e.g., obsessionality, irritability, social withdrawal) and physiological (e.g., bloating, delayed gastric emptying, fatigue) and that may maintain dietary restraint and weight and shape overvaluation (Fairburn et al., 2003). The model also identifies four additional maintaining mechanisms (mood intolerance, interpersonal problems, perfectionism, and core low self-esteem) that in some clients contribute to the cycle of ED symptoms (i.e., weight and shape overvaluation and strict dieting, binge eating and compensatory behaviors).

Mood intolerance describes difficulties with mood regulation, including impulsivity, and has been reported in clients with BN. Such clients have difficulty in dealing appropriately with intense mood states and engage in dysfunctional mood modulatory behavior, such as binge eating (Fairburn et al., 2003). Interpersonal problems are pronounced among some individuals with EDs (Fairburn et al., 2003) and are thought to maintain ED symptoms by undermining self-esteem and intensifying the need to be in control, especially of eating, shape, and weight. Perfectionism is a characteristic feature of those with EDs (e.g., Shafran, Cooper, & Fairburn, 2002), and an overlap often occurs between the ED and other life domains, with clients applying perfectionistic standards to the attempted control of eating, shape, and weight and to other aspects of their lives. Low self-esteem is common among people with EDs, but some individuals hold an unconditional, pervasive negative view of themselves that is thought to maintain ED symptoms as a result of two main processes (Fairburn, 2008). Individuals with intensely low self-esteem may strive especially hard to control eating, shape, and weight to gain some minimal sense of self-worth, and they may feel hopeless about their ability to overcome their EDs.

The CBT–E protocol has two versions: a focused form that centers exclusively on ED psychopathology and a broad form that addresses the additional maintaining mechanisms described earlier (Fairburn, 2008). These two versions of CBT–E have been evaluated empirically in outpatient populations: in a randomized controlled trial (Fairburn et al., 2009) and in two community-based effectiveness trials (Byrne et al., 2011; Fairburn et al., in press). The randomized controlled trial included 154 outpatients with a *DSM–IV–TR* ED but who were not markedly underweight (body mass index [BMI] > 17.5), and therefore none met criteria for AN. At the end of treatment, half of the sample had ED symptom scores within community norms and half reported no binge–purge behaviors, and these improvements were maintained after 1 year. The Byrne et al.'s community-based trial ($N = 125$) reported similar outcomes in a population that included clients with AN (BMI ≤ 17.5). Symptom remission was found in two thirds of those

290

who completed treatment and in 40% of the full sample (i.e., both treatment completers and noncompleters). Therapy completion was low, with only half of the sample completing treatment, although this figure is commensurate with completion rates more broadly reported for EDs (Byrne et al., 2011).

Byrne et al.'s (2011) study tested CBT–E among consecutive referrals to a community outpatient clinic in Australia. Participants had a range of ED diagnoses, including AN. At the end of the study, full remission (cessation of key ED behaviors, BMI ≥ 18.5, not meeting criteria for an ED) was achieved by two-thirds of completers and 40% of the overall sample. Among AN completers, half achieved full remission, a similar proportion to that observed for BN and EDNOS completers. However, among the entire sample (i.e., intention to treat), including treatment completers and noncompleters, only 25% of the AN group achieved full remission, which was significantly lower than the proportions for the BN and EDNOS groups.

In the study by Fairburn et al. (in press), two thirds of AN patients consecutively referred to three community clinics in the United Kingdom and Italy were able to complete outpatient treatment. Of these, the average weight gain over 40 weeks was 16.5 pounds (2.77 BMI points), ED features improved, and there was minimal deterioration over 60-week follow-up. Results from the randomized controlled trial and community studies suggest that CBT–E is a promising treatment for all ED diagnoses in adults.

# Enhanced Cognitive–Behavioral Therapy

CBT–E is structured and time limited, as is its precursor, CBT–BN, although it is more flexible and individualized. Treatment targets the mechanisms that maintain the ED, which are identified at treatment outset by an individualized case formulation of the client's specific ED behaviors and cognitions.

What follows is a brief outline of CBT–E, highlighting the central features of the treatment. It is, however, only an overview, and the reader is encouraged to study the detailed descriptions of CBT–E in one of two books: the treatment guide written by its developer (Fairburn, 2008) and a treatment guide on a similar version of transdiagnostic CBT (Waller et al., 2007). The version of CBT–E described here is the focused version, which has two recommended lengths, short and long. The short course is for individuals who are not underweight and involves approximately 20 sessions over 20 weeks, with the first 8 sessions held twice a week, the next 10 weekly, and the last 3 held every other week. The long course is for those with a BMI of 17.5 or less and involves approximately 40 sessions over 40 weeks. Sessions are held twice a week until patients are consistently gaining weight and then transition to weekly, moving to fortnightly toward the end of weight regain, then to once every 3 weeks toward the end of treatment.

## *Assessment Therapeutic Alliance and Orientation to Treatment*

The assessment procedure usually takes two sessions. The main goal of assessment is to build a positive therapeutic relationship to create a firm foundation for treatment. Counselors achieve this relationship by expressing genuine curiosity about the client's current life, dreams, and fears; interest in helping him or her; instillation of hope; and validation of ambivalence, if present. When working with EDs, this stance is particularly important, because successful treatment involves clients giving up highly valued behaviors and beliefs. Although most clients with an ED will recognize some negative aspects of their condition (often binge eating or excessive preoccupation with controlling food, shape, and weight), they tend to believe that restriction or compensatory behaviors are vital to avoid gaining weight and becoming "fat," thus they fear giving up these behaviors. The high drop-out rate, especially among clients with AN, reflects this fear of change. Acknowledging and validating the valued aspects of clients' EDs are crucial to building rapport, in that a shared understanding is developed and the counselor can work on increasing clients' motivation and courage to change. Clients will be encouraged to move outside their comfort zone in the short term to benefit in the long term by being free of an ED.

The counselor's stance should balance empathy with firmness (Fairburn, 2008; Vitousek, Watson, & Wilson, 1998). Our experience has been that clinicians new to the field of EDs or CBT–E are reluctant to be firm, fearing driving clients away. With the experience of being firm, they realize the importance and benefits. Moreover, therapeutic alliance is high in CBT for EDs when firmness is balanced with empathy (Waller, Evans, & Stringer, 2012), an example of which is the introduction of self-monitoring. The counselor's empathic understanding of how hard it might be to undertake needs to be balanced with a firm expectation of task completion.

Counselors should convey several essential points to clients about what to expect from treatment. CBT–E focuses on the present and the factors currently maintaining the ED cycle. CBT–E is a collaborative therapy, and it is especially suited to work with EDs because it encourages working together openly in a nonjudgmental way that involves clients in all aspects of treatment. It is a very active treatment, with an expectation of between-session work, such as self-monitoring and experimenting with new behaviors (e.g., trying out previously avoided foods). Therapy can be described as a marathon, with the client as the runner; the counselor as the coach, offering strategies and advice; and family and friends as cheerleaders, offering encouragement. The client has to do the hardest work to cross the finish line. Our experience has been that being honest up front about the hard work involved and the commitment of support builds trust and rapport.

It is vital that the counselor convey respect and understanding that change may be highly anxiety provoking, but equally critical that the counselor establish that treatment focuses on change. Establishing nonnegotiable aspects of treatment is important, for example, that the general goal of CBT–E is to normalize eating and reduce ED behaviors. Target behaviors differ among clients but commonly include restricting, binge eating, purging, and excessively exercising. Weight changes may occur: regain in those who are underweight through restriction and loss in those who binge eat without compensatory behaviors. Although weight regain is an overt goal for underweight clients, weight loss should never be a goal in treatment. It is important to ask clients in or above the healthy weight range if they are willing to put weight loss on hold for the duration of treatment (i.e., about 5 months) and give their best effort to overcoming their ED. They should be informed that actively seeking weight loss will interfere with ED treatment and that at the end of treatment, if they are still unhappy with their weight and want to lose weight, they are free to do so and the counselor will facilitate a referral to a registered dietitian with experience in EDs. Our experience has been that very few clients end therapy with this goal; they come to realize that their efforts at weight loss were counterproductive and develop more acceptance of their weight.

## Assessment: Information Gathering

While building rapport, the counselor needs to collect information on what has brought the client into treatment and how he or she can be helped. Apart from the usual demographic information and mental health history that are commonly gathered in a counseling setting, the counselor must focus on specific areas in clients with EDs.

### Eating Patterns

Having some objective data on current behaviors and attitudes is useful. Clients can be mailed a questionnaire to complete before attending or asked to arrive 20 minutes before the initial interview to complete it in the waiting room. We have found it rare that a client will complain or not comply. A useful and free publicly available self-report questionnaire is the Eating Disorder Examination Questionnaire (EDE–Q; Fairburn, 2008; Fairburn & Beglin, 1994), which gives a total (Global) score and four subscale scores (Dietary Restraint, Eating Concern, Shape Concern, Weight Concern), as well as frequency estimates for binge eating, purging, and excessive exercise over the past 28 days.

Whether or not a questionnaire is used, the counselor should ask about current eating patterns. Specific questions should seek to identify binge eating; compensatory behaviors such as fasting or extreme undercating; self-induced vomiting (and the possibility of blood in the vomit); laxative, diuretic, or appetite suppressant misuse; exercise for shape and weight control (frequency and type); and misuse of weight loss drugs (e.g., Alli®). Fluid intake should be assessed because dehydration is a risk in clients who purge, and excessive fluid intake is also a potential risk because it puts an unnecessary burden on the cardiovascular system and kidneys. Further inquiries should cover any dietary rules such as time rules, avoided foods, and portion control or calorie limits.

### Weight

The client's current weight and height should be measured and a BMI calculated; weighing will become a central part of counseling. Previous weight should be assessed, with questions on childhood size (e.g., slim, average, chubby), family build, and lowest and highest (nonpregnant) weight since adolescence (including age at those weights). This information is helpful in estimating where the client's weight might fall naturally without the ED. A recent weight history (over the previous 12 months) should be taken with a particular concern for rapid weight loss. A 5-foot, 6-inch-tall woman weighing 140 pounds (with a BMI of 22.6) may look healthy, until one discovers that 4 months earlier she weighed 200 pounds (with a BMI of 32.3). Commencing outpatient treatment with clients with a BMI lower than 14 is inadvisable, and if a client's weight drops to that level during counseling, then treatment should be suspended and inpatient treatment should be recommended (American Psychiatric Association, 2006; National Institute for Health and Clinical Excellence, 2004).

*Physical Status*

For female clients, a menstrual history should be taken, with age of menarche (first period) and episodes of amenorrhea (loss of periods) or menstrual irregularities. For male clients, hormonal functioning should be assessed by means of questions regarding sexual desire, performance, nocturnal emissions, and early morning erections, with decreased functioning suggestive of hormonal malfunction.

All clients should receive a medical examination from their primary care physician (PCP) before starting treatment and receive regular medical monitoring from their PCP. Although conducting medical monitoring is outside the scope of practice for counselors, it is important that counselors know of any physical conditions (e.g., diabetes, thyroid, celiac disease) and any prescribed or over-the-counter medications and be aware of any risk factors. If the client is diabetic, it is important to assess for insulin misuse to control weight (i.e., underuse).

Medical risk should be monitored throughout treatment, because all EDs carry risk. Ideally, the PCP conducts regular monitoring. However, because many adult patients are reluctant to see their PCP regularly, responsible counselors regularly ask questions about clients' health to guide their treatment or their decision to refer them to their PCP or to the hospital emergency department. PCPs should be alerted to any changes in physical presentation.

It is incumbent on clinicians working with clients with EDs to learn about medical risks in this population (Mehler & Andersen, 2010). Of particular concern (identified at assessment or during treatment) are dizziness or fainting; blood in vomit and frequent vomiting; irregular heart beat or chest pains; and fatigue or weakness (e.g., when climbing stairs), because these are suggestive of medical instability. If the client reports any of these symptoms, the client's PCP should be contacted immediately.

The PCP is responsible for facilitating a hospital admission if warranted. Indications for hospitalization include medical instability; a suicide plan or intent or any psychiatric disorder requiring admission; need for supervision during and after meals and in bathrooms; inability to benefit from outpatient treatment; and need for more structure. Referral to an ED specialist or a higher level of care (e.g., a day treatment program) may be indicated for clients with a more severe symptom presentation. Alternating between levels of care does not rely on weight criteria alone; the client's full clinical and social circumstances should instead be taken into account (American Psychiatric Association, 2006).

## Treatment

What follows is a description of the major components of CBT–E.

### Stage 1

This first stage usually consists of seven sessions, with a focus on behavioral change.

*Psychoeducation.* A large component of CBT–E, especially early in treatment, is psychoeducation. The counselor shares information, encouraging and empowering clients to review the information and reflect on how it might apply to their personal situation, with the aim of increasing motivation to change. This sharing of information for the client's benefit enhances rapport.

Psychoeducation may be given in the assessment phase, if relevant, but is certainly given in the early stages of treatment, whenever indicated. A handout on the main topics to be discussed is available for counselors and clients at http://www.cci.health.wa.gov.au/resources/minipax.cfm?mini_ID=19. These topics are the following:

- *Vicious cycle that maintains the ED*: Dieting sets people up to binge. Overconcern about weight or shape leads to restriction, which leads to hunger and binge eating, which lead to purging or further restriction.
- *Starvation syndrome:* The "Minnesota experiment" (Keys, Brozek, & Henschel, 1959) involved a group of fit young men drafted into the U.S. Army during World War II but who, as conscientious objectors, volunteered to be in a humanitarian program. They had their caloric intake reduced by half for 6 months and experienced not only the expected physical changes, but mental changes too, including preoccupation with food, social withdrawal, irritability, depression, and anxiety. It is important that this piece of psychoeducation be given to people of low weight before constructing their case formulation (see the Formulation section) so that they understand how starvation can account for symptoms and keep them stuck in their ED cycle.
- *Relative ineffectiveness of purging:* The counselor should debunk myths (e.g., vomiting only rids the body of 30%–60% of calories ingested, and laxatives only rid the body of approximately 10%) and highlight dangers (e.g., electrolyte imbalance, gastrointestinal problems, erosion of dental enamel).
- *Health risks of EDs:* The risks pertain especially to cardiac, dental, and bone health.

- *Importance of regular eating:* Regular eating provides structure; keeps blood sugar and metabolism steady; and combats binge eating, overeating, undereating, and grazing.
- *Importance of nutritional variety:* Normal eating from all food groups is important for optimal health.
- *Importance of not weighing frequently:* Weight normally fluctuates from day to day, and counselors are unable to draw conclusions about trends in weight until they have at least four readings; also, clients may misinterpret the number on the scale.
- *Excessive exercise and its potential dangers:* Excessive exercise is especially dangerous to cardiac, dental, and bone health.
- *Metabolism and energy expenditure:* The counselor should review the body's caloric needs to keep vital organs functioning and myths about metabolism.

*Formulation.* The counselor creates a case formulation to develop a shared understanding of what maintains the client's ED—in other words, the vicious cycle of thoughts and behaviors that perpetuate it. Clients find this intervention helpful because they are given an explanation of what keeps their disorder going, and this new insight engages them in the treatment. Creating a map or diagram of the client's ED helps clients take a step back from or helicopter view of their experience of the ED. This development of meta-cognitive awareness, which is useful throughout treatment, creates distance from the ED and the opportunity to reflect on rather than be engulfed by their disordered behaviors and thoughts.

The formulation follows a template (i.e., it is anchored to evidence-based models of ED maintenance), although it is individualized to specific aspects of the client's ED and created using the client's words and terms. Fairburn (2008) provided three basic models: BN, restricting AN, and a mixed model for cases in which binge–purge and restricting behaviors coexist. We recommend being familiar with the three models to create the personalized formulation with ease. Although overvaluation of weight and shape is the central tenet of the theory underpinning CBT–E and the focus of the formulation (but not usually the starting point), it will mean different things to clients. It may be expressed as "I don't want to get fat" or "I must have a flat stomach" or "I must be skinny so people will take care of me." Next, we illustrate the creation of a formulation that follows the mixed model.

*Case vignette.* Sandra, a 19-year-old university student, presented with what her PCP called bulimia. She reported binge eating approximately 3 times per week and compensating by taking as many as 20 laxatives and then fasting the following day. However, after questioning, it appeared that her binges were in fact not large amounts of food and not more than most people would eat; therefore, they did not qualify as binges and she did not meet *DSM–IV–TR* criteria for BN. Her height was measured at 5 feet, 6 inches, and her weight was 115 pounds, giving her a BMI of 18.6. She reported that she had weighed 130 pounds (BMI = 21.0) a year earlier. Her periods were sporadic, and she had not menstruated for 3 months. She reported fatigue and irritability and withdrawal from friends. She was diagnosed with EDNOS.

In creating the formulation, the counselor asked Sandra what she would like to change most, and the answer was "binges, because I lose control, I break my rules." The clinician started by writing "Binge" about two thirds of the way down a piece of paper (this can also be done on a whiteboard). He asked what she did after binge eating and, on hearing that she took laxatives, he drew an arrow down from "Binge" and wrote "Laxatives." He asked whether she would take laxatives if she did not binge. She said, "Of course not," and confirmed that knowing she would be taking laxatives and that "emptying her stomach" allowed her to eat even more. He pointed out how taking laxatives served to reinforce the binge eating and drew an arrow back to "Binge." He then asked the circumstances around her binges. Sandra responded that they usually occurred when she got home in the afternoon. After being prompted about eating patterns earlier in the day, she replied, "I try not to eat lunch. I restrict, I try to eat only certain things," and the counselor wrote, "Try not to eat lunch. Restriction, food rules," and connected it with an arrow down to "Binge." When asked why she did not eat during the day, Sandra replied, "I'm scared of getting fat." The counselor wrote that down and joined it with an arrow to "Restriction, food rules." He then asked about other results of not eating lunch. Sandra replied that she felt irritable and her stomach felt bloated, and she did not like being around people. The counselor reminded Sandra about starvation syndrome and pointed out that this was a clear example of malnutrition playing a part in maintaining her ED. He filled out those symptoms and tied them in with other features in the formulation (see Figure 13.1). Sandra was able to see how her eating patterns created a self-perpetuating cycle.

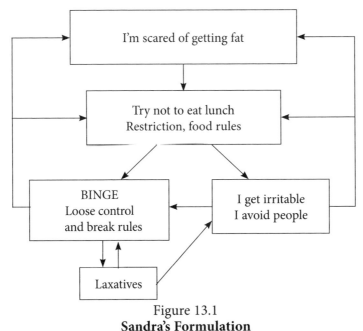

Figure 13.1
**Sandra's Formulation**

*Regular eating.* This behavior is perhaps the most important because it is one of the most effective ways of reducing binge eating (for those who binge). It also addresses the erratic eating commonly seen in clients with EDs and challenges the rules held by many concerning when to eat (or not). The formulation provides a rationale for introducing regular eating, highlighting the chain of events that typically lead to binge eating: attempts to restrict eating and the resulting failure to keep up the restriction. Eating regularly involves eating every 2–4 hours throughout the day: breakfast, morning snack, lunch, afternoon snack, dinner, and an additional evening snack for those who eat their dinner early, have high energy requirements (e.g., athletes), or need to increase their weight.

Clients may be hesitant to eat regularly in a structured way because many restrict early in the day. Therefore, the counselor needs to give a clear rationale and may well need to repeat it. Clients need to understand that regular eating reduces restriction, binge eating, and grazing throughout the day and maintains a steady level of blood sugar (which affects mood) and increased metabolism. We have observed that many clients are persuaded by this last point because most clients want a fast metabolism.

Some clients will need to make changes gradually, for example, introducing a small lunch (if they usually abstain from eating until the afternoon) and then later a breakfast, or leaving 1 hour between snacking (if they are grazing throughout the day) and then increasing the gap to 2 and then 3 hours. Planning meals and snacks, either the night before or at the start of the day, is often helpful. Clients will need strategies to resist eating or binge eating between planned meals and snacks. Counselors can begin to introduce behaviors incompatible with binge eating (e.g., going for a walk without a credit card or cash, calling a friend, playing solitaire on the computer). At this point in treatment all clients, whatever their weight, may choose what they eat while they focus on structuring their eating pattern.

*Self-monitoring.* Because the goal of Stage 1 is for clients to change their pattern of eating, it is vital that they and their counselor are fully aware of food consumed (and when) and what disordered behaviors are occurring (and when). Clients are asked to self-monitor not just food intake (i.e., a food log that they might have completed for a dietitian), but also associated thoughts and feelings. Monitoring must be in real time to enable client awareness of occurrences in the moment and to make changes in the moment. Clients must be encouraged to be honest, with themselves and their counselor, in monitoring records.

Self-monitoring often arouses anxiety in clients that they will (a) become more preoccupied; (b) restrict, binge, or purge more because they can see how much they have consumed; (c) be judged by the counselor; and (d) find it too hard to monitor in real time. Self-monitoring is a challenging task; therefore, it is imperative that counselors believe in its critical function and convey this importance to clients. They must be firm, while empathetically acknowledging clients' concerns about self-monitoring. Counselors should address clients' anxieties and reassure them of the following:

1. Although clients' preoccupation with eating and food may increase in the short term, it will then decrease and allow them to view their eating behaviors neutrally. Monitoring provides them with an opportunity to disengage from eating, become aware of eating patterns, and learn that what they thought was out of their control and awareness (e.g., binges) can be understood and changed with practice and application.
2. Seeing how much they have really consumed in a day can be helpful in shaping or changing eating into more healthy patterns.
3. Counselors are not there to judge or be shocked but to help; they will be working together with the client, much as detectives looking for clues in the monitoring records. The aim is to help clients to gain control over their ED, not to embarrass them.
4. Difficulties in real-time recording can be problem solved in advance. We have found that clients come up with smart strategies such as texting themselves; e-mailing home from their work computer at lunch; and carrying a small card in their pocket when they are out for coffee. There is even an iPhone application that assists with self-monitoring in EDs by giving frequent reminders and feedback, although we have not had experience with its use.

Clients will need to be shown a completed record and instructions to complete their self-monitoring record. The records should be reviewed each session, and this review may take a large portion of the first few sessions to ensure the client is recording in real time, thoroughly, and recording not only behaviors but also feelings and thoughts. Counselors should identify particular patterns (e.g., binges tend to occur after an argument with the mother) and discuss these patterns to help the client make changes. See Fairburn (2008) or www.psych.ox.ac.uk/credo/ for examples of self-monitoring and instructions.

*In-session weighing.* CBT–E requires clients be weighed as part of treatment. Clients should be weighed at the start of the session. Their weight should be logged on a graph (with weight on the $x$-axis and sessions on the $y$-axis) each session, with the weight calculated as a BMI, because BMI seems to be less triggering for clients than weight. We find it helpful to refer to "the number on the scale" rather than "your weight" because it serves to distance clients from the notion of their weight being an integral part of who they are.

Counselors should buy a set of digital scales for their office because it is essential that both the client and the counselor know the client's weight and discuss it in each session. Many clinicians are reluctant to weigh clients. The counselor must understand and believe in the usefulness of in-session weighing and in clients knowing their weight and give a clear rationale: Both people knowing the weight is a necessary part of treatment. Weighing allows for the monitoring of changes that may indicate medical problems. Continued weight loss in underweight clients and precipitous weight loss, even in clients above or in the healthy weight range, should be addressed and clients sent to the PCP for a medical check.

As with self-monitoring, weighing arouses anxiety in clients. Clients with EDs are concerned that their weight will increase if they reduce or stop their disordered behaviors such as restricting, purging, or exercising. In-session weighing allows the client to disconfirm these fears because all changes are tracked and can be interpreted objectively with the counselor's help. Weight monitoring allows examination of the relationship between eating and weight and the opportunity to challenge the overvaluation of weight and shape. Psychoeducation must be provided about normal weight fluctuations and the inability to draw conclusions with less than four consecutive weights.

In-session weighing can also be difficult because many clients with EDs weigh themselves at home, often several times a day, and are wary of relying on once-weekly in-session weighing. It is important to inform clients that frequent weighing results in preoccupation with weight and provides misleading information. Clients tend to interpret any weight fluctuation as a signal to restrict to avoid further weight increase if weight has gone up or to advance weight loss if weight has gone down. Thus, at-home weighing should be discouraged because it is a behavior that maintains dietary restriction. A second difficulty with in-session weighing is that some eating-disordered clients avoid knowing their weight. Because clients with EDs typically overestimate their weight and any weight increases, avoiding weighing becomes problematic because there is no opportunity to disconfirm fears of weight gain. In-session weighing is necessary to address both unhelpful forms of weight-related behavior—frequent weighing and avoidance of weighing.

### Stage 2

Usually at about the eighth session, the client and counselor evaluate how treatment is going. This is a good time to readminister the EDE–Q, if it has been given pretreatment, to assess objective changes in ED symptoms. The progress review has several aims. First, the goal is to identify whether the client is improving with treatment and the status of eating-disordered behaviors, such as binge eating, purging and restriction. Second, an aim in Stage 2 is to assess the client's engagement with CBT–E, in terms of regular eating patterns, compliance with self-monitoring, and cessation of at-home weighing. Third, the counselor works to identify barriers to change, such as depression and low self-esteem. A final goal of this stage is to review and expand on the formulation, incorporating recently acquired information, to plan the remainder of treatment.

*Case vignette.* Larry, a 26-year-old single man with BN, had done reasonably well in Stage 1. He was eating regularly and had reduced binge–purge behaviors from daily to twice per week. His residual binges were only occurring when he felt particularly frustrated at work. The Stage 2 review allowed him and his counselor to identify his mood difficulties, and they decided to work on improving his mood tolerance in Stage 3, in addition to working on his overvaluation of weight and shape.

*Stage 3*

This stage covers the remainder of treatment up to the final two sessions (i.e., Sessions 9–18 in the usual, short version of the treatment). The focus of Stage 3 is on the mechanisms maintaining the client's ED, identified in the formulation at the start of treatment and built on in Stage 2. The most common maintaining mechanisms are overvaluation of weight and shape, mood difficulties, and dietary restraint or rules. These maintaining factors can be addressed in any order.

*Identifying the overvaluation (of controlling weight and shape) and its consequences.* Overvaluation of control over weight and shape will have been identified in the initial formulation, because it is the core maintaining feature of EDs. Yet only at this stage are the consequences of this over-valuation discussed and clients are made aware of the negative effects it has on other areas of their lives.

Construction of a pie chart can illustrate these effects. Clients are asked to list the domains of their life in which they judge their self-worth and rank them in order of importance. Common domains are family, work, weight and shape, and friends. Clients are asked to allocate slices on the pie diagram to reflect the relative importance of each domain. They are often surprised or ashamed at the large size of their weight–shape slice, which reflects the large amount of importance they give to weight and shape in terms of judging themselves over other life domains. This realization often spurs them on to reduce the excessive importance given to weight and shape.

Reducing the importance of weight and shape is one of two strategies for addressing concerns about weight and shape. The other is to enhance the importance of other domains for self-evaluation. Clients are asked to create a new pie chart with slices representing their ideal distribution of life domains on which they would base their self-worth; most will want a more balanced basis for self-evaluation. This new pie chart demonstrates how change might occur—by enlarging certain slices (e.g., friends) or creating a new slice (i.e., introducing a new activity)—and leads to setting specific goals for homework, such as inviting a colleague out for coffee or becoming a volunteer at a pet rescue center.

*Shape checking and avoidance.* Addressing body shape checking is a potent way of reducing the importance attached to weight and shape. One form of body checking, weight checking (weighing) will already have been addressed in Stage 1, and clients should have learned by now that reducing that form of checking reduces their concern about the number on the scale. Clients need to be educated about shape checking and avoidance because they may be unaware of these behaviors and how unhelpful they are. The behaviors maintain a focus on weight and shape and reinforce body dissatisfaction. Clients need to know that although most people check their bodies to some extent (e.g., looking in the mirror to check make-up or taking account of the tightness of clothes), people with EDs check in unusual ways (e.g., looking in mirrors repeatedly, touching their bones, interpreting slightly tight clothes as evidence of being overweight).

**301**

In contrast, some clients may avoid looking at and touching their bodies by covering up mirrors or wearing baggy clothes. This avoidance is unhelpful because it does not allow them to disconfirm their fears about their body shape. Others may do both, switching from avoidance to checking and back. Many clients engage in a different form of checking by comparing themselves with others, usually thinner people, with the result that they feel like failures (i.e., not thin enough). To reduce body checking and avoidance of all kinds, clients must become aware when they are engaging in these behaviors. They will need to record incidents on self-monitoring sheets and work with their counselor on reducing the behaviors.

*Case vignette.* Carla, a 43-year-old single mother, sought counseling for her 7-year-old daughter, who was developing fussy eating habits. It soon became clear that Carla had a 25-year history of an ED (at 5 feet, 5 inches, she weighed 108 pounds, with a BMI of 18.0). After 13 sessions of counseling and having increased her caloric intake and gained 6 pounds (BMI = 19.0), Carla was still obsessed with her body shape. In response to recording each episode of body checking, she became aware of the time she spent checking each day: 2 hours of mirror gazing (front and side views on rising, after going to the bathroom, after her run, before and after meals, when she undressed at night) and personal comparisons of her body shape with students at the college where she taught. Carla was encouraged to reduce mirror gazing and comparisons with young, slim college students. Each week she reduced her mirror gazing by 15 minutes per day until she was only using the mirror for a total of 15 minutes per day. She then conducted a survey, rating every third woman in her age range, which made her realize that most were larger than her. Reducing her checking helped her to feel better about her body and less anxious about eating more and gaining weight.

*Feeling fat.* Another way to challenge the importance of weight and shape is to address the experience of feeling fat, reported by many women but experienced often and particularly strongly by people with EDs. Because the experience is associated with being fat, it reinforces body dissatisfaction and ED behaviors. People with EDs report fluctuations in feeling fat from day to day and even throughout the day. It can best be thought of as a mislabeling of difficult emotions (such as anger or sadness) or a heightened awareness of the body (such as feeling full or bloated after eating). To challenge this phenomenon, clients are asked to record when they experience feeling fat particularly intensely and to identify the context in which they may be mislabeling emotions (such as feeling sad) or bodily sensations (such as thighs rubbing together in very hot weather) as feeling fat.

*Dietary rules.* Dietary rules will have been identified in Stage 1 and most likely have improved with the establishment of regular eating. If clients are still practicing restriction (undereating) or dietary restraint (attempts to restrict), then these behaviors need to be addressed at this point in counseling because they hinder recovery. Clients need to be reminded of the role of dieting and dietary rules in the vicious cycle of EDs. Counselors may need to probe for rules underlying the restriction and the beliefs that shape these rules (e.g., that eating carbohydrates will result in weight gain).

Dietary rules need to be addressed because they tend to be rigid and maintain preoccupation with controlling weight, shape, and eating. The most common rules relate to when (or not) to eat (which will have been challenged with regular eating); how much (or how little) to eat; or what variety of foods to eat. Other rules may include needing to earn food (e.g., after vigorous exercise) and eating less than everyone else. It can be useful to conduct behavioral experiments to test clients' beliefs and fears associated with breaking dietary rules and eating avoided foods.

*Case vignette.* Rob, an 18-year-old college student, had a rule related to avoiding complex carbohydrates because he believed he would gain body fat if he ate bread, rice, or potatoes. His self-monitoring showed that his diet consisted mainly of carrots, tuna, and chicken breasts, although he had recently begun to eat fruit at breakfast. Rob was asked to go to his local supermarket with a notebook and write a list of food items he avoided. He rated how anxious he would be (out of 10) if he ate each food. He then placed the foods in one of three columns: (a) those foods rated 1 to 3 that he avoided but could imagine eating, (b) those rated 4 to 7 that were more anxiety provoking, and (c) those rated 8–10 that were most distressing. He was then asked to plan eating an item from the first list that week. As his first challenge, he chose to address his avoidance by eating half a cup of kidney beans in a salad at lunch on Saturday with his older sister. Setting his experiment in a context in which he felt safe (at home with his supportive sister) enabled him to carry out his plan successfully. He soon progressed to avocado (from his second list) and other anxiety-provoking foods until he felt ready to tackle an item from his third list, a baked potato. Rob learned that he could eat a wide variety of food without changing his body composition (percentage of body fat).

*Moods and events.* Although all people are affected by their moods and the context of their lives, some clients experience a worsening of ED symptoms in response to adverse moods or events. Mood intolerance might be a maintaining mechanism for such clients who use their ED behaviors to control, dampen, or distract them from difficult mood states. Difficulties tolerating moods often become apparent during assessment (when there is a history of self-harm, drug abuse, or alcohol abuse), early in treatment (by current acting out), or by the Stage 2 review (through monitoring records). Problem solving is often sufficient to help clients deal with events that trigger changes in their eating and can be introduced once event-related eating symptoms are identified in self-monitoring records. Clients are encouraged to brainstorm potential responses, list the pros and cons of each potential solution, and choose the most effective option.

Mood-related changes in eating need to be addressed in clients who have difficulty tolerating certain mood states and those who experience intense moods. These clients may be identified as having a history of self-harm or substance abuse. They need to learn to recognize that their reaction to adverse events or mood states escalates rapidly and that these responses can be changed with practice. Providing clients with psychoeducation on the links between emotions, cognitions, and behavior is useful. Counselors will help clients identify a triggering event and their appraisal of that event (cognitions). Clients will then learn to recognize any aversive changes in mood, cognitive appraisal of these changes, and any amplification of emotions. The next step is to identify unhelpful or dysfunctional behavior used to modulate the mood, any resulting changes in the mood, and the cognitive appraisal of the situation. Distress tolerance skills (e.g., distraction) help clients learn alternative strategies to cope with intense moods, and cognitive challenging addresses specific unhelpful thinking styles (e.g., black-and-white thinking).

*Mindsets.* A good time to introduce the concept of an ED mindset is as clients approach the end of treatment and are experiencing improvement in ED symptoms. The experience of good days, relatively free from their previous preoccupation, indicates the weakening of the ED mindset and the mechanisms maintaining the ED. However, clients will likely still experience bad days, when ED behaviors and thoughts recur (e.g., binge eating, preoccupation with calories). The mind can be compared to a DVD player, with many DVDs that get played in the different contexts of clients' lives. In the midst of an ED, the ED DVD gets stuck and continues to play without letup. With improvement in symptoms, the ED DVD gets unlocked for certain periods and then gets reactivated (recurrence of symptoms). Clients can learn to manipulate their ED mindset as they would manage a DVD. A setback can be examined, using monitoring records, to examine the context in which the ED DVD becomes reactivated. Clients learn to deal with the recurrence of the ED mindset by recognizing triggers for its return (the "signature tune" of the ED DVD). They learn to respond to an actual recurrence by doing the right thing ("ejecting" the DVD), by behaving as though they did not have an ED and were not vulnerable to the ED mindset, or by engaging in fun or social activities.

### Stage 4

The last stage of CBT–E is made up of two or three sessions, with a focus on ending counseling and becoming one's own therapist, and has two goals, maintaining gains and preventing relapse. Creating a maintenance plan involves looking back over the counseling sessions to assess progress. It is important to identify what strategies were helpful and need to be continued (e.g., regular eating) and what behaviors need more practice (e.g., increasing the variety of foods). A relapse prevention plan involves identifying potential triggers for relapse (e.g., a friend dieting) and strategies for dealing with setbacks (e.g., eject the ED DVD and focus on establishing healthy routines and challenging ED cognitions). Referring to a lapse or a setback rather than to a relapse is helpful because many clients with EDs have entrenched black-and-white thinking and believe that even one binge means that they have returned to a full ED. Lapses can be approached as challenges to be overcome with the skills clients have learned in treatment. A follow-up or review session approximately 3 months after the end of treatment allows goals to be set and clients to gain confidence in managing their eating themselves.

## Conclusion

In this chapter, we provided counselors with an overview of CBT–E. We described the theory behind the treatment and summarized the preliminary evidence for its effectiveness with the full range of EDs in adults and illustrated the treatment interventions with specific examples. We hope that counselors will be encouraged to read more about CBT–E and use this approach with their clients with EDs.

## Chapter Highlights

- EDs are significant mental health problems with medical aspects and are common, particularly among young girls and women; approximately 15% of women will have a diagnosable ED requiring clinical attention in their lifetime.
- It is probable that counselors will encounter people with EDs in their general practice and that those presenting for other issues, such as anxiety or depression, may have an undetected ED. Therefore, knowing how to screen for EDs and being able to assess and treat these clients is useful.
- CBT–E was developed from the recommended evidence-based treatment for adults with BN, CBT–BN. It was enhanced to make it applicable to all EDs and to address additional maintaining mechanisms (mood intolerance, interpersonal problems, perfectionism, low self-esteem) to the core ED psychopathology.
- CBT–E has proven efficacious in one randomized controlled trial to date and outcomes were essentially replicated in a community-based effectiveness trial.
- CBT–E has four stages: focus on changing behaviors, review, challenging cognitions and body image issues, and maintenance and relapse prevention.
- Easy-to-read treatment guides are available to enhance counselors' understanding of and skills in CBT–E.

## Recommended Resources

### Handouts and Resources

- Centre for Clinical Interventions
    http://www.cci.health.wa.gov.au
  Fact sheets and information packages are available for health professionals, primary care physicians, and clients to download and use.

### Readings

Fairburn, C. G., Cooper, Z., & Shafran, R. (2003). Cognitive behaviour therapy for eating disorders: A "transdiagnostic" theory and treatment. *Behaviour Research and Therapy, 41,* 509–528.

Garner, D. M. (1997). Psychoeducational principles in treatment. In D. M. Garner & P. E. Garfinkel (Eds.), *Handbook of treatment in eating disorders* (2nd ed., pp. 145–177). New York, NY: Guilford Press.

### Treatment Manuals

Fairburn, C. G. (1995). *Overcoming binge eating.* New York, NY: Guilford Press.

Fairburn, C. G. (2008). *Cognitive behavior therapy and eating disorders.* New York, NY: Guilford Press.

Waller, G., Cordery, H., Corstorphine, E., Hinrichsen, H., Lawson, R., Mountford, V., & Russell, K. (2007). *Cognitive behavioral therapy for eating disorders: A comprehensive treatment guide.* Cambridge, England: Cambridge University Press.

# References

American Psychiatric Association. (2000). *Diagnostic and statistical manual of mental disorders (4th ed., text rev.).* Washington, DC: Author.

American Psychiatric Association. (2006). *Practice guideline for the treatment of patients with eating disorders* (3rd ed.). Washington, DC: Author.

Byrne, S. M., Fursland, A., Allen, K. L., & Watson, H. (2011). The effectiveness of enhanced cognitive behavioural therapy for eating disorders: An open trial. *Behaviour Research and Therapy, 49,* 219–226.

Fairburn, C. G. (1981). A cognitive–behavioural approach to the treatment of bulimia. *Psychological Medicine, 11,* 707–711.

Fairburn, C. G. (2008). *Cognitive behavior therapy and eating disorders.* New York, NY: Guilford Press.

Fairburn, C. G., & Beglin, S. J. (1994). Assessment of eating disorders: Interview or self-report questionnaire? *International Journal of Eating Disorders, 16,* 363–370.

Fairburn, C. G., Cooper, Z., Bohn, K., O'Connor, M. E., Doll, H. A., & Palmer, R. L. (2007). The severity and status of eating disorder NOS: Implications for *DSM–V. Behaviour Research & Therapy, 45,* 1705–1715.

Fairburn, C. G., Cooper, Z., Doll, H. A., O'Connor, M. E., Bohn, K., Hawker, D. M., . . . Palmer, R. L. (2009). Transdiagnostic cognitive–behavioral therapy for patients with eating disorders: A two-site trial with 60-week follow-up. *American Journal of Psychiatry, 166,* 311–319.

Fairburn, C. G., Cooper, Z., Doll, H. A., O'Connor, M. E., Palmer, R. L., & Dalle Grave, R. (in press). Enhanced cognitive behaviour therapy for adults with anorexia nervosa: A UK–Italy study. *Behaviour Research and Therapy.*

Fairburn, C. G., Cooper, Z., & Shafran, R. (2003). Cognitive behaviour therapy for eating disorders: A "transdiagnostic" theory and treatment. *Behaviour Research and Therapy, 41,* 509–528.

Fairburn, C., Marcus, M., & Wilson, G. (1993). Cognitive–behavioral therapy for binge-eating: A comprehensive treatment manual. In C. G. Fairburn & G. T. Wilson (Eds.), *Binge eating: Nature, assessment and treatment* (pp. 361–404). New York, NY: Guilford Press.

Hay, P. J., Mond, J., Buttner, P., & Darby, A. (2008). Eating disorder behaviors are increasing: Findings from two sequential community surveys in South Australia. *PLoS ONE, 3,* e1541.

Keski-Rahkonen, A., Hoek, H. W., Susser, E. S., Linna, M. S., Sihvola, E., Raevuori, A., . . . Rissanen, A. (2007). Epidemiology and course of anorexia nervosa in the community. *American Journal of Psychiatry, 164,* 1259–1265.

Keys, A., Brozek, J., & Henschel, A. (1959). *The biology of human starvation.* Minneapolis: University of Minnesota Press.

Le Grange, D., & Lock, J. (2007). *Treating bulimia in adolescents: A family-based approach.* New York, NY: Guilford Press.

Lock, J., Le Grange, D., Agras, W., & Dare, C. (2001). *Treatment manual for anorexia nervosa: A family-based approach.* New York, NY: Guilford Press.

Mehler, P. S., & Andersen, A. E. (2010). *Eating disorders: A guide to medical care and complications* (2nd ed.). Baltimore, MD: Johns Hopkins University Press.

Morgan, J. F., Reid, F., & Lacey, J. H. (1999). The SCOFF questionnaire: Assessment of a new screening tool for eating disorders. *BMJ, 319,* 1467–1468.

National Institute for Health and Clinical Excellence. (2004). *Eating disorders. Core interventions in the treatment and management of anorexia nervosa, bulimia nervosa and related eating disorders.* London, England: National Health Service.

Neumark-Sztainer, D., Wall, M., Larson, N. I., Eisenberg, E., & Loth, K. (2011). Dieting and disordered eating behaviors from adolescence to young adulthood: Findings from a 10-year longitudinal study. *Journal of the American Dietetic Association, 111,* 1004–1011.

Ricca, V., Mannucci, E., Mezzani, B., Di Bernardo, M., Zucchi, T., Paionni, A., . . . Faravelli, C. (2001). Psychopathological and clinical features of outpatients with an eating disorder not otherwise specified. *Eating and Weight Disorders, 6,* 157–165.

Shafran, R., Cooper, Z., & Fairburn, C. G. (2002). Clinical perfectionism: A cognitive–behavioural analysis. *Behaviour Research and Therapy, 40,* 773–791.

Swanson, S. A., Crow, S. J., Le Grange, D., Swendsen, J., & Merikangas, K. R. (2011). Prevalence and correlates of eating disorders in adolescents. Results from the National Comorbidity Survey Replication Adolescent Supplement. *Archives of General Psychiatry, 68,* 714–723.

Vitousek, K., Watson, S., & Wilson, G. T. (1998). Enhancing motivation for change in treatment-resistant eating disorders. *Clinical Psychology Review, 18,* 391–420.

Wade, T., Bergin, J., Tiggemann, M., Bulik, C., & Fairburn, C. G. (2006). Prevalence and long-term course of eating disorders in an adult Australian cohort. *Australian and New Zealand Journal of Psychiatry, 40,* 121–128.

Waller, G., Cordery, H., Corstorphine, E., Hinrichsen, H., Lawson, R., Mountford, V., & Russell, K. (2007). *Cognitive behavioral therapy for eating disorders: A comprehensive treatment guide.* Cambridge, England: Cambridge University Press.

Waller, G., Evans, J., & Stringer, H. (2012). The therapeutic alliance in the early part of cognitive–behavioral therapy for eating disorders. *International Journal of Eating Disorders, 45,* 63–69.

White, S., Reynolds-Malear, J. B., & Cordero, E. (2011). Disordered eating and the use of unhealthy weight control methods in college students: 1995, 2002, and 2008. *Eating Disorders, 19,* 323–334.

## Chapter 14

# Interpersonal Psychotherapy for Clients With Eating Disorders

*Heather L. Waldron, Marian Tanofsky-Kraff, and Denise E. Wilfley*

Interpersonal psychotherapy (IPT) is a brief, triphasic, time-limited therapy that focuses on improving interpersonal functioning and, in turn, psychiatric symptoms by relating symptoms to interpersonal problem areas and developing strategies for dealing with these problems (Freeman & Gil, 2004; Klerman, Weissman, Rounsaville, & Chevron, 1984). IPT was originally developed in the late 1960s by Gerald Klerman et al. (1984) for the treatment of unipolar depression. In the late 1980s, IPT was successfully modified for clients with bulimia nervosa (BN; Fairburn et al., 1991; Fairburn, Peveler, Jones, Hope, & Doll, 1993) and shortly thereafter adapted into a group format for individuals with binge eating disorder (BED; Wilfley et al., 1993, 2002; Wilfley, Frank, Welch, Spurrell, & Rounsaville, 1998; Wilfley, MacKenzie, Welch, Ayres, & Weissman, 2000). IPT has been found to be an effective treatment for BN and BED.

IPT is grounded in theories developed by Meyer, Sullivan, and Bowlby, who postulated that interpersonal functioning is a critical component of psychological adjustment and well-being. Meyer (1957; see also Frank & Spanier, 1995; Klerman et al., 1984) suggested that psychopathology was rooted in maladjustment to one's social environment. Sullivan (1953) believed that individuals could not be understood in isolation from their interpersonal relationships and posited that enduring patterns in these relationships could either encourage self-esteem or result in anxiety, hopelessness, and psychopathology. IPT is also associated with the work of Bowlby (1982), who originated attachment theory. Bowlby emphasized the important link between early attachment and the later development of interpersonal relationships and emotional well-being. He hypothesized that failures in attachment resulted in later psychopathology.

The interpersonal roles and relationships relevant to IPT include the nuclear family, extended family, friendship groups, work setting, and neighborhood or community. The IPT model acknowledges a two-way relationship between social functioning and psychopathology: Social role disturbances can serve as precursors for psychopathology, and psychopathology can result in impairments in one's ability to perform social roles (Bowlby, 1982). Thus, in IPT, interpersonal functioning is recognized as a critical component of psychological adjustment and well-being. We should note that IPT makes no assumptions about the causes of psychiatric illness; however, it does assume that the development and maintenance of some psychiatric illnesses occur in a social and interpersonal context. It also assumes that the onset, response to treatment, and outcomes are influenced by the interpersonal relations between the client and significant others.

In this chapter, we provide an overview of IPT for eating disorders. First, we summarize the theoretical and empirical bases of IPT for the treatment of eating disorders (EDs). Next, we explain the delivery of IPT for EDs, phase by phase, along with a description of the major tenets of the treatment. This description is followed by a case example that illustrates the use of IPT with a client with BED. Finally, we describe future directions, including novel adaptations of IPT and the need for widespread dissemination and implementation of IPT in community settings. Although we review the major tenets of IPT here, more extensive information on IPT, detailing empirical background, theoretical foundation, and strategies and techniques, is provided in a comprehensive book by Weissman, Markowitz, and Klerman (2000).

## Interpersonal Psychotherapy Model of Eating Disorders

A strong body of evidence has supported the interpersonal model of binge eating, which posits that interpersonal problems lead to negative affect, which in turn triggers disordered eating (Ansell, Grilo, & White, 2012; Wilfley, Stein, & Welch, 2005). Individuals with EDs report past difficult social experiences, problematic family histories, and specific interpersonal stressors more often than individuals without EDs (Fairburn et al., 1998; Fairburn, Welch, Doll, Davies, & O'Connor, 1997). The interpersonal model of EDs posits that social problems create an environment in which EDs develop and are maintained as a coping mechanism, serving to reduce negative affect in response to unfulfilling social interactions (Rieger et al., 2010). As a result, EDs may worsen interpersonal problems by increasing social isolation and impeding fulfilling relationships, thereby maintaining the disorder (Rieger et al., 2010). Because negative affect is the most widely reported antecedent to binge eating (Wolfe, Baker, Smith, & Kelly-Weeder, 2009), IPT helps clients acknowledge and express painful affect so that they can better manage negative feelings without turning to food. IPT also seeks to reduce eating pathology by supporting the development of healthy interpersonal skills that can replace maladaptive behaviors and promote a positive self-image.

Much empirical evidence has supported the use of IPT for BN and BED, but the relative lack of research examining the utility of IPT for anorexia nervosa is notable. Indeed, no controlled studies have demonstrated the efficacy of IPT for anorexia nervosa. However, the possibility exists that the IPT model could be applicable to clients with anorexia nervosa because they tend to have deficits in social–cognitive skills that impede their capacity to create and experience validating social interactions (Rieger et al., 2010).

## Evidence Base for Interpersonal Psychotherapy for Bulimia Nervosa

The evidence supporting the effectiveness of IPT for the treatment of BN is ample. To date, cognitive–behavioral therapy (CBT) is the most-researched, best-established treatment for BN (Wilson, Grilo, & Vitousek, 2007). However, IPT is the only psychological treatment for BN that has demonstrated long-term outcomes that are comparable to those of CBT (Wilson & Shafran, 2005). Currently, all controlled studies of IPT for BN have been comparison studies with CBT. Initially, similar short- and long-term outcomes for binge eating remission between CBT and IPT were reported (Fairburn et al., 1993, 1995). In a subsequent multisite study, Agras, Walsh, Fairburn, Wilson, and Kraemer (2000) compared CBT and IPT as treatments for BN. At the end of treatment, clients receiving CBT showed significantly higher rates of abstinence from binge eating and lower rates of purging than those receiving IPT. However, by 8- and 12-month follow-ups, the two treatments no longer differed significantly in outcome. Clients receiving CBT had maintained their progress or slightly worsened, and clients receiving IPT had experienced slight improvements. The initial, more impressive effect of CBT compared with IPT may be partially explained by a relative lack of focus on ED symptomatology in the research version of individual IPT for BN. A potential advantage of IPT may be that many clients with BN perceive the interpersonal focus of IPT as particularly relevant to their ED and to their treatment needs, perhaps more so than a cognitive–behavioral focus on distortions related to weight and shape; indeed, IPT clients rated their treatment as more suitable and expected greater success than did CBT clients. Currently, IPT is considered an alternative to CBT for the treatment of BN (Wilson et al., 2007). Counselors have been recommended to inform clients of the slower response time for improvements compared with CBT (Wilson, 2005). However, we contend that when interpersonal problems are consistently linked to ED symptoms in IPT, response to treatment will likely occur more rapidly.

An emerging literature has provided some insight into predictors of success with IPT for the treatment of EDs. Chui, Safer, Bryson, Agras, and Wilson (2007) reported that although clients in their large multicenter trial responded with higher abstinence rates when randomized to CBT

311

as opposed to IPT, African American female participants showed greater reductions in binge eating episode frequency when treated with IPT than with CBT. This finding suggests that IPT may be particularly appropriate for African American women with BN and speaks to the need for further study of IPT with different racial and ethnic groups. Because therapeutic alliance is associated with treatment outcome, researchers from this same study examined clients' expectation of improvement (Constantino, Arnow, Blasey, & Agras, 2005). They found that expectation of improvement was positively associated with outcome for both CBT and IPT, emphasizing the important role of client expectations in both treatments. Finally, in a study of postremission predictors of relapse, Keel, Dorer, Franko, Jackson, and Herzog (2005) found that for women with BN, worse psychosocial functioning was associated with a greater risk for relapse, which, they posited, may partly help to explain the long-term effectiveness of IPT for BN.

## Evidence Base for Interpersonal Psychotherapy for Binge Eating Disorder

On the basis of IPT's initial success in the treatment of BN (Fairburn et al., 1991), Wilfley et al. (1993, 2000) developed IPT for BED in a group format. During this time, they worked with many clients who presented with chronically unfulfilling relationships, issues that were well suited to be addressed in a group format. Therefore, they adapted new strategies to specifically address such interpersonal deficits. For example, in the current format of group IPT for BED, group members with interpersonal deficits are strongly encouraged to view the group as a "live" social network. This social milieu is designed to decrease social isolation, support the formation of new social relationships, and serve as a model for initiating and sustaining social relationships outside of the therapeutic context (Wilfley et al., 1998). Clients with BED commonly experience shame and self-stigmatization, which potentially contribute to the maintenance of the disorder. Thus, group therapy inherently offers a radically altered social environment for clients with BED, who typically keep shameful eating behaviors hidden from others.

IPT has demonstrated effectiveness in the treatment of BED. As in the case of CBT for BN, CBT for BED has an extensive evidence base establishing specific and robust treatment effects (Devlin et al., 2005; Grilo, Masheb, & Wilson, 2005; Kenardy, Mensch, Bowen, Green, & Walton, 2002; Nauta, Hospers, Kok, & Jansen, 2000; Ricca et al., 2001; Telch, Agras, Rossiter, Wilfley, & Kenardy, 1990; Wilfley et al., 1993). Two randomized trials have compared IPT with CBT and found that IPT has similar effects to CBT in the treatment of BED. The first study (Wilfley et al., 1993) compared group CBT, group IPT, and a wait-list control group. The findings revealed that both treatments were more effective at reducing binge eating than the control group and resulted in similar significant reductions in binge eating in both the short and the long term. The second study (Wilfley et al., 2002) included a substantially larger sample size and demonstrated equivalent short- and long-term efficacy for CBT and IPT in reducing binge eating and associated specific and general psychopathology. Approximately 60% of the clients remained abstinent from binge eating at 1-year and 4-year follow-ups (Hilbert et al., 2012; Wilfley et al., 2002). In contrast to the literature on IPT for BN, CBT and IPT had identical time courses for almost all outcomes in the BED studies.

In a follow-up analysis of treatment predictors of long-term outcome in the Wilfley et al. (2002) study, clients with a greater extent of interpersonal problems at both baseline and midtreatment showed poorer treatment response to both CBT and IPT (Hilbert et al., 2007). An important caveat of this finding, however, is that those individuals with greater interpersonal problems were not surprisingly also those who had more Axis I and Axis II psychiatric disorders and lower self-esteem than those with less severe interpersonal problems. Such individuals are likely in need of more intensive or extended treatment. Supporting this assertion, Markowitz, Skodol, and Bleiberg (2006), in a study of IPT for individuals with borderline personality disorder and comorbid depression, suggested that extending IPT effectively improves the disorder. A preliminary examination of clients in the larger BED cohort indicated that those in IPT maintained reductions in binge eating and disordered eating cognitions at least 5 years posttreatment (Bishop, Stein, Hilbert, Swenson, & Wilfley, 2007). These data may suggest evidence for good maintenance of change for clients with BED who are treated with IPT.

Results from a more recent multisite trial comparing individual IPT, behavioral weight loss treatment, and CBT guided self-help (CBT-GSH) for the treatment of BED have pointed to the importance of making a clear connection between interpersonal problems and binge eating symptoms in the delivery of IPT. Similar to Wilfley et al.'s (2002) trial, in this multisite study the counselors linked interpersonal functioning to disordered eating symptoms throughout the course of IPT. In this study, IPT was rated as most acceptable to clients, and the dropout rate was significantly lower in IPT than in the other two interventions (Wilfley, Wilson, & Agras, 2008). At 2-year follow-up, IPT and CBT-GSH were significantly more effective than behavioral weight loss in eliminating binge eating. Furthermore, compared with the other two treatments, IPT also produced greater reduction in binge episodes for clients presenting with low self-esteem and more disordered eating behaviors and cognitions. CBT-GSH was generally effective only for those with low ED psychopathology. In this trial, compared with Wilfley et al. (2002; see also Hilbert et al., 2007), individuals with more psychopathology showed notably greater improvements in IPT than CBT-GSH. This finding was in concert with Hilbert et al.'s (2007) follow-up data, which suggested that greater disordered eating serves as a moderator in predicting poorer outcome in CBT.

In general, compared with Caucasian participants, individuals of other ethnic minorities demonstrated less retention in the multisite study (Wilfley et al., 2008). Although no treatment by ethnicity effects were found in this regard, attrition for minority participants in IPT was very low and dropout rates by minorities in CBT-GSH were very high. The low enrollment of minority participants across sites prevents us from drawing definitive conclusions. Nevertheless, this pattern aligns with the finding that IPT was particularly effective for African American participants in the previously described multisite study for individuals with BN (Chui et al., 2007). We posit that perhaps the personalized nature of IPT (e.g., problem areas and goals are developed on the basis of each individual's unique social environment) is modifiable to, and thus particularly acceptable to, people of various cultures and backgrounds.

Several recommendations may be drawn from the recent multisite study (Wilfley et al., 2008). CBT-GSH could be considered the first-line treatment for most individuals with BED, and IPT could be recommended for clients with low self-esteem and high ED psychopathology. Alternatively, IPT could be considered a first-line treatment for BED on the basis of several factors: IPT has been shown to be effective across multiple research sites, is associated with high retention across different client profiles (e.g., high negative affect, minority groups), and demonstrated superior outcomes to behavioral weight loss overall and to CBT-GSH among a subset of clients with high disordered eating psychopathology and low self-esteem. Counselors and clients should consider these alternatives when deciding the best approach to treatment. Finally, behavioral weight loss should not be considered a first-line treatment when treating individuals with BED. In summary, the literature suggests that IPT is an efficacious treatment alternative to CBT for BED.

# Considerations When Choosing Treatment Modality

When determining the treatment approach for clients with EDs, the counselor and client should together review the various advantages and disadvantages of using IPT, CBT, or another therapeutic modality. It is crucial for counselors to also explore their own comfort level in terms of their expertise, theoretical knowledge, and propensity to use an interpersonally focused treatment as part of this decision. IPT is a specialty treatment, as is CBT, and should be administered only by trained practitioners. However, it has been argued that experienced counselors who have been trained in other treatment modalities tend to learn IPT quickly and are often able to implement IPT with a high degree of integrity even with minimal training (Birchall, 1999).

To date, although more data exist in support of CBT's efficacy, evolving literature has indicated that IPT may be well suited to clients presenting with or without exacerbated difficulties in social functioning. Although greater problems were associated with poorer outcomes for both CBT and IPT in the Hilbert et al. (2007) study, the moderator effect found in the more recent multisite study (Wilfley et al., 2008)—that clients presenting with greater psychopathology seem to respond well to IPT—suggests that IPT may be well suited to individuals with a broad range of disordered eating and general psychopathology. Moreover, IPT may be enhanced for individuals with exacerbated psychological problems (Markowitz et al., 2006). IPT may also possibly be especially fitting for some minority groups (e.g., African Americans) or specific age cohorts (e.g., adolescents). Last, some clients may express discomfort or difficulties with elements of CBT (e.g., self-monitoring), and IPT should be considered for these individuals.

# Delivering Interpersonal Psychotherapy

Several common, basic concepts exist across all adaptations of IPT, including treatment for EDs. Specifically, adaptations for IPT all focus on interpersonal problem areas and maintain a similar treatment structure. IPT is a time-limited treatment, and its success hinges on the counselor's ability to rapidly identify patterns in interpersonal relationships and link these patterns to eating-disordered symptoms that may have contributed to the onset and maintenance of the disorder. Thus, early identification of the problem area or areas and treatment goals by the counselor and client is crucial. It is paramount to remember that throughout every session, interpersonal functioning should be linked to the onset and maintenance of the ED.

## *Interpersonal Problem Areas*

A primary aim of IPT is to help clients identify and address current interpersonal problems. IPT makes no assumptions about the etiology of an ED and thus focuses on current as opposed to past relationships. Treatment focuses on resolving problems within four social domains that are associated with the onset and maintenance of the ED: interpersonal deficits, interpersonal role disputes, role transitions, and grief (see Table 14.1).

### *Interpersonal Deficits*
Clients with interpersonal deficits are those who are socially isolated or who are in chronically unfulfilling relationships. The goal is to reduce the client's social isolation by helping to enhance the quality of existing relationships and encouraging the formation of new relationships. To help these clients, it is necessary to determine why they have difficulty in forming or maintaining relationships. Carefully reviewing past significant relationships will be particularly useful in making this assessment. During this review, attention should be given to both the positive and the negative aspects of the relationships, as well as an investigation of potentially recurrent patterns in these relationships. Examining the nature of the client–counselor relationship may also be appropriate because it may be the client's only close relationship and it is present to be observed (Wilfley et al., 2005).

### *Interpersonal Role Disputes*
Interpersonal role disputes are conflicts with a significant other (e.g., a partner, other family member, employer, coworker, teacher, or close friend) that emerge from differences in expectations about the relationship. The

Table 14.1
**Interpersonal Psychotherapy Problem Areas and Strategies**

| Problem Area | Description | Strategies and Goals |
|---|---|---|
| Interpersonal deficits | A long-standing history of social isolation, low self-esteem, loneliness, and an inability to form or maintain intimate relationships | Reduce the patient's social isolation by helping to enhance the quality of existing relationships. Encourage the formation of new relationships. |
| Interpersonal role disputes | Disputes with significant other (e.g., partner, family member, coworker, friend) that emerge from differences in expectations about the relationship | Identify the dispute. Weigh options to resolve the dispute. Modify expectations and faulty communication to bring about a satisfactory resolution. |
| Role transitions | Difficulties resulting from a change in life status (e.g., divorce, retirement, moving, diagnosis of medical illness) | Recognize positive and negative aspects of the new role. Mourn and accept loss of the old role. Restore self-esteem by developing a sense of mastery in the new role. |
| Grief | Complicated bereavement after the death of a loved one | Facilitate mourning. Help the patient to find new activities and relationships to substitute for the loss. |

goals of treatment include clearly identifying the nature of the dispute and exploring options to resolve it. Determining the stage of the dispute is important; once the stage of the dispute becomes clear, modifying the client's expectations and remedying faulty communication may be important to bring about adequate resolution. It may be particularly helpful to explore how nonreciprocal role expectations relate to the dispute. If resolution is impossible, the counselor assists the client in dissolving the relationship and in mourning its loss (Wilfley et al., 2005).

### Role Transitions
Role transition includes any difficulties resulting from a change in life status. Common role transitions include a career change (i.e., promotion, firing, retirement, changing jobs), a family change (marriage, divorce, birth of a child, child moving out), the beginning or end of an important relationship, a move, graduation, or diagnosis of a medical illness. The goals of therapy include mourning and accepting the loss of the old role, recognizing the positive and negative aspects of both the old and the new

roles, and restoring the client's self-esteem by developing a sense of mastery in the new role. Key strategies in achieving these goals will include a thorough exploration of the client's feelings related to the role change and encouraging the client to develop new skills and adequate social support for the new role (Wilfley et al., 2005).

## Grief

Grief is identified as the problem area when the onset of the client's symptoms is associated with the death of a loved one, either recent or past. Grief is not limited to the physical death of a loved one. Grief can also result from the loss of a significant relationship or the loss of an important aspect of one's identity. The goals for treating complicated bereavement include facilitating mourning and helping the client to find new activities and relationships to substitute for the loss. Reconstructing the relationship, both the positive and the negative aspects, is central to the assessment of not only what has been lost but also what is needed to counter the idealization that so commonly occurs. As clients become less focused on the past, they should be encouraged to consider new ways of becoming more involved with others and establishing new interests (Wilfley et al., 2005). Making use of this framework for defining one or more interpersonal problem areas, IPT for EDs focuses on identifying and changing the maladaptive interpersonal context in which the eating problem has developed and been maintained.

## Triphasic Structure

IPT for EDs is a time-limited treatment that typically includes 15 to 20 sessions over 4 to 5 months. It can be delivered in an individual or group format. In a group format, clients can use the group as an interpersonal laboratory in which they can practice improved ways of communicating with others. Regardless of format or exact number of sessions, IPT is delivered in three phases. The initial phase involves the examination of a client's interpersonal and ED history to identify the interpersonal problem area or areas associated with BED onset and maintenance. From this history, a detailed plan is formulated that specifies what problem area or areas are most relevant to the client and how changes in interpersonal functioning can be achieved. The intermediate phase of treatment focuses on illuminating connections between symptoms and interpersonal events during the week and implementing strategies to help clients make changes in the identified problem areas. In the termination phase, clients evaluate and consolidate gains, detail plans for maintaining improvements, and outline any remaining work to be completed.

### Initial Phase

The initial phase of IPT consists of standard assessment and diagnosis of BED, identification of interpersonal problem areas, and development of treatment goals. See Table 14.2 for an overview of tasks for the initial session. The counselor conducts a full assessment, including instruments

Table 14.2
**Tasks of Initial Session or Sessions**

- [ ] Discuss chief complaint and eating disorder symptoms.
- [ ] Obtain history of symptoms.
- [ ] Place client in the sick role.
- [ ] Establish whether there is a history of prior treatments for the eating disorder or other psychiatric problems.
- [ ] Assess client's expectations of psychotherapy.
- [ ] Reassure client about positive prognosis.
- [ ] Explain interpersonal psychotherapy and its basic assumptions.
- [ ] Complete an interpersonal inventory (detailed review of important relationships).

- Include discussion of all important individuals in the client's life: family members; relatives; friends, relationships at church, job, social agencies. For each, discuss
  1. frequency and content of interactions,
  2. expectations of both parties, and whether expectations are fulfilled,
  3. satisfying and supportive aspects of relationship,
  4. unsatisfying or stressful aspects of relationship,
  5. things client would like to see change in relationship, and
  6. how the client's eating disorder has affected the relationship. Does the individual know that client is suffering from an eating disorder?

- Has a recent change or conflict in the relationship occurred that might be related to the onset or exacerbation of the eating disorder?
- Provide information regarding the extent of the client's social support network and information regarding potential social supports that client might call on.

- [ ] Present case formulation.

- Identify a specific problem area to focus on and name it.
- Relate the eating disorder to the interpersonal problem area: "Your eating disorder symptoms seem connected to this role transition [describe] you are going through. How does that sound to you?"

- [ ] Agree on treatment contract.

- Primary goal of treatment:

  1. symptom reduction.
  2. improvement in the problem area.

- "In this therapy, we will work on helping you better manage your interpersonal problems. We will try to discover what you want and need in this situation. We will work with you on how to get your needs met and how you can take care of yourself, so you can reduce your eating disorder symptoms."
- Active client role: "In our sessions I want you to be as open and honest about your feelings as you can. Your feelings are important because they will tell us what your needs are." "I will also ask you to work on the issues we discuss between sessions." "Interpersonal therapy is a therapy of change."
- Confidentiality
- Duration and frequency of treatment

such as the Emotional Eating Scale (Arnow, Kenardy, & Agras, 1995), the Inventory of Interpersonal Problems (Horowitz, Rosenberg, Baer, Ureno, & Villasenor, 1988), and the Eating Disorder Examination (Fairburn & Cooper, 1993). The client is then formally diagnosed with BED and assigned the "sick role." The diagnosis helps the client understand that he or she has a known condition that can be treated, and the sick role relieves the client of other responsibilities, granting him or her permission to recover, which is especially helpful to individuals who tend to set aside their own needs to care for and please others. The counselor also explains the rationale for IPT, describing that therapy focuses on identifying and altering current dysfunctional interpersonal patterns related to ED symptomatology.

Next, the counselor conducts an interpersonal inventory, a critical component of IPT, to identify the client's specific problem area or areas. The interpersonal inventory involves a thorough examination of the client's interpersonal history. Although counselors have historically taken as many as three sessions to complete the interpersonal inventory, conducting a longer (approximately 2-hour) first session to complete the entire interpersonal inventory may increase the treatment's effectiveness by allowing clients to get on board early in terms of their understanding of IPT and how their ED fits into the IPT rationale (Wilfley et al., 2000). The interpersonal inventory is essential for adequate case formulation and development of an optimal treatment plan. The clinical importance of investing the time to conduct a comprehensive interpersonal inventory cannot be overemphasized; accurate identification of the client's primary problem areas is often complicated and is crucial to success in treatment.

The interpersonal inventory involves a review of the client's current close relationships, social functioning, relationship patterns, and expectations of relationships. Patterns and changes in interpersonal relationships are explored and discussed with reference to the onset and maintenance of ED symptoms. For each significant relationship, the following information is assessed: frequency of contact, activities shared, satisfactory and unsatisfactory aspects of the relationship, and ways in which the client wants to change the relationship. The counselor also obtains a chronological history of significant life events, fluctuations in mood and self-esteem, interpersonal relationships, and ED symptoms. Throughout this process, the counselor and the client work together to connect life experiences and ED development and symptoms. This exploration provides an opportunity for the client to clearly recognize the relationship between life events, social functioning, and the ED, thereby clarifying the rationale behind IPT. The information obtained from the interpersonal inventory can be put together into a life chart, an exploratory tool that is used to make connections between interpersonal events and the onset and maintenance of the ED. It is a working document used throughout treatment that provides important insights for both the counselor and the client.

On completion of the interpersonal inventory, the counselor and client collaboratively develop an individualized interpersonal formulation, which includes the identification of the client's primary interpersonal problem area. Although some clients may present for treatment with difficulties in several problem areas, the time-limited nature of the treatment necessitates focus on the problem areas that appear to not only affect the client's interpersonal functioning most, but also on those that are most closely linked to the ED. The counselor, with the client's input, should assign one, or at most two, problem areas on which to formulate a treatment plan. We recommend that counselors write out the agreed-on goals and present this written summary to clients because this can be a very effective technique that serves as a treatment "contract" of sorts. This document becomes a collaborative work agreement that may be revised and revisited throughout treatment to assess and plan future progress. The goals developed at this stage will be referenced at each future session and will guide the day-to-day work of the treatment. If more than one problem area is identified, the client can choose to work simultaneously on both or may decide to first address the problem area that seems most likely to be responsive to treatment.

For example, if a client presents with role disputes and interpersonal deficits, the client and counselor might decide to first tackle role disputes, because interpersonal deficits may reflect long-term patterns requiring considerably more time and effort to change. Once the role dispute has been resolved, the counselor and client could then decide how to best address the more entrenched problem of interpersonal deficits. Once the primary problem areas have been identified and the treatment goals have been agreed on, the initial phase of treatment is completed. Forming this contract can help the client and counselor maintain focus on the connection between the ED and interpersonal problem area and guides the client throughout the course of treatment (Wilfley et al., 2002).

### Intermediate Phase

The intermediate phase of IPT is considered the work phase of treatment. The counselor's essential task in this phase is to assist the client in understanding the connection between difficulties in interpersonal functioning and ED symptoms. The counselor uses the strategies specific to the client's problem area to help the client achieve his or her goals. Once strategies for tackling the client's specific problems are identified, the counselor facilitates the client's work on these goals. Each week, the counselor maintains a focus on how the client is working on his or her agreed-on goals between sessions. Clients are encouraged to be responsible for their treatment and to recognize that it requires attention and persistence. Midway through treatment, the client is encouraged to complete a form that reflects on treatment to date and to plan for future gains. The counselor continually encourages the client to identify connections between ED symptoms and interpersonal events during the week and guides him or her in developing strategies to alter the interpersonal context in which ED symptoms occur. Illuminating these connections and altering the interpersonal problems that allowed for the onset and maintenance of the ED will disrupt the binge eating cycle. In the following vignette, a client with interpersonal role disputes talks about the connections he has made between his binge eating and the difficulties he has with his boss:

*Counselor:* How has it gone for you this week with your goals?

*Client M:* What I've realized is that I get a negative feeling when I have had a tough exchange with my boss. I get to a point where I shift into automatic pilot, and my car will drive right into Jack-in-the-Box. And I know that I'm shut down. I have to deal with it on a different level other than eating it. Because that's what I do, I eat it, to numb myself as you said. And whatever makes me get that way, I have to look at that.

*Counselor:* This is great work! One of the things that we discussed as a goal was to be thoughtful about what you are doing during the day and when you are binge eating—being aware of when you find yourself shifting. It's good that you are making that connection between your negative feelings and your binge eating. Now that you have made that connection, how would you like to start working on your interactions with your boss?

Additionally, one of the counselor's most important jobs is to redirect discussions to highlight the connections between binge eating and interpersonal events. Clients may bring up distressing aspects of their ED symptoms and want to engage in extended discussion related to these symptoms. When this occurs, however, the counselor should redirect clients to link their symptoms to the interpersonal context and gently guide them toward discussion of treatment goals. Following is an example of how a counselor can gently, but firmly, help a client get back on track to work on his goals. In doing so, the counselor is able to engage the client in a more meaningful discussion about his relationship with his wife.

*Counselor:* What did you want to work on today?

*Client R:* Well, last week I spent a lot of hours at work, which was really tough for me, so I didn't have a whole lot of hours to eat, which was good. I had an episode Sunday, though. When I finished my work, I went in and started cooking, and I didn't stop until I got a phone call. Thank goodness my friend called me last night because I would've eaten all the way through till this morning.

*Counselor:* It seemed like one of the things you shared with me last week was that eating was a way for you to unwind, you know, destress. Instead of sharing your work stressors with your wife, you'll turn to food.

*R:* Boy, did I unwind, right on the refrigerator, I ate this whole. . . .

*Counselor:* Let me refocus you for a moment back to your goals; how is it coming with sharing more with your wife?

*R:* Good, really good, my wife and I are actually talking quite a bit more. She's not used to that, so she's kind of wondering what's up with me. But then she knows why I'm asking questions and then talking to her more, because of therapy and my goals. She's pretty private herself and doesn't talk a lot, either. So it's weird for us to do that.

*Counselor:* Sounds like it does feel weird, but as we discussed during the beginning of treatment, the more you are able to share your stressors with your wife, the less you will be turning to food when you are stressed. Also, as you share with each other more, it will feel a lot less weird to you and your wife.

*R:* I do think that we are getting a little closer.

During each phase, and especially the intermediate phase, counselors use the following specific strategies to help clients meet their goals:

- *Therapeutic stance:* IPT places importance on establishing a positive therapeutic alliance between counselor and client. The IPT therapeutic stance is one of warmth, support, and empathy. Throughout all phases of the treatment, the counselor is active and advocates for the client rather than remaining neutral. Issues and discussions are framed positively so that the counselor may help the client feel at ease throughout treatment. Such an approach promotes a safe and supportive working environment. Confrontations and clarifications are offered in a gentle and timely manner, and the counselor is careful to encourage the client's positive expectations of the therapeutic relationship. Finally, the counselor conveys a hopeful and optimistic attitude about the client's potential to recover.

- *Focusing on goals:* As a directed, goal-oriented therapy, IPT counselors should maintain a focus each week on how the client is working on his or her agreed-on goals between sessions. Phrases such as "moving forward on your goals" and "making important changes" are used to encourage clients to be responsible for their treatment while also reminding them that altering interpersonal patterns requires attention and persistence. During the course of therapy, unfocused discussions sometimes arise. The counselor should sensitively, but firmly, redirect the discussion to the key interpersonal issues. By explicitly addressing goals each week, the client can work toward necessary changes. This goal-oriented focus has been supported by research on IPT maintenance treatment for recurrent depression, which has demonstrated that the counselor's ability to maintain focus on interpersonal themes is associated with better outcomes (Frank, Kupfer, Wagner, McEachran, & Cornes, 1991). In IPT for EDs, it is essential that the counselor facilitate and strengthen the recognition of connections between clients' problematic eating and difficulties in their interpersonal lives.

- *Making connections:* It is crucial that the counselor assist clients in recognizing, and ultimately becoming more aware of, the connections between eating difficulties and interpersonal events during the week. As clients learn to make these connections, the counselor should guide them to develop strategies to alter the interpersonal context in which the disordered eating symptoms occur. As a result, the cycle of the ED is interrupted. Clients are also encouraged to make connections between interpersonal functioning and positive eating patterns. For example, an individual may recognize that communication improved with a significant other and, as a result, the client did not engage in eating-disordered behaviors. To encourage positive and negative connections, counselors should ask clients about their eating patterns between sessions, whether any changes occurred, and any recognized links between eating patterns and interpersonal functioning.

- *Exploratory questions:* Use of general, open-ended questions often facilitates the free discussion of material, which is especially useful during the beginning of a session. For example, the counselor might open a session by saying, "Tell me about your relationship with your husband." Once this has generated discussion, progressively more specific questioning should follow.
- *Encouraging affect:* IPT's focus throughout the therapeutic process involves affect elicitation and exploration (Wilfley et al., 2000), which is particularly relevant because negative affect is the most widely reported antecedent of binge eating episodes (Wolfe et al., 2009). The IPT counselor should assist clients in (a) acknowledging and accepting painful emotions, (b) using affective experiences to facilitate desired interpersonal changes, and (c) experiencing suppressed affect (Wilfley, 2008; Wilfley et al., 2000).

  *Encourage acceptance of painful affects.* Individuals with EDs often use food to cope with negative affect. Therapy provides an arena to experience and express these feelings rather than using food to cope with them. As the feelings are expressed, it is important for the IPT counselor to validate and help the client accept them (Wilfley, 2008).

  *Teach the client how to use affect in interpersonal relationships.* Although the expression of strong feelings in the session is seen as an important starting point for much therapeutic work, the expression of feelings outside the session is not a goal in and of itself. The goal is to help the client act more constructively (e.g., not binge eating or purging) in interpersonal relationships, which may involve either expressing or suppressing affects, depending on the circumstances. A goal for clients in IPT is to learn when their needs are met by expressing affect and when they are better met by suppressing affect. However, a primary goal is helping clients to identify, understand, and acknowledge their feelings whether or not they choose to verbalize them to others (Wilfley, 2008). The following vignette demonstrates this strategy.

  S. presented as silent and withdrawn at the beginning of the session, which her counselor immediately noticed. Initially, she denied any relationship between her nonverbal behavior and the counselor's observation. The counselor was persistent, and S eventually acknowledged that she was feeling hurt because her father had not acknowledged her son's first birthday. She spent some time clarifying and expressing her feelings of anger and rejection with regard to her own relationship with her father. The issue that emerged in the session was "When do you stop wanting something from a parent that you can never get from them?" Even though she became aware of and expressed many painful feelings regarding her relationship with her father, S's goal was not to go out and express these feelings to her father directly at this time. Instead, S and her counselor began to discuss how she can become more fulfilled and satisfied by working to make other choices in terms of who to turn to for support and care.

*Help the client experience suppressed affects.* Many clients who struggle with BN and BED are emotionally constricted in situations in which strong emotions are normally felt. An example may be the client who is unassertive and does not feel anger when his or her rights are violated. However, a client may feel anger but may lack the courage to express it in an assertive manner. Sometimes clients will deny being upset when it is clear that an upsetting interaction has just occurred. The counselor might say, "Although you said you were not upset, it appears to me that you have shut down since you talked about the situation with your husband." In this way, the counselor will attempt to draw out affect when it is suppressed (Wilfley, 2008).

- *Clarification:* Clarification is a useful technique that can serve to increase the client's awareness about what she or he has actually communicated and to draw awareness to contradictions that may have occurred in the client's presentation of interactions or situations. An example might involve contradictions between the client's affect and speech: "While you were telling me how upset you are about your father, you had a smile on your face. What do you think that's about?"
- *Communication analysis:* The technique of communication analysis is used to identify potential communication difficulties that the client may be experiencing and to assist the client in modifying ineffective communication patterns. In using communication analysis, the counselor asks the client to describe, in great detail, a recent interaction or argument with a significant other. The counselor and client will collaboratively work to identify difficulties in communication that may be affecting the process and outcome of the interaction and to find more effective strategies.
- *Use of the therapeutic relationship:* The premise behind this technique is that all individuals have characteristic patterns of interacting with others. The technique is used by exploring the client's thoughts, feelings, expectations, and behavior in the therapeutic relationship and relating them to the client's characteristic way of behaving or feeling in other

relationships. This technique is particularly relevant to and useful for clients with interpersonal deficits and interpersonal role disputes. Use of this technique offers the client the opportunity to understand the nature of his or her difficulties in interacting with others and provides the client with helpful feedback on his or her interactional style.

## Termination Phase

The purpose of the termination phase is to consolidate gains made throughout treatment and to establish future goals for continued work. The counselor should begin to discuss termination early and clearly and should address any anxiety or grief the client may be experiencing related to the end of treatment. This step is crucial because when feelings of sadness or loss are not acknowledged, they may lead to fears of relapse or an increase in symptoms. In the four to five sessions of the termination phase, clients are encouraged to reflect on the progress and changes they have made during treatment. It is especially important for the counselor to emphasize that clients have begun to successfully manage their relationships and emotions. Individuals with EDs not uncommonly attribute changes in treatment to the counselor rather than to their own hard work, which may erode clients' confidence in their ability for continued success and improvement after treatment. Because there are always goals that are not accomplished within the time frame of IPT, termination should also include a discussion of strategies to prevent relapse and plans for continued work after treatment has ended. Clients should be realistic and predict that setbacks will occur but that with continued effort, change and progress can be sustained. The counselor should guide the client in a discussion of contingencies for handling future problems, because this discussion will bolster feelings of competence. It is vital to assist clients in thinking about warning signs and symptoms that suggest a need for action on their part.

## Case Example

The following case example of Barb illustrates how the phases and techniques of IPT can be used in treatment of BED.

Barb, a 53-year-old cosmetologist, presented for treatment for BED. At the time of the initial intake, she was having three binge episodes a week during which she consumed an unambiguously large amount of food (typically three to four fast food sandwiches within a half-hour) and felt a loss of control. She reported being most likely to binge eat when feeling uneasy and shared that her overeating caused her marked distress. Barb's binge eating began at age 15 and had been followed by years of dieting and weight fluctuations. At 231 pounds, Barb was severely overweight and above the 95th percentile of weight for her age. An investigator-based assessment indicated that she had significant eating psychopathology that included an extreme fear of weight gain and great discomfort in allowing herself or others to see her body. Barb had no other Axis I psychopathology but met criteria for obsessive–compulsive personality disorder with a subthreshold diagnosis of self-defeating personality disorder. Barb had never been in therapy before.

### Initial Phase

Barb met with her counselor to begin the interpersonal inventory and identify her current interpersonal problems. During this initial meeting, the counselor talked with Barb about her diagnosis and instructed her about how taking an interpersonal approach would lead to the amelioration of her binge eating. The counselor also educated Barb about BED and reassured her that her ED was driving her incremental weight gain and out-of-control eating rather than a lack of motivation on her part. After learning about her current symptoms by discussing a recent episode, Barb's counselor skipped back to her very first time binge eating, using it as a frame through which to move forward chronologically in time. In doing so, Barb and her counselor together began to construct a life chart of relationship difficulties that were involved in the onset and maintenance of her binge eating problems (see Table 14.3). Barb had a history of conflict avoidance and a fear of criticism. At age 15, she began a series of failed relationships that she had attempted to hide or glorify to appear as the perfect daughter and to not disappoint her parents. Accordingly, she binge ate when she was alone and used food to "numb out" to manage the feelings that she kept private. Barb's attempts at secrecy and use of food to disconnect from her feelings continued throughout her subsequent marriage. Although her husband had been cruel and verbally abusive, Barb worked hard to "fool everyone for 18 years" into believing that she had a fulfilling relationship because she did not want anyone to think that she had failed in her marriage.

Since her divorce, Barb had been in a live-in relationship but remained emotionally disconnected from her boyfriend. In the same way, she concealed her ED from him, ate very little when they were together, and continued to binge eat when alone. At work, Barb shared that she put in 14-hour days because she felt uncomfortable saying no to her customers' requests to see her before and after business hours. Given the long periods of time she spent on her feet without breaks to eat or rest, Barb clearly disregarded her needs to an extreme degree. Consequently, she found herself binge eating at night (such on her way home from work) to avoid the conflicted feelings she had about her resentment and frustration regarding her workload. Together, Barb and her counselor examined the link between her binge eating and use of food as a primary coping strategy to manage her negative affect states and avoidance of conflict. Given her history of unfulfilling relationships and an inability to effectively manage her interpersonal relationships, the counselor identified interpersonal deficits as her primary problem area.

Toward the end of the third session, Barb and her counselor began to collaboratively identify treatment goals that would assist her in working on her interpersonal deficits. Three goals were identified that related to both Barb's

Table 14.3
**Life Chart for Case Example: Barb**

| Age | Weight or Eating Problem | Relationships | Events and Circumstances | Mood |
|---|---|---|---|---|
| 5 | Normal weight | | Tonsils are removed. | |
| 6 | Begins gaining weight | | | |
| 14 | Concerns about weight; first binge; prescribed amphetamines to lose weight | | Grandfather died. | Feels sad at funeral but does not cry because she thinks it would be a sign of weakness. |
| 15 | | | Sister gets married, borrows money from parents, and files for bankruptcy with her husband. | Perceives parents as being extremely disappointed in sister. |
| 16 | Less concern about weight because "Paul's ex-wife was a lot heavier than me" but begins binge eating | Meets Paul, 23, who works at a gas station. | Does not tell parents about Paul given her father's high-profile job and position in the community. | Comfortable in relationship; fearful of parents' disappointment; worries about their finding out. |
| 18 | Binge eating when alone | Becomes engaged to Paul. Tells sisters, but not parents. | Graduates from high school; goes to beauty school. | |
| | Loses weight | Paul breaks off the engagement. | Abortion | |
| | | | Paul "steals" back the ring (seen on Paul's new girl-friend); throws herself into work as a secretary; is promoted repeatedly. | |

*(Continued)*

Table 14.3 (*Continued*)
**Life Chart for Case Example: Barb**

| Age | Weight or Eating Problem | Relationships | Events and Circumstances | Mood |
|---|---|---|---|---|
| 18 | More comfortable about weight ("Dean's wife was a lot heavier than me"). | Meets Dean, who works as a salesman; Dean says he is separated from his wife, who is pregnant. | Dean's wife pickets her parents' house; parents do not make mention of this. | Does not feel guilty about the relationship |
| | Binge eating when alone ("Food was my only friend when he was away"); never eats when with him. | Lies to family and friends, telling them that they got married. | Moves to Chicago with Dean. | Secrecy (wanting to be "perfect & not disappoint my parents"); homesick |
| | | Spouse of coworker tells her Dean is cheating on her. | Throws Dean out of the house; on his way out, Dean takes her ring from her jewelry box. | |
| 27 | Binge eating as an outlet | Gets pregnant, marries Bob, an alcoholic, who is "cruel and verbally abusive." | Lies to mother that she got pregnant after the wedding; birth of first child. | Compliant, scared |
| 28 | Heaviest point; 265 pounds | Bob occasionally shoves her. | Birth of second child; "I channeled my energy into my daughters." | Hateful |
| 32 | "Eating a lot." | Husband hits her; she stands up to husband only once, to ask him to choose between her and alcohol. | Does not tell anyone ("Nobody had a clue that we didn't have a wonderful marriage"). | Scared |
| | | Bob no longer drinks but continues being verbally abusive. | Continuing Girl Scout troop leader; very active in church | Emotionally distant ("I made it happy for me") |

*(Continued)*

Table 14.3 (Continued)
**Life Chart for Case Example: Barb**

| Age | Weight or Eating Problem | Relationships | Events and Circumstances | Mood |
|-----|-------------------------|---------------|--------------------------|------|
| 39 | | Has sex with husband approximately 2 times a year. | Husband invests $80,000 of their joint money in real estate; all money lost; begins saving "every penny," sending $10,000 to her sister to open a savings account for her; becomes a workaholic. | Fearful husband will hit her; obedient; proud at holding onto her feelings; derives esteem from keeping her trouble from her children and others. |
| 41 | Eating as a way to "hold everything together." | Sexual relationship with Bob ends. Although she does not express anger, Bob yells at her, saying he can do whatever he wants with his money. | | |
| 46 | 260 pounds, blood pressure increasing with increasing weight | | Marital therapy with clergy for 3 months. | |
| 47 | Loses 90 pounds (170 pounds); lowest adult weight | Files for divorce. | | |
| 50 | | Meets current boyfriend. | Mother dies. | Funeral is "a lot less stressful [than my grandfather's] because I knew it was OK to cry." |

*(Continued)*

329

Table 14.3 (*Continued*)
**Life Chart for Case Example: Barb**

| Age | Weight or Eating Problem | Relationships | Events and Circumstances | Mood |
|---|---|---|---|---|
| 51 | | Moves in with current boyfriend. | | Feels satisfied with their relationship. |
| 52 | Binge eating at night. | | Works 14-hour days or longer, not pausing to eat or rest during the day. | |
| 53 | 231 pounds, binges on objectively large amounts of food 3 times a week, binge eating its most frequent ever. | Does not tell any family members she is seeking help. | | |

binge eating and her work to resolve problems with interpersonal deficits. As her first goal, Barb was directed to become more aware of and to learn to identify her feelings when she began to binge eat or feel out of control with her eating. She was told that many people who struggle with binge eating have difficulty identifying and labeling their affective states. Learning to do this would provide her with an extremely useful tool with which to begin to eliminate her binge episodes and, in a preliminary way, to help increase her connections with others. As another goal, Barb was encouraged to begin sharing her feelings with others (especially her boyfriend, with whom she lived) rather than trying to avoid potential conflict. The counselor discussed with her that years of lying to important people in her life as well as engaging in self-deceit to maintain an image of perfection had led to her inability to communicate effectively or manage conflict. Given her history of failing to convey her feelings, wishes, and needs to others, beginning to share her full range of feelings with her boyfriend, daughters, and coworkers would be especially important for her work on her interpersonal problem area. As a final goal, Barb was instructed to find ways to nurture herself rather than spend all of her energy caring for others. Consistent with her problem area, Barb had established a pattern (common among binge eaters) of excessive caretaking for others in her relationships. Barb was encouraged to take better care of herself to break the vicious cycle of self-denial that she had established in her significant relationships. In addition, focusing on herself in relationships would also teach Barb about more effectively negotiating her interactions. Given the inextricable link between her problem area and binge eating, Barb's counselor explained that the exclusive focus on these goals would lead to the elimination of her binge eating.

Before beginning the intermediate phase, Barb began doing important work on her goal of taking care of herself and sharing more with her boyfriend. She also began thinking about ways in which she might be able to reduce her workload. As a result, Barb shared with her counselor that she was feeling better about herself. Barb's counselor marked with her the end of the initial phase and indicated that the structure of the sessions would change (i.e., she would take on more responsibility to talk about her progress on her goals).

### Intermediate Phase

During the second phase of treatment, Barb continued sharing the work she had been doing on her goals in her outside life. Her counselor encouraged her to notice her style of glossing over problems, and Barb continued to receive helpful feedback, both in and out of sessions, about minimizing her feelings. As Barb spoke about her unhappiness during her first marriage, she began to understand that maintaining the facade of a perfect life prevented her from turning to others for assistance. In fact, discounting her own feelings in general prevented her from experiencing her emotions or dealing with her feelings in more adaptive ways. About halfway through treatment, to review progress and plan for the remainder of treatment, Barb and her counselor reviewed her midtreatment goal reflection (see Table 14.4).

Table 14.4
**Midtreatment Goal Reflection for Case Example: Barb**

*Area 1.* Share your feelings with others rather than avoiding conflict. For example, you can practice confronting significant others in your life (e.g., boyfriend, sisters) when you are upset. You can also practice saying no to people, such as your customers at the salon.

| | |
|---|---|
| 1. In what ways have you used treatment to work on this goal? | I've worked on sharing more with my boyfriend. Once, I confronted him when I thought he overreacted to something I said, and I could get through him being upset with me. I'm also talking more with my sisters. I even told my sister that she hurt my feelings. |
| 2. How has work on this goal been connected to decreasing your problems with binge eating? | Instead of eating when I'm upset, I can sometimes talk to him about my feelings. |
| 3. In your social network, what changes have you noticed as a result of your work on this problem? | My relationships are going a little better with my sisters and my boyfriend. |
| 4. In what ways have you been unable to work on this problem? | I still have a hard time not working a lot of hours and saying no to my customers. |
| 5. What specific plan do you have for continuing to work on this problem over the next 10 weeks? | I'll try to set some boundaries with my customers, and I want to share more with my daughters. |

As treatment progressed, Barb had several occasions at work in which she found herself in conflict with others. In session, the counselor used the IPT techniques of clarification, communication analysis, and encouragement of affect to assist Barb in finding ways of negotiating the conflict. After several attempts, Barb was finally able to experience that conflict could be worked through effectively. In addition, Barb began to share more with her sisters, communicate more effectively with coworkers, and set limits with customers by refusing some of their requests. Toward the end of the intermediate phase, Barb was aware of the enormous energy she had spent trying to conceal her problems and was now sharing more with her friends and family. She reported that as a result her relationships were more satisfying, and in fact she and her boyfriend had become engaged.

*Termination Phase*
At the beginning of the termination phase, the counselor spoke with Barb about the subtle shift in treatment focus for the remaining sessions. Specifically, the counselor told Barb that the session marked the beginning of the final or termination phase of treatment. Even though Barb would still be encouraged to push forward on her treatment goals, the counselor told her that they would be spending some of the remaining session time reviewing and consolidating her progress, formally saying goodbye to one another,

and discussing how she could use what she had learned in treatment to manage future interpersonal challenges. Barb used the remaining time during the termination phase to continue taking better care of herself by decreasing her work hours. By the end of treatment, Barb had also begun to have frank discussions with her daughters about their unresolved feelings about his father. In reviewing her progress, Barb was able to acknowledge that over the course of treatment she was able to recognize her feelings and take care of her needs by making more time for herself. Barb also noted that she was able to attend to negative feelings "without feeling as if the world was coming to an end." She shared that as she began to accomplish these goals, her relationships with others began to get better.

At the end of treatment, Barb had stopped binge eating. At a 1-year follow-up visit, Barb had lost 70 pounds from her initial assessment weight and continued to be binge free.

# Future Directions

Several important areas require further study. We first discuss the important next step of determining whether IPT for EDs can be translated from specialty care centers to the primary care setting and other community settings in which counselors may be trained to deliver IPT, thus increasing access to this evidence-based treatment. Additionally, in an effort to continually improve IPT and broaden its utility, we review a newly emerging adaptation of IPT to prevent excess weight gain in adolescents and then propose other research directions, including other applications for IPT.

## Disseminating and Implementing Interpersonal Psychotherapy in Community Settings

Despite the pressing need for intervention and the proven effectiveness of evidence-based treatments such as IPT and CBT for the treatment of EDs, substantial evidence has shown that clients are not receiving these treatments in routine clinical care (Beidas & Kendall, 2010; National Collaborating Centre for Mental Health, 2004; Proctor et al., 2009; Resnick, 2005; Wilfley et al., 2002; Wilson, Wilfley, Agras, & Bryson, 2010). Additionally, even when clients do receive these treatments, they are often not competently delivered (Shafran et al., 2009). This failing was recently highlighted by the director of the National Institute for Mental Health:

> We have powerful, evidence-based psychosocial interventions, but they are not widely available. . . . A serious deficit exists in training for empirically supported psychosocial interventions. . . . Translational research will need to focus not only on "bench to bedside" but also on "bedside to practice." (Insel, 2009, pp. 131–132)

Delays in treatment delivery result in prolonged illness, disease progression, poorer prognosis, and greater likelihood of relapse (Leavitt, 2001).

Given the problems that co-occur with EDs, such as depression, low self-esteem, and social maladjustment, that are also successfully treated using evidence-based therapies for EDs, the opportunity for intervening positively in the lives of this population makes it a public health priority. However, the dearth of systematic research on treating EDs in community mental health centers is notable (Resnick, 2005). A major barrier is that relatively few counselors have been trained to use these treatments competently (Shafran et al., 2009; von Ranson & Robinson, 2006; Weissman et al., 2006). In their large-scale evaluation of barriers to the adoption of new treatments, Cook, Biyanova, and Coyne (2009) identified training issues (e.g., lack of local training and ongoing supervision to refine and integrate skills) as the major reason for the lack of dissemination and implementation. What is urgently needed is a practical, economically feasible means of training counselors to implement empirically supported treatments suitable for widespread use.

## Adapting Interpersonal Psychotherapy for the Prevention of Excessive Weight Gain

A recent and novel adaptation of IPT, IPT for excess weight gain (IPT–WG), has been developed, and is currently being tested, for the prevention of excess weight gain in adolescents who report loss of control (LOC) patterns (Tanofsky-Kraff et al., 2007). *LOC* refers to the sense that one cannot control what or how much one is eating, regardless of the reported amount of food consumed (Tanofsky-Kraff, 2008). LOC eating is common among youths, is associated with distress and overweight (Tanofsky-Kraff, 2008), and predicts excess weight gain over time (Tanofsky-Kraff et al., 2009) and the development of partial- or full-syndrome BED (Tanofsky-Kraff et al., 2011). IPT–WG makes use of IPT for the prevention of depression in adolescents (IPT—adolescent skills training, or IPT–AST; Young, Mufson, & Davies, 2006) and group IPT for BED (Wilfley et al., 2000) and evolved from the unexpected finding that individuals with BED who cease to binge eat tend to maintain their body weight during or after treatment (Agras et al., 1995; Agras, Telch, Arnow, Eldredge, & Marnell, 1997; Devlin et al., 2005; Wilfley et al., 1993, 2002). Therefore, treatment of binge eating among youths has been hypothesized to reduce excess weight gain and prevent full-syndrome EDs during development (Tanofsky-Kraff et al., 2007).

Several factors have suggested that IPT is particularly appropriate for the prevention of obesity in high-risk adolescents with binge or LOC eating patterns. Specifically, youths frequently use peer relationships as a crucial measure of self-evaluation (Mufson, Dorta, Moreau, & Weissman, 2004; Tanofsky-Kraff, 2012). A study by Lemeshow et al. (2008) revealed the importance of perceived social interactions and social standing on body weight gain over time. In this prospective cohort study, adolescent girls who rated themselves lower on a subjective social standing scale were 69% more likely to gain more weight over time than girls who rated themselves on the higher end of the scale (Lemeshow et al., 2008). Furthermore, overweight teens are more likely to experience negative feelings about themselves, particularly regarding their body shape and weight, than normal-weight adolescents (Fallon et al., 2005; Schwimmer, Burwinkle, & Varni, 2003; Striegel-Moore, Silberstein, & Rodin, 1986), perhaps because of their elevated rates of appearance-related teasing, rejection, and social isolation (Strauss & Pollack, 2003). The social isolation that overweight teens report may be directly targeted by IPT.

Several longitudinal studies have found depressive symptoms to predict weight gain and obesity onset in children and adolescents (Anderson, Cohen, Naumova, & Must, 2006; Goodman & Whitaker, 2002; Pine, Goldstein, Wolk, & Weissman, 2001; Puder & Munsch, 2010; Stice, Presnell, Shaw, & Rohde, 2005). Thus, IPT's proven efficacy in decreasing depressive symptoms in adolescents (Mufson, Dorta, Wickramaratne, et al., 2004) may serve to decrease an additional risk factor for excessive weight gain. In addition to reducing depressive symptomatology, IPT is posited to increase social support, which has been demonstrated to improve weight loss and weight maintenance in overweight adults (Wing & Jeffery, 1999) and children (Wilfley et al., 2007). Indeed, data have suggested that low social problems predict better response to weight loss treatment in children (Wilfley et al., 2007).

IPT–WG for adolescents at high risk for adult obesity, delivered in a group format, maintains the key components of traditional IPT: (a) a focus on interpersonal problem areas that are related to the target behavior (in this case, LOC eating); (b) the use of the interpersonal inventory at the outset of treatment to identify interpersonal problems that are contributing to the targeted behavior; and (c) the triphasic structure of the intervention (initial, intermediate, and termination). The primary activities of IPT–WG are to provide psychoeducation about risk factors for excessive weight gain and to teach general skill building to improve interpersonal problems. IPT–WG was founded on Young and Mufson's (2003) IPT–AST and group IPT for the treatment of BED in adulthood (Wilfley et al., 2000). IPT–WG differs from other adaptations in that it was developed specifically to address the particular needs of adolescent girls at high risk for adult obesity because of their current body mass index percentile and report of LOC eating behaviors (Tanofsky-Kraff et al., 2007).

Based on IPT–AST, IPT–WG is presented to teenagers as "Teen Talk" to be nonstigmatizing. Similar to IPT–AST, this preventive adaptation of IPT focuses on psychoeducation, communication analysis, and role playing (Young & Mufson, 2003). Specific interpersonal communications skills are taught, including "Strike while the iron is cold," "Use 'I' statements," "Be specific" (when talking about a problem), and "Put yourself in their shoes" (Young & Mufson, 2003). For IPT–WG, an additional skill, "What you don't say speaks volumes," has been added to teach adolescents how their body language has the ability to affect communication regardless of their words. During the interpersonal inventory, a "closeness circle" (Mufson, Dorta, Moreau, & Weissman, 2004) is used to identify the participant's close relationships. To address developmental differences among participants, girls are assigned to groups on the basis of younger (12–14 years) and older (15–17 years) age. Thus, sessions may be appropriately geared toward the adolescents' developmental level. For instance, younger adolescents, who may be uncomfortable talking about themselves, may respond better to hypothetical situations and games, whereas older teenagers may more readily discuss their own interpersonal issues from the outset.

Based on IPT for BED, IPT–WG focuses on linking negative affect to LOC eating, overeating, times when individuals eat in response to cues other than hunger, and overconcern about shape and weight. Moreover, a timeline of personal eating, weight-related problems, and life events is discussed individually with participants before the group program. Unlike IPT for BED, the problem area of grief is rarely relevant because of the participants' young age but may be included on a case-by-case basis. Similar to both IPT–AST and IPT for BED, IPT–WG is delivered in a group format. IPT–WG consists of 12 weekly sessions, more than IPT–AST (8 sessions), but less than group IPT for BED (typically 20 sessions). Similar to IPT–AST, group size is smaller than in IPT for BED (5 vs. 9 members), enabling counselors to keep adolescents engaged (Tanofsky-Kraff, 2012). Although an effectiveness trial is still underway, preliminary data have suggested that IPT–WG may be a promising intervention for prevention of excess weight gain and BED (Tanofsky-Kraff et al., 2010).

In addition to future research to examine IPT–WG's effectiveness, several other important areas require further study. An important next step is to determine whether IPT for EDs can be translated from specialty care centers to the primary care setting and other typically nonresearch clinical practice milieus in which counselors may be trained to deliver IPT. In an effort to continually improve IPT and broaden its utility, we propose other research directions in the following sections.

## Enhancing Interpersonal Psychotherapy for Bulimia Nervosa and Binge Eating Disorder

As efforts to more frequently and consistently link ED symptoms to interpersonal functioning have evolved in the use of IPT for BED, clinical researchers involved in developing IPT for BN should also consider stressing this link during the delivery of IPT so that it offers the utmost potency. IPT in its current form already seamlessly incorporates aspects of other therapeutic modalities. For example, the collaborative, behavioral formulation during the interpersonal inventory is one of the ways in which IPT more closely resembles the behavioral therapies than it does the supportive or psychodynamic therapies. Therefore, some aspects of CBT may support IPT's efficacy. For example, IPT counselors might wish to use self-monitoring as a method for clients to become more aware of the negative affect surrounding their ED symptoms. Such an approach is already being tested in other treatment modalities. Indeed, Fairburn (2008) and colleagues have found the inclusion of an interpersonal module effective when administering a recently modified version of CBT for EDs, enhanced CBT for EDs.

## Testing Efficacy of Interpersonal Psychotherapy for Anorexia Nervosa

Research examining the utility of IPT for anorexia nervosa is relatively lacking. Indeed, no controlled studies have demonstrated the efficacy of IPT for anorexia nervosa. The IPT model could possibly be applicable to clients with anorexia because they tend to have deficits in social–cognitive skills that impede their capacity to create and experience validating social interactions (Rieger et al., 2010). Research into a possible adaptation of IPT for this population would be extremely useful, given the lack of efficacious evidence-based treatments for this disorder (Bulik, Berkman, Brownley, Sedway, & Lohr, 2007).

## Adapting Interpersonal Psychotherapy Into Adolescent and Child–Parent Formats

Given the robust efficacy of IPT for adolescents with depressive disorders, and the initial promise of IPT–WG (Tanofsky-Kraff et al., 2010), future research should involve additional adolescent adaptations. Adolescence is a key developmental period for cultivating social and interpersonal patterns, which may explain why adolescents appear to relate well to IPT. From its inception, Mufson, Dorta, Moreau, and Weissman (2004) made important adolescent-relevant adaptations to the treatment (e.g., the inclusion of a parent component and the assignment of a limited sick role, because youths are required to attend school and reducing their activities is likely to exacerbate their interpersonal difficulties). Given that this foundation has been established, the use of IPT for adolescents with BN and BED warrants investigation.

Using IPT with younger children may also be effective. A pilot study of family-based IPT for the treatment of depressive symptoms in 9- to 12-year-old children was found to be feasible and acceptable to families (Dietz, Mufson, Irvine, & Brent, 2008). Currently, an effectiveness trial is underway. The moderating influence of social problems on weight loss outcome in a family-based program (Wilfley et al., 2007) has suggested that targeting interpersonal functioning in the nuclear family milieu may serve as a point of intervention for the treatment of eating- and weight-related problems during middle childhood.

# Conclusion

IPT is a specialty treatment that has been shown to be effective in the short and long terms for the treatment of BN and BED. It is a time-limited treatment that targets current interpersonal problems in the areas of interpersonal deficits, interpersonal role disputes, role transitions, and grief to reduce ED symptomatology. The main problem area is determined by conducting a thorough interpersonal inventory. Throughout treatment, linking interpersonal functioning and ED symptoms and achieving progress by referring back to the established problem area and goals are paramount. IPT is now an established treatment for BN and BED and has shown promise for the prevention of excess weight gain in adolescents. No controlled studies have demonstrated the efficacy of IPT for anorexia nervosa. Researchers should continue to examine the use of IPT in additional populations, such as younger children. The time is ripe to disseminate this highly acceptable evidence-based treatment into widespread community practice to increase access to care for clients in need.

# Chapter Highlights

- The IPT model postulates that social problems create an environment in which EDs are developed and maintained.
- IPT reduces eating pathology by supporting the development of healthy interpersonal skills.
- IPT shows comparable effectiveness to CBT for BN and BED.
- No empirical evidence exists supporting the use of IPT for anorexia nervosa.
- Throughout every session of IPT, interpersonal functioning and ED symptoms should be linked.
- IPT focuses on setting goals to address current interpersonal problems in the domains of interpersonal deficits, interpersonal role disputes, role transitions, and grief.
- The interpersonal inventory is of paramount importance and will help to develop the treatment plan that will drive progress from session to session.
- In the termination phase, the clinician should discuss strategies to prevent relapse and continue work after the end of treatment

# Recommended Resources

Clinicians are directed to contact Dr. Wilfley at wilfleyd@psychiatry.wustl.edu for access to the unpublished manual for IPT, *Interpersonal Psychotherapy for Binge Eating Disorder (BED) Therapist's Manual*. For more extensive information on IPT, see the *Comprehensive Guide to Interpersonal Psychotherapy* (Weissman, Markowitz, & Klerman, 2000).

Markowitz and Weissman's recently published *Casebook of Interpersonal Psychotherapy* (2012; Oxford University Press) includes more in-depth clinical guidelines for the use of IPT with patients with BED in both individual and group settings.

The book *Interpersonal Psychotherapy for Group* (Wilfley, MacKenzie, Welch, Ayres, & Weissman, 2000) is an excellent resource detailing the modification of IPT for group settings.

Finally, the International Society for Interpersonal Psychotherapy (http://interpersonalpsychotherapy.org/) provides frequent opportunities around the world for certification in the delivery of IPT for a range of psychological problems.

# References

Agras, W. S., Telch, C. F., Arnow, B., Eldredge, K., Detzer, M. J., Henderson, J., & Marnell, M. (1995). Does interpersonal therapy help patients with binge eating disorder who fail to respond to cognitive–behavioral therapy? *Journal of Consulting and Clinical Psychology, 63,* 356–360.

Agras, W. S., Telch, C. F., Arnow, B., Eldredge, K., & Marnell, M. (1997). One-year follow-up of cognitive–behavioral therapy for obese individuals with binge eating disorder. *Journal of Consulting and Clinical Psycholology, 65,* 343–347.

Agras, W. S., Walsh, B. T., Fairburn, C. G., Wilson, G. T., & Kraemer, H. C. (2000). A multicenter comparison of cognitive–behavioral therapy and interpersonal psychotherapy for bulimia nervosa. *Archives of General Psychiatry, 57,* 459–466.

Anderson, S. E., Cohen, P., Naumova, E. N., & Must, A. (2006). Association of depression and anxiety disorders with weight change in a prospective community-based study of children followed up into adulthood. *Archives of Pediatrics and Adolescent Medicine, 160,* 285–291.

Ansell, E. B., Grilo, C. M., & White, M. A. (2012). Examining the interpersonal model of binge eating and loss of control over eating in women. *International Journal of Eating Disorders, 45,* 43–50. doi:10.1002/eat.20897

Arnow, B., Kenardy, J., & Agras, W. S. (1995). The Emotional Eating Scale: The development of a measure to assess coping with negative affect by eating. *International Journal of Eating Disorders, 18,* 79–90.

Beidas, R. S., & Kendall, P. C. (2010). Training therapists in evidence-based practice: A critical review of studies from a systems–contextual perspective. *Clinical Psychology: Science and Practice, 17,* 1–30.

Birchall, H. (1999). Interpersonal psychotherapy in the treatment of eating disorder. *European Eating Disorders Review, 7,* 315–320.

Bishop, M., Stein, R., Hilbert, A., Swenson, A., & Wilfley, D. E. (2007, October). *A five-year follow-up study of cognitive–behavioral therapy and interpersonal psychotherapy for the treatment of binge eating disorder.* Paper presented at the meeting of the Eating Disorders Research Society, Pittsburgh, Pennsylvania.

Bowlby, J. (1982). *Attachment and loss* (Vol. 1, 2nd ed.). New York, NY: Basic Books.

Bulik, C. M., Berkman, N. D., Brownley, K. A., Sedway, J. A., & Lohr, K. N. (2007). Anorexia nervosa treatment: A systematic review of randomized controlled trials. *International Journal of Eating Disorders, 40,* 310–320. doi:10.1002/eat.20367

Chui, W., Safer, D. L., Bryson, S. W., Agras, W. S., & Wilson, G. T. (2007). A comparison of ethnic groups in the treatment of bulimia nervosa. *Eating Behaviors, 8,* 485–491. doi:10.1016/j.eatbeh.2007.01.005

Constantino, M. J., Arnow, B. A., Blasey, C., & Agras, W. S. (2005). The association between patient characteristics and the therapeutic alliance in cognitive–behavioral and interpersonal therapy for bulimia nervosa. *Journal of Consulting and Clinical Psychology, 73,* 203–211.

Cook, J. M., Biyanova, T., & Coyne, J. C. (2009). Barriers to adoption of new treatments: An Internet study of practicing community psychotherapists. *Administration and Policy in Mental Health and Mental Health Services Research, 36,* 83–90.

Devlin, M. J., Goldfein, J. A., Petkova, E., Jiang, H., Raizman, P. S., Wolk, S., . . . Walsh, B. T. (2005). Cognitive behavioral therapy and fluoxetine as adjuncts to group behavioral therapy for binge eating disorder. *Obesity Research, 13,* 1077–1088.

Dietz, L. J., Mufson, L., Irvine, H., & Brent, D. A. (2008). Family-based interpersonal psychotherapy (IPT) for depressed preadolescents: An open treatment trial. *Early Intervention Psychiatry, 2,* 154–161.

Fairburn, C. G. (2008). *Cognitive behavior therapy and eating disorders.* New York, NY: Guilford Press.

Fairburn, C. G., & Cooper, Z. (1993). The eating disorder examination, 12th ed. In C. G. Fairburn & G. T. Wilson (Eds.), *Binge eating: Nature, assessment and treatment* (pp. 317–360). New York, NY: Guilford Press.

Fairburn, C. G., Doll, H. A., Welch, S. L., Hay, P. J., Davies, B. A., & O'Connor, M. E. (1998). Risk factors for binge eating disorder: A community-based, case-control study. *Archives of General Psychiatry, 55,* 425–432.

Fairburn, C. G., Jones, R., Peveler, R. C., Carr, S. J., Solomon, R. A., O'Connor, M. E., . . . Hope, R. A. (1991). Three psychological treatments for bulimia nervosa: A comparative trial. *Archives of General Psychiatry, 48,* 463–469.

Fairburn, C. G., Norman, P. A., Welch, S. L., O'Connor, M. E., Doll, H. A., & Peveler, R. C. (1995). A prospective study of outcome in bulimia nervosa and the long-term effects of three psychological treatments. *Archives of General Psychiatry, 52,* 304–312.

Fairburn, C. G., Peveler, R. C., Jones, R., Hope, R. A., & Doll, H. A. (1993). Predictors of 12-month outcome in bulimia nervosa and the influence of attitudes to shape and weight. *Journal of Consulting and Clinical Psychology, 61,* 696–698.

Fairburn, C. G., Welch, S. L., Doll, H. A., Davies, B. A., & O'Connor, M. E. (1997). Risk factors for bulimia nervosa: A community-based case-control study. *Archives of General Psychiatry, 54,* 509–517.

Fallon, E. M., Tanofsky-Kraff, M., Norman, A. C., McDuffie, J. R., Taylor, E. D., Cohen, M. L., . . . Yanovski, J. A. (2005). Health-related quality of life in overweight and nonoverweight Black and White adolescents. *Journal of Pediatrics, 147,* 443–450.

Frank, E., Kupfer, D. J., Wagner, E. F., McEachran, A. B., & Cornes, C. (1991). Efficacy of interpersonal psychotherapy as a maintenance treatment of recurrent depression: Contributing factors. *Archives of General Psychiatry, 48,* 1053–1059.

Frank, E., & Spanier, C. (1995). Interpersonal psychotherapy for depression: Overview, clinical efficacy, and future directions *Clinical Psychology: Science & Practice, 2,* 349–369.

Freeman, L. M. Y., & Gil, K. M. (2004). Daily stress, coping, and dietary restraint in binge eating. *International Journal of Eating Disorders, 36,* 204–212.

Goodman, E., & Whitaker, R. C. (2002). A prospective study of the role of depression in the development and persistence of adolescent obesity. *Pediatrics, 110,* 497–504.

Grilo, C. M., Masheb, R. M., & Wilson, G. T. (2005). Efficacy of cognitive behavioral therapy and fluoxetine for the treatment of binge eating disorder: A randomized double-blind placebo-controlled comparison. *Biological Psychiatry, 57,* 301–309.

Hilbert, A., Bishop, M. E., Stein, R. I., Tanofsky-Kraff, M., Swenson, A. K., Welch, R. R., & Wilfley, D. E. (2012). Long-term efficacy of psychological treatments for binge eating disorder. *British Journal of Psychiatry, 200,* 232–237. doi:10.1192/bjp.bp.110.089664

Hilbert, A., Saelens, B. E., Stein, R. I., Mockus, D. S., Welch, R. R., Matt, G. E., & Wilfley, D. E. (2007). Pretreatment and process predictors of outcome in interpersonal and cognitive behavioral psychotherapy for binge eating disorder. *Journal of Consulting and Clinical Psychology, 75,* 645–651. doi:10.1037/0022-006X.75.4.645

Horowitz, L. M., Rosenberg, S. E., Baer, B. A., Ureno, G., & Villasenor, V. S. (1988). Inventory of Interpersonal Problems: Psychometric properties and clinical applications. *Journal of Consulting and Clinical Psychology, 56,* 885–892.

Insel, T. R. (2009). Translating scientific opportunity into public health impact. *Archives of General Psychiatry, 66,* 128–133.

Keel, P. K., Dorer, D. J., Franko, D. L., Jackson, S. C., & Herzog, D. B. (2005). Postremission predictors of relapse in women with eating disorders. *American Journal of Psychiatry, 162,* 2263–2268.

Kenardy, J., Mensch, M., Bowen, K., Green, B., & Walton, J. (2002). Group therapy for binge eating in Type 2 diabetes: A randomized trial. *Diabetic Medicine, 19,* 234–239.

Klerman, G. L., Weissman, M. M., Rounsaville, B. J., & Chevron, E. S. (1984). *Interpersonal psychotherapy of depression.* New York, NY: Basic Books.

Leavitt, M. (2001). Medscape's response to the Institute of Medicine Report: Crossing the quality chasm: A new health system for the 21st century. *Medscape General Medicine, 3,* 2.

Lemeshow, A. R., Fisher, L., Goodman, E., Kawachi, I., Berkey, C. S., & Colditz, G. A. (2008). Subjective social status in the school and change in adiposity in female adolescents: Findings from a prospective cohort study. *Archives of Pediatrics & Adolescent Medicine, 162,* 23–28.

Markowitz, J. C., Skodol, A. E., & Bleiberg, K. (2006). Interpersonal psychotherapy for borderline personality disorder: Possible mechanisms of change. *Journal of Clinical Psychology, 62,* 431–444. doi: 10.1002/jclp.20242

Meyer, A. (1957). *Psychobiology: A science of man.* Springfield, IL: Charles C Thomas.

Mufson, L., Dorta, K. P., Moreau, D., & Weissman, M. M. (2004). *Interpersonal psychotherapy for depressed adolescents* (2nd ed.). New York, NY: Guilford Press.

Mufson, L., Dorta, K. P., Wickramaratne, P., Nomura, Y., Olfson, M., & Weissman, M. M. (2004). A randomized effectiveness trial of interpersonal psychotherapy for depressed adolescents. *Archives of General Psychiatry, 61,* 577–584.

National Collaborating Centre for Mental Health. (2004). *Eating disorders: Core interventions in the treatment and management of anorexia nervosa, bulimia nervosa and related eating disorders* (National Clinical Practice Guideline No. CG9). London, England: British Psychological Society & Royal College of Psychiatrists. Retrieved from www.nice.org.uk

Nauta, H., Hospers, H., Kok, G., & Jansen, A. (2000). A comparison between a cognitive and a behavioral treatment for obese binge eaters and obese non-binge eaters. *Behavior Therapy, 21,* 441–461.

Pine, D. S., Goldstein, R. B., Wolk, S., & Weissman, M. M. (2001). The association between childhood depression and adulthood body mass index. *Pediatrics, 107,* 1049–1056.

Proctor, E. K., Landsverk, J., Aarons, G., Chambers, D., Glisson, C., & Mittman, B. (2009). Implementation research in mental health services: An emerging science with conceptual, methodological, and training challenges [Proceedings Paper]. *Administration and Policy in Mental Health and Mental Health Services Research, 36,* 24–34.

Puder, J. J., & Munsch, S. (2010). Psychological correlates of childhood obesity. *International Journal of Obesity, 34*(Suppl. 2), S37–S43. doi:10.1038/ijo.2010.238

Resnick, J. L. (2005). Evidence-based practice for treatment of eating disorders. In S. E. Cooper (Ed.), *Evidence based psychotherapy practice in college mental health* (Vol. 20, pp. 49–63). New York, NY: Haworth Press.

Ricca, V., Mannucci, E., Mezzani, B., Moretti, S., Di Bernardo, M., Bertelli, M., . . . Faravelli, C. (2001). Fluoxetine and fluvoxamine combined with individual cognitive–behaviour therapy in binge eating disorder: A one-year follow-up study. *Psychotherapy and Psychosomatics, 70,* 298–306.

Rieger, E., Van Buren, D. J., Bishop, M., Tanofsky-Kraff, M., Welch, R., & Wilfley, D. E. (2010). An eating disorder-specific model of interpersonal psychotherapy (IPT-ED): Causal pathways and treatment implications. *Clinical Psychology Review, 30,* 400–410. doi:10.1016/j.cpr.2010.02.001

Schwimmer, J. B., Burwinkle, T. M., & Varni, J. W. (2003). Health-related quality of life of severely obese children and adolescents. *JAMA, 289,* 1813–1819.

Shafran, R., Clark, D. M., Fairburn, C. G., Arntz, A., Barlow, D. H., Ehlers, A., . . . Wilson, G. T. (2009). Mind the gap: Improving the dissemination of CBT. *Behavior Research and Therapy, 47,* 902–909.

Stice, E., Presnell, K., Shaw, H., & Rohde, P. (2005). Psychological and behavioral risk factors for obesity onset in adolescent girls: A prospective study. *Journal of Consulting and Clinical Psychology, 73,* 195–202.

Strauss, R. S., & Pollack, H. A. (2003). Social marginalization of overweight children. *Archives of Pediatrics & Adolescent Medicine, 157,* 746–752.

Striegel-Moore, R. H., Silberstein, L. R., & Rodin, J. (1986). Toward an understanding of risk factors for bulimia. *American Psychologist, 41,* 246–263.

Sullivan H. (1953). *The interpersonal theory of psychiatry.* New York, NY: W.W. Norton.

Tanofsky-Kraff, M. (2008). Binge eating among children and adolescents. In E. Jelalian & R. Steele (Eds.), *Handbook of child and adolescent obesity* (pp. 41–57). New York, NY: Springer.

Tanofsky-Kraff, M. (2012). Psychosocial preventive interventions for obesity and eating disorders in youths. *International Review of Psychiatry, 24,* 262–270. doi:10.3109/09540261.2012.676032

Tanofsky-Kraff, M., Shomaker, L. B., Olsen, C., Roza, C. A., Wolkoff, L. E., Columbo, K. M., . . . Yanovski, J. A. (2011). A prospective study of pediatric loss of control eating and psychological outcomes. *Journal of Abnormal Psychology, 120,* 108–118. doi:10.1037/a0021406

Tanofsky-Kraff, M., Wilfley, D. E., Young, J. F., Mufson, L., Yanovski, S. Z., Glasofer, D. R., & Salaita, C. G. (2007). Preventing excessive weight gain in adolescents: Interpersonal psychotherapy for binge eating. *Obesity, 15,* 1345–1355.

Tanofsky-Kraff, M., Wilfley, D. E., Young, J. F., Mufson, L., Yanovski, S. Z., Glasofer, D. R., . . . Schvey, N. A. (2010). A pilot study of interpersonal psychotherapy for preventing excess weight gain in adolescent girls at-risk for obesity. *International Journal of Eating Disorders, 43,* 701–706. doi: 10.1002/eat.20773

Tanofsky-Kraff, M., Yanovski, S. Z., Schvey, N. A., Olsen, C. H., Gustafson, J., & Yanovski, J. A. (2009). A prospective study of loss of control eating for body weight gain in children at high risk for adult obesity. *International Journal of Eating Disorders, 42,* 26–30. doi: 10.1002/eat.20580

Telch, C. F., Agras, W. S., Rossiter, E. M., Wilfley, D. E., & Kenardy, J. (1990). Group cognitive–behavioral treatment for the nonpurging bulimic: An initial evaluation. *Journal of Consulting and Clinical Psychology, 58,* 629–635.

von Ranson, K. M., & Robinson, K. E. (2006). Who is providing what type of psychotherapy to eating disorder clients? A survey. *International Journal of Eating Disorders, 39,* 27–34.

Weissman, M. M., Markowitz, J., & Klerman, G. L. (2000). *Comprehensive guide to interpersonal psychotherapy.* New York, NY: Basic Behavioral Science Books.

Weissman, M. M., Verdeli, H., Gameroff, M. J., Bledsoe, S. E., Betts, K., Mufson, L., . . . Wickramaratne, P. (2006). National survey of psychotherapy training in psychiatry, psychology, and social work *Archives of General Psychiatry, 63,* 925–934.

Wilfley, D. E. (2008). *Interpersonal psychotherapy for binge eating disorder (BED) therapist's manual.* Unpublished manuscript.

Wilfley, D. E., Agras, W. S., Telch, C. F., Rossiter, E. M., Schneider, J. A., Cole, A. G., . . . Raeburn, S. D. (1993). Group cognitive–behavioral therapy and group interpersonal psychotherapy for the nonpurging bulimic individual: A controlled comparison. *Journal of Consulting and Clinical Psychology, 61,* 296–305.

Wilfley, D. E., Frank, M. A., Welch, R. R., Spurrell, E. B., & Rounsaville, B. J. (1998). Adapting interpersonal psychotherapy to a group format (IPT-G) for binge eating disorder: Toward a model for adapting empirically supported treatments. *Psychotherapy Research, 8,* 379–391.

343

Wilfley, D. E., MacKenzie, K. R., Welch, R. R., Ayres, V. E., & Weissman, M. M. (2000). *Interpersonal psychotherapy for group.* New York, NY: Basic Books.

Wilfley, D. E., Stein, R. I., Saelens, B. E., Mockus, D. S., Matt, G. E., Hayden-Wade, H. A., . . . Epstein, L. H. (2007). Efficacy of maintenance treatment approaches for childhood overweight: A randomized controlled trial. *JAMA, 298,* 1661–1673.

Wilfley, D. E., Stein, R. I., & Welch, R. R. (2005). Interpersonal psychotherapy. In J. Treasure, U. Schmidt, & E. van Furth (Eds.), *The essential handbook of eating disorders* (pp. 137–154). West Sussex, England: Wiley.

Wilfley, D. E., Welch, R. R., Stein, R. I., Spurrell, E. B., Cohen, L. R., Saelens, B. E., . . . Matt, G. E. (2002). A randomized comparison of group cognitive–behavioral therapy and group interpersonal psychotherapy for the treatment of overweight individuals with binge-eating disorder. *Archives of General Psychiatry, 59,* 713–721.

Wilfley, D. E., Wilson, G. T., & Agras, W. S. (2008, September). *A multi-site randomized controlled trial of interpersonal psychotherapy, behavioral weight loss, and guided self-help in the treatment of overweight individuals with binge eating disorder.* Paper presented at the Eating Disorders Research Society, Montreal, Quebec, Canada.

Wilson, G. T. (2005). Psychological treatment of eating disorders. *Annual Review of Clinical Psychology, 1,* 439–465. doi:10.1146/annurev.clinpsy.1.102803.144250

Wilson, G. T., Grilo, C. M., & Vitousek, K. M. (2007). Psychological treatment of eating disorders. *American Psychologist, 62,* 199–216. doi:10.1037/0003-066X.62.3.199

Wilson, G. T., & Shafran, R. (2005). Eating disorders guidelines from NICE. *Lancet, 365,* 79–81. doi:10.1016/S0140-6736(04)17669-1

Wilson, G. T., Wilfley, D. E., Agras, W. S., & Bryson, S. W. (2010). Psychological treatments of binge eating disorder. *Archives of General Psychiatry, 67,* 94–101.

Wing, R. R., & Jeffery, R. W. (1999). Benefits of recruiting participants with friends and increasing social support for weight loss and maintenance. *Journal of Consulting and Clinical Psychology, 67,* 132–138.

Wolfe, B. E., Baker, C. W., Smith, A. T., & Kelly-Weeder, S. (2009). Validity and utility of the current definition of binge eating. *International Journal of Eating Disorders, 42,* 674–686. doi:10.1002/eat.20728

Young, J. F., & Mufson, L. (2003). *Manual for interpersonal psychotherapy—Adolescent skills training (IPT-AST).* New York, NY: Columbia University.

Young, J. F., Mufson, L., & Davies, M. (2006). Efficacy of interpersonal psychotherapy—adolescent skills training: An indicated preventive intervention for depression. *Journal of Child Psychology and Psychiatry, 47,* 1254–1262.

## Chapter 15

# Psychosocial Treatments for Obesity and Aberrant Eating Patterns in Youths

*Kerri N. Boutelle and Stephanie Knatz*

Approximately one third of children in the United States are overweight or obese (Ogden, Carroll, Kit, & Flegal, 2012), which translates to 4 to 5 million children. Children who are obese are at an increased risk for many negative health sequelae in childhood and in adulthood, including orthopedic and endocrine conditions, cardiovascular disease, and cancer and all-cause mortality (Dietz, 1998; Key et al., 2004; Micic, 2001; Must et al., 1999). Additionally, obese children are at an increased risk for psychosocial consequences in childhood and adolescence, including poor self-esteem, teasing and verbal abuse (Jackson, Grilo, & Masheb, 2000; Strauss, 2000; Thompson, Coovert, & Stormer, 1999), and isolation from social networks (Strauss & Pollack, 2003). Hospital costs for obesity-related conditions in youths ages 6 to 17 increased from $35 million in 1979 to $127 million in 2000 (Wang & Dietz, 2002), and the number of hospitalizations among children who are obese nearly doubled from 1999 to 2005 (Trasande, Liu, Fryer, & Weitzman, 2009).

Although aberrant eating behaviors can occur independent of weight, evidence has suggested that binge eating and other aberrant eating behaviors, such as loss of control (LOC) eating, are overrepresented in overweight and obese youths (Eddy et al., 2007; Glasofer et al., 2006; Wilfley et al., 2011), putting those children at greater risk for weight gain. Additionally, youths who report aberrant eating behaviors such as binge eating and LOC eating evidence elevated levels of depression, anxiety, body dissatisfaction, and behavioral problems (Decaluwe & Braet, 2003; Eddy et al. 2007; Glasofer et al., 2006; Goldschmidt, Aspen, Sinton, Tanofsky-Kraff, & Wilfley, 2008; Goossens, Braet, & Bosmans, 2010; Hartmann, Czaja, Rief, & Hilbert, 2010; Hilbert, Rief, Tuschen-Caffier, de Zwaan, & Czaja, 2009; Johnson,

Grieve, Adams, & Sandy, 1999; Morgan et al., 2002; Tanofsky-Kraff, Faden, Yanovski, Wilfley, & Yanovski, 2005), as well as decrements in self-esteem and social functioning (Ackard, Neumark-Sztainer, Story, & Perry, 2003; Berkowitz, Stunkard, & Stallings, 1993; Elliott et al., 2010; Goossens, Braet, Bosmans, & Decaluwe, 2011; Isnard et al., 2003). Considering the high prevalence rates and significant psychosocial and health consequences of obesity and aberrant eating behaviors, it is important that efforts are made to intervene with these youths.

In this chapter, we first describe the current research on obesity and aberrant eating patterns and the theoretical conceptualizations of overeating and obesity in youths. A summary of current treatment approaches for obesity and overeating follows. Last, we provide a case presentation and a summary of key points.

# What Aberrant Eating Patterns Can Promote Overweight in Youths?

Aberrant overeating patterns involve eating for reasons that are not motivated by biological hunger and refer to a range of eating behaviors that involve a lack of ability to regulate food intake, including binge eating, LOC eating, emotional eating, eating in secret, and eating in the absence of hunger (EAH).

## Binge Eating

According to the *Diagnostic and Statistical Manual of Mental Disorders* (4th ed., text rev.; American Psychiatric Association, 2000), *binge eating* is defined as eating an objectively large amount of food and experiencing a sense of loss of control over eating. Both of these criteria (loss of control and objective overeating) must be present to diagnose a binge episode. LOC eating, an aberrant eating behavior that is defined later in this chapter, differs from binge eating because only the experience of LOC is required, with or without the consumption of unambiguously large amounts of food. At this time, prevalence estimates of binge eating are 2% to 40% in youths depending on age and characteristics (e.g., community vs. weight-loss treatment seeking) of the sample studied (Glasofer et al., 2006; Lamerz et al., 2005; Tanofsky-Kraff et al., 2004).

Binge eating disorder, however, is relatively uncommon in youths, with a rate of approximately 1% (Ackard, Fulkerson, & Neumark-Sztainer, 2007; Decaluwe & Braet, 2003). The current fourth text revision of the *Diagnostic and Statistical Manual of Mental Disorders* (American Psychiatric Association, 2000) requires the presence of objective binge eating at least twice a week, on average, for a duration of 6 months for a diagnosis of binge eating disorder (BED) to be made, thus excluding youths who report objective binge eating at a lower frequency or those who report recurrent subjective binge eating. It has been suggested that in the upcoming fifth edition of the *Diagnostic and Statistical Manual,* the frequency threshold for objective binge eating be lowered to once per week, but this change would still exclude individuals reporting subjective binge episodes. Low prevalence rates are likely related to stringent diagnostic criteria that exclude youths who report binge eating at a lower frequency than defined or who only endorse subjective binge eating, defined as LOC eating episodes that are not unambiguously large but are considered large by the respondent. Furthermore, the criteria for BED were developed for adults and thus may not include eating disturbances that may present differently in youth disorders (Marcus & Kalarchian, 2003; Tanofsky-Kraff, Marcus, Yanovski, & Yanovski, 2008).

Cross-sectional data have suggested that a clear relationship exists between binge eating episodes and overweight or obesity in childhood. Among young children, parent reports of a child's binge eating were correlated with the child's overweight status (Lamerz et al., 2005). In a large school-based study, an adolescent's self-report of binge eating in the past month was associated with higher body weight (Field, Colditz, & Peterson, 1997). In another school-based sample, overweight adolescents were more likely to report binge eating than their normal-weight peers (Neumark-Sztainer, Butler, & Palti, 1995). Similar findings have been reported in other adolescent school-based samples using survey methods (Ackard et al., 2003). Children and adolescents with binge eating also tend to have increased psychopathology (e.g., depressive symptoms and disordered eating attitudes) compared with children and adolescents who do not binge eat (Goossens, Braet, & Decaluwe, 2007; Goossens, Soenens, & Braet, 2009; Tanofsky-Kraff, 2008).

Longitudinal studies have shown that binge eating predicts weight gain among youths. Binge eating was associated with weight gain (Stice, Cameron, Killen, Hayward, & Taylor, 1999) and obesity onset (Stice, Presnell, & Spangler, 2002) over a 4-year period in a sample of community youths. In another large community study of youths ages 9 to 14, boys, but not girls, who reported binge eating gained significantly more weight than those who do not binge eat (Field et al., 2003). Among 6- to 12-year-old children who were overweight or who had a parent who was overweight, self-reported binge eating episodes predicted greater increases in body fat mass (Tanofsky-Kraff et al., 2006). Additionally, binge eating predicted depressive symptoms in a community sample of adolescents (Presnell, Stice, Seidel, & Madeley, 2009). However, depressive symptoms were also predictive of eating pathology, suggesting that depressive and binge eating symptomatology may reciprocally influence one another over time.

### *Loss of Control Eating*

LOC eating refers to a perception of eating without the ability to stop. LOC eating can occur with or without episodes of overeating. The notion that the experience of LOC is the most relevant component of a binge episode in comparison to the consumption of objectively large amounts of food is often adopted in studies with youths, likely because of the difficulty involved in making a size criterion determination for youths of different ages because physically developing boys and girls have vastly varying energy needs. For example, the consumption of an entire large pizza by a child or adolescent of any age would likely be considered unambiguously large. By contrast, five slices of pizza eaten by a growing adolescent might be less clear. Furthermore, in younger children, the size of eating episodes may be limited by parental controls, masking how much a child might have eaten given the opportunity.

The prevalence rates of LOC eating range from 4% to 45%, with higher estimates among overweight youths and when rates are self-reported versus assessed in structured interviews (Tanofsky-Kraff, 2008). Youths with LOC eating are more likely to be heavier and have greater fat mass than youths with no LOC episodes (Goossens et al., 2007; Shomaker et al., 2009). Children and adolescents with LOC eating also exhibit greater psychological symptoms, disordered eating cognitions and behaviors (Goossens et al., 2007; Morgan et al., 2002; Tanofsky-Kraff et al., 2004, 2008), and dysfunctional emotion regulation strategies (Czaja, Rief, & Hilbert, 2009) than their counterparts without LOC eating. Prospective data have shown that youths who report LOC eating gain more weight over time than their counterparts without LOC (Tanofsky-Kraff et al., 2009). Thus, accumulating evidence has suggested that the experience of loss of control is a critical aspect of binge eating in youths and may have more predictive and diagnostic validity in comparison to assessing full binge eating episodes that require both over-eating and the experience of LOC. Although both of these eating behaviors have been shown to cause distress in youths who report them, relatively few youths meet criteria for BED, suggesting that diagnostic criteria may need to be modified to better account for the importance of LOC. Furthermore, although it is clear that LOC eating and binge eating occur at greater rates in overweight and obese youths, these behaviors only occur in a subset of overweight and obese youths.

### Eating in Secret or Hiding Food

Eating in secret is an aberrant eating behavior that is included in the diagnostic features of BED. However, very little is known about the prevalence rates of eating in secret among overweight and obese youths. As with many of these behaviors, it may overlap with binge eating, LOC eating, and/or EAH. In a study examining prevalence rates of secretive eating in a sample of overweight adolescents, approximately one third of the sample endorsed at least one episode of secretive eating within the month before the survey (Knatz, Maginot, Story, Neumark-Sztainer, & Boutelle, 2011). Additionally, in another study, 23% of adolescent girls reported eating alone (Vervaet & Van Heeringen, 2000). Prospective data have suggested that eating in secret identifies those who will develop an eating disorder (ED) later on (Fairburn, Cooper, Doll, & Davies, 2005). However, additional data are required to understand the relationship between eating in secret, disordered eating, and overweight and obesity in youths.

## Eating in the Absence of Hunger

EAH was initially described in a longitudinal study of preschool children and their parents (Fisher & Birch, 1999). EAH is assessed using a behavioral paradigm in which children are fed a meal to satiety, after which hunger ratings are obtained to ensure fullness. After a short break, children are offered access to a variety of palatable snack foods in addition to toys and games for 10 minutes. Food consumption during the free-access period is measured. In this section, we describe findings related to EAH in children. EAH in adolescents is not well described in the literature, and more research is needed to understand how this behavior affects older children.

In a preschool study, girls were divided into high- and low-snack-intake groups (based on the free-access session) using a median split based on calories consumed (Fisher & Birch, 2002). In this study, EAH was relatively stable because 68% of girls in the high-intake group at age 5 were also in the high-intake group at age 7. EAH is considered a stable phenotypic behavior in young girls that is equivalent to disinhibited eating in adults (Fisher & Birch, 2002). This may also be true for male children; however, the research has focused on female children because of the higher rates of disinhibited eating and ED psychopathology in adult women compared with men. Several subsequent studies have examined EAH in overweight children and have demonstrated that children who are overweight or at higher risk of becoming overweight eat significantly more than normal-weight, lower risk children in the EAH paradigm (Faith et al., 2006; Fisher & Birch, 2002; Fisher et al., 2007; Francis & Birch, 2005; Moens & Braet, 2007; Shunk & Birch, 2004). In contrast to binge and LOC eating, EAH can occur with or without a cognitive understanding by the child of how much the child ate, and can occur with or without distress in the child (Wolkoff et al., 2011).

## Emotional Eating

*Emotional eating* refers to eating in response to a range of negative emotions, including coping with anxiety, depression, anger, and loneliness (Faith, Allison, & Geliebter, 1997). Emotional eating is relatively common in overweight youths. One study of 55 overweight children (ages 5–13) seeking weight loss treatment found that 63% endorsed the question "Do you ever eat because you feel bad, sad, bored, or any other mood?" (Shapiro et al., 2007). Emotional eating is also associated with LOC eating (Tanofsky-Kraff, 2008). In adolescents, emotional eating is associated with disturbed eating and symptoms of depression and anxiety (Van Strien, Engels, Van Leeuwe, & Snoek, 2005). Studies investigating the relationships between negative mood and LOC eating using laboratory feeding paradigms or ecological momentary assessment have produced mixed results. Some studies have shown that negative affect is associated with a greater likelihood of reporting LOC (Goldschmidt, Tanofsky-Kraff, & Wilfley,

2011), whereas other studies have not supported the relationship between negative mood and LOC (Hilbert et al. 2009; Hilbert, Tuschen-Caffier, & Czaja, 2010). Furthermore, laboratory studies evaluating the association between negative affect and EAH do not support the relationship between negative mood and EAH (Aranda, Swift, & Boutelle, 2011). Longitudinal data have suggested that negative affect predicts binge eating in youths (Stice & Agras, 1998). However, longitudinal, prospective data are needed to determine whether there is, indeed, a predictive relationship between emotional eating and excessive weight gain.

In summary, obesity and aberrant eating patterns in youths are common and are associated with negative physiological and psychological outcomes. Many of these concepts are interrelated and may in fact overlap because researchers are only beginning to uncover these behaviors in youths. For example, parents often report that children who exhibit EAH also engage in a lot of secretive eating. These behaviors may possibly be more appropriately construed as dimensions of early eating disturbances as opposed to discrete categories.

## Theoretical Conceptualization of Obesity and Aberrant Overeating Patterns

During the past few decades, the prevalence of individuals who are overweight and obese has increased substantially in developed societies. The cause of obesity, which is the consequence of an imbalance between energy intake and energy expenditure, is multifactorial, and it develops from the interaction between genotype and the environment. The emergence of this obesity epidemic has gone hand in hand with changes in the environment. Today's environment is considered "obesiogenic," providing increased opportunities for energy intake and decreased opportunity for energy expenditure. For example, children have greater access to unhealthy foods at school and at home, and physical activity has been replaced with sedentary activities such as the use of computers, video games, and other technology. Our understanding of how and why obesity occurs is incomplete; however, it involves the integration of social (e.g., socioeconomic status), behavioral (e.g., consumption of high-calorie foods), cultural (e.g., the overrepresentation of obesity in certain ethnicities and races), physiological (e.g., appetite regulation), metabolic (e.g., resting energy expenditure), and genetic (e.g., genetic dispositions toward obesity) factors (Grundy, 1998). However, ultimately, the treatments that have been developed are still behavioral in nature, focusing on finding ways of changing the energy balance by eating less and exercising more.

Several etiological theories exist regarding the development of aberrant eating patterns. Most of this work has been conducted with adults rather than children or adolescents. The first theory suggests that binge eating is related to escape from negative affect. Escape theory suggests that certain types of self-destructive behaviors, including binge eating, provide an escape from negative affect and painful self-awareness (Baumeister, 1990; Heatherton & Baumeister, 1991). The motivation to escape from self-awareness begins with a comparison of self against high standards or ideals, including expectations that the individual should have the ideal body. This comparison leads to awareness of shortcomings (i.e., not having the ideal body), which leads to negative affect such as anxiety or depression. These emotions evoke cognitive narrowing and ultimately disinhibition regarding overeating. Some support for this model has been reported in the literature (Blackburn, Johnston, Blampied, Popp, & Kallen, 2006). A recent meta-analysis found that high levels of negative affect preceded binge eating, and that further elevations in negative affect followed binge episodes (Haedt-Matt & Keel, 2011).

Another theory suggests that binge eating develops in response to rigid dietary restraint (e.g., limiting food intake; Polivy & Herman, 1985). A perceived lapse in restraint (e.g., eating something that was to be restricted) is interpreted as a failure in control, which leads to the abandonment of restraint and subsequent binge eating (Grilo & Shiffman, 1994). A few longitudinal studies have suggested that dietary restraint predicts the onset of binge eating in childhood and adolescence (Allen, Byrne, La Puma, McLean, & Davis, 2008; Field et al., 2008; Stice & Agras, 1998; Stice et al., 2002). Dieting alone appears to be an insufficient factor in explaining binge eating onset because most dieters never develop binge eating problems (e.g., Fairburn et al., 2005). Moreover, most children have reported initiating LOC eating before any dieting attempts (Tanofsky-Kraff et al., 2005).

Theories have also attempted to integrate both dietary restraint and negative affect in explaining the occurrence of binge eating. The Dual Pathway and Cognitive–Behavioral models are two such models. Although both posit that dietary restraint and negative affect are direct antecedents to binge eating, they differ in terms of the critical feature postulated to promote these precipitants. Although the Dual Pathway model holds body dissatisfaction as the central construct (Stice & Agras, 1998), the Cognitive–Behavioral model proposes that low self-esteem is the central construct that leads to binge eating. Both models have received some support in the pediatric literature (Decaluwe & Braet, 2005; Goossens, Braet, & Bosmans, 2010; Stice, 2001).

Finally, the Cue Reactivity model of binge eating, which is based on learning theory, posits that exposure to food cues elicits cravings, thereby enhancing the likelihood of binge eating (Jansen, 1998). The Cue Reactivity model of binge eating (Jansen, 1994, 1998) suggests that through Pavlovian conditioning, cues such as the sight, smell, and taste of food, as well as rituals for eating, environment in which eating occurs, and affective states and food-related cognitions can elicit physiological responses that are experienced as craving. It is possible that some individuals are more cue sensitive than others and the ability to self-regulate eating in response to food cues is weakened over time or in certain individuals. Research has shown that overweight people exhibit heightened responsiveness to food cues (Ferriday & Brunstrom, 2010; Tetley, Brunstrom, & Griffiths, 2009).

Exposure to the sight and smell of food increases reported hunger (Ferriday & Brunstrom, 2008; Nederkoorn, Smulders, & Jansen, 2000; Oakes & Slotterback, 2000) and initiates cephalic phase responses, including release of insulin, changes in salivation, heart rate, gastric activity, and blood pressure (Nederkoorn et al., 2000; Nederkoorn, Smulders, Havermans, & Jansen, 2004; Overduin, Jansen, & Eilkes, 1997). Enhanced cephalic phase responses are associated with perceived food cravings in adults (Nederkoorn et al., 2000) and with overeating in 8- to 12-year-old obese children (Jansen et al., 2003). One study showed that overweight children tend to be more responsive to food cues than their normal-weight peers (Aspen, Stein, & Wilfley, 2011), which may translate to overeating (Jansen et al., 2003). In sum, although long-term energy imbalance clearly leads to obesity, competing theories exist regarding the etiology of energy imbalance and overeating. Overeating may possibly occur as a result of negative affect, dietary restraint, a heightened responsivity to food and other signals of eating, or some combination of all of these factors. Much more research is needed to further evaluate this and the other models in youths.

# Treatment Approaches Targeting Weight Loss in Overweight and Obese Youths

On the basis of the theories we have described and the premise that long-term energy imbalances result in excess weight gain, several treatments have been developed to target weight loss and aberrant eating patterns in overweight and obese youths. In this section, we review two treatments for weight reduction in overweight and obese youths and provide a case example for behavioral weight loss for pediatric obesity, the current gold-standard treatment for weight loss in children. Last, we review a treatment for aberrant eating patterns that specifically targets binge eating and EAH. As behavioral specialists, counselors play a crucial role as the primary providers of these treatments in a variety of settings including schools, mental health agencies, and community agencies and organizations.

## Behavioral Weight Loss for Pediatric Obesity

Family-based behavioral treatment for weight loss is a family intervention to reduce weight in obese youths. It is delivered to both parents and children and combines nutrition education and exercise with behavior therapy techniques (Epstein, 1996). Behavioral weight loss is a conglomerate of several empirically supported strategies, including parents as active participants in treatment (Epstein, McCurley, Wing, & Valoski, 1990), providing exercise in addition to diet (Epstein, Wing, Penner, & Kress, 1985), providing mastery criteria for behavior change (Epstein, McKenzie, Valoski, Klein, & Wing, 1994), problem solving (Epstein, Paluch, Gordy, Saelens, & Ernst, 2000), and reducing sedentary behaviors (Epstein, Paluch, Gordy, & Dorn, 2000; Epstein, Valoski, Kalarchian, & McCurley, 1995). In addition, this treatment protocol includes separate parent and child groups and individual one-on-one meetings for goal setting and problem solving (Epstein, 1996). Changes in behavior are conceptualized and taught as lifestyle changes and healthy habit acquisition as opposed to a diet. The program encourages healthy weight loss behaviors, primarily enacted by parents so as to avoid resistance and excessive responsibility on the part of the child. Ten-year longitudinal data have shown that one third of children treated with this modality are no longer overweight in adulthood (Epstein, Valoski, Wing, & McCurley, 1990, 1994). Data have also suggested that children who participate in this program do not have an increase in ED symptoms (Brownell & Rodin, 1994; Epstein, Paluch, Saelens, Ernst, & Wilfley, 2001).

### Treatment Description

Behavioral weight loss typically consists of 20 sessions that take place over the course of a 6-month period. The first 16 sessions occur weekly, and the remaining 4 sessions occur biweekly. Sessions consist of hour-long separate parent and child groups that take place simultaneously. In addition to attending the group, each family participates in a family coaching session facilitated by a behavioral coach. The coaching session focuses on setting specific, tailored goals and monitoring and reviewing progress. Group sessions are differentiated by topic and include didactics, experiential learning, and goal setting for parents, whereas the focus in children's groups is on experiential learning and skills acquisition through the use of developmentally appropriate games and activities. Both coaching sessions and group sessions are typically provided by counselors and psychologists with some knowledge or expertise in the area of eating and weight issues. Behavioral weight loss treatments are generally sponsored by and held in medical settings including large hospital organizations and university medical schools. Schools and community agencies are also ideal locations at which to hold these treatments because they may be the most effective way to reach and target overweight and obese youths.

### Psychoeducation

Parental competence is achieved by providing education on dietary information and energy expenditure as they relate to energy balance. Families are taught that the primary inputs contributing to weight loss are caloric intake and physical activity. This principle is taught in the context of what is referred to as the "energy balance," where families learn that to lose weight, an individual must expend more energy than he or she takes in. Correspondingly, the goals of treatment are to increase physical activity and reduce caloric intake.

Families are provided with a child-friendly dietary classification system, referred to as the *traffic light diet*, in which foods are classified by color (red is stop, yellow is slow down, green is go) on the basis of energy density and sugar and fat content. For example, a bag of potato chips is considered a red food because of its high fat content, whereas air-popped popcorn is considered green because of its low fat and sugar content. The traffic light diet is intended to assist families in making food choices that are compatible with weight loss. In addition to learning to classify foods, families learn appropriate portion size, how to count calories, and caloric guidelines for both adults and children.

Additionally, families are taught to increase their physical activity and decrease sedentary activity. Increases in physical activity are achieved through planned physical activity (i.e., going for a run) or lifestyle activity (walking to school). Additionally, screen time is decreased outside of homework needs. Interventionists use the behavioral technique, *successive approximation,* to assist families to meet designated physical activity goals over the course of the first five weeks of treatment. Parents are shaped to a goal of 60 minutes per day, and children are shaped to a goal of 90 minutes per day.

### Behavior Modification Strategies

Parents learn a variety of behavior modification strategies to promote healthy behaviors in their children. In addition to learning behavioral strategies to be implemented at home, behavioral strategies are used within the context of treatment to facilitate weight loss and the promotion of healthy eating and activity habits.

*Self-monitoring.* All group members receive weekly self-monitoring booklets in which daily dietary intake and physical activity are recorded. Both parents and children complete these booklets, which are then reviewed with their behavioral coach. Families are instructed to keep track of caloric intake, number of foods from each color category, physical activity, and sedentary activity on a daily basis. As one of the primary predictors of weight loss, self-monitoring by participants is highly encouraged and time is spent identifying barriers and problem solving to increase the likelihood of successful monitoring.

*Goal setting.* To increase healthy behaviors such as physical activity and reduce unhealthy behaviors such as the consumption of red foods, behavioral coaches set goals with each family that are tracked and reviewed on a weekly basis. Goals are set for the following components of treatment: daily calorie consumption, minutes of physical activity, minutes of sedentary activity, number of red foods consumed, and number of fruits and vegetables consumed. Parents are responsible for keeping track of whether their child met his or her goals, and goals are reviewed in behavioral coaching sessions on a weekly basis.

*Positive reinforcement.* To promote healthy behaviors and motivate children, a behavioral reward system is used in which children earn points for engaging in healthy behaviors and losing weight. Parents are taught to implement the reward system and keep track of their child's progress on a weekly basis. Generally, children have small, medium, and large rewards that can be earned on the basis of the number of points that they have obtained. In addition to rewards, parents are also taught to practice praising behaviors in an effort to reinforce healthy behaviors.

*Stimulus control.* Parents are taught to limit stimuli that promote unhealthy behaviors by restructuring their home environments to reduce the availability of unhealthy foods and reduce the availability and visibility of healthy foods. Parents are advised to eliminate unhealthy foods from the home and increase the accessibility of healthy foods, such as fruits and vegetables. For example, one parent who did not feel comfortable throwing away red foods decided to store them on the highest shelf of her pantry. Every Sunday, she also began cutting up fruits and vegetables and storing them in single-size portions at eye level in her refrigerator so that her child would be more likely to grab these on returning home from school. (For a session-by-session example, please see Table 15.1.)

## Family-Based Treatment of Pediatric Obesity

Another treatment under development is family-based treatment of pediatric overweight and obesity (FBT–PO). FBT–PO is a specific adaptation of family-based treatment for adolescents with EDs (Eisler et al., 1997; Le Grange, Crosby, Rathouz, & Leventhal, 2007; Lock, Couturier, & Agras, 2006). Family-based treatment for EDs is a compelling intervention for youths who are obese because of its disease-based model, its explicit focus on blame reduction, and its focus on moving away from a child-directed personal responsibility paradigm and toward environmental change. Most important, it capitalizes on and strengthens parents' capacities to function as agents of change in health-related behaviors. Research has shown that most efficacious interventions include parental involvement to some degree (Jelalian & Saelens, 1999); however, there is no one-size-fits-all model of family treatment. Thus, FBT–PO modulates the quantity and quality of parental involvement on the basis of the child's developmental stage. In addition, although drawn from an ED intervention, FBT–PO recognizes that obesity is not a psychiatric condition. The level of parental control in the early stages of treatment for anorexia nervosa, for example, is more extreme and speaks to the psychologically driven reduced insight and judgment in the patient (see Chapter 17, this volume). In contrast, FBT–PO allows for more parent–child collaboration in health-related decision making, the level of which is determined not by severity of illness but by developmental stage. The changes to be made in the home are also broadly health promoting and are appropriate for all family members, including nonoverweight siblings. Families are provided with information on appropriate dietary intake and given recommendations on caloric intake and physical activity. Behavioral weight loss strategies such as self-monitoring are also used to assist with weight loss. The intervention is practical, but focuses primarily on restructuring parenting styles and family member coalitions so that implementation of changes is possible. Thus, FBT–PO is first and foremost a psychological family therapy intervention.

### Treatment Description

FBT–PO takes place over the course of a 24-week period during which families are seen for 16 visits. Treatment occurs in three phases during which the child or adolescent transitions to more developmentally

Table 15.1
**Example Treatment Session Outline for Behavioral Weight Loss**

| Session | Group Aims | Behavioral Coaching Aims |
|---|---|---|
| 1. Introduction | Session guidelines<br>Childhood obesity<br>  psychoeducation<br>Structure of program | Graph weight.<br>Review behavioral goals for<br>  treatment.<br>Introduce self-monitoring.<br>Introduce point system. |
| 2. Healthy eating | Traffic light plan<br>Calorie goals<br>Using the food reference<br>  guide | Graph and review weight<br>  change.<br>Provide feedback on self-<br>  monitoring.<br>Introduce nine behavioral<br>  goals. |
| 3. Motivation system<br>  and parenting skills | Positive parenting<br>Modeling<br>Reward system | Graph and review weight<br>  change.<br>Child begins to accrue<br>  points for meeting behav-<br>  ioral goals.<br>Continue providing feed-<br>  back on self-monitoring.<br>Points earned become con-<br>  tingent on weight loss.<br>Topic review |
| 4. Making your home<br>  environment healthy | Restructuring the home food<br>  environment | Graph and review weight<br>  change.<br>Review points earned.<br>Topic review |
| 5. Red and green<br>  physical activity | Define "red" and "green"<br>  activity.<br>Set activity goals.<br>Provide information on<br>  benefits of physical activity. | Graph and review weight<br>  change.<br>Review points earned.<br>Topic review |
| 6. Behavior chains | Antecedents and consequences<br>  of unhealthy eating behaviors<br>How to identify a behavior<br>  chain and break it | Graph and review weight<br>  change.<br>Review points earned.<br>Topic review |
| 7. Healthy shopping on<br>  a budget/choosing<br>  foods wisely | Cooking tips<br>Meal planning practice activity<br>Shopping wisely | Graph and review weight<br>  change.<br>Review points earned.<br>Topic review |
| 8. High-risk situations<br>  (parties, holidays,<br>  and vacations) | Holiday planning<br>Staying healthy during school<br>  breaks and vacation | Graph and review weight<br>  change.<br>Review points earned.<br>Topic review |

*(Continued)*

Table 15.1 *(Continued)*
## Example Treatment Session Outline for Behavioral Weight Loss

| Session | Group Aims | Behavioral Coaching Aims |
|---|---|---|
| 9. High-risk situations (school lunches, restaurants, and fast food) | Parenting strategies around restaurants and fast food Eating at restaurants | Graph and review weight change. Review points earned. Topic review |
| 10. Emotion or stress and eating | Link between emotions, stress, and eating Recognizing hunger cues Relaxation strategies | Graph and review weight change. Review points earned. Topic review |
| 11. Lifestyle activity | Brainstorming barriers and possible solutions Activity scheduling | Graph and review weight change. Review points earned. Topic review |
| 12. Problem solving | Preplanning Problem-solving skills (SOLVE/STEPS) | Graph and review weight change. Review points earned. Topic review |
| 13. Relapse prevention | Defining a lapse and relapse Constructing a relapse prevention plan | Graph and review weight change. Review points earned. Topic review |
| 14. Staying motivated with more physical activity | Ways to make physical activity more consistent Helping children be more active Activity planning and scheduling | Graph and review weight change. Review points earned. Topic review |
| 15. Review and planning healthy habits | Review key concepts Making healthy behaviors a habit | Graph and review weight change. Review points earned. Topic review |
| 16. Teasing and body image | Body image and self-esteem Media and body image Teasing and strategies to use with children | Graph and review weight change. Review points earned. Topic review |
| 17. Open forum | Open discussion | Graph and review weight change. Review points earned. Topic review |
| 18. Responsibility | Discussing responsibilities of parents and children | Graph and review weight change. Review points earned. Topic review |

*(Continued)*

Table 15.1 *(Continued)*
**Example Treatment Session Outline for Behavioral Weight Loss**

| Session | Group Aims | Behavioral Coaching Aims |
|---|---|---|
| 19. Ordering right in the real world | Mock restaurant and practicing ordering | Graph and review weight change. |
| | How to make healthy decisions at restaurants | Review points earned. Topic review |
| 20. Graduation | Parent discussion | Graph and review weight change. |
| | Graduation ceremony | Review points earned. |
| | | Review discharge and relapse plan. |

*Note.* SOLVE = stop, outline, list, view, execute/evaluate; STEPS = stop, think, evaluate, perform, self-praise/self-assessment.

appropriate autonomy over eating and physical activity and session focus shifts from weight-related issues to broader issues related to child and adolescent development. The first eight sessions occur weekly, with the remainder of the sessions occurring biweekly. Weight is obtained at the start of each session and is graphed so it can be visually presented to the family during the session. The proportion of session time and responsibility over therapeutic tasks such as self-monitoring is dependent on the child's age, as noted earlier.

*Phase 1.* During the first phase of treatment, the primary objectives are to position the family to support the child and to relay information and behavioral strategies necessary to achieve weight loss, including self-monitoring and information pertaining to dietary intake and physical activity and common causes of obesity (genetic and environmental). Several strategies are used to position the family appropriately so that they are able to support their child in weight loss, including the reduction of blame and the promotion of self-efficacy and parental unity. To attain collaboration from the family, the therapist frames the child's weight status as a crisis that requires immediate mobilization.

A family meal is conducted at the second session to assess parental feeding styles and dietary intake. Families are given direct feedback by the therapist on ways in which the meal could be improved, both nutritionally and in terms of parenting styles used to promote healthy behaviors. Families remain in Phase 1 of treatment until children are no longer gaining weight (optimally losing weight), self-monitoring is being completed, and parents feel confident in their ability to implement family-level, health-promoting changes in the home.

*Phases 2 and 3.* Phase 2 of treatment is intended to transfer the appropriate amount of independence and control around eating and physical activity behaviors back to the child. Autonomy is dependent on age and is negotiated with parents; however, during this phase, parental involvement should decrease and children's self-efficacy in managing health-promoting behaviors is promoted. During Phase 2, education about dietary intake and physical activity continues, with particular focus placed on barriers encountered by the family. Phase 3 focuses on developing a maintenance plan that the family can follow to ensure continuity of health-promoting behaviors. Other issues that affect weight should also be addressed in these two phases, including binge eating, psychosocial factors related to weight and appearance, and lapses and relapses.

## Treatments Targeting Aberrant Eating Patterns in Youths

Of note, interpersonal therapy for the prevention of excessive weight gain (Tanofsky-Kraff, 2008; Wilfley et al., 2007) focuses on improving LOC and emotional overeating by improving interpersonal functioning and relationships. We do not discuss the model in this chapter; please see Chapter 14 on interpersonal therapy for a review.

The regulation of cues (ROC) treatment program, developed by Boutelle and colleagues (see Boutelle & Tanofsky-Kraff, 2010, for review), targets obese children and adolescents who engage in EAH. The ROC program is based on Schachter's (1971; Schachter & Rodin, 1974) externality theory of obesity, which states that obese people are more reactive to external cues to eat (time, presence and quality of food, situational effects, etc.) and less sensitive to internal hunger and satiety signals than their lean counterparts. The two main tenets of Schachter's theory, increased sensitivity to food cues and decreased sensitivity to internal cues, are used to target specific mechanisms to reduce overeating when not biologically hungry. Another treatment that focuses on reducing eating in the absence of hunger is the regulation of cues (ROC) treatment program. ROC, developed by Boutelle et al. (2011), represents an integration of multiple strategies in an effort to target overeating in a comprehensive manner. ROC integrates the Children's Appetite Awareness Training Program to improve awareness of hunger and satiety cues with cue-exposure treatment to improve self-regulation in response to food cues. The Children's Appetite Awareness Training Program is aimed at enhancing awareness of hunger and fullness signals and at teaching children to use these signals to guide decisions about eating (Craighead & Allen, 1996). ROC integrates the Children's Appetite Awareness Training Program treatment with a cue-responsivity program (Boutelle et al., 2011). The cue-responsivity program, initially developed as a stand-alone treatment, teaches children to resist eating in response to cravings that are elicited by external food cues. External food cues are prompts in the environment that are associated with eating such as the presence of food, food characteristics (sight, smell, or taste of food), and certain environments or cognitive and affective states associated with eating. Examples of external cues that may elicit a craving include the smell of popcorn at the movie theater or the presence of brownies at a party.

In addition to these strategies, ROC also includes psychoeducation about common reasons for overeating, skills training, and behavioral strategies borrowed from behavioral weight loss treatments.

ROC is delivered in 12 weekly group sessions that require the attendance of both the overweight child and at least one parent. ROC has been successfully conducted with both children and adolescents, ranging from age 8 to age 16. This treatment is designed for the subset of overweight and obese youths who engage in aberrant eating behavior, such as those described earlier in the chapter. Parents and children receive separate group sessions so that information can be delivered to the children in a developmentally appropriate manner. Similar to the children's group, parents receive psychoeducation and skills acquisition training; however, parent groups are also intended to promote positive parenting and incorporate the delivery and practice of parenting skills. The first five sessions focus on appetite awareness training, and the last seven sessions focus on reducing responsivity to external cues and combating cravings. Each parent and child session introduces a common reason for engaging in EAH and a corresponding skill. Common reasons for EAH are introduced as "tricky hungers" in an effort to teach parents and children to differentiate between cravings and physiological hunger. Each session begins with an experiential exercise targeting appetite awareness (Sessions 1–5) and cue responsivity (Sessions 6–12). Apart from the experiential exercises, parent sessions are predominantly didactic. Conversely, child sessions are intended to be experiential, with the majority of group time devoted to practicing the skills taught. The three main components of the ROC treatment program are outlined next.

*Appetite awareness training.* Appetite awareness training is taught and practiced over the first five sessions. Children and parents are introduced to a scale referred to as the *hunger meter* that describes physical and cognitive signs and symptoms at varying levels of hunger and fullness. The hunger meter is a 5-point Likert scale ranging from *starving* (1) to *stuffed* (5) and is intended to assist group members in identifying varying degrees of hunger and satiety. Group members are then instructed on guidelines relating to eating and restraining based on the hunger meter scale. For example, group members are taught to avoid the extremes of the scale by eating every 2 to 3 hours. The scale is then used during eating episodes as a self-monitoring tool. Group members are introduced to the hunger meter in the first session and begin actively monitoring levels of hunger and fullness using the scale during the second group session. Parents and children bring meals to group during these sessions and practice hunger monitoring in session, as well as for all meals eaten outside of session. To facilitate this, parents and children are given monitoring booklets on a weekly basis that require that ratings be conducted before, during, and after meals for three meals and two snacks per day.

*Cue exposure.* Cue exposure is conducted with the intent of training parents and children to be less responsive to the presence of palatable foods, and it is practiced in the next seven sessions. Cue exposure treatment trains individuals to avoid eating palatable foods in their presence when they are not physically hungry. Exposure treatment is conducted to unpair the association between the sight, smell, and taste of food and the consumption of food. Group members learn the basic tenets of Pavlovian conditioning, and exposures are conducted with the intent of teaching participants to tolerate high cravings in the presence of craved foods until the cravings deteriorate. Both parents and children construct a list of seven highly craved foods and bring these foods to session to use them for the exposures. Children are introduced to the "Volcravo," a craving volcano that is used to measure the intensity of cravings. The 5-point Volcravo rating scale is used to measure cravings during exposures. Exposures occur during the last 15 to 20 minutes of parent and child sessions, during which group members rate the intensity of their cravings over 30-second intervals. During exposures, participants are instructed to hold, smell, and taste the food. Group leaders then use various prompts to ensure that group members continue to focus on the food while they continue to monitor changes in craving levels without eating any more of the food. Children and parents are then instructed to practice at-home exposures, incorporating other external cues, such as triggering environments, social contexts, or both during which periods of EAH usually occur.

*Skills training.* Children and parents learn common reasons for overeating and EAH, presented as "tricky hungers," over the course of the 12-week period. A corresponding skill is used and practiced with each tricky hunger. Skills taught include distraction, activity substitution, relaxation, mindful eating, media awareness, and cost–benefit analyses. Children and parents are asked to keep track of tricky hungers experienced and skills used in their self-monitoring booklets with the intention of enhancing their awareness of reasons for overeating.

Over the course of treatment, parents learn behavioral management techniques intended to promote healthy behaviors in their children. Behavioral strategies that are taught to parents in ROC include improved communication through daily meetings, positive reinforcement of healthy behaviors, behavior modeling to promote healthy behaviors, and controlling and eliminating unhealthy food stimuli to minimize responsiveness to external cues. In addition, parents are encouraged to construct a motivation system that rewards their children for engaging in program-related behaviors (such as self-monitoring). (For a session-by-session outline, see Table 15.2.)

## Case Example: Behavioral Weight Loss

Lanie was a 10-year-old overweight girl who attended behavioral weight loss treatment with her mother, Pamela. On beginning treatment, Lanie weighed 103 pounds, placing her at the 94th percentile of weight for kids

Table 15.2
**Example Treatment Session Outline for Regulation of Cues**

| Session | Tricky Hunger | Coping Skill | In Vivo Experience |
|---|---|---|---|
| 1. Introduction | NA | NA | |
| 2. Hunger monitoring, parenting skills | Ignoring fullness | Prescribed eating, move to reduce tricky hungers | Hunger monitoring during meal |
| 3. Cue-related eating | Getting too hungry | Stimulus control | Hunger monitoring during meal |
| 4. Emotional eating | Feeding your moods | Physiological skills | Hunger monitoring during meal |
| 5. Biological risks for overeating, mindless eating | Eating too fast | Delay, mindfulness | Hunger monitoring during meal |
| 6. Cravings, Pavlovian conditioning | Eating because it's there | Activity substitution, imagery | Cue exposure |
| 7. Media education | Media and marketing tricks | Home exposures | Cue exposure |
| 8. Abstinence violation effect, making decisions | Who cares response | Decision balance, superhero | Cue exposure |
| 9. Boredom, redirecting behavior | Eating for entertainment | Distraction | Cue exposure |
| 10. Assertiveness training | Eating because other people are | Assertiveness, cruising | Cue exposure |
| 11. Dichotomous thinking | Food rules | Thought skills | Hunger and cue exposure |
| 12. Planning for high-risk situations, relapse prevention, goals | NA | NA | Hunger and cue exposure |
| 13. Review, relapse prevention | NA | NA | Hunger and cue exposure |
| 14. Next steps | NA | NA | Graduation buffet practice |

*Note.* NA = not applicable.
Source is Kerri Boutelle, PhD. Results of initial study were published in Boutelle et al. (2011).

her age and height. Lanie and Pamela attended 19 of the 20 treatment sessions, where they participated in separate parent and child groups, in addition to a joint behavioral coaching session. At the start of treatment, Pamela described her family as a "Costco family," admitting that she did not cook and that most of their family meals consisted of frozen foods bought at Costco, including frozen chicken nuggets and frozen pizza bites.

In the first parent session, Pamela openly discussed her concern over Lanie's weight and admitted that their family's diet was not the healthiest, citing time and financial constraints as the major reasons. She worried that eating healthy required financial means that her family did not have but described herself as very motivated to change her family's eating habits in an effort to help Lanie avoid health problems in the future. She reported that Lanie did not appear concerned with her weight, probably because of her young age, but expressed concern over Lanie's self-esteem being affected by her weight once she hit her teenage years. A typical day of eating for Lanie included a bowl of sugary cereal for breakfast, a peanut butter and jelly sandwich with chips and juice for lunch, and chicken nuggets with French fries for dinner.

Lanie and Pamela were asked to keep food logs after the first session of treatment in log books, referred to as *habit books*, that were distributed to the groups. At Session 2, they were introduced to the traffic light diet and met with their individual coach to review their habit books. Lanie and Pamela quickly discovered that most of their diet consisted of red foods, foods that are high in fat and sugar and that are considered to contribute to weight gain. They initially expressed disappointment and discouragement in realizing that the foods that they ate regularly were considered to be unhealthy. Lanie sadly turned to her mom and asked, "Does this mean I never get to have chicken nuggets again?" Their coach, Jack, explained that the goal of the program was not to completely eliminate red foods, but to cut down on them and find healthier alternatives, referred to in the program as *green foods*. They then discussed ways to prepare chicken so that it would not be considered a red food. Together, Jack, Pamela, and Lanie explored food options and found other ways of preparing chicken that were healthier. Pamela and Lanie agreed to try baking chicken over the next week. During this session, Jack also set goals for both Pamela and Lanie that would help them lose weight. Lanie and Pamela were asked to work toward reducing the number of red foods eaten per week, increase the number of fruits and vegetables to five servings per day, and record everything in their habit books. A daily calorie goal of between 1,000 and 1,200 was also set for Lanie to lose a half a pound or more on a weekly basis.

Over the next 5 weeks, Lanie lost 5.2 pounds. Throughout this time, Pamela and Lanie worked really hard to get in the habit of recording their food intake in their habit books and replacing red foods with green foods so that it was easier for Lanie to meet her calorie goal of 1,000 to 1,200 per day. Lanie and Pamela attributed much of their success to revamping the foods in their house. Lanie talked excitedly about how much she enjoyed the "red food detective game," a game assigned to the family after Session 3, where they were tasked to identify and label all red foods in their homes with red-dot stickers. During this game, Pamela and Lanie discovered that their breakfast cereal was a red food, as were many of the snack foods in their home. Pamela explained that instead of removing all of the red foods from her home as recommended, she decided to store them on the highest shelves in her pantry. She and Lanie then came to an agreement that Lanie would be allowed to have a serving of the red-food cereal once per week and that they would make sure to work it into their weekly red-food limit.

Pamela explained how she felt unable to throw away the boxes of cereal and other red foods because of their cost, but proudly explained how she had found an alternative way to make the red foods less available, by making them inaccessible and placing limits on Lanie's consumption of these foods. Lanie's daily intake changed drastically over this time, with a typical day now including a low-sugar cereal with skim milk for breakfast, a lean turkey sandwich with mustard and lettuce, applesauce (no sugar added) and fresh fruit for lunch, a chicken and vegetable stir-fry for dinner, and fresh fruits, carrot sticks, and sliced cucumbers for snacks.

Throughout this time, Pamela and Lanie also worked on making sure that they were writing all foods in their habit books. Because Lanie was bringing the same lunch to school on a daily basis, Pamela and Lanie recorded her lunch in her habit book the night before. They also developed a new habit of writing down her dinner foods while they were still seated at the table, right after they finished eating. Lanie and Pamela found it difficult to complete their habit books at first but began to use old habit books to copy information about their foods because they were mainly eating similar meals from week to week. By the 5th week, Lanie's habit book was being completed thoroughly, with Pamela's help.

To keep Lanie motivated, Pamela was keeping track of how well Lanie was meeting her goals (described earlier), and Lanie earned points on a weekly basis for each goal that she met. Lanie's first reward was a trip to Build-a-Bear with her mother and sister after earning 15 points for meeting her goals. In addition to providing rewards, Pamela was also learning to praise Lanie for positive behaviors that she was engaging in, such as making healthy choices when they dined out.

Pamela was also responsible for filling out her own habit book and meeting a daily calorie goal, in addition to keeping track of green and red foods. Pamela attributed much of Lanie's success to the fact that she and the rest of her family were participating in the changes with Lanie. During their daily meetings, where they would review habit books and Pamela would help Lanie calculate calories and portion sizes of the food she had eaten, Lanie and Pamela would also plan dinners and other meals for themselves and the rest of the family. Pamela felt that involving the whole family avoided Lanie's feeling singled out and provided Lanie with a sense of self-efficacy in being responsible for teaching her siblings about the program.

In summary, by the end of the first 5 weeks, Lanie and her mother had mastered recording foods and related information (calories, portion sizes, number of red and green foods) in their habit books, restructured their home food environment to eliminate unhealthy (red) foods and increase healthy (green) foods, implemented a reward system to motivate Lanie, and were consistently meeting the program goals.

Between Sessions 5 and 10, Lanie lost another 3 pounds. With more time in the program, Lanie and Pamela worked with their behavioral coach, Jack, to identify problem scenarios and come up with solutions to avoid Lanie's getting off track. During this time, the parent group was focused on problem-solving skills and identifying patterns of unhealthy behaviors. Pamela and Lanie noticed that the days on which Lanie did not meet her calorie goal tended to be days on which the family had an event that resulted in eating outside of the home. Birthday parties were common events for Lanie that often led to exceeding her calorie goal. Lanie and Pamela began to discuss these events during their daily meeting time and learned to plan ahead to prepare for these high-risk situations. For example, when Lanie was invited to a birthday party, the two of them would sit down the week before and discuss the food that would likely be at the party. Pamela would then ask Lanie what she thought she would want to have at the party. For one birthday party that they planned on attending, they guessed that there would be pizza, chips, soft drinks, and cake. Together, they decided she would have one slice of pizza and a small slice of cake. They then calculated the number of red-food servings that this meal would be and made sure to allot properly throughout the week so that Lanie could eat these foods without exceeding her weekly red-food goal. On the day of the event, they calculated the number of calories of this meal and ate accordingly before the party to ensure that Lanie would not go over her daily calorie goal. They also devised a "secret sign" that Pamela and Lanie could use to signal each other if they saw each other not following the program. Sure enough, Lanie was able to attend the party, eat the foods that she had planned, and still lost weight at the following session because of their effective planning.

By the end of Session 10, Pamela and Lanie described feeling as though the changes that they had been making were becoming habitual and no longer felt effortful. They began to struggle with continuing to complete their habit books, reporting that they were aware of what they were eating throughout the day without having to write it down. Jack encouraged them to continue to complete their habit books by reviewing them weekly and problem-solving on barriers to recording. He also pointed out that Lanie's rate of weight loss had slowed considerably, paralleling their not completing their habit books. Between Sessions 13 and 16, Lanie's weight was more or less steady. In seeing this, they were able to make a commitment to continue to complete them for the remainder of the treatment program. Between Sessions 10 and 20, Lanie lost 2.8 more pounds, resulting in a total of 11 pounds lost over the course of treatment. By the end of the treatment program, her weight was 92 pounds, placing her at the 84th percentile of weight for kids her height and age. Lanie's weight loss moved her from being on the cusp of the over-weight–obese line to a weight that was within the normal weight range for children her height and age. In addition to Lanie's weight loss, Pamela also lost 15.8 pounds over the course of treatment.

# Chapter Highlights

- Obesity and aberrant eating behaviors are associated with physiological and psychological risks.

- Binge eating, LOC eating, emotional eating, eating in secret, and EAH should be assessed by clinicians.
- Models of aberrant eating behaviors can assist in developing treatment targets.
- Behavioral weight loss for youths is an evidence-based treatment that has been shown to be effective in reducing weight in overweight and obese children.
- Family-based treatment of pediatric obesity is a treatment targeting weight loss that is currently under development.
- Two treatments for aberrant eating behaviors in youths, interpersonal therapy for the prevention of weight gain (reviewed in Chapter 14) and the regulation of cues intervention, are evidence-based treatments that specifically target aberrant eating behaviors in overweight and obese youths and may ultimately lead to weight loss.

## Recommended Resources

Boutelle, K. N., Zucker, N. L., Peterson, C. B., Rydell, S. A., Cafri, G., & Harnack, L. (2011). Two novel treatments to reduce overeating in overweight children: A randomized controlled trial. *Journal of Consulting and Clinical Psychology, 79,* 759–771.

Epstein, L. H., Myers, M. D., Raynor, H. A., & Saelens, B. E. (1998). Treatment of pediatric obesity. *Pediatrics, 101,* 554–570.

Epstein, L. H., Valoski, A., Wing, R. R., & McCurley, J. (1990). Ten-year follow-up of behavioral, family-based treatment for obese children. *JAMA, 264,* 2519–2523.

Tanofsky-Kraff, M., Marcus, M. D., Yanovski, S. Z., & Yanovski, J. A. (2008). Loss of control eating disorder in children age 12 years and younger: Proposed research criteria. *Eating Behaviors, 9,* 360–365.

Wilfley, D. E., Tibbs, T. L., Van Buren, D. J., Reach, K. P., Walker, M. S., & Epstein, L. H. (2007). Lifestyle interventions in the treatment of childhood overweight: A meta-analytic review of randomized controlled trials. *Health Psychology, 26,* 521–532.

## References

Ackard, D. M., Fulkerson, J. A., & Neumark-Sztainer, D. (2007) Prevalence and utility of *DSM–IV* eating disorder diagnostic criteria among youth. *International Journal of Eating Disorders, 40,* 409–417.

Ackard, D. M., Neumark-Sztainer, D., Story, M., & Perry, C. (2003). Overeating among adolescents: Prevalence and associations with weight-related characteristics and psychological health. *Pediatrics, 111,* 67–74.

Allen, K. L., Byrne, S. M., La Puma, M., McLean, N., & Davis, E. A. (2008) The onset and course of binge eating in 8- to 13-year-old healthy weight, overweight and obese children. *Eating Behaviors, 9,* 438–446.

American Psychiatric Association. (2000). *Diagnostic and statistical manual of mental disorders* (4th ed., text rev.) Washington, DC: Author.

Aranda, B., Swift, E., & Boutelle, K. N. (2011, April). *Disentangling cues to eating in the absence of hunger: Mood versus hedonic associations.* Paper presented at the Academy of Eating Disorders.

Aspen, V. A., Stein, R. I., & Wilfley, D. E. (2011). An exploration of salivation patterns in normal weight and obese children. *Appetite, 58,* 539–542.

Baumeister, R. F. (1990). Suicide as escape from self. *Psychological Review, 97,* 90–113.

Berkowitz, R., Stunkard, A. J., & Stallings, V. A. (1993). Binge-eating disorder in obese adolescent girls. *Annals of the New York Academy of Science, 699,* 200–206.

Blackburn, S., Johnston, L., Blampied, N., Popp, D., & Kallen, R. (2006). An application of escape theory to binge eating. *European Eating Disorders Review, 14,* 23–31.

Boutelle, K. N., & Tanofsky-Kraff, M. (2010). Treatments targeting aberrant eating patterns in overweight youth. In D. Le Grange & J. Lock (Eds.), *Eating disorders in children and adolescents: A clinical handbook.* New York, NY: Guilford Press.

Boutelle, K. N., Zucker, N. L., Peterson, C. B., Rydell, S. A., Cafri, G., & Harnack, L. (2011). Two novel treatments to reduce overeating in overweight children: A randomized controlled trial. *Journal of Consulting and Clinical Psychology, 79,* 759–771.

Brownell, K. D., & Rodin, J. (1994). The dieting maelstrom: Is it possible and advisable to lose weight? *American Psychologist, 49,* 781–791.

Craighead, L. W., & Allen, H. N. (1996). Appetite awareness training: A cognitive behavioral intervention for binge eating. *Cognitive and Behavioral Practice, 2,* 249–270.

Czaja, J., Rief, W., & Hilbert, A. (2009). Emotion regulation and binge eating in children. *International Journal of Eating Disorders, 42,* 356–362.

Decaluwe, V., & Braet, C. (2003) Prevalence of binge-eating disorder in obese children and adolescents seeking weight-loss treatment. *International Journal of Obesity and Related Metabolic Disorders, 27,* 404–409.

Decaluwe, V., & Braet, C. (2005). The cognitive behavioural model for eating disorders: A direct evaluation in children and adolescents with obesity. *Eating Behaviors, 6,* 211–220.

Dietz, W. H. (1998). Health consequences of obesity in youth: Childhood predictors of adult disease. *Pediatrics, 101,* 518–525.

Eddy, K. T., Tanofsky-Kraff, M., Thompson-Brenner, H., Herzog, D. B., Brown, T. A., & Ludwig, D. S. (2007) Eating disorder pathology among overweight treatment-seeking youth: Clinical correlates and cross-sectional risk modeling. *Behavior Research and Therapy, 45,* 2360–2371.

Eisler, I., Dare, C., Russell, G. F. M., Szmukler, G., Le Grange, D., & Dodge, E. (1997). Family and individual therapy in anorexia nervosa: A 5-year follow-up. *Archives of General Psychiatry, 54,* 1025–1030.

Elliott, C. A., Tanofsky-Kraff, M., Shomaker, L. B., Columbo, K. M., Wolkoff, L. E., Ranzenhofer, L. M., & Yanovski, J. A. (2010). An examination of the interpersonal model of loss of control eating in children and adolescents. *Behaviour Research and Therapy, 48,* 424–428.

Epstein, L. H. (1996). Family-based behavioural intervention for obese children. *International Journal of Obesity and Related Metabolic Disorders, 20,* 14–21.

Epstein, L. H., McCurley, J., Wing, R. R., & Valoski, A. (1990). Five-year follow-up of family-based behavioral treatments for childhood obesity. *Journal of Consulting and Clinical Psychology, 58,* 661–664.

Epstein, L. H., McKenzie, S. J., Valoski, A., Klein, K. R., & Wing, R. R. (1994). Effects of mastery criteria and contingent reinforcement for family-based child weight control. *Addictive Behaviors, 19,* 135–145.

Epstein, L. H., Paluch, R. A., Gordy, C. C., & Dorn, J. (2000). Decreasing sedentary behaviors in treating pediatric obesity. *Archives of Pediatrics & Adolescent Medicine, 154,* 220–226.

Epstein, L. H., Paluch, R. A., Gordy, C. C., Saelens, B. E., & Ernst, M. M. (2000). Problem solving in the treatment of childhood obesity. *Journal of Consulting and Clinical Psychology, 68,* 717–721.

Epstein, L. H., Paluch, R. A., Saelens, B. E., Ernst, M. M., & Wilfley, D. E. (2001). Changes in eating disorder symptoms with pediatric obesity treatment. *Journal of Pediatrics, 139,* 58–65.

Epstein, L. H., Valoski, A. M., Kalarchian, M. A., & McCurley, J. (1995). Do children lose and maintain weight easier than adults: A comparison of child and parent weight changes from six months to ten years. *Obesity Research, 3,* 411–417.

Epstein, L. H., Valoski, A., Wing, R. R., & McCurley, J. (1990). Ten-year follow-up of behavioral, family-based treatment for obese children. *JAMA, 264,* 2519–2523.

Epstein, L.H., Valoski, A., Wing, R.R., & McCurley, J. (1994). Ten-year outcomes of behavioral family-based treatment for childhood obesity. *Health Psychology, 13,* 373–383.

Epstein, L. H., Wing, R. R., Penner, B. C., & Kress, M. J. (1985). Effect of diet and controlled exercise on weight loss in obese children. *Journal of Pediatrics, 107,* 358–361.

Fairburn, C. G., Cooper, Z., Doll, H. A., & Davies, B. A. (2005). Identifying dieters who will develop an eating disorder: A prospective, population-based study. *American Journal of Psychiatry, 162,* 2249–2255.

Faith, M. S., Allison, D. B., & Geliebter, A. (1997). Emotional eating and obesity: Theoretical considerations and practical recommendations. In S. Dalton (Ed.), *Obesity and weight control: The health professional's guide to understanding and treatment* (pp. 439–465). Gaithersburg, MD: Aspen.

Faith, M. S., Berkowitz, R. I., Stallings, V. A., Kerns, J., Storey, M., & Stunkard, A. J. (2006). Eating in the absence of hunger: A genetic marker for childhood obesity in prepubertal boys? *Obesity, 14,* 131–138.

Ferriday, D., & Brunstrom, J. M. (2008). How does food-cue exposure lead to larger meal sizes? *British Journal of Nutrition, 100,* 1325–1332.

Ferriday, D., & Brunstrom, J. M. (2010). "I just can't help myself": Effects of food-cue exposure in overweight and lean individuals. *International Journal of Obesity, 35,* 142–149. doi:10.1038/ijo.2010.117

Field, A. E., Austin, S. B., Taylor, C. B., Malspeis, S., Rosner, B., Rockett, H. R., . . . Colditz, G. A. (2003). Relation between dieting and weight change among preadolescents and adolescents. *Pediatrics, 112,* 900–906.

Field, A. E., Colditz, G. A., & Peterson, K. E. (1997). Racial/ethnic and gender differences in concern with weight and in bulimic behaviors among adolescents. *Obesity Research, 5,* 447–454.

Field, A. E., Javaras, K. M., Aneja, P., Kitos, N., Camargo, C. A., Jr., Taylor, C. B., & Laird, N. M. (2008). Family, peer, and media predictors of becoming eating disordered. *Archives of Pediatrics & Adolescent Medicine, 162,* 574–579.

Fisher, J. O., & Birch, L. L. (1999). Restricting access to foods and children's eating. *Appetite, 32,* 405–419.

Fisher, J. O., & Birch, L. L. (2002). Eating in the absence of hunger and overweight in girls from 5 to 7 y of age. *American Journal of Clinical Nutrition, 76,* 226–231.

Fisher, J. O., Cai, G., Jaramillo, S. J., Cole, S. A., Comuzzie, A. G., & Butte, N. F. (2007). Heritability of hyperphagic eating behavior and appetite-related hormones among Hispanic children. *Obesity, 15,* 1484–1495.

Francis, L. A., & Birch, L. L. (2005). Maternal influences on daughters' restrained eating behavior. *Health Psychology, 24,* 548–554.

Glasofer, D. R., Tanofsky-Kraff, M., Eddy, K. T., Yanovski, S. Z., Theim, K. R., Mirch, M. C., . . . Yanovski, J. A. (2006). Binge eating in overweight treatment-seeking adolescents. *Journal of Pediatric Psychology, 32,* 95–105.

Goldschmidt, A. B., Aspen, V. P., Sinton, M. M., Tanofsky-Kraff, M., & Wilfley, D. E. (2008). Disordered eating attitudes and behaviors in overweight youth. *Obesity, 16,* 257–264.

Goldschmidt, A. B., Tanofsky-Kraff, M., & Wilfley, D. E. (2011). A laboratory-based study of mood and binge eating behavior in overweight children. *Eating Behaviors, 21,* 37–43.

Goossens, L., Braet, C., & Bosmans, G. (2010). Relations of dietary restraint and depressive symptomatology to loss of control over eating in overweight youngsters. *European Child & Adolescent Psychiatry, 19,* 587–96.

Goossens, L., Braet, C., Bosmans, G., & Decaluwe, V. (2011). Loss of control over eating in pre-adolescent youth: The role of attachment and self-esteem. *Eating Behaviors, 12,* 289–295.

Goossens, L., Braet, C., & Decaluwe, V. (2007). Loss of control over eating in obese youngsters. *Behavior Research and Therapy, 45,* 1–9.

Goossens, L., Soenens, B., & Braet, C. (2009). Prevalence and characteristics of binge eating in an adolescent community sample. *Journal of Clinical Child & Adolescent Psychology, 38,* 342–353.

Grilo, C. M., & Shiffman, S. (1994) Longitudinal investigation of the abstinence violation effect in binge eaters. *Journal of Consulting and Clinical Psychology, 62,* 611–619.

Grundy, S. M. (1998). Multifactorial causation of obesity: Implications for prevention. *American Journal of Clinical Nutrition, 67*(3, Suppl.), 563S–572S.

Haedt-Matt, A. A., & Keel, P. K. (2011). Revisiting the affect regulation model of binge eating: A meta-analysis of studies using ecological momentary assessment. *Psychological Bulletin, 137,* 660–681.

Hartmann, A. S., Czaja, J., Rief, W., & Hilbert, A. (2010) Personality and psychopathology in children with and without loss of control over eating. *Comprehensive Psychiatry, 51,* 572–578.

Heatherton, T. F., & Baumeister, R. F. (1991). Binge eating as escape from self-awareness. *Psychological Bulletin, 110,* 86–108.

Hilbert, A., Rief, W., Tuschen-Caffier, B., de Zwaan, M., & Czaja, J. (2009). Loss of control eating and psychological maintenance in children: An ecological momentary assessment study. *Behavior Research and Therapy, 47,* 26–33.

Hilbert, A., Tuschen-Caffier, B., & Czaja, J. (2010). Eating behavior and familial interactions of children with loss of control eating: A laboratory test meal study. *American Journal of Clinical Nutrition, 91,* 510–518.

Isnard, P., Michel, G., Frelut, M. L., Vila, G., Falissard, B., Naja, W., . . . Mouren-Simeoni, M. C. (2003). Binge eating and psychopathology in severely obese adolescents. *International Journal of Eating Disorders, 34,* 235–243.

Jackson, T. D., Grilo, C. M., & Masheb, R. M. (2000). Teasing history, onset of obesity, current eating disorder psychopathology, body dissatisfaction, and psychological functioning in binge eating disorder. *Obesity Research, 8,* 451–458.

Jansen, A. (1994). The learned nature of binge eating. In C. Legg & D. A. Booth (Eds.), *Appetite: Neural and behavioral bases* (pp. 193–211). London, England: Oxford University Press.

Jansen, A. (1998). A learning model of binge eating: Cue reactivity and cue exposure. *Behavior Research and Therapy, 36,* 257–272.

Jansen, A., Theunissen, N., Slechten, K., Nederkoorn, C., Boon, B., Mulkens, S., & Roefs, A. (2003). Overweight children overeat after exposure to food cues. *Eating Behaviors, 4,* 197–209.

Jelalian, E., & Saelens, B. E. (1999). Empirically supported treatments in pediatric psychology: Pediatric obesity. *Journal of Pediatric Psychology, 24,* 223–248.

Johnson, W. G., Grieve, F. G., Adams, C. D., & Sandy, J. (1999). Measuring binge eating in adolescents: Adolescent and parent versions of the questionnaire of eating and weight patterns. *International Journal of Eating Disorders, 26,* 301–314.

Key, T. J., Schatzkin, A., Willett, W. C., Allen, N. E., Spencer, E. A., & Travis, R. C. (2004). Diet, nutrition and the prevention of cancer. *Public Health Nutrition, 7,* 187–200.

Knatz, S., Maginot, T., Story, M., Neumark-Sztainer, D., & Boutelle, K. (2011). Prevalence rates and psychological predictors of secretive eating in overweight and obese adolescents. *Childhood Obesity, 7,* 30–35. doi:10.1089/chi.2011.0515.Knatz.

Lamerz, A., Kuepper-Nybelen, J., Bruning, N., Wehle, C., Trost-Brinkhues, G., Brenner, H., . . . Herpertz-Dahlmann, B. (2005). Prevalence of obesity, binge eating, and night eating in a cross-sectional field survey of 6-year-old children and their parents in a German urban population. *Journal of Child Psychology and Psychiatry, 46,* 385–93.

Le Grange, D., Crosby, R. D., Rathouz, P. J., & Leventhal, B. L. (2007). A randomized controlled comparison of family-based treatment and supportive psychotherapy for adolescent bulimia nervosa. *Archives of General Psychiatry, 64,* 1049–1056.

Lock, J., Couturier, J., & Agras, W. S. (2006). Comparison of long-term outcomes in adolescents with anorexia nervosa treated with family therapy. *Journal of the American Academy of Child & Adolescent Psychiatry, 45,* 666–672.

Marcus, M. D., & Kalarchian, M. A. (2003). Binge eating in children and adolescents. *International Journal of Eating Disorders, 34*(Suppl.), S47–S57.

Micic, D. (2001). Obesity in children and adolescents—A new epidemic? Consequences in adult life. *Journal of Pediatric Endocrinology and Metabolism, 14,* 1345–1352.

Moens, E., & Braet, C. (2007). Predictors of disinhibited eating in children with and without overweight. *Behavior Research and Therapy, 45,* 1357–1368.

Morgan, C., Yanovski, S., Nguyen, T., McDuffie, J., Sebring, N., Jorge, M., . . . Yanovski, J. A. (2002). Loss of control over eating, adiposity, and psychopathology in overweight children. *International Journal of Eating Disorders, 31,* 430–441.

Must, A., Spadano, J., Coakley, E. H., Field, A. E., Colditz, G., & Dietz, W. H. (1999). The disease burden associated with overweight and obesity. *JAMA, 282,* 1523–1529.

Nederkoorn, C., Smulders, F., Havermans, R., & Jansen, A. (2004). Exposure to binge food in bulimia nervosa: Finger pulse amplitude as a potential measure of urge to eat and predictor of food intake. *Appetite, 42,* 125–130.

Nederkoorn, C., Smulders, F. T., & Jansen, A. (2000). Cephalic phase responses, craving and food intake in normal subjects. *Appetite, 35,* 45–55.

Neumark-Sztainer, D., Butler, R., & Palti, H. (1995). Eating disturbances among adolescent girls: Evaluation of a school-based primary prevention program. *Journal of Nutrition Education, 27,* 24–31.

Oakes, M., & Slotterback, C. (2000). Self-reported measures of appetite in relation to verbal cues about many foods. *Current Psychology, 19,* 137–142.

Ogden, C. L., Carroll, M. D., Kit, B. K., & Flegal, K. M. (2012). Prevalence of obesity in United States, 2009–2010. *National Center for Health Statistics Brief, 82,* 1–7.

Overduin, J., Jansen, A., & Eilkes, H. (1997). Cue reactivity to food- and body-related stimuli in restrained and unrestrained eaters. *Addictive Behaviors, 22,* 395–404.

Polivy, J., & Herman, C. P. (1985). Dieting and binging: A causal analysis. *American Psychologist, 40,* 193–201.

Presnell, K., Stice, E., Seidel, A., & Madeley, M. C. (2009). Depression and eating pathology: Prospective reciprocal relations in adolescents. *Clinical Psychology & Psychotherapy, 16,* 357–365.

Schachter, S. (1971). Some extraordinary facts about obese humans and rats. *American Psychologist, 26,* 129–144.

Schachter, S., & Rodin, J. (1974). *Obese humans and rats.* Washington, DC: Erlbaum/Halsted.

Shapiro, J. R., Woolson, S. L., Hamer, R. M., Kalarchian, M. A., Marcus, M. D., & Bulik, C. M. (2007). Evaluating binge eating disorder in children: Development of the Children's Binge Eating Disorder Scale (C-BEDS). *International Journal of Eating Disorders, 40,* 82–89.

Shomaker, L. B., Tanofsky-Kraff, M., Elliott, C., Wolkoff, L. E., Columbo, K. M., Ranzenhofer, L. M., . . . Yanovski, J. A. (2009). Salience of loss of control for pediatric binge episodes: Does size really matter? *International Journal of Eating Disorders, 43,* 707–716.

Shunk, J. A., & Birch, L. L. (2004). Girls at risk for overweight at age 5 are at risk for dietary restraint, disinhibited overeating, weight concerns, and greater weight gain from 5 to 9 years. *Journal of the American Dietetic Association, 104,* 1120–1126.

Stice, E. (2001). A prospective test of the dual-pathway model of bulimic pathology: Mediating effects of dieting and negative affect. *Journal of Abnormal Psychology, 110,* 124–135.

Stice, E., & Agras, W. S. (1998). Predicting onset and cessation bulimic behaviors during adolescence: A longitudinal grouping analysis. *Behavior Therapy, 29,* 257–276.

Stice, E., Cameron, R. P., Killen, J. D., Hayward, C., & Taylor, C. B. (1999). Naturalistic weight-reduction efforts prospectively predict growth in relative weight and onset of obesity among female adolescents. *Journal of Consulting and Clinical Psychology, 67,* 967–974.

Stice, E., Presnell, K., & Spangler, D. (2002). Risk factors for binge eating onset in adolescent girls: A 2-year prospective investigation. *Health Psychology, 21,* 131–138.

Strauss, R. S. (2000). Childhood obesity and self-esteem. *Pediatrics, 105,* 15.

Strauss, R. S., & Pollack, H. A. (2003). Social marginalization of overweight children. *Archives of Pediatrics & Adolescent Medicine, 157,* 746–752.

Tanofsky-Kraff, M. (2008). Binge eating among children and adolescents. In E. Jelalian & R. Steele (Eds.), *Handbook of child and adolescent obesity* (pp. 41–57). New York, NY: Springer.

Tanofsky-Kraff, M., Cohen, M. L., Yanovski, S. Z., Cox, C., Theim, K. R., Keil, M., . . . Yanovski, J. A. (2006). A prospective study of psychological predictors of body fat gain among children at high risk for adult obesity. *Pediatrics, 117,* 1203–1209.

Tanofsky-Kraff, M., Faden, D., Yanovski, S. Z., Wilfley, D. E., & Yanovski, J. A. (2005). The perceived onset of dieting and loss of control eating behaviors in overweight children. *International Journal of Eating Dis-*

orders, *38*, 112–22.

Tanofsky-Kraff, M., Marcus, M. D., Yanovski, S. Z., & Yanovski, J. A. (2008). Loss of control eating disorder in children age 12 years and younger: Proposed research criteria. *Eating Behaviors, 9,* 360–365.

Tanofsky-Kraff, M., Yanovski, S. Z., Schvey, N. A., Olsen, C. H., Gustafson, J., & Yanovski, J. A. (2009). A prospective study of loss of control eating for body weight gain in children at high risk for adult obesity. *International Journal of Eating Disorders, 42,* 26–30.

Tanofsky-Kraff, M., Yanovski, S. Z., Wilfley, D. E., Marmarosh, C., Morgan, C. M., & Yanovski, J. A. (2004). Eating-disordered behaviors, body fat, and psychopathology in overweight and normal-weight children. *Journal of Consulting and Clinical Psychology, 72,* 53–61.

Tetley A., Brunstrom J., & Griffiths P. (2009). Individual differences in food-cue reactivity: The role of BMI and everyday portion-size selections. *Appetite, 52,* 614–620.

Thompson, J. K., Coovert, M. D., & Stormer, S. M. (1999). Body image, social comparison, and eating disturbance: A covariance structure modeling investigation. *International Journal of Eating Disorders, 26,* 43–51.

Trasande, L., Liu, Y., Fryer, G., & Weitzman, M. (2009). Effects of childhood obesity on hospital care and costs, 1999–2005. *Health Affairs, 28,* 751–760.

Van Strien, T., Engels, R. C., Van Leeuwe, J., & Snoek, H. M. (2005). The Stice model of overeating: Tests in clinical and non-clinical samples. *Appetite, 45,* 205–213.

Vervaet, M., & Van Heeringen, C. (2000). Eating style and weight concerns in young females. *Eating Disorders, 8,* 233–240.

Wang, G., & Dietz, W. H. (2002). Economic burden of obesity in youths aged 6 to 17 years: 1979–1999. *Pediatrics, 109,* 81–81.

Wilfley, D., Berkowitz, R., Goebel-Fabbri, A., Hirst, K., Ievers-Landis, C., Lipman, T. H., . . . Van Buren, D. (2011). Binge eating, mood, and quality of life in youth with type 2 diabetes: Baseline data from the TODAY study. *Diabetes Care, 34,* 858–860.

Wilfley, D. E., Tibbs, T. L., Van Buren, D. J., Reach, K. P., Walker, M. S., & Epstein, L. H. (2007). Lifestyle interventions in the treatment of childhood overweight: A meta-analytic review of randomized controlled trials. *Health Psychology, 26,* 521–532.

Wolkoff, L. E., Tanofsky-Kraff, M., Shomaker, L. B., Kozlosky, M., Columbo, K. M., Elliott, C. A., . . . Yanovski, J. A. (2011). Self-reported vs. actual energy intake in youth with and without loss of control eating. *Eating Behaviors, 12,* 15–20.

## Chapter 16

# Dialectical Behavior Therapy for Clients With Complex and Multidiagnostic Eating Disorder Presentations

*Anita Federici and Lucene Wisniewski*

There is a great deal of interest in and discussion about how to improve treatment for clients with complex and multidiagnostic eating disorders (EDs) and, specifically, how dialectical behavior therapy (DBT) might be applied. In the past decade, numerous book chapters and articles have been published on the topic (see review by Bankoff, Karpel, Forbes, & Pantalone, 2012; Safer, Telch, & Chen, 2009). Most of the literature describes treatment adaptations (specifically 20 weeks of DBT skills training) for individuals with bulimia nervosa (Safer, Telch, & Agras, 2001) and binge eating disorder (Safer, Robinson, & Jo, 2010; Telch, Agras, & Linehan, 2001) who present with low or moderate illness severity. Thus, therapists treating clients with primary bulimia nervosa and binge eating disorder (e.g., those with moderate illness severity and little or no diagnostic comorbidity) are directed to these resources.

The treatment of clients with complex EDs and multiple problems is, however, more complicated. The literature to date has recommended more comprehensive treatment models for clients with chronic anorexia nervosa and for clients with multiple problem behaviors (Ben-Porath, Wisniewski, & Warren, 2009; Chen, Mathews, Allan, Kuo, & Linehan, 2008; Kröger et al., 2010; Palmer et al., 2003). Detailed descriptions outlining the rationale and use of DBT for complex clients with comorbid Axis I and II disorders have previously been published (Fox, Federici, & Power, 2012; Wisniewski, Bhatnagar, & Warren, 2009; Wisniewski & Kelly, 2003; Wisniewski, Safer, & Chen, 2007). Thus, in this chapter we expand on several key foundational concepts described in the literature in an effort

375

to provide further guidance to clinicians working with multidiagnostic and complex ED presentations. After a brief review of the affect regulation model and the rationale for using DBT with this population, we focus the bulk of the chapter on the therapeutic stance, ways to prioritize multiple problem behaviors, strategies to increase commitment, and methods to manage therapy-interfering behaviors.

# Dialectical Behavior Therapy for Complex Eating Disorder Presentations: Rationale and Overview

DBT is a comprehensive treatment intervention that is celebrated for its success in treating suicidal and self-injurious behaviors in a population once considered treatment resistant (e.g., individuals with borderline personality disorder; Linehan, 1993a). The past decade alone has witnessed the rapid growth and application of DBT to a wide variety of mental disorders. Randomized trials have shown that DBT is associated with fewer hospital admissions, lower rates of substance abuse and angry outbursts, increased client commitment to therapy, fewer dropouts, and decreased therapist burnout (see reviews by Lynch, Trost, Salsman, & Linehan, 2006; Robins & Chapman, 2004). Applied in its standard format, DBT involves a 1-year commitment to weekly individual therapy, group skills training, telephone skills coaching, and a therapist consultation team (Linehan, 1993a, 1993b). DBT uses a combination of behavioral principles, cognitive modification techniques, Eastern meditative practices, and acceptance-based strategies, with the aim of helping clients eliminate impulsive and self-destructive behaviors while building a life worth living (Harned, Banawan, & Lynch, 2006).

## Affect Regulation Model and Biosocial Theory

DBT is based on an affect regulation model. From this perspective, problematic and self-destructive behaviors (e.g., self-injury, food restriction, vomiting) are primarily caused by deficits in one's ability to adaptively regulate emotion (Harned et al., 2006; Linehan, 1993a). Individuals with emotion regulation deficits typically have difficulty experiencing or tolerating emotions, accurately identifying various feeling states, and adaptively communicating their emotional needs. Without the ability or skills to regulate emotions in a reliable and consistent manner, emotionally sensitive individuals often feel unstable and unsure of their needs and often have difficulty in relationships. Thus, symptoms become a way of reducing emotional distress (Chapman, Gratz, & Brown, 2006). Individuals with EDs consistently report that symptoms provide relief from emotions that are perceived as threatening or overwhelming or that exceed existing coping abilities (Haynos & Fruzzetti, 2011; Heatherton & Baumeister, 1991). Symptoms such as binge eating and purging have been described as coping strategies, physical escapes, and ways of withdrawing from emotional pain and discomfort (Cockell, Zaitsoff, & Geller, 2004). Similarly, food restriction and excessive exercise often subdue intense emotions by providing a sense of numbness, control, or self-soothing or by their ability to generate positive feelings (Overton, Selway, Strongman, & Houston, 2005).

Linehan (1993a) proposed that emotion regulation deficits are the result of two interconnected systems: (a) a biological vulnerability to emotions and (b) chronically invalidating environments. According to this theory, some individuals are naturally (or biologically) more sensitive to their emotions from birth. Their genetic temperaments are such that they tend to have a low emotional threshold, respond to situations with greater emotional intensity, and take longer to return to baseline once activated. Clinicians who work in the ED field are well acquainted with the pervasiveness of emotion regulation deficits in their clients. Studies have shown that individuals with EDs have difficulty accurately recognizing and labeling emotional states in themselves and others (Bydlowski et al., 2005), have greater difficulty accepting their emotions, and report greater affect dysregulation than control groups (Svaldi, Griepenstroh, Tuschen-Caffler, & Ehring, 2012).

A biological emotional sensitivity alone, however, may not be predictive of problem behavior. The risks increase when an emotionally sensitive person is repeatedly exposed to an invalidating environment (Linehan, 1993a). Invalidating environments communicate subtly or overtly that an individual's feelings and internal experiences are in some way incorrect, unacceptable, or otherwise inappropriate. Instead of providing nurturance for and tolerance of individual differences, such environments dismiss, punish, or otherwise fail to accept the experiences or needs of the individual. Over time, some individuals cope by dismissing or judging their own emotions, doubting their internal feelings and gut reactions, and ultimately never learning self-acceptance or ways to adaptively manage their emotions and needs.

## Treatment Description and Overview

The treatment and interventions described in this chapter are based on the empirical literature reviewed in the preceding section as well as more than 10 years of our program development and clinical practice. We initially applied the standard outpatient DBT model (e.g., once-weekly individual DBT plus skills training and telephone coaching) with this population; however, our experiences indicate that once-weekly therapy is not sufficient to achieve symptom interruption and more sustainable behavior change for these particular clients. It is very difficult for even the most skilled clinician to effectively treat a client with a chronic and multidiagnostic ED presentation alone in outpatient practice. Additionally, we have observed that applying the standard DBT model, which does not include empirically supported ED interventions (e.g., weight monitoring, food exposures, meal planning), often results in little or no change to core ED symptoms. Our experience to date has suggested that treatment for this unique population requires the following components: (a) a more concentrated treatment dose (i.e., more than once-weekly individual therapy to start) that includes a treatment team, consisting of individual therapy, skills group training, nutrition, psychiatry, and medicine; (b) attention to motivational issues; (c) daily goal setting and accountability; (d) targeting of behaviors that interfere with treatment delivery; (e) meal planning, food exposure, and weight and medical monitoring; and (f) comprehensive skills training, particularly in the area of emotion regulation.

With these goals in mind, we have developed an innovative and intensive outpatient treatment model that blends the standard DBT model with empirically supported ED interventions (e.g., psychoeducation, meal planning and preparation, in vivo food exposures, monitoring of weight and medical stability, and cognitive modification of maladaptive ED-related thoughts). For a full description of the program, please see Federici, Wisniewski, and Ben-Porath (2012). In brief, most of the program is delivered in a group format and includes two DBT skills training groups per week. Consistent with the DBT model, skills groups begin with a mindfulness exercise, followed by homework review, teaching of new skills, and establishing new homework assignments with attention to potential obstacles to skill practice. Clients are also required to attend weekly individual DBT therapy, as well as to attend weekly appointments with the staff dietician and team psychiatrist. All clients have access to, and are expected to use, telephone skills coaching. All therapists attend a weekly consultation team meeting. The core intensive outpatient program runs Monday through Friday from 8:00 a.m. to 11:00 a.m. Clients who require a higher level of care because of symptom severity may attend our extended day treatment hours from 11:00 a.m. to 2:00 p.m. to have access to greater meal support and skills training. Clients are expected to limit the amount of time in day treatment to decrease dependency on treatment and encourage the development of activities beyond the treatment setting.

Our program is designed for clients who have not responded adequately to standard ED treatments such as cognitive–behavioral therapy–based day treatment, inpatient treatment, or residential programming. Given the empirical support for standard ED programming and given the experimental nature of our current treatment, clients who have never tried traditional, empirically supported ED treatments are referred to such programs first. In addition, clients must meet one or more of the following criteria: (a) presenting with a comorbid Axis I or Axis II disorder, (b) struggling with pervasive emotion dysregulation, or (c) demonstrating significant therapy-interfering behaviors that typically disrupt standard ED interventions. In many cases, clients who present with severe medical instability or dangerously low body weight may be referred to inpatient treatment or hospitalization for refeeding or medical stabilization before entry into our program. Such cases are based on a clinical team decision, given that many of our patients have had countless inpatient treatments only to lose the weight that was gained during hospitalization soon after discharge.

# Selected Strategies for Clients With Complex and Multidiagnostic Eating Disorder Presentations

In this section, we describe four key DBT interventions and their application to patients with EDs who also present with multiple problem behaviors. Using case examples and scripted dialogues, we review (a) therapist stance and patient assumptions, (b) facilitation of client commitment to treatment, (c) prioritization of multiple problem behaviors, and (d) implementation of contingency management strategies. Although these four interventions are foundational, we want to highlight that they are only a part of the full DBT treatment approach that we use in our treatment program. The full treatment involves the use of validation, structural, stylistic, and additional change strategies that can be found in Linehan's (1993a) original text as well as Koerner's (2012) more recent publication.

## *Therapist Stance and Assumptions About Patients*

Whether a counselor is working at a higher level of care or in an outpatient setting, the therapeutic stance in DBT is foundational and essential to successful treatment delivery. In DBT, individual therapists (and the entire treatment team) make a commitment to practice a nonjudgmental, dialectical stance in their practice. They also accept the DBT assumptions about clients, therapy, and therapists (Table 16.1) and use them to guide their clinical decisions (Koerner, 2012; Linehan, 1993a). Using these assumptions can be challenging when working with clients who display such behaviors as purging three times per day, water loading to artificially increase weight before being weighed, and maintaining a dangerously low body weight. Therapists may feel anxious about the client's physical health and frustrated at a perceived lack of behavioral change. Their initial response might be to label the client's behaviors as manipulative or as proof that she or he is unmotivated. Similarly, therapists might communicate disapproval nonverbally (e.g., a look of frustration, short or curt answers). Instead, from a DBT perspective, discussing these behaviors would be important, including therapists' reactions to them, in a matter-of-fact manner free of judgment and assumptions. A nonjudgmental position moves away from labeling experiences, emotions, thoughts, and behaviors as good or bad. Instead, everything simply is as it is. Maintaining a nonjudgmental stance models adaptive behavior for the client, lessens emotion dysregulation (on the part of both client and therapist), and helps to maintain a strong working alliance. The therapist's nonjudgmental response to even the most egregious behaviors will be quite different from how people typically respond to the client, which serves to decrease polarization and increase collaboration and openness on the part of the client.

Additionally, all members of the DBT team agree to adopt a dialectical worldview. To do so means to accept that no one person has a lock on the

Table 16.1
### Dialectical Behavior Therapy (DBT) Assumptions About Clients, Therapy, and Therapists

Assumptions about clients
- Clients are doing the best they can.
- Clients want to improve.
- Clients cannot fail in DBT.
- The lives of suicidal clients (and those with multidiagnostic eating disorder presentations) are unbearable as they are currently being lived.
- Clients must learn new behaviors in all relevant contexts.
- Clients may not have caused all of their own problems, but they have to resolve them anyway.
- Clients need to do better, try harder, or be more motivated to change.

Assumptions about therapy and therapists
- The most caring thing therapists can do is to help clients change.
- Clarity, precision, and compassion are of the utmost importance in the conduct of DBT.
- The relationship between therapists and clients is a real relationship between equals.
- Therapists can fail to apply the treatment effectively. Even when applied effectively, DBT can fail to achieve the desired outcome.
- Therapists who treat individuals with pervasive emotion dysregulation need support.

*Note.* From *Doing Dialectical Behavior Therapy: A Practical Guide* (p. 22), by K. Koerner, 2012, New York, NY: Guilford Press. Copyright 2012 by the Guilford Press. Reprinted with permission.

absolute truth. Instead, the team agrees to accept that multiple opinions, experiences, and truths can coexist. In DBT, rather than getting stuck when the team is polarized, the team works to celebrate differences in opinion and recognize them as opportunities to find new solutions. For instance, a skills group leader may state in a team meeting that she or he is feeling frustrated by a client's lack of progress and poor attendance in skills group. The dietician might report feeling similarly burnt out by the same client's argumentative style during meals. The individual therapist, however, might argue that the client has been working very hard to get to treatment on time, has reduced the overall number of absences over the past month, and has made progress in other domains such as weight gain and reduced self-injury. From a dialectical stance, the question is not about who is right and who is wrong; rather, the question is what is valid about each person's perspective and how does the team develop a treatment plan that includes all valid points. The same tensions arise quite frequently with clients. A client may want to live and want to die at the same time. Another client can hold the desire to start a family alongside her wish to starve herself to death. Although the urge might be to challenge one thought as maladaptive, a dialectical position acknowledges the validity in both points of view and seeks to find a synthesis. Change (whether on a team or with a client), therefore, occurs as the result of the synthesis between opposing forces.

Finally, those working within the DBT framework also agree to adopt a consultation-to-the-client approach. DBT strongly emphasizes teaching clients to take greater responsibility for their actions and their lives, which can be an especially difficult position for therapists to take when working with multidiagnostic clients who present with severe ED symptoms (e.g., low body weight, medical instability) and other life-threatening behaviors (e.g., recurrent self-injurious behavior). A therapist's initial urge, especially a therapist who subscribes to the medical model, might be to coordinate treatment, talk to the family, communicate the client's needs to other team members, and problem solve on behalf of the client. These practices are common in many inpatient hospital settings. In the consultation-to-the-client approach, however, therapists do not speak for or act on behalf of their clients; instead, clients are encouraged to take primary responsibility for themselves and adopt a more proactive stance. Although circumstances may certainly call for treatment providers to advocate for their clients (such as when the client's life is in imminent danger and he or she is not willing to contract for safety or use skills), it is essential that therapists not treat clients as fragile or incapable of acting skillfully. Our approach, rather than solving clients' problems, calls for therapists to help clients learn new ways of managing their life circumstances. This approach might mean only speaking with the family or other treatment providers with the client in the room, having the client call the dietician during a session to schedule an appointment, or role playing with the client on how the client can get his or her needs met with other team members.

### Getting a Commitment

Before treatment can begin, pretreatment issues need to be addressed. To begin intensive treatment, the client and therapist must agree on treatment goals (e.g., a commitment to change, a commitment to initial therapy goals) and on the nature of the treatment (e.g., eliminating life-threatening behavior, engaging in food exposures, attendance rules). This phase of treatment is essential and especially important for clients who have a history of multiple, unsuccessful treatment attempts because of ongoing therapy-interfering behaviors, severe emotional dysregulation, or other Axis I or II pathology. Often, and in spite of the treatment history, when clients with severe ED symptoms present to a treatment setting, the urge is to quickly admit them into the program. The urge makes sense. Sitting across from a client who is visibly emaciated and who may be medically unstable is frightening. The therapist may feel pressure from family members or other health care providers to begin treatment immediately. It is, however, important to recognize that in DBT, the commitment or pretreatment phase is active treatment. Moreover, our experience has been that rushing clients with multidiagnostic ED presentations into treatment often backfires. Without agreement on treatment goals and how therapy-interfering behaviors will be managed, the client is likely to re-create past treatment experiences, staff are likely to feel frustrated and burnt out, and the likelihood of premature termination or lack of progress is increased. In our clinic, we have observed that taking time to work on commitment and resisting the urge to rush these particular clients into treatment leads to greater therapy collaboration and less therapy-interfering behavior.

In our program, clients must be willing to commit to three nonnegotiable criteria. The first is a willingness to eliminate life-threatening behaviors, including suicidal and self-injurious acts as well as ED symptoms that are imminently life threatening. Given that treatment is based on building a life worth living, therapy cannot proceed if a client is not willing to make this commitment. Second, clients must be willing to work on reducing ED behaviors. Although this sounds obvious, many clients we have treated are more interested in reducing self-injury or mood problems and less motivated to gain weight or stop excessive exercising. It is important to help the client understand that building a life worth living and a life with less dysregulation while also engaging in disordered eating behaviors will be difficult, if not impossible. Finally, clients must be willing to participate in the program for a minimum of 6 months. We have found that making sustainable symptom change in this patient population using shorter treatment (e.g., 3 months) is difficult. We have also observed that making an explicit agreement to participate in treatment enrollment for a specified period of time helps to keep clients connected longer. During this phase, the therapist weaves in information about treatment (e.g., the biosocial theory, how weight and meal plans are managed, contingency management for therapy-interfering behaviors, the consultation-to-the-client approach). Intensive therapy does not begin unless the client and therapist can agree on initial treatment goals and the process of change.

Although great emphasis is placed on what the client needs to do to work with the therapist, highlighting that treatment is a partnership and a collaborative effort is important. The therapist also makes specific commitments to the client. For example, the therapist agrees to attend all sessions on time, to be prepared, to offer off-hours skills coaching by telephone, to seek regular consultation to ensure the provision of adherent and effective treatment, and to treat the client with respect. It is important to highlight the things to which both client and therapist will both be agreeing should they decide to work together.

### Key Points in Facilitating Client Commitment

1. Have a strong working knowledge of how to use the DBT commitment strategies. Linehan (1993a) identified seven core commitment strategies designed to increase the client's motivation to engage in treatment. Although reviewing each technique in detail is beyond the scope of this chapter, the reader is directed to review Linehan's (1993a) original writing and Koerner's (2012) expertly written descriptions of the topic.

2. Meet the client where she or he is as opposed to trying to get the client to meet the therapist's wants or needs. For example, instead of pointing out to the client all the behaviors and things that are problematic and in need of change, the therapist can identify what the client is willing to acknowledge as problematic. For example, at a first session, a client may not be particularly motivated to attend treatment but may be interested in finding a way to stop her parents from insisting that she work on her recovery.

3. Emphasize that the goal is to build a life worth living, in contrast to emphasizing that the goals are strictly ED related. It is easy for clients and therapists to focus exclusively on the details of symptom interruption. Although it is true that one must reduce or eliminate self-destructive and impulsive behaviors to have a life worth living, the therapist must help clients understand that they are committing to something much bigger than symptom change. Getting a strong commitment to build a less chaotic, more independent, and possibly more satisfying life helps clients to see the bigger picture. Once the client buys into the model of engaging in treatment to build a life worth living, discussions can then focus on how to do it (e.g., increasing weight, decreasing self-injury).

4. Commitment strategies are designed for use throughout treatment. For clients with multiple problem behaviors, the desire and willingness to change will wax and wane over time. It is important to be able to use a variety of commitment strategies flexibly over time to keep clients engaged and motivated to work on their treatment and life goals.

### Getting in Control: Treatment Targets

The treatment of an ED is complicated on its own. When clients present with additional diagnoses and problem behaviors, therapists can quickly feel overwhelmed by the sheer number of therapy targets. In this section, we describe how DBT facilitates organization, order, and progress when multiple problem behaviors need to be addressed, as in the following case example.

#### Case Example

Daniele would often show up at the clinic for her individual therapy appointments quite early. Because she had been a client at the center before, she was familiar to most staff members and many current clients. Daniele liked to spend time talking with the front desk staff, hugging people she knew when they walked by, or listening to her iPod in the waiting room. In an early session, Daniele wore big sunglasses and a hoodie and was very interested in talking with the therapist about the therapist's background and personal interests. She did not want to discuss self-harming behaviors, was not interested in gaining weight (in spite of her current body mass index of 16.5), and did not agree with the doctor who told her she was hypokalemic (e.g., had a dangerously low potassium level). Her half-completed diary card indicated that she had high urges for suicide and that she had vomited every day over the past week. Daniele's parents had left the therapist a voice message stating that they were concerned about their daughter's ability to continue her job as a nanny because they had noticed increased self-injury as well as problems with concentration. As Daniele drops into the chair across from the therapist, she swings her legs over the arm of the chair and says that she needs to rest because she is hung over from drinking last night.

### Structuring the Session

Trying to determine how to structure a 50-minute session with a client such as Daniele is typically overwhelming and confusing for practitioners. Without guiding principles, sessions often get off track, and life-threatening behaviors may or may not be addressed. As are clients, clinicians are doing the best they can given their level of training and theoretical knowledge; however, that might mean that a clinician with expertise in substance abuse might choose to focus on the previous night's drinking episode. Another therapist with expertise in EDs may focus on the restriction and vomiting, and another clinician with experience in family systems therapy might target the phone call from Daniele's parents.

DBT provides a road map for clinicians working with clients such as Daniele. The DBT treatment hierarchy prioritizes multiple problem behaviors and offers a framework for both the client and the therapist to follow as they navigate treatment together. In DBT, any behavior that could lead to the death of the client must be targeted in session. Such Target 1 behaviors include suicidal and self-injurious behaviors (e.g., cutting, burning, scratching) as well as ED symptoms that could imminently lead to death (e.g., ipecac abuse in a low-weight bradycardic client or purging behaviors in a client with electrolyte imbalances). A larger discussion about where specific ED symptoms fall on the treatment hierarchy can be found elsewhere (Wisniewski et al., 2007). In Linehan's (1993a) formulation, therapy cannot continue if the client is dead; thus, any behavior that could cause death must be addressed. A common experience is that the client may not agree with the therapist that a particular behavior is life threatening. In the preceding case example, Daniele believed that her low potassium was a chronic condition that was not concerning. Other clients may argue that scratching behaviors are not imminently life threatening. "I didn't scratch that hard" or "I wasn't planning to kill myself" are common assertions. The vignette presented later highlights ways one might manage such statements.

After life-threatening acts, the therapist addresses Target 2 behaviors, defined as any behavior that interferes with treatment delivery. The stance here is "How can you get better if you can't get the treatment that you need?" If a client diagnosed with diabetes could not get his or her insulin, that issue would be a major problem. It is the same for clients with EDs. Behaviors such as arriving late to sessions, not paying for therapy, omitting the presence of symptoms, water loading before being weighed, or losing concentration in session because of inadequate food intake are considered Target 2 behaviors and must be addressed.

The third category in the treatment hierarchy involves behaviors that interfere with quality of life. These behaviors include symptoms or life circumstances that do not fall into the first two categories (e.g., substance abuse, other ED symptoms, a fight with a boyfriend, losing one's job). Note that clients often want to talk about Target 3 issues regardless of the presence of Target 1 and Target 2 symptoms. One client we treated had a significant trauma history and was most motivated to work on her symptoms of posttraumatic stress disorder. The problem was that the frequency and intensity of her self-injury and food restriction would increase dramatically whenever she tried to think or talk about the trauma. From a DBT stance, the client needed to first be able to demonstrate that she was able to adaptively regulate her emotions and not engage in life-threatening behaviors before targeting the trauma symptoms. Note also that where on the treatment hierarchy a symptom lies will not always be clear. Some behaviors straddle the border between two categories, and the therapist must carefully consider at which level such behaviors will be targeted. Consultation with the team is often necessary to determine where more complicated behaviors fall on the treatment hierarchy.

In the following vignette, the therapist works with Daniele to sort through the many presenting issues and to structure the therapy session:

*Therapist:* Hey! So great to see you. It looks sunny out there today [warm genuine communication]—not great, I guess, if you have a hangover [irreverent, nonjudgmental stance].

*Daniele:* Yeah, it's gorgeous but my head is pounding.

*Therapist:* Doesn't sound like fun. So . . . I'd love to set our agenda for today. How about taking off those sunglasses and swinging your legs back around so we can get started? [direct communication, targets therapy-interfering behavior, said nonjudgmentally]

*Daniele:* (Reluctantly swings legs forward and sits up. Pauses and does not take off sunglasses; instead looks at therapist.)

*Therapist:* (Sees that client has paused and decides to extinguish behavior by looking down at her notes, waiting for the client to take off sunglasses. The moment Daniele removes the glasses:) Great! It's so much nicer for me when I get to see your eyes [reinforces adaptive behavior verbally and behaviorally by increasing warmth and communication as soon as desired behavior occurs]. So where's that diary card? [Quickly moves to set the structure for the session.]

*Daniele:* (gives a wry smile and hands a half completed diary card to the therapist)

*Therapist:* (scanning the diary card) Yikes (frowns). This is only half filled out. Can you take a minute to fill in the rest before we go on? [aversive response to extinguish therapy-interfering behavior]

*Daniele:* (Rolls her eyes, takes the diary card back, and completes it.)

*Therapist:* Fabulous. Thanks. (takes diary card back) [reinforces adaptive behavior] (scanning the diary card) I feel like there are so many things to talk about today [self-involving self-disclosure] What about you? What do you want to put on our agenda? [collaborative stance]

*Daniele:* I don't know. My parents are all upset about me working. They want to talk with you about it.

*Therapist:* Yeah, glad you brought that up. They left me a voice message about that and I wanted to talk about it with you. Sounds like that needs to go on our agenda.

*Daniele:* I guess so.

*Therapist:* Okay—are you up for writing our items on the board? [asks client to note agenda items on the white board in the office; assesses willingness and motivation]

*Daniele:* Sure. (Gets up and starts writing on the board.)

*Therapist:* Awesome [matter-of-fact tone; reinforces adaptive behavior]. What else?

*Daniele:* I don't know. I guess you'll want the usual update on symptoms?

*Therapist:* Absolutely. I see here (referring to the diary card) that you've had at least one episode of vomiting every day over the past week (pauses) and there were two episodes on both Saturday and Sunday (looks up at client who nods in agreement). Ugh. [Leans back in her chair away from the client; aversive contingency.] And I am also noticing really high urges for suicide on Friday night (frowns).

*Daniele:* Yeah. It was a rough weekend.

*Therapist:* Sounds like it was really hard [genuine, validating tone]. I really want to hear what happened. Let's add those two things to our agenda (client writes them on the board). What else? (Client shrugs.) Are there any other symptoms you've had over the past week that aren't on the diary card [direct, nonjudgmental tone]?

*Daniele:* No, all the symptoms are there.

*Therapist:* Okay. Love that you are so open about reporting symptoms [reinforces adaptive behavior]. How about the drinking last night. I thought your goal was no alcohol this month? (Client huffs and adds it to the agenda, therapist nods and smiles at the client to reinforce her willingness to identify targets.) One more thing to add related to the time you spend socially out in the waiting room [nonjudgmental stance].

*Daniele:* (frowning) Wow. This feels like a lot.

*Therapist:* Yeah—I'm with you [validates client's sense of feeling overwhelmed]. Are you willing to go on with the session [commitment strategy]?

*Daniele:* Do I have a choice? (said half-smiling)

*Therapist:* Yes! You always have a choice. If this feels like too much, we can end for today [freedom to choose strategy].

*Daniele:* (sheepishly) No, let's go on.

*Therapist:* (leans toward client) Okay, great. I was hoping you might make that choice [winks at client; reinforces adaptive behavior].

Alright, quick test. Can you identify which of those behaviors on the board are Target 1, 2, and 3? [Keeps client on her toes and actively engaged in agenda setting.]

*Daniele:* Oh god. Fine. This is Target 2, this is Target 1.... (Client writes on white board, finishes, and sits back down.)

*Therapist:* You are on fire! Great job [reinforces adaptive behavior]. I'm with you on all of them except the vomiting. You have that as Target 3 but I was thinking of it as Target 1.

*Daniele:* Why? I thought it was quality-of-life stuff.

*Therapist:* Well, it might be if it wasn't directly related to the low potassium. Vomiting when you are hypokalemic bumps it up to Target 1.

*Daniele:* Right (stands and corrects it on the board).

*Therapist:* Okay (both client and therapist look at agenda on board). We have to target the life-threatening stuff for sure as well as the therapy-interfering behaviors. How about we try to stay super focused so we have some time near the end of the session to talk about the issue with your parents and babysitting [sets agenda and asks client for collaboration].

*Daniele:* Okay.

*Therapist:* Great [reinforcement]—can you keep an eye on the time with me so we stay focused?

Note that in this case example, the therapist uses several strategies to structure the session. She collects the diary card from the client and establishes an agenda for the session in the first 5 minutes. When the client has multiple problem behaviors, taking time at the beginning of each session to identify what needs to be discussed on the basis of the treatment hierarchy is absolutely essential. It is important that the therapist does not get into a discussion about each issue while setting the agenda. The therapist should simply name the issues and organize them first. It can be tempting to start talking about a topic, especially ones that are life threatening, as soon as they are named ("You vomited every day last week. What was going on that your symptoms increased?"). Engaging in discussions before collecting all relevant information often results in items being missed, not having enough time to discuss everything, or learning about more serious behaviors (e.g., high urges for suicide) toward the end of the session when little time is left.

The therapist in the preceding example also engages the client in the agenda-setting process. Getting the client to collaborate and become actively involved with agenda setting and time keeping is an important exercise. It strengthens the client's learning and understanding of DBT, helps the client take greater responsibility in the session and build organizational skills, and facilitates a greater sense of partnership between therapist and client. Finally, even in this brief exchange, the therapist weaves in commitment strategies (freedom to choose) and a dialectical, nonjudgmental stance (all behaviors are discussed in a matter-of-fact tone, and the therapist also alternates between validating the client's emotions with pushing for change) and opportunities to reinforce adaptive behavior and extinguish maladaptive behavior (both verbally and nonverbally).

It is essential that therapists adhere to the treatment hierarchy. First, it communicates the severity of the client's symptoms. Second, it can work to shape the client's behavior. Clients will quickly learn that they can gain more therapy time talking about what they want to talk about if they work on eliminating self-injury or ED-related medical instability. In our consultation work, we have found that therapists often fear that this approach may drive symptoms underground (e.g., that clients will lie about the frequency or occurrence of a symptom to avoid talking about it). Our stance has been to address this directly with the client (as a Target 2 behavior) using commitment strategies along with the strength of the therapeutic relationship, as follows:

> *Daniele:* Well, whatever, I think this hierarchy thing is stupid. It doesn't make me want to be honest with you (seems annoyed, rolls her eyes).
>
> *Therapist:* It can definitely be a hard thing to follow sometimes [said non-judgmentally and with empathy] (pauses) and it makes me sad that you might choose to withhold information from me [frowns slightly; gives direct communication with self-disclosure of therapist's emotions].
>
> *Daniele:* Well, I don't want to lie to you, but I don't want to spend the whole session talking about medical instability. I've got bigger problems that I want to figure out.
>
> *Therapist:* Definitely glad to hear that you don't want to lie to me [reinforcing adaptive behavior], and we need to target the fact that your vomiting behaviors are driving your potassium levels too low. (pauses) I so want to talk about other things with you, too [said with warmth and genuineness], and yet, here's the thing . . . if you are dead or end up in the hospital because of the hypokalemia, that's really going to interfere with our chances of ever talking about those other things you want help with.
>
> *Daniele:* Ugh. Just saying that makes me not want to tell you everything.
>
> *Therapist:* Are you trying to make me work extra hard today (said with irreverence and a slight smile)? Here's the deal. If you want to lie to me, I can't stop you. I hope you choose otherwise but at the end of the day I am not going to know for sure whether or not you are holding back on me [nonjudgmental stance emphasizing freedom to choose].
>
> *Daniele:* Like I said, it's not that I want to lie to you, it's just that I think it's stupid sometimes that we have to spend so much time on it.
>
> *Therapist:* I'm glad you can be open with me now about how you feel. That helps me [reinforces adaptive behavior]. Again, it's your choice [freedom to choose]. In my experience, it all comes out in the wash at some point (pauses) and that would really hurt our relationship. It would be really hard for me to know that you held back [self-disclosing statement]. If you want to take that chance, that's your choice. Ready to move on?

As the therapist, getting in control of multiple problem behaviors is hard work. Identifying therapy issues with the client in a direct and non-judgmental manner, including therapy-interfering behaviors as they arise (e.g., the urge to withhold information, as in the preceding case) helps to keep the client and therapist on track. We also strongly recommend that therapists regularly review cases in the team consultation meeting to ensure that therapists are adhering to the hierarchy and to provide guidance when sessions start to feel overwhelming.

## Shaping Behavior: Contingency Management Strategies

Consistent with the DBT model, contingency management procedures are central to our program. To use these strategies effectively, however, clinicians must be well versed in the principles and application of learning theory (e.g., classical and operant conditioning). In essence, contingency management strategies are designed to reinforce adaptive behavior and extinguish maladaptive behavior. Their application is based on the knowledge that the consequences of a behavior (e.g., people laugh when I tell a joke) influence the probability of the behavior occurring again in the future (e.g., more joke telling). Thus, it is possible to increase or decrease the frequency of a behavior by influencing its associated consequences. In the previous example with Daniele, when she hesitates to take off her sunglasses, the therapist looks down at her notes as an aversive contingency (e.g., the consequence of keeping your sunglasses on during the therapy session is decreased attention from the therapist). Contingency management strategies may be subtle, as in a slight withdrawal of warmth (e.g., sitting back from the client or shifting to a more serious tone of voice) or more overt (e.g., directly talking about life-threatening ED behaviors when they occur). The selection of what strategy to use when is dependent on the therapist's intimate knowledge of what is reinforcing to a particular client. What works for one client may not work for another. Likewise, what works for one client in one circumstance may not work for the same client in a different circumstance. For instance, withdrawal of warmth when a client refuses to talk about a therapy-interfering behavior will be more effective with an individual who craves attention and affection from the therapist than someone who dislikes such attention and prefers more distance. It may take some time to determine what contingency will shape a given client's behavior.

Take for example our experience with Jill, a young woman who presented with an 8-year history of anorexia nervosa, binge–purge type, and comorbid borderline personality disorder with recurrent episodes of self-injury. Before her participation in the DBT program, efforts to change Jill's symptoms were largely unsuccessful. In particular, her self-injury often resulted in discharge from standard ED programs, which felt that they were not equipped to manage her multiple problem behaviors. During the initial commitment phase with Jill, she quickly developed a strong attachment to her individual DBT therapist and often requested more time with her beyond their weekly 50-minute sessions. In an effort to shape the client's behavior, the pair agreed to the following contingency: For every full week (e.g., 7 consecutive days) the client abstained from engaging in any self-injurious behavior, she would "earn" an extra 20 minutes with the individual therapist. If she engaged in self-injury, however, she would only have their 50-minute session, at least half of which would be spent completing a detailed chain analysis of the targeted behavior (an aversive contingency for the client, who disliked speaking about self-injury). At the time of this writing, Jill has not engaged in any episodes of self-injury in 14 weeks. She attributes her willingness and ability to meet this goal to a highly reinforcing contingency.

All people are shaped by the behaviors of others and the environment that surrounds them. DBT requires that therapists remain mindful of how they influence their clients and how their clients influence them and use that information to guide treatment planning. For example, in reviewing a case in our consultation team, we realized that one of our therapists had decreased her focus on explicitly targeting weight gain (e.g., following up on weekly weight goals, weighing the client at the start of each session, conducting a chain analysis of episodes of restriction) in her sessions with a client with anorexia. We discovered that the therapist had been influenced by the client's behavior of either crying or dissociating every time the subject was broached. Similarly, one of our dieticians recognized that, as a result of a patient's angry outbursts and hostility, she had stopped addressing episodes of therapy-interfering behaviors during meal times (e.g., tearing apart food in small pieces, ongoing negative comments about her meal plan). To be clear, from a DBT standpoint, such behaviors are not regarded as manipulative; rather, they are understood as the client's best efforts (albeit maladaptive) to get their needs met (e.g., to not gain weight or follow their meal plan). As with all people, clients' behaviors are merely the result of a lifetime of learning and reinforcement. If people respond by backing away or decreasing their emphasis on change when the client cries, dissociates, or becomes angry, then the client will likely continue to engage in these processes to get his or her needs met. DBT therapists observe and describe the behavior nonjudgmentally and use it as data to help move the client closer to his or her treatment and life goals:

*Therapist:* Ah, so I notice just now you reacted with an angry comment when I asked you not to cut your food into small pieces [uses behaviorally specific information nonjudgmentally].

*Jill:* (glares at therapist and has an angry tone of voice) Don't tell me what to do. I'm eating my food just fine.

*Therapist:* (with softness and directness) Yikes. When you stare at me like that it really makes me want to back off [nonjudgmental, radically genuine response targeting therapy-interfering behavior]! Hmmm. I know your goal in coming into this program was to be able to go out with your friends and not feel like your eating disorder took center stage. I'm assuming that is still your goal . . . yes? [commitment strategy of linking to prior commitments; refrains from making assumptions about the client's behavior.]

*Jill:* (reluctantly) Yes.

*Therapist:* OK. Good to know. So my commitment to you is to help you meet that goal, which means observing and describing [therapist generalizes mindfulness skills] times when you engage in ED behavior during meals. Is there a way we can do that together without you shooting daggers at me with your eyes? [said with irreverence and a slight smile; therapist targets motivation and commitment.]

*Jill:* Fine (huffs but refrains from breaking her food into smaller pieces and instead takes a bigger bite).

*Therapist:* You rock. Now, as you finish, tell me more about that movie you saw last night [reinforces adaptive behavior and moves on].

## Weekly Goal Sheet

Given the importance of contingency management with this population, we developed a weekly worksheet (see Figure 16.1) to be used collaboratively by client and therapist. The worksheet is organized around the treatment hierarchy and prompts clients to set concrete and achievable goals in each of the targeted areas (e.g., a weight goal, a therapy-interfering behavior goal). For each goal, clients are also asked to identify a corresponding contingency and reward. Therapists are recommended to help clients set their own contingencies. In our experience, and once clients have been fully oriented to these procedures and how they will help the client meet their life goals, clients are far more skilled and knowledgeable about what will shape their own behavior then therapists are.

In our program, the weekly goal sheet is completed in a 90-minute goal-setting group at the end of each treatment week to prepare clients for the week ahead. Clients are instructed to complete the worksheet to the best of their ability before the group. If they have not done so, it is treated as a therapy-interfering behavior and named as such. Clients are free to discuss all the goals in the group with the exception of their weight goals, which are reviewed and discussed in greater detail with the individual therapist and treatment team as needed.

## Key Points in Contingency Management Procedures

1. *Orient the client.* A therapist is more likely to help the client make changes when he or she fully understands and buys into the goals and procedures. DBT is a comprehensive therapy with many moving parts; therapists sometimes forget to explain to clients why they are doing what they are doing. Transparency is an integral part of the DBT model. Before using contingency management strategies, it is important to teach clients about learning theory, thoroughly explain the rationale for using contingencies to change behavior, and link the use of these strategies to their treatment and life goals. It is also essential to orient clients to what will happen when they do not want to follow a contingency (see Point 3). In our program, we first use a

392

**Meal Plan Goal/s:**
Weekday: _____
Weekend: _____

**Food Exposure Goal/s:**
Weekly: _____
Daily: _____

**Weight Goal/s:**
1. _____

**Life-Threatening Behaviors Goal/s:**
1. _____

**Therapy Interfering Behaviors Goal/s:**
1. _____
2. _____

**Quality of Life/Other Goal/s:**
1. _____
2. _____

**Appointment Goals:**
(e.g., PCP, EKG, nutrition)
1. _____
2. _____

**Insurance/Payment Goals:**
1. _____

**Contingencies/Natural Consequences:**
1. _____
2. _____

1. _____
2. _____

1. _____

**Contingencies/Natural Consequences:**
1. _____

1. _____
2. _____

**Contingencies/Natural Consequences:**
1. _____
2. _____

1. _____
2. _____

1. _____

**Rewards:**
1. _____
2. _____

1. _____
2. _____

1. _____

**Rewards:**
1. _____

1. _____
2. _____

**Rewards:**
1. _____
2. _____

1. _____
2. _____

1. _____

_____
*Clinicial Signature*

_____
*Client Signature*

Figure 16.1
**Sample Client Goal Plan**

blend of commitment and dialectical strategies to increase the client's willingness to meet the contingency. If a client is still unwilling to follow through, despite our best efforts, we nonjudgmentally name the behavior as therapy interfering, and clients may not return to the program until they have met with their individual therapist to discuss motivation and commitment issues and complete a chain analysis.

2. *Be collaborative.* Ideally, contingencies are the result of a cooperative, nonjudgmental conversation between therapist and client. Even in situations in which there are program limits (e.g., a client must gain 1–2 pounds per week on an inpatient unit), helping the client identify what might work for him or her in a given circumstance is important. The idea here is to link contingency management procedures to the client's goals. For example, with Jill a therapist might explicitly connect the plan of reinforcing adaptive behavior with more therapist contact to the client's larger goal of developing stronger, healthier relationships in general. Of particular note is the use of the consultation-to-the-client approach, discussed earlier. Identifying needs, setting concrete goals, and learning to be accountable are skills that therapists need to help clients master. Clients with multiple problem behaviors are often less skilled at organizing multiple competing demands and problem solving in ways that help them build a life worth living. The weekly goal group and corresponding goal worksheet target such skill deficits and help clients take greater responsibility for their actions and their lives.

3. *Follow through.* The therapist must follow through on a contingency once it is set. Often, clients want to change or forego their contingency in the heat of the moment. This response is normal for everyone. It is incredibly difficult to change well-ingrained habits (e.g., smoking, procrastinating, swearing), and people often do not like to meet the contingencies when they struggle (e.g., they put off putting money into the "swear jar" like they said they would). The therapist's job is to hold patients to their contingencies. In our program, we set goals with corresponding contingencies and rewards (see Figure 16.1) at the end of each week. Clients are oriented to the fact that the contingencies set on Friday are held and cannot be changed until the following Friday, at which time we will review the effectiveness and suitability of the plan.

4. *Know your limits and when to flex them.* In the example of Jill, it was within the therapist's limits to extend her sessions with the client by 20 minutes when she met the goal of no self-injury for the week before. Therapists (and clinical environments) will differ with respect to limits. Some therapists would not be able or willing to extend a session. Choosing contingencies requires awareness of one's own limits as well as the limits of the therapeutic milieu, when applicable. Some contingencies may be beyond the control of the client and therapist. For example, on an inpatient ED unit, the program contingency for

not meeting the weekly 1- to 2-pound weight goal for several weeks might be to add a nasogastric tube. Likewise, natural contingencies are at play. A client who chooses not to gain weight might lose the ability to return to college because of medical instability, or a client who decides to withhold information about symptoms from his or her therapist might face the natural contingency of burning out the therapist or treatment team (e.g., the therapist feels frustrated with the client; the team starts to feel that they are not able to effectively treat the client). A strong consultation team will help each of its members to set contingencies with their clients that will reduce (not add to) burnout as well as support therapists when they flex their limits to help shape a client behavior.

## Conclusion

We presented the rationale for and use of DBT with clients with complex and multidiagnostic ED presentations who have not responded to standard ED treatments. To provide a foundation and initial starting point for therapists working with this particular population, we outlined the application of four specific DBT strategies (therapist stance, commitment building, prioritizing multiple problem behaviors, and contingency management). Our recommendation is that clinicians working in this field obtain training and consultation in both the treatment of EDs and the application of DBT. We are currently conducting research to evaluate the efficacy of our program. Clinicians interested in learning more about this model are encouraged to review the materials in the Recommended Resources section as well as those listed in the References section.

## Chapter Highlights

- Clients with complex and multidiagnostic ED presentations have unique treatment needs.
- Comprehensive DBT models that include individual DBT therapy, skills training, telephone skills coaching, and a therapist consultation team may be a more effective treatment approach for difficult-to-treat clients.
- Therapist stance is key. A nonjudgmental, dialectical approach is particularly helpful in facilitating a strong therapeutic alliance and increasing treatment retention and client collaboration.
- Allocate time for pretreatment commitment work. Ensure that clients want to engage in the therapy process, that they fully understand the nature of the commitment, and that therapist and client both agree to work together toward common goals.
- Use of the treatment hierarchy to structure sessions and prioritize multiple problem behaviors is central to effective treatment.
- Comprehensive knowledge and the ability to apply behavioral principles is essential (e.g., contingency management).

- Consultation and supervision are essential. Therapists treating complex and multidiagnostic clients with EDs need support to ensure adherence to the treatment model and to reduce burnout.

# Recommended Resources

## Readings

Federici, A., Wisniewski, L., & Ben-Porath, D. (2012). Description of an intensive dialectical behavior therapy outpatient program for multidiagnostic clients with eating disorders. *Journal of Counseling & Development, 90,* 330–338. This article is in a special issue on the prevention and treatment of eating disorders.

Koerner, K. (2012). *Doing dialectical behavior therapy: A practical guide.* New York, NY: Guilford Press.

Linehan, M. M. (1993a). *Cognitive behavioral treatment of borderline personality disorder.* New York, NY: Guilford Press.

Linehan, M. M. (1993b). *Skills training manual for treating borderline personality disorder.* New York, NY: Guilford Press.

Wisniewski, L., & Ben-Porath, D. D. (2005). Telephone skill-coaching with eating-disordered clients: Clinical guidelines using a DBT framework. *European Eating Disorders Review, 13,* 344–350.

Wisniewski, L., Safer, D., & Chen, E. Y. (2007). Dialectical behavior therapy for eating disorders. In L. A. Dimeff & K. Koerner (Eds.), *Dialectical behavior therapy in clinical practice* (pp. 174–221). New York, NY: Guilford Press.

## Web Sites

- Behavior Tech
  http://behavioraltech.org/ol/
  Online learning in key areas such as managing therapy-interfering behaviors, skills training, validation strategies, and chain analysis.
- Practice Ground
  http://www.practiceground.org/
  Online learning community that offers Web-based courses, discussions, articles, and teaching tools to help clinicians learn, strengthen, and generalize their skills using evidence-based practices.

# References

Bankoff, S. M., Karpel, M. G., Forbes, H. E., & Pantalone, D. W. (2012). A systematic review of dialectical behavior therapy for the treatment of eating disorders. *Eating Disorders, 20,* 196–215 doi:10.1080/10640266.2012.668478

Ben-Porath, D. D., Wisniewski, L., & Warren, M. (2009). Differential treatment response for eating disordered patients with and without a comorbid borderline personality diagnosis using a dialectical behavior therapy (DBT)-informed approach. *Eating Disorders, 17,* 225–241. doi:10.1080/10640260902848576

Bydlowski, S., Corco, M., Jeammet, P., Paterniti, S., Berthoz, S., Laurier, C., & Chambry, J. (2005). Emotion-processing deficits in eating disorders. *International Journal of Eating Disorders, 37,* 321–329. doi:10.1002/eat.20132

Chapman, A. L, Gratz, K. L, & Brown, M. Z. (2006). Solving the puzzle of deliberate self-harm: The experiential avoidance model. *Behavior Research and Therapy, 44,* 371–394. doi:10.1016/j.brat.2005.03.005

Chen, E. Y., Matthews, L., Allan, C., Kuo, J. R., & Linehan, M. M. (2008). Dialectical behavior therapy for clients with binge-eating disorder or bulimia nervosa and borderline personality disorder. *International Journal of Eating Disorders, 41,* 505–512. doi:10.1002/eat.20522

Cockell, S., Zaitsoff, S., & Geller, J. (2004). Maintaining change following eating disorder treatment. *Professional Psychology: Research and Practice, 35,* 527–534. doi:10.1037/0735-7028.35.5.527

Federici, A., Wisniewski, L., & Ben-Porath, D. (2012). Description of an intensive dialectical behavior therapy outpatient program for multidiagnostic clients with eating disorders. *Journal of Counseling & Development, 90,* 330–338.

Fox, J. R. E., Federici, A., & Power, M. J. (2012). Emotions and eating disorders: Treatment models. In J. R. E. Fox & K. P. Goss (Eds.), Eating and its disorders (pp. 315–337). Chichester, England: Wiley. doi:10.1002/9781118328910.ch21

Harned, M. S., Banawan, S. F., & Lynch, T. R. (2006). Dialectical behavior therapy: An emotion-focused treatment for borderline personality disorders. *Journal of Contemporary Psychotherapy, 36,* 67–75. doi:10.1007/s10879-006-9009-x

Haynos, A. F., & Fruzzetti, A. E. (2011). Anorexia nervosa as a disorder of emotion dysregulation: Evidence and treatment implications. *Clinical Psychology Science & Practice, 18,* 183–202. doi:10.1111/j.1468-2850.2011.01250.x

Heatherton, T. E., & Baumeister, R. E. (1991). Binge eating as escape from self-awareness. *Psychological Bulletin, 110,* 86–108. doi:10.1037//0033-2909.110.1.86

Koerner, K. (2012). *Doing dialectical behavior therapy: A practical guide.* New York, NY: Guilford Press.

Kröger, C., Schweiger, U., Sipos, V., Kliem, S., Arnold, R., Schunert, T., & Reinecker, H. (2010). Dialectical behavior therapy and an added cognitive behavioral treatment module for eating disorders in women with borderline personality disorder and anorexia nervosa or bulimia nervosa who failed to respond to previous treatments: An open trial with a 15-month follow-up. *Journal of Behavior Therapy & Experimental Psychiatry, 41,* 381–388. doi:10.1016/j.jbtep.2010.04.001

Linehan, M. M. (1993a). *Cognitive behavioral treatment of borderline personality disorder.* New York, NY: Guilford Press.

Linehan, M. M. (1993b). *Skills training manual for treating borderline personality disorder.* New York, NY: Guilford Press.

Lynch, T. R., Trost, W. T., Salsman, N., & Linehan, M. M. (2006). Dialectical behavior therapy for borderline personality disorder. *Annual Review of Clinical Psychology, 3,* 181–205. doi:10.1146/annurev. clinpsy.2.022305.095229

Overton, A., Selway, S., Strongman, K., & Houston, M. (2005). Eating disorders—The regulation of positive as well as negative emotion experience. *Journal of Clinical Psychology in Medical Settings, 12,* 39–56. doi:10.1007/s10880-005-0911-2

Palmer, R. L., Birchall, H., Damani, S., Gatward, N., McGrain, L., & Parker, L. (2003). A dialectical behavior therapy program for people with an eating disorder and borderline personality disorder: Description and outcome. *International Journal of Eating Disorders, 33,* 281–286. doi:10.1002/eat.10141

Robins, C. J., & Chapman, A. L. (2004). Dialectical behavior therapy: Current status, recent developments, and future directions. *Journal of Personality Disorders, 18,* 73–79. doi:10.1521/pedi.18.1.73.32771

Safer, D. L., Robinson, A. H., & Jo, B. (2010). Outcome from a randomized controlled trial of group therapy for binge eating disorder: Comparing dialectical behavior therapy adapted for binge eating to an active comparison group therapy. *Behavior Therapy, 41,* 106–120. doi:10.1016/j. beth.2009.01.006

Safer, D. L., Telch, C. F., & Agras, W. S. (2001). Dialectical behavior therapy for bulimia nervosa. *American Journal of Psychiatry, 158,* 632–634. doi:10.1176/appi.ajp.158.4.632

Safer, D. L., Telch, C. F., & Chen, E. Y. (2009). *Dialectical behavior therapy for binge eating and bulimia.* New York, NY: Guilford Press.

Svaldi, J., Griepenstroh, J., Tuschen-Caffler, B., & Ehring, T. (2012). Emotion regulation deficits in eating disorders: A marker of eating pathology or general psychopathology? *Psychiatry Research, 197,* 103–111. Retrieved from http://www.ncbi.nlm.nih.gov/pubmed/22401969

Telch, C. F., Agras, W. S., & Linehan, M. M. (2001). Dialectical behavior therapy for binge eating disorder. *Journal of Consulting and Clinical Psychology, 69,* 1061–1065. doi:10.1037//0022-006X.69.6.1061

Wisniewski, L., Bhatnagar, K. C., & Warren, M. (2009). Using dialectical behavioral therapy for the treatment of eating disorders: A model for DBT enhanced CBT. In I. Dancyger & V. Fornari (Eds.), *Evidence-based treatments for eating disorders: Children, adolescents, and adults.* New York, NY: Nova Science.

Wisniewski, L., & Kelly, E. (2003). The application of dialectical behavior therapy to the treatment of eating disorders. *Cognitive and Behavioral Practice, 10,* 131–138. doi:10.1016/S1077-7229(03)80021-4

Wisniewski, L., Safer, D., & Chen, E. Y. (2007). Dialectical behavior therapy for eating disorders. In L. A. Dimeff & K. Koerner (Eds.), *Dialectical behavior therapy in clinical practice* (pp. 174–221). New York, NY: Guilford Press.

397

## Chapter 17

# Family-Based Therapy for Children and Adolescents With Anorexia

*Kim Hurst and Shelly Read*

Anorexia nervosa (AN) is a severe psychiatric disorder that usually occurs in adolescence, with an average age of onset of 17 years (Steiner et al., 2003; Wentz, Gillberg, Anckarsa, Gillberg, & Rastam, 2009). The prevalence of AN is estimated at 0.3%, with rates increasing over the past century, particularly in young women ages 15–24 years (Hoek, 2006). The causes of AN are generally considered to be multifactorial (Wonderlich, Lilenfeld, Riso, Engel, & Mitchell, 2005). Research has shown that adolescence is an illness-specific risk period for the onset of AN, especially among girls (Steiner et al., 2003). For many, navigating adolescence can present minor difficulties. Others, however, may experience more challenges during this developmental period. In particular, entering into puberty can be a very emotional, stressful, and confusing time in which significant physical and emotional changes take place (Killen et al., 1992). Stress has been suggested to amplify the negative feelings an adolescent has about him- or herself, leading to a preoccupation with weight and shape concerns (Sharpe, Ryst, Hinshaw, & Steiner, 1997). This increase in body dissatisfaction may contribute to a rise in dieting behaviors (Sassaroli & Ruggiero, 2005), which are linked with eating disorders (EDs).

AN is often considered a long-term illness with an average duration of 5 to 7 years (Beumont & Touyz, 2003). Research has indicated, however, that many young people achieve full recovery from the illness (Strober, Freeman, & Morrell, 1997). AN has a profound impact on the lives of individuals and their families (Robin, Siegel, & Moye, 1995; Wallin & Kronvall, 2002), with the highest mortality rate of any psychiatric illness; approximately 10% to 20% of those with AN die within 20 years of onset (Katzman, 2005). Predictions are that about one half of the deaths are due to suicide and one half are due to secondary physical complications of anorexia, particularly cardiac failure (Herzog et al., 2000). Given the severity and complexity of AN, effective treatment that aims to prevent protracted length of illness and reduces potential morbidity and mortality is essential.

Over the past 25 years, empirical evidence has accumulated suggesting that family-based interventions are effective outpatient treatments for children and adolescents with early-onset AN. Maudsley family-based treatment (FBT) is currently the most promising treatment for adolescents with anorexia (Bulik, Berkman, Brownley, Sedway, & Lohr, 2007; Treasure, Claudino, & Zucker, 2010). Therefore, in this chapter we describe using FBT for adolescents with AN. First, we review the history of how AN has been conceptualized within the family context over time, and then we summarize the empirical evidence and key theoretical underpinnings of FBT. Finally, we provide a review of the treatment phases encompassed in FBT and demonstrate the application of the treatment through the use of a case study. Our aim is to orient the reader to the application of the approach, both theoretically and practically. Recommended resources, readings, and details of the FBT manual are included.

## Family Factors Implicated in the Pathogenesis of Anorexia

In the past, families often encountered blame for their child's AN, and this idea was perpetuated by an archive of historical research that implicated family dynamics as part of the presentation of EDs (Charcot, 1889; Morgan & Russell, 1975), with the earliest of these suggesting that the family was in fact at the root of EDs such as AN (Lasègue, 1873). Numerous authors (Bruch, 1962; Harris, Brown, & Bifulco, 1986; Schmidt, Tiller, & Treasure, 1993; Selvini-Palazzoli, 1974) described differences in parental care and high levels of dysfunction in those families in which a child was diagnosed with an ED compared with those in which a child was not. Others have suggested that anorexia is associated with a controlling and authoritative nature in the mother–daughter relationship (Bruch, 1962). As a result of these early theories, parents were often excluded from treatment.

Much of the research during the 1960s and 1970s explored whether a particular family pattern was a necessary precondition of the pathogenesis of anorexia or occurred as a consequence of the illness. Minuchin et al. (1975) and Selvini-Palazzoli (1974) observed similar familial characteristics in families with children diagnosed with anorexia; they tended to be conflict avoidant, family members were seen to be enmeshed, and often generational boundaries were blurred They theorized that the child had a crucial role in perpetuating the family's avoidance of conflict, which reinforced anorexic symptoms. This was the start of a critical shift in thinking: that instead of excluding parents, including parents in treatment would actually facilitate improved outcomes by therapeutically targeting the avoidance of family conflict (Blinder, Chaitin, & Goldstein, 1988).

400

In the 1980s and 1990s, researchers began to express a lack of interest in the cause of anorexia (Dare et al., 1995; Eisler, 1995) and moved away from an active exploration of the family as the primary determinant of anorexia. Regardless of how the illness arose, researchers agreed that the symptoms become intertwined with family relationships, causing the entire family to experience suffering and distress (Weme & Yalom, 1996). Researchers began to emphasize behavioral recovery rather than insight and understanding of the disorder (Haley, 1973). This idea had implications in developing a family-based intervention that would markedly improve the long-term outcome of patients with anorexia.

# Empirical Evidence Supporting Family-Based Treatment

FBT was developed in the 1980s by Christopher Dare (1985) and colleagues at the Maudsley Hospital in London and was later manualized in 2001 (Lock, Le Grange, Agras, & Dare, 2001). FBT uses the family as a key resource for recovery by mobilizing the parents to take control of the young person's anorexic behaviors. There have been five randomized controlled trials and several uncontrolled studies using FBT.

The first trial compared FBT with individual supportive therapy after an initial hospitalization to restore weight (Russell, Szmukler, Dare, & Eisler, 1987). The theoretical underpinning for this research was that families of patients with anorexia were rigid and dysfunctional, and food and eating were used as the focus of family problems (Dare et al., 1995). Therapy was required to correct this family disturbance by taking a structural approach in strengthening the parental dyad and focusing on mealtime behavior as an illustration of this. Intervention also focused on improving family communication and directly dealing with avoided conflict. The conception was that both younger and older patients should be able to be treated in the same way (Dare et al., 1995; Russell et al., 1987). The results of this first trial demonstrated that the response to family therapy lay in illness factors (age of onset, illness duration, and presence of bulimic symptoms) and if parents directed high levels of criticism toward the child with anorexia, the family was more likely to drop out of family therapy.

Delivery combinations (Eisler et al., 2000; Le Grange, Eisler, Dare, & Russell, 1992) and treatment dose (Lock, Agras, Bryson, & Kraemer, 2005) have also been investigated. Standard FBT was compared with a modified version in which the young person and parents were seen separately, and results were similarly positive. A shorter treatment dose (10 sessions) was compared with the standard 20 sessions, and both interventions were found to be equally effective. Clients with more persistent and severe eating-related obsessional thinking and nonintact families were noted to benefit from the longer dose of treatment. Moreover, FBT appears to be just as positive for children as it is for adolescents (Lock, Couturier, & Agras, 2006). In addition, research follow-ups at 2 and 6 years revealed that results were similarly enduring as those of the original trial conducted by Russell et al. (1987; see also Eisler, Simic, Russell, & Dare, 2007; Lock, Le Grange, Forsberg, & Hewell, 2006).

The most recent trial, a large study of 121 participants, compared manualized FBT with an active treatment: adolescent-focused individual therapy (Lock et al., 2010). At the end of treatment, no significant difference was found in full remission rates between the treatment groups, with 42% for FBT and 23% for adolescent-focused therapy; however, the FBT group had better outcomes at the 6- and 12-month follow-ups. Although both treatments led to improvement, the results from this study indicated that FBT appeared to improve physical health more quickly than individual therapy, as evidenced by higher body mass index percentiles in participants at the end of treatment and at 6- and 12-month follow-up points. This result is particularly pertinent given the potential physical consequences of anorexia. In addition to the trials we have mentioned, dissemination of FBT beyond the treatment development sites in the United States, United Kingdom, and Australia appears to have been successful (Couturier, Isserlin, & Lock, 2010; Ellison et al., 2012; Loeb et al., 2007; Paulson-Karlsson, Engstrom, & Nevonen, 2009; Wallis, Rhodes, Kohn, & Madden, 2007).

The American Psychiatric Association (2006) practice guidelines for EDs specified FBT as an evidence-based treatment for children and adolescents. The U.K. National Collaborating Centre for Mental Health guidelines (2004) indicated that family interventions that directly treat the ED should be offered to children and adolescents. Support for other outpatient psychological treatments for adolescents are currently lacking (Lock & Gowers, 2005). Further research to determine who is more likely or unlikely to respond to treatment is required, but early response demonstrated via weight gain has been found to be the best predictor of remission at treatment end (Doyle, Le Grange, Loeb, Doyle, & Crosby, 2010). For a more comprehensive review of the research, please refer to Hurst, Read, and Wallis (2012).

# Maudsley Family-Based Treatment

### Theoretical Underpinnings of Family-Based Treatment

The FBT model is unique in that it integrates theoretical ideas from several established family therapy approaches including structural, narrative, strategic, and Milan systemic (Rhodes & Wallis, 2009). Family therapy approaches hold that individuals are best understood within the context of relationships and through assessment of the interactions within an entire family (Corey, 2005). FBT purports that parents' involvement in their child's therapy is vitally important for ultimate success in treatment. A key feature of FBT is that parents need to take an executive position and work together to defeat AN (Lock et al., 2001). This idea is drawn from structural family therapy's understanding that clear boundaries between the parent and the sibling subsystems are essential to healthy family functioning (Minuchin et al., 1975).

FBT takes the position that the child with AN is not functioning at his or her appropriate developmental level (i.e., has regressed). Normal adolescent behavior is seen as having been arrested by the presence of AN (Lock et al., 2001). Therefore, the child is not viewed as being in control of his or her behavior; instead, the AN controls the child. FBT asks parents to compensate for this discrepancy between chronological age and illness-influenced developmental state by temporarily taking charge of their child's eating until the ED recedes. FBT also uses the narrative therapy technique of externalization (White & Epston, 1990). Externalization is used to separate the client from the anorexia. Through this separation, the family can begin to perceive the AN in a different way and commence helping without blaming and judging the young person for his or her behavior.

An agnostic view of AN etiology is undertaken in FBT, which is drawn from strategic family therapy (Haley, 1973). The factors that produce or predispose one to AN (Madanes, 1981) are not considered a focus of FBT. Treatment therefore does not concentrate on uncovering the reasons why AN has occurred but rather refocuses the family on finding solutions to remove the affected child from the grip of the illness (Lock et al., 2001). FBT encourages the family to find solutions to fight the AN, and the counselor therefore resists an expert stance and instead defers to the parents' expertise (Rhodes, 2003). The idea of neutrality is drawn from Milan systemic family therapy (Boscolo, Cecchin, Hoffman, & Penn, 1987), which views the family as a homeostatic system in which direct pressure for change is likely to be met with counterpressure to maintain the system in an unchanged balanced state (Boscolo et al., 1987; Selvini-Palazzoli, 1974). To avoid this, the FBT counselor assists the family in generating ideas through the use of questioning techniques rather than by being directive (Lock et al., 2001). Therefore, in FBT the counselor maintains a neutral stance in relation to how the family will take charge of AN but departs from the Milan neutrality in that weight gain and normal eating are an urgent, nonnegotiable requirement of treatment (Lock et al., 2001).

## Treatment Phases

FBT is an intensive outpatient treatment that proceeds through three clearly defined phases. Approximately 20 to 24 treatment sessions occur over a 12-month period. Phase 1 of treatment, referred to as *refeeding the patient,* focuses on the dangers of severe malnutrition associated with anorexia, weight restoration, and a return to normal eating. Sessions are scheduled weekly, and the counselor coaches the parents to unite in their endeavor to refeed their child in a firm but warm and consistent way (Lock et al., 2001). During this phase, a family meal is conducted during which the counselor can observe how the family interacts around eating and can assist the parents around the issue of their child's food refusal (Lock et al., 2001). Externalization of the anorexia and aligning the young person with his or her siblings so they can provide additional support and encouragement are also key tasks in this phase.

Phase 2, referred to as *negotiations for a new pattern of relationships,* focuses on encouraging the parents to assist their child to take back some control and responsibility over food and eating again. Sessions are scheduled once every 2 or 3 weeks, and steady weight gain continues. In this phase, less persuasion by parents is required around eating. Phase 2 centers on carefully negotiated trial periods in which the young person becomes more responsible for his or her eating, and sessions also include an exploration of the relationship between adolescent developmental issues and anorexia (Lock et al., 2001).

Phase 3 of treatment is referred to as *adolescent issues and termination* and is scheduled monthly. At this point, the young person's weight is stable, and the self-starvation has abated. This phase sees a shift in direction toward the impact anorexia has had on the young person. FBT asserts that anorexia interrupts the path of regular adolescent development, and the counselor's task is to facilitate the adolescent to establish a healthy identity that is no longer enmeshed with anorexia (Rhodes, 2003). Because the initial crisis is over, the parents are able to refocus on their relationship as a couple. The termination session explores the family's experience of therapy, with the counselor instilling confidence in the family that they can proceed with likely success if future problems arise.

Now we discuss the FBT treatment phases in greater detail, using examples from a case study. We provide specific examples of questions and techniques the counselor can use during treatment, based on the FBT treatment manual by Lock et al. (2001), Rhodes and Wallis (2009), and our clinical experience in delivering this treatment. The following information should not be considered a replacement for using the FBT treatment manual and participating in training and supervision of the model; rather, it serves as an additional complementary resource.

## Case Example

Kelly was a 16-year-old girl presenting with her first episode of AN. At initial presentation, she weighed 101 pounds, was 5 feet, 4 inches, tall, and had an ideal body weight of 75%. She also had an 8-month history of amenorrhea. At assessment, Kelly was medically compromised and required immediate admission to a hospital. She had a 5-week pediatric admission that included nasogastric tube refeeding and cardiac monitoring because of tachycardia (her pulse rate was 35 beats per minute). Kelly was discharged at 118 pounds (85% ideal body weight), and the family began FBT in line with the three phases described in the Maudsley FBT manual (Lock et al., 2001).

## Medical Evaluation and Treatment

As in the case of Kelly, patients with anorexia are subject to a variety of physical and medical complications related to weight loss and malnutrition, and therefore treatment must include ongoing medical and physical management (Katzman, 2005). During FBT, the counselor should consult frequently with the medical professionals involved in the case. Initially, patients may require intensive medical monitoring (i.e., weekly or more) and in some cases hospitalization; these decisions should be made in collaboration with medical professionals. When working with Kelly and her family, we liaised with the medical team treating her in the hospital and were involved in discharge planning to ensure continuity of care between inpatient and outpatient settings. Later, we focus further on decision making surrounding when to consider hospital versus community treatment.

## Assessment

Lock et al. (2001) recommended setting up a separate assessment session before the commencement of FBT. Our experience has been that conducting an assessment session can provide a great platform to better understand the dynamics of the family and the potential barriers to treatment. In addition, it provides an opportunity to spend time explaining what the treatment involves and why it is the best option for the family's child. Ideally, if a young person is in the hospital for medical stabilization, this session would occur toward the end of discharge. If the young person does not require hospitalization, it would be included as a part of a broader intake and assessment that occurs in the outpatient setting.

### Engagement

The first part of the session is spent explaining that FBT is a family-based treatment and that the family needs to ascertain whether it is the treatment for them. In FBT, the tone adopted by the counselor is very important; the counselor conveys the seriousness of the child's illness to the family in a warm but grave manner, both to raise their anxiety and to engage them in treatment (Lock et al., 2001). Next, it is important to engage with each family member, in hierarchical order, asking about work, school, and how each person spends his or her free time. This process assists in making each person feel included and part of the therapeutic process from the beginning.

### Assessing Onset

Tracking the onset of the illness is important because it helps the counselor to understand the way that the anorexia developed over time within the family system and the manner in which the weight loss occurred (such as restriction, excessive exercise, laxative use, etc.). Questions may include, "When did you first notice X was losing weight?" "When did you first notice things weren't quite right?" and "What was happening around the time that the weight loss first started?" The young person may be asked, "How did the anorexia make you lose weight?" and "What things did it make you do?"

Getting a sense of what exactly was happening within the family system at that time is also important; for example, was a separation or divorce in progress? Was the family under considerable financial pressure? Was the family dealing with some kind of traumatic event or situation? Exploring the impact past issues have had or continue to have on the family can provide valuable information about the way the family has coped with and managed AN until now. Frequently, these past issues have either diverted attention away from the developing ED or overwhelmed the family to the point that they are unable to take action against the AN (Rhodes & Wallis, 2009).

> Kelly had an 8-month history of increased physical exercise, restricted oral intake, and subsequent weight loss (35 pounds). Her weight loss had occurred by reducing meal portion size, eliminating food groups from her diet, increased involvement in cooking and food preparation, frequent self-weighing, and social withdrawal from peers and family. She also experienced body image disturbance, preoccupation with achieving weight loss, calorie counting, averting thoughts of hunger, and increased anxiety. Kelly identified several psychosocial stressors that she felt contributed to her mental state and low mood, including ongoing conflict and bullying from her school peers. Her parents initially noticed changes in Kelly's mood; before the onset of AN, she was a cheerful, bright adolescent, but this changed as a result of anorexia, and at assessment she presented with low mood and increased irritability and was very tearful. Her parents' concerns were heightened when Kelly stopped menstruating.

## Effects of the Anorexia on Psychosocial and Family Function

The key processes in this part of the assessment are to assess how central the anorexia has become in the family's life. How affected are the family dynamics? How helpless does the family feel? To assess this, the counselor can ask the parents exactly how things have changed within the family since the emergence of anorexia. The counselor can ask the parents to think back to 1 or 2 years before the onset and reflect on the differences with regard to food and eating within the family. The discussion not only assists the counselor to better understand the development of the illness but also assists the parents to reflect on how much ground anorexia has taken.

During this part of the interview, it is also important to assess the risk of self-harm and suicidality and comorbid symptomatology (such as obsessive–compulsive disorder) and ask whether the family has a history of mental illness and, more specifically, eating issues. In addition, this is a good time to assess the young person's general level of functioning by asking about his or her school performance and social skills. For example, does the young person have any friends? Does he or she see friends outside of the school setting? Is the young person passing his or her classes in school? The kind of information gathered at this stage is demonstrated in the following case example.

> At assessment, Kelly's mother explained that she and her daughter had initially begun arguing about food and that it increased gradually over time to the point at which there was tension and distress at every meal. Kelly's dad was very tearful and stated that he felt such grief for the loss of his daughter, stating that Kelly seemed like a totally different child. He also stated that he was very aware of how this situation was affecting their younger daughter Sarah. Kelly's mother stated that she missed the closeness that she used to have with Kelly, noting that they used to spend a lot

of time together, but that Kelly was now isolating herself from the whole family and telling them that she hated them or did not want to be around them. Younger sister Sarah stated that she tried to stay out of all the arguments regarding food and kept herself busy with other activities as a way of managing how hard things were at home.

## Ways Parents Have Tried to Help

The aim in this part of the session is to assess the family's attempted solutions and strengths with regard to challenging anorexia, as well as exploring issues that may restrain successful treatment. For example, knowing whether parents have a conflict-avoidant parenting style is vital because challenging anorexia is likely to involve a lot of conflict. The counselor may ask a question such as "How realistic do you think it is that you will be able to beat anorexia without conflict?" Another useful statement, illustrated next, may be "You need to be willing to temporarily lose your relationship with your child to save her life."

At assessment, Kelly's parents, Jane and Peter, explained that they had initially tried to help Kelly by keeping things calm at meal times when possible, so instead of fighting about eating they would sit with her quietly until she was finished. They had encouraged her to eat foods that she liked, cooked her favorite dishes, and used reward systems. They reported that these strategies worked initially, but not in the longer term, with food refusal increasing. Jane and Peter also stated that they had stopped Kelly from doing all exercise (both secretive and planned) and had been to see a general practitioner and a pediatrician. At assessment, they stated that they were feeling panicked and desperate watching their daughter waste away and did not know what to do next.

## Provide a Rationale for Treatment

Once the counselor has reached this final part of the assessment session, it is time to create intensity and parental anxiety to assist with engaging them in treatment. The counselor explains the treatment approach, including the need for parental control (at least in the initial stages), the lengths to which the parents will need to go to save their child, and the importance of sibling support. The counselor also explains that although hospitalization alone does not cure anorexia, it is a necessary option at times for medical resuscitation and refeeding. It is important to note that if the young person is medically compromised, he or she will of course need to be hospitalized, but that it will only be temporary, and recovery will come about at home with them. We have found that explaining the limitations of individual therapy at this point is also important so that the parents understand that according to the evidence, FBT is their child's best chance to recover. While creating anxiety in session, the counselor also acknowledges that the family will have his or her support every step of the way and that FBT is the best treatment option available. It is useful to finish this section of the interview by stating that the family needs to be 99.9% sure that they want to engage in the therapy approach before commencing it because of the commitment it requires from all family members (Rhodes & Wallis, 2009).

One of the first requirements for treatment is that every family member needs to attend every session. The theoretical justification for having everyone present is to assist in the counselor's assessment of the family and to maximize the opportunity to help the whole family (Eisler et al., 1997; Le Grange et al., 1992; Minuchin et al., 1975; Russell et al., 1987; Selvini-Palazzoli, 1974). Another supposition is that the family members know and love the child the best, have the most invested in the child's recovery, and are therefore the best resource to get the child well.

### Explore Potential Challenges
The final step in the assessment process is to assess the strengths and family restraints that help prepare for the start of therapy (Rhodes & Wallis, 2009). A useful question to ask is, "If we were to go through with this treatment and it was a success, what do you think you would say were your biggest challenges personally in participating in this treatment?" This question orients the counselor to the potential challenges and areas to be aware of in commencing FBT.

## Therapeutic Goals and Intervention

The structure of the sessions throughout the three phases of treatment follows a similar course. At the beginning of each session, the counselor meets briefly with the client and uses this time to obtain the weight measurement and inquire whether there is anything the young person would like to address in the family session. After this brief 5- to 10-minute period of interaction, the rest of the family joins the session, the young person's weight is plotted on a graph for everyone to see, and progress is discussed (Lock et al., 2001).

### Phase 1: Refeeding the Client
Phase 1 is characterized by persistence and tenacity within the family that creates an atmosphere in which the AN cannot survive. Treatment targets weight restoration and normal eating above all other considerations. In this first phase of treatment, Sessions 1 and 2 are distinctly important and are therefore discussed in detail.

*Session 1.* According to Lock et al. (2001), this session "sets the tone for the entire first phase of treatment" (p. 46). There are three main goals to achieve in Session 1:

1. Engage the family in the therapy.
2. Obtain a history of how the anorexia is affecting the family.
3. Obtain preliminary information about how the family functions.

Session 1 highlights are described next.

After Kelly was weighed, the family joined the session, and her weight progress was illustrated via a weight graph. Kelly's weight had increased, and her parents were congratulated on their efforts. If weight loss had occurred, the information would be used to reinvigorate the parents in their efforts to refeed their daughter (Lock et al., 2001).

The counselor explained that discovering why the ED occurred would not be the focus; rather, the first goal was motivating the parents to take action against the anorexia. This goal was achieved by increasing their anxiety about the devastating effects the anorexia was having on their entire family. The counselor balanced stressing the seriousness of the illness while emotionally containing family members, for example, "Kelly is desperately unwell and you may need to go to extraordinary measures to get her well."

The next task is to gain an understanding from each family member of the effects the anorexia has had on them, both individually and as a family. Circular questions are effective in attaining this information because this technique "draws connections and distinctions" (Brown, 1997, p. 109) between family members. To understand the effects, the counselor begins by questioning the parents and then the children from oldest to youngest (in line with structural family therapy). Questioning in this way draws attention to the family hierarchy. The circular questions in the following case example have been drawn from Rhodes and Wallis (2009):

The counselor asked Peter, "If I was to ask your wife what effect the anorexia has had on her, what do you think she'd say?" Peter stated that he believed his wife had experienced increased stress and worry as a result of the anorexia entering the family, particularly over the lack of control she had over the situation. Jane agreed and stated that she thought her husband's main concern was the increase in conflict within the family and the impact this was having on familial relationships. Both parents stated that they were worried that the focus on Kelly's illness left them little time to attend to their other daughter's needs. Sarah agreed, but stated that she understood why her parents temporarily needed to focus more on Kelly.

Families often come to treatment with intense feelings of guilt and blame associated with the onset of the ED. The counselor's role is to address these feelings by ensuring that the family understands that guilt is one of the anorexia's methods of deception and often results in disempowering the family (Rhodes & Wallis, 2009). Exploration of guilt is demonstrated as follows:

The counselor asked the family, "Who is most likely to have been targeted by the anorexia to feel guilt? Who in the family can argue against this?" Both Jane and Kelly stated that they had been targeted by anorexia and were feeling guilty, Jane because she felt she should have seen the warning signs of the ED earlier, and Kelly because she felt she was causing her family a lot of distress. Peter stated that he also experienced feelings of guilt because he was overweight and was worried that it had led to the development of his daughter's ED. Kelly denied that this was the case and told her parents that they were not to blame. In the same way, Kelly's parents assured her that she did not cause the ED herself.

In Session 1, it is also important for the anorexia to become the target of the intervention rather than the young person. Throughout the session, the counselor assists the family to externalize illness by "stressing that the child has little control over her illness" (Lock et al., 2001, p. 52).

> The counselor asked the parents, "If you had to rate it out of 100%, how much do you feel the anorexia has been in charge of Kelly and how much has Kelly been in charge of it?"

Out of 100%, both parents felt the anorexia had been 95% in charge of Kelly and she had been in charge only 5%.

This exercise highlights to parents just how little control their child has over the anorexia and how they cannot expect the child to manage it on his or her own, but rather how as parents they need to step in and take charge. The counselor then inquires about what each family member has observed the illness make the young person do, which is useful for targeting these behaviors. If any critical comments are made toward the young person, the counselor needs to address them in the session immediately via externalization. For example, the counselor might say, "It's awful that the anorexia made Kelly throw her food out when she so desperately needs it." Externalization is further demonstrated in the case example:

> It was revealed that Kelly was engaging in secret exercise, body checking and constantly weighing herself. At meal times, she would eat extremely slowly and on occasion had been caught trying to hide food in her pockets. The parents indicated that Kelly would yell and cry at mealtimes, making it difficult for them to manage because they did not like seeing Kelly upset. The counselor reassured the parents by reminding them that conflict was going to occur and that it was unavoidable in the battle to fight the anorexia and get their daughter well. It was important for the counselor to empathize with the client: "Kelly, it is terribly sad that this awful illness has disrupted your life to this extent and has left you without much control."

The final component of the first session requires the counselor to charge the parents with the task of refeeding by emphasizing that the family is the best resource for this task.

> In the session, Kelly's counselor stated, "We have talked about the seriousness of anorexia and the fact that this will be a huge challenge for your family. We know that it is a horrific illness with concerning statistics and that family treatment is the best option to get your child well. Recovery happens at home. It is your job as parents to fight the anorexia for Kelly, because it is an illness she cannot fight herself. It's going to be your job to make sure she is eating enough and that all the tricks and behaviors of AN are managed to get her through this. It may be necessary for Kelly to take time off school and for you not to go to work for the first few weeks of treatment to establish refeeding. I have every confidence that you can do this, because before anorexia she was healthy. You know how to feed your children.

The session concludes with instructions for the parents to bring a meal to the next session, which is usually scheduled within a few days of Session 1.

The counselor might say, "Next session I want you to bring a meal to eat together as a family. I want you to choose something for Kelly that will reverse the effects of starvation."

*Session 2: Family Meal.* Three main goals are to be achieved during the family meal (Lock et al., 2001):

1. Continue the assessment of the family structure and its likely impact on the parents' ability to successfully refeed their child.
2. Provide an opportunity for the parents to experience success in refeeding their child.
3. Assess the family process specifically during eating.

This unique session provides a firsthand opportunity for the counselor to observe the family's processes during a meal and how the anorexia has disrupted family interaction. The counselor explains to the family that the purpose of the meal is to get the young person to eat one more mouthful than the anorexia wants him or her to. The parents are asked to reflect on how things have changed with the emergence of the anorexia; in this way the parents are used as the therapeutic agents of change (Rhodes, 2003). This process not only assists the counselor to better understand the development of the illness, but also assists the parents to reflect on how much ground anorexia has taken.

> Kelly's parents reported that the kinds of foods they purchased had changed (e.g., healthier low-fat options and no junk food) as a result of the anorexia. Kelly had become controlling about how and when food was prepared and had taken over cooking the evening meal. Previously, the family had eaten the evening meal together, but more recently Kelly had been eating her meal separate from the family at an earlier time.

The counselor can then encourage the parents to consult their parental instincts regarding changes to the client's eating routine. The counselor should refrain from taking over the parents' role by being overcontrolling or overdirecting them; instead, the counselor needs to allow them to make the decisions and work out strategies. All families differ in the way in which they approach the family meal session, and there is no right or wrong way. For example, some parents use verbal encouragement from the moment the food is presented to their child, and others may wait to observe whether their child will commence the meal on his or her own, prompting only when required. Regardless of parents' approach during the family meal session, a point is usually reached at which the young person refuses to eat any more, and this point is when the counselor coaches the parents to be consistent and firm in their requests to get their child to eat. The counselor instructs the parents to take charge and to avoid detailed negotiations with the child. For example, the counselor might say, "Ask Kelly to put some food on her fork and raise it to her mouth. Ask Kelly to take a mouthful. Don't negotiate with her." With the counselor's coaching, the parents are asked to minimize the differences in how they approach getting their child to eat and unite consistently from that point onward. Some of the strategies Kelly's parents used to get her to eat were to sit on either side of her during the meal, remain calm during times of distress, and balance firm and clear instructions with empathy and respect. The anorexia is externalized to help manage parental frustration with what appears to be stubbornness and disobedience. Peter stated, "Kelly, Mom and I can see how hard the anorexia is making this for you, but we are going to help you through this, because starving is not an option."

In addition to parental guidance, Lock et al. (2001) identified sibling support as important to recovery. If the young person has no siblings, the counselor should explore with the family who else could provide this additional support, for example, his or her best friend could be invited to join some of the therapy sessions. Kelly's sister was involved in the treatment process, as described next.

> While parental empowerment continued, Kelly's sister Sarah was encouraged to provide direct support and be sympathetic to Kelly's plight. Sarah was asked to refrain from helping her parents with eating; instead, she was encouraged to recognize how difficult it was for her sister. During the family meal session, Sarah praised her sister and gave her a hug when she was upset.

The session concludes with the counselor providing a summary of the family's strengths and reiterating the need for ongoing vigilance and immediate action.

*Sessions 3 to 10.* The remainder of Phase 1 is about keeping the family focused on refeeding and achieving weight gain. The counselor reviews progress with refeeding by tracking exactly what happened during specific meal times, including difficult ones. Kelly's progress and the counselor's interventions during these sessions are described as follows:

> Kelly's parents encountered difficulties when they did not agree on foods and refeeding strategies before mealtimes. The counselor assisted Kelly's parents with accessing their expertise in creating high-density meals while reminding them that their daughter's illness was still dangerous to her. Given Kelly's recent admission to the hospital, her parents were highly motivated to ensure their daughter would regain health and would not lose weight. Before beginning FBT, Kelly had been involved in decision making regarding food choices, which left her vulnerable to the influence of anorexia. Regular attempts at negotiating and arguing with her parents about food choices often resulted in Kelly refusing to eat. Her parents decided that to ensure weight gain occurred, Kelly would need to consume six meals a day, consisting of the three main meals and three snacks. In addition, Kelly's parents decided that until they observed consistent weight gain, they needed to make all decisions around the type, volume, and variety of food consumed rather than negotiating or giving choices. Her parents also agreed that meal times would

need to be fully supervised, so that anorexia would not encourage Kelly to restrict her intake if left alone.

Kelly's eating became the parents' central priority, and as such the family's routine needed to be adjusted. Kelly's parents took leave from work for 2 weeks to focus on the refeeding and supervision of their daughter.

The most innovative idea the family used to tackle the issue of avoided foods was to attend a different restaurant each week. Kelly would be required to order from the menu something she had previously enjoyed before the emergence of anorexia and consume the meal in its entirety. Although Kelly found the experience difficult initially, she later reported that being surrounded by other people enjoying food made it easier for her to begin to find pleasure in food again.

Sarah was able to alleviate Kelly's anxiety around upcoming meals by distracting her with conversation and listening to music. Kelly also found that her sister's praise and encouragement during mealtimes made it easier for her to consume her meal rather than give in to anorexia.

The main challenge for the family during Phase 1 was managing secret exercise. The parents' strategy to manage it was to increase supervision and add to Kelly's oral intake when secret exercise was uncovered. The parents decided that Kelly would be required to consume an extra snack immediately after the discovery of secret exercise.

After seven sessions, Kelly's weight reached 116 pounds (95% ideal body weight), and her parents were no longer struggling to manage her behaviors. Kelly demonstrated a consistent pattern of weight gain and was eating without conflict under parental supervision. Her parents reported feeling more in charge of the anorexia, and Kelly appeared less captured by the anorexia, so treatment moved into Phase 2.

## Phase 2 (Negotiations for a New Pattern of Relationships)

Lock et al. (2001, p. 175) stated that several criteria should be met when considering transition into Phase 2 of therapy:

1. The child's weight should be at a minimum of 87% of ideal body weight.
2. Conflict and negotiation around food and eating should have decreased significantly, and the parents should no longer be experiencing significant struggles with getting their child to eat regular and appropriate meals.
3. Parents should feel empowered in the refeeding process, as evidenced by the family demonstrating relief that they can take charge.

In Phase 2, the counselor creates a shift in the mood of the sessions by being more hopeful and optimistic in his or her manner, in contrast to the sober and solemn disposition demonstrated in Phase 1. This shift in the counselor's demeanor reflects the family's success with weight restoration and reinforces that the counselor has faith in the parents and their ability to refeed their child. The therapeutic aim of this phase is to assist the parents to hand over control of eating to their child in an age-appropriate way and for them to support the child to meet this challenge (Lock et al., 2001). The counselor continues to provide support to the parents regarding food and eating issues, with the additional focus on the young person exploring the difference between anorexic and adolescent thinking. Sessions become less circumscribed and structured, and parents become more empowered, trusting in their own ability because of previous success rather than requiring direct coaching (Rhodes, 2003; Rhodes & Wallis, 2009).

In handing control back to the patient, it is often useful to start by carefully negotiating a trial period of fading parental management to see whether the adolescent can cope with this change. In session, the counselor develops a mutually agreed-on handing-over process with the parents that includes the client's input. In the example of Kelly, her parents initially let her have some say over food choices, then progressed to letting her serve some of her own meals (under supervision), and eventually gave her the opportunity to eat alone for one to two meals per day while her parents supervised the main meal. It was done in a very graduated way, and each new step toward independence was carried out logically, following success at the last step and increased confidence for both Kelly and her parents that she could manage more independence without succumbing to the influence of anorexia.

Phase 2 is also the time to encourage the adolescent to restart engagement with the outside world (e.g., socializing with peers, dating). The counselor also assists the parents with planning any gradual return to exercise, including their thoughts about increasing calories and managing injuries or risk to bones. In speaking to the young person, the counselor focuses on what is in it for him or her as the young person takes more control of the anorexia (e.g., getting teenage life back). Another example of working toward the aims of Phase 2 may be to encourage the parents and adolescent to problem solve a plan regarding eating out with friends, including exactly which foods the adolescent will have and where. Signs of regression or weight loss may occur if the client is given more autonomy than he or she is ready for, which is not uncommon. If weight loss continues, it may be necessary to reinstate Phase 1.

> During Phase 2, Kelly demonstrated no dietary restrictions dictated by anorexia, and she was able to attend school full time, engage in exercise, and continue to gain weight. The enjoyment of being with friends and the reduced worry and conflict within the family assisted Kelly in beginning to negotiate adolescence without the anorexia. Kelly also reestablished relationships with her peers and began to socialize with them regularly. These changes occurred gradually over time, and with each new step Kelly gained the confidence to move on to something more. With the Phase 2 goals achieved, treatment progressed to Phase 3.

## Phase 3 (Adolescent Issues and Termination)

Lock et al. (2001, p. 209) stated that the major goals for Phase 3 are

1. to establish that the adolescent–parent relationship no longer requires the symptoms as an idiom of communication,

2. to review adolescent issues with the family and to model problem solving of these types of issues, and
3. to terminate treatment.

Therapy moves into Phase 3 once the young person's weight is stable at between 90% and 100% of his or her ideal body weight and the young person is managing food and eating independently. At the beginning of Phase 3, the counselor reviews the progress made by the family. The counselor presents a minilecture on adolescence, and the family generates a list of issues for discussion. Because this phase is relatively brief, the family prioritizes the issues they feel are most important to address. Any issues raised in Phase 1 or 2 that were deferred because of the focus on refeeding and weight restoration should be included. If other significant concerns are present at this stage, the counselor may need to organize a separate course of adolescent family therapy.

During Phase 3 sessions, the counselor facilitates discussion between the parents and the adolescent to resolve each issue raised and maintains a focus that conceptualizes each issue as a normal part of adolescent development. The counselor's role is to empower the parents to approach each of the issues rather than provide solutions for them. At this point in therapy, the counselor can also assist the family to think about a return to normal life (i.e., how things were within the family before anorexia). Posing questions about other aspects of life can create the space for the parents to move their sole focus from their daughter and anorexia to priorities that would have existed had the illness not come into the family (Rhodes & Wallis, 2009). Phase 3 is also the time to plan for potential future issues. The counselor does this by helping the family predict what the issues might be and generate ideas about how they could resolve them.

> During Phase 3, Kelly worked hard on establishing an identity that was not entwined with anorexia and her body image, and she instead became more aligned and engaged with her peers. She began to become more autonomous by obtaining part-time employment and entered into a romantic relationship with a same-age peer. Kelly also began pursuing vocational interests and engaged in a training program. During this phase, Kelly's weight was stable (118–123 pounds, 100% ideal body weight), and her menstruation cycle returned. Her parents began to reinvest in their lives and relationship after the intensity of refeeding. Kelly's parents were now able to spend time together as a couple and engage in activities they had previously enjoyed, such as going out to dinner and the movies together.

### Termination of Therapy

It is important to review each family member's individual experience of the therapy and to give everyone an opportunity to say goodbye. The counselor's role is to express confidence in the family's ability to manage any future problems that may arise (Garven & Rhodes, 2011).

In the termination session, Kelly reported that she felt relieved that her parents had taken charge of food and eating and believed that if it had not occurred she would not have recovered as quickly. Her parents stated that treatment had strengthened their family's relationships and reestablished the unity of their parenting team. They also stated that they felt that as difficult as the journey to fight anorexia had been, therapy had been highly supportive and empowering.

## Levels of Care: Community Versus Hospital Treatment

As stated previously, FBT is an outpatient treatment. We have also noted that anorexia is a serious condition that encompasses many potential medical complications and a high rate of mortality. Given these factors, it is sometimes necessary for clients to be admitted to either a pediatric–medical or a psychiatric unit. Our experience in working with this particular client group has been that it is not only preferable but necessary to work collaboratively as part of a multidisciplinary team that includes a medical professional (e.g., general practitioner, pediatrician, or psychiatrist). Liaising with these professionals is imperative in ensuring that the young person is medically well enough to be at home and to be treated on an outpatient basis (American Psychiatric Association , 2006).

There may also be times when although a young person is medically stable, the family insists that they are not coping well either practically or emotionally, and a hospitalization is needed for respite. Our preference is to avoid this when possible because it can give the message that the family cannot cope and needs to hand their child over to professionals. It goes against the philosophical underpinnings of FBT, which purport that parents are the experts on their own children, have the most invested in their recovery, and are therefore the best people to bring about recovery. Circumstances still exist, however, in which exceptions need to be made, perhaps in a single-parent family in which there is little support or in which parents have limited capacity because they are dealing with their own physical or psychological issues. For these reasons, there are no hard-and-fast rules about when an admission should be considered, unless the young person is medically unstable. If the counselor is unsure, it is best to consult with the rest of the treating team and the family to discuss the best way forward.

## Practice Challenges With Family-Based Therapy

Although ongoing research evidence is mounting that suggests FBT should be the first-line treatment for children and adolescents presenting with anorexia, as counselors working with this model we have identified several practice challenges in our daily practice. The first and possibly most stressful challenge the family and the counselor can face is when weight gain is very slow or nonexistent in Phase 1 (Wallis, Rhodes, Kohn, & Madden, 2009). Numerous reasons exist as to why this may occur, and careful questioning assists the counselor in eliminating each potential cause and uncovering the reason for lack of progress. For example, parents may be preparing, serving, and supervising all meals, but their child may be secretly exercising outside of meal times when unsupervised. Questioning needs to be methodical and curious, exploring each potential hypothesis that would explain limited success. The first step in reinvigorating the family is to help them learn how to detect and prevent potential covert behaviors as they move toward change. Ensuring that the parents are in an executive role and working together is essential, as is sibling support for the young person (Ellison et al., 2012). The counselor must understand in great detail how much control the parents are exerting over food and anorectic behaviors, their level of persistence, and their level of fear about conflict surrounding food (Hurst et al., 2012).

Fatigue in the family can also present a challenge in therapy, and it is common because of the relentlessness of AN. The serious nature and sometimes protracted illness duration can lead families to become fatigued with the ongoing day-to-day challenges caused by AN. It is not uncommon for parents to feel that they are on top of anorexic behaviors and then discover that their child is being influenced in some new way to eliminate calorie intake and stall progress. Constant conflict around food and eating is also very exhausting for families to cope with on a daily basis. The counselor's role in these situations is to validate feelings of frustration and exhaustion while balancing the need for parents to continue to stay motivated. It is essential to provide hope and to reinvigorate the parents when they are feeling depleted, reiterating that as exhausted as they are, they have to persevere to save their child's life. We have also found that in this situation, drawing on the experience of other families with whom we have worked can be useful to normalize their feelings of fatigue at this stage of treatment and explain that it will improve as they get on top of AN.

Another practice challenge can be implementing FBT with older adolescents, who had been moving toward individuation from their parents before the onset of anorexia. In most cases of adolescent-onset anorexia, the young person has actually regressed developmentally and needs to be cared for rather than continuing to be independent. Engaging in FBT can create challenges of adjustment not only for the young person, but also for the parents in renegotiating their role as parents of a child with serious illness, during which the child needs to be treated (temporarily) as a much younger child and taken care of rather than moving toward the independence of adulthood. The counselor reminds both the young person and the parents that this temporary interruption of autonomy is vital, explaining that once the young person is well again, he or she will return to the previous developmental path.

Conversely, once the young person is moving into Phase 2 of FBT, some parents may be paralyzed by the fear that their child will regress if he or she is given back control. In these situations, the counselor can assist by reviewing and amplifying the successes that the parents have achieved in Phase 1, empathize with their fears, and help them see that progress will stall if they do not move forward to a more normal developmental situation for their child. Starting with a small experiment often helps things move forward with a manageable level of anxiety for everyone, for example, allowing the young person to manage her or his own morning tea or afternoon snack independently for a week or perhaps preparing her or his own breakfast. Through such an experiment, the young person has the opportunity to demonstrate that he or she has learned about the type and volume of foods needed to maintain weight, and the parents learn to trust that their child can manage greater independence in eating (Hurst et al., 2012).

In addition, single-parent families can present different challenges when delivering FBT. Research has demonstrated that FBT is as effective for this family constellation, but it has been proposed that they may require a longer duration of treatment (Lock et al., 2005). Single-parent families sometimes have more limited resources than intact families in which both parents are available. They may therefore experience exhaustion more frequently because they carry the load of responsibility alone. The counselor needs to be conscious not to be drawn into a coparenting role but instead encourage the parent to recruit other adults in his or her life who can support the parent through this process in lieu of a partner. We have often involved an aunt or grandparent in sessions if they are quite involved in the adolescent's life.

Finally, working with families affected by AN can evoke feelings of distress, frustration, and anxiety within the counselor. Because of this, self-reflection and supervision are essential. Discussing transference issues in supervision can assist the counselor to maintain the fidelity of the model and ensure that the core tenets of FBT remain central to treatment.

## Conclusion

Anorexia is a serious psychiatric illness that has a significant impact not only on the young person but also on his or her entire family. Numerous medical complications can arise as a result of anorexia and, with the highest mortality rate of any psychiatric illness, the need for effective treatment is paramount. FBT provides an evidence-based approach to outpatient treatment that supports the family in taking responsibility for helping their adolescent without blaming her or him for developing the illness. By working through the three phases of treatment, the medical, psychological, and family issues are addressed in a sequential way that can lead to sustainable recovery. The case study of Kelly demonstrates that parents can shift from feeling panicked and disempowered at the beginning of treatment to feeling confident in their abilities as parents to cope in the future. Although FBT can be highly effective, it is not suitable for every case of adolescent anorexia, and it is not without its challenges for the family and counselor. Having the support of a multidisciplinary team is essential in managing both the medical risks and the therapeutic challenges anorexia presents.

# Chapter Highlights

- When using FBT, the view of anorexia and its etiology is agnostic.
- FBT assumes that the adolescent is embedded within the family.
- In FBT, parents' involvement in therapy is vitally important.
- Separation of the client from the anorexia (externalization) is imperative. The target of the intervention is the anorexia, not the child or family. The adolescent is not viewed as being in control of her or his behavior; rather, the anorexia controls the adolescent.
- In FBT, the adolescent with anorexia is seen as regressed, functioning not on an adolescent level but instead on that of a much younger child who is in need of a great deal of help from the parents.
- The counselor's task (at least initially) is to keep the parents focused on refeeding their adolescent so as to free her or him from the control of anorexia.
- In FBT, hospitalization is viewed only as a temporary solution.
- In FBT, structural changes in the family are made to defeat anorexia.
- Therapists resist the expert stance, instead deferring to the family for solutions. The counselor uses the family's resourcefulness to bring about recovery.
- Medical safety precedes other adolescent issues.

# Recommended Resources

### For Counselors

Lock, J., Le Grange, D., Agras, W. S., & Dare, C. (2001). *Treatment manual for anorexia nervosa: A family-based approach.* New York, NY: Guilford Press

Rhodes, P., & Wallis, A. (2009). The Maudsley model of family therapy for anorexia nervosa. In S. J. Paxton & J. P. Hay (Eds.), *Interventions for body image and eating disorders: Evidence and practice* (pp. 58–74). Melbourne, Victoria, Australia: IP Communications.

Rhodes, P., & Wallis, A. (Eds.). (2011). *A practical guide to family therapy: Structured guidelines and key skills.* East Hawthorn, Victoria, Australia: IP Communications.

### For Parents

Alexander, J., & Le Grange, D. (2009). *My kid is back: Empowering parents to beat anorexia nervosa.* Melbourne, Victoria, Australia: Melbourne University Press

Collins, L. (2005). *Eating with your anorexic: How my child recovered through family based treatment and yours can too.* New York, NY: McGraw–Hill.

Lock, J., & Le Grange, D. (2005). *Help your teenager beat an eating disorder.* New York, NY: Guilford Press.

# References

American Psychiatric Association. (2006). *Treatment of patients with eating disorders* (3rd ed.). Washington, DC: Author.

Beumont, P. J. V., & Touyz, S. W. (2003). What kind of illness is anorexia nervosa? *European Child and Adolescent Psychiatry, 12,* 20–24.

Blinder, B. J., Chaitin, B. F., & Goldstein, R. S. (1988). *The eating disorders.* New York, NY: PMA.

Boscolo, L., Cecchin, G., Hoffman, L., & Penn, P. (1987). *Milan systemic family therapy: Theoretical and practical aspects.* New York, NY: Harper & Row.

Brown, J. (1997). Circular questioning: An introductory guide. *Australian and New Zealand Journal of Family Therapy, 18,* 109–114.

Bruch, H. (1962). Perceptual and conceptual disturbances in anorexia nervosa. *Obstetrical & Gynecological Survey, 17,* 730–732.

Bulik, C. M., Berkman, N. D., Brownley, K. A., Sedway, J. A., & Lohr, K. N. (2007). Anorexia nervosa treatment: A systematic review of randomized controlled trials. *International Journal of Eating Disorders, 40,* 310–320.

Charcot, J. M. (1889). *Clinical lectures on diseases of the nervous system.* London, England: New Sydenham Society.

Corey, G. (2005). *Theory and practice of counseling and psychotherapy* (7th ed.). Belmont, CA: Thomson Learning.

Couturier, J., Isserlin, L., & Lock, J. (2010). Family-based treatment for adolescents with anorexia nervosa: A dissemination study. *Eating Disorders, 18,* 199–209.

Dare, C. (1985). The family therapy of anorexia nervosa. *Journal of Psychiatric Research, 19,* 435–443.

Dare, C., Eisler, I., Colahan, M., Crowther, C., Senior, R., & Asen, E. (1995). The listening heart and the chi square: Clinical and empirical perceptions in the family therapy of anorexia nervosa. *Journal of Family Therapy, 17,* 31–57.

Doyle, P. M., Le Grange, D., Loeb, K., Doyle, A. C., & Crosby, R. D. (2010). Early response to family-based treatment for adolescent anorexia nervosa. *International Journal of Eating Disorders, 43,* 659–662.

Eisler, I. (1995). Family models of eating disorders. In G. Szmukle, C. Dare, & J. Treasure (Eds.), *Handbook of eating disorders: Theory, treatment and research.* London, England: Wiley.

Eisler, I., Dare, C., Hodes, M., Russell, G., Dodge, E., & Le Grange, D. (2000). Family therapy for adolescent anorexia nervosa: The results of a controlled comparison of two family interventions. *Journal of Child Psychology and Psychiatry, 41,* 727–736.

Eisler, I., Dare, C., Russell, G., Szmukler, G. I., Le Grange, D., & Dodge, E. (1997). Family and individual therapy in anorexia nervosa: A five-year follow-up. *Archives of General Psychiatry, 54,* 1025–1030.

Eisler, I., Simic, M., Russell, G., & Dare, C. (2007). A randomised controlled treatment trial of two forms of family therapy in adolescent anorexia nervosa: A five-year follow-up. *Journal of Child Psychology and Psychiatry, 48,* 552–560.

Ellison, R., Rhodes, P., Madden, S., Miskovic, J., Wallis, A., Baillie, A., . . . Touyz, S. (2012). Do the components of manualized family-based treatment for anorexia nervosa predict weight gain? *International Journal of Eating Disorders, 45,* 609–614.

Garven, R. & Rhodes, P. (2011). The final session. In P. Rhodes & A. Wallis (Eds.), *Working with families: A practical guide.* Melbourne, Australia: IP Communications.

Haley, J. (1973). *Uncommon therapy: The psychiatric techniques of Milton H. Erickson.* New York, NY: Norton.

Harris, T. O., Brown, G. W., & Bifulco, A. (1986). Loss of parent in childhood and adult psychiatric disorder: The role of lack of adequate parental care. *Psychological Medicine, 16,* 641–659.

Herzog, D. B., Greenwood, D. N., Dorer, D. J., Flores, A. T., Ekeblad, E. R., Richards, A., . . . Keller, M. B. (2000). Mortality in eating disorders: A descriptive study. *International Journal of Eating Disorders, 28,* 20–26.

Hoek, H. W. (2006). Incidence, prevalence and mortality of anorexia nervosa and other eating disorders *Current Opinion in Psychiatry, 19,* 389–394.

Hurst, K., Read, S., & Wallis, A. (2012). Anorexia nervosa in adolescence and Maudsley family-based treatment. *Journal of Counseling & Development, 90,* 339–345.

Katzman, D. K. (2005). Medical complications in adolescents with anorexia nervosa: A review of the literature. *International Journal of Eating Disorders, 37,* 52–59.

Killen, J. D., Hayward, C., Litt, I., Hammer, L. D., Wilson, D. M., Miner, B., . . . Shisslak, C. (1992). Is puberty a risk factor for eating disorders? *American Journal of Diseases of Children, 146,* 323–325.

Lasègue, E. C. (1873). On hysterical anorexia. *Medical Times and Gazette, 2,* 265–266.

Le Grange, D., Eisler, I., Dare, C., & Russell, G. F. (1992). Evaluation of family treatments in adolescent anorexia nervosa: A pilot study. *International Journal of Eating Disorders, 12,* 347–357.

Lock, J., Agras, W. S., Bryson, S., & Kraemer, H. (2005). A comparison of short- and long-term family therapy for adolescent anorexia nervosa. *Journal of the American Academy of Child & Adolescent Psychiatry, 44,* 632–639.

Lock, J., Couturier, J., & Agras, W. S. (2006). Comparison of long-term outcomes in adolescents with anorexia nervosa treated with family therapy. *Journal of the American Academy of Child & Adolescent Psychiatry, 45,* 666–672.

Lock, J., & Gowers, S. (2005). Effective interventions for adolescents with anorexia nervosa. *Journal of Mental Health, 14,* 599–610.

Lock, J., Le Grange, D., Agras, W. S., & Dare, C. (2001). *Treatment manual for anorexia nervosa: A family-based approach.* New York, NY: Guilford Press.

Lock, J., Le Grange, D., Agras, S. W., Moye, A., Bryson, S. W., & Booil, J. (2010). Randomized clinical trial comparing family-based treatment with adolescent-focused individual therapy for adolescents with anorexia nervosa. *Archives of General Psychiatry, 67,* 1025–1032.

Lock, J., Le Grange, D., Forsberg, S., & Hewell, K. (2006). Is family therapy useful for treating children with anorexia nervosa? Results of a case series. *Journal of the American Academy of Child & Adolescent Psychiatry, 45*, 1323–1328.

Loeb, K. L., Walsh, B. T., Lock, J., Le Grange, D., Jones, J., Marcus, S., . . . Dobrow, I. (2007). Open trial of family-based treatment for full and partial anorexia nervosa in adolescence: Evidence of successful dissemination. *Journal of the American Academy of Child & Adolescent Psychiatry, 46*, 792–800.

Madanes, C. (1981). *Strategic family therapy.* San Francisco, CA: Jossey-Bass.

Minuchin, S., Baker, B. L., Rosman, B., Liebman, R., Milman, L., & Todd, T. (1975). A conceptual model of psychosomatic illness in children: Family organisation and family therapy. *Archives of General Psychiatry, 32*, 1031–1038.

Morgan, H. G., & Russell, G. M. (1975). Value of family background and clinical features as predictors of long-term outcome in anorexia nervosa: Four-year follow-up study of 41 patients. *Psychological Medicine, 5*, 355–371.

National Collaborating Centre for Mental Health. (2004). *Eating disorders: Core interventions in the treatment and management of anorexia nervosa, bulimia nervosa and related eating disorders.* London: British Psychological Society & the Royal College of Psychiatrists.

Paulson-Karlsson, G., Engstrom, I., & Nevonen, L. (2009). A pilot study of a family-based treatment for adolescent anorexia nervosa: 18- and 36-month follow-ups. *Eating Disorders, 17*, 72–88.

Rhodes, P. (2003). The Maudsley model of family-based treatment for anorexia nervosa: Theory, practice and empirical support. *Australian and New Zealand Journal of Family Therapy, 24*, 191–198.

Rhodes, P., & Wallis, A. (2009). The Maudsley model of family therapy for anorexia nervosa. In S. J. Paxton & J. P. Hay (Eds.), *Interventions for body image and eating disorders: Evidence and practice* (pp. 58–74). Melbourne, Victoria, Australia: IP Communications.

Robin, A. L., Siegel, P. T., & Moye, A. (1995). Family versus individual therapy for anorexia: Impact on family conflict. *International Journal of Eating Disorders, 17*, 313–322.

Russell, G. F., Szmukler, G. I., Dare, C., & Eisler, I. (1987). An evaluation of family therapy in anorexia nervosa and bulimia nervosa. *Archives of General Psychiatry, 44*, 1047–1056.

Sassaroli, S., & Ruggiero, G. M. (2005). The role of stress in the association between low self-esteem, perfectionism, and worry, and eating disorders. *International Journal of Eating Disorders, 37*, 135–141.

Schmidt, U., Tiller, J. M., & Treasure, J. (1993). Setting the scene for eating disorders: Childhood care, classification and course of illness. *Psychological Medicine, 23*, 663–672.

Selvini-Palazzoli, M. (1974). *Self-starvation: From the intrapsychic to the transpersonal.* London, England: Chancer Press.

Sharpe, T. M., Ryst, E., Hinshaw, S. P., & Steiner, H. (1997). Reports of stress: A comparison between eating disordered and non-eating disordered adolescents. *Child Psychiatry and Human Development, 28,* 117–132.

Steiner, H., Kwan, W., Shaffer, T. G., Walker, S., Miller, S., Sagar, A., Lock, J. (2003). Risk and protective factors for juvenile eating disorders. *European Child & Adolescent Psychiatry, 12,* 38–46.

Strober, M., Freeman, R., & Morrell, W. (1997). The long-term course of severe anorexia nervosa in adolescents: Survival analysis of recovery, relapse, and outcome predictors over 10–15 years in a prospective study. *International Journal of Eating Disorders, 22,* 339–360.

Treasure, J., Claudino, A., & Zucker, N. (2010). Eating disorders. *Lancet, 375,* 583–593.

Wallin, U., & Kronvall, P. (2002). Anorexia nervosa in teenagers: Change in family function after family therapy, at 2-year follow-up. *Nordic Journal of Psychiatry, 56,* 363–369.

Wallis, A., Rhodes, P., Kohn, M., & Madden, S. (2007). Five-years of family based treatment for anorexia nervosa: The Maudsley Model at the Children's Hospital at Westmead. *International Journal of Adolescent Medicine and Health, 19,* 277–283.

Wallis, A., Rhodes, P., Kohn, M., & Madden, S. (2009). The family based treatment of anorexia nervosa at Children's Hospital, Westmead: Implementation, experience and practice challenges. In D. Bennet, S. Towns, E. Elliot & J. Merrick (Eds.), *Challenges in adolescent health: An Australian perspective* (pp. 141–152 ). Sydney, New South Wales, Australia: Nova.

Weme, J., & Yalom, J. D. (1996). *Treating eating disorders.* San Francisco, CA: Jossey-Bass.

Wentz, E., Gillberg, C., Anckarsa, H., Gillberg, C., & Rastam, M. (2009). Adolescent-onset anorexia nervosa: 18-year outcome. *British Journal of Psychiatry, 194,* 168–174.

White, M., & Epston, D. (1990). *Narrative means to therapeutic ends.* New York, NY: W. W. Norton.

Wonderlich, S. A., Lilenfeld, L. R., Riso, L. P., Engel, S., & Mitchell, J. E. (2005). Personality and anorexia nervosa. *International Journal of Eating Disorders, 37,* 68–71.

## Chapter 18

# A Relational–Cultural Approach to Working With Clients With Eating Disorders

*Heather Trepal, Ioana Boie, Victoria Kress, and Tonya Hammer*

Vivian, a 30-year-old recently divorced lesbian African American woman, struggles to raise her child and deal with numerous life stressors. Vivian has battled bulimia for the past 15 years, but the additional crises of getting a divorce and coming out as a lesbian have made it especially difficult to manage the disorder. She also works full time while pursuing a doctoral degree, all of which add to her stress.

Vivian began experimenting with bulimia in high school after the weight gain she experienced secondary to puberty began to bother her. On scholarship, she attended exclusive private schools—for high school and college—and was surrounded by predominately White women whom she perceived to be thin and prettier than her. She reported always feeling different from the other girls and ashamed of her weight. She learned from other girls how to purge to help control her weight, which led to her feeling more accepted.

After 7 years of marriage, her husband—who had at times been physically and verbally abusive—responded with anger to her coming out as a lesbian. In addition, her family now barely speaks to her, and they are embarrassed by and generally hostile toward her. Some of her friends have also disconnected from her, which has left her feeling rejected and lonely. Around the time of her divorce, Vivian had a brief romantic relationship with a woman at work, but it ended with Vivian feeling embarrassed and hurt.

Vivian finds herself feeling increasingly misunderstood and alienated and thus marginalized from her family, her culture, and society in general. As her sense of loneliness escalates, so does the bulimia. Navigating numerous stressful life events including her self-perceived relational failures, raising a child, and going to school have left her feeling overwhelmed. Vivian feels unable to

425

manage her feelings of isolation, shame, and guilt. She feels lonely and raw and is beginning to feel hopeless about her future. As we discuss the application of relational–cultural theory (RCT) to working with clients with eating disorders (EDs), we illustrate some of the main concepts using Vivian's case.

Feminist interpretations of the origins, development, and maintenance of mental health concerns, including EDs, have focused on the contributions of gender roles, cultural variables, and issues of power, privilege, and marginalization (Eriksen & Kress, 2008). As an extension of feminist therapies, RCT is a theoretical approach that suggests that the need for connection and context, instead of individuation, is the foundation of development. These needs are also central to understanding mental health disorders' etiology, maintenance, and treatment. RCT "hopes to better represent both women's and men's psychological experience as it seeks transformation of chronic disconnection into connection and empowerment of individuals of both genders and for society as a whole" (Jordan, 2010, p. 24). In this chapter, we provide an overview of RCT, followed by recommendations for using relationally focused counseling for EDs via both prevention and individual counseling.

# Relational–Cultural Theory Overview

Although we do not cover the entire scope of RCT in this chapter, a few concepts are necessary to understand the application of RCT to EDs.

## Relational Competence

According to RCT, growth occurs in—and through—relationships and connections with others. In healthy relationships that foster growth, people are able to experience change; thus, one of the goals of RCT is to develop relational competence, as opposed to traditional theories in which the goal is autonomy or individuation. If in fact relational competence is not present and the relationships are unhealthy, the result can be chronic isolation and a detriment to development.

## Connections Versus Disconnections

Another important tenet of the RCT approach is that people experience a desire for connections to others; however, despite this desire, and on the basis of their individual relational templates and sociocultural histories, they use strategies for disconnection to maintain their emotional safety in relationships, which in RCT is referred to as the *central relational paradox* (Jordan, 2010, p. 28). The central relational paradox is basically that although people desire connection, they do everything they can to protect themselves by distancing themselves from the very relationships they desire.

## Relational Images

Relational images represent inner constructions of the roles and expectations individuals have for themselves in relationships on the basis of previous relationships (Miller & Stiver, 1997). These mental templates are developed early in life, are carried over throughout the life span, and are based on the outcomes of other relationships in the person's life, including relationships with primary caregivers or other intimate relationships. If these images are positive, then the individual will be able to develop healthy relationships and maintain an authentic sense of self. If, however, relational images are based on empathic failures or unmet expectations, then they could possibly lead to chronic disconnection and the need to develop coping strategies or strategies of disconnection as protective maneuvers. We describe these strategies later in the chapter.

## Cultural Context and Controlling Images

According to this approach, considering a client's cultural context is also important. *Cultural context* refers to all of the intersections of a client's identity (e.g., race, sex, gender, class, ability, spiritual tradition, affectional orientation). Sometimes, aspects of a clients' identity will help them access membership in the dominant social group. Other times, different aspects of their identity will afford them membership in a nondominant social group. Each of these identities may intersect and have an impact on clients as they go through their day. It is especially important to examine clients' cultural contexts as they relate to controlling images. For example, if an aspect of a client's identity does not match the "right" controlling image, then the client can feel marginalized and disempowered—as though he or she is less than, or not as good as, those images the dominant society deems valuable.

From an RCT perspective, controlling images have been described as those that the dominant culture values and imposes on others (Walker, 2005). In addition to relational images, according to RCT, controlling images also have an impact on an individual's relational competence and development. Specifically, *controlling images* have been defined as "images constructed by the dominant group that represent distortions of the nondominant group being depicted, with the intent of disempowering them" (Jordan, 2010, pp. 102–103). They can especially influence and undermine internal thoughts and feelings related to body image (Hammer, 2009). Hill Collins (2000) warned that these images are "designed to make racism, sexism, poverty, and other forms of social injustice appear to be natural, normal, and inevitable parts of everyday life" (p. 69).

## Growth-Fostering Relationships

According to RCT, people move toward relational competence if they develop healthy relational templates that can empower the person to confront the controlling images. Relational competence results in the development of healthy growth-fostering relationships, which results in feelings of zest, empowerment, increased clarity, a greater sense of self-worth, and a desire for more connections, or the "five good things" (Miller, 1986, p.

3). Finally, in direct contrast, chronic isolation or disconnection results in "five bad things": a depletion of energy, helplessness or immobility, confusion, diminished self-worth, and a turning away from relationships (Dooley & Fedele, 2004). Disconnection such as this can lead to the development of a variety of mental health concerns, including EDs, which is why an understanding and application of RCT can be beneficial in the treatment of EDs.

### Relational-Cultural Theory and the Counseling Relationship

Finally, from an RCT standpoint, the counseling relationship is collaborative and focuses on mutual empathy (i.e., when both parties in a relationship are affected by one another) and authenticity (Jordan, 2010; Miller & Stiver, 1997). According to Duffey and Somody (2011), in RCT, *authenticity* "refers to the capacity to represent ourselves honestly in relationships" (p. 229). As clients are able to practice self-empathy, examine their strategies for disconnection, and experiment with relationships in counseling, counselors can use authenticity and express honest compassion for their clients' experiences. As such, clients can forge new relational templates for growth-fostering relationships that can be transferred to relationships outside of counseling.

# Why Use Relational–Cultural Theory in Eating Disorder Treatment?

RCT provides a respectful and dynamic framework for approaching clients with EDs. Additionally, RCT highlights the cultural contexts that are essential to understand in the treatment of EDs. Furthermore, RCT has been identified as an approach that works well in conjunction with other treatments for working with clients with ED (Sanftner, Tantillo, & Seidlitz, 2004; Tantillo, MacDowell, Anson, Taillie, & Cole, 2009; Tantillo & Sanftner, 2003), including those mentioned in Chapters 13 to 17 in this text. Specifically, Tantillo and Sanftner (2003) found short-term relational group therapy based on the RCT model to be equally as effective in treating bulimia and depressive symptoms as short-term cognitive–behavioral group therapy. To better understand why RCT is appropriate and effective in working with clients with EDs, disconnections and mutuality are two areas that must be explored.

### Relational-Cultural Theory as a Strategy for Disconnection

Disconnections can be explained as routine challenges in relationships. These disconnections or challenges can include disagreements or arguments as well as ongoing relational patterns. Strategies of disconnection often begin as attempts to self-protect (Miller & Stiver, 1997). For example, when a person has a relationship in which the other party is unable to respond to her needs, she becomes a chameleon of sorts and develops strategies to protect herself in the relationship. Often, this means becoming—or representing herself—in a way that is acceptable to the other person, despite how she really feels. Eventually, she grows increasingly unable to access her own thoughts and feelings. Subsequently, she becomes unwilling and unable to represent her authentic self with others for fear of being ignored and devalued (Miller & Stiver, 1997). In time, if these relational ruptures are not repaired, these disconnections between self and others become increasingly isolating.

EDs have been linked to a need for a sense of control (American Psychiatric Association, 2000) and have been presented as a coping strategy (Brewerton, 2007). As such, it makes sense to conceptualize EDs as a strategy for disconnection; through disconnection with others, one simplifies one's world and achieves a perceived sense of control (Trepal, Boie, & Kress, 2012). EDs can also be rooted in a sense of disconnection with one's body secondary to not feeling as though one lives up to idealized media images of beauty. For example, images in the media often portray models who are tall and thin. If people compare their body with those images and feel or believe that their body is different from or not equal to those idealized images, they may feel disconnected—or separate—from their body as a result. From an RCT perspective, EDs are aptly framed as "disease[s] of disconnection" (Tantillo, 2006, p. 86).

Moreover, when EDs serve as a means to disconnect, ED behaviors present an opportunity to disconnect from pain and to temporarily find emotional and physical safety. Behaviors associated with EDs can distort reality and further distance people from themselves and others. People are not able to be fully aware of their bodily sensations (e.g., hunger, thirst) and feelings (e.g., anger, grief, anxiety) when they are disconnected from themselves. In addition, it is possible to distract—or disconnect—oneself from relational pain (e.g., fighting, confronting someone) when one is consumed with managing an ED.

Many different strategies used by those who have EDs result in a sense of disconnection from others, and these strategies include blaming others, criticizing, withdrawing, and isolating (Hartling, Rosen, Walker, & Jordan, 2000). Isolation in particular may be an important relational consideration because EDs often involve private rituals and behaviors (American Psychiatric Association, 2000). Similar to other forms of self-harm, the isolation created by the ED is cyclical (Trepal, 2010). For example, a person may retreat to manage overwhelming emotions (e.g., feeling out of control, stress, anger) and practice behaviors associated with his or her ED (e.g., binging, purging, ingesting nonfood objects or substances, excessive exercise). After using various disconnection strategies, individuals may feel a sense of guilt and shame at having used these coping strategies. When they disclose these behaviors to others, or when others discover them, they can be pushed back into isolation and out of actual connection.

## Mutuality

Specifically, the RCT concept of mutuality (e.g., awareness of, connection to, and impact on another) is an essential concept in understanding the role of EDs within the context of relationships. In relationships in which mutuality is present, there is room for both parties' growth. According to Miller and Stiver (1997), people whose early relationships lacked mutuality are more likely to struggle with psychological issues, including EDs. If early emotional templates suggest that one's ideas, thoughts, feelings, and experiences are not important (i.e., they are devalued or ignored) or if these relationships are marked by chronic and irreparable disconnections, people may assume that it is better to disguise aspects of themselves to maintain their safety in relationships.

Some research support exists for the idea that low levels of mutuality in relationships can affect ED symptoms. For example, in one study women with EDs self-reported lower mutuality in relationships with friends and romantic partners than did a non-ED control group (Sanftner et al., 2004). Tantillo and Sanftner (2003) also found that clients who self-reported low mutuality in relationships with their parents had more severe ED symptoms.

# Applying Relational–Cultural Theory to Eating Disorder Treatment

Through the theoretical lens of RCT, we focus on ED treatment in two areas, prevention and individual treatment. RCT is well suited to addressing EDs because the therapeutic relationship in RCT focuses not only on collaboration and mutual empathy but also on authenticity in the relationship. In addition, it is helpful for deconstructing and addressing the disconnections that result from a client's relationship and sociocultural contexts. In this section, we address prevention and individual-level ED treatment.

## Prevention

Prevention efforts rely "most heavily on providing information to increase understanding, enhance attitudes, and promote functional behavior while attempting to minimize resistance" (Choate & Schwitzer, 2009, pp. 165–166). The elements discussed in this section can be incorporated in ED prevention with an RCT focus and may benefit students and clients who are already experiencing problems but who have not yet developed EDs.

### Cultural Psychoeducation
Although psychoeducation regarding ED can be an important component of prevention efforts, an RCT approach broadens the focus to the roles of gender, power, privilege, and oppression in development. Walker (2002) suggested that societal power involves those aspects of difference in social identities that the dominant culture values or devalues, including race, sex, gender, physical ability, spirituality, and class, among others (p. 2). According to the controlling image in current society, if a person is the right weight and body shape, relationships will be both possible and fulfilling. Unexamined, these harmful images can cause problems when people experience a cognitive dissonance between their real bodies and

430

the idealized, unattainable, controlling images that the dominant society supports (Trepal et al., 2012, p. 350).

From an RCT prevention perspective, counselors can first talk with clients about their experiences with societal discrimination, exclusion, and trauma related to many aspects of the clients' physical characteristics, including body shape, size, weight, height, and skin color. They can also help them to begin the process of critiquing dominant cultural values and expanding the range of options that are available for clients to be true to their own values. Approaches such as media literacy (Levine & Piran, 2001; Levine, Piran, & Stoddard, 1999), in which students and clients become active and involved consumers of media, can be used to identify, evaluate, deconstruct, and resist images (for examples, see Choate & Curry, 2009).

Second, prevention programs need to aim at promoting positive body image while incorporating culturally relevant values and traditions. One such example is the Beloved Body Soul (2011) program promoting English, Spanish, and bilingual psychoeducation on women's body image. Similar curricula could be used in both community mental health and school counseling settings by including cultural values and traditions relevant to both majority and especially minority groups of men and women in the area of body acceptance. Group curricula can be tailored to member needs on the basis of multiple cultural dimensions, including ethnicity, sexual preference, spirituality, socioeconomic status, national origin, attractiveness, ableism, and body shape and size.

A third area of RCT prevention focus is to promote a counterdialogue for the current thinness-as-health cultural narrative. Along these lines, two emerging critical perspectives are the Health at Every Size (Bacon, 2010) and Fat Acceptance paradigms (National Association to Advance Fat Acceptance, 2012). Weight acceptance, focusing on health, not on appearance, is highly related to increased body satisfaction and decreased drive for thinness (which then decreases dieting, which lowers risk for EDs and obesity). Prevention efforts can focus on health and self-acceptance regardless of whether an individual meets a culturally imposed standard of thinness. As an example, school and mental health counselors can try activities such as having their students, clients, or groups experiment with remaining "fat-talk free" for a certain amount of time. In this activity, people are instructed to pay attention to the times (both internally and externally) when they participate in "fat talk" (e.g., commenting negatively on their own bodies or others' bodies, focusing on weight and size, vilifying certain foods relative to weight and size, and using physical activity related to weight and size). Often, students and clients will report that they are unable to engage in a fat-talk free way of life for long. This activity can promote fruitful discussion on the issue, including examining ways in which the culture promotes a thin ideal and dissatisfaction with real bodies.

### Prevention Through Connection

Hartling (2004) asserted that prevention through connection is an important reframing of traditional prevention efforts that emphasize individualistic approaches. Prevention efforts for disorders such as substance abuse have focused on "teaching information or skills to increase an individual's ability to stand alone, think independently, be self-sufficient, and resist peer-pressure—that is, prevention through self-sufficiency, disconnection, or separation" (Hartling, 2004, p. 199). At times, this approach may be useful (e.g., disconnecting from substance-abusing peers). RCT prevention efforts focus less on individualized strategies and more on relational approaches. Thus, from an RCT perspective, effective prevention efforts must take multiple forms of connection into account, including connection to self, others, and the larger community. According to Trepal et al. (2012),

> building and strengthening community knowledge of and response to ED is a vital prevention component. Prevention through connection initiatives can include intervening at the individual, community (e.g., school, agency), and larger system (e.g., government) levels; all of these initiatives—to some extent—overlap and inform one other. Individual-level prevention programs should present tangible information for developing coping skills, de-stigmatizing mental health services, and maximizing the use of counseling services and related resources. (Trepal et al., 2012, p. 351).

Each of these avenues can contribute to a sense of community building around the topic of EDs. Thus, recognizing that enacting societal change on their own might be impossible, individuals are not expected to act alone (or suffer in silence) and can be encouraged to form connections with others around these issues.

In addition, groups can emphasize social support, which can be highly influential in helping people who have an ED make meaningful change. An example of a more individual-level, long-term prevention program that can be helpful is the Tri Delta Reflections: Body Image Program, a peer-led prevention program involved with sororities around the United States (see Chapter 11, this volume). Other prevention programs that highlight cultural psychoeducation, media literacy, and prevention through connection are Fat Talk Free (Tri Delta Sorority, 2011), an initiative to encourage women to de-emphasize discussing weight and negative body talk and Celebrating Eating Disorders Awareness Week (National Eating Disorders Association, 2011), which focuses on EDs and body image issues prevention while reducing the stigma surrounding EDs and improving access to treatment.

# Individual Treatment Strategies

Adapted from relational treatment models (Trepal et al., 2012), goals for incorporating relationally focused individual counseling strategies include (a) fostering self-empathy, (b) increasing understanding of EDs, and (c) renovating relational images related to EDs.

## *Self-Empathy With Clients With Eating Disorders*

Before clients can progress toward relational competency and healthy relationships, they need to develop a better understanding of self (Nakash,

Williams, & Jordan, 2004) and ultimately self-empathy. Jordan (1991) described self-empathy as a process of developing empathy for one's own experiences without criticism or blaming. Counselors can assist clients in assessing their self-empathy. Some examples of questions to assess self-empathy are the following:

- How do you view yourself and your behavior, feelings, and varied experiences?
- In what ways are you disconnected from yourself and your emotional and cognitive experiences?
- How do you view yourself in relation to others?
- How do you experience your body and emotions related to social norms? (Trepal et al., 2012)

Developing and fostering self-empathy is arguably difficult when faced with relational oppression. This type of oppression involves marginalization of and discrimination against nondominant groups by dominant ones. Relational oppression especially helps dominant groups to retain control over the connections within the larger culture, including connections to self (leaders and visible others do not look like the nondominant group) and others (institutions are not welcoming to the nondominant group). According to RCT, relational oppression can create further disconnection (Miller & Stiver, 1997). As the dominant group exerts power over others, those who are on the margins may be affected by these dynamics (Ruiz, 2005). As such, the degree to which clients perceive, understand, and internalize the "isms" in their lives, including race, ethnicity, gender role, socioeconomic status, and historical context, should be examined (Talleyrand, 2010).

Men struggling with ED may be further marginalized for having what is commonly referred to as a "woman's issue" (Maine & Bunnell, 2008, p. 189; see also Chapter 2, this volume). In Western society, men are encouraged to be self-reliant and independent. They may be at a cultural disadvantage when it comes to expressing their needs in relationships. Using this approach to counseling men with ED, counselors can assist men in examining society's messages, informed by the gendered ways in which men are socialized to value power, dominance, and status (Maine & Bunnell, 2008, pp. 188–189).

## Strategies for Fostering Self-Empathy

Counselors can use various approaches to foster self-empathy with clients. For example, externalizing techniques such as recognizing, naming, and identifying self-destructive behaviors (i.e., the ED) can be helpful. This type of approach removes the behavior from the person, freeing the client to develop a new relationship with the ED. Moreover, by asking the client to give the ED influence a descriptive name that is then used to refer to it or using other activities such as having the client draw a picture of it or write a letter to it, the counselor can further encourage the separation of the self (e.g., worth) of the person from his or her self-destructive behavior (i.e., the ED).

Once the client has begun to step away from the ED, he or she is able to begin the process of developing self-empathy. Useful techniques include having a client's observing self express compassion for his or her experiencing self. For example, the counselor can ask clients to reflect on their experience as though they were observing themselves from across the room or as though their experience belonged to a friend instead of themselves (Jordan, 2010). This technique can reduce self-critique and blame by taking another perspective. Self-affirmations (e.g., "I am choosing to let go, and as such I am taking control" or "I respect myself and others") can also be useful tools for enhancing a sense of self-compassion. Finally, clients should be encouraged to honor their vulnerability. It can be both difficult and humbling for clients to attempt change, particularly when examining and learning to have empathy for themselves (see also Box 18.1).

All of these techniques can help clients understand that they are not the problem, the ED is the problem (White & Epston, 1990) and may reduce feelings of shame. Ultimately, the goal is to empower clients' sense of personal agency, deepen their awareness of the influence of the ED, and enhance their ability to make successful changes (Hoffman & Kress, 2008).

Counselors must remember that the ED serves a protective, preserving function for the client (Banks, 2006). The ED disconnection strategies protected the client; thus, the process of ameliorating the ED behaviors is not easy. According to Trepal et al. (2012),

> Centering all of one's energy and attention on an eating disorder allowed the person to narrow his or her world and focus; all that mattered was the eating-related concerns (e.g., weight, calories, exercise). The risks associated with self-honesty, self-love and care, and opening one's self to others were mollified by the eating disorder. Thus, the eating disorder and other self-harming behaviors served as a barrier between the person and others. When these barriers are removed, clients will likely feel more vulnerable and fearful and, therefore, may want to retreat these comfortable, self-harming, disconnecting behaviors. Counselors are advised to express compassion for clients and their experiences and to honor the pace at which they take the risk of more deeply connecting with themselves and others. (p. 352)

When clients begin to explore self-empathy, they may be ready to master other relational challenges. For clients to be prepared to work on these challenges, they need to have an increased understanding of the function that the ED serves in their lives.

### Increasing Understanding of Eating Disorders

According to Tantillo (2004), clients with ED will be able to

> let go of eating disorder symptoms as [they are] able to (a) identify the connections between [their] relationships with food and [their] relationships with the self and others, and (b) develop mutually empathic and empowering relationships with others inside and outside the therapy office. (p. 53) (See also Box 18.2).

> ## Box 18.1 Application to Vivian's Case
>
> ***Goal:*** Foster client self-empathy.
>
> ***Strategies:*** Externalization, self-affirmation, honoring vulnerability
>
> As indicated in Vivian's case study, she finds herself feeling increasingly misunderstood and alienated and thus marginalized from her family, her culture, and society in general. Furthermore, she is experiencing chronic isolation and is overwhelmed by her feelings of shame and guilt associated with, in part, her ED. Strategies including externalization, self-affirmation, and honoring her vulnerability would possibly prove beneficial.
>
> Although she has some ambivalence about whether the ED is her friend or her foe, she does identify that it has at times been harmful. Vivian is invited to process and explore the ways in which the ED encourages her to disconnect from her feelings and thoughts. To foster self-empathy, Vivian is invited to name and identify the ED influence. She is asked to have her observing self express compassion for her experiencing self. Vivian chooses to name the ED Marie (the name of a girl who bullied her in grade school). Vivian is encouraged to paint a picture of Marie that captures and conveys her toxic influence. She is then encouraged to write a letter to Marie in which she describes the ways Marie keeps her from being authentic about her own feelings and experiences.
>
> In this letter, Vivian is able to convey that Marie seduces her and encourages her to isolate and engage in secretive behaviors. At the time, the isolation feels safe and comforting, but the resulting binging and purging and emptiness that follows results in her feeling worse about her situation. Over four to five sessions, Vivian is able to slowly recognize the ED, Marie, as a seductive foe as opposed to a friend. She is able to see the ways in which Marie has kept her isolated from herself and from others in an attempt to control her. Gradually, Vivian begins to feel more empowered, and the ED influence is viewed as less of a friend.

As clients are able to begin the process of developing self-empathy, they can also examine the connections between their relationships and their ED behaviors, in both relational and behavioral terms.

Jordan and Dooley (2000) identified relational challenges as routine times when it is difficult to be authentic in relationships. A therapeutic opportunity exists when clients feel the pull of such a challenge and, instead of using disconnection strategies, they are encouraged to remain in connection. Counseling can provide a context within which clients can learn about relational challenges associated with EDs, focusing on exploring disconnections from self and others. Counselors can help clients to identify their relational challenges and common unproductive disconnection strategies (Trepal et al., 2012).

### Renovating Relational Images

The final goal in relationally focused counseling is examining and renovating relational images from the client's past. As stated earlier, these relational expectations determine beliefs and expectations about future

> ### Box 18.2 — Application to Vivian's Case
>
> **Goal:** Increase understanding of eating disorders.
> **Strategies:** Examine connections between relationships with food and self and others.
>
> From the initial start of Vivian's journey with bulimia, she experienced a distinct connection between her relationship with food, herself, and others. This connection was evidenced, for example, by the sense of connection she felt when the girls at her school taught her how to purge to help control her weight. She felt connected to the girls through the process. However, it was an inauthentic connection, not only with other individuals but also with her own body.
>
> In counseling, Vivian is encouraged to develop an understanding of the relationship between the ED, herself, and others. Using a large piece of paper, a timeline is constructed on which she is invited to detail when the ED entered her life and what events were occurring at that time. In the context of her relationships (connections and disconnections), the ED dynamics are explored via the timeline. Vivian is able to identify what relationship and self-struggles she was having when the ED began. She is also able to link her relationship struggles with escalations in ED symptoms.
>
> Vivian is then invited to brainstorm a list of people in her life who are supportive and loving. Next, she is asked to make a list of people who are neutral forces in her life. Finally, she is asked to generate a list of those people in her life who are toxic. These three lists are discussed, and she is encouraged to draw on supportive others and monitor interactions with those who are toxic. She also explores the kinds of people and relationships she would like to invite into her life. Guided imagery is used as a technique to help her visualize and connect with the experience of inviting healthy relationships into her life and pushing toxic relationships away.

relationships (Miller & Stiver, 1995, p. 3). Counselors can assist clients in examining these relational images by exploring their early experiences. Cultural expectations of beauty, thinness, and attractiveness (i.e., controlling images) often interfere with the development and maintenance of positive relational self-images and may be explored. Individuals with EDs perceive that they cannot attain this image; therefore, they disconnect from themselves. Counselors can address negative images related to how their relationships with others will play out because their appearance is not what they had imagined (e.g., they cannot attract a romantic partner or sustain a romantic relationship because they believe their body is not perfect).

In addition, addressing relational images in the family of origin is also important. Sanftner, Ryan, and Pierce (2009) argued that attending to the impact of multiple relationships (e.g., parents, romantic partners) in clients' lives may be an important factor related to addressing body image dissatisfaction and potentially preventing the development of more severe ED symptoms (p. 276). Counselors can ask questions to investigate relational patterns. For example, parents' or siblings' early comments regarding body type or eating habits may be explored. It is also important for counselors to explore how effectively clients engage in conflict, which can uncover whether the client can present his or her needs to others (Jordan, 2010). According to Jordan (2010), questions such as "If I am [fill in the blank], then the other person will [fill in the blank]" may be useful for garnering this information (p. 36).

Although exploring and analyzing relational images from the past is important, RCT also purports that new experiences provide opportunities to expand these images (Miller & Stiver, 1995). As clients are further able to practice negotiating current relationships, it is important to help them to examine their disconnection strategies (including ED behaviors), which were at one time self-preserving. Counselors can begin this process by exploring when and how the clients disconnect.

According to RCT, it is important to normalize routine disconnections and to help clients learn to represent their own needs and views to others when in conflict (Miller & Stiver, 1997). An important task is to help clients maintain connection; when clients feel the pull of disconnection, they can learn to remain in connection (rather than using strategies for disconnection). Clients can be encouraged to explore, develop, and practice new coping skills and relational strategies that encourage remaining in connection with others while avoiding a reliance on ED behaviors. Depending on the outcome, clients can be supported in practicing new ways of being in conflict that allow both parties in the relationship to practice mutual empathy (i.e., using *I* statements, trying to listen from the other's point of view; see also Box 18.3). Finally, it is important to remember that in an attempt to self-protect, clients may retreat to their old disconnection strategies (Trepal, 2010). Counselors should emphasize to clients that change is not always a linear process (Banks, 2006).

---

**Box 18.3  Application to Vivian's Case**

*Goal:* Renovate relational images.
*Strategies:* Examine images in family of origin, images in the media, and images from other significant relationships.

Vivian finds herself struggling with media images of what it is to be beautiful, what it is to be feminine, and what it is to be African American. In the intersection of these identities, she also struggles with her family's expectations for her in relationship to them. Struggling to develop her identity in the midst of the messages she receives externally, Vivian uses the ED not only as a mechanism of control and coping, but also as what she sees as a possible means to meet those expectations. In counseling, Vivian is encouraged to name and actively resist disempowering and destructive messages in the media. She is also supported in exploring relational images related to her family of origin and significant others, particularly those involving the expectations that she might have in relationships (if I _____, then the other person will _____).

# Conclusion

EDs are complex and can pose many unique challenges to those who suffer from them and to those engaged in their recovery process. RCT is a theoretical approach that takes into account the importance of having a relational and cultural focus in counseling. RCT is emerging as a culturally sensitive approach to extend and enhance current ED prevention and treatment frameworks. According to the RCT perspective, EDs are rooted in disconnection from self and others (Tantillo, 2006). By taking a relational–cultural approach, several prevention and intervention strategies can be used, such as the ones outlined earlier. Some of these include understanding the cultural and relational impact on EDs and the relationship with ED, understanding and working through disconnections, fostering self-empathy and renovating relational images related to the maintenance of the ED cycle, such as those used in Vivian's case.

Because people with EDs often isolate from others and have a difficult time being authentic to who they are, the emphasis that RCT places on helping clients to deepen their sense of connection to themselves and others may be therapeutic. Through RCT's emphasis on examining the strategies that are used to disconnect from one's self, clients may become better aware of their emotions, thoughts, and patterns of disconnection. Last, RCT provides a culturally and relationally sensitive lens for examining the role of gender, ethnicity, socioeconomic status, and affectional orientation in examining the effects of power and marginalization in individuals' lives, as examined in Vivian's story.

Although RCT may be a helpful approach to treating EDs, it is important that counselors tailor their approach to the client's unique treatment needs. Whether used as a stand-alone framework or to complement other treatment approaches, RCT highlights the need for a better understanding of the relational and cultural factors influencing the development and maintenance of ED symptoms.

# Recommended Resources

Beloved Body Soul. (2011). *Preventing eating disorders in the Latino community*. Retrieved from http://belovedbodysoul.com/presentations/preventing-eating-disorders-in-the-latino-community/
Health at Every Size
www.lindabacon.com
Jean Baker Miller Training Institute at the Wellesley Centers for Women http://www.jbmti.org/
Jordan, J. V. (2010). *Relational–cultural therapy*. Washington, DC: American Psychological Association.
Tri Delta Sorority. (2011). *The Center for Living, Learning and Leading: Fat talk free*. Retrieved from http://thecenter.tridelta.org/our-programs/reflections-body-image-program/fat-talk-free-week

# References

American Psychiatric Association. (2000). *Diagnostic and statistical manual of mental disorders* (4th ed., text rev.). Washington, DC: Author.

Bacon, L. (2010). *Health at every size: The surprising truth about your weight.* Dallas, TX: BenBella Books.

Banks, A. (2006). Relational therapy for trauma. *Journal of Trauma Practice, 5,* 25–47.

Beloved Body Soul. (2011). *Preventing eating disorders in the Latino community.* Retrieved from http://belovedbodysoul.com/presentations/preventing-eating-disorders-in-the-latino-community/

Brewerton, T. D. (2007). Eating disorders, trauma, and comorbidity: A focus on PTSD. *Eating Disorders, 15,* 285–304. doi:10.1080/10640260701454311

Choate, L. H., & Curry, J. (2009). Addressing the sexualization of girls through comprehensive programs, advocacy, and systemic change: Implications for professional school mental health professionals. *Professional School Counseling, 12,* 213–221.

Choate, L., & Schwitzer, A. (2009). Mental health counseling responses to eating-related concerns in young adult women: A prevention and treatment continuum. *Journal of Mental Health Counseling, 31,* 164–183.

Dooley, C., & Fedele, N. M. (2004). Mothers and sons: Raising relational boys. In J. V. Jordan, M. Walker, & L. M. Hartling (Eds.), *The complexity of connections: Writings from the Stone Center's Jean Baker Miller Training Institute* (pp. 220–249). New York, NY: Guilford Press.

Duffey, T., & Somody, C. (2011). The role of relational–cultural theory in mental health counseling. *Journal of Mental Health Counseling, 33,* 223–242.

Eriksen, K., & Kress, V. E. (2008). Gender and diagnosis: Struggles and suggestions for counselors. *Journal of Counseling & Development, 86,* 152–162.

Hammer, T. R. (2009). Controlling images, media, and women's development: A review of the literature. *Journal of Creativity in Mental Health, 4,* 202–209. doi:10.1080/15401380903084936

Hartling, L. (2004). Prevention through connection: A collaborative approach to women's substance abuse. In M. Walker & W. B. Rosen (Eds.), *How connections heal: Stories from relational–cultural therapy* (pp. 197–215). New York, NY: Guilford Press.

Hartling, M., Rosen, W., Walker, M., & Jordan, J. V. (2000). *Shame and humiliation: From isolation to relational transformation* (Work in Progress No. 88). Wellesley, MA: Stone Center Working Paper Series.

Hill Collins, P. (2000). *Black feminist thought: Knowledge, consciousness, and the politics of empowerment* (2nd ed.). New York, NY: Routledge Press.

Hoffman, R., & Kress, V. E. (2008). Narrative therapy and non-suicidal self-injurious behavior: Externalizing the problem, and internalizing personal agency. *Journal of Humanistic Counseling, Education and Development, 47,* 157–171.

Jordan, J. V. (1991). Empathy and self-boundaries. In J. Jordan, A. Kaplan, J. Miller, I. Stiver, & J. Surrey (Eds.), *Women's growth in connection* (pp. 67–80). New York, NY: Guilford Press.

Jordan, J. V. (2010). *Relational–cultural therapy.* Washington, DC: American Psychological Association.

Jordan, J. V., & Dooley, C. (2000). *Relational practice in action: A group manual.* Wellesley, MA: Wellesley College, Stone Center.,

Levine, M. P., & Piran, N. (2001). The prevention of eating disorders: Toward a participatory ecology of knowledge, action, and advocacy. In R. Striegel-Moore & L. Smolak (Eds.), *Eating disorders: Innovative directions in research and practice* (pp. 233–254). Washington, DC: American Psychological Association.

Levine, M. P., Piran, N., & Stoddard, C. (1999). Mission more probable: Media literacy, activism, and advocacy as primary intervention. In N. Piran, M. P. Levine, & C. Steiner-Adair (Eds.), *Preventing eating disorders: A handbook of interventions and special challenges* (pp. 1–25). Philadelphia, PA: Brunner/Mazel.

Maine, M., & Bunnell, D. (2008). How do the principles of the feminist relational model apply to treatment of men with eating disorders and related issues? *Eating Disorders, 16,* 187–192. doi:10.1080/10640260801887428

Miller, J. B. (1986). *Toward a new psychology of women.* Boston, MA: Beacon.

Miller, J. B., & Stiver, I. P. (1995). *Relational images and their meanings in psychotherapy* (Work in Progress No. 74). Wellesley, MA: Stone Center Working Paper Series.

Miller, J. B., & Stiver, I. (1997). *The healing connection.* Boston, MA: Beacon.

Nakash, O., Williams, L. M.., & Jordan, J. V. (2004) *Relational–cultural theory, body image and physical health* (Wellesley Centers for Women Working Paper No. 416). Wellesley, MA: Stone Center, Wellesley Centers for Women.

National Association to Advance Fat Acceptance. (2012). *About us.* Retrieved from http://www.naafaonline.com/dev2/about/index.html

National Eating Disorders Association. (2011). *National Eating Disorders awareness week.* Retrieved from http://www.nationaleatingdisorders.org/programs-events/nedawareness-week.php

Ruiz, E. (2005). Hispanic culture and relational cultural theory. *Journal of Creativity in Mental Health, 1,* 33–55. doi:10.1300/J456v01n01_05

Sanftner, J. L., Ryan, W. J., & Pierce, P. (2009). Application of a relational model to understanding body image in college men and women. *Journal of College Student Psychotherapy, 23,* 262–280. doi:10.1080/87568220903167182

Sanftner, J. L., Tantillo, M., & Seidlitz, L. (2004). A pilot investigation of the relation of perceived mutuality to eating disorders in women. *Women & Health, 39,* 85–100. doi:10.1300/J013v39n01_05

Talleyrand, R. M. (2010). Eating disorders in African American girls: Implications for counselors. *Journal of Counseling & Development, 88,* 319–324.

Tantillo, M. (2004). The therapist's use of self disclosure in a relational therapy approach for eating disorders. *Eating Disorders, 12,* 51–73.

Tantillo, M. (2006). A relational approach to eating disorders multifamily therapy group: Moving from difference and disconnection to mutual connection. *Families, Systems, & Health, 24,* 82–102. doi:10.1037/1091-7527.24.1.82

Tantillo, M., MacDowell, S., Anson, E., Taillie, E., & Cole, R. (2009). Combining supported housing and partial hospitalization to improve eating disorder symptoms, perceived health status, and health related quality of life for women with eating disorders. *Eating Disorders, 17,* 385–399. doi:10.1080/10640260903210172

Tantillo, M., & Sanftner, J. (2003). The relationship between perceived mutuality and bulimic symptoms, depression, and therapeutic change in group. *Eating Behaviors, 3,* 349–364. doi:10.1016/S1471-0153(02)00077-6

Trepal, H. (2010). Exploring self-injury through a relational-cultural lens. *Journal of Counseling & Development, 88,* 494–499.

Trepal, H., Boie, I., & Kress, V. (2012). A relational cultural approach to working with clients with eating disorders. *Journal of Counseling & Development, 90,* 346–356.

Tri Delta Sorority. (2011). *The Center for Living, Learning and Leading: Fat talk free.* Retrieved from http://thecenter.tridelta.org/our-programs/reflections-body-image-program/fat-talk-free-week

Walker, M. (2002). *How therapy helps when the culture hurts* (Work In Progress No. 95). Wellesley, MA: Stone Center Working Paper Series.

Walker, M. (2005). Critical thinking: Challenging developmental myths, stigmas, and stereotypes. In D. Comstock (Ed.), *Diversity and development: Critical contexts that shape our lives and relationships* (pp. 47–66). Belmont, CA: Brooks/Cole.

White, M., & Epston, D. (1990). *Narrative means to therapeutic ends.* New York, NY: W. W. Norton.

# Index

*Figures and tables are indicated by f and t following page numbers.*

## A

Abraham, S., 212

ACA. *See* American Counseling Association

Acculturation process, 49, 51–52, 55–56

Adolescents. *See* Children and adolescents

Affect regulation model, 323–324, 376–377

African Americans. *See also* Race and racial issues

anorexia nervosa among, 50

binge eating disorder among, 45, 47, 50

body type acceptance among, 5

bulimia nervosa among, 50, 312

counseling implications for, 55

eating disorders among, 46–47, 52, 53

obesity among, 45, 46–47, 170

Agenda-setting in counseling, 383–389

Agras, W. S., 248, 311

Ahluwalia, J. S., 269

Alexander, L. E., 246

Altabe, M., 4

Amenorrhea, 92

American College of Sports Medicine, 245

American Counseling Association (ACA)

on client autonomy, 74

on counselor self-awareness, 70

on ethical decision-making, 77, 80–82

on interdisciplinary team conduct, 72

on scope of competence, 71

American Indians, eating disorders among, 108

American Psychiatric Association, 72, 402

American Psychological Association, 27

American School Counselor Association (ASCA)

on ethical standards, 72

*National Model* of, 121, 123, 125, 128

programs promoted by, 120

ANAD. *See* National Association of Anorexia Nervosa and Associated Disorders

Andersen, A. E., 33

Anorexia nervosa (AN)

in children and adolescents and, 399–401, 417–418. *See also* Family-based treatment (FBT)

client competence and, 75–76

clinical interviews and, 98–99

*DSM* criteria for, 50, 91, 92, 129

hospitalization for, 74–75, 416

interpersonal psychotherapy for, 311, 337

mortality rates and, 69, 221, 399–400

parental influence on, 400, 407

prevalence of, 202, 287, 399

racial considerations in, 50

risk factors for, 26

treatment goals for, 72–73

women and, 22

Anxiety disorders, 104, 149, 349

Appel, A., 128

Appetite. *See also* Eating in absence of hunger (EAH)

awareness training, 360

body image concerns and, 206–207

ASCA. *See* American School Counselor Association

443

*(Continued)*

(*Continued*)